CONNECTIONS

an integrated reader and rhetoric

for college writing

Kendall Hunt
ublishing company

Donald C. Jones
University of Hartford

Kerry L. Beckford
Tunxis Community COllege

Cover image © Shutterstock, Inc.

www.kendallhunt.com
Send all inquiries to:
4050 Westmark Drive
Dubuque, IA 52004-1840

Copyright © 2015 by Kendall Hunt Publishing Company

ISBN 978-1-4652-8348-1

Printed in the United States of America

TABLE OF CONTENTS

PREFACE FOR INSTRUCTORS

Approach

The goals of this textbook are ambitious. This textbook aims to teach students to read insightfully, think critically, and write analytically about their cultures and themselves. To fulfill these goals, this book includes two introductory chapters, seven instructional chapters, and five thematic chapters. Each of the introductory and the thematic chapters involves students in challenging yet accessible topics, but this textbook does not just expect students to get involved with the thematic chapters. It also provides instructional chapters to teach them *how* to do so. Each of these chapters presents the key concepts and effective strategies of college-level reading and writing.

The two introductory chapters introduce these ambitious goals of college-level literacy. With the subtitle "Connecting the Thematic and the Instructional Chapters," each chapter presents subject content for writing and suggests rhetorical instruction for advanced literacy, and professors can use either chapter to engage students in sustained inquiry. Chapter 1 emphasizes reading and writing equally, and Chapter 2 concentrates on the writing process. Both explain the pedagogy of this textbook and the format of the thematic chapters.

The instructional chapters teach college-level literacy explicitly. Each chapter begins by asking students to consider what they already know about reading, writing, rhetoric, or research. Then, as students engage in each chapter's instruction and application, they will expand their knowledge of these literacies. Chapters 3 and 4, for example, teach students to read actively and to manage the writing process effectively.

The thematic chapters promote further inquiry of compelling issues. The themes range from family and cities to energy and education. Each chapter presents students with diverse perspectives, represented by compelling written and visual texts. This array of perspectives invites students to render, explore, and analyze their thoughts, feelings, and beliefs on compelling issues. This inquiry is guided through the practice of three common forms of critical thinking.

The explicit instruction of critical thinking demystifies academic inquiry. Three common forms of critical thinking are presented: the analysis of **multiple perspectives, cultural influences,** and **historical trends.** For some students, the consideration of multiple perspectives must begin with the more concrete recognition of various participants in a conflict or a debate. Once students learn to recognize who is involved—a participant—they next can pursue the less obvious question of what is believed—a perspective. Next the more abstract questions of when and why these beliefs are held can be posed so students learn to analyze historical trends and cultural influences.

Scope

The topics of the thematic chapters are diverse, engaging, and related. They include:

10. Family Forms and Roles
11. Education and Outcomes
12. Cities and Suburbs
13. Energy and Sustainability
14. Literacy and Technology

These chapters progress from concerns familiar to most students, like family and education, to other, more abstract ones, such as energy use and computer technologies. The later chapters will enhance student awareness of these seemingly less immediate but still pressing concerns.

The thematic chapters teach college-level critical thinking. The post-reading questions of each text include specific queries that are identified as involving the analysis of multiple perspectives, cultural influences, and historical trends. Through this explicit instruction of critical thinking and its repeated practice, no student will be left behind to sink; instead all are taught how to swim along the currents of academic inquiry.

These chapters can be used separately or jointly. After assigning one of the assignments in the first chapter, an instructor can shift students' attention to another topic, such as family or education. Or some chapters can be connected, such as when students examine social networks in Chapter 1, they can continue to the study of the effects of technology on literacy in Chapter 14. Or the growth of the suburbs in Chapter 12 can be connected to our great dependence on oil in Chapter 13.

The instructional chapters address the demands of college-level literacy. The subjects of these chapters include:

3. The Reading Process
4. The Writing Process
5. Writing Assignments
6. Argument and Rhetoric
7. Academic Honesty and Its Conventions
8. Research Methods and Motives
9. Professional Writing and Workplace Texts

Each of the thematic chapters includes direct references to these chapters so students are taught how to excel on the reading and writing tasks assigned. Thus, students will experience this textbook as an integrated whole; they will be able to connect the instructional chapters to the thematic content.

Reading Process: Students will learn many strategies of advanced literacy. Most college writing assignments depend on strong reading comprehension. This chapter includes revealing questions about student memories of learning to read and their most recent reading instruction. Most students will recall vivid moments of learning to read during elementary school, but they struggle to remember more advanced reading instruction. These memories will arouse the students' curiosity and prepare them to assess their current reading habits. Students then learn to engage in such active reading strategies as highlighting, annotating, and double-entry notes.

Writing Process: Students will learn *how* to write well. The writing process movement of Peter Elbow, Janet Emig, Donald Murray, and others is four decades old, but many students still have not learned its fundamental lesson of using a gradual, multifaceted method of writing. This chapter teaches the writing process explicitly and encourages students to vary their process according to their writing tasks. The invention, or prewriting, of ideas and phrases is taught as an initial activity that precedes the drafting of a difficult text. This chapter also emphasizes the later parts of the writing process by treating revising and editing as two distinct and equally important steps. Students will learn not only how to write well but also to vary their process according to their writing tasks.

Writing Assignments: Students will examine writing as a product as well as a process. One problem at the start of the writing process movement was the excessive shift from a product orientation to a focus on process. Students, however, need to learn about the ends as well as the means of writing. They must consider the different conventions of various kinds of writing as well as why they sometimes differ. For instance, students are asked to consider why the first person is used in most narratives but rarely employed in a lab report. There are good reasons for these different conventions so students will be encouraged to consider this discursive variation.

Argument and Rhetoric: Students will learn to appreciate and expand their persuasive powers. Starting with familiar examples, such as arguing over a weekend curfew, students will learn that rhetoric involves, as Aristotle stated, the discovery of the available means of persuasion. This chapter teaches students to recognize and employ the key concepts of rhetoric, such as the rhetorical triangle and the three rhetorical appeals. It also includes more contemporary concepts, such as Kenneth Burke's notion of identification, and these terms are taught through application to engaging examples.

Academic Honesty: Students are taught to appreciate the reasons for as well as the various forms of documentation. Rather than present rules, this chapter frames this issue as one of convention, a matter of accepted practices. Using the concepts of communal dependence and individual assertion, the conventions of paraphrase, quotation, attribution, citation, and elaboration are presented. Then various kinds of plagiarism are explained, and the debates over intellectual property and paper mill purchases are presented.

Research Methods and Motives: Students will learn that a research essay represents a culmination of much of their literacy instruction. The research essay is presented as a synthesis of other reading and writing activities, not an entirely separate and often dreaded assignment. Through references to other instructional chapters, students are taught, for example, to read their research sources critically and to advance an argument persuasively. Students also learn to engage in the full range of research activities. These activities are presented in a sequence, but alternate orders also are acknowledged. The headings within this chapter mean that different students (or their professors) can tailor this instruction to their preferred order of activities for completing research essays.

Professional Writing and Workplace Documents: Students are taught to expand their writing repertoires to include workplace texts. Some students who struggle with academic assignments flourish as writers of more practical documents, such as memos and brochures. This chapter breaks down the false dichotomy between academic and workplace writing by relating, for instance, the thesis and introduction of a standard essay to a memo's subject and executive summary. This chapter also presents very direct applications of key rhetorical concepts, such as writer, message, and audience.

Features

Every thematic chapter has the same features, and they include:

- **An engaging introduction**
- **A first freewrite on the students' initial beliefs**
- **A series of six historical and contemporary readings**
- **A headnote for each reading**
- **A set of eight post-reading questions**
- **Two visuals**
- **Two more freewriting possibilities**
- **Two final writing assignment sequences**

The first two chapters offer an explanation of these features. These brief explanatory comments are intended to demystify the reasons for the first freewrite on students' experiences, the headnotes preceding reading selections, the post-reading questions, and the rest of this textbook's apparatus. Some students will benefit, for instance, from learning about the value of reading a headnote before tackling a challenging text. This textbook takes the time to explain what seems obvious to a professor but might not be understood by some students.

The introduction and first freewrite of each chapter are designed to arouse student interest. The introduction can be used to promote an engaging class discussion of the two primary topics of each chapter. The twofold nature of each chapter means that they can be used in various ways; for example, in Chapter 10, students can focus on the legally accepted forms of American families today or the traditional roles of parents in these groups. The first freewrite is designed to elicit the initial beliefs of students on the chapter topic. These assumptions are not dismissed as derivative cultural reproductions or fixed as unalterable individual positions. Instead, they are treated as the starting points to be enriched, complicated, contradicted, and affirmed by the readings and the activities of each chapter.

The readings include historical, contemporary, and visual texts. The historical readings present other perspectives and help students gain some critical distance on their own viewpoints. The contemporary readings present multiple perspectives and immerse students in some of the ongoing debates of modern society. The visual texts reinforce the comprehension, analysis, and interpretation of the print texts in each chapter. These readings also range from literature and history to sociology and journalism so that students will encounter many of the texts they will be asked to read across the curriculum.

The headnotes and post-reading questions suggest interesting approaches to each reading selection. The headnotes include information about the author and the text's original publication so students can read rhetorically by considering speaker, audience, and message. The post-reading questions offer an array of approaches to each text. As explained in the first two chapters, the post-reading questions in every subsequent chapter progress from **Close Reading** questions to **Analytical Writing/Discussion** queries and then on to **Further Options**, which often suggest connections with other readings in the same or another chapter.

The activities in each chapter can be used in various ways. For example, one instructor could use some of the **freewriting possibilities** to enrich the thematic exploration. These freewrites, however, are placed in the middle and at the end of each chapter so another professor could skip over them to create a quicker unit using several readings and a compelling visual or two. Again with the **post-reading questions**, an instructor could assign only one or two to discuss a text briefly, whereas another teacher could use several to create a pre-reading discussion, more thorough textual analysis, and a post-reading writing assignment.

Every thematic chapter ends with two final assignment sequences. With these two final essay questions, a professor or a student can choose one assignment or the other to complete a chapter. For example, a student can write about equal opportunity or government policies in Chapter 12 on cities and suburbs. The final assignments ask students to assert their now more informed opinions, and they are taught to develop their essays gradually. Students are encouraged to analyze the final question as well as review various readings before starting to draft their responses. This gradual, process-oriented approach will enable more students to excel on their final essays.

The instructional chapters teach much more than "basic" skills. Each chapter relies on familiar examples and public issues to explain key concepts. These concepts are highlighted with bold lettering and are presented in a list for review at the end of each chapter. Every chapter also refers to several theorists so students learn that the academic study of reading, writing, and rhetoric has a long and rich tradition. As students become more capable readers, writers, and rhetoricians, they will be joining academic disciplines that date back to ancient Greece and are as current as today's bloggers.

The instructional chapters engage students in the construction of knowledge. Rather than talk *at* students, each chapter talks *with* students to scaffold their current knowledge into greater understanding. Addressing students as "you," these dialogic chapters make sophisticated concepts, theorists, and practices accessible to their intended audience. Knowledge, as John Dewey asserted, is not a brick; it cannot be handed to students. Genuine knowledge instead must be developed by learners engaged in instruction, application, and reflection, carefully guided by their teachers.

Structure

The first two thematic chapters provide an essential start to this textbook because each assignment introduces the critical reading, writing, and thinking abilities expected at college. A professor can choose to start with either Chapter 1 or 2, and each one explains the structure of the subsequent thematic chapters. These two chapters are shorter versions of the later thematic chapters so students can progress through one of them quickly. In addition to making explicit connections to the other instructional chapters, these two chapters can by connected by subject to the thematic chapters. For example, Chapter 1 can be connected to Chapter 14, and Chapter 2 can be linked to any one of the thematic chapters by asking students to focus their personal narratives on the upcoming chapter's theme, such as by assigning personal narratives on education, to create a smooth transition to Chapter 11.

The rest of a one-semester writing course can be devoted to a few of the thematic chapters and several of the instructional chapters. Students could engage in, for example, an in-depth study of energy and sustainability from Chapter 13, perhaps enriched by several readings on the growth of suburbs from Chapter 12. Or a professor could assign two chapters in two units of equal duration, such as by studying family in Chapter 10 and education in Chapter 11, as part of a semester-long examination of identity formation.

Students with two required writing courses can continue their examination of the chapter's themes, such as by adding Chapter 13 on cities and writing a research essay in a year-long study of identity formation. These synergies among various chapters mean that students will develop the depth of knowledge to be able to write well.

The instructional chapters can be tailored to meet the needs of a class or a particular subset of students. A professor can select from the seven chapters to provide the most appropriate instruction for large or small groups of students. This tailoring of instruction can continue within these chapters because headings divide each one into several discrete segments. Then specific instruction, for example, on active reading strategies or invention methods can be provided from Chapters 3 and 4. Or more advanced students can learn to employ the rhetorical appeals or evaluate online sources from Chapters 6 and 8.

E Supplement

For each thematic chapter, students can increase their knowledge through the additional texts suggested in the e supplement. Using the access code, students can find links to these online resources and learn more about the topics they want to pursue. For each chapter (1, 2, and 10–14), at least six additional readings and/or videos are provided. Professors can use some of these resources, especially the videos, to enrich their classroom instruction.

Acknowledgments

We want to thank Kathy McCormick, Sherry Horton, Charles Lipka, and other colleagues who helped develop some of the central concepts of this textbook. We also are indebted to Donna L. Coffey, Michelle Huston, Kerri Provost, Sue Aliberti, Irene Papoulis, Peter Elbow, Beth Richards, and Sally Terrell who supported our efforts and provided invaluable feedback. We benefited from the generous support of Angela Lampe, Katie Kotz, and Sara McGovern of Kendall Hunt.

Donald C. Jones
University of Hartford
Associate Professor, English
Ph.D. University of New Hampshire
Rhetoric and Writing

Kerry L. Beckford
Tunxis Community College
Instructor, English
M.F.A. Pine Manor College
Creative Nonfiction

NOTE TO STUDENTS

This textbook is designed to build upon the many language and literacy skills you already have developed in school and at home. These abilities will vary among you and your classmates. Some students may be confident and capable readers and writers, in part, because the language practices in their homes approximate the academic discourses of college study. Other students may be less confident readers or writers, but they already are very adept at critical thinking. They can analyze a controversial issue in a social studies class or a complex problem their team or family must solve. Still other students may have the rich linguistic skills of speaking another language and a heightened awareness of cultural differences. All of these diverse resources create a rich foundation for the students in a college writing course to continue their development. Using this textbook, you can develop further your critical reading, writing, and thinking skills—the abilities upon which so much of college success depends.

This textbook offers you both high expectations and clear explanations. Drawing upon your current knowledge and personal experiences, you will be expected to read challenging texts, write convincingly in various forms, and think critically about issues that are relevant to both your life and your studies. If you take a look at the table of contents, you will find that the themes of the reading chapters range from Family and Education and Cities to Sustainable Energy and Digital Literacy.

The thematic chapters will immerse you in contemporary discussions of compelling topics. You will be invited to explore your initial opinion because each chapter begins with an engaging introduction and a first writing activity. Then the main readings will encourage you to expand, enrich, complicate, and even contradict your first thoughts and feelings. The readings also range from personal memoirs and literature to historical and sociological texts, and this array of texts will prepare you for reading the diverse texts you will be assigned in other courses.

After each reading selection, you will find a set of questions that progress from close reading to analytical writing/discussion and on to further options. This progression is designed to elicit increasingly complex responses from you and your classmates. By reading some of the text selections and answering some of their post-reading questions, you will develop a more informed perspective. Then at the end of each chapter, each final assignment sequence asks you to assert your deeper understanding insightfully and persuasively. However, as the word "sequence" suggests, you will be taught how to develop this final paper gradually. In other words, you will not be left in a sink-or-swim situation; instead you will learn how to follow the currents of academic reading, writing, and thinking.

The final assignment sequences are just one of the many explanations provided so you will be able to fulfill the high expectations of this textbook. The first two chapters explain the format of the subsequent thematic chapters and encourage you to make connections to the instructional chapters. For example, for each reading, the purpose of the headnotes before each text and the format of the post-reading questions are explained. With the connections made to the instructional chapters, you will learn how to excel at college-level literacies.

The seven instructional chapters will teach you how to read critically, write insightfully, argue persuasively, cite properly, and much more. Each of these instructional chapters is divided into shorter segments with headings so you and your professor can tailor the use of this helpful information for your greatest benefit. The key concepts of each chapter are marked in bold and then listed at the end so you can review them. These chapters also refer to some of the key theorists because we want to show that you are becoming a member of an academic discipline as old as the study of rhetoric in ancient Greece and as current as the writing of today's bloggers.

Like this note, these chapters defy the usual prohibition against addressing the reader as "you." The second-person pronoun is used so *you* will be engaged in a dialogue about reading or research, drawing upon your current beliefs on how to read closely or research effectively. These chapters are designed to talk *with* you rather than *at* you.

You are reading the final copy of many drafts, and this book is the result of our work with literally hundreds of students. Although we can't quote or acknowledge every one, we want to thank the countless students who have contributed to our teaching and to this effort. We hope you will enjoy using this textbook.

Donald C. Jones,
University of Hartford

Kerry L. Beckford,
Tunxis Community College

Introductory Chapters

PART 1

Living in This Digital Era

Connecting the Thematic and Instructional Chapters

As explained in our Note for Students, we have created two versions of this initial chapter. In each one, we will explain some of the key features of this textbook, using these italicized comments. The first chapter focuses on reading as well as writing and offers a condensed version of the subsequent thematic chapters (10–14). The second chapter concentrates on writing and encourages you to draw more deeply on your own experiences. Both chapters present the critical reading, writing, and thinking abilities that will be developed in the rest of this book, and much of your college education will depend on these abilities. Each chapter starts with several quotations on the theme.

I sometimes suspect that we're seeing something in the Internet as significant as the birth of cities. It's something that profound and with that sort of infinite possibilities. It's really something new, it's a new kind of civilization.

—*William Gibson (1995)*

For college students, many of whom have moved away for the first time, the ability to stay in touch … with high school acquaintances … [minimizes] the distress caused by the loss of old friends.

—*Nicole B. Ellison, Charles Steinfield, and Cliff Lampe (2007)*

The idea of a world where everybody has a say and nobody goes unheard is deeply appealing. But what if all of the voices that are piling on end up drowning one another out?…. I don't want our young people aggregated, even by a benevolent social-networking site…. [I don't want them to] become a mob.

—*Jaron Lanier (2010)*

Texting has become like blinking: the average person, regardless of age, sends or receives about 400 texts a month. . . The average teen processes an astounding 3,700 texts a month. . . [This creates] a whole new mental environment, a digital state of nature where … few people will survive unscathed.

—*Tony Dokoupil (2012)*

Introduction

As factories grew and railroads started to cross the United States, Henry David Thoreau expressed a profound distrust of these nineteenth century developments; he declared:

> You never gain something but that you lose something.

Although most of us do not share Thoreau's skepticism of railroads and factories, we too may have our doubts about the latest technologies. We often judge the new through the framework of the old, such as when the first cars were seen as "horseless carriages." Then we struggle to appreciate the value of the latest advancement, while others may see only the good in the newest technologies. Thoreau, however, asked us to consider both the benefits and the drawbacks of these inventions.

Our ambivalent reactions to new technologies—deep skepticism or great expectations—continue today with the advances of computers and the Internet. As you probably know, the Internet was created as a U.S. Department of Defense project in the 1970s, and then this digital system was adopted quickly by scholars, advertisers, and many others. Now with the development of the more participatory forms of the Internet, such as social networks like Facebook, what is known as the Web 2.0 has been heralded as the greatest communication medium of all time. It has been praised for its potential to transform democracy and end oppression. However, one of the original developers of the Internet and the person who coined the term "virtual reality," Jaron Lanier now has grave doubts about Web 2.0 technologies. He considers the Internet to be a dangerous medium of conformity, social control, and mob mentality.

So much has changed in one generation. College students in the 1970s who were typing their papers on manual machines soon found themselves learning to use personal computers, e-mail messages, websites, and social networks during the next three decades. Many of these "digital immigrants" moved to these new electronic environs with some trepidation, while many of their children or grandchildren, who are the college students and young adults of the twenty-first century, take these new technologies for granted. They grew up with computers in their classrooms, and many have never used or even seen a manual typewriter. These "digital natives" may not have ever stopped to question their use of these technologies because they always have been present in their lives.

Whether you are a digital native or immigrant, this chapter asks you to consider these digital technologies carefully. You, however, will not be expected to condemn or accept every aspect of the computers and the Internet. Instead we will ask you to examine the particular advantages and the specific drawbacks of our reliance on the Web 2.0 and its related devices, such as cell phones and iPods. Your answers will develop from your experiences, the beliefs of your classmates, and the knowledge you gain from the reading selections of this chapter.

The readings, visual texts, freewriting, and final assignment of this chapter are designed to develop the reading and writing abilities necessary for college-level study. You will learn more about these college literacies through the connections made to the instructional chapters (3–9). After each of the readings, you will find a set of questions that also are presented in the thematic chapters (10–14). These post-reading questions are divided into close reading, analytical writing, and further option queries. Some questions will also teach you to engage three forms of critical thinking: examining multiple perspectives, analyzing cultural influences, and tracing historical trends. Writing responses to some of the post-reading questions and discussing more of them will prepare you to complete the formal essay of the final assignment. This final writing assignment will ask you to assert your own, more informed perspective on computers, the Internet, and social networks in particular. This chapter asks: **What do you think we have gained and lost as we live in this digital era?**

In Chapter 3 on the Reading Process, we explain that comprehending a challenging text involves a gradual construction of meaning (see p. 76 for more). This construction often draws on your prior knowledge of the topic so after the introduction of each chapter, we will ask you to pause and consider what you already know and feel about a subject. To elicit your thoughts and feelings, we will ask you to use what is known as freewriting. This technique is like letting yourself talk informally on the page. Rather than trying to compose complete sentences in perfect paragraphs, you can begin developing your thoughts more easily and "freely" by asserting them in quickly written phrases and often in a rambling order. Freewriting is not intended to be a final effort; instead it can be a very productive start of writing that can be revised and edited later (for more on freewriting, see p. 85 of Chapter 4).

Freewrite 1: Initial Impressions

Before you read about some young people going "unplugged" from the latest digital technologies and media, please consider your own experiences with, or your friends' use of, some of the following examples:

- Cell phones and text messages
- E-mail and instant messaging
- Blogs and tweets
- The Internet and websites
- Facebook and other social networks

Through discussion and/or freewriting, answer some of the following questions: Which of these digital media do you or your friends enjoy using the most? Which ones have ever become problematic for you or others? If you had to forego the use of some of these media, which ones would you be most or least likely to abandon and why?

In addition to considering your own initial thoughts and feelings on a topic, another effective strategy for the gradual construction of meaning is to preview a text. This skimming through a text before you read it closely can involve examining the title, reading the headnote on the author and the publication, and checking the headings in a longer text. This short reading does not include headings, but many of the texts in the subsequent chapters are divided into more manageable sections by their headings. For more on previewing a text and other reading comprehension strategies, see Chapter 3 on the Reading Process.

YOUNG AND UNPLUGGED: DIGITAL NATIVES IN RETREAT

by Bella English

In this story for a lifestyle section of the *Boston Globe*, Bella English presents a group of young adults who have decided to live without computers and the Internet at home. Although their reasons vary, all of them believe their lives are better without access to the Web and other digital technologies. English is a frequent contributor to the *Boston Globe*, and this article originally was published on April 25, 2009.

There's a television in Cara and Alan Kalf's Arlington living room, but it's stashed in a corner, its screen turned resolutely to the wall. It's used only for the occasional DVD - or as a favorite perch for the family cat.

As for music, the couple listens to record albums - remember those? - on a turntable or on one of the old jukeboxes Alan has restored. There's no Internet connection in the household. Cara has an iPod she uses only when traveling. She also has a cellphone: "But I don't always answer it. Sometimes I leave it in my coat pocket. I forget about it."

The couple aren't elderly Luddites terrified by technology. She's 27; he's 31. They are members of a small cohort: the young and unplugged. While their friends, relatives, and colleagues have every gadget known to mankind, the Kalfs have made a conscious decision not to blog, tweet, or instant message. They e-mail only when necessary. And they say they're better off without all that stuff.

According to the Pew Research Center's Internet & American Life Project, 96 percent of adults who work use the Internet, e-mail, or have a cellphone. Of workers and nonworkers alike, only 14 percent are "off the grid," with no online access or cellphone, and they tend to be older, low-income women. Nearly 40 percent of Americans use wireless mobile devices such as BlackBerrys. Almost a quarter of Americans use social networking sites such as Facebook.

Dr. Peter Whybrow, head of the Department of Psychiatric and Biobehavioral Sciences at UCLA's School of Medicine, says the preoccupation with high-tech tools is understandable. "By nature we are curious creatures and we love trinkets and novelties," he says. But the fast pace of technology has created a glut of gadgets - and a slight backlash.

"A small group of people are reacting to what is overload," Whybrow says. "They are fascinated by this initially… but after a while, they find it erodes time as opposed to saving time, and time is the only thing we've really got that is our own. If you become consumed by new technology and forget you are fundamentally creatures of the natural world, you do end up diminishing your life."

The Kalfs would agree with that. "We make it difficult for ourselves to access the Internet so we don't spend time just hanging out on it," says Cara, who teaches eighth-graders in Stoneham. Instead, they have more time for reading, for hobbies - and for each other.

"Worshiping at the church of the pixel comes at the expense of real-life experience," says Alan, who teaches biology at Lexington Christian Academy. His students are aghast at the fact that he doesn't watch TV. But by limiting their use of technology, they have freed up time for activities they love. She works on craft projects. He restores old jukeboxes, pinball machines, and furniture.

Not having Internet access can be inconvenient, but if they feel an urgent need for a computer, they go to her parents' house. They don't miss the sensory overload they had when they watched television and spent more time online. "It's not that I don't like doing these things," Alan says. "It's that I like them too much, and have a hard time setting limits. And then I feel frustrated at the end of the evening when I haven't accomplished or learned anything."

Instead, the couple listens to music and radio shows. They read a lot. They're involved in church activities. They cook from scratch and have friends over for dinner. They love board games. They play music: Cara the guitar, Alan piano, organ, and Dobro.

The Kalfs realize that few people their age limit their use of high-tech gadgets. "Sometimes friends think it's weird," Cara says. She recently told her brother-in-law that she was sure there were others like her and her husband. "Yeah, the Amish," he replied.

But there are a few others, and they're closer than Pennsylvania Dutch country. Anna Raassina and Stephen Seaward of Brookline have neither a television nor a microwave. Both 23, they gave up Facebook a couple of years ago. They don't IM. Because they're in college - senior philosophy majors at UMass-Boston - they must have computers, but once they finish, they plan to pack them away.

"I feel a little bit like a prisoner to it," Seaward says. "It's very useful - there's no denying that - but I think we also lose something. The more things become fast-paced, the less able we are to understand complex arguments, to concentrate on long artworks, like a symphony, or read a long novel."

As a demographic group, the couple would be considered "digital natives," or those in their mid-teens to mid-20s who have grown up in a highly technical, online world of video games, text messaging, websites, and social networking. But Seaward says his mother limited the time he spent using the Internet, watching television, and playing video games.

"I'm not a Luddite," he says. "I don't go off into the woods somewhere. I know how to do all this stuff." He had an iPod, but after it went through the washing machine in his pants pocket, he didn't replace it. He doesn't have a car; he takes the T. There's no microwave, he says, because "it doesn't do anything that my stove or oven don't do."

Rebecca Norman, 22, lives in an apartment with two other seniors at UMass-Amherst. They have no television. Norman sends texts only if it's urgent. She tried Facebook briefly but opted out. "I find the whole thing very voyeuristic," says Norman, who grew up in Newton. Instead, she writes letters - on stationery she makes - and uses the telephone to keep in touch. E-mail is reserved for academic or job-related missives.

Her friends wonder why she's not on Facebook. "They think I'm just trying to be a contrarian," she says, "but I tell them I'm not trying to make a statement. I just prefer not to have it in my life." She says she'd rather spend her spare time reading and working on art projects. Even her middle-age mother and her 80-year-old grandfather are on Facebook, as are her two sisters. But there's one advantage to not having it, she says: "My sisters have had to deal with whether or not to friend our mom."

Close Reading Questions

1. Cara Kalf acknowledges that she may be considered "weird." Why do you (or do you not) find it difficult to understand her decision to forego using a cell phone and the Internet?

2. What is a "digital native," and what vivid memories do you have of learning to use some digital media?

Analytical Writing/Discussion

3. Alan Kalf, Stephen Seaward, and Rebecca Norman offer different reasons for abandoning digital technologies. What are some of their reasons and whose reasons do you find most or least difficult to understand? (Multiple Perspectives)

4. Do you think the great number of Americans who use digital media make it more or less likely for a few to choose the opposite? Why? (Cultural Influences)

5. As you probably know, Stephen Seaward's reference to going "off into the woods" alludes to Henry David Thoreau's retreat to Walden Pond in the nineteenth century. Since the 1800s, do you think it has become easier or harder for an individual to refuse to conform to the majority and why? (Historical Trends)

Further Options

6. In this reading, Cara Kalf mentions the Amish and Stephen Seaward refers to a Luddite. Research one or both of these references. In what ways do you think they are similar to or different from the young and unplugged people today?

In the set of questions above, the close reading queries prompt you to notice key details and explore their significance. Your professor may ask you, or you may choose, to skim them before you start reading the text. The next set of questions for analytical writing and discussion encourage you to read even more critically and insightfully. Some questions are labeled as the three forms of critical thinking that are used throughout this book: multiple perspectives, cultural influences, and historical trends. Each of these forms is explained below.

Multiple Perspectives

The consideration of multiple perspectives asks you to distinguish several different viewpoints and examine what exact beliefs each perspective involves. This examination does not mean that you have to abandon your own perspective entirely, only that you seek to clarify and expand your initial position by being open, at least initially, to considering alternative viewpoints. For as the philosopher John Stuart Mill stated, "He who knows only his side of an argument knows little."

When faced with a question on multiple perspectives, such as number three for "Young and Unplugged," it may be tempting to object: "How can I know what they were thinking?" and it is true that we sometimes cannot be certain about others' viewpoints. Yet we often engage in just this kind of analysis, such as when we wonder, "What's up with her?" For instance, when a parent reacts with sudden anger or a friend is too subdued, we ask and often answer, "Where is he coming from?" Then we speculate not about a literal place but about his perspective, her viewpoint, someone's take on a situation. We engage in this kind of critical thinking not only in our daily lives but also in academic study. We try to interpret a literary character's assumptions or analyze a historical figure's motivations. We wonder, for example, does Huck Finn believe in racial inferiority as Twain's novel begins? Was the abolition of slavery Abraham Lincoln's primary motive for fighting the Civil War?

To consider various viewpoints, it may be helpful to create a chart such as the following one for "Young and Unplugged":

On the Use of Digital Technologies

96% of Americans

Cara Kalf

Alan Kalf

Stephen Seward

Rebecca Norman

What exactly does each person believe? It may be useful to rely on a quotation from the reading to help you determine each perspective.

Cultural Influences

As we examine other perspectives, we often start to wonder not only what was someone else thinking but why did he or she have this viewpoint. We will refer to this consideration as the analysis of cultural influences, meaning what beliefs support a viewpoint. Again you will be engaged in conjecture, but it is not just idle speculation because we can draw some reasonable inferences. For instance, most Americans like to emphasize their individuality, yet the cultural influences on this viewpoint can be analyzed. Literary characters like Huck Finn, comic book heroes such as Superman, and famous Americans like Sojourner Truth all stress the supposed uniqueness of our individual identities. Widespread cultural practices, such as every student being graded separately in most schools, also promote an individualistic concept of the self. In other words, our widespread belief in individualism, paradoxically, is promoted by many elements of American culture. As diagrammed below, many influences affect our development and help to shape our individual identities:

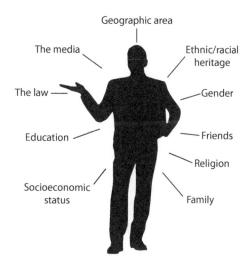

A famous theorist named Louis Althusser has explained an individual's relationship with society by stating that each person is "interpellated," is drawn into a culture. This process of interpellation begins when we are very young; long before we are aware that our attitudes about race, gender, wealth, pleasure, and so much more are being influenced by society. Yet these cultural influences do not necessarily control every individual, making each person develop the exact same perspective. Instead, as another important thinker named Michel Foucault has theorized, the many influences of a culture are complex and sometimes even contradictory. We, therefore, have some freedom of choice from among these many influences.

Question four on "Young and Unplugged" asks you to consider cultural influences. Perhaps the level of education influences some of these dissenters, such as when Stephen Seward worries about being less able to "understand a complex argument, to concentrate on… a symphony or read a long novel." The opinion of Rebecca Norman's friends that she is "trying to be a contrarian" may make it harder for her to resist digital media. Or do you think it makes her resistance more appealing?

Historical Trends

Another form of critical thinking common to much of academic inquiry is the analysis of historical trends. As the term suggests, this analysis examines how a perspective changes or remains the same over time. For example, some typical academic questions include Does Huck's perspective on Jim change as they journey down the Mississippi River? Or in *The Scarlet Letter*, does Hester remain steadfast in her love for the minister? During the Civil War, did President Lincoln ever waver in his conviction that our nation could not be divided? Several of the people featured in this reading also place their perspectives in a historical context by referring to the Luddites, Henry David Thoreau ("I don't go off into the woods somewhere"), and the Amish. Understanding the continuity of today's "young and unplugged" viewpoint with past critics of technology can both strengthen their position and reveal some of its weaknesses.

One way to analyze historical trends is to draw a timeline and add several perspectives over time:

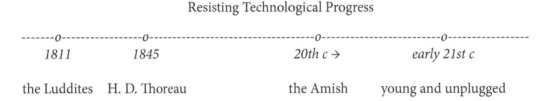

Resisting Technological Progress

```
-------o-----------------o----------------------------------o-----------------------o-----------------
  1811              1845                                  20th c →              early 21st c

  the Luddites   H. D. Thoreau                        the Amish        young and unplugged
```

Then, as reading question 5 asks, some of the similarities and differences among these viewpoints can be analyzed.

The Further Options questions invite you to make connections between readings, to apply certain principles of rhetoric, or to engage in some helpful research. Since the Further Options question above suggests some analysis of historical trends, let us offer some sample research with the next two short readings.

THE LUDDITES

by Stephen E. Jones

> In the following reading, the violent acts and desperate motives of the Luddites are explained. This movement broke out in 1811 in England in response to new technologies for the manufacture of cloth, which had been produced by skilled tradesmen. The reading comes from *Against Technology: From the Luddites to Neo-Luddism* by Steven E. Jones, a book published in 2006.

The Luddites of 1811 to 1812 smashed machines. They did so in protest and to sabotage specific owners' looms and finishing shops. They did *not* voluntarily give up technologies of convenience or status, as do many neo-Luddites today. They rarely issued anything like philosophical statements. Mostly they wrote threatening letters and composed celebratory ballads. They picked up sledgehammers and other lowly tools as well as guns and other weapons, then marched through the darkness to sabotage the machines that promised increased productivity in their trades. They did so in order to make a point and to stop the use of the machines. Luddite direct action can be seen as taking from the relatively rich in order to give back (or keep) what was due to the workers (many of whom were poor). For doing this, the Luddites faced execution by hanging (and indeed some of them were hanged in the end) and they became legendary, their odd name eventually becoming a parable for anti-technology ideas and feelings as well as actions.

The name Luddite seems to have first been used in print in December 1811, in a newspaper account in the *Nottingham Review* about a group of protesting stocking-knitters in Nottinghamshire, who were presumably already calling themselves Luddites or at least naming themselves followers of Ned Ludd or General Ludd. Soon the term was also adopted to describe textile workers in Yorkshire and Lancashire, who began to organize themselves, to act in bands or secret groups, in order to take direct action against those they accused of violating the fair and customary practices of their trade, sometimes putting them out of work and generally profiting from changes in their social and economic conditions by deploying new kinds of machinery....

With their faces blackened or wearing masks like bandits, sometimes in women's clothing or other forms of disguise, and armed with sledgehammers, axes, pikes, and, on occasion, guns, the Luddites showed up at houses to seize arms (for further raids) or to destroy a machine-owner's property and goods. On occasion they harmed but more commonly merely threatened the owners or their families. Their signature act was to break "obnoxious," offending "frames" — kinds of knitting or cloth-finishing machines that, while efficient in terms of labor and costs, were making many of their jobs redundant and producing inferior cloth, thus harming their reputations and the reputation of their skilled trade as a whole. They were protecting their trade — which, more than a job, was a culture, an economy, and a group of coworkers, a labor "gang," their social identity in the community as well as a technique or set of practices.

Their actions, which became known as "ludding," spread during 1812, moving from the stocking knitters in Nottingham to skilled cloth-finishers (or croppers, those who cropped the nap of the cloth to make it smooth and ready to sell) in the West Riding of Yorkshire and then to other workers elsewhere in the North of England. An organized network may have been behind this expansion, or unconnected groups may have copied the example and name of the first Luddites. The net result was perceived as a movement or conspiracy, with only the degree of conscious organization in question. Luddism increased for a year or so, was squelched by government prosecutions and hangings, and then resurged briefly in 1816 to 1817.

THE AMISH

by Jamie Sharp

In the following reading, Jamie Sharp explains the religious and practical reasons that the Amish avoid many modern technologies. Located in Pennsylvania and many other parts of the country, the Amish live separately from mainstream Americans, though their lives often are intertwined with other citizens through commercial ventures. Sharp wrote this text in 1999, while he still was a college student.

FIGURE 1 An Amish buggy.

With their plain style of dress, straw hats, suspenders, and buggies, it is not difficult to see why so many of us perceive the Amish as having a hatred of technology. In reality, the Amish do not despise technology and even have incorporated many technologies into their culture. Other technologies, however, have been rejected completely or used within certain limitations as a result of deep religious beliefs and the rules that guide and maintain their distinct culture…. The most important factor of Amish life is Gelassenheit, or submission to the will of God…. By giving up individuality and any thought of selfishness, they embrace God's will by serving others and submitting to Him.

The Amish feel that Gelassenheit should permeate every facet of their existence, and even be apparent in their material possessions. Consequently, they will only selectively use modern technologies…. The Amish believe that using lanterns and the buggies typifies their lifestyle of simplicity and modesty. Any technology that does not uphold the Gelassenheit principles is banned from use. Electricity is seen as a connection with the outside world and violates the Amish principle of separation from society. Electricity also promotes the use of household items, such as the television, that allow the outside, "English," values of sloth, luxury, and vanity to infiltrate the household. Automobiles are not often used because they degrade the Gelassenheit principle of a small, close-knit community. The Amish fear, with good reason, that these modern transportation technologies will cause them to spread apart, much like most modern American families. Also, the Amish fear that the automobile will promote competition among themselves. They worry that the car will become a status symbol and promote vanity, which is in direct violation of the Gelassenheit value of modesty. The telephone is banned from the household because, much like the automobile, it promotes a separation of community. Instead of taking a carriage or walking to a friend's house, the Amish feel that they would be tempted to simply stay home and speak on the phone. In order to uphold Gelassenheit, many modern technologies have been banned from regular use.

Rather than provide a full range of questions, let's concentrate on historical trends in these two readings:

Analytical Writing/Discussion

1. Why do you think the current rejection of digital media can or cannot be connected to the Luddites or the Amish? What details of these earlier examples suggest a strong similarity with or a significant difference from Cara and Alan Kalf or the other unplugged young adults?

2. By placing the current rejection of digital media in a historical context, what strengths or weaknesses of this position do you believe are revealed?

3. Did some of this historical context change your own viewpoint? If so, how? *Note that your perspective too can be analyzed as changing over time or remaining the same.*

Each thematic chapter (10–14) will consist of three historically focused readings and then three more contemporary ones. Before we turn to three additional readings to present an array of contemporary perspectives, we will offer another opportunity for freewriting.

Freewrite 2: Facebook Users

Let's tap into your knowledge of Facebook, or if you are not one of its users, let you develop more understanding of this social networking site. Using either your own Facebook page plus those of your "friends" or by asking an acquaintance to show you some Facebook pages, what do you think are some of the typical characteristics of Facebook pages? You may want to focus this design description on a particular group, such as certain students at your college or a group based on a particular interest. What do you think these design features and content suggest about these users of Facebook?

Below is the first of three contemporary readings on cultural influences. It, however, is not only a text that originates from a print source; instead it includes one of the many other kinds of texts found online: a transcript of a radio interview of a writer, which is followed by an excerpt from the author's book (as found online). As you read this text, you may want to try reading with a pen in hand and writing comments in the margins; for more on annotating a text, see p. 78 of Chapter 3.

HAMLET'S BLACKBERRY: TO SURF OR NOT TO SURF?

by National Public Radio

> The following reading combines a 2010 National Public Radio report on William Powers and an excerpt from his book titled *Hamlet's BlackBerry: A Practical Philosophy for Building a Good Life in the Digital Age.* In this transcript and excerpt, Powers traces the problem of information overload into the past and considers the advantages as well as the drawbacks of our connected lives. Before his book, Powers first wrote a 75-page essay titled, "Hamlet's Blackberry: Why Paper Is Eternal," which was presented and published as part of the Discussion Paper Series at Harvard University. For an excerpt from that essay, see p. 354 in Chapter 14 of this textbook.

Do you find yourself checking Facebook as soon as you wake up in the morning? Do you answer e-mails on your Blackberry while surfing the Web? Even as you read this article, is your right index finger twitching on the mouse, just itching to click on something new?

If so, welcome to the 21st century. Without even realizing it, we've signed up for a life in which we're all connected, all the time. Whether or not this is a good thing is the subject of *Hamlet's Blackberry*, a new book by William Powers based on an essay he penned in 2007.

Early in the book, Powers describes a scene that should strike many as familiar: He is standing at a crosswalk in the middle of Manhattan, alongside five or eight other people—all of whom are staring intently at some digital device.

"Here I was in New York, the most fantastic city in the world—so much to look at, to see and hear, and everybody around me essentially wasn't present," he tells NPR's Mary Louise Kelly. "These gadgets are wonderful, and they do fantastic stuff for us all day long, but to miss out on your surroundings all the time, which I think we increasingly do—I really question that."

But Powers' book is not a Luddite manifesto. The writer may question the way we use our gadgets, but he certainly doesn't condemn it. ("With a few keystrokes, I can bring up an old manuscript from the British Museum. That is miraculous," he says.) He does, however, recognize the downside of constantly being flooded with new information—or what he calls the "conundrum of connectedness."

"We don't have any gaps, any breaks in which to make sense of it; do something new, creative with it; enjoy it," he says.

Among the things that suffer from our overconnectedness, Powers says, are relationships.

"If we're constantly toggling between people on Facebook and texts and all these new ways of connecting all day long, and we never have a sustained connection, it's not really connectedness," Powers says. "It's sort of the opposite of connectedness."

His aim in *Hamlet's Blackberry* is to help teach people how to connect more wisely. To that end, Powers looked to the past, where he found several precedents to both the current information age and the anxiety that has come with it.

The Roman philosopher Seneca, for example, was plagued by the connectedness that came along with living in the capital of a vast empire.

"There was noise and there was business," Powers says. "There was more work, there was paperwork—it was papyrus work at the time, but it was paperwork. There was bureaucracy. There was just a lot of information incoming."

Another major figure Powers examines actually developed his own strategies for coping with overstimulation. In William Shakespeare's *Hamlet*, the titular Danish prince is visited by the ghost of his murdered father, who informs Hamlet that his murderer is none other than Hamlet's uncle.

"Hamlet is so overwhelmed by this news, this new piece of information, that he's not sure what to do with it," Powers says.

So Hamlet reaches into his pocket and pulls out his "tables," an object Powers describes as a sort of proto-electronic planner. Powers says that in the Elizabethan Age, tables were a new gadget designed to help people bring order to their lives.

"It was basically an erasable, plaster-like surface inside of a little booklet," he says. "You could write notes during the day and then wipe them away clean at night."

In other words, even denizens of the late 16th century had a method for dealing with information overload.

But how are we of the 21st century supposed to cope with that same problem?

In the book excerpt that accompanies the radio transcript online, Powers examines the advantages as well as the problems of our digital connections:

From *Hamlet's Blackberry*

Today we're always just a few taps away from millions of other people, from endless information and stimulation. Family and friends, work and play, news and ideas—sometimes it seems everything we care about has moved to the digital room. So we spend our days there, living in this new ultra-connected way.

We've been at it for about a decade now, and it's been thrilling and rewarding in many ways. When the whole world is within easy reach, there's no end of things to see and do. Sometimes it feels like a kind of a paradise.

However, there's a big asterisk to life in this amazing place. We've been doing our best to ignore it, but it won't go away. It comes down to this: We're all busier. Much, much busier. It's a lot of work managing all this connectedness. The e-mails, texts, and voicemails; the pokes, prods, and tweets; the alerts and comments; the links, tags, and posts; the photos and videos; the blogs and vlogs; the searches, downloads, uploads, files, and folders; feeds and filters; walls and widgets; tags and clouds; the usernames, passcodes, and access keys; pop-ups and banners; ringtones and vibrations. That's just a small sample of what we navigate each day in the room. By the time you read this there will be completely new modes of connecting that are all the rage. Our tools are fertile, constantly multiplying.

As they do, so does our busyness. Little by little, our workdays grow more crowded. When you carry a mobile device, all things digital (and all people) are along for the ride. Home life is busier too. Much of what used to be called free time has been colonized by our myriad connective obligations, and so is no longer free.

It's easy to blame all this on the tools. Too easy. These tools are fantastically useful and enrich our lives in countless ways. Like all new technologies, they have flaws, but at bottom they can't make us busy until we make them busy first. We're the prime movers here. We're always connected because we're always connecting.

Beyond the sheer mental workload, our thoughts have acquired a new orientation. Of the two mental worlds everyone inhabits, the inner and the outer, the latter increasingly rules. The more connected we are, the more we depend on the world outside ourselves to tell us how to think and live. There's always been a conflict between the exterior, social self and the interior, private one. The struggle to reconcile them is central to the human experience, one of the great themes of philosophy, literature, and art. In our own lifetime, the balance has tilted decisively in one direction. We hear the voices of others, and are directed by those voices, rather than by our own. We don't turn inward as often or as easily as we used to.

In one sense, the digital sphere is all about differentiating oneself from others. Anyone with a computer can have a blog now, and the possibilities for self-expression are endless. However, this expression takes place entirely within the digital crowd, which frames and defines it. This makes us more reactive, our thinking contingent on others. To be hooked up to the crowd all day is a very particular way to go through life.

For a long time, there was an inclination to shrug all of this off as a mere transitional issue, a passing symptom of technological change. These are early days, we tell ourselves. Eventually, life will calm down and the inner self will revive. There's a basic wisdom in this hopeful view. It's never a good idea to buy into the dark fears of the techno-Cassandras*, who generally turn out to be wrong. Human beings are skillful at figuring out the best uses for new tools. However, it can take a while. The future is full of promise, but we have to focus on the present, how we're living, thinking, and feeling right now.

Close Reading Questions

1. What scene from New York City troubles Powers? Why do you (or do you not) share his concern with this example of our connected lives?

2. What exactly was Hamlet's table, and how did it function like a preelectronic planner or Blackberry?

3. To avoid the label of a Luddite, Powers acknowledges some of the benefits as well as the drawbacks of our constantly connected lives. According to Powers, what are some of these positives and negatives? (Multiple Perspectives)

Analytical Writing/Discussion

4. What examples from the past does Powers relate to our problem of connectedness? Do these two examples from the past make our current problem seem more or less urgent to you and why? (Historical Trends)

5. According to Powers, what effect is our constant connectedness having on our way of thinking, our sense of self? Why do you agree or disagree with Powers that this effect probably will be temporary? (Cultural Influences)

Further Options

6. As explained in Chapter 6 on Rhetoric, identification involves a writer trying to relate to an audience's experiences and beliefs. Once this identification has been made, an audience is more likely to accept a writer's argument. Does the first paragraph of this interview transcript ("Do you find yourself checking Facebook . . ?") create this identification with you? If so, does this identification make you more willing to be persuaded by Powers? (For more on identification, see p. 103 in Chapter 6.)

---

*In Greek mythology, Cassandra is a prophet of doom who predicted the downfall of her city during the Trojan War.

WHY I DESPISE FACEBOOK

by Tom Hodgkinson

Tom Hodgkinson acknowledges the public popularity and the economic success of Facebook, but he remains skeptical of its effects on its users. This British writer instead promotes a more relaxed attitude toward life, such as in the magazine *The Idler*, for which he serves as the editor and a frequent contributor. This essay originally appeared on January 18, 2008 in the English newspaper titled *The Guardian* so some British spellings are used.

There is no way of denying that as a business, [Facebook] is pure mega-genius. Some net nerds have suggested that its $US15 billion valuation is excessive, but I would argue that if anything that is too modest. Its scale really is dizzying, and the potential for growth is virtually limitless. "We want everyone to be able to use Facebook," says the impersonal voice of Big Brother on the website. I'll bet they do. It is Facebook's enormous potential that led Microsoft to buy 1.6% for $US240 million. A recent rumour says that Asian investor Lee Ka-Shing, said to be the ninth richest man in the world, has bought 0.4% of Facebook for $US60 million.

The creators of the site need do very little [but] fiddle with the program. In the main, they simply sit back and watch as millions of Facebook addicts voluntarily upload their ID details, photographs and lists of their favourite consumer objects. Once in receipt of this vast database of human beings, Facebook then simply has to sell the information back to advertisers, or, as [Mark] Zuckerberg puts it in a recent blog post, "to try to help people share information with their friends about things they do on the web." And indeed, this is precisely what's happening. On November 6 [2007], Facebook announced that 12 global brands had climbed on board. They included Coca-Cola, Blockbuster, Verizon, Sony Pictures and Conde Nast. All trained in marketing spin of the highest order, their representatives made excited comments along the following lines:

"With Facebook Ads, our brands can become a part of the way users communicate and interact on Facebook," said Carol Kruse, vice-president, global interactive marketing, the Coca-Cola Company.

"We view this as an innovative way to cultivate relationships with millions of Facebook users by enabling them to interact with Blockbuster in convenient, relevant and entertaining ways," said Jim Keyes, Blockbuster chairman and CEO. "This is beyond creating advertising impressions. This is about Blockbuster participating in the community of the consumer so that, in return, consumers feel motivated to share the benefits of our brand with their friends."

"Share" is Facebookspeak for "advertise." Sign up to Facebook and you become a free walking, talking ad[vertisement] for Blockbuster or Coke, extolling the virtues of these brands to your friends. We are seeing the commodification of human relationships, the extraction of capitalistic value from friendships.

Now, by comparison with Facebook, newspapers, for example, begin to look hopelessly outdated as a business model. A newspaper sells advertising space to businesses looking to sell stuff to their readers. But the system is far less sophisticated than Facebook for two reasons. One is that newspapers have to put up with the irksome expense of paying journalists to provide the content. Facebook gets its content for free. The other is that Facebook can target advertising with far greater precision than a newspaper. Admit on Facebook that your favourite film is *This Is Spinal Tap*, and when a Spinal Tap-esque movie comes out, you can be sure that they'll be sending ads your way.

It's true that Facebook recently got into hot water with its Beacon advertising program. Users were notified that one of their friends had made a purchase at certain online shops; 46,000 users felt that this level of advertising was intrusive, and signed a petition called "Facebook! Stop invading my privacy!" to say so. Zuckerberg apologised on his company blog. He has written that they have now changed the system from "opt-out" to "opt-in." But I suspect that this little rebellion about being so ruthlessly commodified will soon be forgotten: after all, there was a national outcry by the civil liberties movement when the idea of a police force was [made] in Britain in the mid-19th century.

Futhermore, have you Facebook users ever actually read the privacy policy? It tells you that you don't have much privacy. Facebook pretends to be about freedom, but isn't it really more like an ideologically motivated virtual totalitarian regime? [Zuckerberg] and the rest have created their own country, a country of consumers.

Now, you may, like [Zuckerberg] and the other new masters of the cyberverse, find this social experiment tremendously exciting. Here at last is the enlightenment state longed for since the Puritans of the 17th century sailed away to North America, a world where everyone is free to express themselves as they please, according to who is watching. National boundaries are a thing of the past and everyone cavorts together in freewheeling virtual space. Nature has been conquered through man's boundless ingenuity. Yes, and you may decide to send [Facebook] investor [Peter] Thiel all your money, and certainly you'll be waiting for the public [stock] flotation of the unstoppable Facebook.

Or you might reflect that you don't really want to be part of this heavily funded program to create an arid global virtual republic, where your own self and your relationships with your friends are converted into commodities on sale to giant global brands. You may decide that you don't want to be part of this takeover bid for the world.

For my own part, I am going to retreat from the whole thing, remain as unplugged as possible, and spend the time I save by not going on Facebook doing something useful, such as reading books. Why would I want to waste my time on Facebook when I still haven't read Keats' *Endymion*? And when there are seeds to be sown in my own backyard? I don't want to retreat from nature, I want to reconnect with it. Damn air-conditioning! And if I want to connect with the people around me, I will revert to an old piece of technology. It's free, it's easy and it delivers a uniquely individual experience in sharing information: it's called talking.

Close Reading Questions

1. Why does Hodgkinson consider Facebook to be an incredibly successful business? According to the author, what exactly it Facebook selling and to whom?

2. Why does Hodgkison think Facebook is much more effective at selling advertisements than newspapers? How does the comparison of Facebook with newspapers change (or not) your own thinking about the purpose of each one?

3. Why does Hodgkinson consider November 6, 2007 to be a crucial day in the development of Facebook? Why do you agree or disagree with Hodgkinson's critique of this moment? (Historical Trends)

Analytical Writing/Discussion

4. Why do you or do you not share Hodgkinson's concerns about the privacy policies of Facebook? What exactly are his concerns and how do you react to them?

5. In his final paragraphs, Hodgkinson presents two perspectives on Facebook. Which one do you find to be more accurate and why? (Multiple Perspectives)

Further Options

6. Others, such as the Luddites and the Amish, resisted what they considered to be "new" technologies. Why does Hodgkinson's resistance strike you as similar to or different from that of the Luddites and the Amish? For more on these two groups, see pp. 10–12 of this chapter. (Cultural Influences)

The last question above asks you to make a connection between two readings, and this synthesis of sources is a key feature of college-level reading and writing in many courses. Each thematic chapter will contain two visuals and one will be a chart for your consideration. What do you think is especially noteworthy in the growth of Facebook?

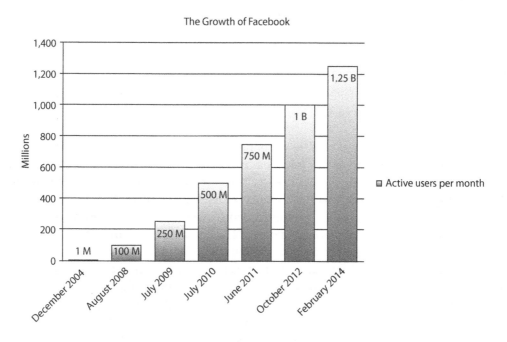

FIGURE 2   The Growth of Facebook

The last reading is a longer text so it includes headings that you can use to preview the text. The post-reading questions include a full set of eight queries: three close reading, two analytical writing, and two further questions. A set of eight questions will follow the readings in the subsequent thematic chapters (10–14), yet we do not expect your professor will assign every one. Instead by answering a few and discussing others, you will be able to engage in a thorough examination of each reading.

FACEBOOK: WHAT'S NOT TO LIKE?

by Robert Lane Greene

In this final reading of this chapter, Robert Lane Greene examines recent trends of this social network and ponders the future of Facebook. Greene is a correspondent for *The Economist*, a weekly paper for business news and international politics as well as the author of *You Are What You Speak*. It seems appropriate that this reading was published online on the site More Intelligent Life on December 30, 2012 (http://moreintelligentlife.com).

What is Facebook, anyway? The most obvious point of historical comparison is the social networks that preceded it. First there was Friendster, the flirt-and-forget site of the first half of the 2000s. Then everyone dumped Friendster for MySpace, and MySpace was bought by News Corp for $580m. Its value soared to $12 billion, and the received wisdom was that MySpace would take over the world. Then it didn't, and News Corp sold it for $35m, because someone else had finally got social networking right. Started by Mark Zuckerberg in 2004, Facebook went from a Harvard dorm room to the rest of teenage America's bedrooms to hundreds of millions of people all around the world—even parents and grandparents. Along the way, Facebook has fuelled revolutions in the Middle East, and inspired an Oscar-winning movie. Other social networks can only try to build out from the few niches it hasn't already filled. Facebook is the undisputed champion of the world.

But the real comparison is not with other social networks. To give real credit to its achievement today and its ambitions for the future, it can only be said that Facebook's true competitor is the rest of the entire internet.

The internet allows three things, broadly speaking: access to content (video, music, things to read), self-expression (blogs, Twitter) and communication (e-mail, chat, Skype). Facebook competes with it on all these fronts. By one estimate, one minute in every seven spent online, anywhere in the world, is spent on Facebook. To express themselves, users have Status Updates. For content, they can find photos, videos, music, news stories, recipes, book reviews and much more. And for communication, of course, there are your friends and Friends. More and more, the point of Facebook is to do almost anything you would do anyway, but with your friends, online. Facebook is an internet within the internet, so dominant that both it and other technology companies are realising that it is far easier to join forces than to fight.

Take Spotify. This Sweden-based company is on the way to being the first music-sharing service getting right what Napster and others once tried and failed: to get people to pay small amounts to listen to music online, or to put up with ads. What do you do about Spotify, if you're Facebook? Time spent on Spotify could drag users away. So Facebook's approach is make Spotify users Facebook users. If your cousin Bob is on Spotify, you and his 234 other Friends can see that he is listening to "Somebody That I Used to Know," and listen along if they want to. Far from competing with Facebook, Spotify enhances it—and the other way round.

Twitter, with its micro-blogging, would seem to be a direct Facebook competitor. It is smaller, with 383m users in January 2012, but growing faster, and its use by celebrities and journalists, plus its role in the Arab uprisings, has made it the social network to watch. So how does Facebook feel about Twitter? "We shouldn't be competing with almost any of these people." So says Andrew ("Boz") Bosworth, Facebook's 30-year-old director of engineering. Barrel-chested and talking a mile a minute, Bosworth is visibly enthusiastic one second, cheerfully irritated with what he sees as misconceptions the next: his catchphrase seems to be "I don't want to tell you what to write, but if I were writing your article…"

Bosworth is not only happy about working with the likes of Twitter, he is exuberant. He cites Facebook's partnership with Skype: "You wanna specialise in video calling? Awesome!" But you and your company would be well advised to work with a certain platform that begins with "Face" and ends with "book." "If you're a start-up today, you can leverage the world's largest social network. For free. Why would you want to do the really hard thing, which is recreate a social network, when what you can do is focus on the technology you want to build, and use the one that already exists?"

The prospect of access to Facebook's billion has brought in ever more partners. Pinterest, an online pinboard growing faster than Facebook or Twitter did in their infancy, is a partner. So is GoodReads, where people can talk about the books they've read and want to read. Online gaming, facilitated by Facebook, helped power a four-year-old games company, Zynga, to a $1 billion ipo in July 2011. Facebook's offer to potential competitors is "grow with us, not at our expense."

This highlights a key feature of Facebook: it is the anti-Apple. Apple's products are designed down to their molecules so that you never forget who made them. The colours, fonts and distinctive shapes give Apple an ever-present personality. This reflects the top-down, "we know best" culture cultivated for decades by the brilliant authoritarian Steve Jobs.

Facebook could not be more different. "'Authority' is just not a word here," Bosworth says with a laugh. "It's not a thing we use." Of course if Mark Zuckerberg, the billionaire 27-year-old founder, has an idea, others will listen. But so will they listen to the junior-most developer who wants to make something new. One forum for this is the Hackathon. The boombox that interrupted my interview was, I later heard, carried by Roddy Lindsay, a Facebook developer, marching around the halls in a cape for the traditional Hackathon commencement. At the Hackathon, developers join together under one rule: you cannot work on what you normally work on. If that sounds like Google, with its 20% rule, this is a lot more raucous. They fire up new ideas, toss out old ones, collaborate, blow off steam and make things. Most won't work. Some will: the Spotify app that allows users to listen along with their friends came from a Hackathon. The culture of "why not this too?" keeps the giant growing and constantly changing.

In contrast with its spectacular power, Facebook shows an unintimidating face to the world. The bland blue design is more like a default blog template than the biggest website ever. The plain lower-case logo looks almost sorry to bother you. Tiffani Jones Brown, who oversees the writing of much of the text on the site, says that its personality must be nothing more than "simple, human, clear and consistent." The music app is called…Music. The photos app is called Photos. The message service is called Messages. Everything on the site is to be written so that an 11-year-old can read it—even though Facebook likes its users to be at least 13.

All this is by design. Bosworth says "You didn't come to Facebook because we're so awesome. You came to Facebook because your friends are awesome. They're doing interesting things and you want to know about it. Time that you're spending conscious of Facebook as a thing probably means we made a mistake." The obvious contrast, again, is with the even bigger company up the road. "Your Apple product might actually still be fun without your friends. Facebook is just the most boring product on the internet without your friends."

A Global Community

Whether this is naivety or modesty, the world is certainly not bored by Facebook. It is not merely an empty place where friends come to hang out, or an open platform other companies can plug their technologies into. Facebook's reach can be seen in raw numbers: the 850m users, the 8 billion chat messages a day, the billion photos uploaded every four days. But it is not just a technological marvel, a youth movement or a business story. After just eight years of existence, Facebook is the biggest social phenomenon since the telephone.

The Facebook community looks more and more like the world itself. Technology has traditionally been seen as a male preserve. Programming, gaming, message boards, the early days of blogging, all call to mind a male nerd in a black T-shirt. But Facebook was at near gender parity from the start. Now, female users write 60% of comments and share 70% of the pictures. Among American Facebookers, 18% of females update their status at least once a day, according to the Pew Internet & American Life Project, while just 11% of males do so. Women and girls are simply keener social networkers than men and boys. This makes Facebook's decision to keep its whizz-bang technology out of users' faces not just a clever bit of design, but a canny strategic decision.

Which they increasingly do, not just across the gender divide but around the world. Around 80% of Facebook users are outside the United States and Canada, and this while being banned in China. (For a point of comparison, about 63% of iPhones were sold outside America in the last quarter of 2011.) Russia and Vietnam are among the rare countries where another social network is bigger. Despite its American DNA, Facebook was so prominent in the Arab spring that when Wael Ghonim, the Egyptian activist whose imprisonment became a cause célèbre, was asked where the next revolution would be, he replied: "Ask Facebook." Tiffani Jones Brown says that one of her most complicated jobs is keeping Facebook's "clear, human, simple" tone across the many different languages and cultures Facebook is reaching.

Finally, Facebook is growing older—and not just one year older each year, either. As the habit spreads upwards from kids to their parents, the median age has steadily climbed, although Facebook prefers not to say by how much. This is a challenge for its designers, who want to present a simple experience to new users, while also appealing to those who expect their favourite sites to be buzzy and innovative. As growth continues to "the second billion" Bosworth breezily mentions, Facebook will be used on slower devices with slower connections, making it harder than ever for it to work equally well for everyone.

As Facebook reaches further into every corner of our lives, it also engenders confusion, annoyance and concern. The litany of complaints is familiar. "People are going to be so busy writing about their lives that they forget to live them," as a friend complains to me, is perhaps the most typical. This "Facebook isn't real life" trope spans many sub-complaints. The word "friend" is being devalued by having hundreds upon hundreds of "Friends." Users' pages are not a genuine portrait, but a careful selection of photos and updates that amount to an illusion. People should be enjoying their vacation, not taking hundreds of pictures of it and putting them on Facebook. People should spend more time curling up with real books, not waste time bragging about what they read via GoodReads. The birthday messages that pour in because Facebook told your "Friends" it was your birthday are no substitute for real friends who actually remember. And so on.

Facebook is now competing with older and older technologies. The voice call over the telephone is a competitor, says Gabe Trionfi, a user-experience researcher for Facebook. But he sees no problem with this. He leans over his laptop to perform a search of public posts for "Feeding 2am." This produces a list of posts of women nursing their children in the middle of the night, Facebooking on their phones with their free hand. This is something no one would have done on the phone before. Mothers, with babies to their breasts, are reaching out to their sisters. Could anything be more human?

Another piece of evidence that Facebook is no longer just an internet company is another old technology it is challenging: the car. Ford, which participated in a Hackathon with Facebook, is trying to integrate it into its cars via Ford Sync, its hands-free entertainment and communication system. And well might the car try to catch up with the social network. American teenagers are no longer getting drivers' licences as early as they once did. Getting a licence immediately after your 16th birthday used to be nearly automatic for those in car-owning households; in 1988, 45% of 16-year-olds got a licence. By 2008, that number had fallen to just 30%. The rising cost of petrol and insurance will have played some role in this, but surely Facebook has too: it makes young people feel less cut off, just as it brings together friends or relatives on different continents. Cue, again, the complaints that people are too busy social networking to live "real life."

Bosworth is merrily impatient with these complaints. "The things people complain about in real life, it's like they rediscovered them on Facebook. It's like gossip never existed before, as if your history never followed you around before. I'm not saying there's not some differences—but these aren't Facebook problems, they're just fundamentally human problems." The philosophy is simple, he says: "Humans talk. Maybe we should let them talk online."

So "talking" is neither good nor bad. But Facebook means that what people are saying will never again be far away. Long ago, everyone was in regular physical contact with most of the people they would ever know. Everyone knew everyone's business, but "everyone" was not many people. Then urbanisation, cramming together people from far-flung places, allowed us to vanish into the crowd. Now Facebook is mashing today's vast crowds into the small town of old, making a world that is both exhilarating and unsatisfying, with more people than ever to keep up with, and more people than ever keeping tabs on you. One study of many on the phenomenon of "Facebook anxiety" produced a simple but striking finding: people's moods were depressed after reading their Facebook news feed, compared with a control group. One of the researchers attributed this to the fact that most status updates are positive. Reading an endless stream of mostly upbeat news from friends can cast your life in a bad light.

But that is far from fair to the full spectrum of life on Facebook. Life's hardships are lived socially too. There are groups for people with MS and HIV. A group brings together those with Asperger's Syndrome and their families. Characteristically, they share both problems and the neurological differences of which many "Aspies" are dead proud. Obsessions are compared—baseball, cooking, dinosaurs, telephone boxes—and commonalities unearthed: many Aspies, it turns out, love Lego, and creations are gleefully shared.

When a call for help goes out, Facebook becomes the world's biggest megaphone. I discovered this after hearing news of a rangy blond jock I'd played American football with in high school. Will was diagnosed with cancer in 2009, the year his first child was born; he was 34. Since then, the "Support Will Jones" public group on Facebook has racked up 1,500 members. Will has posted triumph, setback, triumph, setback and triumph. Around 900 people have offered him their prayers. When there has been good news, people have plied him with congratulations, which look heart-rendingly premature now. Two years later, Will is still alive, but tumours continue to reappear and require treatment. In "real" life, friends might have moved on or lost heart – it is crushingly hard to support someone with cancer over three years offline. But on Facebook 44 people cheered Will's latest piece of good news. If Facebook makes it too easy to express the vapid or insipid, it also allows us to go on benefiting from the far-flung relationships they might otherwise have let go cold.

Facebook's staff eagerly point to a June 2011 study of 2,200 American users of social-networking sites. Far from confirming that Facebook atomised and isolated its users, the Pew Internet & American Life Project found that they had about 9% more strong offline social ties than non-users. (The effect was similar for other non-Facebook networks like Twitter and LinkedIn, and it held up when demographic variables were controlled for.) Facebook users were more likely to agree that "most people can be trusted". And they have more diverse social networks—counter to the claim that social networking facilitates social bubbles.

They are more politically engaged: Pew found that frequent Facebook users were two and a half times as likely as others to attend a political rally, and 57% more likely to try to influence someone to vote. These numbers were not controlled for demographics, so they do not show that Facebook causes political engagement. But a study by Facebook's own data team did find that Facebook gets people to vote. In America's 2010 congressional elections, a box showed most Facebook users the names of some friends who had voted. (Some users were shown no box, or a different box that simply exhorted them to vote, to provide control groups.) Cameron Marlow, one of Facebook's data scientists, says that the study found that as many as a million people, out of a total turnout of 91m, may have voted who otherwise would not have.

As David Kirkpatrick, author of "The Facebook Effect" (2010), puts it, "Ordinary people, if they are pissed off, will use Facebook to communicate it to the world. It is the easiest tool they have ever had." To overwhelm an opponent's Facebook page, posting angry comments faster than they can be deleted, is a new kind of activist victory. Kirkpatrick ticks off a list of stories in his inbox, delivered that day by a Google Alert for the words "Facebook protest", running through a dozen—from the life-and-death to the mundane. He notes that Twitter played a special role in catalysing protests that had already begun in the Arab spring. But "the alert to follow the Twitter feeds starts on Facebook." Could people even revolt against Facebook on Facebook? As Kirkpatrick notes (and Bosworth also told me), the news feed, Bosworth's own baby, was wildly unpopular when it was introduced in 2006. How did Facebook know people were angry? Angry comments spread like brushfire, through the news feed. "If it's increasing usage," Kirkpatrick says, "they disregard the protest."

So is there no sense in which Facebook has changed our lives for the worse? Kids drink and misbehave and then put the inevitable photos on Facebook, embarrassing themselves and even hurting career prospects. Fights between family members are seen by hundreds of outsiders. Lovers canoodle for the entire online public. Changing views of privacy are probably the domain in which critics have the most defensible point. A generation is growing up saturated with the idea that nothing is too personal to put online.

Relationships can now begin and end on Facebook. As I was writing this article, an old friend found his girlfriend sex-chatting with an ex (via Gchat, not Facebook). Whether he would stay with her or not was quickly resolved, when his status was publicly changed to Single, as every one of his "Friends" instantly found out in their news feeds. (The kids, and Facebook's staff, call this "making it 'Facebook official'.") My friend asked me to Unfriend the ex. With mixed feelings, I did this thing, this verb that did not exist ten years ago.

A week later, a second close friend also broke up with his on-and-off girlfriend of five years. In their last stint together he had never become Friends with her, for fear of the endless drama. ("Why is she writing on your wall?...", and so on.) But I was Friends with her. Should I Unfriend her, I asked, trying to get familiar with the rules of "Facebook official". No, he said. He didn't want to hurt her needlessly.

The Future of Facebook

Will a backlash against "too much information" ever hit Facebook? Around 75 years ago, the world's biggest threat was totalitarian governments, which would throw citizens into prison not just for public opposition but for private "thought crimes". The right to a private life was a core part of freedom. Today, Facebook is a weapon against oppression—ask the former presidents of Egypt and Tunisia. But it also allows a world in which people have joined to become a modern, hip, social kind of voluntary Big Brother themselves, putting more data about themselves in each other's (and Facebook's) hands than Hitler or Stalin could ever have dreamed of. The comparison is absurd, of course; Facebook is a happy money-making company in California, reliant on our consent, not an evil government in Moscow or Berlin. But privacy nudniks cannot be wholly laughed off when they say people are losing valuable, time-worn habits of discretion.

Facebook has already added the ability to sort Friends into Close Friends and Acquaintances, so that not everyone has to share everything with colleagues or clients. But a potential rival has built its entire service around this concern. Google+, launched officially last September, had reached 90m total registrations by February (although Google will not say how many use the site monthly, the direct comparison to Facebook's 850m or so monthly users).

Vic Gundotra, a senior vice-president at Google, says that when he was researching the prospects for Google+, people repeatedly raised mocking air-quotes when describing their Facebook "Friends". Google+ is built around "Circles", customisable by users, so that they can easily share only among close friends, family, co-workers, people who watch "True Blood" on television, or some other common characteristic. Facebook allows segmentation like this in various ways too, but Circles are core to Google+, built around the insight that not everything should be shared with everybody. Two-thirds of content shared on Google+ is shared with limited circles rather than being made public.

Google has good reason for taking on the social-networking giant, as Facebook seeks to integrate nearly every activity users might fancy. Google too has built an entire ecosystem of products: search, phones, e-mail, chat, photo-sharing, music, books, and now Google+. Apple, too, has Facebook in its sights; the new version of its operating system, Mountain Lion, closely integrates Twitter, but has no such easy Facebook functionality. Twitter is cute and unthreatening; Facebook's ever-expanding universe menaces Apple's, with its iPhone, iPad, iCloud, iTunes, iMovie, iBooks and more. As Google's Gundotra says, there are only so many hours in the day. Time spent with eyeballs on your company's products is money. Apple, Google and Facebook are increasingly competing to offer a complete world to their users.

Even if Facebook should fall—as Friendster and MySpace rose and fell—its reverberations will be lasting. Google made the internet navigable. Apple made it portable, through intuitive, brilliant devices. Now Facebook has made it social, raising a generation that will never again expect things to be otherwise.

Facebook has not replaced social life. It has tightened the social fabric, in a way that fits many people, and which many just as clearly chafe against. The social ills ascribed to it are, by and large, not new. Once people suffered from hysteria and melancholy; in the modern age, they have anxiety and depression. Once they suffered gossiping and bullying; now it's "Facebook official" drama and cyber-bullying. Once they could envy the greener grass on their neighbour's side; now it's "Facebook anxiety" about his (or, more likely, her) online photos. Once they wondered if their social lives were fulfilling enough; now they suffer FOMO—fear of missing out—and get to see all the pictures from the party they weren't invited to. New labels for old problems. But these problems are larger-looming and becoming ever-present for the millions who can't get enough of their social networks. And unplugging from Facebook to get a month's or a year's peace is an increasingly cranky-looking decision. For the majority of Facebookers who can't leave the site alone, its ubiquity means that the good and the bad, the joys and the miseries of the social world will never again leave them alone either. "Like" it or not.

Close Reading Questions

1. Greene asks and answers, "what is Facebook, anyway?" Which of his many responses do you agree or disagree with the most and why?

2. What does Greene think is the best comparison to be made for Facebook? Why do you think this is or is not the best way to understand Facebook?

3. Why does Greene consider Facebook to be the "anti-Apple" in its business model? Which business model do you believe will ultimately be most successful and why? (Multiple Perspectives)

Analytical Writing/Discussion

4. Which of the drawbacks of Facebook that Greene presents do you think is most significant and why? Then why do you agree or disagree with Andrew Bosworth's "impatience" with some of these complaints? (Cultural Influences)

5. Which of the benefits of Facebook that Greene presents do you think is most significant and why? (Cultural Influences)

6. Using a timeline, sketch the contributions of several of the Internet corporations presented in this reading: Friendster, MySpace, Apple, Facebook, Google, Twitter, Skype, and so on. Which of these contributions do you think will have the most lasting impact on the twenty-first century and why? (Historical Trends)

Further Options

7. As explained in Chapter 6 on Rhetoric, it is important to acknowledge that the opinions of others may have some validity, to make what is known as a concession (see p. 103). What are some of the key concessions that Greene makes to the critics of Facebook, and why do you think his concessions are effective or not in persuading a reader to finally "like" Facebook?

8. Both Greene and Hodgkinson assert the importance of humans talking, but they differ on the benefit of doing so online. The noted media writer Marshall McLuhan stated, "The medium is the message." In other words, how we communicate (the medium) matters as much as what we communicate (the message). In what ways—good or bad—do you think the medium of Facebook affects our communication with each other and therefore our relationships as well?

Before you turn to the final assignment, each chapter will offer you another opportunity for freewriting and discussion.

Freewrite 3: Quotation Response

Sometimes less is more when it comes to comprehending a text. Rather than grapple with the entire text, you may develop more understanding from working with a smaller section. From one of the three contemporary readings, select what you consider to be a key quotation. Then respond to it, such as by explaining why you think this quotation is significant, how your own experiences demonstrate or contradict this assertion, or why you agree or disagree with the writer. Note that this informal writing in response to a specific quotation is similar to the double-entry notes explained on p. 80 of Chapter 3.

The ability to synthesize several texts in an extended essay is a fundamental ability for college and beyond. Each chapter, therefore, ends with a final assignment in which you are asked to write a formal essay in response to several of the readings of the chapter. This assignment includes a sequence designed to make your effort more manageable. Your professor may alter, or give you the opportunity to change, this assignment sequence.

Final Assignment 1: When to Use and When Not to Use

Cara Kalf and others in the first reading made a deliberate choice to be "unplugged" at home. As the author Bella English explains, the reasons to forego the Internet in these homes vary, but all believe that their lives are better without these digital influences. The rest of the texts in this chapter present diverse viewpoints on this issue, and now it's time for you to add your opinion.

Essay Question

Imagine someone who does not share your enthusiasm or your hesitation for using the Internet and related digital devices, such as cell phones and iPods. How can you convince this person that there are certain times when it is enjoyable and beneficial to use or not to use some of these technologies? What does this person believe, and what evidence might alter his or her perspective? In other words, what does he or she not understand about your preference for using digital devices or being unplugged?

Write a formal and extended essay to answer this question. Be sure to include specific references and direct quotations from several readings in this chapter (see Chapter 7 on Academic Honesty on quoting and citing properly). Be sure to not only support your informed perspective but also to anticipate and answer some of the possible objections of those who do not already agree with you. Your task is to assert your opinion and persuade others to consider it carefully.

Freewrite 4: Assignment Analysis

Before you try to start answering this complex question, analyze its parts. Reread the questions above and underline several phrases that represent key parts of the larger answer you will be developing. Then pick two or three of these phrases and freewrite your immediate impressions: What do you think right now? Then, pause to look for connections, contradictions, and omissions within your first response: what else do you want to discuss, what else do you want to add, and/or what order of your ideas is developing? Finally, consider the audience of your essay: who does not agree with you already, and why might they disagree? (For more on freewriting and other invention strategies, see Chapter 4 on the Writing Process.)

Reading Review

Once you have sketched some of your initial ideas, review some of the readings to find specific details and persuasive evidence to support, enrich, and possibly complicate your response. Here are some readings and post-reading questions that you may want to consider:

1. Freewrite 1
2. English, Analytical Writing Question 3
3. Jones/Sharp, Analytical Writing Question 2
4. Freewrite 2
5. Powers, Close Reading Question 3
6. Hodgkinson, Analytical Writing Question 4
7. Greene, Analytical Writing Questions 4 and 5
8. Freewrite 3

Feel free to include other readings and post-reading questions. You also may want to review the suggestions for writing persuasively in Chapter 6 on Rhetoric as well as practice the peer response described in Chapter 4 on the Writing Process.

Additional Source Suggestions

In the e-supplement of this textbook, there are several sources that will help you deepen your understanding of digital life and strengthen your final assignment. These sources include videos as well as readings, and they present multiple perspectives, historical trends, and cultural influences on living digitally. To access these materials, see the code on the inside front cover of this textbook, which will lead you to the website for additional sources.

* * *

This chapter, like the subsequent thematic ones (10–14), emphasizes reading as much as writing. You have been asked to write in response to several texts and then write a final essay that synthesizes the sources and presents your informed perspective. You have been asked to place what seemed to be the personal choice of a few young adults to forego Facebook and other digital technologies in larger cultural and historical contexts. Throughout this book, we assume neither that an individual can ever be entirely free from all cultural influences nor that society always predetermines a person's thoughts, feelings, and actions. We instead assume that a back and forth, or dialectical, relationship exists between self and society. In other words, culture affects a person's perspective, but an individual also can have an impact on his or her viewpoint and those of others as well. In fact, a college education and its training in reading and writing in particular, can be considered a means to have more control over your life and your society.

Examining a Personal Conflict

Connecting the Thematic and Instructional Chapters

As explained in our Note for Students, we have created two versions of this initial chapter. In each one, we will explain some of the key features of this textbook, using these italicized comments. This chapter concentrates on writing and encourages you to examine more deeply your own experiences. The first chapter focuses on reading as well as writing and offers a condensed version of the subsequent thematic chapters (10–14). Both chapters present the critical reading, writing, and thinking abilities that will be developed in the rest of this book, and much of your college education will depend on these abilities.

> Had it been my purpose to seek the world's favor, I should have put on finer clothes.... But I want to appear in my simple natural everyday dress, without strain or artifice; for it is myself I portray.
>
> —*Michel Montaigne, on writing personal essays (1580)*

> [Students who are] unable to find words to render their experiences... are radically impoverished [because this writing] mirrors back to themselves a sense of their experiences from a little distance.
>
> —*Peter Elbow (1991)*

> It is essential for any writer who wants to speak to a general audience... to write in a manner that welcomes any reader. . . . Writers must trust that readers are ready to receive our words— to grapple with the strange and unfamiliar or to know again what is already known in new ways.
>
> —*bell hooks (1999)*

> Is it part of human consciousness to seek and create narrative?
>
> —*Sven Birkerts (2010)*

Introduction

In this chapter, we will ask you to write what are termed first-person essays or nonfiction narratives. We will combine those terms and refer to this assignment as a personal narrative. You will be asked to write about a significant conflict in your life and present it as a story showing a sequence of events, actions, and words. In addition to presenting this sequence, this narrative also should include your thoughts, feelings, and insights; these impressions will add some significance to your tale. Then a reader will not only understand what happened in this conflict but why it is significant for you and others.

This twofold focus on yourself and others may seem difficult to develop. First, rather than avoid the first person, the writer of a personal essay must focus on the self. As Henry David Thoreau, the author of *Civil Disobedience* and *Walden*, explained,

> In most books, the I, or first person is omitted… We commonly do not remember that it is after all, always the first person that is speaking. I should not talk so much about myself if there were anybody else whom I knew as well.

Yet second, as the more recent writing theorist Donald Murray asserted, one may write *for* oneself but one should not write *to* oneself only. Instead writers like Thoreau and Murray must keep their readers in mind and welcome their audience, as another writer named bell hooks advocates. The best of today's blogs demonstrate this combination of personal experience and public relevance. These digital texts are but the latest examples in the long tradition of personal narratives.

This tradition of first-person essays includes such key figures as Michel Montaigne, Henry David Thoreau, and Virginia Woolf. Montaigne, a sixteenth-century French writer, launched into his essays by asking "What do I know?" and he followed that question into an exploration of human nature, often using himself as the central example. Centuries later, Thoreau and Woolf asked what does one need to live well. Thoreau's answer was a life of simplicity and Woolf's was a space for women to think freely. Even more recently, diverse writers like James Baldwin, E. B. White, Alice Walker, Amy Tan, Richard Rodriquez, Annie Dillard, David Sedaris, and Mary Karr have explored the events, emotions, and expectations of their lives.

Some writing teachers and theorists have doubted the value of asking college students to write personal narratives. Peter Elbow believes that it is vital for students to learn to render their experiences and then to reflect upon them. David Bartholomae, on the other hand, counters that so many of our supposedly "personal" experiences are dictated by our cultures. Students, therefore, should begin by questioning their society, rather than reproducing it. This chapter, however, provides careful guidance for you to analyze as well as narrate your experiences; you will be asked to think critically about your society as well as yourself. Such self-awareness and cultural examination are integral to the long tradition of first-person essays and nonfiction narratives.

Along with the debate over personal narratives among writing theorists, professors in other disciplines have promoted their value. For example, two psychology professors named Kitty Klein and Adriel Boals found that asking undergraduates to write about a difficult experience improves their memory overall. Making sense of these events led to significant increases in these students' working memory, meaning their ability to recall and organize information in general. The medical school at a leading university also relies on personal narratives to improve these future doctors' skills. The Program in Narrative Medicine at Columbia University trains medical students to "recognize, absorb, interpret, and be moved by stories of illness." This program was developed because "effective medical practice needs to replace hurried impersonal care with careful listening, empathic attention, and personal fidelity." We too believe that learning to write, read, and appreciate personal narratives is one way, though not the only way, to advance such intellectual traits as detailed recall, sensitive understanding, and critical analysis.

This chapter puts writing under the proverbial microscope, asking you to examine your current practices and to learn ways to write with even more confidence and competence. We will offer you a sequence of possible activities from which you, working with your professor, can choose. This chapter also will teach you to engage in several forms of critical thinking that are common to many academic subjects, such as art history, chemistry, English, engineering, and sociology. We will present and then ask you to engage in three forms of critical thinking, which we will refer to as examining multiple perspectives, analyzing cultural influences, and tracing historical trends. As we will explain, you already engage in these forms of critical thinking so we want you to learn to apply them to many of your academic writing assignments.

The writing assignments, sample readings, suggested strategies, and final assignments of this chapter are designed to develop the writing (and reading) abilities necessary for college-level study. You will learn more about these college literacies through the connections made to the instructional chapters (3–9). After each of the sample narratives by published authors, you will find a set of questions that also are presented in the thematic chapters (10–14). These post-reading questions are divided into close reading, analytical writing, and further option queries. This chapter asks: **As you narrate and analyze a personal conflict, what can you learn about yourself and your culture?**

In Chapter 4 on the Writing Process, we explain that composing a challenging text involves a gradual construction of meaning (see p. 85 for more). This construction often draws on your prior knowledge of the topic so after the introduction of each chapter, we will ask you to pause and consider what you already know and feel about a subject. To elicit your thoughts and feelings, we will ask you to use what is known as freewriting. This technique is like letting yourself talk informally on the page. Rather than trying to compose complete sentences in perfect paragraphs, you can begin developing your thoughts more easily and "freely" by asserting them in quickly written phrases and often in a rambling order. Freewriting is not intended to be a final effort; instead it can be a very productive start of writing that can be revised and edited later (for more on freewriting, see p. 85 of Chapter 4).

Freewrite 1: Genre and Convention

Before you start writing your own personal narrative, we want you to pause and consider the nature of this assignment. Most students learn to write five-paragraph essays before they come to college; you probably know the drill: an introduction, three body paragraphs, and a conclusion—right? Now let's consider what a reader will expect as she starts to read your draft; can you contrast a personal narrative with a five-paragraph essay? What are some of the expected features of each form of writing? How does what a reader expects of each assignment differ?

The following start of a personal narrative demonstrates why it is important to distinguish this assignment from a five-paragraph essay; a student began his first draft with an introduction like

> *In the summer of my freshman year, I learned a valuable lesson. My soccer coach wanted me to play defense, but I had always been an offensive player who loved to score goals. My conflict taught me to be a better teammate.*

This student states his focus exactly and sums up his conflict neatly, but as the opening of a personal narrative, this introduction tells a reader too much too soon. This criticism initially confused this student writer because he had been taught to write precisely this kind of an introduction… for a five-paragraph essay.

When some students have discussed the differences between these assignments, their responses have included the following:

Personal Narrative	Five-Paragraph Essay
more flexible structure	*fixed structure*
engaging opening	*intro paragraph*
multiple paragraphs of various length	*three body paragraphs with topic sentences*
events presented	*ideas explained*
showing details	*supporting info*
order by chronology	*organize three topics*
end with significance	*sum up main points*

Of course, the students didn't always phrase these contrasts so precisely, but we have done so following the conventions of a textbook. Note in our example, how conventions help to determine what is expected and written. To sum up the differences between a narrative and a five-paragraph essay, we will assert that a personal narrative enables a reader to experience an event whereas a five-paragraph essay allows a reader to understand an idea. In other words, the first is more concrete and subjective, and the second is more abstract and objective. With this emphasis on the writer's thoughts, feelings, and actions, a personal narrative should include the first person, which most teachers forbid in a five-paragraph essay. This exclusion of "I" from this kind of essay matches its purposes, but so too does the use of the first person in a narrative essay. This reversal of the "rule" against "I" does not mean that your high school teacher or your current writing professor is wrong; instead it demonstrates that different writing tasks have different conventions (for more on tasks, see Chapter 5).

Part One: A Personal Narrative

Here's the first of the two main assignments of this chapter:

> Write a narrative essay about a significant conflict in your life. This conflict can be a direct confrontation between you and a friend, a family member, or an authority figure, such as a teacher or a coach. It also could be a quieter, less obvious tension between you and others or within yourself. Remember that a personal narrative tries to make sense of these events so the conflict should not be one that is too recent or too painful for you to recall and later too difficult for you to examine critically. You also should be ready to share drafts of this narrative with at least a few classmates.

We hope you already have some possible topics in mind or perhaps you have jotted them down in writing. Below we will provide a sequence of possible activities to guide you through the writing process, and these possibilities will address

- Topic selection
- Detail collection
- Subject focus

- Tentative organization
- Preliminary drafting
- Textual analysis
- Draft revision
- Final editing

We also know that some students like to have a clearer image of what it is expected before they are ready to proceed. Let us stress that this is just one sample and many other topics and variations of a personal narrative are possible; you'll find several other sample narratives below. However, let's get started with the following sample essay.

In each chapter, you will find a series of readings presented with headnotes that contain information on the author and the publication. Skimming the headnote as well as the title will help you begin the gradual construction of meaning from a text. For more on previewing a text and comprehending a text, see Chapter 3 on the Reading Process. After this narrative, we will present several close reading questions, and we will add questions for analytical writing and further options to the subsequent readings.

PASSING

by Toi Derricotte

In this narrative, Toi Derricotte explores her racial identity and the reactions of others to her ambiguous appearance. In her essays and poems, Derricotte examines various aspects of her identity, such as her multiracial heritage, her struggles as a woman, and her fascination with taboo subjects, such as death. This essay from 1997, originally titled "The California Zephyr" is from one of Derricotte's most acclaimed works, *The Black Notebooks: An Interior Journey.*

I'm sure that most people don't go around all the time thinking about what race they are. When you look like what you are, the external world mirrors back to you an identity consistent with your idea of yourself. However, for some like me, who does not look like what I am, those mirrors are broken, and my consciousness or lack of consciousness takes on serious implications. Am I not conscious because, like others, I am just thinking of something else? Or is it because I don't want to be conscious? Am I mentally "passing"?

All my life I have passed invisibly into the white world, and all my life I have felt that sudden and alarming moment of consciousness when I remember I am black. It may feel like I'm emerging too quickly from deep in the ocean, or touching an electric fence, or I'm like a deer stuck in the headlights of an oncoming car. Sometimes in conversation with a white person who doesn't know I'm black, suddenly a feeling comes over me, a precursor—though nothing at all has been said about race—and I either wait helplessly for the other shoe to drop, try desperately to veer the conversation in another direction, or prepare myself for a painful distinction. My desire to escape is indistinguishable from my desire to escape my "blackness," my race, and I am filled with shame and fury. I think the first time I became conscious of this internal state was when I was fifteen, on my way cross country on a train, the California Zephyr.

The first day out, a young white man sat in the seat beside me. We had had a pleasant conversation, but at night when I grew tired, I asked him to go back to his seat so that I could stretch out. He said, "If you saw what's sitting in the seat next to me, you'd know why I can't go back." Of course, I knew without looking back what he meant, and as I stood up and turned around to see, I felt that now familiar combination of sickening emotions: hope that my sense of the situation was incorrect - in effect preferring to distrust my own perceptions and fear that it wasn't, that my tender feelings for this man, and his feelings for me, were in mortal danger. If I spoke, I would make myself vulnerable. At the very least, he would categorize me in the same way he had categorized the other black person. If I didn't, I would be a coward, a betrayer of my people.

It seemed to me that even deeper than laws, than institutional practices, it was his invisible thoughts that hurt me. In fact, it seemed that, in a way, it is the combined thoughts, conscious and unconscious of all of us that hold the machinery of racism, and in small remarks such as these, I am able to grasp, because *I* am allowed entry into it, a world of hatred so deep and hidden that it is impossible to address. This juncture of communication may seem so small an event in the history of racism, and of such indeterminate origins, that it hardly worthy of speech. But it is precisely in such moments that I sense the local and engendering impulse, the twisted heart that keeps us locked in separate worlds of hate. It makes me despair of any real intimacy between blacks and whites.

I turned around and, sure enough, there was a black man, a soldier sitting in the seat. I said, very softly, "If you don't want to sit next to him, you don't want to sit next to me." I had hoped he'd be too stupid or deaf to understand. But he grew very quiet and said, after a few minutes, in a voice even softer than mine, "You're kidding."

"No," I said.

"You're kidding."

Each time he said it, he grew quieter. He excused himself. He may have slept in the bathroom. Every other seat was taken, and when I looked back to see if he was sleeping next to the soldier, the seat was empty.

The next morning, he found me on the way to breakfast and profusely apologized. "Please let me buy your breakfast," he said. I was lonely and wanted company, but I felt I had to punish him. I thought punishment was the only way he would gain respect for black people, and I felt the most effective kind of punishment was not verbal confrontation—which probably would only confirm his stereotypes of hostile blacks—but cool withdrawal. I had to punish myself, too, for I didn't want the pain of loneliness and alienation. I wanted and needed company, I liked him. But I felt in order to cut myself off from him, I had to cut off my feelings of tenderness and trust.

The last night on board, just before we were to arrive I looked back and saw him sleeping beside the soldier. Perhaps he had gotten sick of sleeping in the bathroom. Or perhaps my suffering had done some good.

Close Reading Questions

1. Why do you think that Derricotte has (or has not) chosen an engaging conflict?

2. What details are most or least compelling to you?

3. As Derricotte alternates between actions and thoughts, why do you think the organization of her narrative is or is not effective?

In this chapter, we will present some of the key parts of the writing process to help you develop your own personal narrative on an important conflict. Although we will present a sequence that starts with topic selection and detail collection, you may want to return to these steps later on. Or you may want to consider the order carefully only after you have started to draft. We do not intend our sequence to be a rigid progression that every student must follow exactly. Your topic choice, your writing habits, and your professor's suggestions will influence your process.

Topic Selection and Detail Collection

As you turn your attention back to your own personal narrative, please note that your conflict does not have to be sensational; you are not applying for a chair-throwing talk show or a headline-making reality television program. A conflict involves an opposition, but it does not always mean a loud argument or a physical confrontation. In the past, students have chosen to write about many diverse topics, ranging from athletic struggles, artistic fears, and authority confrontations to tragic losses, difficult choices, and disappointed ambitions.

As you develop this narrative, it will be shared with and discussed by at least a few of your classmates so don't pick a subject that you cannot imagine allowing another student to read about. There is a fine line between the personal and the private, and you and your instructor will have to determine where exactly that line lies. Your professor also may ask every student to write a narrative about a common theme, such as education, to link this assignment with your later work in another thematic chapter, like Chapter 11 on American high schools.

You should choose your topic carefully because you will be devoting several weeks to this chapter. Good topics depend on knowledge and interest. Avoid a topic in which you were not really involved in the conflict because you may not have enough knowledge to write well. Yet you also should avoid a conflict in which you were a central figure if that event already is settled in your mind, for you soon will lose interest in it. Both knowledge and interest are essential.

As explained in Chapter 4, brainstorming, clustering, and freewriting can be used to generate an array of potential topics (see pp. 85–88). Once you have collected several topic possibilities, you will not be required to share all of these choices, but the topic you choose should not be too private to share with others. Use one or more of the following methods: brainstorming, clustering, and/or freewriting, generate at least four topics below:

<u>Some Possible Topics</u>

Once you have gathered some likely topics, pick at least two and try to collect what Donald Murray terms a "necessary abundance" of details. Using brainstorming or another invention method, gather as many details, phases, and connections as you can in several minutes. Be receptive to many ideas now, and only later should you try to judge them. These details will enable you to *show*, as the old adage goes, rather than to *tell* your audience about your conflict.

Topic One   Topic Two   Topic Three

Your professor may ask you to explain some of your topics and details to another classmate or two. Obviously, if you cannot discuss a topic for several minutes, you either need to develop it more or move on to another one. A likely topic is one that you feel you have enough to write about (knowledge) as well as a desire to understand the conflict better (interest).

Focus and Order

Once you have made a preliminary decision on your topic, you may want to sum it up in a sentence or two:

I think my conflict is about _____, and the primary conflict is between _____ and _____ .

Some of you, however, may struggle to assert your focus so soon. If you have been able to collect a necessary abundance of details and your topic still interests you, keep going. Once you have worked on an order and drafted a few pages, your focus probably will be clarified. As we will explain below, sometimes we have to "write to learn" (see p. 37). With your focus in mind, you may want to go back and collect more details, perhaps by focusing on your audience and their needs. Writing often involves a tension between a writer and a reader: What does the writer want to say? vs. What can a reader understand? For example, is a conflict with a friend or teacher based on some previous moment of distrust? Or was a decision to leave a clique or quit a team influenced by an outsider? Try considering both what you want to say and what a reader needs to know to help you collect more details.

Since a narrative shows events rather than explains ideas, try imagining what we will call "scenes." These scenes resemble the panels of a graphic novel or the storyboard of a movie; they are frames filled with crucial details. What are three main scenes of your narrative? You can begin with the opening event or a central moment, then add two more.

Creating an Order

Scene One   Scene Two   Scene Three

Here's a sample of one student's scene planning. This student, Aliza Leavitt, decided to write about her conflict over her college choice, a struggle that she realized had been developing for several years.

Three Scenes:

Early Choices	College Visit	Application Process
always knew what	really loved it	unbearable stress
I wanted to be yet	advertising major	rejection fears
it changed every year	beautiful campus	accepted at 6 of 7
archeologist	college banner	best birthday
architect	over my bed	present yet!

Which details attract your attention as a reader? Which ones need to be developed more so you can understand them better? Do any seem unnecessary to you? What questions would you want to ask Aliza if she were one of your classmates? Next, your professor may ask you to apply some of these questions to your own scenes and/or to those of a classmate.

Drafting

Although we already have suggested a significant amount of writing, completing a draft may require more concentration for a more sustained period. This sustained concentration can be promoted or hindered by the time and place of writing. Many professional writers prefer to wake early to write; some reach for their favorite pen at a desk, whereas others settle with keyboard into a comfortable chair. Some students write late at night in a busy dorm room, while others need a quiet library corner at midday. Like so much of the process of writing, there is no single method that enables every writer to succeed. It, however, is important to choose a time and place that does not distract you from writing. For example, many writers like music as part of their drafting environment, yet as they settle into drafting, this music soon becomes "gray" background noise. Many songs may pass, but they go virtually unheard. Music and other elements of our writing environment, such as instant messaging, should be used to maintain our focus or take a planned break, but they should not disrupt the concentration needed to write well.

We already have mentioned that some students are able to write a first draft quickly and sometimes without engaging in much of the preliminary writing suggested above. These students usually have been turning their topics over in their minds, and they already have planned much of their writing, at least unconsciously. Other students, of course, are much less prepared to draft so here's an example of Aliza's early drafting:

The last tour we went on before school started was to [University #1]. From the moment we got out of the car, I really loved it there. They had an advertising major, which many places did not, and that was something I was looking for. The school itself was beautiful, and I loved the atmosphere. It seemed like a perfect match for me, and it really could be the place I would end up spending my four years. For months after, a blue and gold banner hung over my bed.

The beginning of senior year came too quickly, and it wasn't long before we started sending out applications. The stress on all of us from parents, teachers, and guidance counselors was almost unbearable at times. Important deadlines were looming, and the dreaded thought of not getting into any schools was something my friends and I joked about all the time, but we were all secretly afraid of. Even though I knew where I wanted to go, I ended up applying to seven schools, just in case. After getting into six and being waitlisted at another, I had nothing to complain about. I got into my top 3 schools. I really only cared about one school though, and I happened to get that acceptance letter the day before my birthday. I was so excited to open the envelope and tell my mom as soon as she got home from work. She was so happy for me, and I thought that would be it.

As you probably suspect, Aliza's college search is far from over, and your reaction to this drafting demonstrates what we will term *peer response*. These reactions by other students involve more than editing suggestions, instead they are assertions of a reader's engagement with a text (or difficulty getting engaged). It is almost always better to begin responding to a draft by being positive: What do you think are some of the most effective, showing details that enable a reader to experience this event? Then shift from this specific praise to areas that may need some revision: Do any parts of this draft seem less effective to you and why? For instance, does Aliza sometimes lapse into telling her impressions rather than showing them for her reader? If there are any parts that you do not understand, can you state this problem as a question, as in "What did you mean when you said…?" Based on your own, possibly similar, experiences with college decisions, what vivid details can you suggest to Aliza? (For more on peer response, please see p. 89 in Chapter 4.)

Your professor may ask you to submit a complete, revised and edited, draft for grading. If so, please see pp. 88–91 on revising and editing in Chapter 4. Let us also suggest that you may want to turn your attention to your professor's grading criteria. He or she may provide you with a grading rubric, and it can be very helpful to make sure that your expectations match those of your professor. It's so frustrating to be surprised by a low grade, and often when such a disappointment occurs, a student's assumptions about the assignment do not match a teacher's expectations. To avoid this frustrating gap, you can try describing the traits of an excellent personal narrative from beginning to end. What would you say are some of the outstanding features of an "A" paper? What would a reader expect from the top of page one to the bottom of the final page?

The Features of Excellence in a Personal Narrative

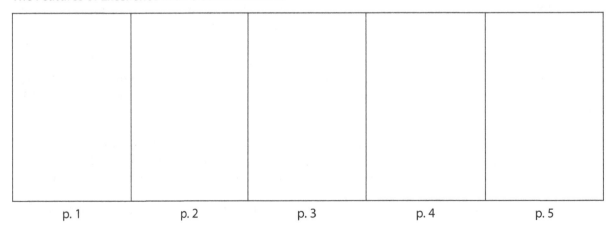

| p. 1 | p. 2 | p. 3 | p. 4 | p. 5 |

Please consult with your professor, but students in the past have asserted that these features include an engaging title and opening, a clear focus, showing details, fine phrases, an effective order, proper emphasis on main events, appropriate word choice, thoughtful reflection, a strong ending, and thorough editing. Of course, it is easier to name these features than to fulfill them, but it is even harder to fulfill expectations that have not been realized!

When you submit your narrative, most college professors also will expect you to follow the conventional page format of one-inch margins, double-spaced lines, indented paragraph breaks, and numbered pages. Most will ask you to include, on the top of the first page, essential details like your name, the course number, and the date or the assignment number. Some may ask you to include what is termed a *running header* of your name and page number at the top of each page. You may be asked to submit your paper electronically instead of or in addition to a hard copy, and most professors appreciate a staple or paper clip to keep the pages of the hard copy in order and to make it easy to handle many student papers.

Your professor may ask you to engage in only some of the subsequent analysis of your narrative, or due to time constraints, your professor may ask you to proceed to one of the later chapters. If time permits, you can learn to practice much of the critical thinking and analytical writing required in most college courses through this further focus on your narrative.

You also may gain some insights on your own narrative by taking a look at Aliza's complete draft. We have numbered the paragraphs for easier discussion.

Aliza's draft:

The Finish Line

1. College is something that most people start dealing with in the middle of high school. However, in my case, I started thinking about college in middle school. The whole concept was so interesting to me. I don't know why, but maybe it is because I'm the oldest of four siblings. Like most oldest children, I thought it would be exciting to do something I had no experience with yet.

2. I've always known what I've wanted to be when I grew up, even though what I've wanted has changed a few times over the years. When I was younger, I wanted to be an archeologist (mainly because I had a really cool social studies teacher who did the same thing). A few years later, I decided that I wanted to be an architect, and after that phase, I finally settled on something I had always been interested in, business and advertising. I loved thinking about the future and what it would bring.

3. I've never really had a "dream school" like some kids do. I didn't come from a line of Cornell or Harvard graduates, and there wasn't a particular school that I was expected to attend, so I was on my own to narrow the thousands of options down to one. Naturally, like my changing career interests, my top college picks changed as well.

4. The first college I visited was in 10th grade while on the way back from visiting relatives, and it was so exciting. Walking around the campus that day against the backdrop of the sparkling Hudson River was so different, and much better than being stuck in the same old high school hallways. . . . It was a whole different world. We went to the bookstore after the tour, and I bought a sweatshirt and told my mom "this is where I'm going." At first, it was probably the excitement of it all, but this phrase became very familiar to her and seemed to pop up after every college tour that we would go on.

5. The last tour we went on before school started was to [University #1]. From the moment we got out of the car, I really loved it there. They had an advertising major, which many places did not, and that was something I was looking for. The school itself was beautiful, and I loved the atmosphere. It seemed like a perfect match for me, and it really could be the place I would end up spending my four years. For months after, a blue and gold banner hung over my bed in my room.

6. The beginning of senior year came too quickly, and it wasn't long before we started sending out applications. The stress from parents, teachers, and guidance counselors was almost unbearable at times. Important deadlines were looming, and the dreaded thought of not getting into any schools was something my friends and I joked about all the time, but we were all secretly afraid of. Even though I knew where I wanted to go, I ended up applying to seven schools, just in case. After getting into six and being waitlisted at another, I had nothing to complain about. I really only cared about one school though, and I happened to get that acceptance letter the day before my birthday. I was so excited to open the envelope and tell my mom as soon as she got home from work. She was so happy for me, and I thought that would be it.

7. The weeks came when it was time for the financial aid letters to be awarded. I'm not a genius, but my slightly above average grades in high school and good SAT scores managed to get me some scholarship money that I was so grateful for. Growing up with a single parent in a one-income household is something I knew would have an impact on college. The question was never if I could go at all, but how it would be made affordable. I knew that college came with a hefty price tag. The price of school is something that limits so many students' chances of going to college and getting an education. Looking back, I realize my good luck had to break some time, and the day came when the one place I wanted to go to didn't offer me nearly enough money in scholarships. We were all shocked, seeing as all of the other schools I had been accepted to, I would be able to attend financially. The full cost of [University #1] just wasn't feasible for my family.

8. Watching my mom go to a job everyday that she's never really loved, to provide the best for my sister and I, is something I'm so grateful for. She has always put us first and that means so much to me. There's always been a part of me that has wanted to work hard and make something of myself to thank her for all she's done. I guess that's one reason why college means so much to me.

9. It took a while to come to terms with the situation; I was so disappointed. Until then I thought getting in would be my biggest challenge. I always knew money would be a factor, but never a deciding one. Even though my mom never said no, it would have been personally hard for me to go, knowing what I would be leaving behind. I was left with a huge decision. I could go to this school, but in turn put myself and my family into a huge amount of debt, or I could find another option. I knew that I really had no choice, but having my heart set on one thing for the good portion of a year was tough to get over.

10. Over the next month I struggled with this decision; I knew what I had to do. So, the search started over again, which was a little strange as I was looking at the other colleges I had been accepted to. I spent a lot of time looking at my other options. We even went to a few more open houses to take one last look around.

11. I decided on [University #2]. I found out a lot of things I didn't know when I quickly filled out a free application one day in September (which is literally the only reason I'm here today). With one of the best business schools around, I realized there was nowhere else I should be.

It's almost ironic that I ended up at a school I knew hardly anything about when applying and didn't go to the place I had invested so much of my time into. Even though [University #2] wasn't my first choice, looking back I can't believe I would have wanted to go anywhere else! Now the banner in my room is red and white, and I wouldn't have it any other way. Everything happens for a reason, as my mom likes to say. She's right.

12. Eventually, most conflicts come to a resolution. For me, it took a while, but I ended up realizing that I made the right decision. And while not all conflicts have happy endings, this one did, but that doesn't mean there weren't some bumps along the way. It's the way we deal with conflicts that determines how they turn out.

13. Once in a while, while I'm walking around campus, I think about what it would be like had I ended up at [University #1]. It's never for long, but the thoughts are still there. How would it be different? Would I be different? Would I be happy or happier than I am here? These thoughts don't stick around too long; I really am content with how things worked out in the end. Through it all, I've learned a lot about myself and how I handle difficult situations. I had always seen planning for college as a race and getting in as a finish line. I realize now that it's only just the beginning.

As in each of thematic chapters (10–14), we will pause in the middle of this one and offer an opportunity to freewrite on your efforts so far.

Freewrite 2: Peer Response

Reading and reacting to the drafts of others can help you gain some perspective on your own writing. Your professor may ask you to engage in peer response to a classmate's draft so you may want to practice such helpful responding by reacting to Aliza's draft. Through freewriting and/or discussion, answer some of the following questions:

- What do you think are some of the more effective parts of Aliza's draft?
- When do you lose interest in her draft or have trouble understanding?
- In your own words, how would you sum up her conflict?

For more on peer response, see p. 89 of Chapter 4.

Part Two: An Analytical Revision

This second assignment asks you to revise your narrative by analyzing your perspective on this conflict as well as examining the viewpoints of some other participants. Your final paper should present not only what happened but also to help a reader understand why this conflict occurred. Again, you will not be expected to complete this task all at once; instead you will be offered a sequence of several possibilities.

If you have read and responded to Toi Derricotte's narrative or Aliza's draft, it will be easy for you to complete the first step of this assignment: the identification of the conflict's participants. Then this seemingly obvious question leads to some complexity if you consider whether there are any other participants, including indirect ones, in each narrative. Who else can you consider to be involved in these conflicts?

Derricotte's Narrative	Aliza's Narrative
narrator	narrator
young man	her mom
_____?	_____?
_____?	_____?
_____?	_____?
_____?	_____?

As with your initial collecting of details, be receptive to many ideas now and save any hard judgments for later. When this question on participants is posed, there usually is a weighty pause, and then a student will suggest others are involved. However, this suggestion often is made with a tentative question (rather than a confident answer), such as "Couldn't you consider Aliza's teachers an important participant in her desire to attend college?" Then a line of many other participants quickly forms. Who else do you think can be considered, even indirectly, to be participants in these conflicts?

You probably have added the sleeping soldier and the young man's family as participants in Derricotte's conflict and for Aliza, you may have considered not only her teachers but also her classmates who are stressed over their college choices. Let us emphasize that every idea you develop at this point does not have to be included in your revision; generating as many possibilities now will allow you to be more critical and insightful later on. Who else can you add to our list for Aliza? Then can you create a similar list of participants for your own narrative? Who are the most obvious participants as well as some indirect ones in your conflict?

Aliza's Narrative	Your Narrative
narrator	_____?
her mom	_____?
teachers	_____?
classmates	_____?
guidance counselor	_____?
_____?	_____?

Multiple Perspectives

The consideration of multiple perspectives asks you to distinguish several participants' viewpoints and examine what exact beliefs does each perspective involve. This examination does not mean that you have to abandon your own perspective entirely, only that you seek to clarify and expand your initial position by being open, at least initially, to alternative viewpoints. For as John Stuart Mill stated, "He who knows only his side of an argument knows little."

When faced with the examination of multiple perspectives, it may be tempting to object, "How can I know what they were thinking?" and it is true that we sometimes cannot be certain about others' viewpoints. Yet we often engage in just this kind of analysis, such as when we wonder, "What's up with her?" For instance, when a parent reacts with sudden anger or a friend is too subdued, we ask and often answer, "Where is he coming from?" Then we speculate not about a literal place but about his perspective, her viewpoint, someone's take on the situation. We engage in this kind of critical thinking not only in our daily lives but also in academic study. We try to interpret a literary character's assumptions or analyze a historical figure's motivations. We wonder, for example, does Huck Finn believe in racial inferiority as Twain's novel begins? Was the abolition of slavery Abraham Lincoln's primary motive for fighting the Civil War? Using one of your own experiences, this assignment is designed to help you handle many of the forms of critical thinking involved in academic inquiry.

Again for this second assignment, we will offer several possibilities, and, working with your professor, you can decide which ones you will complete. To continue this analysis of perspectives, can you describe the viewpoints of several participants in your conflict? Where do you think they were coming from? It may be helpful to create a chart as Aliza did below:

Aliza's Conflict:

Participants	Perspectives
Aliza -	I should go to the best college what is the "right" school for me?
her mother -	a college education is important my daughter will find her way
classmates -	we aren't geeks, but we study hard what if no one accepts me?
guidance counselors -	our top students go to good colleges college acceptance = school success
admission officers -	we accept the best our college = your career success

Your Conflict:

Participants	Perspectives

Another more creative possibility is to explore someone's perspective by imagining a dialogue with another participant or an internal debate within one person. For example, what might a less academic-oriented friend say to Aliza as she worried about her college choice? Or what might be Aliza's own back-and-forth thoughts as she fretted over her financial aid problems?

Aliza:

Other perspective:

Aliza:

… and so on

Let yourself have fun and even be funny in this dialogue, such as letting the final line in Aliza's dialogue come from her friend: "I can't believe you've had that blue banner over your bed since last year!" Sometimes when we allow our thoughts to flow, we can create fine phrases and strong insights.

Published authors of personal narratives often include multiple perspectives in their tales. For example, the following narrative by Rick Bragg explores various perspectives on his mother and Southern culture.

MEMORIES OF ALABAMA AND A MOTHER

by Rick Bragg

In this excerpt from his memoir, Rick Bragg presents many vivid impressions of his impoverished childhood in Alabama and what seems to be true about his mother. Note the multiple perspectives on place and parents presented. The author is a New York Times correspondent and a Pulitzer Prize winner. His memoir, titled *All Over but the Shoutin,'* was published in 1997.

My mother and father were born in the most beautiful place on earth, in the foothills of the Appalachians along the Alabama-Georgia line. It was a place where gray mists hid the tops of low, deep-green mountains, where redbone and bluetick hounds flashed through the pines as they chased possums into the sacks of old men in frayed overalls, where old women in bonnets dipped Bruton snuff and hummed "Faded Love and Winter Roses" as they shelled purple hulls, canned peaches and made biscuits too good for this world. It was a place where playing the church piano loud was near as important as playing it right, where fearless young men steered long, black Buicks loaded with yellow whiskey down roads the color of dried blood, where the first frost meant hog killin' time and the mouthwatering smell of cracklin's would drift for acres from giant, bubbling pots. It was a place where the screams of panthers, like a woman's anguished cry, still haunted the most remote ridges and hollows in the dead of night, where children believed they could choke off the cries of night birds by circling one wrist with a thumb and forefinger and squeezing tight, and where the cotton blew off the wagons and hung like scraps of cloud in the branches of trees.

It was about 120 miles west of Atlanta, about 100 miles east of Birmingham, close to nothin' but that dull red ground. Life here between the meandering dirt roads and skinny blacktop was full, rich, original and real, but harsh, hard, mean as a damn snake. My parents grew up in the 1940s and 1950s in the poor, upland South, a million miles from the Mississippi Delta and the Black Belt and the jasmine-scented verandas of what most people came to know as the Old South. My ancestors never saw a mint julep, but they sipped five-day-old likker out of ceramic jugs and Bell jars until they could not remember their Christian names.

Men paid for their plain-plank houses and a few acres of land by sawing and hand-lifting pulpwood onto ragged trucks for pennies a ton. They worked in the blast furnace heat of the pipe shops, loaded boxcars at the clay pits and tended the nerve gas stockpiles at the army base, carrying caged birds to test for leaks. They coaxed crops to grow in the up-country clay that no amount of fertilizer would ever turn into rich bottomland, tried in vain to keep their fingers, hands and arms out of the hungry machinery of the cotton mills, so that the first thing you thought when you saw an empty sleeve was not war, but the threshing racks. The summers withered the cotton and corn and the tornado season lasted ten months, making splinters out of their barns, twisting the tin off their roofs, yanking their tombstones out of the ground. Their women worked themselves to death, their mules succumbed to worms and their children were crippled by rickets and perished from fever, but every Sunday morning The Word leaked out of little white-wood sanctuaries where preachers thrust ragged Bibles at the rafters and promised them that while sickness and poverty and Lucifer might take their families, the soul of man never dies.

White people had it hard and black people had it harder than that, because what are the table scraps of nothing? This was not the genteel and parochial South, where monied whites felt they owed some generations-old debt to their black neighbors because their great-great- grandfather owned their great-great-grandfather. No one I knew ever had a mammy. This was two separate states, both wanting and desperate, kept separate by hard men who hid their faces under hoods and their deeds under some twisted interpretation of the Bible, and kicked the living shit out of anyone who thought it should be different. Even into my own youth, the orange fires of shacks and crosses lit up the evening sky. It seems a cliche now, to see it on movie screens. At the time, it burned my eyes.

It was as if God made them pay for the loveliness of their scenery by demanding everything else. Yet the grimness of it faded for a while, at dinner on the ground at the Protestant churches, where people sat on the springtime grass and ate potato salad and sipped sweet tea from an aluminum tub with a huge block of ice floating in it. The pain eased at family reunions where the men barbecued twenty-four hours straight and the women took turns holding babies and balancing plates on their knees, trying to keep the grease from soaking through on the one good dress they had. The hardness of it softened in the all-night gospel singings that ushered in the dawn with the promise that "I'll have a new body, praise the Lord, I'll have a new life," as babies crawled up into the ample laps of grandmothers to sleep across jiggling knees. If all else failed, you could just wash it away for a while, at the stills deep in the woods or in the highly illegal beer joints and so-called social clubs, where the guitar pickers played with their eyes closed, lost in the booze and the words of lost love and betrayal. They sang about women who walked the hills in long black veils, of whispering pines, and trains.

It was the backdrop and the sound track of our lives. I was born into it in the summer of 1959, just in time to taste it, absorb it, love it and hate it and know its secrets. When I was a teenager, I watched it shudder and gasp and finally begin to die, the pines clear-cut into huge patches of muddy wasteland and the character of the little towns murdered by generic subdivisions and generic fast-food restaurants. The South I was born in was eulogized by pay-as-you-pray TV preachers, enclosed in a coffin of light blue aluminum siding and laid to rest in a polyester suit, from Wal-Mart.

I watched the races fall into an uneasy and imperfect peace and the grip of the poverty ease. There was reason to rejoice in that, because while I was never ashamed to be a Southerner there was always a feeling, a need, to explain myself. But as change came in good ways, I saw Southernness become a fashion, watched men wear their camouflage deer-hunting clothes to the mall because they thought it looked cool, watched Hank Williams and his elegant western suits give way to pretty boys in ridiculous Rodeo Drive leather chaps. And I thought of my granddaddy Bobby Bragg, gentler than his son in some ways, who sat down to dinner in clean overalls, a spotless white shirt buttoned to the neck and black wingtip shoes.

Only the religion held. It held even though the piano players went to music school and actually learned to read notes, even though new churches became glass and steel monstrosities that looked like they had just touched down from Venus. It held even though the more prosperous preachers started to tack the pretentious title of "Doctor" in front of their name and started to spend more time at seminars than visiting the sick. It held even though the Baptists started to beat drums and allow electric guitar, even though-Jesus help us-the Church of Christ conceded in the late 1970s that it was probably not a mortal sin if boys went swimming with girls. It held. God hung in there like a rusty fishhook…

The first memory I have is of a tall blond woman who drags a canvas cotton sack along an undulating row of rust colored ground, through a field that seems to reach into the back forty of forever. I remember the sound it makes as it slides between the chest-high stalks that are so deeply, darkly green they look almost black, and the smell of kicked-up dust, and sweat. The tall woman is wearing a man's britches and a man's old straw hat, and now and then she looks back over her shoulder to smile at the three-year-old boy whose hair is almost as purely white as the bolls she picks, who rides the back of the six-foot-long sack like a magic carpet.

It is my first memory, and the best. It is sweeter than the recollection I have of the time she sat me down in the middle of a wild strawberry patch and let me eat my way out again, richer than all the times she took me swimming in jade-colored streams and threw a big rock in the water to run off the water moccasins. It is even stronger than the time she scraped together money for my high school class ring, even though her toes poked out of her old sneakers and she was wearing clothes from the Salvation Army bin in the parking lot of the A&P. It was not real gold, that ring, just some kind of fake, shiny metal crowned with a lump of red glass, but I was proud of it. I was the first member of my family to have one, and if the sunlight caught it just right, it looked almost real.

But it is the memory of that woman, that boy and that vast field that continues to ride and ride in my mind, not only because it is a warm, safe and proud thing I carry with me like a talisman into cold, dangerous and spirit-numbing places, but because it so perfectly sums up the way she carried us, with such dignity. We would have survived on the fifty-dollar welfare check the government decided our lives were worth. The family could have lived on the charity of our kin and the kindness of strangers. Pride pushed her out into the cotton field, in the same way that old terror, old pain squeezed my daddy into a prison of empty whiskey bottles.

I asked her, many years later, if the strap of the sack cut deeper into her back and shoulders because I was there. "You wasn't heavy," she said. Having a baby with her made the long rows shorter, somehow, because when she felt like quitting, when she felt like her legs were going to buckle or her back would break in two, all she had to do was look behind her. It gave her a reason to keep pulling.

Like I said, it is a perfect memory, but too perfect. It would have been easy for me to just accept the facade of blind sacrifice that has always cloaked her, to believe my momma never minded the backbreaking work and the physical pain as she dragged me up and down a thousand miles of clay. I wish I could just accept the myth that she never went to see me or my brothers play basketball or baseball because she was too tired, and not because she was ashamed of her clothes. I would like to believe she didn't even notice how her own life was running through her hands like water. But the truth is she did know, and she did think about it in the nighttime when her children were put to bed and there was no one left to keep her company except her blind faith in God and her own regret.

There is a notion, a badly mistaken one among comfortable people, that you do not miss what you never had. I have written that line myself, which is shameful to me now. I, of all people, should know better, should know that being poor does not make you blind to the riches around you; that living in other folks' houses for a lifetime does not mean a person does not dream of a house of his or her own, even if it is just a little one.

My mother ached for a house, for a patch of ground, for something. When I was a young man and we would take drives through town, she stared at the homes of others with a longing so strong you could feel it. She stared and she hoped and she dreamed until she finally just got tired of wanting.

The only thing poverty does is grind down your nerve endings to a point that you can work harder and stoop lower than most people are willing to. It chips away a person's dreams to the point that the hopelessness shows through, and the dreamer accepts that hard work and borrowed houses are all this life will ever be. While my mother will stare you dead in the eye and say she never thought of herself as poor, do not believe for one second that she did not see the rest of the world, the better world, spinning around her, out of reach.

In fact, poor was all she had ever witnessed, tasted, been. She was not some steel magnolia thrust into an alien poverty by a sorry man, but a woman who grew up with it, whose own mother would just forget to eat supper if there wasn't enough to go around. Her sisters wed men who worked hard, who bought land, homes and cars that did not reek of spilt beer. Through their vows, and some luck, they made good lives and had good things that had never been worn or used before. Momma, bless her heart, picked badly, and the years of doing without spun a single, unbroken thread through her childhood, her youth, her middle age, until the gray had crept into her hair.

Close Reading Questions

1. What are some of the sensory details (sight, sound, etc.) of the setting that Bragg describes seem most vivid to you?

2. What is Bragg's first memory of his mother, and why do you think he considers it to be the best?

Analytical Writing/Discussion

3. Bragg presents many impressions of individuals and kinds of people. Who are six of the dozen or more participants that Bragg portrays? What are the distinct perspectives of at least four of these participants? You may want to answer this question using a chart as shown on p. 43.

4. In this brief reading, the author presents many subjects ambivalently, meaning as having more than one quality, such as good and bad. What does Bragg consider to be both the positive and the negative changes in the South during his childhood? Why do you agree or disagree with Bragg's evaluation of some of these changes?

5. What are some of the multiple perspectives Bragg presents about his mother? In other words, what seems to be valid and what really is true about her actions and attitudes?

Cultural Influences

As we examine other perspectives, we often start to wonder not only what was someone else thinking but why did he or she have that viewpoint. As we ask what beliefs support that perspective, we are engaged in what we will term an *examination of cultural influences*. Again you will be engaged in conjecture, but it is not just idle speculation because we can draw some reasonable inferences. For instance, most Americans like to emphasize their individuality, yet the cultural influences on this viewpoint can be analyzed; reasonable inferences can be drawn. Literary characters like Huck Finn, comic book heroes such as Superman, and famous Americans like Sojourner Truth all stress the supposed uniqueness of our individual identities. Widespread cultural practices like every student being graded separately in most schools also promote an individualistic concept of the self. In other words, our widespread belief in individualism paradoxically is promoted by many elements of American culture. As diagrammed below, many influences affect our development and help to shape our individual identities:

A famous theorist named Louis Althusser has explained an individual's relationship with society by stating that each person is "interpellated," is drawn into a culture. This process of interpellation begins when we are very young; long before we are aware that our attitudes about race, gender, wealth, pleasure, and so much more are being influenced by society. Yet these cultural influences do not necessarily control

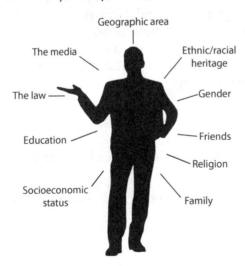

Geographic area

The media

Ethnic/racial heritage

The law

Gender

Education

Friends

Religion

Socioeconomic status

Family

every individual, making each person develop the exact same perspective. Instead, as another important thinker named Michel Foucault has theorized, the many influences of a culture are complex and sometimes even contradictory. We, therefore, have some freedom of choice from among these many influences.

To understand multiple ideologies and their development, the circle diagram of cultural influences can be applied to a specific conflict. For example, how do some popular television shows now depict Southern culture, an issue of Rick Bragg's personal narrative? Or, let's switch to Aliza's topic: the college search process. At most high schools, when you enter the guidance counselor's office, how is college choice portrayed? What else influences most students' desire to attend college? Do you think the alternative of a "gap year" of traveling or interning after high school is likely to become more popular?

As with writing a compelling narrative, insightful analysis depends on specific details and vivid examples. For instance, as Aliza engaged in this analysis, at one point she suddenly laughed with the insight that she had kept the last four years' copies of *The US News and World Report's* special edition on "America's Best Colleges." Not only had she kept them, she also had stacked them on the nightstand next to her bed! How's that for a revealing specific of the cultural pressure on students to pick the "right school"?

You may want to create a messy brainstorm, a neat chart, or carefully phrased prose, but can you analyze some of the cultural influences on several perspectives in your conflict?

Participants	Perspectives	Cultural Influences

Here's part of what Aliza wrote about the cultural influences on her perspective:

When I first found out that I probably wouldn't be able to go to [my first choice], I was so disappointed. I thought that I would be missing out on my only opportunity to get a great education.... My mom was a lot more optimistic than I was at that time. She knew it wasn't the end of the world. I took [my financial aid problem] a lot harder than my mom because I had such a narrow perspective on it. I had set myself up [to find the "right school"]. . . . There were a lot of reasons, personal and cultural, that influenced my thoughts. I was really looking forward to getting out of high school and starting college. As much as I loved high school, I didn't cry on graduation day like some of my friends. I was excited to move on.

I think that most students applying to colleges feel competitive with their friends (on some level). Many of my friends talked about going to schools in Texas, Michigan, California, and even Hawaii. All of their plans sounded so exciting, but I didn't want to be too far from home so I was limited to the New York and New England area.... I found some of the best colleges in the Northeast so I wouldn't be discouraged about not going far away; still, I was a bit jealous of my friends' choices. . . . The media plays up the idea of going to an Ivy League school. I think that's why so many students feel pressure to attend the "best" schools.

Can you continue Aliza's analysis with some more specific examples on the cultural influences on college choice? Beyond the great example of *The US News and World Report* on top colleges, how else is finding the "right school" stressed in American culture?

Cultural Influences on College Choice

parents' expectations

competition with friends

US News on top colleges

_____ ?

_____ ?

_____ ?

Now you also can examine the cultural influences that may have affected the participants in your narrative. Try answering the following questions:

- In your narrative, what is the most obvious conflict? AND what is the most significant conflict? (Note the answers to these two questions may or may not be the same.)

- Who are the direct participants in the most important conflict? Who are other indirect but possibly influential participants?

- At the time of the conflict, what was your perspective? How did it differ from at least one other perspective?

- Why was your viewpoint different from others? In other words, what beliefs, experiences, and cultural influences affected each perspective?

If you'd like to see a published author engaged in the examination of cultural influences, read the following nonfiction essay:

DON'T CALL ME MARIA

by Judith Ortiz Cofer

As a child, Judith Ortiz Cofer grew up listening to the stories of her grandmother. As a writer, Ortiz Cofer tells her own tales of growing up and living in two sometimes clashing cultures: Puerto Rican and American. A prolific and acclaimed writer, she also examines the tensions between patriarchal oppression and female empowerment. Originally titled "The Myth of the Latin Woman," this narrative from 1993 appeared in a collection of essays called *The Latin Deli*.

On a bus trip to London from Oxford University, where I was earning some graduate credits one summer, a young man, obviously fresh from a pub, spotted me and as if struck by inspiration went down on his knees in the aisle. With both hands over his heart he broke into an Irish tenor's rendition of "Maria" from West Side Story. My politely amused fellow passengers gave his lovely voice the round of gentle applause it deserved. Though I was not quite as amused, I managed my version of an English smile: no show of teeth, no extreme contortions of the facial muscles—I was at this time of my life practicing reserve and cool. Oh, that British control, how I coveted it. But Maria had followed me to London, reminding me of a prime fact of my life: you can leave the Island, master the English language, and travel as far as you can, but if you are a Latina, especially one like me who so obviously belongs to Rita Moreno's gene pool, the Island travels with you.

This is sometimes a very good thing—it may win you that extra minute of someone's attention. But with some people, the same things can make you an island – not so much a tropical paradise as an Alcatraz, a place nobody wants to visits. As a Puerto Rican girl growing up in the United States and wanting like most children to "belong," I resented the stereotype that my Hispanic appearance called forth from many people I met.

Our family lived in a large urban center in New Jersey during the sixties, where life was designed as a microcosm of my parents' casas on the island. We spoke in Spanish, we ate Puerto Rican food bought at the bodega, and we practiced strict Catholicism complete with Saturday confession and Sunday mass at a church where our parents were accommodated into a one-hour Spanish mass slot, performed by a Chinese priest trained as a missionary in Latin America.

As a girl, I was kept under strict surveillance, since virtue and modesty were, by cultural equation, the same as family honor. As a teenager I was instructed on how to behave as a proper senorita. But it was a conflicting message girls got, since the Puerto Rican mothers also encouraged their daughters to look and act like women and to dress in clothes our Anglo friends and their mothers found too "mature" for our age. It was, and is, cultural, yet I often felt humiliated when I appeared at an American friend's party wearing a dress more suitable to a semiformal than to a playroom birthday celebration. At Puerto Rican festivities, neither the music nor the colors we wore could be too loud. I still experience a vague sense of letdown when I'm invited to a "party" and it turns out to be a marathon conversation in hushed tones rather than a fiesta with salsa, laughter, and dancing—the kind of celebration I remember from my childhood.

I remember Career Day in our high school, when teachers told us to come dressed as if for a job interview. It quickly became obvious that to the barrio girls, "dressing up" sometimes meant wearing ornate jewelry and clothing that would be more appropriate (by mainstream standards) for the company Christmas party than as daily office attire. That morning, I had agonized in front of my closet, trying to figure out what a "career girl" would wear because, essentially, except for Marlo Thomas on TV, I had no models on which to base my decision. I knew how to dress for Sunday mass, and I knew what dresses to wear for parties at my relatives' homes. Though I do not recall the precise details of my Career Day outfit, it must have been a composite of the above choices. But I remember a comment my friend (an Italian-American) made in later years that coalesced my impression of that day. She said that at the business school she was attending the Puerto Rican girls always stood out for wearing "everything at once." She meant, of course, too much jewelry, too many accessories. On that day at school, we were simply made the negative models by the nuns who were themselves not credible fashion experts to any of us. But it was painfully obvious to me that to the others, in their tailored skirts and silk blouses, we must have seemed "hopeless" and "vulgar." Though I now know that most adolescents feel out of step much of the time, I also know that for the Puerto Rican girls of my generation that sense was intensified. The way our teachers and classmates looked at us that day in school was just a taste of the culture clash that awaited us in the real world, where prospective employers and men on the street would often misinterpret our tight skirts and jingling bracelets as a come-on.

Mixed cultural signals have perpetuated certain stereotypes—for example, that of the Hispanic woman as the "Hot Tamale" or sexual firebrand. It is a one-dimensional view that the media have found easy to promote. In their special vocabulary, advertisers have designated "sizzling" and "smoldering" as the adjectives of choice for describing not only the foods but also the women of Latin America. From conversations in my house I recall hearing about the harassment that Puerto Rican women endured in the factories where the "boss men" talked to them as if sexual innuendo was all they understood and, worse, often gave them the choice of submitting to advances or being fired.

It is custom, however, not chromosomes, that leads us to choose scarlet over pale pink. As young girls, we were influenced in our decisions about clothes and colors by the women—older sisters and mothers who had grown up on a tropical island where the natural environment was a riot of primary colors, where showing your skin was one way to keep cool as well as to look sexy. Most important of all, on the island, women perhaps felt freer to dress and move more provocatively, since, in most cases, they were protected by the traditions, mores, and laws of a Spanish/Catholic system of morality and machismo whose main rule was: *You may look at my sister, but if you touch her I will kill you.* The extended family and church structure could provide a young woman with a circle of safety in her small pueblo on the island; if a man "wronged" a girl, everyone would close in to save her family honor.

This is what I have gleaned from my discussions as an adult with older Puerto Rican women. They have told me about dressing in their best party clothes on Saturday nights and going to the town's plaza to promenade with their girlfriends in front of the boys they liked. The males were thus given the opportunity to admire the women and to express their admiration in the form of *piropos*: erotically charged street poems they composed on the spot. I have been subjected to a few piropos while visiting the Island, and they can be outrageous, although custom dictates that they never cross into obscenity. This ritual, as I understand it, also entails a show of indifference on the woman's part; if she is "decent," she must not acknowledge the man's impassioned words. So I do understand how things can be lost in translation. When a Puerto Rican girl dressed in her idea of what is attractive meets a man from the mainstream culture who has been trained to react to certain types of clothing as a sexual signal, a clash is likely to take place. The line I first heard based on this aspect of the myth happened when the boy who took me to my first formal dance leaned over to plant a sloppy overeager kiss painfully on my mouth, and when I didn't respond with sufficient passion, said in a resentful tone: "I thought you Latin girls were supposed to mature early"—my first instance of being thought of as a fruit or vegetable—I was supposed to *ripen*, not just grow into womanhood like other girls.

It is surprising to some of my professional friends that some people, including those who should know better, still put others "in their place." Though rarer, these incidents are still commonplace in my life. It happened to me most recently during a stay at a very classy metropolitan hotel favored by young professional couples for their weddings. Late one evening after the theater, as I walked toward my room with my new colleague (a woman with whom I was coordinating an arts program), a middle-aged man in a tuxedo, a young girl in satin and lace on his arm, stepped directly into our path. With his champagne glass extended toward me, he exclaimed, "Evita!"

Our way blocked, my companion and I listened as the man half-recited, half-bellowed, "Don't Cry for Me, Argentina." When he finished, the young girl said: "How about a round of applause for my daddy?" We complied, hoping this would bring the silly spectacle to a close. I was becoming aware that our little group was attracting the attention of the other guests. "Daddy" must have perceived this too, and he once more barred the way as we tried to walk past him. He began to shout a ditty to the tune of "La Bamba"— except the lyrics were about a girl named Maria whose exploits all rhymed with her name and gonorrhea. The girl kept saying, "Oh, Daddy" and looking at me with pleading eyes. She wanted me to laugh along with the others. My companion and I stood silently waiting for the man to end his offensive song. When he finished, I looked not at him but at his daughter. I advised her calmly never to ask her father what he had done in the army. Then I walked between them and to my room. My friend complimented me on my cool handling of the situation. I confessed to her that I really had wanted to push the jerk into the swimming pool. I knew that this same man—probably a corporate executive, well-educated, even worldly by most standards—would not have been likely to regale a white woman with a dirty song in public. He would perhaps have checked his impulse by assuming that she could be somebody's wife or mother, or at least *somebody* who might take offense. But to him, I was just an Evita or a Maria: merely a character in his cartoon-populated universe.

Because of my education and my proficiency with the English language, I have acquired many mechanisms for dealing with the anger I experience. This was not true for my parents, nor is it true for the many Latin women working at menial jobs who must put up with stereotypes about our ethnic group such as: "They make good domestics." This is another facet of the myth of the Latin woman in the United States. Its origin is simple to deduce. Work as domestics, waitressing, and factory jobs are all that's available to women with little English and few skills. The myth of the Hispanic menial has been sustained by the same media phenomenon that made "Mammy" from *Gone with the Wind* America's idea of the black woman for generations; Maria, the housemaid or counter girl, is now indelibly etched into the national psyche. The big and the little screens have presented us with the picture of the funny Hispanic maid, mispronouncing words and cooking up a spicy storm in a shiny California kitchen.

This media-engendered image of the Latina in the United States has been documented by feminist Hispanic scholars, who claim that such portrayals are partially responsible for the denial of opportunities for upward mobility among Latinas in the professions. I have a Chicana friend working on a Ph.D. in philosophy at a major university. She says her doctor still shakes his head in puzzled amazement at all the "big words" she uses. Since I do not wear my diplomas around my neck for all to see, I too have on occasion been sent to that "kitchen," where some think I obviously belong.

One such incident that has stayed with me, though I recognize it as a minor offense, happened on the day of my first public poetry reading. It took place in Miami in a boat-restaurant where we were having lunch before the event. I was nervous and excited as I walked in with my notebook in my hand. An older woman motioned me to her table. Thinking (foolish me) that she wanted me to autograph a copy of my brand new slender volume of verse, I went over. She ordered a cup of coffee from me, assuming that I was the waitress. Easy enough to mistake my poems for menus, I suppose. I know that it wasn't an intentional act of cruelty, yet of all the good things that happened that day, I remember that scene most clearly, because it reminded me of what I had to overcome before anyone would take me seriously. In retrospect I understand that my anger gave my reading fire, that I have almost always taken doubts in my abilities as a challenge—and that the result is, most times, a feeling of satisfaction at having won a convert when I see the cold, appraising eyes warm to my words, the body language change, the smile that indicates that I have opened some avenue for communication. That day, I read to that woman, and her lowered eyes told me that she was embarrassed at her little faux pas, and when I willed her to look up at me, it was my victory, and she graciously allowed me to punish her with my full attention. We shook hands at the end of the reading, and I never saw her again. She has probably forgotten the whole thing, but maybe not.

Yet I am one of the lucky ones. My parents made it possible for me to acquire a stronger footing in the mainstream culture by giving me the chance at an education. And books and art have saved me from the harsher forms of ethnic and racial prejudice that many of my Hispanic *compañeras* have had to endure. I travel a lot around the United States, reading from my books of poetry and my novel, and the reception I most often receive is one of positive interest by people who want to know more about my culture. There are, however, thousands of Latinas without the privilege of an education or the entrée into society that I have. For them life is a struggle against the misconceptions perpetuated by the myth of the Latina as whore, domestic or criminal. We cannot change this by legislating the way people look at us. The transformation, as I see it, has to occur at a much more individual level. My personal goal in my public life is to try to replace the old pervasive stereotypes and myths about Latinas with a much more interesting set of realities. Every time I give a reading, I hope the stories I tell, the dreams and fears I examine in my work, can achieve some universal truth which will get my audience past the particulars of my skin color, my accent, or my clothes.

I once wrote a poem in which I called us Latinas "God's brown daughters." This poem is really a prayer of sorts, offered upward, but also, through the human-to-human channel of art, outward. It is a prayer for communication, and for respect. In it, Latin women pray "in Spanish to an Anglo God / with a Jewish heritage," and they are "fervently hoping / that if not omnipotent, / at least He be bilingual."

Although several challenging questions are provided below, we do not expect a professor to assign or a student to be asked to answer every one thoroughly, such as in a homework assignment due as class begins. Instead one of the pleasures of a good class discussion is for students to respond to a question or two and then develop expanded answers and insights through conversation and collaboration.

Close Reading Questions

1. In addition to Ortiz Cofer herself, who would you identify as some of the other main participants in her conflict?

2. How would you describe the perspectives of some of the participants, such as Ortiz Cofer's parents and her Anglo teachers? (Multiple Perspectives)

Analytical Writing/Discussion

3. How did the varied customs related to fashion create misunderstandings between Puerto-Rican girls like Ortiz Cofer and her Anglo classmates? What are some of the primary influences on your own fashion choices, and when, if ever, have they created a "cultural clash" for you? (Cultural Influences)

4. How do influences within Puerto-Rican culture both promote and protect a teenage female's sexuality? Why do you think some of your own cultural influences represent (or do not represent) a similar self-contradiction?

5. Ortiz Cofer both describes and disrupts some "pervasive stereotypes." What do you think are some of the cultural influences of society today that still maintain or oppose such ethnic stereotypes?

Historical Trends

Another form of critical thinking common to much of academic inquiry is the analysis of historical trends. As the term suggests, this analysis examines how a perspective changes or remains the same over time, in history. For example, some typical academic questions on historical trends include: Does Huck's perspective on Jim change as they journey down the Mississippi River? Or in *The Scarlet Letter*, does Hester remain steadfast in her love for the minister? During the Civil War, did President Lincoln ever waver in his conviction that our nation should not be divided? Or from the example of Cofer's examination of cultural influences presented above, we could shift to historical trends by asking a question like: To what degree do you think stereotypes about Latina women have changed or remained the same over the last few decades? Understanding the continuity of today's perspectives with those of the past can reveal both the progress a person or a society has made and the problems that still persist.

One way to analyze historical trends is to draw a timeline and add several perspectives over time. Here's an example using Huck Finn's relationship with Jim:

Huck's Attitude Toward Jim

```
-------o-----------------------------o--------------------------------o------------------------o-------
```

at the start   the raft trip begins   Huck lies for Jim   the ending

Then, some of the changes and continuities in Huck's perspective can be analyzed.

When Aliza completed this analysis, she traced her evolving perspective:

```
---o----------------------------------o--------------------o------------o---------------------o--------
```

at age 14   16   17   months later   now at 18

at 14, already excited about college, knew I would go

at 16, started looking at specific colleges online, wanted to find the best one for me

at 17, after the campus visit, I knew it was the right school

months later, so happy when I was accepted! Then when the disappointing letter on financial aid arrived, I felt panic and anger. After a few weeks, I knew I had to pick from my other good choices.

at 18, content at this college -- how I study matters more than where I study.

Then she analyzed these changes more by writing:

Looking back, I think my thoughts and feelings have changed a lot. I had built up college choice to be such an important thing. . . . I went from being devastated [by the financial aid problem] to understanding that it wasn't the end of the world if I couldn't go there. Everything began to change when I [stopped] being so focused on the one negative aspect of my six choices. Not going [there] didn't mean that I would not succeed. It didn't mean that I would be miserable somewhere else. I could get a really good education and have a good time at many of the places I had been accepted to.... My new perspective became much more similar to the way my mom was looking at things all along. She knew everything would be ok; she even wrote me an e-mail one day when I was struggling to narrow down my remaining options that said, "Don't worry, you WILL end up at a good school." I was making everything a lot more stressful than it had to be and she saw that. I was so disappointed at first because I had been so enthusiastic about going to [my top choice].

Using either your age or references to days and months, you too can analyze in historical trends, perhaps by first drawing a timeline describing the perspective at each point:

Participant's Name _____

------------o------------------------o------------------------o------------------------o------------------

First Perspective:

Second:

·

·

Final Perspective:

You also can examine these perspectives and their changes or continuities over time by answering the following questions:

- What was your perspective or those of others before the conflict began?
- As your conflict developed, how did your perspective or those of others change or remain the same? At what point in time?
- Immediately after the conflict as well as long afterward, did these viewpoints shift? If so, from what to what, for whom, when, and why?
- Finally, now at this present time, what is your perspective or those of others?

For a published example of the analysis of historical trends, please read the following essay.

MOTORCYCLE TALK

by Thomas Simmons

> As a child, Thomas Simmons learned to love motion and machines, and as an adult, he still rides a motorcycle and flies a small airplane. In the following narrative, he examines his relationship with his father through their shared interest in a motorcycle. This personal story is excerpted from his memoir from 1991 titled *The Unseen Shore, Memories of a Christian Science Childhood.*

My father, who suffered from so many private griefs, was not an easy man to get along with, but in one respect he was magnificent: he was unfailing in his devotion to machines of almost any variety. When he chose to, he could talk to me at length on the virtues of, say, the 1966 Chevrolet four-barrel carburetor or the drawbacks of the Wankel rotary engine. Talking, however, was not his strongest suit: he was a man of action. As he liked to point out, talking would never make an engine run more smoothly.

On weekends sometimes, or on his rare summer days of vacation, he would encourage me in my first and last steps toward automotive literacy. He would allow me to stand beside him as he worked on the car, and when he needed a simple tool—a crescent wrench or needlenose pliers—I would be allowed to hand them to him. And when I was 12, he and my daring mother bought me a motorcycle.

It was a 50cc Benelli motocross bike—neither new, nor large, nor powerful, nor expensive. But it gave form and life to my imaginings. No longer did I have to confine myself wistfully to magazine photos of high-speed turns and hair-raising rides through rough country. I had the thing itself—the device that would make these experiences possible, at least to some degree.

And, although I did not know it at the time, I also had a new lexicon [set of terms]. The motorcycle was a compendium of gears and springs and sprockets and cylinder heads and piston rings, which between my father and me acquired the force of more affectionate words that we could never seem to use in each other's presence.

Almost immediately the Benelli became a meeting ground, a magnet for the two of us. We would come down to look at it—even if it was too late in the day for a good ride—and my father would simply check the tension of the chain, or examine the spark plug for carbon, or simply bounce the shock absorbers a few times as he talked. He'd tell me about compression ratios and ways of down-shifting smoothly through a turn; I'd tell him about my latest ride, when I leaped two small [mounds] or took a spill on a tight curve.

More rarely, he'd tell stories of his youth. His favorite, which he recounted in slightly different versions about four times a year, had to do with the go-kart he built from scrap parts in his father's basement during the Depression. It was by any account a masterful performance; he managed to pick up a small, broken gasoline engine for free, and tinkered with it until it came back to life. The wheels, steering gear, axles, chassis—all were scrounged for a few cents, or for free, from junkyards and vacant lots in and around Philadelphia.

Winter was in full swing when my father had his go-kart ready for a test-drive; snow lay thick on the ground. But he'd built the go-kart in his father's large basement, and given the weather he felt it made sense to make the trial run indoors. His engineering skills were topnotch. Assembled from orphan parts, the go-kart performed like a well-tuned race car. My father did what any good 13-year-old would have done: he got carried away. He laid on the power coming around the corner of the basement, lost control, and smashed head-on into the furnace. It was a great loss for him. The jagged wood and metal cut and bruised him; he had destroyed his brand-new car. Far worse was the damage to the furnace. In 1933 such damage was almost more than the family finances could sustain. Furious, my father's father called him names, upbraided him for his stupidity and irresponsibility, and made him feel worthless. Years later, as he would tell this story to me, my father would linger over those words—"stupid," "irresponsible"—as if the pain had never gone away.

In these moments he and I had a common stake in something. Though he might not know whether I was reading at the eighth-grade level or the twelfth-grade level—or whether my math scores lagged behind those of the rest of the class—he was delighted to see that I knew how to adjust a clutch cable or stop after a low-speed, controlled skid. These skills were a source of genuine adventure for me, and I came to life and he observed my progress.

But this was only part of our rapport with the motorcycle. My father found few occasions to be overtly tender with the family, but he could be tender with a machine. I began to notice this in the countless small adjustments he regularly made. His touch on the cranky carburetor settings for gas and air was gentle, even soothing; as least it seemed to soothe the motorcycle, which ran smoothly under his touch but not under mine.

I found that, from time to time, this tenderness buoyed me up in its wake. If my father was, in his dreams, a flat-track mechanic, then I was his driver: he owed me the best he could give me; that was his job. This dream of his bound us in a metaphor which, at its heart, was not so different from the straight-forward love another child might have received from a more accessible father. I did not know this then, not exactly. But I knew, when we both hovered over the Benelli's cylinder head or gearbox, adjusting a cam or replacing a gasket, that he would not have worked on this machine for himself alone.

Yet there was a secret to our new language, a secret that only slowly revealed itself. What we shared through the motorcycle contradicted most of our other encounters in the family. It was almost as if we lived in another world when we came together over this machine, and for a time I hoped that world might be the new one, the ideal on the horizon. I was wrong. The bands of our words were strong, but too narrow to encompass the worlds rising before me.

Almost without knowing it I began to acquire other vocabularies—the tough, subtle speech of girls, the staccato syllables of independence, the wrenching words of love and emptiness. In this I began to leave him behind. He could not talk of these things with me. He remained with his engines, and long after I had ceased to ride it, he occasionally would open the gas jets, prime the carburetor, and take the motorcycle for a spin around the block.

But as it seems that nothing is ever wholly lost, this vocabulary of the garage and the flat-track speedway has a kind of potency, a place in the scheme of things. When, recently, I had dinner with my father, after not seeing him for nearly a year, we greeted each other with the awkwardness of child cousins: we hardly knew what to say. I had almost given up on the possibility of prolonged conversation until I happened to mention that my car needed a new clutch. Suddenly we were safe again, as we moved from the clutch to the valves on his souped-up VW and the four-barrel carburetor on the '66 Chevrolet Malibu, still pouring on the power after all these years. We had moved back to the language of our old country. And though one of us had journeyed far and almost forgotten the idioms, the rusty speech still held, for a time, the words of love.

Close Reading Questions

1. In what specific ways does the purchase of the motorcycle change the narrator's relationship with his father? What quotations from the text support your response? (Historical Trends)

2. What childhood story does the father repeat several times? Why do you think he would retell this tale?

3. What topics and terms bring the narrator and his father closer together? What topics and terms keep them separated? (Multiple Perspectives)

Analytical Writing/Discussion

4. Using both evidence from the text and speculation based on your own knowledge, how would you describe the father's viewpoint, and what do you think may have influenced his perspective? (Cultural Influences)

5. Over the years, how does the narrator's attitude toward his father's mechanical abilities change and/or remain the same? Similarly, how does his attitude toward his father's character change and/or remain the same? (Historical Trends—although only one specific reference to age is made, try drawing a timeline using such points as before the motorbike, its purchase at age 12, soon after its purchase, a few years later, and many years later.)

Further Options

6. As you look back over the sample narratives that you have read in this chapter (by Derricotte, Braggs, Ortiz Cofer, and/or Simmons), in what ways do you think these personal narratives are similar and different in their content and/or their style?

The ability to synthesize several texts in an extended essay is a fundamental ability for college and beyond so each thematic chapter, therefore, ends with a final assignment. This assignment includes a sequence designed to make your effort more manageable, and your professor may alter, or give you the opportunity to change, this assignment sequence.

Final Assignment: An Analytical Revision of What Happened and Why

As suggested by the examples of Aliza's analysis of her narrative, you probably will understand your conflict better, and perhaps differently, as you analyze its participants and their perspectives. This analysis will enable you, or even compel you, to revise your narrative. The final assignment of this option is for you to revise your narrative by adding some of your analysis:

> In a carefully drafted, revised, and edited final copy, narrate and analyze a significant conflict from your own life. You do not have to be a central figure of this conflict, but you should be a direct participant. In addition to presenting your perspective on this conflict, you also should examine the viewpoints of some of the other participants and analyze why some of these perspectives developed and differed.

> Rather than just expect you to complete this revision, we will offer some suggestions on how to revise your draft.

Revision as Reseeing

Just as analysis often involves going back to collect more ideas, revision may require you to return to focus and order. Sometimes students realize that the focus of their narratives has changed. A classmate of Aliza named Heather, for example, realized that her similar conflict over college choice was actually about another related issue. During her analysis of her conflict, Heather realized that she saw New York City, where one college was located, as a center of boundless opportunities. Her mother, however, considered this city to be a place of many dangers, especially for a young woman far from home. Heather then revised her narrative by focusing on these differences in perspectives and explaining her mother's fears about allowing her daughter to attend college in New York.

In "Passing," Toi Derricotte too adds insightful analysis to her vivid narration of a train ride. If you look back at "Passing," you can notice how Derricotte alternates between a specific event, the train ride in paragraph three, and critical thinking, the "machinery of racism" in four. Again in her final paragraphs, Derricotte seamlessly combines another moment, breakfast with a reflection on sympathy, suffering, and withdrawal.

The challenge of revision for Aliza and Heather was for each writer to combine the new insights of their analyses with the events of their original narratives. They had to revise, which literally means, when you consider its prefix of "re-", to see their previous drafts again and anew. Rather than just dump the explanatory insights at the end of their narratives, these students had to refocus and reorder their previous drafts.

Back in the section on focus, we asked you to answer

My conflict is about _____ , and the primary conflict is between _____ and _____ .

At that time, we conceded that you might not be able to answer this prompt fully, and we knew then but did not admit that for at least some students, your initial answer might change later. As you have been engaged in analysis, your focus may have changed as it did for Heather and your understanding of the conflict may have increased as for Aliza.

During this process of analysis and revision, what we as writing teachers find crucial and many students find exciting is the fact that you, as the narrative writer, still have the freedom and responsibility for revising your draft. Revision in this assignment does not mean completing only what the teacher tells you to do in order to get a better grade. Instead, like Heather, you will have to decide what you want to focus on in your revision. You will have to decide how you want to revise your narrative and what you want your reader to "see" in the new draft.

Checking Your Order and Emphasis

Even with a clearer focus in mind, it is not always easy to revise your narrative because you will have to decide not only where to add the insightful analysis but also where to condense and cut the previous draft. In the sometimes circular process of writing, this reorganization requires you to stand back and consider again the order and emphasis of your narrative. One way to create this critical distance on your narrative is to try outlining after drafting (see p. 87 in Chapter 4 for more explanation). Most students are taught to outline before they draft, but many struggle to do so effectively. Some students, however, find that outlining *after* drafting can be very beneficial.

On a new page or screen, state the focus of your previous draft and then assert the planned focus of your revision, even if they are exactly the same. If they differ, then stating both will help you reconsider your previous draft. Next, number the paragraphs of the original narrative, and then outline what is the purpose of each one. What is each paragraph about?

Narrative Focus: _____

New Focus: _____

1. Introductory scene
2.
3.
4.
5.

Next you can freewrite and/or discuss with a classmate what you have learned from this analysis.

Freewrite 3: Revision Plans

Try answering some of the following questions as you consider your revision:

- How has your understanding of the conflict been changed, enriched, or complicated?
- What parts of the previous draft will you use again?
- What parts need to be altered, expanded, condensed, or cut?
- What new scenes or details need to be added and where?
- Do you need to make any changes in order and where?
- To fulfill your "new" focus, how should your original paragraphs and new ideas be organized?

You already may have started to consider where to add some of the insights from your analysis, but to encourage yourself to make even more additions, try to layer onto your outline some of the information from your analysis. You may want to grab a different colored pen or use another font to add these analytical insights to your outline. Of course, using another pen or font is just another suggestion for you to try. Let us stress, you do not have to follow every recommendation we make. Our goal is for you to find a combination of strategies that work for you.

Here is a sample of this outlining after drafting based on Aliza's analysis:

	Narrative Outline	**Revision Plans**
1.	College choice intro	revise final sentences
2–4	Different choices	
5.	Visit to university #1	ADD high school emphasis on college
6.	Rejection fear yet accepted!	
7.	Financial aid problem	
8.	Mother's example	
9.	Difficult decision over debt	explain more
		ADD mother's perspective
		ADD media stress on college
		ADD my new perspective
10.	Struggle to choose	
11.	University #2 chosen	
12.	Retrospection on #1	
13–14.	Conclusion on the finish line	change order and condense

Once you have planned your revision using some of these activities, you still have to actually write the revised draft, but your plan lets you concentrate on drafting.

Computers too make revision so much easier, especially if you have kept your narrative drafts and analyses in clearly labeled files. Now you can cut and paste from those files to create a revised copy. You also can do the same using the low-tech strategy of scissors and tape. Using the scissors, cut a clean copy of your original narrative apart into separate paragraphs and spread them out before you on a table. Next, cut apart sections of your analysis and literally tape them into place among the narrative paragraphs. Some students like the physical and spatial activity of this scissor and tape approach, while others can think and create more efficiently with the desktop cutting and pasting from several computer files. Again, you need to find the methods that work for you on this assignment.

Just as there are differences in the conventions of a narrative and a five-paragraph essay, you may find that the more informal phrasing used in your narratives differs from the more formal terms used in your analysis. Try to avoid any abrupt changes in the phrasing, the diction, of your revision. Then your new draft will seem like a coherent text and not some bumpy combination. To add the insights of analysis, try using some of the following phrases that will help you maintain the less formal, less academic tone of a personal narrative:

Multiple Perspectives -	He believed that …
	She didn't understand …
	Everyone in their group assumed …
Cultural Influences -	My friend probably was affected by …
	Her decision may have been influenced …
	It didn't help this conflict that he watched …
Historical Trends -	At that time, she felt …
	He later realized …
	Their attitude changed when …
	Looking back, I now understand …

To conclude your revision, you may want to rely on historical trends by explaining: What is your current perspective? As you look back, what do you now understand about this conflict and some of its participants? As you reflect on this conflict, how do you now react when you see others involved in a similar conflict?

Here is Aliza's revision that maintains many of her details and much of her original order. To aid discussion, we have numbered the paragraphs, presented her revisions in bold, and added comments on her revision.

Aliza's revision:

The Finish Line

1. College is something that most people start dealing with in the middle of high school. However, in my case, I started thinking about college in middle school. **My fascination with this idea played a big part in my life, or else I probably wouldn't have struggled**

as much as I did when deciding where to go to school. [new phrasing in a condensed introduction]

2. I've always known what I've wanted to be when I grew up, even though what I've wanted has changed a few times over the years. When I was younger, I wanted to be an archeologist (mainly because I had a really cool social studies teacher who did the same thing). A few years later, I decided that I wanted to be an architect, and after that phase, I finally settled on something I had always been interested in, business and advertising. I loved thinking about the future and what it would bring.

3. I've never really had a "dream school" like some kids do. I didn't come from a line of Cornell or Harvard graduates, and there wasn't a particular school that I was expected to attend, so I was on my own to narrow the thousands of options down to one. Naturally, like my changing career interests, my top college picks changed as well.

4. The first college I visited was in 10th grade while on the way back from visiting relatives, and it was so exciting. Walking around the campus that day against the backdrop of the sparkling Hudson River was so different, and much better than being stuck in the same old high school hallways. . . . [I thought] this was college and I was finally here. We went to the bookstore after the tour, and I bought a sweatshirt and told my mom "this is where I'm going". At first, it was probably the excitement of it all, but this phrase became very familiar to her, and seemed to pop up after every college tour that we would go on.

5. The last tour we went on before school started was at [University #1]. From the moment we got out of the car, I really loved it there. Compared to some of the other places we had visited, the campus was so open and beautiful. **Nestled quietly next to the mountains, I immediately loved the atmosphere and having visited right at the end of summer, everything was still green and full of life. Everyone just looked so happy.** They had the advertising major I was looking for, which many places did not. It seemed like a perfect match for me, and it really could be the place I would end up spending my next four years. For months after, a blue and gold banner hung over my bed in my room. [new showing details]

6. The beginning of senior year came too quickly, and it wasn't long before my friends, classmates and I started sending out applications. The stress from parents, teachers, and guidance counselors was almost unbearable at times. **Coming from one of the best public high schools in the area, our high school's reputation for education and college preparation could never be escaped. My guidance counselor once told us that by just going to our school, our applications would look better, which was something we found hard to believe. College was always made to be a pretty big deal, and planning for it wasn't just something that started at the end of junior year; it started right away. On our family information nights, we sat with our parents and listened to lectures about interviewing and how to write "the perfect college essay" from local admissions counselors. Last year marked the "highly anticipated" introduction of a new personalized college planning website that the school would be the first in the area to utilize (freshmen now are being strongly encouraged to explore this site). In the years I was in high school, a number of students from my graduating class and those older than me had been admitted to Harvard, Yale, Cornell, and Notre Dame. The guidance office used to have a big map with little push pins showing where all of our graduates were going. College was drilled into our heads from day one.** [cultural influences added]

7. Important deadlines were looming, and the dreaded thought of not getting into any schools was something my friends and I joked about all the time, but we were all secretly

afraid of. **We had all seen the movie Accepted, where the characters decide to create their own college when nowhere else had accepted them, and as funny as the concept was, we promised ourselves not to end up in their position.** So, even though I knew where I wanted to go, I ended up applying to seven schools, just in case. After getting into six and being waitlisted at another, I had nothing to complain about. I really only cared about one school though, and I happened to get that acceptance letter the day before my birthday. I was so excited to open the envelope and tell my mom as soon as she got home from work. She was so happy for me, and I thought that would be it. [cultural influences added]

8. Then, the weeks came when it was time for the financial aid letters to arrive. I'm not a genius, but my slightly above average grades in high school and good SAT scores managed to get me some scholarship money that I was so grateful for. Growing up with a single parent in a one-income household is something I knew would have an impact on my college education. The question was never if I could go at all, but how it would be made affordable. I knew that college came with a hefty price tag. The price of school is something that limits so many students' chances of going to college and getting an education. Looking back, I realize my good luck had to break some time, and the day came when the one place I wanted to go didn't offer me nearly enough money in scholarships. We were all shocked, seeing as all of the other schools I had been accepted to were very generous with their scholarship and aid money. The full cost of [University #1] just wasn't feasible for my family.

9. Watching my mom go to a job everyday that she's never really loved, to provide the best for my sister and I, is something I'm so grateful for. She has always put us first and that means so much to me. There's always been a part of me that has wanted to work hard and make something of myself to thank her for all she's done. I guess that's one reason why college means so much to me.

10. It took a while to come to terms with the situation; I was so disappointed. Until then I thought getting in would be my biggest challenge. I always knew money would be a factor, but never a deciding one. Even though my mom never said no, it would have been personally hard for me to go, knowing what financial difficulty I would be creating for her. **My younger sister will be starting college in a few years, which also factored into my situation.** I was left with a very difficult decision. I could go to this school, but in turn put myself and my family into a **huge debt**, or I could find another option. I knew that I really had no choice, but having my heart set on one thing for the good portion of a year was tough to get over. [slight changes in phrasing]

11. **For me, at that time, not going to [University #1] seemed like the end of the world. My view of the situation was so narrow that I didn't realize that I did have other options. . . . . My mom, on the other hand, had a different view on the whole situation. [Her] generation grew up in a different world than we are living in today. The world was moving at a much slower pace then. The amount of advertising wasn't nearly as substantial as it is now. In my mom's case, she wrote letters to a few colleges asking for catalogues, and then had to write another letter asking to set up a tour, months in advance. I, however, got my first college catalogue in the mail from a place hours away I had never heard of. I checked the box to be put on an extensive mailing list when I took the PSAT, something I later regretted. Only a week later I was receiving up to 50 emails a week from colleges trying to compete for my attention.**

12. My mother reminded me that there also wasn't the amount of magazines, books and movies dedicated to "getting your kid into college." I am the self-admitted owner of the past four issues of <u>U.S News & World Report's</u> annual installment of America's Best Colleges. In fact, there are literally thousands of these types of books and magazines published each year, which says something about our society's view on the importance of a college education.

13. Since my mom wasn't the main target of all the pressure that is put on today's youth, she was able to see that not going to my first choice of school didn't mean I wouldn't succeed in life; I would be fine at any "good" college. [cultural influences added]

14. Over the next month I struggled to pick another college; **I really did have other perfectly good options**, but I just didn't see that at the time. So, the search started over again, looking at the other colleges I had been accepted to, which was a little strange. **I had already decided on [University #1] in my mind and in doing so, I had ruled out the other places I had been accepted by finding their faults (which is the normal process). Now, I had to somehow go back and find the hidden qualities I had previously passed over. This was really difficult.** We even went to a few more open houses to take one last look around. [details added on historical trends]

15. Finally, I decided on [University #2]. I found out a lot of things I didn't know when I quickly filled out a free application one day in September (which is literally the only reason I'm here today). With one of the best business schools around, I realized there was nowhere else I should be. It's almost ironic that I ended up at school I knew hardly anything about when applying and didn't go to the place I had invested so much of my time into. Even though [University #2] wasn't my first choice, looking back I can't believe I would have wanted to go anywhere else! Now the banner in my room is red and white, and I wouldn't have it any other way. [paragraph deleted]

16. Once in a while, while I'm walking around campus, I think about what it would be like had I ended up at [University #1]. It's never for long, but the thoughts are still there. How would it be different? Would I be different? Would I be happy or happier than I am here? These thoughts don't stick around too long; I really am content with how things worked out in the end. Looking back at it all, I realize now that getting a good education is more important, not where I study. I had always seen planning for college as a race and getting in as a finish line. I realize now that it's only just the beginning.

We have presented Aliza's revision with numbered paragraphs for easy reference. What parts of her revision seem stronger to you? Did you notice that she added a few more showing details about the campus in paragraph five? Do you think any more showing details could and should be added to paragraph five? Has she added the analysis to her original narrative smoothly? Does her analysis in paragraphs 6, 11, and 12 on the cultural influences that "drill" college choice into students seem effective to you? Does the contrasting perspective of her mother make the change in Aliza's perspective seem believable to you? Has she created enough vivid scenes or are more possible? What did you think of her ending? You may want to use Aliza's revision as a sample to practice peer response before you provide feedback for a classmate.

We chose Aliza's paper to serve as the primary sample of this chapter for three reasons. First, many first-year students have experienced a conflict over college choice. Second, Aliza's revision method of primarily adding to her original narrative makes her changes easy to understand. Third, her good effort can be improved even further, giving you the opportunity to suggest how the final draft could have become an even better paper. For instance, some students like Aliza's ending, but others object that it is a little too neat: "A finish line … just the beginning." Some readers also wish that Aliza had reflected even more on the issue of her conflict. Just as Derricotte considers suffering and racism beyond her particular experience, Aliza could have reflected more on the implications of the college pressures felt by most high school students. For instance, does the unrelenting pressure to be accepted by the "right school" place too much emphasis on getting good grades and not enough on learning itself in high school?

Editing the Final Draft

Donald Murray once quipped that a draft is never done, just due. With more time and energy, we often can keep working on a text, but a deadline must be met so the writing process must end. However, before that effort ceases, it is important to not only revise but also edit, and please note that these are two different activities.

Aliza's good revision can be edited further. Consider, for example, the problem in the following phrase from paragraph nine:

> . . . *to provide the best for my sister and I*

Although we sometimes may say "my sister *and I*" as the pronoun in a sentence like this one, this phrase should be written as "my sister and me." We can hear this correction if we focus on the pronoun choice "I/me" by removing the other person and saying "provide for I" and "provide for me." Then the grammatically correct phrasing of "to provide the best for my sister and me" can be discerned.

Editing can be dismissed as nitpicking, but proper spelling, grammar, and punctuation actually make it easier for a reader to comprehend your writing. Consider two examples of a misplaced modifier in Aliza's revision. In paragraphs five and six, she states,

> *Nestled quietly next to the mountains, I immediately loved the atmosphere and having visited right at the end of summer, everything was still green and full of life.*

> *Coming from one of the best public high schools in the area, our high school's reputation . . . could never be escaped.*

Aliza does not mean to assert that she is "Nestled quietly next to the mountains," and she probably is referring to herself as someone "Coming from one of the best public high schools." These problems with a phrase modifying the subject of a sentence can be corrected easily to improve a reader's comprehension. The first example could be edited and improved to become:

> *Compared to some of the other colleges we had visited, the campus seemed so open and beautiful. Several buildings were nestled quietly next to the mountains, and I immediately loved the setting. Since we visited at the end of summer, everything was still green and full of life.*

Doesn't the elimination of the misplaced modifier and the other changes in sentence structure make this passage easier to read and understand? How would you correct the second example? Although it may be difficult to eliminate every editing problem, once you notice a repeated error, try focusing on it for a while. Perhaps you will notice and be able to improve a few more sentences, such as the following one from paragraph fifteen:

With one of the best business schools around, I realized there was nowhere else I should be.

→ *With one of the best business schools around, this university feels like the right place for me.*

Take the time to edit carefully, and a reader will be able to understand your writing better.

Additional Source Suggestions

In the e-supplement of this textbook, there are several sources that will help you deepen your understanding of narrative writing and strengthen your final assignment. These sources include videos as well as readings, and they present more information on narrative and academic writing. To access these materials, see the code on the inside front cover of this textbook, which will lead you to the website for additional sources.

***

Just as we asked you to consider the traits of a strong narrative in the first main assignment, here are the main expectations for the final assignment:

- A vivid, focused narrative
- The analysis of multiple perspectives
- A smoothly ordered and properly edited revision

In addition to presenting the general steps of the writing process from collecting to editing, we also have suggested some activities for writing a narrative in particular. For example, we have suggested that you plan several scenes and organize your draft. We also have presented three forms of analysis that are used frequently in academic inquiry: multiple perspectives, cultural influences, and historical trends. Your instructor may ask you to write what are termed "process notes" so you reflect on these assignments and become more aware of your writing process and college-level writing. For more on process notes, see p. 93 of Chapter 4.

In the two main parts of this assignment, our goals have been for you to learn to

- Practice the writing process more fully
- Pursue a topic based on your interest and knowledge
- Assume a writer's freedom and responsibility
- Fulfill the conventions of a particular genre
- Engage in the critical thinking of most college studies

This assignment emphasizes the writing process, and the subsequent thematic chapters (10–14) involve reading as much as writing. For some students, it is better to focus on one of these related tasks first. Yet reading has been implicit, such as when you have been asked to comprehend and respond to the sample narratives by Aliza and others. Although you have been the primary source of the narrative and its analytical revision, you also have been encouraged to interact with others by discussing the published narratives and responding to each other's drafts. What seemed to be a personal conflict has been expanded and enriched by these interactions. On a more abstract level, you have been asked to place your conflict in a larger social context as you have considered reader expectations and examined cultural influences. Throughout this chapter and the rest of this book, we assume neither that an individual can ever be entirely free from all cultural influences nor that society always predetermines a person's thoughts, feelings, and actions. We instead assume that a back-and-forth, or dialectical, relationship exists between self and society. In other words, culture affects a person's perspective, but an individual also can have an impact on his or her viewpoint and those of others as well. In fact, a college education and its training in reading and writing in particular, can help you exert more control over your life and your society.

Instructional Chapters

PART 2

The Reading Process

CHAPTER 3

If you have started to read this textbook, you are a capable reader. As we will explain below, throughout much of history you would have been considered to be highly literate. As a successful student, you already can read many kinds of texts and for many different purposes. If you are like many of our students, each day you read such diverse texts as campus signs (Smith Hall), text messages (c u l8ter?), Facebook updates (studying 2nite), website info (Registration Schedule), textbook chapters (Principles of Macroeconomics), and literary texts (*The House on Mango Street*). Yet just as some students do not consider themselves to be "real" writers, you may be balking at our classification of you as an able reader. Note, however, that you not only read many texts every day but also vary your reading process depending on your purpose.

There may be as many reasons for reading as there are volumes in your college library, but our purposes can be reduced to a few broad categories:

Reading for **enjoyment**

Reading for **information**

Reading for **action**

Reading for **interpretation**

Whether it's reading a text message or a favorite website, you probably never stop to consider how you read for enjoyment, you just do it. This easy process of reading distinguishes pleasurable reading from interpreting an academic text for most students. We can't deny that interpretation often requires more effort, and let us stress, more *deliberate* effort. Reading a textbook chapter for information or a novel for interpretation makes us work harder and proceed more slowly, and for most of us, harder and slower means less enjoyment. When you turn to these more difficult kinds of reading, you probably alter your process. You don't expect to comprehend quickly; instead you work harder by taking mental or written notes. If this effort becomes too hard and the pace too slow, our reading may bog down and then we later may claim, "I read it, but I don't remember much." Unfortunately, this claim usually leads to classroom frustration and perhaps course failure.

Most professors believe that college students *should* be able to understand and interpret assigned readings. Yet the very use of *should* reveals that not every student *can* fulfill these expectations. The purpose of this chapter is to help you close this gap between the ideal (*should*) and the actual (*can*). In this chapter, we have used headings to create smaller segments in order to increase your comprehension. We will offer you many strategies, but we don't expect your reading process will always include each one. Instead, you will have to determine when a strategy will help you fulfill your purpose.

Memories and Goals

Let's begin with your current assumptions and actions when you are asked to read a difficult text. Please answer the following questions through writing and/or discussion:

- What is one of your most vivid memories of learning to read?
- What is one of your most memorable recollections of reading instruction?

Our own responses to the first question include a grade school book about a boy's adventures riding his horse out west and the comfort of reading a novel in a warm bed on a Saturday morning. You too may recall a favorite book or place to read. Or perhaps you remember your sense of accomplishment when you could transform the marks on the page into spoken words and later when you were able to finish a long book, such as a Harry Potter novel. Most students have more difficulty answering the second question about reading instruction. They try to recall a reading lesson from elementary school.

The memorable responses to the first question and the vague recollections to the second reveal a problematic concept of reading itself. When students believe that they have not been taught to read since grade school, this belief suggests that reading only involves decoding letters like C-A-T and recognizing words like "cat." These skills, which are known as phonetic and sight reading, are two crucial lessons of early literacy instruction, but by high school and college, reading consists of much more than **letter decoding** and **word recognition**. What else do you think college students are expected to do when they are asked to read a textbook or a novel? What do you think we expect as you are reading this page?

- Decoding letters (**phonetic reading**)
- Recognizing words (**sight reading**)
- _____
- _____
- _____
- _____?

You may have used some slightly different phrases to assert some of the additional aspects of reading listed below, but it is important that you understand this list and can distinguish what is usually termed "basic" or "functional" literacy from "advanced" or "critical" literacy.

Functional Literacy	Advanced Literacy
Decoding letters	**Comprehending meaning**
Recognizing words	**Applying information**
	Interpreting ideas
	Analyzing an argument
	Connecting to other texts and/or contexts

Two historians of literacy, Daniel Resnick and Lauren Resnick, explain that the **standard of literacy** was much lower in colonial America. If a colonist in New England could pronounce a biblical passage and/or sign his or her name, he or she was deemed to be literate. Using this minimal standard of literacy, approximately two-thirds of male colonists in New England were considered to be literate, yet many women received very little literacy training and almost every African-American was denied instruction in seventeenth-century America. Thus, using even this low standard, no more than half of these colonists were considered to be literate. By the end of the nineteenth century, the standard of literacy had increased, but only 7% of Americans graduated from high school, so less than a third of the population met this higher measure of literacy. Today, our standard is not only much higher, but a much larger segment of our society is expected to not only comprehend but also interpret complex texts. By 2000, three-quarters of 18-year-olds graduated from high school, although their diplomas did not always guarantee full literacy. The No Child Left Behind Act of 2001 (NCLB) sets the goal of 100% fulfillment of high school literacy standards by 2014. Thus, if one looks back over history, our literacy standards have been a moving target and an ever-greater number has been expected to meet them. In this era of online texts, our twenty-first century standard of literacy has been raised even higher, for we are expected to be able to decipher visual texts as well. For instance, how does the following graph illustrate the history of literacy standards and their fulfillment?

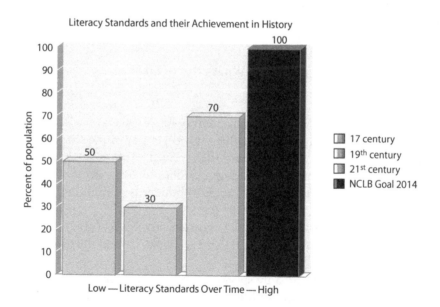

Some may doubt that it is possible for a nation to educate a great majority of its citizens to reach advanced literacy. Some scholars, such as Mike Rose, have conceded that educational and economic inequalities may make this lofty goal difficult to achieve, yet Rose also considers this ambition to be "an extraordinary social experiment: the attempt to provide education for all members of a vast pluralistic democracy." By coming to college, your classmates and you have become part of this great democratic experiment.

However, when some students struggle to comprehend their reading assignments, some professors will utter, "They *should…* " in exasperation because the students' abilities do not equal the professors' expectations. Yet this gap between ability and expectation can be closed. Let's continue with one more question on your reading habits that will be followed by a demonstration of your reading process. Through writing and/or discussion, answer this additional question:

- What conditions are conducive for you to read well? In other words, when and where do you like to read a difficult text?

There probably will be some variety in the responses by you and your classmates. Some probably will like to read in complete silence while sitting upright at a desk in the morning. Others will prefer a comfy chair with some background music on at night. The only response we will question is conditions that disrupt our concentration, like trying to read while on Facebook. Concentration is a crucial condition of reading, but it is not always enough to enable us to comprehend a difficult text. The strategies used also affect our comprehension so let's consider them next, but you may want to pause and consider what you have read so far.

Your Process in Action

Using excerpts from reading from chapters one and two, we want you to read these passages and then reflect on your reading process:

From Chapter 1:

Facebook: What's Not to Like?

by Robert Lane Greene

What is Facebook, anyway? The most obvious point of historical comparison is the social networks that preceded it. First there was Friendster, the flirt-and-forget site of the first half of the 2000s. Then everyone dumped Friendster for MySpace, ... and the received wisdom was that MySpace would take over the world. Then it didn't,.... Started by Mark Zuckerberg in 2004, Facebook went from a Harvard dorm room to the rest of teenage America's bedrooms to hundreds of millions of people all around the world....

But the real comparison is not with other social networks. To give real credit to its achievement today and its ambitions for the future, it can only be said that Facebook's true competitor is the rest of the entire internet.

The internet allows three things, broadly speaking: access to content (video, music, things to read), self-expression (blogs, Twitter), and communication (e-mail, chat, Skype). Facebook competes with it on all these fronts. By one estimate, one minute in every seven spent online, anywhere in the world, is spent on Facebook. To express themselves, users have Status Updates. For content, they can find photos, videos, music, news stories, recipes, book reviews, and much more. And for communication, of course, there are your friends and Friends ... Facebook is an internet within the internet, so dominant that both it and other technology companies are realising that it is far easier to join forces than to fight....

From Chapter 2:

Don't Call Me Maria

by Judith Ortiz Cofer

This media-engendered image of the Latina in the United States has been documented by feminist Hispanic scholars, who claim that such portrayals are partially responsible for the denial of opportunities for upward mobility among Latinas in the professions....

One such incident that has stayed with me, though I recognize it as a minor offense, happened on the day of my first public poetry reading.... I was nervous and excited as I walked in with my notebook in my hand. An older woman motioned me to her table. Thinking (foolish me) that she wanted me to autograph a copy of my brand new slender volume of verse, I went over. She ordered a cup of coffee from me, assuming that I was the waitress. Easy enough to mistake my poems for menus, I suppose. I know that it wasn't an intentional act of cruelty, yet of all the good things that happened that day, I remember that scene most clearly, because it reminded me of what I had to overcome before anyone would take me seriously. In retrospect, I understand that my anger gave my reading fire, that I have almost always taken doubts in my abilities as a challenge....

Every time I give a reading, I hope the stories I tell, the dreams and fears I examine in my work, can achieve some universal truth, which will get my audience past the particulars of my skin color, my accent, or my clothes.

Now that you have read both texts, use writing and/or discussion to answer the following questions:

- Which text did you find harder to read and why?
- What strategies did you use to read the easier text and the more difficult one?
- What are 2–3 important ideas of the "easier" text?
- What are 2–3 important ideas of the "harder" text?

Many students usually find the first piece by Greene harder to read than the second one by Cofer. They explain that the "story" of her experiences as a Latina is easier to follow than the analysis of Facebook in Greene. Even though many of these students' own personal experiences differ greatly from those of Latina, the comparisons with and the contrasts to their experiences make this reading easier for them to comprehend. Other students, however, assert that they prefer the "facts" in the first reading. This group usually dislikes reading too many "flowery" details. Neither preference is wrong, but each will affect a reader's comprehension of a text. Those who prefer a story and a personal connection may struggle with a chapter on macroeconomics, and those who dislike flowery details may find it hard to finish reading a novel. We bring ourselves, meaning our preferences, our experiences, and our knowledge to a text, and when our preferences don't match a text, we may struggle unless we alter our expectations and strategies.

It, therefore, is important to recognize what kind of text we are being asked to read because reading is an interactive process between the reader and the text. When our expectations don't match a text, we usually will struggle until we alter them. For example, once we realize that Greene offers an analysis of Facebook, we are more ready to comprehend this text. Determining the kind of text we are being asked to read helps us decide consciously what reading strategies to use.

A Crucial Assumption

As explained below, there are many strategies for advanced literacy, but let us stress now they all depend on your assumptions about the process of reading. One of our students named Frank once summed up a problematic assumption about reading when he declared one day,

> I must not be a very good reader; I don't get the meaning all at once.

Frank did not lack the intelligence to read well; instead his assumption that reading involves **immediate and complete comprehension** prevented him from succeeding with difficult texts. Have you ever felt like Frank? What doesn't he understand about reading yet?

If we disagree with Frank and deny that reading always involves "all at once" comprehension, reading becomes a **gradual construction of meaning**. We can demonstrate this slower process by showing how we start to understand Greene's analysis of Facebook. Our thoughts reveal a messier, more gradual method:

> Ok, what am I supposed to be reading? Something about Facebook, but what's with the opening question? There's no story so where is this going? I probably should read with a pen in hand like my professor keeps saying. Yea, but what should I mark? I could be like the guy in my lit. class who highlights almost all of the page in yellow. What's the point of coloring the page? Hmm, first, it says that Friendster and MySpace rose and fell before Facebook took over social networking - duh! So does he think Facebook will fail too? Now he says that Facebook should be compared with the rest of the Internet so what can and can't you do with Facebook? I'd say everything and anything online; Facebook has bought another upstart. Maybe that's what Greene means when he says Facebook should be compared with the rest of the Internet. If Facebook wants to 'join forces' instead of fighting as Greene states, then he is arguing that Facebook wants to become the dominant force of all of the Internet!

As these thoughts reveal, reading a difficult text takes time; sometimes our minds may wander a bit, but once we understand one part and gain a sense of the overall purpose, these insights lead us on to more comprehension. Once we can understand or "see" some of the proverbial trees as well as the forest, we gradually construct meaning from the text.

During this gradual construction of meaning, reading and writing no longer have to be opposite activities. We don't have to read once and then write in one draft. Instead we can start to read, take a few mental notes or write down an idea, read on and understand more, write another idea … and on this process goes. As meaning is constructed, reading and writing become parallel and even complementary processes. Although we must admit, even some skilled readers may not be aware of or be able to articulate how they engage in these twin literacies so well. Yet again, if we do not identify and explain the strategies of reading explicitly, less skilled readers like Frank will feel that there is some secret to success, or, even worse, they just aren't smart enough to be skilled readers.

Some Effective Strategies

As a matter of convenience, we will provide some handy names for the following strategies, but the activities matter more than their labels. Many reading theorists and teachers like to refer to five fundamental strategies of comprehension as SQ3R. This acronym stands for Survey, Question, Read, Recall, and Review. However, to stress that reading involves all five of these strategies, we will refer to the third activity as Engage, and alter two other terms as well to clarify those strategies (Preview for Survey and Respond for Recall). When you are trying to read a difficult text for information, you can construct meaning gradually by

Previewing, Questioning, Engaging, Responding, and Reviewing

Let us stress that you do not always have to engage in every one of these strategies, and we will acknowledge that very skilled readers do not practice each one consciously. Like very prolific writers that brainstorm briefly and draft quickly, skilled readers employ some of these strategies intuitively while most of us have to learn to use them deliberately. All of them are the "secrets of success" that you can learn to use as needed.

Preview

Most of us preview a text in the most basic way; we flip from the first page to the last one to see how long the reading is. Previewing a reading (or surveying as it also is known) can involve a bit more than determining the number of pages. Before you settle down to read an assignment from front to back, try skimming over the text, noticing some of its most obvious features, such as the three things in Greene. Textbooks are designed for this skimming so notice the reading's organization, such as the headings and sections. Ask yourself: what are the main sections, and what does the entire text seem to be about? Like a good student essay, most texts will assert a thesis in the first few paragraphs, and many academic articles begin with an abstract that summarizes the main points. You also should determine what kind of text you will be reading: is it primarily a narrative, an exposition, an argument, etc? (For more on the various kinds of writing, see "Tasks" in Chapter 5, p. 95.) Previewing a challenging text is like watching another athlete or musician get ready to perform; you want to know what you will be facing.

Question

We often don't stop to question a text until we feel overwhelmed and then we ask, "What is this reading about?" or declare, "Why do I have to read this?" Both of these questions can help us avoid such frustration if we pose them *before* we start to read the entire text. If we assume that every aspect of the text has a purpose, we can ask and prepare to seek answers to questions like why does Greene switch from comparing Facebook with previous social networks to comparing it with the rest of the Internet? Or what does Judith Ortiz Cofer mean by her title—what happens when she is seen as another Maria, another Latina? The headings or illustrations of a reading also can arouse our curiosity. We can ask what is the relationship between, say, the second and third heading or we can wonder if an image represents a major figure and if a chart depicts an important trend. Even if a text lacks headings or section breaks, we can wonder, how will this 10- or 20-page text be organized? You also should consider your professor as well as the text. Consider why does the professor want you to read this text, and what does he or she expect you to be able to do in response to the text? For example, if the professor wants you to learn new information so you can repeat it in class, you probably should read with a pen or a highlighter in hand. Yet, if the expectation is that you should be ready to interpret, criticize, or apply a reading, you can use more of the techniques for textual engagement presented below.

Engage

We decided to not refer to this part as the "Read" of SQ3R, because reading involves more than this strategy. We "engage" with a text as we start to read each sentence and paragraph carefully and closely. During this concentrated effort, our attention may wander so there are several techniques we can use. As you know, one option is to mark the text by **highlighting** or **underlining** main ideas. Another option to be even more active is **annotating** the text. These comments written in the margins can include an outline of key points, a comment on a pattern, an objection to an opinion, or a question for later consideration.

Here's an example of engaging with a text through underlining and annotating Cofer's conclusion of her stories of being a Latina:

This <u>media-engendered image of the Latina</u> in the United States has been documented by feminist Hispanic scholars, who claim that such portrayals are <u>partially responsible for the denial of opportunities for upward mobility</u> among Latinas in the professions. . . One such incident that has stayed with me, though I recognize it as a minor offense, happened <u>on the day of my first public poetry reading</u>. . . I was nervous and excited as I walked in with my notebook in my hand. An older woman motioned me to her table. Thinking (foolish me) that she <u>wanted me to autograph</u> a copy of my brand new slender volume of verse, I went over. She <u>ordered a cup of coffee from me,</u> <u>assuming that I was the waitress.</u>	*ex. - Modern Family* *stereotypes → opportunities denied* *big moment!* *bigger embarrassment!* *I'd be so upset!* *vivid example of problem*

After being told by most high school teachers NOT to write in your books, the benefit of buying or renting your college books is that you CAN annotate them. There's no gain in the resale value for keeping the pages clean because the buyback price usually doesn't depend on your markings. If you cannot annotate a text, such as for an assigned library reading, you can jot down the same comments on Post-it notes, in your notebook, or with your computer. It's easy to imagine that in the near future, most college students will engage with digital copies of assigned readings through interactive software. For now, we can mark most texts with pen in hand.

Unless we consider medieval manuscripts that lack word spacing and paragraph indenting, we tend to take the format of print texts for granted. We rarely stop to consider the benefits of the "white space" formatting to separate letters and main ideas. We also fail to notice that when we pick up a novel, we read each line from left to right and the page from top to bottom. However, when we engage with digital texts, we should consider its format as much as its content. Even more than a textbook or a newspaper, a digital text, such as a website, is organized spatially into discernable sections of meaning. The homepage of a website presents its main topics in a menu located at the top or in the left margin. The first block of text presents the key details, and the subsequent paragraphs are as concise as possible and separated by white space to focus attention and minimize eye strain. Elaborations of meaning are indicated by arrows to later pages or links to other sites. Colors and images are other features of the format designed to attract attention and reinforce content. Thus, as we engage with websites and other digital texts, we should notice the format as well as the content: What information is placed in the most prominent positions of top and left? What has first priority in the menu, and what is subordinated? What information is displayed prominently and highlighted with color, and what details are relegated to later pages or links?

Respond

Once you have completed a first-to-last page reading of a difficult text, you can continue your gradual construction of meaning by responding to the text through discussion, diagram/illustration, and double-entry notes. Through interactive programs, such as a class chat room, you can discuss a text with a classmate online before class, and some professors may require these electronic exchanges. Of course, you also can meet a classmate and ask, "Hey, what did you think of that reading?" Either form of **discussion** can help you determine what are some of the key details and the central premise of an assigned reading. For students who are visual learners, creating a **diagram** of a reading or imagining an **illustration** (or two) for the main ideas will increase your comprehension of a difficult text. Here's an example of diagramming from Greene:

What is Facebook, anyway? The most obvious point of historical comparison is the social networks that preceded it. First there was Friendster, the flirt-and-forget site of the first half of the 2000s. Then everyone dumped Friendster for MySpace, … and the received wisdom was that MySpace would take over the world. Then it didn't,…. Started by Mark Zuckerberg in 2004, Facebook went from a Harvard dorm room to the rest of teenage America's bedrooms to hundreds of millions of people all around the world….

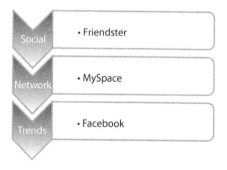

Double-entry notes are an even more active form of response. As their name suggests, the notes are "double" because you don't just copy down main ideas of a text. Instead you take notes by writing out at least part of a key passage and then, in another column, you write a response to it. The very act of copying down a key passage—whether by typing or handwriting—makes you pay more attention to the author's words, and the second column is a space for you to write some of your thoughts. Ideally, your response should consist of more than a summary or a personal connection, although both are essential parts of comprehension. Your response can also include a question, a link to another part of the same text, or a placement of this reading in the larger context of your course. Here's one more example from Cofer:

I went over. She ordered a cup of coffee from me, assuming that I was the waitress. Easy enough to mistake my poems for menus, I suppose. I know that it wasn't an intentional act of cruelty, yet of all the good things that happened that day, I remember that scene most clearly, because it reminded me of what I had to overcome before anyone would take me seriously. In retrospect I understand that my anger gave my reading fire, that I have almost always taken doubts in my abilities as a challenge. . . Every time I give a reading, I hope the stories I tell, the dreams and fears I examine in my work, can achieve some universal truth which will get my audience past the particulars of my skin color, my accent, or my clothes.	*I find it hard to believe that the woman could mistake Cofer for a waitress, but she did! Unbelievable. I like how Cofer is understanding ("Easy enough"), but she also admits her anger at that moment. Even better she uses her anger to dispel the woman's prejudice. She meets the challenge head on, but is it a challenge that can ever be overcome entirely? Are Cofer's stories, dreams, and fears enough to make all of her audiences "get past" her ethnicity and their own prejudices? What does it take to dispel bias, to end discrimination?*

This response in double-entry notes does not have to be perfectly phrased; instead you can use the quick phrasing of brainstorming and freewriting to "write to learn" (for more on writing to learn, see Chapter 4, p. 85). As you write a response to a reading, these twin literacies become, as we stated above, parallel and complementary activities. As you are creating double-entry notes, where does reading end and where does writing begin? It's not always easy to discern.

Review

As you finish reading a text, you can review by looking back over your marked text to reinforce your comprehension. This look back is similar to our reconsideration of any important event. You also may want to review a text before a class when you know a professor expects you to participate in a discussion or as you start to prepare to write a more formal assignment. Of course, if you turn to a previously read assignment and find marked pages and some notes, it will be much easier to say something "smart" and write insightfully.

Thus, these strategies are more effective for comprehension and more efficient for time. With our apologies to a well-known advertising campaign, we will assert,

> *Annotating a reading-greater effort*
>
> *Responding to a text-better grades*
>
> *Enjoying your reading process-priceless!*

It may seem that you usually are asked to read for academic purposes like comprehension and interpretation, but many of your professors also hope that you will read for action, such as applying a key concept to a new circumstance, and even for pleasure, like enjoying a challenging poem. Few of us enjoy our first encounter with a difficult poet like Emily Dickinson or a complex report on a technical problem, such as a flawed bridge design. However, by using some of the strategies for active and gradual comprehension, we hope you will be able to declare, in contrast to Frank's quotation above, that you "get it!" You *will* have the ability to comprehend difficult texts, just as many of your professors think you *should*.

Key Terms and Concepts

Before you finish with this chapter, here is a list of key concepts; which ones can you explain easily, and which ones do you need to review?

Reading purposes
    for enjoyment
    for information
    for action
    for interpretation

Functional literacy
    Decoding letters (phonetic reading)
    Word recognition (sight reading)

Advanced literacy
    Comprehending meaning
    Interpreting ideas
    Applying information
    Analyzing an argument
    Connecting to other texts and/or contexts

Standard of literacy

Immediate comprehension vs.
    Gradual comprehension

Reading strategies
    Preview
    Question
    Engage
        Highlighting
        Underlining
        Annotating
    Respond
        Discussion
        Diagram
        Illustration
        Double-entry notes
    Review

The Writing Process

CHAPTER 4

For most high school graduates, writing sometimes can be a relatively easy task. Most of us can write a "to-do" list, reply to an electronic message, or draft a five-paragraph essay without too much difficulty. However, at other times, most of us struggle to write well. We may struggle to complete the literary analyses, lab reports, and persuasive papers we are expected to write. As we try to explain, for instance, a literary character, we may find ourselves staring at a blank screen or crumpling sheet after sheet of half-started pages. Why is writing sometimes so easy yet at other times so difficult?

This is a crucial question for a college student to consider since you will be asked to write many assignments. One tempting answer to these difficulties is to doubt yourself as a writer: "I must not be very good, smart enough, a *real* writer …." Yet these doubts can lead to a self-defeating cycle of apathy ("why try?"), procrastination ("not now") and failure ("oh no"), and then even more self-doubt. No one, however, should spend four years at college in this cycle of doubt, despair, and defeat.

To understand why writing sometimes is easy yet on other occasions so challenging, let's distinguish between two specific examples: texting an electronic reply and drafting a literary analysis. Beyond "easy" and "hard," what else do you think distinguishes these two kinds of writing? What differences can you add to the list below?

Texting a Reply	Analyzing a Novel
easy	hard

You probably added "fun" to one column, but does the enjoyable always have to be matched with easy? A crucial difference you may not have considered is that these two examples represent two very different processes of thinking and writing. Texting a friend is usually so easy because most likely you already know what you want to say (unless a difficult situation like a break-up is involved). Yet when it comes to analyzing a character in a novel, like Huck Finn's attitude toward Jim or Hester Prynne's love in *The Scarlet Letter*, we usually do not know what we want to say. Thus, we can add to our list an important distinction:

Texting a Reply	Analyzing a Novel
easy	hard
know what to say	need to figure it out

As we exchange text messages with a friend, such as in

"where r u?"

"goin 2 class"

"wanna have lunch"

"ya, at 12"

we don't stop to think (at least not for long) about what we want to say (except for that breakup again). This kind of writing goes straight from our thoughts and onto the screen—easy! We record what we are thinking, what we already know.

Analyzing Huck or Hester is—pardon the pun—another story; we usually do not know what we want to say. Is Huck a racist or not? Is Hester a fool for loving the minister? Such complicated questions involve much more than just recording what we think. If we try to write this literary analysis like we text a reply, we almost always will be doomed to frustration and failure. These problems develop because our first thoughts, phrases, and order are not ready to be our final draft. These difficulties, however, do not mean that a writer is destined to fail and just not smart enough. These problems instead reveal that some writing tasks require a different approach, another kind of writing process.

Let's consider how we would write the exception noted above: the break-up message. If someone is really heartless, he or she may text the first thought that comes to mind: "don't wanna see you; we're thru." Even with its rhyme, this probably isn't the best message to send. Most of us instead would practice what we want to say and how we would phrase it using our minds, our mouths, and our fingertips: "I need some space" (what a stupid cliché), "maybe we need a break" (better but too sudden), "spending every Saturday night together …" and on we would go. We would use writing to clarify our thinking, to see what we want to say. Unless we hit send immediately, writing lets us see our thoughts and imagine a reader's reactions. Or if we ask a friend about our not-yet-sent message, if we seek a peer response to a draft as described below, we can even learn how some readers might react and then revise as needed (for more on what is known as peer response, see p. 89 below).

Although completing a more difficult writing task requires greater effort, we can, in fact, use writing itself to make this assignment easier. As long as we do not assume that we already should know what we want to say, writing can become a useful tool rather than a frustrating struggle. This alternative approach to writing will require more writing, but it also will be more effective.

Texting a Reply	Analyzing a Novel
easy	hard
know what to say	need to figure it out
writing as recording one draft	writing as thinking in several steps

You probably have been taught about the **writing process**, but have you been convinced to really try it? To write a difficult paper, we can slow down the process and separate at least some of the steps we try to complete all at once in a first-*and*-final-no-time-to-revise-gotta-get-it-done draft. The steps of the writing process can be described as

- **Collect** ideas and phrases (invention)
- **Focus** on a main topic/idea
- **Order** the ideas (arrangement)
- **Draft** sentences and paragraphs
- **Revise** a draft
- **Edit** a final copy

Some writing theorists have used other terms to describe these steps of the writing process, such as prewriting, writing, and rewriting. Or back in elementary school, your teachers may have talked about a "sloppy copy." Our description is based on Donald Murray's theory, but we have added two terms from ancient rhetoric: **invention** and **arrangement** (see Chapter 6 for more on rhetorical theory). Invention refers to the initial collection of ideas ("What the heck can I say about Huck and Jim?") and arrangement refers to the organization of those ideas once we have decided on a focus, a thesis ("As they travel down the Mississippi River, Huck slowly recognizes Jim's humanity.")

Although these six steps may seem like much more work than sitting down to "get it done," they actually make writing easier if you are trying to draft a challenging paper. To explain how more steps can be easier, let us add another writing theorist's analogy. Linda Flower has compared writing with juggling, and the trick to learning to juggle is to start with only one ball or two. Even when a skilled juggler is handling three balls or more, she really concentrates on only one or two at any time. Thus, it's easier for most of us to separate the writing process into several distinct steps, and focus on only one or two at a time. This alternative approach to writing reduces the number of steps we have to handle at one time so we can concentrate better and work more efficiently. You already may practice some of these steps, but we will explain each one and some related strategies below. We also will divide our explanations into several smaller segments, as marked by our headings, so this information will be easier to read and comprehend.

Three Initial Steps

As we start to write, we usually have to collect information, establish a focus, and create an order before we draft. Sometimes we complete these steps almost intuitively, and at other times, we must handle each one with a deliberate effort.

Collecting

- **Brainstorm**—jot down a list of ideas as you think of them
- **Cluster**—diagram your initial ideas by linking some with lines
- **Freewrite**—think onto the page by writing quickly and imperfectly

What unites these varied strategies is their ease. We can let ourselves "blurt" out words while writing just as we often do while chatting, emailing, and texting. We can permit ourselves to collect ideas without worrying if our thoughts are perfect or our phrases are eloquent. As another writing theorist named Peter

Elbow explains, we don't need to heed our critical self yet; we let our creative self "talk" onto the page or screen. We can plan to return to these collected ideas later for critical judgment.

Focusing

Once we have collected some ideas, we have to find a focus, determine our purpose. Sometimes a **thesis** is assigned (Prove Huck is not …), but usually in college writing, you will have to determine your purpose on the subject given, your answer to the question posed. Although some of us shy away from controversy, a thesis has to make a deliberate claim, state an assertion someone else can reasonably disagree with (Huck is a racist when he …). Of course, not all writing begins with an explicit thesis (In this essay I will …). Some kinds of writing, such as a narrative, have a clear focus, but this purpose is not revealed immediately; instead it is shown throughout a narrative.

A reader of a narrative comes to this text with different expectations than the audience of a literary analysis or a lab report. To be successful, themselves a writer will have to fulfill these expectations (or break them for a very deliberate reason) because as Donald Murray also explained, "Writers may write *for* themselves, but they do not write *to* themselves." Even most diarists or bloggers have an audience in mind as they write. Two more theorists, Patricia Bizzell and James Berlin, therefore, have insisted that writing is a social process as well as an individual one. In other words, as a writer completes these steps, this process is influenced by audience expectations and writing conventions; writing is an **individual** *and a* **social process**.

> Writers may write
> <u>for</u> themselves,
> but they do not
> write <u>to</u> themselves.

Ordering:

To create an effective order, most writers have to shift from thinking about what they know to considering what a reader needs to learn if they are to understand our knowledge. Although a brainstorming list may spring quickly from our minds, we usually need to reorganize these thoughts if we are to communicate with others effectively. Some of the most common patterns for creating an effective order are

- **Chronological**: present an event by following its time sequence
- **"In medias res"**: follow the ancient pattern of beginning in the middle of the action, and then backtracking to the beginning before presenting the rest of the sequence
- **Problem to solution**: explain a difficulty and then present a remedy
- **Cause and effect**: describe a crucial factor and its result

Can you add any other organizational patterns? You may want to add two other common kinds of high school writing: pro/con and compare/contrast patterns.

Some kinds of writing, such as lab reports, already have a fixed order and for a good reason. This order allows another researcher to replicate an experiment exactly because science depends on the confirmation of experimental results. There are other, already established organizational patterns, such as the pro/con order, that help us produce satisfying results. Some writing tasks, however, do not have such fixed orders so it can be very beneficial to outline after a first draft has been completed. Most of us have been instructed to outline before we begin drafting, but outlining afterwards can help us judge and revise a first draft. But wait, we are getting ahead of ourselves; we need to discuss drafting next.

The Most Obvious Step

Drafting

As we draft, we try to turn our intentions into communication; we try to make our meaning clear enough to stand apart from ourselves. We try to reach a reader to whom we cannot explain face-to-face what we meant to say. To reach our audience, we turn our thoughts into phrases, sentences, and paragraphs. A handbook can help you transform ideas into written language on each of these levels, so let us offer some general advice. First, each of these levels represents a place to bog down and become frustrated with writing. Stumbling over word choice, also known as **diction**, can block even the best of writers (should I refer to Hester as *devoted* or *deluded* in her love?). Some decisions of diction can determine an entire analysis, but it usually is better to keep thinking and drafting even when the perfect word isn't at your fingertips. Let a less-than-perfect word suffice and mark it for later consideration and correction. The final draft of your paper, of course, must have grammatically correct and pattern-pleasing sentences. Again, your sentence structure, or **syntax**, may be less than perfect in a first draft. Bruce Ballenger, the author of several books on writing, argues that we sometimes have to write badly to write well. If you learned to write a "sloppy copy" in grade school, you probably know what he means. Perfection or even pretty good usually requires more than one attempt.

Paragraphs, as you know, are the building blocks of a paper. The old rule of thumb is that each paragraph should be organized around one main idea. Another way to consider paragraphing is to think about white space: those areas of a page or screen not filled with letters or images. A reader's eye and mind need white space to remind her or him to pause, complete one idea, and prepare for another one. The white space of an indentation as a new paragraph begins does so much for a reader with so little visually. It's easy to notice the importance of white space if you have ever tried to read a medieval manuscript. These texts usually lack paragraphs and sometimes even spaces between words. The modern equivalent would be a poorly designed web page jammed with information or even a page of a college student's paper that lacks any indentations. A paragraph longer than a page almost always can be and should be broken into two or more paragraphs.

To double check our order, we can outline after a first or partial draft has been written. Number each paragraph of the draft and identify its topic. This additional effort again can help us write better; follow the outline in your mind. Does it seem sensible to start with 1, follow with 2, and then continue with 3, 4, and 5? Or would 4, 2, and then 3 be better? Once we realize that 1, 4, 2, and 3 is better, often 5, 6, and 7 will follow easily.

It's important to note that the writing process so far has been presented as though it were a fixed set of steps: first, collect; second, focus; third, order; fourth, draft. Although these fixed steps make it easier to explain the writing process, the reality of writing often involves more than marching up a set of steps once. Instead, we may, for example, create a draft and go back to check our order. Then a new order may lead to a sharper focus so more details may have

First Order	Better Order
1	1
2	4
3	2
4	3, 5, 6, 7

to be collected, and on the complex process of writing will go. Although writing often is a messier process than these four fixed steps (plus revision and editing), we have to be able to separate these steps so we can handle the demands of a difficult task. Once we can distinguish these steps, we may be able to discern why we sometimes get stuck in the middle of the process. Most of us have become bogged down, for instance, in the middle of completing a first draft. We are going along smoothly and suddenly we get stuck; we don't know how to start the next paragraph. We can keep drafting and drafting that next sentence, but we know that none of them are any good. Or our minds and fingertips may just stop, and we end up staring at a blank page or screen for too long. Yet if we understand the various steps, then we may realize that the best way to proceed is to go backward briefly. Perhaps we are stuck while drafting because our order is wrong or we haven't collected enough ideas for the next section. If we understand the separate steps of this process, we have a better chance of overcoming our moments of frustration. Once a first draft is complete, devoting some time to editing is essential, and a day or more for revision is even better.

Two Later Steps

Once we have drafted some complete sentences and organized paragraphs, we usually need to revise and edit.

Revising

Having the time to revise, to *really* revise, depends on starting the initial steps of the process long before the due date. It is tempting to assume that this extended process of writing takes too much time.

However, if you have ever spent three, four, or more hours working on a last-minute-gotta-get-it-done first *and* final draft, can you imagine distributing the same number of hours over several days? Starting early and collecting for 20 or 30 minutes, then seeking a focus for those ideas the next day can actually be a much more efficient and effective approach. Consider an athletic or musical ability that you excel at; did you learn to throw that ball or play that instrument all at once? Even now, do you practice separate parts of this ability for hours before you try to demonstrate your great proficiency to others? Why not approach writing just as you accomplish one of your talents?

Revision, like drafting, can occur on many levels, ranging from the entire draft to a single sentence or phrase. Some of the rhetorical concepts presented in

All-Nighter	A Gradual Process
a struggle	Monday: collect
from	30 min.
10 pm to	Tues: focus and
2 am on	order 20 min.
Thursday	Wed: draft 70 min.
night	reorganize 10 min.
into Friday	Th: revise, edit, print, and
due 8 am =	proofread 80 min. =
4 hours	3 1/2 hours

Chapter 6 can aid you in your revision. For example, the rhetorical triangle can help you reconsider the draft overall: What is your purpose and for what audience? The three rhetorical appeals can also help you "re-see" your draft. Have you established an effective relationship with your intended audience (ethos)? Have you arranged your ideas and evidence in a logical order (logos)? Have you evoked from your reader the emotions that match your purpose (pathos)? You also can revise on the smaller scale of a paragraph, sentence, or phrase. A good handbook will offer many helpful suggestions for revision, but it's also easy to be overwhelmed by so much advice.

Like athletes or musicians who keep track of their typical difficulties, most writers can revise better when they are aware of what kinds of improvements their writing usually needs. Teachers regularly identify weaknesses that require revision as they grade, but some students check their grade and turn toward their next assignment. Taking the time to look back at the comments on a graded paper, however, helps student writers improve their next efforts. Saying "Gee, I got a C" should not be a student's only reaction to a graded paper.

In addition to reviewing previous papers, **peer response** is another beneficial guide for revision. However, a response by another student must consist of more than superficial praise ("I really liked it") or dismissive critiques ("You lost me on page three; it wasn't very good"). Helpful peer response provides, just as its name suggests, a reader's reaction to a draft: where is the text effective (or not) and why? These responses are about meaning rather than grading or editing. Most of us need some training to become comfortable and competent with peer responding, but we can learn to use and even enjoy a trusted reader's reactions. This training can involve responding to anonymous sample texts, peer papers, and/or published writing as well as working in paired partners, small groups, and full class discussions.

Response guidelines are as varied as writing assignments, but here is a general response format that will fit almost any draft:

Strengths

Identify what phrases, sections, and/or features you find to be most effective and memorable. Be very specific, as in, "I can really imagine the scene on the top of page two when you used the phrase …" or "The analysis on page three is very good because …." Note the importance of explaining why as well as what.

Focus

Describe what you think is the purpose of the paper. In a sentence or two, answer: What do you think the writer is trying to accomplish?

Weaknesses

Admit when you, as a reader, were confused by some phrases or lost interest in certain sections. Again, be specific and concentrate on your reactions as a reader, for example, "By the bottom of page three, I wasn't sure if you still were trying to …." You also can phrase these concerns as questions, such as "Can you tell me more why you felt this way?" Avoid statements that explicitly criticize the draft as in "The ending wasn't very good" because these judgmental assertions do not help a writer understand why a section is weak; concentrate on your reactions as a reader.

Editing

Notice a few minor editing problems and correct them, such as by adding a missing apostrophe or helping with a misspelled word. However, you are not responsible for making every edit or even identifying each one. Mark the first few, and then assert that "This draft needs a thorough editing. It started to be difficult for me to concentrate on your meaning because there are many errors involving _____ (spelling, punctuation, etc.)." As a sample of student writing, Aliza's narrative can be used to practice peer response.

For more overtly persuasive writing, the following guidelines can help you assess the strengths and weaknesses of a draft:

Interest: How does the writer try to attract the attention of a reader who does not already agree with his or her viewpoint?

Thesis: What does the writer want to convince the reader to believe?

Supports: What evidence does the writer use to prove the validity of the thesis?

Objections: What counterarguments can be anticipated and answered?

Audience and Tone: Who is the writer trying to convince? To reach this intended audience (and not just those who already agree), what tone should be used? What tone will alienate an initially skeptical reader?

These response guidelines for persuasive writing can be practiced by responding to texts by professional writers, such as those by Tom Hodgkinson and Deborah Meier in Chapters 1 and 11. Every page of this book has been reviewed by several preliminary readers, and we have made many revisions based on their responses.

When readers engage in peer response, the responders should almost always begin with positive comments, and this praise must be specific ("I thought p. 2 middle was very vivid because the details …" and "One of your best supports was …"). Then identify the focus or the thesis of the draft ("I think you are trying to …"). Thus far, the writer should listen more than reply to the response in order to demonstrate his receptiveness. Then as the response turns toward more problematic sections, a discussion should develop. The writer should not immediately resist the response ("You don't understand that …") because then most responders will stop providing specific and sincere comments. If the writer listens well at first and signals her willingness to follow the responder, she later can start to imagine possible revisions ("Maybe I should say …" or "What if I explained next …?"). As writers, we sometimes forget that what we meant to say is not always the same as what appears on the page for a reader; fortunately peer response can reveal this gap between intention and comprehension. As revisions are discussed, peer response becomes more constructive than critical so many writers learn to enjoy rather than fear reader feedback. These sessions ideally transform students concerned with deadlines and grades into writers concentrated on meaning and form.

Reader as Peer Responder	Writer of Draft-In-Progress
Start with positive comments.	Stay quiet and listen well.
Be specific and sincere.	Don't argue immediately.
Turn from strengths to weaknesses.	Keep accepting a reader's reactions.
Stress your reactions as a reader.	Start discussing possible revisions.
End with editing suggestions.	Assume the responsibility for editing the entire draft.

Editing

Like revision and response, editing is a later step in the writing process that can be completed best if the deadline is not looming ("It's due in six hours and I need some sleep!"). A frustrated student writing for a grade may find editing to be one last chore, but when expression, communication, and comprehension are the goals, editing can be a satisfying last step. Like revision focused on repeated problems, editing is easier if you are aware of your frequent errors. Keep a list in your notebook or put a sticky note on your computer to remind yourself of your repeated errors. Then you can use the "Find" function to search for some of these errors, such as homonym misspellings like "then" and "than" that spell check will not detect. Spelling and grammar checks will reveal some editing problems so don't ignore the red and green squiggles of spelling and grammar checks, yet don't depend on them too much. Old-fashioned methods like consulting a print dictionary and reading a draft aloud can also help you complete the edits that a final draft deserves.

Timed Essays

We started this chapter by presenting the writing process with two extreme opposites: a quick text message and a gradually written assignment. Yet time, thought, and process clash in the messy middle of these two extremes, such as when you have to write an in-class, timed essay. Here's a typical essay question for an American history exam:

> Although slavery sometimes is considered to be the primary reason for the Civil War, what were several other significant causes of this conflict? In a well-organized essay, explain slavery as one of at least three causes of this war.

What would you do to answer this essay question? Consider both your thoughts as well as your actions: "To answer this question, I would …."

Although the pressure of a timed essay may make you launch immediately into drafting the opening sentences of your essay, it usually is easier to condense but still follow the separate steps of the writing process. First, can you collect some ideas on the causes of the conflict? (Note as well the related step of determining what exactly the assignment is asking you to do; for more, see Chapter 5 on Writing Assignments.) Through some quick thinking and/or brainstorming notes, you might consider, "Let's see, slavery and … other causes? States rights and what else? Apart from slavery and states rights, another reason was economic tensions: Southern raw materials and Northern manufacturing. Anything else?" and on your thinking, brainstorming, and collecting might go. Then you could determine your focus ("I'll stress economic differences") and your order ("Start with slavery; I'll need some details like the Dred Scott decision. Then states rights and then end by emphasizing economic tensions.")

After a few minutes of this planning, it would be easy to start drafting if you knew the trick of turning the question into your introduction:

> *Slavery sometimes is considered the primary reason for the Civil War, but the issue of abolition was only one of several, sometimes related but not always connected causes. In addition to slavery, the controversies over states rights and economic policies transformed the once United States into a house divided.*

Then it would be time to pull the format of the five-paragraph essay out of your writer's toolbox. This format is not the only wrench you'll need for college writing, but it is a very useful one for timed essays. And if you are asked to explain four or five factors, just add another body paragraph or two. With these ideas already collected, it would be easier for you to plan coherent paragraphs (one cause per section-right?) and draft your answer. Don't forget to use a few topic sentences ("States rights also contributed to this conflict . .") and explicit transitions ("The divisions created by the debate over states rights were exacerbated by other regional differences: economic priorities.").

To have enough time to emphasize these economic differences, you would have to monitor the 30 or 40 minutes allotted for this essay. After about 20 minutes, it would be time to turn to the third cause. You would have had to explain the first two causes quickly and avoided writing too much about one reason, slipping from focused analysis into rambling summary. Then to complete this essay, you would have to add an explicit conclusion, one that does not just repeat the introduction's ideas and phrases. Instead you would want to add a final thought without branching off into a new topic entirely. For example, you might end with

Slavery, states rights, and economic differences all led to the Civil War. The fact that historians may emphasize one cause over another demonstrates that they engage in interpretation as much as factual researching and reporting. The causes of this struggle are the subject of an endless debate.

Ideally you would have a few minutes remaining as those final words are drafted. Although you probably could not revise much of this timed essay, you should proofread and edit so use the last few minutes to look for your typical errors. As with writing a homework assignment gradually over several days or more, it actually is more efficient to answer a timed essay by tackling each step separately: collect, focus, order, draft, edit (and possibly revise a little).

Completing a 40-minute, In-class Exam Essay

2–3 min.	Read the essay question more than once.
2–3 min.	Determine the essay's required form and features.
4–5 min.	Collect ideas and phrases for your answer.
2–3 min.	Organize your ideas into an effective order.
2–3 min.	Turn the main question into your introduction.
	Start drafting and avoid overwriting as you begin.
12–15 minutes	Monitor your time and develop each section adequately. Use paragraphs, topic sentences, and explicit transitions.
2–3 min.	End with an enriching conclusion.
4–5 min.	Review the draft, edit, and, if possible, revise as needed.

When faced with an exam essay, a short assignment, or a major paper, you can learn to control your writing process, and such control depends on your knowledge of the many steps of writing. Like a violinist who is aware of the angle of his bow or a hurdler who notices the extension of her first foot, most skilled writers understand and can articulate many aspects of their writing process or, we really should say, processes of writing. We want you to distinguish writing about what you already know well and can phrase easily from writing when you still need to figure out your thoughts and word them carefully, which is a more gradual process. Skilled writers, like any talented artist or athlete, know some shortcuts, but they also know when to use them *and* when not. This entire chapter can be summed up in the following sentences: *The quick is not always the easiest, and the easy is not always the most effective. An effective writing process, however, is usually the most satisfying one.*

Writing Process Reflections

To help you reflect on your writing process, you may be asked to write "process notes" and/or discuss the comments of some professional writers on their approaches.

The following questions can help you look back on your writing process; choose a few and write a page of **process notes**:

- *In what ways was your writing process for this assignment similar to or different from your usual writing practices in high school?*
- *How did you collect ideas? What strategies from brainstorming to premature drafting were productive or frustrating for you?*
- *How did you pick a topic and/or decide on your focus for an assigned topic?*
- *Why did you find it easy or hard to create an order for your reader to follow?*
- *What reader did you have in mind as you created this order?*
- *What expectations did you assume your intended reader had about your paper's content, order, and format?*
- *When was it easy or difficult for you to draft phrases, sentences, and paragraphs?*
- *When and why did you have to go back to an earlier step in the writing process?*
- *How did you revise your first draft?*
- *With more time and energy, what is another revision you would have liked to complete?*
- *If you engaged in peer response, what in particular was beneficial (or not)?*
- *What errors from a previous paper did you need to edit in this assignment? How did you edit this paper?*

Some Key Terms and Concepts

Before you finish with this chapter, see below the list of key concepts. Which ones can you explain easily and which ones do you need to review?

Writing process
  Collect/invention
    Brainstorm
    Cluster
    Freewrite
  Focus
    Thesis
  Order/Arrangement
    Chronological
    "in medias res"
    Problem to solution
    Cause and effect
    Pro/Con
    Compare/Contrast
  Draft
    Diction
    Syntax
  Revise
    Peer response
  Edit
  Process notes
  An individual *and* a social process

Writing Assignments

In high school, you probably wrote many five-paragraph essays, and exposition in general may have been emphasized. Yet this emphasis on exposition—explaining an event, a concept, or a text—can make the transition to college writing difficult for some students. They may not realize, at least initially, that many assignments involve other tasks, such as analysis and argument.

When a student fails to recognize or can't fulfill the expected task of a writing assignment, the results usually are frustration ("What am I supposed to do?") and disappointment ("Why did I get a D?!"). It's important that you understand the range of writing you will be expected to complete at college and learn to ask several key questions about every writing assignment you receive.

When an assignment is given, almost every student will ask or wants to ask, "When is it due?" and "How long should it be?" However, there are several other equally important questions to ask about each assignment:

- What is the primary task?
- What sources should be used?
- What conventions should be followed?
- What specialized terms, if any, should be included?

Some students do consider these questions before they tackle an assignment, but let's examine them fully.

What Tasks

College writing assignments involve many tasks; in addition to **exposition**, the other kinds of assignments, also known as **modes of discourse**, include

- **Description**
- **Narration**
- **Analysis**

- **Comparison and contrast**
- **Synthesis**
- **Argument**

Using your own words, how would you define each task? If a classmate were to ask you about a writing assignment, how would you explain the main task and distinguish it from other ones? For example, what would you say that analysis means? How does exposition differ from narration or argument?

Ideally, every writing assignment should use these exact terms to identify the task or tasks a student is expected to fulfill in a writing assignment. Some professors, however, use other words and phrases to state their expectations; what do you think a professor expects if an assignment were to use the following phrases?

> interpret the significance
>
> recount an important event
>
> summarize the main idea and several key points
>
> defend your position
>
> explain similarities and/or differences

The tasks implied by some of these phrases may seem obvious to you and your classmates; did most of your class assume that the first phrase requires analysis and the second involves narration? Yet does the third ("summarize") suggest exposition or analysis? The primary tasks of the last two probably seem to be argument ("defend") and compare/contrast ("similarities and/or differences"), but would you disagree with a classmate if he or she thought that both of those assignments also involve analysis?

"Analysis" is one of those words that we may try to take for granted. Yet some students awkwardly refer to "analyzation" so they probably are uncertain of what this task requires. What exactly should a college student do when analysis is assigned? The etymology of "analysis" suggests a "breaking into parts," and, to analyze an event or text, you have to distinguish some of the pieces of the whole. Yet what should you do next to avoid only explaining each part?

Analysis also involves discerning some pattern among those pieces. The analysis of a poem, for example, requires a reader to notice the rhyme pattern, the word choice, and the imagery. Then this interpretation could show how these parts work together to create a certain effect, such as a somber mood. The analysis of a historical event would require a similar identification, for instance, of several causes, and the demonstration of a cause–effect relationship. Usually, historical analysis also is tentative rather than absolute (e.g., *To what degree* do you think President Lincoln fought the Civil War in order to abolish slavery?). Thus, analysis involves not only the breaking down of the whole into parts and connecting some of the pieces into a significant pattern but also weighing one cause or trend against another (Lincoln's other reasons for war).

Although such analysis may seem to be difficult, it is something we do all the time, such as when we encounter an upset friend or an angry family member. We usually ask what is causing that emotion, we wonder if they are more troubled by this or that, and we weigh whether they will be calmed if we respond one way or another. A leading educator named Gerald Graff believes that most students have a "hidden intelligence," meaning they already know how to engage in complex intellectual tasks like analysis, but they may find it difficult to complete this task on an academic subject.

Although it's easier to discuss these tasks separately, most college writing assignments will involve more than one genre. Consider, for example, the basic lab report of many science classes. It usually contains:

- An introduction that states the problem
- A list that catalogs of materials and equipment
- A procedure that presents each experimental step in correct order
- A results section that describes the outcomes, often with charts or graphs
- A discussion that interprets the significance of the results
- A conclusion that affirms or revises the original hypothesis and suggests further experimentation

Some lab reports also include a title page, an abstract, a reference list, and an appendix or two. The basic parts listed above involve a great deal of exposition, but what other tasks does this assignment require? When, for example, does the author of a lab report also have to engage in analysis and argument? The analysis presented in the discussion section leads to an argument that is summed up in the conclusion.

A lab report is only one example of many, usually quite complex, college writing assignments. Now we want you to pause and consider the various writing assignments of your college education. In your current college courses as well as your future study in a major, what different kinds of writing assignments do you think you will be assigned as you complete courses in the humanities (e.g., literature and philosophy), the social sciences (psychology and sociology), and the sciences (biology, chemistry, plus mathematics)? Over the next few years of your undergraduate education, your range of writing assignments may include but not be limited to the following:

- Personal narratives
- Expository essays
- Textual summaries
- Reading responses
- Literary analyses
- Poetry and fiction
- Creative nonfiction
- Opinion pieces
- Comparisons and contrasts
- Arguments
- Syntheses
- Research papers
- Lab reports
- Memos and proposals
- Websites and blogs
- Personal statements
- Application letters

Many of these assignments will involve not only various tasks but also diverse sources and conventions. However, before you read on, can you pause to consider the various kinds of papers you have been assigned to write this semester and/or last term? What tasks are suggested on your course syllabi and/or specific assignments?

What Sources and Which Conventions

As you reread an assignment, consider what **sources** you are expected to use. Many college writing assignments will require you to rely on one or more of the following sources:

- Personal experiences and/or observations
- Personal interviews and/or surveys
- Textbook and/or class notes
- Newspaper and/or magazine articles
- Scholarly articles and/or books
- Films and/or videos
- Blogs and/or websites

For more information on how to access some of these sources and evaluate their content, see Chapter 8 on Research Methods and Motives.

For some students, the difficulty of finding good sources is surpassed by their confusion over the diverse **conventions** of various writing assignments. It may seem to some students that one professor tells them to do this but another instructor says to do that. There usually are some good reasons for these differences, but they need to be discussed explicitly. For example, let's examine a lab report in relation to a narrative (as assigned in Chapter 2): In what ways do the conventions of these two assignments differ? In what ways, if any, are they similar? In other words, how are you expected to write in each assignment?

At first, no writing tasks may seem to be more different than a narrative and a lab report. Don't English professors want flowery language while scientists value straightforward facts? Yet these assignments are not as different as they first appear. Each assignment has a main focus, includes detailed information, creates a cause-and-effect sequence, and leads readers to a final thought. Here is a list of some of their fundamental similarities as well as their apparent differences:

Narrative	Lab Report
get the reader interested	state the problem and the hypothesis
show with vivid details	list all materials
create a compelling order	present each step
identify characters, including "I"	avoid the first person "I"
reveal the consequences of key actions	discuss the results
provide some greater meaning	conclude on its significance

One of the most obvious contrasts between these two assignments is the subjective nature of a narrative and the objectivity of a lab report. In a narrative, "I" often is used to present sensory experiences, but in a lab report, the convention is to avoid the first person, so experimental details are presented using the passive voice. Rather than state "I weighed the item and found that it was 1.2 g," the writer of lab reports employs the passive voice to state "The item was weighed, and its mass was 1.2 g." While a narrative includes sensory details like "the gorgeous sunshine warmed my hands," a lab report definitely would not mention "the pretty blue flame of the Bunsen burner"!

To understand the reasons for these differences in conventions, we must consider their results. A narrative allows the reader to imagine the writer's experience through vivid details, and the lab report is detailed yet detached because the experiment is supposed to be reimagined and even re-created by the readers. Anyone who follows the lab's procedure properly should reach the same results. Thus, the different conventions of a subjective narrative and a more objective lab report are a matter of **rhetorical means and ends**. Sometimes writers use different means, such as the first person "I" or not, to reach the same ends: reader comprehension, audience understanding.

What Terms and Why

Every academic discipline has its own specialized **terms**, its own jargon. For example, the average person would define a "line" as a mark from here to there; some are straight but others, wavy. Yet this word means much more when art students learn to study a painter's use of "line" or when math students are taught that in non-Euclidean geometry, parallel lines can cross. At college, a "line" can have several, very specialized meanings.

It's natural to resist these complicated terms and ask why can't we just use plain language and talk simply? Consider, however, whatever sport or hobby you enjoy. Why do baseball pitchers talk about two and four seamers? Or why do motorcyclists refer to "entering the apex" of a turn and quilters talk about "stitch in the ditch"? Every group has its own jargon, so what are some of the specialized terms of your major? In other words, what are some of the key terms and phrases your professors use in class and expect you to include in your speech and writing? Here are some quick examples from diverse disciplines:

- History: political legitimacy
- Philosophy: ontology
- Communication: relational processes
- Chemistry: covalent bonds
- Computer sciences: downward compatibility
- Economics: organizational behavior
- Music: cadence
- Engineering: structural dynamics
- Education: hidden curriculum

As students struggle with the use of terms like these, it is easy and tempting to dismiss them as words no one uses in the "real" world. Yet in the "real" world of professionals, many of these terms *are* used every day. These terms are central to your education, or as a writing theorist named Mike Rose states,

> You could almost define a university education as an initiation into a variety of powerful ongoing discussions. . . . The more comfortable students become with this kind of influential talk, the more they will be included in further conversations, ... which virtually defines them as members of an intellectual community.

Thus, it is crucial to consider: Do academics use these terms to impress students? Or do they use them, like motorcyclists and quilters who refer to "the apex" and "the ditch," as convenient labels for complex concepts?

The use and misuse of specialized terms depends upon **audience**. What happens when an expert uses a specialized term while addressing a general audience and yet while speaking with another expert? Depending on one's audience, jargon can be elitist and exclusionary or quick and convenient for bikers, quilters, and academics. To avoid the negative effects of jargon on a general audience, many writers rely on **embedded definitions** in their writing, such as when they refer to exposition, or explaining, in the same sentence. By slipping in, or embedding, quick definitions like "explaining" for exposition, a general reader can follow an expert's language. For students writing for professors, embedded definitions serve another important purpose: they demonstrate to the instructor that the student is not just mimicking the "big words" of **academic discourse** but is able to use them knowledgeably.

Key Terms and Concepts

Before you finish with this chapter, here is a list of key concepts; which ones can you explain easily, and which ones do you need to review?

Tasks/modes of discourse
    Exposition
    Description
    Narration
    Exposition
    Analysis
    Comparison/contrast
    Synthesis
    Argument

Sources
    Conventions
    Rhetorical means and ends

Terms
    Audience
    Embedded definitions

Academic discourse

Argument and Rhetoric

CHAPTER 6

Rhetoric dates back to ancient Greece, making many of its concepts more than two millennia old. It's tempting to dismiss a theory so ancient: How can rhetoric, meaning the art of persuasion, still be relevant? Yet many aspects of the human condition have not changed that much over the last twenty-or-so centuries. We still find ourselves disagreeing with others, wanting to win an argument, or needing to persuade another person. Our challenge continues to be, as it has been for centuries: Can we learn to use rhetoric well? In this chapter, we will use some familiar experiences to explain how we can understand and create arguments better in our daily lives as well as in college reading and writing assignments.

Argument is a fundamental form of college-level reading and writing. Much of high school instruction involves reading an explanation of an event in a textbook and writing an exposition of a concept, but college reading and writing often involve arguments. For instance, college students often are asked to not only explain an event or a concept but also argue why *this* analysis or interpretation is better than *that* one.

Let's start with an argument that you probably can easily imagine; you may have engaged in this kind of argument recently: a teenager and a parent differing over a weekend curfew. In one version of this argument, the teen and the parent recognize their differences ("Be home by 11." then "How about 1?") and start to trade accusations ("You never let me…" and "Don't be childish…"). This argument usually ends with a door slammed, a party missed, or a curfew violated. This version matches the concept of argument that many of us have when we are asked to imagine one: a verbal battle between two or more people.

On a daily basis, we encounter others or find ourselves engaged in these angry clashes, such as when a roommate complains about a noisy alarm clock, classmates disagree during a discussion, or a student decides to end an online friendship. These disputes may be brief, but they often end with more anger than agreement: "You'd better turn off that alarm…", "That's a ridiculous statement…", and "You're off my list; leave me alone." It's easy for us to slip into these clashes as the media surrounds us with aggressive disputes: Guests on daytime television insult each other, sports radio callers rip into a coach, and politicians trade charges during a debate. As Gerald Graff asserts, the very word "argument … conjures up an image … of acrimonious warfare." As we argue, we usually "make enemies ... yet rarely change each other's minds."

Two theorists named George Lakoff and Mark Johnson have analyzed the development of these war-like arguments. When a difference of viewpoints is recognized, we exaggerate these differences so those who disagree with us become our "enemies." Then we characterize them as jerks, idiots, and other words not fit for print in a textbook, so they *have* to be defeated. The war must be won; there can be no compromise. If a rule has to be bent a bit, well so be it. If this were the only kind of argument possible, we'd have to end this chapter right now because we all know how to conduct these martial arguments.

Fortunately, our example of a curfew dispute can result in another kind of argument. Can you imagine a more positive version? One that doesn't end with loud voices and a door slammed?

Weekend Curfew

A Teen   *A Parent*

Of course, many positive variations are possible, but here's one. Once the difference in time is recognized ("Do I have to be home by 11 or 1?"), each person could acknowledge the other's position. The teen could acknowledge the parent's concern that driving late at night can be more dangerous, and the parent could recognize the teen's desire for greater independence. As the parent and teen acknowledge each other's position instead of exaggerating their differences, a more positive outcome becomes much more likely. The teen can overcome the parent's fears by admitting, "I know that late night driving can be more dangerous, but you know I'm a good driver." The parent can acknowledge and even appeal to the teen's independence: "I know you want to spend time with your friends before you head off to college, but can you help me avoid worrying about you so much?" These recognitions of the other's concerns could create a better outcome, though a little compromise by both may be necessary: "Okay, I'll leave the party before midnight, and I'll call you if I'll be home later than midnight." Although it sometimes is very satisfying to crush the other side in an argument, this compromise not only makes both sides feel more content, it also makes them more likely to seek a more productive resolution when the next argument arises. The positive result of this curfew argument also suggests the original meaning of argument. In Latin, "argumentum" means "to make clear," not name calling or chair throwing. As we argue, we can try to make our positions clear to others and ourselves. Then everyone can decide better what positions we will and will not alter in order to resolve some difference of opinion.

The theories of rhetoric, which date back to the Greeks, can help us "make clear" the best ways to resolve an argument. As the Athenians of ancient Greece tried to establish their fledgling democracy, they argued over who should be considered a citizen and what is the best kind of leader. Aristotle and others like Gorgias tried to understand and teach the most effective methods of argumentation by developing theories of rhetoric. Aristotle defined **rhetoric** as "the discovery of the available means of persuasion." By using the best of these possible methods, the ancient Greeks tried to resolve their societal differences through oral arguments instead of physical aggression. Ever since, we have been disagreeing at home, at work, in classrooms, and in government, but rhetoric can teach us how to make the most persuasive arguments so anger, regret, and violence can be avoided.

The Rhetorical Triangle

We will use our example of a curfew conflict to demonstrate the first and most fundamental concept of their ancient theories: the **rhetorical triangle**.

Message/Purpose

Speaker/
Writer

Audience/
Reader

When a **speaker** considers his **audience** as well as his **message**, it prevents an impulsive assertion of his position ("I wanna stay out late."). This attention to audience makes a speaker balance what she wants to say with how it will be heard ("Yes, driving at midnight can be dangerous, but ..."). The Greeks had names for these "Yes" and "but" strategies: **concession** and **refutation**. Most teens are very good at refuting a parent's argument, but some do not precede this counterargument with a concession, by admitting that the parent may have a valid point. Such a concession usually will gain some goodwill from the parent that, in turn, may make this elder more likely to listen to the teen's response ("... but you know I'm a safe driver."). Of course, the parent may offer his or her own concession and refutation ("Yes, I know you're a good driver, but it's other drivers out late at night that scare me."). Now at least both parties have agreed on what is the real issue: How great are the dangers of other drivers late at night? You probably can imagine how this argument might continue: The parent wants to protect the child, and the teenager counters that a parent can't always be protective, the child has to go forth into the world.

Next, if some of the principles of effective argumentation are used, the results may be less divisive and more satisfying. These principles may even help some of you stay out later next summer.

Three Appeals

Our example of the curfew conflict also demonstrates three other crucial concepts of rhetoric. You probably can imagine listening to this verbal dispute so let us represent it in writing with the ALL CAP SHOUTING of text messaging. Can you hear a teen shouting, "BUT MOM you don't need to WORRY"? This impulsive assertion also could be expressed as "Mom, I know you worry, but ...." This difference of expression involves not only what is said but also how it is said, and the latter reveals the role of a speaker's character in an argument. The ancient Greeks referred to the influence of a speaker's character as **ethos**, and it is one of what they called the three rhetorical appeals. The other two appeals are by feelings, emotions—**pathos** and by reason, logic—**logos**. As with the rhetorical triangle, the Greeks liked to think in threes, in triads, and the three appeals can be listed as

1. *ethos – the appeal by character*
2. *pathos – the appeal by emotion*
3. *logos – the appeal by reason*

Let us explain each one briefly.

Ethos

Former President Ronald Reagan is the epitome of this appeal. Both his supporters and his critics called him the "Teflon President" because nothing negative ever seemed to stick to him. Many voters liked his character so much that they easily accepted his arguments ("Tear down that wall") and they ignored his mistakes (the Iran-Contra scandal). President Reagan is a perfect example of Aristotle's explanation of ethos: "Persuasion is achieved by the speaker's personal character, when the speech is so spoken as to make us think him credible. We believe good men more fully and readily than others."

A modern theorist named Kenneth Burke coined the term **identification** to explain the appeal by character further; he asserted, "You persuade a man only insofar as you can talk his language by speech, gesture, ton[e], … [and] attitude, *identifying* your ways with his" (italics added). Consider, for example, a teen in the curfew argument who concedes, "I know you worry Mom, but I'd like to spend some time with my friends before college" versus one who exclaims, "You never let me …." The second speaker already has lost this argument because that comment shows the very immaturity that the parent fears will endanger the teen. In contrast, the first speaker presents the poise that the parent hopes will keep the child safe.

One last point about ethos and identification: Despite the old saying "When in Rome do as the Romans do," a speaker's character does not have to match that of the audience exactly. In fact, we cringe when a parent tries to talk and dress like a teen or when a student mirrors the middle-age manner of an older teacher. Ethos only requires that the audience connects with a speaker's language and demeanor so she is considered likeable and credible. Then the audience is more ready, as Aristotle explained, to believe the appeals made by pathos and logos.

Pathos

This appeal depends on the emotions aroused in the audience. Like President Reagan, Barack Obama was elected because he stirred feelings of optimism in voters. Like Reagan's slogan of "It's morning in America," Obama emphasized change and hope to an electorate ready for both. He made Americans feel confident and capable. Pathos depends less on the emotions shown by the speaker and more on the feelings evoked from the audience.

Perhaps the best way to demonstrate this distinction between the emotions of speaker and audience is through a counterexample. When a teen exclaims, "But MOM, you NEVER let me …" the outrage of the speaker may not be matched by a similar feeling of unfairness in a parent. Instead it's liable to provoke anger from a listener upset by the teen's self-centered demands. The mistake of confusing a speaker's emotions with those of an audience is a common one. We even have phrases ready to catch this error; we turn to another listener and reject this "sob story" or ask a speaker if he isn't "laying it on a bit too thick?"

Sometimes the most effective emotional appeal is made by an understated assertion. Rather than model feelings for an audience, a subdued speaker can create the conditions for the desired emotional reaction of the audience. In Shakespeare's play *Julius Caesar*, you may recall Mark Antony's famous speech in which he asserts that he has come "to bury Caesar, not to praise him." Then in a solemn voice, he catalogs many of this murdered leader's best traits. The grief he has brought to "bury" this fallen leader provokes exactly the anger he wants from the crowd. This emotion turns the crowd against Brutus and the other conspirators, just as Antony intended. When it comes to pathos, sometimes less feeling expressed by the speaker can create more emotion for the audience.

Logos

As we already have explained, techniques, like concession and refutation, can create a series of logical premises that can bring an audience to a desired conclusion. These series can proceed from specific examples to general principles or follow the reverse pattern. Perhaps you already know the names of these patterns from a writing or a philosophy course. **Inductive reasoning** presents several specific examples to prove a general principle, such as when someone argues that he knows three people who were in car accidents as they were texting while driving so he concludes that texting behind the wheel is dangerous. **Deductive reasoning**, on the other hand, begins with a general principle like drivers should avoid unnecessary risks and applies it to a specific example, such as texting while driving, in order to conclude that drivers should not text behind the wheel. Can you outline these two examples of inductive and deductive reasoning?

Inductive Reasoning	Deductive Reasoning
Singular Example:	General Principle:
Specific Example:	Particular Case:
Conclusion:	Conclusion:

The Greeks created names for these two patterns of logic as well as two more specific forms of deductive reasoning that we still use today: syllogism and enthymeme.

A **syllogism** is a three-step, logical series built on what we can explain informally as an "if this and if that, then …… ." pattern. You probably know this famous example of a syllogism:

A Famous Syllogism

All men are mortal.

Socrates is a man.

Socrates is mortal.

Another way to understand a syllogism is to imagine a listener's reactions: "All men are mortal"—that's true, "Socrates is man"—okay, so "Socrates is mortal"—who could deny that conclusion?! Yet syllogisms sometimes seem a bit too obvious, a little too drawn out for an audience to stay interested in the reasoning.

An **enthymeme** reduces the three steps of a syllogism (1. if this, and 2. if that, then 3. conclusion) to only two. It provides a premise and depends upon the audience to supply the next step so the desired conclusion will be reached. The two-step process of an enthymeme can be diagrammed as

An Enthymeme's Two-Step Logic

1. If this (and an audience knows that)
2. Then the conclusion is. . .

In another Shakespearean play, *The Merchant of Venice*, the protagonist creates a memorable enthymeme that reduces the three-step syllogism on Socrates's mortality to a two-step argument for the humanity of a Jewish character named Shylock. In a climatic scene, Shylock protests his poor treatment by others when he exclaims, "If you cut a Jew, does he not bleed?" Through this enthymeme, Shylock makes the following appeal through deductive reasoning:

Shakespeare's Enthymeme

1. If wounded people suffer and bleed (Shylock will bleed when cut)
2. Then Shylock is as human as his tormentors

Enthymemes, of course, are only effective if the audience can supply the second premise. However, when they do, they will reach the conclusion sought by the speaker based on what seems to be on their own logic. Then an audience is more convinced because they are involved in, and not just following, an argument's reasoning process.

One possible flaw in the use of enthymemes is when an argument appeals only to those who already agree with the speaker. Consider, for example, those on both sides of the abortion debate. As they refer to "a woman's choice" or "the right to life," each side expects the audience to assume that the rights of the mother or the fetus are paramount so the desired conclusion on abortion as being right or wrong is reached. Of course, those who do not already agree could respond that some choices aren't good or a mother's life matters too. The abortion issue has become so contentious because some on both sides engage in what is known as **preaching to the choir**. Appealing to those with the same views as yours is a great campaign strategy to mobilize one's supporters, but it is a much less effective strategy when one must convince others and create a consensus.

Another potential problem in logical appeals is that we sometimes argue, as another theorist named Stephen Toulmin asserts, backward, meaning we develop our arguments in reverse. Rather than start with the facts of a dispute, we often start with the outcome we want to reach and then gather the evidence to support that result. Toulmin, therefore, calls the desired outcome of an argument the **claim** for which one gathers **evidence** or what he termed the data. However, if we only collect the facts that support our position, we end up making one-sided arguments that can be countered easily. Toulmin, therefore, urged that as we develop an argument, we should anticipate possible counterarguments, or rebuttals, to our claim. This **rebuttal** may force us to modify, to qualify our claim, such as by making an absolute claim into a conditional one: "Yes, it's not always the case, but I still will argue that it usually is true that ...." It's easy to imagine an advocate of male superiority making such a **qualification**, or modification of one's claim, after the physical strength of top female athletes has been raised as a rebuttal to his original claim of absolute male dominance.

To test your knowledge of these appeals, here are three more statements by a parent in the curfew conflict. What appeal do you think is primarily being used in each one? Ethos, pathos, or logos?

- "It's a fact that there are many more fatal car accidents after midnight."
- "I'd never forgive myself if you were hurt in a late night crash."
- "I've been driving for thirty years, and I've seen too many teens make stupid driving mistakes."

We think these three statements rely primarily on logos in the first, pathos in the second, and ethos in the third. Of course, these appeals sometimes overlap so you could argue that the second involves the speaker's character, or ethos, as well as pathos.

Since ethos is based on the speaker, pathos with audience, and logos with message, we can sum up our explanation of the three appeals be layering them onto the rhetorical triangle:

Thus, a persuasive speaker tries to project a credible ethos, which makes the audience more receptive to certain emotions as well as the logic of her message.

Three Kinds of Argument

The ancient Greeks, and Aristotle in particular, loved to categorize; we already have suggested that there are several ways to categorize various kinds of arguments. We have distinguished between positive and unproductive arguments as well as between aggressive arguments (win–lose) and conflict compromises (win–win). In what other ways do you think various kinds of arguments can be classified?

Kinds of Arguments

One other way to categorize arguments is to consider arguing over facts, over causes, and over effects ("Is it true that …?", "Why did this happen …?", and "What will the result be if …?"). Of course, these three kinds of argument overlap because, for example, an argument over causes involves the results, the effects.

Despite Aristotle's love for categories and his desire to create absolute classifications, the three kinds of arguments from ancient rhetoric are not airtight categories. Yet these classic categories are easy to recall and use, and they will help you focus and develop an argument. Even better, during the heat of an argument, these categories will encourage you to anticipate and counter the arguments made by others. Thus, they will help you discover, as Aristotle's definition of rhetoric states, the available means of persuasion.

The Greeks created a three-part classification of arguments based on time and topic. For Aristotle and other ancients, the three kinds of argument are **forensic** arguments focused on the past and on the topics of blame and guilt, **epideictic** arguments focused on the present and the topic of values, and **deliberative** arguments focused on the future and the topic of actions.

Three Kinds of Argument	Time	Topic
forensic	past	blame/guilt
epideictic	present	values
deliberative	future	best action

Some theorists also refer to epideictic arguments (pronounced ep-i-DAKE-tic) as **demonstrative** ones because a speaker demonstrates his or her values.

Let's use an argument more significant than a curfew conflict to illustrate these categories, yet it is an issue related to those parent-teen clashes: the legal drinking age. How would you develop an argument over this issue using each one of these three kinds?

Three Arguments over the Drinking Age	Time	Topic
forensic		
epideictic		
deliberative		

A forensic argument over this issue would focus on the past and blame, such as who is responsible for teen drinking and driving accidents: the alcohol companies that promote their products in advertisements aimed at young adults, those who sell alcohol to underage drinkers, or those teens who drink and drive.

An epideictic, or demonstrative, argument would focus on the present and values, such as should we care more about keeping kids safe or teaching teens to be mature? Epideictic arguments over values tend to be framed as absolute ones with no grey area; we **either** care about children's safety *or* teens' maturation.

To break through this either/or dispute, one can shift to a deliberative argument. Then, in a future-oriented argument, one could approach this contentious issue by arguing over the best action, such as *when* should teens have legal access to alcohol so they can avoid tragedies and learn to drink responsibly. This shift from present values to future actions would involve an argument, such as on whether or not the legal drinking age should be lowered back to 18 or perhaps 19.

The shift to a deliberative argument makes a resolution that both sides can accept more likely. The future action could be to enact, as with teen driving licenses in many states, some sort of graduated access policy. This deliberative argument could be for gradual access to alcohol. Then, for instance, this access could be developed gradually, such as

- At age 17, teens legally could consume alcohol in their parents' homes.

- At 18 or 19, teens could purchase alcohol in a bar and restaurant (where others are liable for serving to excess so they would prevent it).

- At 20 or 21, teens could purchase alcohol for private use.

This deliberative argument will hinge on gradually promoting teens' independence while maintaining adult supervision. Thus, deliberative arguments often end in compromise. In contrast, epideictic arguments often produce no-win stalemates, and forensic arguments yield win-lose outcomes.

To test your understanding of these three kinds of arguments, here are three more assertions about the issue of teen drinking. What kind of argument do you think each one primarily represents: forensic, epideictic, or deliberative?

- We need to improve teen alcohol education by eliminating the scare tactics.

- Seat belts and air bags, not the drinking age of 21, have caused the decrease in teen deaths in car accidents over the last decade.

- If parents really love their children, they will keep their teens away from alcohol.

We think these three examples primarily consist of a future-oriented deliberative argument in the first statement, a past-focused forensic one in the second, and a present-oriented epideictic argument over values in the third. However, as with the three appeals, these categories are not absolute. They are not like three bins set apart so items can be sorted into them easily. The third example, for instance can be considered a deliberative argument if you emphasize the future action ("keep . . . teens") over the present values ("really love"). This emphasis, however, will alter the rest of the argument made ("How can we best keep teens . . . ?" versus "Do parents love their teens enough to . . . ?"). Despite the ambiguity of some arguments, these categories can help you determine what is your focus and how to develop your argument.

Here's one last way to help you distinguish the three classic kinds of arguments: consider where they frequently occur.

Three Kinds	Time	Topic	Setting
forensic	past	blame/guilt	courtrooms
epideictic	present	values	campaigns
deliberative	future	best action	government

As the last column of our chart now shows, forensic arguments often occur in legal courtrooms ("Did he do it?"), epideictic ones dominate political campaigns (pro-life or pro-choice?), and deliberative arguments usually are stressed in our legislative government (school reform?).

Just as the location of an argument corresponds with the kind of argument made, so too does the kind of argument often match the result. For instance, a forensic argument over guilt almost always ends with a win/lose result. An epideictic argument over values usually results in a divisive debate in which some values are deemed right and others, wrong. A deliberative argument over an action can lead to more compromises, especially when each side feels pressured to address an urgent problem ("We can't just keep arguing; we have to do something."). Thus, it often is important to decide in advance what kind of argument you want to have; it may well determine much of the outcome.

Two Other Approaches to Argument

Stasis Theory

Although the ancient Greeks developed many of the fundamental concepts and theories of rhetoric, many others have continued to develop its principles. For example, the Romans refined a form of forensic argument known as stasis theory, which courtroom lawyers to this day still practice. A modern version of this theory provides a sequence of four questions with which to argue almost any courtroom case:

1. **What happened? (argument of fact)**
2. **What is the nature of this event? (argument of definition)**
3. **What is the quality of this event? (argument of evaluation)**
4. **What is the best response to this event? (argument of recommendation)**

Let's shift from our earlier example of a curfew conflict to a potentially even more divisive event at a school: a physical confrontation between a teacher and a student. If a principal had to address this confrontation, this administrator—or perhaps a lawyer for the school district—could use the four questions of stasis theory in order to understand this event and decide how to react better.

The first question asked would be an **argument of fact**: **What happened?** Who was the first person to physically confront the other person? How did the physical actions then escalate? Who grabbed, punched, or tackled whom? Who suffered what physical injuries?

Whoever seems to deserve more blame in this conflict is likely to shift from this factual argument to the next question. This person's ultimate goal in a forensic argument would be to show that although he/she may have initiated the physical aggression, this person does not deserve the final blame for this fight. Thus, if the teacher or student must admit that he/she grabbed the shirt of the other person or threw the first punch of this confrontation, the next question would be about the nature of those actions.

The second question concerns whether or not, for instance, the teacher grabbing the shirt of a belligerent student should be categorized as an act of physical aggression that every school district forbids. The teacher or the lawyer representing him or her would ask, **"What is the nature of this event?"** This **argument of definition** focuses on whether or not this seemingly aggressive gesture instead was a protective gesture. Was the teacher trying to ensure his/her own safety, or perhaps the teacher grabbed the student's shirt in order to draw this student from another who seemed ready to fight. In this circumstance, the nature of the teacher's action is transformed from an unprofessional act of aggression to a responsible gesture of protection: exactly what a teacher should do for a student.

If the student believes that the teacher did not act to protect the student or even for self-protection, this next question would be over **"What is the quality of this event?"** This **argument of evaluation** might examine exactly how the teacher grabbed the student's shirt. The student or a lawyer then would try to evaluate that grasp by arguing that the teacher took the front of the student's shirt into two fists, lifted the shirt's collar up to the student's chin, and knocked the student backward. Thus, this intimidating grasp was not a protective gesture but an aggressive one. The quality of this action, of course, would help to determine whether the teacher's initial action should be defined as an appropriate response or unprofessional aggression.

Once the quality of the teacher's and/or the student's physical actions have been judged, the final question creates an **argument of recommendation** over **"What is the best response to this event?"** With this question, a forensic argument shifts to a deliberative one. Once a hearing or trial reaches a conclusion about blame, the issue of punishment must be faced. If this case reached a courtroom, a judge or jury would have to decide, for instance, whether the teacher should be fined, fired, decertified, and/or imprisoned or if the student should be suspended, expelled, prosecuted, and/or incarcerated. The findings from the first three questions on blame would result in some sort of recommendation.

Here are two more events for you to apply stasis theory. Imagine a parent comes home to find two preteen children and a broken plate or window. Or imagine that the stockholders of a company learn from the business's lavish-spending president that bankruptcy must be declared. How might the parent and children or the stockholders and the company president argue according to stasis theory?

Fact: What happened? _____

Definition: What is its nature? _____

Evaluation: What is its quality? _____

Recommendation: What is the best response? _____

As these two examples and the teacher-student fight suggest, a stasis argument usually ends with a win–lose result. The next approach to argument is designed to deliberately promote a win–win outcome through a less combative process.

Rogerian Argument

Developed by psychologist Carl Rogers, this alternative style of argument can help people resolve their differences so that both sides are satisfied with the outcome. A Rogerian argument involves two or more people that differ in their opinions, but their positions cannot be as fixed as those in a forensic argument. This alternative begins by seeking areas of agreement between the two sides. The first question to be posed is not "How do we differ?" but **"What common ground, if any, exists between our positions?"**

Consider, for an example, the ongoing controversy over gun control in America. Two individuals or groups may differ because one believes that Americans have an absolute right to bear arms while the other believes that the possession of weapons by citizens must be regulated to ensure more public safety. It's easy to imagine a divisive debate over this issue with lines like:

A Divisive Debate over Gun Control

"Citizens have the right to bear arms."

"No, guns kept at home are too dangerous."

"But hunting is an American tradition."

"Who needs a machine gun?!"

"Guns don't kill; people DO!"

This argument could continue with the voices becoming louder and angrier as positions are "defended" and opponents are "attacked." The Rogerian alternative is designed to avoid such antagonism among adversaries.

A Rogerian argument over gun control would begin, as stated above, by seeking areas of agreement rather than "squaring off" in fixed positions. The participants would ask "What do *all* of us believe?" and **"Is there any common ground between our positions?"** Through discussion, both sides could realize they want people to be kept safe.

A Rogerian Argument over Gun Control

Common Ground

"Although we may differ in our means, our ends are the same. We want people to be safe. We want innocent citizens to be protected from harm."

After the two sides recognize their differences, the first step, as shown above, is to seek some basic, shared belief.

The second step is for each side to explore the other position through sincere questions. These inquiries serve as an invitation for elaboration: "**Can you tell me more about your belief?**" The intent of these questions must be in the spirit of learning more about the other position, not setting a trap for the other side. How might each side on gun control encourage the other one to explain more? Consider these questions posed by the speaker indicated:

Elaboration Questions

Pro-gun person: *"What types of guns do you think the average citizen should not be allowed to purchase?"*

"How stringent do you think gun permit regulations should be?"

Antigun person: *"How should a homeowner handle a weapon when he is trying to stop an intruder?"*

"What are the best ways to store weapons in a home?"

These questions are intended to allow the other side to elaborate on their perspective, yet they also may lead both sides to confront the complexities of the topic.

Next, a participant in a Rogerian argument should repeat the opposing viewpoint in a respectful manner. This response should demonstrate that one has listened with understanding and empathy. These responses are intended to build trust rather than tension between the two sides. Imagine, for example, if the participants in an argument over gun control were to comment:

Listening and Restating

Pro-gun person: *"I hear you saying that it is tragic when a distraught person grabs a gun, and in a moment of anger or despair, this person kills a loved one. Even worse are the cases of children playing with an unlocked gun and accidentally shooting someone."*

Anti-gun person: *"The news often has terrible reports of home invasions. When a homeowner can retrieve a weapon from the locked storage that you mentioned and protect the family and values, it's a much better outcome than a robbery and other horrible crimes."*

These comments may have to continue for a while to make the two sides willing to step back from their initial divisions ("Who needs …?" and "Guns don't kill …").

The final step of a Rogerian argument comes when the two sides realize that some sort of complex and usually imperfect solution is possible. The gun control controversy, for example, has led to more restrictions on gun purchases as well as more freedom to carry a concealed weapon.

Complex Solutions

We agree that stricter laws should keep guns out of the hands of criminals but citizens should have the right to own carefully stored weapons.

Cynics may find it hard to believe that Rogerian arguments can accomplish much, yet these steps have helped to solve labor disputes and perhaps even a few curfew conflicts in America. They also have helped to bring peace to Northern Ireland and South Africa. The main steps of Rogerian theory are as follows:

1. Recognize differences but be willing to alter one's initial position.

2. Seek common ground with the other side.

3. Explore the opposing viewpoint through sincere questions.

4. Practice listening with empathy and restate the other opinion accurately.

5. Pursue new, complex, and often imperfect solutions.

Let's return to the conflict over the teacher and the student who engaged in some kind of physical confrontation. Rather than seek the win–lose outcome of stasis theory, let's shift from the courtroom setting of a forensic argument to the office of a mediator trying to prevent a lawsuit. How do you think this mediator could foster a Rogerian argument on this issue? What would the teacher and the student each have to do differently in order for a win–win resolution to be achieved?

Student-Teacher Conflict

Recognize Differences

Seek Common Ground

Ask Exploratory Questions

Listen Well and Restate

Pursue Complex Solutions

We would like to add several other key concepts, but we fear that we will overwhelm at least some of our readers if we do. Let us instead provide the final list of key terms, and then we will add a few more concepts of rhetoric and argument.

Key Terms and Concepts

Before you finish with this chapter, here is a list of the key concepts; which ones can you explain easily, and which ones do you need to review?

Rhetoric
  Aristotle's definition and ethics

The rhetorical triangle
  Speaker/writer
  Message/purpose
  Audience/reader

Three rhetorical appeals
  Ethos
    Identification
  Pathos
  Logos
    Premise
    Evidence

Concession
Refutation
Rebuttal
Qualification
Inductive reasoning
Deductive reasoning
Syllogism
Enthymeme
Preaching to the choir

Three kinds of argument
  Forensic
  Epideictic/demonstrative
  Deliberative

Two more kinds of argument
   Stasis theory
      Argument of fact
      Argument of definition
      Argument of evaluation
      Argument of recommendation

A few more key concepts (see below):
Canon
   Invention
   Arrangement
   Style
      Antithesis
      Chiasmus
      Synecdoche
Memory
Delivery

Rogerian argument
   Common ground
   Elaboration questions
   Listening and restating
   Complex solutions

Logical fallacies
   Ad hominen attack
   Bandwagon appeal
   Circular logic
   Correlation vs. causation
   Distracted logic/red herring
   Either/or—dichotomy
   Hasty generalization
   Non sequitur
   Slippery slope
   Straw man argument

A Few More Key Concepts

In the following supplement to this chapter on argument, we want to present some other key concepts of rhetoric. See the list above, and, working with your professor, you can determine when you will study this additional knowledge of rhetoric and argument.

   The Roman rhetorician Cicero summed up the process of creating an effective argument, and his rhetorical **canon** includes:

Invention: determining what are the available means of persuasion

Arrangement: creating the order of the persuasive evidence and appeals

Style: using the appropriate language to reach an audience

Memory: using one's knowledge of rhetoric to speak persuasively

Delivery: presenting an argument effectively

   Although Cicero described rhetoric as "A good man speaking well," neither this definition nor Aristotle's definition fully addresses the issue of ethics in argumentation. During **invention**, a speaker or writer develops many possible ways to argue for one's opinion. However, just because part of an argument is "available," should it be used? For example, should a candidate use an embarrassing detail from his opponent's past, such as a drunken driving arrest at age 22, to discredit him or her? Aristotle's definition of ethos again provides little guidance, for he explains the appeal by character as "Persuasion is achieved by the speaker's personal character, when the speech is so spoken as to *make us think him credible.* We believe good men more fully and readily than others" (italics added). On the one hand, Aristotle seems to insist that a speaker should be a "good man," but on the other, he acknowledges that ethos is a matter of appearance: "to make us think him credible." Thus, ethos and ethics are not necessarily one in the same.

Like Murray's concept of ordering during the writing process, **arrangement** refers to the most effective organization of an argument. Aristotle believed that most arguments should follow a general pattern of the rhetorical appeals organized as

Ethos first, Logos next, and Pathos last

Of course, a writer's credibility and likeability depend on subject knowledge and audience emotions so ethos can never be separate entirely from logos and pathos. Aristotle, however, insisted that a speaker's initial concern must be to appeal by ethos.

The ancients urged speakers to be clear, vivid, and appropriate in their language. They also developed many word patterns to create a **style** that would help sway an audience. There are many more figures than we can present, but here are three of the most common ones:

Antithesis

This phrasing places two ideas side-by-side. In a divisive argument, you can use this figure to assert, "You're either with us or you're against us." During the Vietnam War, those who opposed the protestors used antithesis to argue "America, Love It or Leave It."

Chiasmus

This figure (pronounced kee-AZZ-muss) reverses the first phrase to assert a compelling second phrase. The most famous example probably is President Kennedy's declaration: "Ask not what your country can do for you, but what you can do for your country." Perhaps you have seen another example on a birthday card for an older person: "Rather than counting the years, make the years count."

Synecdoche

This phrasing (pronounced si-NEK-do-ke) uses a part to represent the whole. For instance, Homer announces the return of the hero's ship by referring to Odysseus's sails reaching port.

The fourth part of Cicero's canon, **memory**, seems like the hardest one to transfer from speaking to writing. It seems to us to refer to a speaker's ability to recall a prepared argument, but for the ancients, this concept meant much more than our current sense of memorizing. Memory meant a storehouse, a treasure house of rhetorical knowledge. Skilled orators would travel mentally through this treasure house each day so they could "visit" any room of their rhetorical knowledge when they needed to do so. For example, rhetoricians have developed a set of reasoning errors that they should avoid and will expose when others commit one of these **logical fallacies**. Here are ten of the most common examples of this faulty logic:

Logical Fallacies

Ad Hominen Attack

This fallacy occurs when the advocate of an opposing view is criticized. The person, rather than the opinion, becomes the focus of this attack, such as when a political debate shifts from a policy argument to the denigration of "free-spending Democrats" and narrow-minded Republicans."

Bandwagon Appeal

This flaw replaces reason with popularity, and then one asserts, "But everyone else is …." Of course, the quick counterargument is "If everybody else is jumping off a bridge … ?"

Circular Logic

This fallacy confuses a claim and its evidence. Then only one point ends up being repeated, as in "She's too good for him because he's not nice (or smart) enough." This argument fails to explain why nice (or smart) is equivalent to good. Instead the speaker assumes that this criteria is obvious so he or she "begs the question," meaning in this case, the central question of what makes a good match is never addressed.

Correlation Versus Causation

This logic assumes that because two events occur, the first must be the reason for the second. For example, proponents of music education sometimes argue that because many music students earn good grades, the study of music must make children smarter. This causal argument fails to consider that smart children may be more likely to be interested in music. Correlation does not prove causation.

Distracted Logic

This flaw introduces irrelevant information into an argument. If we can continue our "good enough" dating example from above, it's easy to imagine someone adding, "Yea, and he's not even a member of our group." Yet whether or not he belongs to a social circle has no relevance to this argument. Such distraction is also known as a "red herring" from the old fox-hunting trick of dragging a dead fish across a path to deflect the dogs from their prey and keep the hunt going longer.

Either/Or Fallacy

This argument pits two extreme opposites against each other and denies that any middle ground is possible. In the abortion debate, each side can assert, "we value life and you don't." This dichotomy, however, fails to recognize that instead of just one life, at least two lives are involved in this difficult issue.

Hasty Generalization

This fallacy makes a general claim from insufficient evidence. Prejudice depends on this misuse of inductive reasoning, for it claims that since a few members of a group display some flaw, then every member has this defect. For instance, "My friend's son just lost his third cell phone; children today are so careless."

Non Sequitur

This is another flaw based on a faulty connection between claim and evidence. Political ads often show candidates with their families, but there is not necessarily any relationship between being a caring parent and an effective leader. The English translation of this term is "it does not follow."

Slippery Slope

This fallacy involves a dubious cause-and-effect relationship. It assumes that from a debatable position, next something bad will happen, and the worst will follow: for example, in an argument over controversial books: "If we let children read this novel, they will have immoral thoughts, and then they will act in immoral ways." Those who make such assertions fail to consider that such books can be taught as cautionary tales against undesirable actions.

Straw Man Argument

This flaw creates a caricature of an opposing viewpoint. From our gun control example, those against all restrictions could characterize their opposition as "those naïve liberals who want only the bad guys to have weapons." Once the opposition has been built conveniently out of straw, they are easy to knock down. This fallacy, however, leaves the actual position of the other side still standing and the argument unresolved.

By storing these logical fallacies and many other rhetorical concepts in your memory, you will be able to argue and react to arguments made by others more effectively.

For speech, the **delivery** of an argument involves voice tone and volume as well as facial expressions and physical gestures. In writing, Cicero's fifth and final canon involves the visual presentation of information, such as through font, margins, spacing, bullets, white space, images, and more. Academic writing relies on a very direct and spare delivery, but the memos, brochures, and reports of the workplace usually require a more elaborate delivery of information (for more on document design, see Chapter 9 on Professional Writing).

Academic Honesty and Its Conventions

Having a good friend disagree with you is a difficult situation. Can you recall an instance when a friend doubted one of your choices or opposed one of your beliefs? Despite the bond between you two, this friend suggested that you might be mistaken and asserted another option or opinion ("It might be better if you …" or "I see it differently …"). Then to be persuasive, he or she had to provide some evidence ("Because I learned that …"). Even when this information was given, you may have resisted it ("How do you know that?") or failed to understand its implication ("But what does that mean?"). If your friend didn't name the source ("Someone in the hallway said …") or explain the implications fully (It's obvious that …"), you may have stopped trusting him or her. This friendship was weakened, at least for a while.

This disagreement among friends is like the development of knowledge in an academic discipline, which is the real topic of this chapter. Like friends, academics try to handle their disagreements by asserting an opposing viewpoint, providing supporting information, identifying sources, and explaining the significance. Let us add one more wrinkle, sometimes it's hard to pin down exactly how these disagreements develop. Did some misunderstanding of what everyone thought was known cause the disagreement or did the friend start it by stating an opposing perspective? This is one of those chicken-and-the-egg questions that probably are best left as a constant tension between the two. In other words, disagreements develop through a group's reliance of what is known, **communal dependence**, and one person's expression of a different opinion, **individual assertion**. With these two handy terms: individual assertion and communal dependence, we will explain how and why students and scholars can and should maintain their academic honesty. Simply put, trust among academics or friends—once broken—can be very hard to restore.

Academic Honesty and Its Conventions

You may be surprised that we didn't start this chapter with the dreaded P-word: plagiarism; we will save that issue for later. Instead let us demonstrate an individual assertion. We think any explanation of academic honesty should start with why the conventions of academic honesty exist and how easy they are to fulfill.

We will be referring to the **conventions** of academic honesty rather than its rigid rules ("You must … or else …"). By conventions, we mean expected actions, like what a family assumes everyone will do on a holiday such as Thanksgiving. Academic honesty is less a matter of what some authorities have determined is illegal—a rule not to be broken—and more a matter of what "we" usually do—a convention to be followed if you want to be seen as one of "us." The proper quoting and citing of sources show that you are ready and able to participate in an academic community. They are part of what every college student should know how to do, but sometimes these expectations are not explained sufficiently. To support our assertion that academic honesty involves understanding some easy-to-fulfill conventions, we will explain communal dependence and individual assertion. As you'll see below, we will provide some supporting evidence of our own, identify our sources, and elaborate on our evidence. We will explain by *doing* and not just *telling*.

Communal Dependence and Signal Phrases

For younger students, the question of why conventions like quotations and citations are used can be answered with "Because someone else said it first." Yet this is not enough of an explanation for most college students. A better answer is that academic writers quote and cite their sources in order to place their new ideas in the context of what is already known. By acknowledging this dependence, an academic anticipates and answers a skeptical reader's queries ("Why do you think that …?"). Anticipating such skepticism, an academic writer places quotation marks around her reliance on the exact words by another writer. We, for example, can quote one leading theorist on the communal quality of academic knowledge: it "is an artifact created by a community of knowledgeable peers" (Bruffee 646). As just demonstrated, one easy way to indicate the source of a **quotation** is to place the author's last name and the page number in a **citation** at the end of the sentence. The period is placed after the parenthesis because the citation is part of that sentence. As you may realize, we are using the citation system of the Modern Language Association (also known by its acronym MLA), and this association includes those in the humanities, such as historians, philosophers, and literary critics. (Later we will distinguish MLA citations from two other systems.)

As you probably know, **paraphrased ideas** and **little known facts** as well as exact quotations should be cited. Yet since this information from another writer is not repeated word-for-word, a citation may not demonstrate clearly enough the extent of an academic's dependence on others. Consider the following example as a section of a student's paper:

> Sample Paraphrase: If students are to master the knowledge of a particular discipline, it is not enough for teachers to ask them to repeat this knowledge on a test. Teachers also need to engage students in discussions of this information and require them to utter the key terms of this discipline. For students can only think and know in the ways they can talk and write (Bruffee 642).

The citation clearly marks the information in the final sentence as paraphrased from Bruffee, yet in this example, where do you think the writer's dependence on this source begins? It's hard to tell, isn't it? In fact, the first and second sentences also are paraphrased ideas so a parenthetical citation isn't always enough to indicate fully a writer's reliance on a source. To clarify the extent to which a source has been used, an academic writer can employ what is known as a **signal phrase** or an **attribution**. As shown below, an attribution like According to Kenneth Bruffee, signals that a writer is relying on a source. Note too that when the author's last name is included in the signal phrase, the citation contains only the page number.

Example with Attribution Added (**in bold**):

According to Kenneth Bruffee, if students are to master the knowledge of a particular discipline, it is not enough for teachers to ask them to repeat this knowledge on a test. Teachers also need to engage students in discussions of this information and require them to utter the key terms of this discipline. For students can only think and know in the ways they can talk and write (642).

Even if you had not heard of the term signal phrase before, you probably can add several more to our list:

Some Signal Phrases
According to Smith,
Muñoz explains,
As Wang argues,
.
.
.

With an attribution to "signal" that the next information comes from another writer, the extent of this writer's reliance on a source is clear; it's marked from the signal phrase to the parenthetical citation. When an academic writer follows these conventions, he says, in essence, to others in his academic community: "Here's how I know this information," and this indication serves as more than a defensive gesture: "Look, I'm not making this up." These conventions also act as an implicit invitation for praise: "Wow, she has read so much." Thus, a writer can solicit a reader's admiration by acknowledging her dependence on others, but this dependence is not enough in itself to be an effective academic writer.

Citations and Individual Assertions

When an academic writer provides some quoted or paraphrased information, a reader may not understand how this information relates to his opinion ("What does that mean?"). A writer, therefore, should explain its significance after the citation and not rush on to more cited material immediately. A reader may not be convinced if a writer only repeats what others have said on page after page until the required length has been reached. Consider this combination of the information cited from Bruffee above:

According to Kenneth Bruffee, if students are to master the knowledge of a particular discipline, it is not enough for teachers to ask them to repeat this knowledge on a test. Teachers also need to engage students in discussions of this information and require them to utter the key terms of this discipline. For students can only think and know in the ways they can talk and write (642). Knowledge "is an artifact created by a community of knowledgeable peers" (Bruffee 646).

In this example, the student writer is showing her dependence on what others know without making her own assertion. The very conventions of academic honesty seem to have trapped this student, but knowing how to support, cite, and elaborate create the means for this writer's escape. For the space for individual assertion also exists *after* a citation, as shown with the writing in bold below:

Example with Assertion Added (**in bold**):

According to Kenneth Bruffee, if students are to master the knowledge of a particular discipline, it is not enough for teachers to ask them to repeat this knowledge on a test. Teachers also need to engage students in discussions of this information and require them to utter the key terms of this discipline. For students can only think and know in the ways they can talk and write (642). **Sometimes students are able to get good grades for repeating information that they do not really understand. Discussing a subject and employing the terms used by experts can help students develop a deeper understanding. Through such active study of a subject, students demonstrate** that knowledge "is an artifact created by a community of knowledgeable peers" (Bruffee 646).

Just as an attribution signals to a reader "Here comes some cited info," the writing *after* a citation is read by other academics as "Okay, let's see what she is going to say about that writer's idea." The space *after* one citation and *before* the next attribution provides the room for the writer's own opinions, insights, interpretations, and arguments. Here's a continuation of the example from above; note the two sections **in bold**:

According to Kenneth Bruffee, if students are to master the knowledge of a particular discipline, it is not enough for teachers to ask them to repeat this knowledge on a test. Teachers also need to engage students in discussions of this information and require them to utter the key terms of this discipline. For students can only think and know in the ways they can talk and write (642). **Sometimes students are able to get good grades for repeating information that they do not really understand. Discussing a subject and employing the terms used by experts can help students develop a deeper understanding of their topic. Through such active study of a subject, students demonstrate** that knowledge "is an artifact created by a community of knowledgeable peers" (Bruffee 646). **As he promotes this image of a collaborative community, Bruffee, however, fails to consider the degree to which academics add to a discussion by disagreeing with and rejecting outright the assertions made by their colleagues.**

As suggested by this writer's critique of Bruffee's concept of a collaborative community, the interaction between writers is not always gentle cooperation. In addition to amiable agreement, an academic writer can contradict, limit, clarify, extend, or redirect what others already have stated. In fact, some scholars have characterized the primary academic response as one of opposition: "While most think X, I argue Y" (Graff 55). Whether a writer follows or refutes cited info, each response to other writers serves the ultimate purpose of academic writing: acknowledging and then resolving a disagreement through communal dependence and individual assertion.

Attributions: Signaling More than a Source

An academic writer can keep repeating the same signal phrase throughout his paper: "Smith says ..." then "Muñoz says ..." and even later "Wang says," but such repetition should be avoided on the grounds of sheer boredom. Yet, there is an even better reason to vary the signal phrases used. The wording of an attribution can signal not only a cited source, but also the kind of assertion that a writer will make after it. For example, what do you expect a writer's reaction to a quotation will be based on these three different signal phrases?

Three Different Attributions
Smith states,
Smith assumes,
Smith claims,

From our longer list below, which ones might a writer use to suggest her support of the source material? To imply her doubt? Which ones do you frequently use? Which ones can you use to improve a reader's readiness for your individual assertions?

acknowledges	emphasizes
advocates	errs
affirms	explains
argues	insists
asserts	justifies
believes	laments
claims	pleads
contends	reports
counters	recommends
demands	rejects
denies	states
doubts	urges

The phrasing of an attribution, like the conventions of quoting and citing, helps a writer persuade a reader. It is another rhetorical choice made by a writer. Plagiarism, on the other hand, occurs when a writer exerts too little control over source information.

The Dreaded P-Word

By the time you reached college, you probably knew that **plagiarism** is an act of academic dishonesty because a writer fails to acknowledge his or her reliance on the writing of others. Yet, this basic understanding may not be enough to prevent problems for some students. Often the devil is in the details, so let's consider some of the mistakes that can be made: what do you think are some of the various ways a student, deliberately or not, can commit plagiarism?

Several Kinds of Plagiarism
.
.
.
.
.

You probably listed some of the forms we will discuss below, so we will be brief on each one. We will provide some examples and then explain some additional conventions of academic writing.

Deliberate Copying is usually an act of desperation. A student may have waited too long before beginning an assignment, and as the clock ticks past midnight, he may be tempted to grab the words of another for use in his paper. This example matches one of the etymologies of plagiarism: from Latin, *plagiarius*—a kidnapper. A plagiarist "kidnaps" the words of another for his own profit or engages in what is typically termed **intellectual theft**, meaning the stealing of another writer's ideas and/or phrases for one's own gain.

Imagine if a student, for instance, is writing about scientific inquiry, and she copies the quotation by Bruffee we used above:

Plagiarism Example:

Scientists increase their discipline's knowledge by working from the results of experiments by others. Thus, for scientists, knowledge is an artifact created by a community of peers.

These sentences would raise the suspicions of many professors because the wording "an artifact created by…" is not a phrase that most students would use. Thus, deliberate copying usually is not very difficult for many professors to detect, and, even worse, it is easy for a student to avoid. In a minute or two, this student could have added quotation marks and the citation needed for academic honesty to be maintained:

Copying Corrected:

Scientists increase their discipline's knowledge by working from the results of experiments by others. Thus, for scientists, "knowledge is an artifact created by a community of … peers" (Bruffee 642).

Even though the student has omitted the word "knowledgeable," this otherwise exact wording should be quoted and cited. The omission of a word (or several words) is shown by what is known as an **ellipsis** ("of … peers"), and let us repeat that the period follows the citation because the citation is a part of that sentence.

Sloppy Notes and/or **Careless Drafting** can lead to less deliberate but still unacceptable plagiarism. When a student scribbles down notes without marking quotations or recording page numbers, this seemingly minor problem can cause a major one later on. For as a student drafts a paper, she can't recall what information has been quoted or possibly even where it came from. As she drafts, this writer also may work so rapidly from her notes that she fails to dist

Again, it does not require that much time to indicate

We previously quoted Graff on "While most think
writers as he stresses the frequent opposition a write.
Academe, Graff acknowledges his dependence on not on
reaction. He asserts,

> In *Lives on the Boundary* Mike Rose cites fellow compo
> that "when stuck, student writers should try the followin₃
> have said _____, a close and careful reading shows that ___

Graff uses a footnote instead of a parenthetical citation beca
and we will explain three different ones below. If Graff were to
would appear as ". . . shows that _____" (Bartholomae qtd. in Rose   ...ould
read this citation as "Bartholomae is quoted by Rose on page 189 of

It's also worth noting that Graff states that "Rose *cites* fellow com₁   ...e presents this quotation (italics added). Quoting and citing are so related that these two   ...nough slightly different in
meaning, can be used as interchangeable synonyms.

Cutting and Pasting is also known as "patchwork plagiarism." It happens when a student opens
several sources, usually those online, and then as the name suggests, cuts and pastes several sentences
from one writer with those of other writers. Like copying, this form of plagiarism is deliberate, and it too
can be corrected by adding attributions and citations. Yet this correction is incomplete unless a student
asserts her agreement, elaboration, skepticism, etc., *after* the citation and *before* the next signal phrase.
For instance, if we continue our example based on Bruffee:

Cut and Paste/Patchwork:

Knowledge is an artifact created by a community of peers, yet this collaboration often involves
arguing Y when most people think X.

This example demonstrates another etymological association of the word plagiarism: from the Latin *plaga*
for "net," which is related to *plak*, meaning "to weave." A student engaged in cut and paste plagiarism is
only weaving other writers' words together, but he risks being caught in a dishonest net of his own making! In the corrected version below, the student writer is controlling the source material rather than just
repeating it. Notice the additional assertions by the student marked in bold.

Corrected Version:

**Discussing a subject and employing the terms used by experts can help students develop a
deeper understanding of their topic. Through such active study of a subject, students demonstrate that** knowledge "is an artifact created by a community of knowledgeable peers" (Bruffee
646). **As he promotes this image of a collaborative community, Bruffee, however, fails to consider the degree to which academics add to a discussion by disagreeing with and rejecting
outright the assertions made by their colleagues. For Gerald Graff asserts, academics often
respond to each other by opposing what has been said.** In *Clueless in Academe*, Graff characterizes the typical academic discussion as "While most think X, I argue Y" (55).

Note too that the first time a writer
In any subsequent references to
Paper Mill Purchases
an Internet site, or "pa
honesty, that t
claimer that
in small
academ

... is mentioned, his or her **full name** is provided, as in "Gerald Graff." ... this writer, only the **last name** is used.

... may be the most dishonest form of plagiarism. Buying a complete paper from ... per mill," cannot be explained away as an accident. It is an intentional act of dis- ... however, try to obscure these intentions. They offer papers for sale but add a dis- ... ese papers should be used only as a research aid. The disclaimers, however, usually appear ... print, and they often are contradicted by suggestions that students are not responsible for this ... mic dishonesty. Blame is shifted, as Kelly Ritter explains, to "professors for not creating new writing ... assignments, ... [and universities for requiring] needless general education courses" (620). Once blame has been shifted away from plagiarizing students, it may be very tempting for them, as one site urges, to "Download your Workload" (*School*).

Once a paper is conceived as a commodity to be obtained so apparently pointless work can be avoided, the concept of plagiarism as intellectual theft becomes less clear. Ritter explains this confusion:

> Even when students understand that taking the intellectual and artistic property of others is *wrong*, they might not clearly understand why it is wrong when said product is for *sale* on the Internet. When students ... see writing as a "product" designed to fulfill the distinct purpose in a college course, how far must those students leap to arrive at the conclusion that, like many other items in our culture offered online for sale, this product, too, can be bought? ... [T]he consumer-minded student, unable to distinguish authorship from ownership, might wonder where is the "stealing" in this transaction. (615)

When a paper is purchased, the theft occurs not so much from its original writer, whose individual identity is erased on a seemingly authorless website, but through the misrepresentation of effort made when the paper is submitted for course credit. The fraudulent claim that the student has made the intellectual effort to produce this paper and earn course credit constitutes theft from the academic institution and, in essence, from the student's classmates who have made this effort.

With the long quotation from Ritter above, note the convention of using an **indented, block quotation** to present four or more lines of quoted material. These longer quotations are indented rather than indicated with quotation marks, and the parenthetical citation follows the period of the final sentence.

MLA and Other Citation Systems

Just as students can rationalize their use of paper mills as victimless purchases, they also can become cynical about proper citation when they are overwhelmed by the multiple systems ("MLA, APA, or Chicago! Why can't they all just agree on one way?"). This frustration, however, also offers a glimpse at why these different systems exist. Academics in various disciplines have some good reasons for not agreeing on one citation system; their assumptions about knowledge often inform what distinguishes their conventions from others.

As we have explained, the **Modern Language Association (MLA)**, system of citation places the author's last name and the page number (when available) in parentheses at the end of a sentence, as in (Smith 22). Unlike their colleagues in the humanities, many academics in the social sciences use the

American Psychological Association (APA), system of citation. Their convention differs from that of MLA because when a writer's name is not provided with a signal phrase, the parenthetical citation includes the publication date of the source followed by the page number, as in (Smith, 2007, p. 22). Note that in addition to including the date, the page is marked with p., and each item is separated by commas. APA differs from MLA because psychologists and others, such as sociologists, consider themselves to be social scientists. They want to indicate that they are using the most current information, as indicated by the publication date. In the humanities, it is much more acceptable for a literacy critic, for instance, to rely on a classic scholarly study published several decades ago. Like the great works of literature, this scholarship has "stood the test of time" so the date of its publication is not as important for someone in the humanities. Thus, the differences in the examples listed below suggest the different assumptions about scholarly knowledge held by academics in the humanities versus those in the social sciences.

MLA Parenthetical Citation	APA Parenthetical Citation
(Smith 22).	(Smith, 2007, p. 22).

These differences continue when a signal phrase is used; APA places the citation right after the writer's name, and a paraphrase of a general idea from the text does not include the exact page number.

MLA Parenthetical Citation
Smith argues that . . . paraphrase (22).

APA Parenthetical Citation
Smith (2007) argues that . . . paraphrase.

A third citation system, known as **Chicago**, relies on footnotes that are placed at the end of a sentence.

Chicago Footnotes
Smith argues that . . . paraphrase.[1]

The fact that these citation systems are not rules, but conventions, is shown again by their gradual changes over time. For example, the 2009 version of MLA changed the formatting of what is known as **a works cited list**, which is provided at the end of a paper. MLA includes detailed information on each source, and the kind of source is identified as "Print" or "Web." An Internet source also includes the publisher (or *n.p.* if no publisher is known), the publication date (or *n.d.* if no date is known), and the date accessed.

For both kinds of sources, this information enables a reader to check a writer's reliance on other authors. A reader, for example, may want to check the context of a quotation (so don't alter it!), learn other facts related to the data presented, and understand the cited author's argument better. A works cited page makes it easy for a reader to do so by listing each source and using the author's last name (when known). Here, for example, is the MLA works cited listing for the four sources used in this chapter:

Works Cited:

Bruffee, Kenneth. "Collaborative Learning and the 'Conversation of Mankind.'" *College English* 46.7 (Nov. 1984): 635–52. Print.

Graff, Gerald. *Clueless in Academe*. New Haven: Yale, 2003. Print.

Ritter, Kelly. "The Economics of Authorship: Online Paper Mills. Student Writers, and First-Year Composition." *College Composition and Communication* 56.4 (June 2005): 601–31. Print.

SchoolSucks.com. *n.p. n.d.* Web. 10 June 2014.

The first and third sources demonstrate the format for the works cited **documentation** of an article; the second, a book; and the fourth, a website. There are many other formatting conventions, such as the italicization of book titles and the quotation marks for an article title, so most academic writers keep a convenient site, such as easybib.com, on their desktop or the latest version of a handbook on their desk. The most recent copy of a handbook has to be consulted because lately it seems as though some citation conventions change almost annually.

With repeated use, it's not hard for most academics to recall the general patterns of, say, MLA citation and documentation, but the listing of an authorless article found in an edited collection posted on the Web usually sends most to a how-to citation source. We have explained the reasons for the main conventions, but we will encourage you to consult a source on the particular details of diverse examples of citation and documentation. Like doing what a family expects on Thanksgiving, your use of the expected citation system indicates your readiness to participate in an academic community. On the night before a paper is due, these conventions may seem like one more thing you have to do, but when you submit the paper, your fulfillment of these expectations shows that you know how academics talk-the-talk.

Key Terms and Concepts

Before you finish with this chapter, here is a list of the key concepts; which ones can you explain easily and which ones do you need to review?

Academic honesty
Communal dependence
Individual assertion
Conventions
    Quotations
    Paraphrased ideas
    Little-known facts
    Citation
    Signal phrase or attribution
        Full name/last name

Ellipsis
Indented, block quotations
Documentation/work cited list
Citation systems
    Modern Language Association
    American Psychological Association
    Chicago
Plagiarism
    Intellectual theft
    Deliberate copying
    Sloppy notes and careless drafting
    Cutting and pasting/
        Patchwork plagiarism
    Paper-mill purchases

Research Methods and Motives

CHAPTER 8

In the last week, you probably have tried to check a fact or learn more about a subject. What information have you sought? How did you try to find it, and was this effort successful?

Most students have little trouble answering these questions. They have checked a sports score or some news. They have sought the definition of a difficult term or details on a topic of interest. Yet when a professor utters the word "research," a few students will groan, at least inwardly. If the word "paper" is added to this utterance, as in a "research paper," some of these groans will become audible—why? Although many students frequently seek information, why do some dread an academic "research" assignment? Through freewriting and/or class discussion, please consider this issue:

What images, feelings, and/or memories come to mind when you recall working on a research paper?

When some students were asked to reflect on their experiences, they recalled:

Research means finding out what other people have said on an assigned topic until you have enough to fill up the required number of pages.

8:30 would turn into 10:30 then 12:30, then sleep. I would always get up at 4 a.m. to finish and there I was again, the same position, the same mess, the same procrastination, and the same frustration.

Yet all of these recollections are not so negative; some students described research and writing research papers differently:

I chose to research the daily lives of Romans. While I usually don't like research papers, I liked this one because the topic was interesting to me. I really did want to learn more about it.

A smile usually comes to my face because I enjoy researching. Then I come to a place where I need a detail to back up what I believe, and I sort through the material to find the perfect fact or quotation. Slowly the paper starts to piece itself together from ideas I had never thought of until I researched my topic.

We believe that interest and commitment distinguish the second set of students from the first. Although curiosity may have "killed the cat," according to the old saying, it breathes life into research. This vitality continues as students become committed to their topics. These students have a point they want to prove and an audience they want to persuade. Of course, every research topic may not excite the interest of each student, but we will explain below some ways to get interested in a topic.

Some of the initial hesitation some students may feel toward a research paper may stem, in part, from their anxiety about the effort involved. Fortunately, this concern can be decreased by, assuring you that you already possess many of the skills required and helping you understand the series of tasks to be completed. A research paper combines almost all of the reading and writing abilities presented in this textbook. If you have succeeded so far, there is no reason to doubt that you can have further success. As you will see, we will be referring to many of the abilities from previous chapters. For example, a research paper will involve active reading strategies, like annotating a text and taking double-entry notes. Along with that assurance of your abilities, we will outline many of the necessary tasks. However, we must acknowledge that you and/or your professor may choose to change the order of some of these efforts. Some students like to pose a precise question before they begin researching their topic, while others like to explore a topic widely before they narrow their focus. Such differences make it harder for us to present a detailed sequence. In the left column below, we have created an overview of our research advice, but we want to stress it is only one possible order. In the right column, we have suggested an alternative, and other variations exist.

One Sequence of Research	An Alternative Order
exploring research topics	exploring research topics
finding search terms	posing a research question
seeking sources	seeking sources
posing a research question	finding search terms
engaging with your sources	engaging with your sources
evaluating your sources	evaluating your sources
asserting a tentative thesis	conducting further research
starting to draft	introducing & asserting a thesis
conducting further research	drafting
finalizing your thesis	concluding
introducing and concluding	revising before the deadline
revising before the deadline	editing the almost final draft
editing the almost final draft	

Which sequence would you rather follow and why? What, if any, further changes would you like to make? Along with insisting that more than one order may be possible, we will suggest that you may want to read this chapter gradually, such as by using the headings to follow a sequence that will be most effective for you. We have to follow some order in this chapter, so let's start with how you can get interested in a topic, whether it is chosen or assigned.

Getting Interested

Using the theme of the education chapter, let's imagine being assigned a terrible topic. How would you react if you were assigned the following topic:

High School Desks

At first, this seems like an impossible topic. What could be interesting about desks? And yet, if you stop to think about what seems to be a hopelessly dull topic, can you get involved with it, at least as a possible topic for another student? How can this subject become an interesting one?

In the past, students have suggested some intriguing possibilities; these suggestions include the changing sizes and designs of desks, the development of left-handed ones, their patterns of arrangement and what that reveals about teaching methods, the annual budget for desk repair and replacement in a large school district, various attempts to make desks graffiti-proof, and perhaps the most original idea: the total weight of chewing gum placed under desktops each year, and what that amount suggests about student apathy! We promise that we will not assign any of those topics here or in the education chapter, but they demonstrate that **interest** can turn even what seems to be a dull topic into an intriguing issue for research.

The forms of critical thinking and persuasive reasoning presented in this textbook offer other ways to get interested in a topic:

Multiple Perspectives: Each reading chapter suggests several debates on its theme, and each debate depends, of course, on the differences among various viewpoints. You can become interested in a topic by asking: What do other people believe about this subject? What do they think is true or right? For example, in Chapter 10, we show that there are different perspectives on what should or should not be considered to be an American family today. Also, what are the proper roles of mothers and/or fathers in these families? Or back in the first chapter, we presented the unusual viewpoint of young adults who have decided to forego modern computer technologies, such as social networks like Facebook. Trying to understand why someone holds a particular belief can not only arouse your interest but also lead you to the next approach.

Historical Trends: Asking how a current opinion relates to past viewpoints can pique our interest. For instance, the current claim in education that every student should meet certain standards of learning (and be tested until they reach that mark) becomes even more debatable when you learn that, in 1893, educators were wondering if school standards and methods should be "differentiated" for various kinds of students (see Chapter 11). This historical trend could lead to a research question like: For what reasons and in what ways should student be tracked (or not) by their academic abilities?

Cultural Influences: Wondering what other beliefs support a specific viewpoint can make a topic come alive. For example, the development of suburban areas depended on changes in government regulations, such as on zoning and bank lending. These changing regulations made the growth of suburbs possible, but they also had a negative impact on many urban areas (see Chapter 12). These cultural influences could lead to a research question like: To what degree should government housing and development policies be neutral in their effects, or to what degree should they be designed to favor certain areas or specific groups?

We have offered a few examples from some of the thematic chapters. Can you now develop some other research topics? You can focus on what intrigues you or what topics might interest some of your classmates:

	Multiple Perspectives	Historical Trends	Cultural Influences
Ch. 1 Technology			
Ch. 10 Family			
Ch. 11 Education			
Ch. 12 Cities			
Ch. 13 Energy			
Ch. 14 Literacy			

Some of the rhetorical concepts in Chapter 6 on Argument can also help you become more interested in a topic.

Inductive Reasoning: Starting with specific examples can lead you to a broader question. For example, in Chapter 14, Nicholas Bilton quotes several studies that show that computer technologies are harming our minds and more (see p. 361). Then one can start to wonder: Why are the negative effects of computers? Are they really harmful?

Deductive Reasoning: Beginning with a general principle on a topic can also lead you to an engaging issue. For instance, from Chapter 11 on education, most of us would agree with the general principle that every child in America deserves an equal chance to be educated. The system of mastery testing so "no child is left behind" is based on this principle, but is annual testing the best way to promote greater academic achievement by every group of students?

Let's continue with the topic of education and consider the three kinds of arguments.

Arguments over Blame, Values, and Action: If some students are not learning enough, should their teachers or their parents be blamed (a forensic argument over blame)? Or should we try to place more emphasis on academic achievement than on athletic victories (an epideictic argument on values)? Or should teachers use passive teaching methods, like lecturing, less and active ones more (a deliberative argument over actions)?

Becoming Committed

Along with getting interested in a topic, **becoming committed** to your subject will help you sustain your research efforts. To test your commitment to a topic, try completing the following statement through writing and/or discussion:

> On the topic of _____, I want to learn more
> about _____.

If you repeat only the same words in the second blank, you may not have enough interest in this research. Or, if what you want to learn heads off in many different directions, your commitment may be spread too thin.

A second test for your research topic is to consider the consequences of your effort. Again, try completing the following assertion through writing and/or discussion:

What I hope to learn on this topic will be significant

to _____ (whom?) because _____ (why?).

If you can't yet answer these questions, it doesn't mean that your research won't succeed. However, you will have to tackle these rhetorical questions of audience (whom?) and purpose (why?) at a later time. Let us stress that your commitment to your topic does not have to be totally fixed at this time; it probably will change as your research progresses. Yet the fact remains: your research must be supported by your interest and your commitment. If you ultimately don't care about your topic, who will?

Search Terms

As you begin to seek sources, the success of this effort will depend on the search terms you use. You probably have experienced the frustration of the following story. A student decided to research the trend of interracial marriages in relation to the chapter 10 on American families. He wanted to learn more about the increasing number of such marriages as well as the difficulties and the successes of these families. He typed "interracial marriages" into a recommended database (Academic Search Premier). Then the dreaded message appeared: "No items match this search request." How, he wondered, can this be? No sources on interracial marriages; that's impossible!

Search engines and databases look for exactly what they are told to seek, so a researcher sometimes must experiment with various search terms. It turned out that when the frustrated student tried searching for "marriage and race," he found exactly the sources he had been seeking. Since so much depends on your **search terms**, it's a good idea to keep a list of the various terms you use.

You can also avoid some of this experimentation by consulting the **Library of Congress Subject Headings (LCSH)**. These subject headings, meaning search terms, were established so all American libraries use the same terms to organize sources. You'll find them on the back of the title page of any book, and many databases rely on them as well. Checking the LCSH in your library or online can eliminate the frustration of a fruitless search. One good source, such as a book, may reveal the best search terms for your topic. A reference librarian will also help you, so don't hesitate to ask them for help with your search terms or any other aspect of your research.

Another key component of search terms is the use of words like AND, OR plus quotation marks. These words are known as **Boolean operators**; they are named after George Boole who created this system to "operate" searches. As you can imagine, combining two terms with AND means that both terms must be subjects in a source, but OR means that either term will lead to a source. Search terms in quotation marks mean that sources must have that exact phrase.

The sooner you gain control over your search terms, the sooner you can start reading widely on your topic.

Seeking Sources and Reading Widely

As you become committed to a specific research topic, you can learn more about this interest by **reading widely** on it using various kinds of sources. At the start of this chapter, we asked you to consider how you checked a fact or sought some information. Now can you consider:

What are some of the different kinds of sources you can use for your research?

There, of course, is a rich array of sources you can consult.

We can rely on popular **search engines**, such as Google, bing, and Ask.com, but keep in mind that the sponsor links or matches that appear at the top of the search results are paid placements. Just like tempting foods placed at the end of supermarket aisles, these "sponsored" results have been placed there by companies that have paid a fee for their prominence. There also are general but more **scholarly databases**, such as Academic Search Premier, JStor, and Lexis Nexis. These databases do not have paid placements, and they offer more authoritative, expert sources. There also are particular databases for almost every academic discipline. Various colleges and universities subscribe to certain academic databases so you may need to ask your professor which ones are best for your research (and this is especially true for research in upper-level courses).

Other online sources include blogs and Wikipedia entries. Both, however, are the subject of some debate. Some blogs offer expert opinions, while others are less informed, so a reader has to have some knowledge on a subject in order to discriminate between the two (see more on source evaluation below). Various Wikipedia articles vary in their quality as well: the best ones include rich resources linked in supporting notes while the worst ones make some professors forbid their use. Again it is wise to ask your professor about appropriate sources for your assignment.

Let's not forget print sources, such as books, journals, magazines, and newspapers. When you are looking through the stacks for one promising book, one pleasant surprise may be that you will find an even better source on the same shelf. Newspapers and magazines can be first, very beneficial sources because they often provide overviews and identify experts. Academic journal articles, which usually appear in print as well as online, are written by scholars so they will lead you to current debates and key terms on your topic. You may not be ready to read a journal article during your first foray into research on an unfamiliar subject, but your wide reading should include them a little later on. Why?

One last point: the presence on the Internet of full-text sources that originally were published as print sources obscures the traditional bias for hard copy sources over online ones. Now entire books and scholarly articles can be found online. Where a source is found matters less than our evaluation of its credibility, which we will address below. Many researchers, but not all, still find it easier to comprehend difficult texts by reading printed copies. It is not that we cannot comprehend online texts, but our habits of skim reading Facebook and other website pages may be too quick for our desire to understand and annotate texts.

Here is a list of some of the different kinds of sources we can consult as we begin to read widely. By habit, we may be drawn to some kinds more than others, but which sources do you think are most likely to provide the best information? Consider your current research topic (or a recent one), and make a conscious choice: With which sources should (or did) you start, and which ones should (or did) you consult later?

- Books
- Magazines
- Newspapers
- Dictionaries

- Encyclopedias
- Academic journals
- Reference guides
- Government documents
- Blogs
- Websites
- Wikipedia

Posing a Primary Research Question

At some point, you will probably want to and/or be asked to pose a precise research question. As we explained above, some students will be ready to pose this query as soon as they are interested in a topic, but others will want to wait. Our initial phrase of "At some point …" has been chosen very carefully, but let us explain posing a research question now.

Most college-level research assignments will ask you to do more than summarize several sources on a topic. Rather than this research report, you will be asked to assert a thesis and support it using evidence from your research. This paper is more of an argument, and it requires a researcher to select and synthesize information from several sources. To distinguish this kind of research-based writing, we will refer to it as a research essay (versus a research report).

Your **research question** will help you focus your search for information, yet its exact answer will be determined in the future. This question should not be phrased as a simple yes or no query or suggest only a report that summarizes information on a topic. To demonstrate these kinds of questions, let us continue with more examples from the familiar subject of education. Which questions suggest the developed argument of an essay, a yes/no response, or the broad summary of a report?

Some Sample Research Questions

1. *Does participation in high school athletics affect a student's academic achievement?*
2. *How can high school students be motivated to learn more?*
3. *What are the best ways to reduce bullying in high schools?*

All of these topics could be developed into informative and persuasive research essays, but as each question is phrased above, we think that the third question most obviously suggests a thesis-driven, opinionated essay. The phrase "best ways" indicates more than a report on several approaches to this problem; this research essay will debate which one is most effective.

On the basis of its phrasing, the first question implies a broad yes/no response, and the second one suggests a report on several methods of motivation without much judgment among them. However, all is not lost because both questions can be revised into better ones. For example, the first one can be rewritten as:

#1 Revised: What are the most effective programs to increase academic achievement by high school athletes?

Again, "at some point" you may want to pose several smaller, more specific questions for your research efforts. For instance, if a student wanted to research the best ways to reduce school bullying, what are ten specific questions that would have to be researched and answered?

Primary Research Question: What is the most effective way to reduce bullying in schools today?
Ten Secondary Questions:
1.

2.

3.

4.

5.

6.

7.

8.

9.

10.

Of course, ten is an arbitrary total; we could have requested seven or twelve, but if you can only pose two or three specific questions to guide your research further, you probably should read and think about your topic more.

Some of the first questions we can imagine posing are

- What percent of public high school students feel they have been bullied?

- What types of students are targeted most frequently for harassment?

- How many cases of bullying are reported each year now versus 10, 20, and 30 years ago?

Those are our first reactions, and what questions can you add? Then which ones do you think can be answered with relative ease and using what kind of sources? If you cannot generate a list of ten or more specific questions on your topic, you may need to reconsider the focus of your research. To sum up your efforts so far, your professor may ask you, or you may choose to write a research plan, which can include your topic, your interest, your primary and secondary research questions, and some likely sources.

Engaging with Your Sources

Once you pose several secondary research questions, you can shift from leafing through your likely sources to **engaging** with them more actively. As you start to **annotate sources** and **take notes**, you may find it helpful to keep your reason for research in mind. Try writing your primary research question on the first page of your notes from a source or on a sticky note attached to your computer monitor. This reminder may help you avoid straying too far from your topic. Of course, in some cases, you may choose to change your topic, perhaps in consultation with your professor.

We will also suggest that you should record the publishing information for a source as you start taking notes. For a book, record the author(s), title, place of publication, publisher, and copyright. For most shorter texts, note the author, title, source title, date, and page numbers (plus volume and issue numbers for some magazines or journal articles). For websites, record the author(s) if known, the title, the URL address, and the date accessed (in case the site is altered). It is much easier to gather this information as your research begins rather than at the end of your writing process. Thus, a page of notes, whether typed or handwritten, can start with the following information:

Primary Question: *What programs have proven to be most effective at bullying in high schools, and why are they effective?*

Source Info: *"Anti-bullying policies target staff in schools." American School Board Journal, June 2010, Vol. 197 Issue 6, p.12*

p. 12: As of 2010, forty-one states have laws against bullying in schools. Some districts in Iowa and California are passing laws that are explicitly against bullying by teachers and other staff members

my reaction: *I'm surprised that in 2010, every state did not have laws against students bullying their peers. I never would have thought that a law against teachers bullying others would be necessary, but it seems like a good idea. It stops a few bad ones and makes all teachers set a good example for students.*

p. 12: In Broward County, Florida, students are encouraged to report bullying in several ways, such as in person, by phone, via email, or in a text message. This encouragement led to a 4% increase in reports.

As shown in our example, it's also better to record specific page numbers with your notes. Ideally, this information addresses not only your broad primary question but also some secondary questions. Of course, if you are starting to take notes on a less familiar topic, your notes may not be so precise. These notes are a step beyond the annotations explained in Chapter 3 on Reading (see p. 78), and it's only one more step to create **double-entry notes** also described in Chapter 3. Double-entry notes combine important information from a source with your immediate reaction to these facts, figures, and details (see pp. 80–81). With these responses, you are prepared to add an assertion after some cited information so that you can make the research information support your thesis.

Evaluating Your Sources

After you have taken notes from a few sources, you probably will be able to tell that one source is not only better for your research but also seems to be more accurate, more authoritative. To avoid information that seems too biased or unreliable, you can **evaluate your sources**. This evaluation may sound difficult, for how can a student judge the published writing of an expert? Yet we often do something very similar when we meet a new person. We ask ourselves, "Can I trust him?" and "Is her opinion biased?" We can ask similar questions about any research source.

Questions for Source Evaluation:

- How well does the author demonstrate his or her expertise by citing other sources?

- Is the information current or out of date?

- Does the author include opposing viewpoints? Does the author include the strongest or weakest version of this opposition?

- How thoroughly does the author respond to opposing views?

- As the author engages in a public debate and/or a scholarly discussion, is she or he mentioned or cited by others, which suggests her or his expertise?

- Where was the author's work published?

- Was this work reviewed by others before it was published?

- Who is the intended audience of this publication?

- Is this publication source primarily interested in spreading knowledge or earning some gain?

You and/or your professor may want to add other questions to this list. It is important for you to evaluate your sources because your readers will be evaluating you; they will be judging your ethos, your character as the writer of a research essay (for more on ethos, see Chapter 6, p. 103).

Asserting a Tentative Thesis

When we asked you to make a commitment to your topic, you stated what you wanted to learn and why you thought this topic was significant. You may not have been able to answer each of those questions perfectly, but it was important that you advanced beyond only announcing your topic. If you haven't already done so, it is an appropriate time for you to develop your opinion further in a **tentative thesis**, and it may be easier to do so by engaging in freewriting or discussion. Rather than surrounding yourself with your notes and sources immediately, try responding to the following prompts more informally, as if someone asked you what you are thinking about your topic before class started:

> *What have you started to believe about your topic?*

> *What do you want others to understand about this issue?*

In a casual conversation, we rarely discuss what everyone already believes (what's the point?); instead we talk about what is debatable. In a research essay too, you should add your opinion to the published sources by agreeing with some writers but disagreeing with others. For example, in Chapter 12, the readings differ as they defend and criticize suburban living. Why do you consider the development of surburbia to be a great benefit or a large problem for the United States?

Once you have a sense of what position you want to assert, the next challenge is to sum it up in a few succinct sentences. The phrasing of this thesis is important because it provides both you and your audience with a sense of the purpose of your essay. Consider this example based on the readings of the chapter on cities and suburbs:

Since the 1950s, American suburbs have flourished with the support of government policies, yet this development has come at the expense of those who were left behind in neglected urban areas. Such inequality in government regulation is not compatible with the democratic ideals of this nation.

Don't worry; your thesis is just a tentative one so you can modify it later on.

One good way to get feedback on your thesis is to share it with several classmates. This can be done through e-mail, a discussion board, or the whiteboard in your classroom. Create a list of several theses, and label them with numbers instead of students' names. Then ask everyone to identify some of the stronger theses by their numbers and explain why they seem so strong: What purpose does each one assert? Who might disagree and why? How might the writer try to answer that disagreement?

Next turn to some of the weaker theses and identify them by number. Rather than discuss what is wrong with each one ("Number 2 is weak because …"), focus on how each one can be improved ("Number 8 can be improved by creating a more debatable purpose like …").

Once you have developed a strong, though still tentative, thesis, you probably will be ready to start drafting at least some of your essay.

Starting to Draft

As you turn from taking notes to **drafting your paper**, it will be important to keep your audience in mind: you are trying to convince a reader who does not already agree with you. Chapter 6 on Argument has many suggestions on how to reach an uncertain audience or even an opposing one. Let us repeat one suggestion on **organizing your draft**: you can follow the classic advice on the arrangement of the three rhetorical appeals. In your opening paragraphs, appeal by your ethos, your character as a writer and a researcher. Then turn to logos and provide logical supports for your position. Don't be afraid to acknowledge some of the sound objections that others might raise, and qualify your argument by admitting, for example, that in some cases your position may have to be modified. Finally, don't forget to appeal by pathos, meaning to the audience's emotions. Make sure they understand why your opinion is important, such as by showing what effect it will have on the lives of particular people. Let us stress that this is only one of many possible ways to arrange your argument; the key is to have some clear reasons for the order of your research essay.

If you are not just trying to fill up the required number of pages of a research report, you should be able to explain that your essay starts here, goes on to this, and proceeds to that … because …. Working with your professor, you can decide whether you will outline your essay before, during, or after drafting. However, at some point, you should check the order of your draft and be able to explain it to yourself and others.

As you are drafting, you should also practice the conventions of **academic honesty**. As explained in Chapter 7, you should cite the sources used for quotations, paraphrases, and little-known information. Yet your essay should not consist solely of cited material; you should also help a reader understand the meaning and appreciate the purpose of cited material, such as by using signal phrases and interpretative elaborations. As explained in Chapter 3, double-entry notes make it especially easy to add elaborations on cited information (see p. 80).

Let us add an unusual simile to explain your relationship with your readers: they are like special guests at a gathering on your topic. At this gathering, you would not just meet them at the door and tell them to talk to your sources; instead you would lead these special guests to this source and introduce them, then introduce them to that source in order to create a compelling and convincing evening for this audience.

Although it may seem like a hassle to start citing sources while you are drafting, it is even harder to go back and add citations later to an almost final draft. Even worse is trying to correct citation problems once the issue of academic honesty has been raised; when citing, sooner is better.

Conducting Further Research

If you start drafting after you have asserted a tentative thesis, one benefit is that you will often develop a feeling for where your research is strong and where you still need to learn more. This further research can lead you to the authoritative citations within an already good source, to **specialized academic databases**, and into **government documents** (as mentioned above on sources). It also may lead you to engage in some firsthand research, such as by conducting a survey, an interview, or an observation.

Have you ever started to answer a **survey** and quit before you finished? Let that experience inform the design of your own survey. It should not require too much time, and the questions should be relatively easy to answer. For example, you may want to ask several multiple-choice or 1- to 5-scale questions and then add a longer response question or two. Survey questions should also use neutral phrases, rather than steer the respondent toward one answer. To seek a widespread and representative array of respondents, you can distribute and collect your surveys in person or rely on an online survey instrument, such as those available at surveymonkey.com.

A good **interview** depends on the expertise of the person questioned. Yet with all of the experts on a college campus and/or available online, it is not difficult to find a good subject. As with a survey, your questions should not reveal your own bias. Instead you want to elicit this person's knowledge through probing but inviting queries. The actual interview can be conducted in person, by phone, or electronically. An e-mail interview has the advantage of providing a written record of the exchange, yet the subtleties of voice tone and physical gestures are lost. A phone or face-to-face interview provides those benefits, but you will have to use a tape or video recorder to create a record of the interview. Such recordings can be made only with the explicit consent of the interview subject.

The same consent must be secured for an **observation**, such as by visiting a school for research on an education-related topic. Again, the observer has to be careful to minimize the influence of his or her perspective, such as a researcher focusing on only the flaws of a class based on lecture or discussion. As with a good interview, the researcher has to have a focus prepared but must also be flexible enough to follow a surprising response when it is made.

After any one of these three forms of firsthand research, it is helpful to reflect upon the results as soon as possible, such as by freewriting on their significance. These results can be reinforced through further research to check if others have made similar findings in published research. As your own expertise grows, you will be ready to engage in further research using more specialized and authoritative sources.

Finalizing Your Thesis

As you draft and research further, you may find that you want to alter your initial thesis. Such revisions usually reveal the strengths of your research. As you understand a topic better, you will be more able to confront the complexities of your topic. You now may want to include some qualification of your argument or be ready to preview your main points in your thesis. Yet as you **finalize your thesis**, you probably should check the development of your argument as well. Do your order and emphasis still match your thesis?

Introducing and Concluding

Do we dare refer to "At some point ..." again? Some writers can't imagine starting a draft without creating an introduction first. Others prefer to jump into the middle of a draft and write. Regardless of your preference, you will want to concentrate on your introduction at some point because, like most first impressions, your audience's reaction to your opening will be important.

This **introduction** should lead your readers to your thesis and prepare them to follow your argument. Below we have started a list of several options for an introduction. What other possibilities can you add?

Introduction Options
– a personal experience
– an illustrative anecdote
– a case study
– a revealing fact or figure
– a complicated example
– a provocative question
– a compelling scene
– a general principle
– a 'big picture' description
–
–

If you can impress your audience with your experience, knowledge, or insight, you will have succeeded in the crucial appeal by the writer's character, by ethos (see Chapter 6, p. 103). Then they will be more receptive to the rest of your essay.

Although it may seem to defy common sense, a good way to write one effective introduction is to draft two or more. Working with more than one approach will make you more conscious and critical of the first impression each one makes. Once you have drafted two or more introductions, you can ask a peer to read each one and explain why this or that is preferred. This explanation may lead you to additional revisions of one, the combination of two, or the use of another later in your essay. Even students who already have one good introduction often find that this doubling of their efforts improves some aspect of their draft. Try it!

Ideally, an effective **conclusion** yields the final conviction of your readers. They finish feeling that "She's so right" or "I agree with him." However, repeating all of the ideas of your essay may not be the best approach. Reminding a reader of a main point or two is fine, but you don't have to rehash your entire essay. Here is another list of options. What other possibilities can you add?

Conclusion Options

– explain the significance of your viewpoint
– describe the impact of other choices
– return to the essay's title or an introductory idea
– extend the thesis in a what-is-next step
– end with a compelling quotation and explain its relevance
–
–
–

As explained above, many persuasive conclusions appeal to our emotions more than our logic. This final appeal to pathos can make an audience not only understand but also eager to act on an issue.

Revising before the Due Date

In Chapter 4 on the writing process, we encouraged you to start early enough so you will have time to **revise**, to *really* revise. We explained that revision can occur on many levels, such as from paragraph order to sentence structure. To revise your research essay, you should also check your use of source information. Have you cited all quotations, paraphrases, and little-known facts? Have you offered some attributions to help guide a reader's understanding of this cited information? Have you varied the phrasing of those signal phrases? Have you elaborated on much of this information? Have you avoided large sections filled with only source material or very little source material?

It may be easier to ask a peer or tutor to help you review your draft with such questions in mind. Your professor may provide you with some review questions (or ask you to help create them).

Here is a general list of **peer review questions** that can be adapted to your particular research assignment:

Some Questions for Draft Review

- Do the title and the introduction get the intended audience interested in this essay? Why or why not? If not, what title and introduction could be used to interest a reader?

- Does the opening give the reader a clear sense of the thesis and not just of the topic? Is the thesis debatable, meaning who can disagree and on what? If necessary, how can the thesis be improved?

- After the thesis, does the writer provide general information that an unfamiliar reader may need to understand the topic? Does the writer seem to know some of the key terms and crucial distinctions of this issue?

- What are two of the strongest research sections of this draft? Why is each section effective, especially in relation to the essay's thesis?

- What is one section that seems to be less effective? For example, does the writer seem to be just filling a page with facts? How can this section be improved?

- Does the draft seem to follow a smooth and logical order? What is the general order, meaning from this to that, then on to what and so on?

- Does the writer use diverse sources, and where are they combined, meaning synthesized, well? Or where might more of this synthesis be done?

- Does the writer anticipate and answer possible objections?

- What research, if any, is still needed?

- Does the paper end well? Why is or isn't the conclusion effective?

- Is the research presented properly with citations for direct quotations, paraphrased information, unique phrases, and little-known facts?

- Does any section seem to need a citation so the writer will not be accused of plagiarism?

- How well does the writer elaborate after cited information?

- Does the final list of sources include only sources actually cited? Are they presented in the proper format?

- Has the final draft been proofread for editing errors?

Editing the Almost-Final Draft

If you are not drafting desperately hours before your deadline, the day before the deadline ideally should be reserved for revising *and then* editing. In Chapter 4, we suggested that you should edit an almost-final draft by keeping a list of your **common errors** in mind (see p. 91). You may also want to remind yourself of the exact conventions of the **citation system** you are employing and double-check your fulfillment of these conventions (see pp. 126–128 in Chapter 7). Again, your professor may provide you with editing and citing guidelines; even though it is easier said than done, try to give yourself the time to fulfill them.

As you may already know or will experience soon, there is great satisfaction in researching and writing a strong essay on a topic to which you are committed.

Key Terms and Concepts

Before you finish with this chapter, here is a list of the key concepts; which ones can you explain easily and which ones do you need to review?

Research topics
    Getting interested
    Becoming committed
Search terms
    Library of Congress Subject Headings
    Boolean operators

Seeking sources
   Search engines
   scholarly databases
Posing a research question
   Research essay vs. research report
   Primary and secondary questions
Engaging with your sources
   Annotating
   Taking notes
   Double-entry notes
Evaluating your sources
Asserting a tentative thesis
Starting to draft
   Organizing your essay
   Practicing academic honesty
Conducting further research
   Specialized academic databases
   Government documents
   Survey to conventions
   Survey
   Interview
   Observation
Finalizing your thesis
Introducing and concluding
Revising before the deadline
   Peer review questions
Editing the almost final draft
   Common errors
   Citation conventions

Professional Writing and Workplace Documents

Most students come to college knowing that they will be asked to write many papers. They expect that they will be writing literary analyses chapter summaries, research essays, and lab reports. In addition to these forms of academic writing, many students will also be writing some career-oriented documents, especially in their senior year of college. Majors in engineering and architecture will be asked to write project proposals, seniors in marketing and accounting will be assigned business plans, and students in science and education will learn to write grant applications. Even English majors may find themselves composing a memo about the next edition of the department's literary magazine. At many colleges and universities, it is possible to have a minor or a second major in career-oriented **professional writing**.

Although you may not be familiar with the term "professional writing," you already have had many experiences with these texts. You probably have used instructions to help you assemble new purchases and read colorful brochures about charitable organizations. Memos may have informed you about new work policies, and reports may have influenced your opinions on corporations.

It is ironic that when professional texts succeed, they usually go unnoticed by their audiences. Instead, readers focus on the product purchased or the new policy. Thus, a good way to demonstrate the importance of professional writing is to ask you to notice what happens when one of these texts fails. Consider the example of a set of instructions that baffled you. When have you been frustrated by poorly written instructions? As you tried to follow a step or decipher a diagram, how did you feel? Did you return the purchase, vowing never to buy that brand again?

Here's a more dramatic example of the importance of professional writing. NASA suffered a terrible tragedy in 1986 when the space shuttle Challenger exploded soon after liftoff. There were seven astronauts on this flight, including the first civilian in space, a teacher from New Hampshire named Christa McAuliffe. As we later learned, several engineers had written a series of memos to warn the managers that a disaster was possible. Unfortunately, these memos failed to convey the severity of the situation, and on January 28, 1986, the Challenger space shuttle was launched. As the rockets lifted the shuttle, one engineer turned to another and said that they had "just dodged a bullet" (Vaughn 572). The shuttle, however, exploded several seconds later, less than two minutes into the flight. As the nation was watching the first teacher fly into space, all seven astronauts were killed as a terrible line of smoke crossed the sky.

The most obvious cause of this disaster was the flawed design of the O-rings that sealed large sections of the rocket boosters together. However, this loss of life, equipment, and a nation's confidence could have been avoided if several crucial memos had been written and read better. Tragically, as a presidential commission concluded, "Had these matters been clearly stated, … the launch of 51-L might not have occurred" (Mathes and Stevens 380). Thus, professional writing was also central to this disaster.

Most professional writing, of course, does not have such life and death consequences, and as we have conceded, it is easy to overlook most *successful* examples of instructions, brochures, memos, and reports. Even in the workplace, some employees believe that "writing up results" and "pushing paper" are not "*real*" work." Professional writing, however, contributes much more than creating a written record of work activity. As the authors of "Writing at Exxon ITD" found in their study of workplace writing, these documents helped to set priorities, identify difficulties, establish procedures, organize collaborators, and disseminate solutions (Paradis, Dobrin, and Miller 290–94). In other words, workplace writing promotes critical thinking, effective communication, and good solutions among colleagues.

In this study, the authors found that professional writing also affects individual careers. Workplace documents help employees demonstrate their contributions to an organization, and new employees who excel at professional writing are often placed on the fast track for advancement in their careers. Why? Because their supervisors rightly assume that those who write well will also be able to describe problems, explain outcomes, and organize others. In short, they will be effective managers. Not interested in management? Consider the careers of many musicians and painters whose creativity is often supported through grants and residencies. To gain this financial support, these artists must be able to articulate their creativity in a grant proposal or a residency application.

In this chapter, we will introduce four shorter forms of professional writing:

- A memo
- A flyer
- A resume
- An application letter

Using these examples, we will present several crucial concepts that help distinguish workplace writing from most academic papers. Finally, we will ask you to consider the relationship between professional and academic writing. Let's start with an actual memo from the Challenger disaster.

Memo

Like the five-paragraph essay of academic writing (introduction, three body paragraphs, and conclusion), a memo has a set format. As you may know, a memo begins with its audience, author, date, and topic:

To:

From:

Date:

Subject:

With this opening, let us stress that the rhetorical triangle is at work again (writer-audience-purpose), and, at least for the first three items, little thought seems to be required to complete them.

To: ___, **From:** ___, **Date:** ___. The "**Subject**" too seems easy enough to add … until we consider the Challenger space shuttle disaster further.

In hindsight, it is easy to understand why the managers overlooked the potential disaster even though the engineers tried to communicate their concerns. When the first evidence of a seal problem was noticed, two engineers visited an O-ring supplier and another manufacturer, and, afterward, they wrote a memo to explain what they had learned. They listed the subject as:

Subject: Visit to ___ Corporation and ____ Company (names deleted)

Although the subject describes what the engineers did, meaning their experiences, it fails to convey their purpose to the audience. In other words, they did not focus their readers' attention on what they had learned about the O-rings from these visits. Since they did not consider their audience sufficiently, they also never fulfilled what should have been the ultimate goal of this memo: convincing the managers to pay more attention to the seal problems.

In addition to failing to employ the rhetorical triangle effectively, the engineers also presented their visits as a story. The memo is organized as a narrative of some of the events that occurred during the trip instead of as an analysis of the results. Thus, the writing task is as misguided as the purpose of this memo (for more on tasks, see Chapter 5). The first paragraph of the memo stated:

The purpose of this memorandum is to document the results of a visit to ____ Corporation by ____ and ____ on February 1, 1979 and also to inform you of the visit made to ____ Company by ____ on February 2, 1979. The purpose of the visits was to present the O-ring seal manufacturers with details concerning the large O-ring extrusion gaps being experienced on the space shuttle solid rocket motor clevis joints and to seek opinions regarding the potential risks.

Then the second paragraph continued this narrative structure and focused on the details of the first visit:

The visit on February 1, 1979 to ___ Corporation by ___ and ___ was very well received. Company officials _____ attended the meeting and were presented with the SRM clevis joint seal test data by Mr. ____ and Mr. ____ . After considerable discussion, company representatives declined to make immediate recommendations because of the need for more time to study the data.

Even with these excerpts shortened by the omission of many names, has your attention started to fade from this story? If so, you'll wish that the managers had been able to focus on the next sentence in which the engineers explained that the O-ring suppliers had:

- Voice[d] concern for the design ….

Then in the third paragraph, they added that the second manufacturer too had:

- Expressed surprise that the seal had performed so well …

When these warnings are presented in stark isolation above, these two assertions are chilling. Yet these expressions of "concern" and "surprise" were never heeded by the managers. Buried in the middle of the second and third paragraphs of this poorly written memo, these warnings were never understood so a tragedy was not averted.

The full text of this memo is presented in an appendix at the end of this chapter (see pp. 161–162). Through discussion and/or writing, your professor may ask you to revise some or all of this memo. This revision will require you to consider some of the following questions:

- How would you phrase the subject, and what is the likely reaction of your primary audience to that phrasing?

- How would you change the narrative organization of this memo?

- What consequences of the O-ring problems need to be stated?

- How could you improve the rhetoric to ensure that the managers would understand more of this crucial information?

As the first question about the subject demonstrates, this revision will require you to think critically about purpose and audience. You will have to find the right balance between alarming the audience and alienating them. If your subject line seems to them to be too dramatic, the audience may doubt your credibility, your ethos, and dismiss your warning. Thus, this memo will also have to be effective rhetorically.

The first paragraph of a memo is similar to the introduction of a five-paragraph essay: it states the main idea. Then, the second paragraph of this memo should explain the topic in greater detail, but brevity is crucial for your audience: a busy manager. Most professional writing is as brief as possible, and one way to be concise is to use what are known as **bullets**, which are indented and isolated assertions. You have seen bullets used throughout these chapters, such as those used on the previous page to highlight the "concern" and "surprise" of the seal manufacturers. As shown below, bullets can be phrased as complete sentences or as fragments. Ideally, they should be presented as **parallel phrases** so each one has the same structure. For example, each one can begin with a noun or a verb as shown below:

- The design …
- The seal …
- The gap …

or

- Raises concerns …
- Compromises safety …
- Violates standards …

The Revision of a Flawed Memo

Here is a space for you to revise the Challenger memo and communicate the engineers' concerns more effectively:

To: Space Shuttle Managers (actual names not used)
From: _____ (your name)
Date: February 6, 1979
Subject:

Remember that you should state the purpose of the memo in the first paragraph, then present the crucial information in the next two paragraphs and analyze the significance of these details for your readers. Be concise in your phrasing and use bullets to focus attention on the most important statements. Of course, every memo will not have such dire importance, but the expected format and concise words of professional writing may determine the success of a literary magazine, a new business, or a health campaign.

A Flyer

Now let's switch from the dramatic example of a failed space flight to one found on your college campus. The entrances and bulletin boards of many college buildings are layered with flyers for this club and that event. These seemingly simple texts rely on several traits found in most professional writing, such as white space, font choice, and font size.

As its name suggests, **white space** refers to blank areas of a document, and it eases our comprehension of words and images. As shown by this page, white space indicates the start of a new paragraph. You may have never noticed as your eyes pass over the indentation of a new paragraph, but the white space encourages us to pause and think about the main idea(s) of the last paragraph and prepare for a new topic in the next. As with other flawed examples, we especially notice white space when a text lacks these areas, such as when an enthusiastic child writes a page of uninterrupted sentences or when we try to read a medieval manuscript in which every space of their precious pages are filled with words or images. The lack of white space dulls our comprehension. In contrast, when white space is used well, it highlights key information, such as in the bullets already demonstrated for the Challenger memo:

- Voice[d] concern for the design …
- Expressed surprise that the seal had performed so well …

Our eyes are drawn to the phrases surrounded by white space, and we are more likely to understand this information.

White space can be combined with **font choice and size** in a flyer so important information is emphasized. As the entrance of a building on your campus probably reveals, every flyer does not fulfill its purpose of informing students. Consider this example of a flyer:

This flyer presents all of the necessary information, but can you imagine what probably would happen as you glanced at it while walking by a bulletin board? Yes, you're likely to keep going and not comprehend

ALPHA CHI
Book Drive

Come donate your old K-12th
grade level books and support
literacy at local schools!
Fiction and Nonfiction books will
be accepted!
(Please, NO encyclopedias
or self-help books)

<u>Drop your old books off</u> : At our
table in Caldwell: Smith Lounge
Feb. 15, 17, 22 & 24 12:15-1:45 p.m.
<u>OR:</u>
At our Drop Box in the library near the
front desk from Feb. 14-25

the mass of words presented. There are simply too many words on this flyer, and they are presented without enough white space. To revise this flyer, you will have to consider some of the following questions:

- Where should the appealing image be located to break up the excessive text?
- How can some phrases be worded more concisely?
- Is the font (Lucinda Calligraphy) easy to read?
- Have can font choice and size, **text margins, italics, bold, and underlining** be used more effectively?
- What information is obvious to a student on campus, and what needs to be explained more fully?

We won't claim that the following revision is the best one possible, but in what ways is it an improvement on the original one?

This revision uses fewer words and provides much more white space. The font has been changed to Arial typeface, which is easier to read, and the most important idea: **BOOK DRIVE** is presented in the

Alpha Chi Honor Society
Book Drive
Support literacy at local schools!

Please donate your used books
Fiction and Nonfiction for grades K-12

Collection Sites :
Our Drop Box in the **Library**
Feb. 14-25 (near the front desk)
and
Our Table in **Smith Lounge**, CSU
Feb. 15, 17, 22, & 24, 12:15–1:45 pm

largest letter size and entirely in capitals; the second main idea of "**Please donate** …" is presented in letters almost as large. The audience is urged to "Support literacy" in order to motivate them to join this worthy cause. The sponsoring group, the Alpha Chi Honor Society, has been fully identified to avoid confusion with a fraternity or sorority. Placing the image in the middle of the flyer separates the main ideas from the details of the donations desired and the collection sites. What do you think of the new phrasing of the two lines under the image? How has font size also been used differently in these lines? Underlining and bolding have been used to stress the locations and dates. Can you suggest any further revisions, and upon what rhetorical principles do these revisions depend? (See Chapter 6 for more on rhetoric.)

A Resume

Another format of professional writing that depends on concise phrasing and white space is a **resume**. From the French language, this noun is pronounced "**re**-zu-may" (in contrast to the verb "resume," which is pronounced "re-**zoom**"). A resume is a summary of one's job qualifications that is sent to an employer along with an application letter. Usually one page in length, a resume presents a job applicant's qualifications in a brief, skimmable format. Once again, the headings of this format make it seem easy to complete … until you consider whether or not this text will actually be read by its intended audience.

Imagine an employer trying to hire a new person: she has dozens of applications to sort through and probably little time to do so. Each applicant has submitted a resume accompanied by a letter, and the employer wants to hire the most qualified person *and* return to her other responsibilities as soon as possible.

The applicant needs to convince this busy employer that he or she is the person who should be hired. A resume provides essential information in a standard format, yet the goal of each applicant is to stand out from the rest. Although colors and graphics may seem like a good idea, their use would also reveal an applicant's ignorance of the standard practices of most professions. Instead, what distinguishes an applicant, especially a recent college graduate or a current student, is their educational achievements and relevant experiences. Thus, this information must be presented in a way that highlights her or his qualifications; the typical format of a resume includes the following **headings**:

- **Contact information** (name, address, telephone, and email address)
- **Education** (ordered from most recent to past)
- **Experiences** (paid and volunteer, again in reverse order)
- **References** (to be provided upon request)

Depending on the position being sought, a resume writer may also include some or all of the following information:

- **Objective**
- **Honors and awards**
- **Internships, activities, and skills**

What you decide to include in a particular resume, of course, will depend on the position being sought and how you will present yourself for that opening. In other words, the third corner of the rhetorical triangle, the writer, will be crucial. For example, a resume to gain employment at a clothing store in the mall will differ from one for a job at a summer camp, and both of these will vary from a resume for your first full-time position after college, working, for example, as a professional writer, probably related to your major. Do you want to be perceived as a diligent and personable worker eager to sell clothes at the mall or as a caring and dedicated person ready for the fun and long hours of a summer camp? Or as an accomplished student who has earned special awards in your major and minored in professional writing? Thus, as with a memo or a flyer, you will have to make some careful rhetorical decisions and fulfill a standard format when you write a resume.

Here is one version of the usual format of a resume:

Francisco Alvarez

Box 623
University of Hartford
200 Bloomfield Avenue
West Hartford, CT 06117
860-923-1111
falvarez@hartford.edu

Objective   To obtain a position as a professional writer for an art gallery

Education
University of Hartford
- *Bachelor of Arts*, Art History, Minor in Professional Writing (2014)
  Senior Project: Calder and Miro: A Comparative Study
- Relevant Coursework in Minor: Business Communication, Grants and Proposals, Visual Literacy, and Advanced Rhetorical Theory

Experience
Wadsworth Athenaeum, Hartford, CT
Intern, 2012-13
- Prepared original content for museum website and print documents
- Managed databases of donors and volunteers
- Assisted in fundraising events

Mark Twain House, Hartford, CT
Volunteer, summer 2012
- Assisted with office communication
- Conducted tours

Special Skills   *Computer*: Mac, Windows, Adobe InDesign
Language: English and Spanish

Activities   **Writing Center**, University of Hartford
Tutor, 2011-2013

International Festival, University of Hartford
Organizer, 2011-2012

References   Available upon request from Career Center, University of Hartford

---

The formatting of this resume helps an employer assess an applicant quickly. This text is organized vertically with the most important information, such as name and objective, presented first. Then, headings, bold and italicized lettering, bullets, and white space all are used to create an easily discernible pattern of information. For example, the "Education" heading presents the name of the student's university, his major, and relevant studies. Then, this pattern of using bold or italicized lettering continues in the "Experience" section and subsequent sections. Only relevant "Skills" and "Activities" are listed, and the stock phrase of "Available upon request … " is used for References. Other variations on this particular format are possible, but each one should be designed to enhance a reader's comprehension of the applicant's qualifications. Every resume should address the rhetorical situation of the applicant and the position sought.

Application Letter

When you apply for employment, an **application letter** accompanies a resume, and this letter is designed to introduce you and elaborate on some of your qualifications. As you read the following example of an application letter, please consider the rhetorical situation of an applicant trying to distinguish himself or herself. Which features do you think fulfill that purpose?

April 17, 2012
Mrs. Christina Wang
Director, Wallace Gallery
190 Main Street
West Springfield, MA 01089

Dear Mrs. Wang:

I am writing to apply for the recently advertised position of professional writer and website manager for the Wallace Gallery. My qualifications match the stated responsibilities, making me eager to apply for this position.

As the enclosed resume indicates, my education includes both a major in art history and a minor in professional writing. I possess both the requisite background in the arts as well as the specialized training in writing brochures, business communication, and websites. My senior thesis on Calder and Miró matches the emphasis on the modernist art of your gallery. One of my writing projects involved developing a website to promote the annual showcase of senior art students at my university. To view this and other examples of my professional writing, please go to my online portfolio that can be found at http://www.hartford.edu/falvarez.

My experiences as an intern and a volunteer have prepared me to make a seamless transition to the workplace. My internship at the Wadsworth Atheneum involved the development of web content, as your position requires. Working collaboratively, I created many of the web pages of the 2012–2013 special exhibitions of Vermeer's paintings and Remington's sculptures. I also have managed databases and prepared communications for arts organizations, such as the Mark Twain House. Thus, I am very familiar with the daily tasks and special projects of arts management.

Confidential reference letters are available from Career Services at my university so please let me know if you would like to receive them. I recently consulted your current website, and I look forward to discussing its features and your position. I can be contacted at 860-545-6721.

Sincerely,

Francisco Alvarez

Francisco Alvarez

As a busy employer scans this letter and many others, he or she will be engaged by this application (or not) within a minute or two. Use the standard format of a **business letter** (as shown), and be explicit and concise in the opening paragraph. Mention the exact position because there may be more than one available. Then the reader's attention is directed to the resume by a discussion on the applicant's **qualifications** in the next two paragraphs. An applicant's fit with the position will determine whether the educational or workplace experiences are addressed first. It is essential to lead with one's strengths and connect them to the position (e.g., "My senior thesis … the emphasis on modernist art …"). Then the array of qualifications is presented so the applicant matches the employee needed. Finally, the letter closes with the standard paragraph on **references** and **contact information**. Hopefully, as the employer finishes reading this letter and resume, the applicant's name and number are circled so an interview can be scheduled!

Your professor may ask you to write or discuss an application letter for a professional position related to your major. If you are a first-year student, you may not yet be able to imagine writing this letter, but that difficulty can guide you in your college education. Along with fulfilling the requirements of your major and general education, let your goals also include the development and the articulation of the skills that your dream job will demand. As we asserted at the start of this chapter, effective writing skills will be required for many positions so let's end this chapter by considering how can you get, as we say, from here to there.

From Academic to Professional Writing

As stated at the start of this chapter, during your senior year of college, you probably will start to make the transition from academic writing to professional writing. You may be asked to write a memo, a proposal, or an application. Some students, however, make this transition without ever stopping to consider the relationship between academic and professional writing. Without this understanding, they may be bewildered by some of the changes in expectations. Consider these two examples from "Writing at Exxon ITD."

- A young engineer composed a 75-page report on an experiment, yet when he submitted this great effort to his supervisor, it was rejected. The supervisor told the writer to reduce the document to five pages plus a data sheet.

- Another engineer wrote an economic analysis totaling eight single-spaced pages in length. Yet, it too was criticized for being too long and delaying the recommendation until the end of the analysis.

In the second example, the writer explained that he wanted to show the logic that led to his recommendation, but his supervisor wanted the recommendation on the first page followed by details on its implementation. He rejected the lengthy explanation, asserting that "If he's wrong. ….. He'll hear from us" (302). In other words, this new employee had better be right in his reasoning, and, if he wasn't, then and only then would he be asked to explain his thought process. The supervisor did not want to read through the employee's lengthy explanation; he just wanted his subordinate to be right.

Both of these new employees were caught in the transition from college to workplace writing, and it is easy to understand why. They were still writing as they had been taught at college. This is not to say that their professors were wrong to teach them to write lengthy lab reports and other extended forms of academic writing. However, these students had never considered the similarities of and the differences between academic and professional writing. This comparison and contrast will sharpen your understanding of both and strengthen your ability to write each one.

Let's begin with an obvious difference between most academic writing and most professional writing. As in the example of the 75-page report and the five-page revision demonstrates, most academic writing involves elaboration while professional writing usually requires brevity. We will use this difference to start this analysis. How else can you compare and contrast academic and professional writing?

	Academic Writing	Professional Writing
Comparisons:		
Contrasts:	elaborate	brief

At first, it may be easier to contrast these two forms of writing, especially for students who don't really enjoy writing academic papers. You may be one of these students who dislikes academic writing because it makes you "tear things apart" and "use big words." In other words, it is analytical and abstract, while workplace documents, like memos and brochures, are more functional (they get things done) and concrete (they focus on specifics).

Before we add those contrasts to our chart, please turn to what may strike you as the more difficult question:

How are academic and professional writing similar?

In this chapter, we have asserted that, like academic writing, professional writing requires critical thinking. To revise the flawed Challenger memo or to write an effective resume, the writer had to consider the rhetorical situation carefully. The revised flyer shows that a writer has to think critically about where to place an image and how to use font size to emphasize a main idea. But is any critical thinking required, for instance, to write a simple set of steps 1 through 10 instructions? At first glance, it does not seem so; a writer just has to describe what one does to assemble a product just purchased. Yet the example of flawed instructions reveals that the writer must think long and hard about how the instructions might be misunderstood by a reader. A professional writer has to have a clear comprehension of how the product should be used as well as what the audience does and does not know. This critical thinking and clear comprehension are shown by that moment of insight when one overcomes a flawed set of instructions. The frustrated customer exclaims, "Why didn't they explain it this way?" or "Why would they assume I knew that!"

If professional as well as academic writing involves critical thinking, effective rhetoric, and clear comprehension, then why are they so different in length? Most academic papers are extended elaborations of an idea, and most professional texts are terse assertions of an action. In other words, as some college seniors demand, "Why did I spend four years writing 5, 10, and 20-page papers if my boss is going to want a three-paragraph memo or a two-sided brochure? Why was I assigned long papers to prepare me to write concise documents?"

The comment by the new employee's supervisor quoted above helps to unravel this apparent contradiction: "If he's wrong. …. He'll hear from us." The goals of an employer usually are very different from those of a professor. Your professors ask you to present your understanding in great detail so they can evaluate your learning and teach you further. An employer does not want to devote much time on a subordinate's clear comprehension and critical thinking because, as the old saying goes, time is money. An employer's goals of action and profit are very different from an educator's aims of learning and teaching. Your boss wants results, while your professor seeks learning.

Yet, let's not make these distinctions too sharp. Some workplace writing combines the attributes of academic and professional writing. For instance, an annual report by a corporation presents information in elaborate detail to inform stockholders and potential stockholders of their sound investment. However, this document also is designed to be much easier to skim than an academic essay. A busy investor can glance at the report's headings and choose to read certain sections more thoroughly. Thus, academic and professional writing may not be as different as they first seem to be; nevertheless, there are some significant differences and good reasons for them.

	Academic Writing for Instruction	Professional Writing for Profit
Comparisons:	clear comprehension	clear comprehension
	critical thinking	critical thinking
	effective rhetoric	effective rhetoric
Contrasts:	elaborate	concise
	analytical	functional
	abstract	concrete

By referring to the rhetorical triangle once again, we can conclude on why these differences exist. The contrasts between professional and academic writing depend on their differences of writer, audience, and purpose:

	Academic Writing	Professional Writing
Writer:	Student	Employee
Audience:	Professors	Coworkers
	Classmates	Customers
Purpose:	Teaching	Action
	Learning	Profit

Despite these differences, neither side is wrong. Instead, the traits of academic and professional writing are right for each one because their ultimate goals are different.

Key Terms and Concepts

Before you finish this chapter, here is a list of the key concepts. Which key terms can you explain easily, and which ones do you need to review?

Professional Writing
  Memo
    To:
    From:
    Date:
    Subject:
    Concise paragraphs
    Bullets
    Parallel phrases
  Flyer
    White space
    Font choice and size
    Text margins, italics, bold, and underlining
  Resume
    Headings for easy skimming
    Contact information
    Education
    Experience
    References
    Objective
    Honors and awards
    Internships, activities, and skills
  Application Letter
    Business format
    Qualifications
    References
    Contact information
  Relationship with academic writing
    Contrasts and comparisons
    Writer, audience, and purpose

Works Cited:

Mathes, J.C. and Dwight W. Stevens. "The Challenger Disaster." *Designing Technical Documents*. New York: MacMillian, 1991. 377-405. Print

Paradis, J., Dobrin, D., and Miller, R. "Writing at Exxon ITD." Eds. L. Odell and D. Goswami. *Writing in Non-Academic Settings*. New York: Guilford Press, 1985. 281-307. Print.

Vaughn, Diane. *The Challenger Launch Decision*. Chicago: University of Chicago Press, 1996. Print

Appendix

Example of a Flawed Challenger Memo

February 6, 1979

To: _____
From: Mr. _____
Subject: Visit to _____ Corporation and _____ Company

The purpose of this memorandum is to document the results of a visit to _____ Corporation by _____ and _____ on February 1, 1979 and also to inform you of the visit made to _____ Company by _____ on February 2, 1979. The purpose of the visits was to present the O-ring seal manufacturers were details concerning the large O-ring extrusion gaps being experienced on the Space Shuttle Solid Rocket Motor clevis joints and to seek opinions regarding the potential risks.

The visit on February 1, 1979 to _____ Corporation by _____ and _____ was very well received. Company officials _____ attended the meeting and were presented with the SRM clevis joint seal test data by Mr. _____ and Mr. _____ . After considerable discussions, company representatives declined to make immediate recommendations because of the need for more time to study the data. They did, however, voice concern for the design, stating that the SRM O-ring extrusion gap was larger than that covered by their experience. They also stated that more tests should be performed with the present design. Mr. _____ promised to contact MSFC for further discussions is a few days. Mr. _____ provided Mr. _____ and Mr. _____ with the names of two consultants who may be able to help. We are indebted to the _____ Corporation for the time and effort being expended by their people in the support of this problem, especially since they have no connection with the project.

The visit to the _____ Company on February 2, 1979, by Mr. _____ was also well received; _____ Company supplies the O-rings used in the SRM clevis and joint design. Representatives met with Mr. _____ and were provided with the identical SRM clevis joint data as was presented to _____ Company on February 1, 1979. Reaction to the data by _____ officials was essentially the same as that by _____ Corporation. They also expressed surprise that the seal had performed so well in the present application. Company experts would make no official statement concerning reliability and potential risk factors associated with the present design; however, their first thought was that the O-ring was being asked to perform beyond its intended design and a different type of seal should be considered. The need for additional testing of the present design was also discussed and it was agreed that tests that more closely simulate actual conditions should be done. _____ officials will study the data in more detail with other Company experts and contact MSFC for further discussions in approximately one week. _____ Company has shown a serious interest in assisting MSFC with this problem and their efforts are much appreciated.

Mr. _____

In addition to the problems of the subject, the buried warnings, and the narrative structure of this memo, there are two other features worth noting. First, this memo is an odd combination of the formats of both a memo and a letter. Second, despite this formatting, the memo ends with an effective plan for action ("additional testing … actual conditions"). Unfortunately, these tests were never conducted because their need was not communicated clearly enough.

Thematic Chapters

PART 3

Family Forms and Roles

CHAPTER 10

[The word] family has an especially significant social history.... In none of the pre-seventeenth century senses, can we find the distinctive modern sense of a small group confined to immediate blood relations.... Yet it is clear that between the seventeenth and nineteenth centuries the sense of the small kin-group, usually living in one house, came to be dominant.

—*Raymond Williams (1977)*

Middle-class and working-class families alike developed a belief that married women should not work outside the home. The special responsibility of men for breadwinning made sense in the early nineteenth century.... It followed from the demands of physical strength and dealing with strangers in the new industrial setting.

—*Peter Stearns (1977)*

The very nature of white institutions works against the black extended family as it attempts to fulfill its collective responsibilities and functions within the context of Afro-American values. [Imagine] what black college freshmen go through trying to explain the income of their multiple extended family parents ... to college financial aid officers.

—*Joseph White (1984)*

If the decade of the 1950s was the "heyday" of the nuclear family, it was also a historical aberration. The social stability of the 1950s was less the result of that decade's family forms or values than its unique socioeconomic and political climate.

—*Stephanie Coontz (1995)*

Introduction

Many of us take family for granted; it's the group of people with whom we have lived and grown up—right? Family seems like such an obvious subject that it deserves little attention and even less academic study. Yet most colleges and universities offer courses that focus on the family from diverse angles: the history of family structures, the communication styles of effective parents, and the genetic inheritance of terminal illnesses. Over the last three centuries, the form and function of families have changed so greatly in the United States that many contemporary families would seem very strange to past generations, just as their family structures would strike many of us as unusual today.

Colonial families, for example, often consisted not only of parents and children, but also of other relatives, indentured servants, apprentices, and journeymen. Most of the members of colonial families lived in the same dwelling, and they regularly ate their meals together. These families were less defined by blood relationships and more by household membership; in fact, the word family was a synonym for household in the English spoken during the sixteenth and seventeenth centuries. Because the male head of this household and his assistants often worked and lived in the same dwelling, there was little distinction between a father's economic and domestic roles. He frequently treated his children like workers and his helpers like children. Apprentices, for example, had to promise not only to work for their master but also to obey his commands concerning their conduct. Would you want to live in a family under these conditions? What might be some of the advantages or disadvantages over your family life today?

Since colonial times, the size of U.S. families has steadily decreased. In 1790, most families had seven or more members living in one house. By 1890, less than half of all families were as large, and many had only three members. The definition of family, however, had changed as well; servants and apprentices were no longer considered family members. By 1970, three-quarters of all U.S. families had three members or fewer in the same household. Multiple factors account for this: Grandparents frequently no longer lived with their adult children; some couples chose to have fewer children or none at all; many divorces created single-parent families; and young adult children moved into their own households at an earlier age, often before marriage. By 2000, the number of people in American households had reached the lowest average ever—fewer than three people. More than a quarter of all Americans lived alone at the start of the twenty-first century.

With these differences in numbers, there also have been more complex changes in the roles of family members. For example, while we take for granted that most mothers naturally want to bond with their babies soon after birth, this was not always the case. In colonial times, when many babies did not survive birth or did not live beyond age two, mothers delayed forming emotional bonds with their babies because their survival was too uncertain. Only since the late nineteenth century, with its significant decrease in infant mortality, have mothers been expected to nurture their infants emotionally soon after birth.

The role of fathers has also changed. When the United States was primarily an agrarian society, fathers worked on farms with their wives and children. With the industrialization and urbanization of the United States in the nineteenth century, the location of men's work moved from home workshops and farm fields to factories and offices. As the primary economic providers of their families, fathers had to labor long hours while separated from their wives and children.

As these historic changes suggest, multiple and often conflicting perspectives now exist on what is a family, and what is the expected role of each member. Every reading in this chapter provides a snapshot of a perspective in what is a much larger family album. This chapter is not intended to be a definitive history of the family in the United States. It instead is designed to make you question your own assumptions and those of others about what a family is, has been, and will be. This chapter encourages you to ask and answer these questions about the family's form and function by requiring you to consider your beliefs in relation to readings that offer past and present perspectives.

The three historical readings present three different genres: analysis, autobiography, and fiction, which represent the array of texts you will be asked to read at college. This first reading by the historian Tamara Hareven may surprise you as you learn how different some families were two centuries ago. Then the literary works by Frederick Douglass and Mary Wilkins Freeman reveal some of the nineteenth-century efforts to change family and society. In the two contemporary readings, diverse family issues are examined, such as gender roles, child discipline, cross-racial adoptions, and single mothers. Each of these issues is subject to an ongoing debate, which you will be asked to join.

These texts, along with the reading questions, freewriting activities, and visual elements of this chapter, are designed to develop the reading and writing abilities required for academic study. After each reading, you will find a set of questions that are divided into Close Reading Questions, Analytical Writing/ Discussion, and Further Options. Some questions involve the same investigation of multiple perspectives, cultural influences, and historical trends that were introduced in Chapter 1 or 2. Answering some and discussing more of the post-reading questions will better prepare you to complete the final assignments options. These final writing assignments will ask you to assert your own, more informed perspective on the American family. This chapter asks: **What do you think should be the accepted form(s) of the family and the proper role(s) of each member?**

Freewrite 1: Initial Impressions

Before you turn to the first reading, try to develop some images and ideas of your own. Your professor may ask you to freewrite on one or more of the following suggestions; you may be asked to discuss some as well.

Images: The modern British poet Christopher Isherwood compared himself to a camera as he began to collect ideas for his poetry. He wrote, "I am a camera with its shutter open, quite passive, recording, not thinking…. Some day all of this will have to be developed carefully, fixed [and] printed." Like Isherwood, can you open your mind's shutter, your creative camera, to capture several images of your family? Rather than creating a posed group portrait with everyone standing still, shoulder to shoulder, saying "cheese," try to get some "candid" shots that create some realistic images of your family life. Freewrite one or two descriptive images that record a moment of your family members in action and that reveal their roles within your family.

Analysis: Through further writing and/or discussion, analyze the significance of your descriptive images by answering one or more of the following questions:

- Whom did you include or exclude in your images? Why?

- What is the expected role of each member of your family?

- How do these roles match those expected by society in general? How do they differ?

- What internal and external forces can pull this family together and push it apart?

- How would you define the contemporary American family? What is a family?

THE NINETEENTH-CENTURY RETREAT: FAMILY AND HOME

by Tamara K. Hareven

During the nineteenth century, urbanization and industrialization fundamentally changed the lives and homes of American families, such as the colonial family described in the introduction to this chapter. This relocation of many families

from rural to urban and then to suburban areas, as well as
the transfer of many jobs from farms to factories, altered the
roles of husbands and wives. Tamara Hareven traced this history of the family in such books as *Family Time and Industrial
Time* (1982) and *Families, History and Social Change*(1999).
This article was originally published in 1991.

The concept of the home as the family's haven and domestic retreat emerged only about one hundred fifty years ago, and was, initially, limited to the urban middle classes. In order to understand the development of the home as the family's abode, as a reality and as an ideal, it is necessary to examine the relationship between household, family, and home as they changed over time.

First, the ideal Western family of the past, in which three generations co-resided harmoniously in the same household, has been proven to be a myth. It is part of what William Goode referred to as the classic ideal of "Western nostalgia."[1] Actually, historians of the family have identified the persistence of a nuclear household structure in Western Europe since the sixteenth century, and in the United States since the times of settlement. More recently, historians have found that a nuclear household structure has predominated in England and Italy since the twelfth century.

The persistence of a nuclear household pattern in Western society has significant implications for our understanding of the role of the home and its emergence as a way of life and a symbolic concept. Membership in a nuclear household rested on the principle of residential separation of the generations. Marriage meant the establishment of a separate household by the new couple, even if the older generation was living nearby. In rural society, aging parents often lived on the same land with their married children, but still in separate households. This commitment to the separate residence of the family of origin and the family of procreation should not be misconstrued as a commitment to privacy. Contrary to prevailing myths, preindustrial households rarely included relatives other than the members of the nuclear family, but they often contained unrelated individuals whose presence in the household reflected the various special functions that the family held.[2]

In preindustrial society, there was a significant difference between the family's domicile—the household—and the home as it became idealized later in Western European and American society. In addition to serving as the family's place of residence and the focus for the family's various domestic activities, such as eating, sleeping, and child rearing, the household was the site of a multiplicity of activities. It served as the site of production, as a welfare agency and correctional institution, as an educational institution, and as a place for religious worship. Rather than catering strictly to the needs of the family, the household served the entire community, by taking in dependent members who were not related to the family and by helping maintain the social order.

Accordingly, household membership was not restricted to individuals related by ties of blood and marriage. The household also contained unrelated individuals, such as servants, apprentices, boarders and lodgers, and "unfortunates" from the community, such as orphans, the elderly, the sick and infirm, delinquents, and mentally ill who were placed with families by the local authorities. Even though extended kin were not present in the household as a general pattern, household membership was sufficiently flexible to accommodate extended kin at certain points over the family's cycle, especially when aging parents were too frail to live by themselves and needed to coreside with their children....

Sociability vs. Privacy

The family in preindustrial society was characterized by sociability rather than privacy. As Philippe Aries has emphasized, by contrast to the conception of the home in contemporary society as a private retreat from the outside world, in preindustrial society the family conducted its work and public affairs inside the household. Households were teeming with various activities, and family members, even couples, could hardly retreat into privacy within the crowded household space. The head of the household's various business associates and other individuals actively involved in the family's economic or social activities were often present in the household. Aries provides a vivid description of life in the "big house" in preindustrial France and England. As long as family life was characterized by sociability, the household did not serve strictly as the family's private retreat. Rather, the family's public and private activities were inseparable, and the family's domestic life was often conducted with strangers present....[3] Spaces within the "big house" were not differentiated into family space and public space. No rooms were specifically designated as bedrooms. Beds stood in public areas of the house, and family members slept behind curtains while social activities including outsiders were going on in other parts of the same room. Similarly, in colonial America, bedchambers were not separate or private. Individuals and couples had to share beds with relatives or with unrelated individuals. Colonial American court records, especially those dealing with divorce, abound in various such graphic descriptions, all confirming the lack of privacy that families and unrelated individuals experienced when residing together....

The concept of the home as a private retreat first emerged in the lives of bourgeois families in eighteenth-century France and England, and in the United States among urban, middle-class families in the early part of the nineteenth century. Its development was closely linked to the new ideals of domesticity and privacy that were associated with the characteristics of the modern family—a family that was child-centered, private, and in which the roles of husband and wife were segregated into public and domestic spheres, respectively. The husband was expected to be the main breadwinner and worker outside the home and the wife a full-time housekeeper and mother. This new separation of domestic and public spheres led to the rearrangement of the family's work and living patterns within the home. While earlier, all family members, including children, worked together, or participated in various activities, even if they did not work, in the new setting the world of work became separate from family activities.[4] Family time became restricted primarily to the home, and leisure became an important aspect of domestic life. Reading, embroidering, viewing art, and listening to music had become important pastimes in the home.

Following the removal of the workplace from the home as a result of urbanization and industrialization, the household was recast as the family's private retreat, and home emerged as a new concept and existence. Eventually, other agencies took over the functions that had been earlier concentrated in the family. Factories and business places took over the work and production functions of the family, schools took over the family's formal educational functions, and asylums and correctional institutions took over the family's functions of welfare and social control. The separation of the workplace from the household and the transfer of various other functions and activities of the family to outside institutions resulted in the emergence of the home as a specialized site for the family's consumption, child rearing, and private life. The display of the family's domestic lifestyle through the architectural style of the home and its furnishings and appointments became of extreme importance in the self-characterization of the urban middle-class family in Western Europe and in the United States....[5]

In the private home that emerged in the middle of the nineteenth century, household membership had become restricted to the nuclear family, except for servants. Unlike in earlier periods, apprentices, boarders or lodgers, and dependent community members virtually disappeared from middle-class households. Even the role and social origins of servants changed in relation to the new functions of the home and the family. In preindustrial households, the servants were "lifecycle" servants—young people who were sent to serve in other people's households for educational purposes as much as for service. Such exchanges usually occurred within the same community. On the other hand, servants in nineteenth-century families were usually migrants or immigrants to the city, whose main function was to work in middle-class or upper-class households. For the majority of young women servants, domestic service was still restricted to a life-cycle stage but was now clearly defined as a form of employment rather than as a temporary residence for purposes of socialization.

The Domestic Role of Middle-Class Women

In this new domestic regime, it became inappropriate for middle-class women to work outside the home. "Our men are sufficiently moneymaking. Let us keep our women and children from the contagion as long as possible," wrote in 1832 one of the main advocates and advisers on the cult of domesticity, Sara Josepha Hale, editor of *Godey's Lady's Book* in 1832. Women's main responsibility and all their energies now had to focus on the home and the family, and especially on children. Homemaking became an occupation in itself, one that demanded physical and material resources, planning, and the persistent following of changing fashions. As one writer in mid-century put it, a house "is not only the home center, the retreat and shelter for all the family, it is also the workshop for the mother. It is not only where she is to live, to love, but where she is to care and labor. Her hours, days, weeks, months and years are spent within its bounds; until she becomes an enthroned fixture, more indispensable than the house itself." Homemaking was idealized as part of the cult of domesticity, and was accorded special social status. The complicated tasks of home management required specific advice in how-to-do-it manuals and etiquette books.[6]

Women were expected to be the perfect designers, executors, and custodians of the new domestic retreat. Housework and cooking became, therefore, extremely significant for the maintenance of the perfect home, which, in turn, was viewed by reformers as indispensable for the nation's prosperity and survival. Even the most trivial tasks were considered to be of utmost importance. "It is within your power to create a domestic haven in the lowliest cottage," wrote Daniel Wise. Various magazines, especially *Godey's Lady's Book*, as well as numerous cookbooks and advice books, provided guidance aimed at enabling housewives to achieve perfection in their domestic tasks....[7]

A variety of new appliances and gadgets made their way into the home from the middle of the nineteenth century on. These inventions became important not only as labor-saving devices but as status symbols of the efficient, well-ordered home. Initially, the most important invention was the cooking stove, which replaced open-hearth cooking. The stove revolutionized cuisine, and opened up a new range of possibilities in the simultaneous preparation of a variety of dishes on the top of the stove, rather than the one-pot meals cooked in the hearth. In addition, a whole slew of gadgets and implements, such as apple corers and slicers, vacuum cleaners, laundry strainers, and other devices appeared on the market and made their way into the middle-class home. Ruth Schwartz Cowan claims that these new appliances, rather than saving housewives' time, actually caused "more work for mother," because they provided the opportunity for more complex preparations which required increased time and labor investment on the women's part, and a decrease in the involvement of men in household work....[8]

New Designs for Family Life

The new specialization in the functions of the home and the family also necessitated corresponding architectural designs. Architects joined the trend by busily developing blueprints for new styles of homes that were to accommodate the new domestic lifestyle. The domestic architecture that emerged in the United States in the middle of the nineteenth century, featuring Gothic revival cottages, Italianate villas, and bracketed cottages that were published in builders' guides between 1840 and 1860, translated the domestic ideal into architecture in several ways: These cottages were aimed at segregating the home from the outside world, thus securing privacy for the family. Within the home, spaces were organized in a manner that separated the family's private activities from the public ones such as receiving guests. The parlor became a central space for the family's social activities and entertainment. The kitchen, which had been previously outside, was brought inside, alas, into the basement or the back of the house. Nevertheless, the kitchen became an important component of the home. The parlor was decorated by the family's heirlooms, portraits, lace and embroidery, shadow boxes, and artwork....

In his analysis of the new spaces designed in the domestic architecture which emerged in the middle of the nineteenth century, Clifford Clark concluded that "the design of the second floor, with its emphasis on creating a separate space for each member of the family ... implies that the family was not an organic unit but rather was made up of separate, unique individuals who each had a specific role to play...." Interaction within the family, like the public interaction with guests, was to take place primarily in specifically designated areas—the dining room, porch, and back parlor (family room). In these areas, family interaction became organized around certain rituals—meals, musical events, and games. Clark concluded that the design of the house implied that "the family was an organization which was not an end in itself, but rather a vehicle for promoting the development of each of its members."[9] The new domestic style required two types of privacy: privacy of the family from the community, and privacy of family members from each other within the home.

While the ideal middle-class domestic home is linked in the contemporary popular image with suburbs, as suggested above, initially the ideals of domesticity were played out in the city. The new middle-class home was designed as a response to urbanization as a retreat from the world of work and from the hustle-bustle of urban life. At the same time, it depended on urban services, conveniences, and public activities in order to achieve domestic refinement....But as the nineteenth century progressed, the ideals and lifestyle of domesticity were transferred to the suburbs and became identified with suburban living....

The development of domesticity as a suburban phenomenon, which flourished in the late nineteenth century, according to Margaret Marsh, was a response to the masculine domestic ideal, which by that point in time emphasized the virtues of a suburban retreat from the pressures of city life: "The new domestic ideal centered firmly in the suburbs, represented family pride, family identity and togetherness in face of an urban society that promised individual achievement, anonymity and excitement." By the eve of World War II, she claims, "a new suburban domestic ideal had materialized—an ideal that both reorganized domesticity to make it independent of the notion of separate masculine and feminine spheres and one which redefined the suburbs to emphasize 'place' more than the ownership of property."[10] As urban life became more bewildering, because of a high concentration of immigrants and poverty, domestic life in the suburbs had become idealized as an escape from the city.

The new domesticity in the suburbs led to the isolation of women and children from urban life, and eventually to the entrapment of women in suburban domestic lifestyles....Philippe Aries introduced this question when he lamented the loss of the "big house" and the isolation of the modern family in its domestic retreat: The modern family ... cuts itself off from the world and opposes to society the isolated groups of parents and children. All the energy of the group is expended in helping the children to rise in the world, individually and without any collective ambition, the children rather than the family.[11]

The suburban form of domesticity had become entrenched in American society and predominated until the 1960s, despite various challenges by feminist reformers, especially Charlotte Perkins Gilman, who advocated the establishment of urban residential hotels with communal dining rooms for families so that working women would be free of housekeeping chores. Gilman expected that these apartment hotels would enable women to pursue professional careers along with motherhood without being confined to child-rearing and domesticity....For people who preferred suburban life, Gilman also recommended a suburban counterpart to the apartment hotel, which involved the grouping of several residential houses, all kitchenless but interconnected by covered walkways with a central eating house.[12]

Beyond the Middle Class

When discussing these trends, it is important to remember that the separation of the home from the outside world occurred initially in the lives of a small segment of the population, namely, the urban middle classes. In rural families, and in urban working-class families, the home was viewed less as a specialized retreat, and was open to a multiplicity of functions and activities as it had been in preindustrial society. Significantly, at the very time when middle-class women were being discouraged from pursuing gainful employment, working-class women and children were being recruited as the primary labor force of the industrial revolution. Even after working-class families began to emulate middle-class domestic lifestyles and furnishings, they continued to use the household space in a more diversified and complex way than the middle class. In rural families, the household continued to serve as the site of production in agriculture as well as in domestic industries. Family members worked side by side in related tasks, and there continued to be little separation between domestic life and work life....

In working-class homes, there was little separation between domestic life and work life. The world of work spilled over into the household. In the major cities, "homework," such as garment finishing, engaged all family members in the household. Under such circumstances, the space in the home was used creatively, and was arranged and rearranged to fit the various functions of the family as they came up. At supper time, bundles of garments or other sewing materials were removed from the table so that family members could eat their supper. Beds for lodgers or boarders, or for children were opened up in the hallway or in the kitchen in the evening and were folded back again in the morning....

Families that had attained higher standards of living made a special effort to have a parlor or its semblance. "In one three-room house, where there were seven children, a room which had in it a folding bed, a wardrobe, the carriage where the baby slept in the daytime, and the sewing machine, was referred to with pride as the 'front room,' a phrase with a significance quite beyond its suggestion of locality." Residents invested much money and energy in making the front room the center of family life. "Here in the evening the family gathers about the soft coal or gas grate, while the mother sews and one of the older children plays to the father. Such 'front rooms' are the scenes of those simple festivities which enliven existence in this town." The family scenes and activities described here represent on a more modest scale the activities of middle-class families in the parlor or in the family room. In the four-room houses, the family ate in the kitchen....[13]

Even in the poorest tenements in New York's West Side, residents made a special effort to appoint and decorate their shabby and crowded dwellings. Mary White Ovington, one of the founders of the National Association for the Advancement of Colored People, was impressed by the efforts of black families to decorate a "home," sometimes with "cheap pictures, photographs, cards, vases, little ornaments," that the women, many of whom had been engaged in domestic service, received from their employers. These items, which their employers were happily rid of, nevertheless gave "an air of home likeness to the place." Ovington, who had visited many tenements of this kind, was moved by their residents' hospitality and homelike atmosphere:

The Negroes' homes are often sadly cluttered, but they are rarely bare and ugly. With this love of pretty things goes a desire to live with something of form in the arrangement of the rooms and in the ordering of the meals. When breakfast or dinner comes you will almost always find the table set. I have been surprised to find in the most modest homes that the meal carried with it the air of a social function; the mother would use many dishes though she must take the time from her laundry work to wash them.14

Similarly, the poor Jewish home in which writer Alfred Kazin grew up in Brownsville, New York, left a lasting impression on his subsequent life. In that home the kitchen was the center of family life, and the various objects within became an unforgettable source of his identity:

> The kitchen held our lives together. My mother worked in it all day long, we ate in it almost all meals except the Passover seder, I did my homework and first writing at the kitchen table, and in winter I often had a bed made up for me on three kitchen chairs near the stove…. A large electric bulb hung down the center of the kitchen at the end of a chain that had been hooked into the ceiling; the old gas ring and key still jutted out of the wall like antlers. In the corner next to the toilet was the sink at which we washed, and the square tub in which my mother did our clothes. Above it, tacked to the shelf on which were pleasantly ranged square, blue-bordered white sugar and spice jars, hung calendars from the Public National Bank on Pitkin Avenue and the Minsker Progressive Branch of the Workman's Circle; receipts for the payment of insurance premiums, and household bills on a spindle; two little boxes engraved with Hebrew letters. One of these was for the poor, the other to buy back the Land of Israel.[15]

In their effort to impress American ideals of domesticity on immigrants, social reformers left nothing to chance. A 1909 textbook for teaching English to foreigners incorporated a lesson about the ideal home:

> This is the family, in the sitting-room.
>
> The family is made up of the father, the mother, and the children.
>
> That is the father who is reading.
>
> The father is the husband.
>
> That is the mother who is sewing.
>
> The father and mother are the parents.
>
> The sister is playing the piano.
>
> The brother is standing beside her.
>
> The family makes the home.[16]

Despite the differences between the middle class and the working class and between native born and various ethnics in the family's use of the home, as the twentieth century progressed, the significance of "home" in American society cut across all classes. For working-class as well as for immigrant families, heading one's own household was identified with autonomy. Establishment of a separate household by a newly formed family, as well as the maintenance of household headship in the later years of life, were sacred values and markers of autonomy in American society….

Conclusion

In this brief examination of the emergence of the home as the family's domestic abode in reality and in ideal in Western society, I have tried to emphasize that in the past the family's place of residence—the household—did not always carry the symbolic meaning of "home"; that, indeed, home was the invention of the middle class and was closely related to the emergence of the family as a private, emotional entity. By contrast to the middle class, working-class families continued to maintain greater flexibility and diversity in the use of their domestic space and ways of life. By the twentieth century the ideals of "home" had assumed powerful meaning in the domestic life of working-class families as well. Middle-class styles of consumption and furnishing permeated working-class families....Working-class and immigrant families responded to these influences selectively: they adopted those aspects that suited their needs and their budgets, and blended them into their traditional culture, which they retained.

The privacy of the home and the family have become central concerns in Western civilization. Some historians, like Christopher Lasch, have claimed that the family's private haven has been invaded excessively by modern bureaucracies and by the helping professions. Others, like Philippe Ariès and Richard Sennett, have emphasized the negative consequences of the family's retreat into domesticity and privacy, and its repressive impact on the individual. The first major critics of middle-class domesticity, however, were the women themselves, who had to carry out the high domestic ideals defined for them by the advocates of domesticity in the nineteenth century. Women responded to the pressures to create and maintain an ideal home in isolation from the rest of the world by taking the ideals of domesticity into the larger society, and by investing their energies in various reform movements and purity crusades.

NOTES

[1]William Goode, *World Revolutions and Family Patterns* (New York: Free Press, 1963), p. 6.

[2]John Demos, *A Little Commonwealth: Family Life in Plymouth Colony* (New York: Oxford University Press, 1970); Peter Laslett, "Characteristics of the Western Family Over Time," in Peter Laslett, ed., *Family Life and Illicit Love in Former Generations* (Cambridge: Cambridge University Press, 1977).

[3]Philippe Aries, *Centuries of Childhood: A Social History of Family Life*, trans. R. Baldick (New York: Vintage Books, 1962).

[4]Barbara Welter, "The Cult of True Womanhood 1820–1860," *American Quarterly* 18 (1966): 151–174; Mary Ryan, *Cradle of the Middle Class: The Family in Oneida County, New York 1790–1865* (New York: Cambridge University Press, 1981); Carl Degler, *At Odds: Women and the Family in America from the Revolution to the Present* (New York: Oxford University Press, 1980).

[5]Michelle Perrot, *A History of Private Life, vol. 4, From the Fires of the Revolution to the Great War*, trans. Arthur Goldhammer (Cambridge: Harvard University Press, 1990); Dolores Hayden, *The Great Domestic Revolution: A History of Feminist Designs for American Homes, Neighborhoods and Cities* (Cambridge: MIT Press, 1981).

[6]On domestic-advice literature, see: Welter, "Cult of Domesticity"; Kathryn Kish Sklar, *Catherine Beecher: A Study of Domesticity* (New Haven: Yale University Press, 1973). For domestic-advice literature of the first half of the nineteenth century, see Lydia Sigourney, *The Western Home and Other Poems* (Philadelphia: Parry & McMillan, 1854); *Godey's Lady's Book* (Philadelphia, 1840–60); Lydia Maria Child, *The Mother's Book* (Boston, 1831); Ann Kuhn, *The Mother's Role in Childhood Education: New England Concepts, 1830–1860* (New Haven: Yale University Press, 1947): 35.

[7]Daniel Wise, *Bridal Greetings: A Marriage Gift* (New York, 1850), p. 84; quoted in Kirk Jeffrey, "The Family as a Utopian Retreat from the City: The Nineteenth Century Contribution," *Soundings: An Interdisciplinary Journal* 55 (Spring 1972): 35.

[8]Ruth Schwartz Cowan, *More Work for Mother* (New York: Basic Books, 1983).

[9]Clifford Edward Clark, Jr., "Domestic Architecture as an Index: The Romantic Revival and the Cult of Domesticity in America, 1840–1870," *Journal of Interdisciplinary History 7* (Summer 1976): 33–56. Andrew Jackson Downing, *Cottage Residences: A Series of Designs for Rural Cottages and Villas* (New York, 1842); *Godey's Lady's Book* published a series of revival designs, see George L. Hersey, "Godey's Choice," *Society of Architectural Historians Journal 17* (1959); see also Clifford Edward Clark, Jr., *The American Family Home* (Chapel Hill: University of North Carolina Press, 1986).

[10]Margaret Marsh, "From Separation to Togetherness: The Social Construction of Domestic Space in American Suburbs, 1840–1915," *Journal of American History 76* (1989): 506–527.

[11]Aries, *Centuries of Childhood*, p. 404.

[12]Charlotte Perkins Gilman, *Women and Economics*; quoted in Hayden, *Grand Domestic Revolution*, p. 189.

[13]Margaret F. Byington, *Homestead: The Households of a Mill Town* [1910] (Pittsburgh: University of Pittsburgh Press, 1974), 55–56.

[14]Mary White Ovington, "The Negro Home in New York," *Charities 15* (October 7, 1905): 25–26.

[15]Alfred Kazin, *A Walker in the City* (New York: Harcourt, Brace & World, 1951), pp. 65–66.

[16]Sara R. O'Brien, *English for Foreigners* (Boston, 1909), p. 55.

Close Reading Questions:

1. According to Hareven, American families have not always been the way you probably have assumed. What was the structure and purpose of the family before the nineteenth century?

2. Early in the nineteenth century, middle-class homes originally existed primarily in cities. For what reasons did urban middle-class homes later migrate to the suburbs? Then how did urban and rural working-class homes compare to these suburban, middle-class homes? (Cultural Influences)

3. Why does Hareven assert that suburban living led to "the entrapment of women"? Why do you agree or disagree with her assertion?

Analytical Writing/Discussion:

4. After the Industrial Revolution, the household became "the family's private retreat." What changes in the design of homes promoted this greater privacy for family members? What do you think were the benefits and drawbacks of these forms of privacy in the home? (Multiple Perspectives)

5. How did the "cult of domesticity" for nineteenth-century women increase the division of labor by gender in families? Using the example of a family you know well, to what degree do you think that these divided family roles for men and women still exist today? (Historical Trends)

6. The emergence of household appliances in the mid-nineteenth-century home became "status symbols of the efficient, well-ordered home." Using references to this text, to what degree do you think these devices simplified or complicated the household labor of mothers? Using references to the modern family, why do you think this trend of household appliances and labor has continued or changed?

Further Options:

7. Hareven explains that as the nineteenth family changed, so too did the architectural design of middle-class homes. Considering the now popular open floor plans that combine the kitchen, dining room, and living room in one large space, what do you think this design suggests about families today?

8. Hareven discusses concepts of family, home, and household that might seem antiquated to a twenty-first-century reader. Using methods discussed in Chapter 3 on Reading, such as double-entry journaling or highlighting, make note of the concepts that even now apply to American families, homes, and households. Why do you think some of those concepts have not changed in over a century?

FIGURE 1   An image of a nineteenth-century American family: Captain William T. Shorey and family, Oakland, CA, 1898. In the following reading, note how Frederick Douglass employs nineteenth-century assumptions about family to oppose slavery.

Courtesy of National Park Service

FAMILIES ENSLAVED

by Frederick Douglass

As an escaped slave, Frederick Douglass joined the aboli-
tionist movement and quickly became one of the leading

figures of this antislavery movement. To oppose those who claimed that enslaved Africans in the United States were intellectually and morally inferior, Douglass wrote eloquent speeches and essays to prove his own rationality and slavery's brutality. He, however, had to elicit sympathy as much as horror from his primarily Northern, "white" audience. This reading is excerpted from Douglass' first autobiography, *The Narrative of the Life and Times of Frederick Douglass,* which was published in 1845.

I was born in Tuckahoe, near Hillsborough, and about twelve miles from Easton, in Talbot county, Maryland. I have no accurate knowledge of my age, never having seen any authentic record containing it. By far the larger part of the slaves know as little of their age as horses know of theirs, and it is the wish of most masters within my knowledge to keep their slaves thus ignorant. I do not remember to have ever met a slave who could tell of his birthday. They seldom come nearer to it than planting-time, harvest-time, cherry-time, spring-time, or fall-time. A want of information concerning my own was a source of unhappiness to me even during childhood. The white children could tell their ages. I could not tell why I ought to be deprived of the same privilege. I was not allowed to make any inquiries of my master concerning it. He deemed all such inquiries on the part of a slave improper and impertinent, and evidence of a restless spirit. The nearest estimate I can give makes me now between twenty-seven and twenty-eight years of age. I come to this, from hearing my master say, some time during 1835, I was about seventeen years old.

My mother was named Harriet Bailey. She was the daughter of Isaac and Betsey Bailey, both colored, and quite dark. My mother was of a darker complexion than either my grandmother or grandfather.

My father was a white man. He was admitted to be such by all I ever heard speak of my parentage. The opinion was also whispered that my master was my father; but of the correctness of this opinion, I know nothing; the means of knowing was withheld from me. My mother and I were separated when I was but an infant—before I knew her as my mother. It is a common custom, in the part of Maryland from which I ran away, to part children from their mothers at a very early age. Frequently, before the child has reached its twelfth month, its mother is taken from it, and hired out on some farm a considerable distance off, and the child is placed under the care of an old woman, too old for field labor. For what this separation is done, I do not know, unless it be to hinder the development of the child's affection toward its mother, and to blunt and destroy the natural affection of the mother for the child. This is the inevitable result.

I never saw my mother, to know her as such, more than four or five times in my life; and each of these times was very short in duration, and at night. She was hired by a Mr. Stewart, who lived about twelve miles from my home. She made her journeys to see me in the night, travelling the whole distance on foot, after the performance of her day's work. She was a field hand, and a whipping is the penalty of not being in the field at sunrise, unless a slave has special permission from his or her master to the contrary—a permission which they seldom get, and one that gives to him that gives it the proud name of being a kind master. I do not recollect of ever seeing my mother by the light of day. She was with me in the night. She would lie down with me, and get me to sleep, but long before I waked she was gone. Very little communication ever took place between us. Death soon ended what little we could have while she lived, and with it her hardships and suffering. She died when I was about seven years old, on one of my master's farms, near Lee's Mill. I was not allowed to be present during her illness, at her death, or burial. She was gone long before I knew any thing about it. Never having enjoyed, to any considerable extent, her soothing presence, her tender and watchful care, I received the tidings of her death with much the same emotions I should have probably felt at the death of a stranger.

Called thus suddenly away, she left me without the slightest intimation of who my father was. The whisper that my master was my father, may or may not be true; and, true or false, it is of but little consequence to my purpose whilst the fact remains, in all its glaring odiousness, that slaveholders have ordained, and by law established, that the children of slave women shall in all cases follow the condition of their mothers; and this is done too obviously to administer to their own lusts, and make a gratification of their wicked desires profitable as well as pleasurable; for by this cunning arrangement, the slaveholder, in cases not a few, sustains to his slaves the double relation of master and father.

I know of such cases; and it is worthy of remark that such slaves invariably suffer greater hardships, and have more to contend with, than others. They are, in the first place, a constant offence to their mistress. She is ever disposed to find fault with them; they can seldom do any thing to please her; she is never better pleased than when she sees them under the lash, especially when she suspects her husband of showing to his mulatto children favors which he withholds from his black slaves. The master is frequently compelled to sell this class of his slaves, out of deference to the feelings of his white wife; and, cruel as the deed may strike any one to be, for a man to sell his own children to human flesh-mongers, it is often the dictate of humanity for him to do so; for, unless he does this, he must not only whip them himself, but must stand by and see one white son tie up his brother, of but few shades darker complexion than himself, and ply the gory lash to his naked back; and if he lisp one word of disapproval, it is set down to his parental partiality, and only makes a bad matter worse, both for himself and the slave whom he would protect and defend.

Every year brings with it multitudes of this class of slaves. It was doubtless in consequence of a knowledge of this fact, that one great statesman of the south predicted the downfall of slavery by the inevitable laws of population. Whether this prophecy is ever fulfilled or not, it is nevertheless plain that a very different-looking class of people are springing up at the south, and are now held in slavery, from those originally brought to this country from Africa; and if their increase will do no other good, it will do away the force of the argument, that God cursed Ham, and therefore American slavery is right. If the lineal descendants of Ham are alone to be scripturally enslaved, it is certain that slavery at the south must soon become unscriptural; for thousands are ushered into the world, annually, who, like myself, owe their existence to white fathers, and those fathers most frequently their own masters.

I have had two masters. My first master's name was Anthony. I do not remember his first name. He was generally called Captain Anthony—a title which, I presume, he acquired by sailing a craft on the Chesapeake Bay. He was not considered a rich slaveholder. He owned two or three farms, and about thirty slaves. His farms and slaves were under the care of an overseer. The overseer's name was Plummer. Mr. Plummer was a miserable drunkard, a profane swearer, and a savage monster. He always went armed with a cowskin and a heavy cudgel. I have known him to cut and slash the women's heads so horribly, that even master would be enraged at his cruelty, and would threaten to whip him if he did not mind himself. Master, however, was not a humane slaveholder. It required extraordinary barbarity on the part of an overseer to affect him. He was a cruel man, hardened by a long life of slaveholding. He would at times seem to take great pleasure in whipping a slave. I have often been awakened at the dawn of day by the most heart-rending shrieks of an own aunt of mine, whom he used to tie up to a joist, and whip upon her naked back till she was literally covered with blood. No words, no tears, no prayers, from his gory victim, seemed to move his iron heart from its bloody purpose. The louder she screamed, the harder he whipped; and where the blood ran fastest, there he whipped longest. He would whip her to make her scream, and whip her to make her hush; and not until overcome by fatigue, would he cease to swing the blood-clotted cowskin. I remember the first time I ever witnessed this horrible exhibition. I was quite a child, but I well remember it. I never shall forget it whilst I remember any thing. It was the first of a long series of such outrages, of which I was doomed to be a witness and a participant. It struck me with awful force. It was the blood-stained gate, the entrance to the hell of slavery, through which I was about to pass. It was a most terrible spectacle. I wish I could commit to paper the feelings with which I beheld it....

As to my own treatment while I lived on Colonel Lloyd's plantation, it was very similar to that of the other slave children. I was not old enough to work in the field, and there being little else than field work to do, I had a great deal of leisure time. The most I had to do was to drive up the cows at evening, keep the fowls out of the garden, keep the front yard clean, and run of errands....

I was seldom whipped by my old master, and suffered little from any thing else than hunger and cold. I suffered much from hunger, but much more from cold. In hottest summer and coldest winter, I was kept almost naked—no shoes, no stockings, no jacket, no trousers, nothing on but a coarse tow linen shirt, reaching only to my knees. I had no bed. I must have perished with cold, but that, the coldest nights, I used to steal a bag which was used for carrying corn to the mill. I would crawl into this bag, and there sleep on the cold, damp, clay floor, with my head in and feet out. My feet have been so cracked with the frost, that the pen with which I am writing might be laid in the gashes.

We were not regularly allowanced. Our food was coarse corn meal boiled. This was called mush. It was put into a large wooden tray or trough, and set down upon the ground. The children were then called, like so many pigs, and like so many pigs they would come and devour the mush; some with oyster-shells, others with pieces of shingle, some with naked hands, and none with spoons. He that ate fastest got most; he that was strongest secured the best place; and few left the trough satisfied.

I was probably between seven and eight years old when I left Colonel Lloyd's plantation. I left it with joy.... The ties that ordinarily bind children to their homes were all suspended in my case. I found no severe trial in my departure. My home was charmless; it was not home to me; on parting from it, I could not feel that I was leaving any thing which I could have enjoyed by staying. My mother was dead, my grandmother lived far off, so that I seldom saw her. I had two sisters and one brother, that lived in the same house with me; but the early separation of us from our mother had well nigh blotted the fact of our relationship from our memories. I looked for home elsewhere, and was confident of finding none which I should relish less than the one which I was leaving. If, however, I found in my new home hardship, hunger, whipping, and nakedness, I had the consolation that I should not have escaped any one of them by staying.

Close Reading Questions:

1. According to Douglass, when an African-American slave has been fathered by a "white" master, what are some of the terrible effects on many members of this family?

2. How does Douglass argue that the Biblical defense of slavery was becoming obsolete in the nineteenth century? (Historical Trends)

3. Douglass calls attention to his own literacy when he refers to "the pen with which I am writing" later as an adult. With specific references to the text, what do you consider to be some of Douglass's most eloquent descriptions? What effect do they have on you and why?

Analytical Writing/Discussion:

4. As Douglass describes the horrors of slavery, he portrays some situations in very graphic detail. With what details do you think he convinced his nineteenth-century Northern readers of the horrors of slavery, and what details do you think might have overwhelmed some of them? (Multiple Perspectives)

5. Douglass portrays himself as a child denied basic knowledge and material comforts that most Americans now take for granted. What effects do you think Douglass's description of these deprivations might have had on his diverse readers, including those who opposed slavery as well as those who supported it?

6. Many eighteenth- and nineteenth-century defenders of slavery referred to this ownership of one person by another as the "benign institution," one that helped rather than harmed Africans by supposedly civilizing them. Based on your knowledge of the nineteen-century ideal of the family from reading Hareven's "Retreat," how do you think Douglass uses his readers' beliefs about family—the desired relationships between mothers, fathers, and children—to challenge the allegedly "benign institution" of slavery? (Cultural Influences)

Further Options:

7. As explained in Chapter 6 on Argument, a speaker or writer almost always tries to appeal to some of the values of the audience he or she is trying to persuade. Given your assumptions about Northern "white" Americans in the nineteenth century who read Douglass' autobiography, what values does Douglass portray to establish a bond with his audience?

8. Some literary scholars have worried that as Douglass wrote his autobiography, he became "enslaved" to the values of the readers he wanted to reach. For instance, a leading scholar of African-American literature named Houston Baker has voiced his concern that "Determined to move beyond subservient status, cut off from alternatives.... Douglass adopted a system of symbols that seemed to promise him an unbounded freedom." Why do you think that such assimilation can result in the destruction of an identity as much as the enrichment of one's sense of self?

THE REVOLT OF "MOTHER"

by Mary Wilkins Freeman

Mary Wilkins Freeman was a prolific writer of thirteen novels and many more short stories. She struggled to support her family as her husband provided less and less. Once when her writing was praised by a critic, she modestly replied, "[I] wrote my little stories about the types [of people] I knew." In this short story published in 1891, Freeman demonstrates her knowledge of a hard-working nineteenth-century farm family through her use of a regional dialect and her portrayal of the complex relationship between "Father" and "Mother." This relationship changes, along with the names used to refer to these two characters, over the course of this story. Freeman received little acclaim as a writer during her lifetime, but contemporary critics have hailed her as much more than the author of "little stories."

"Father!"

"What is it?"

"What are them men diggin' over there in the field for?"

There was a sudden dropping and enlarging of the lower part of the old man's face, as if some heavy weight had settled therein; he shut his mouth tight and went on harnessing the great bay mare. He hustled the collar on to her neck with a jerk.

"Father!"

The old man slapped the saddle upon the mare's back.

"Look here, father, I want to know what them men are diggin' over in the field for, an' I'm goin' to know."

"I wish you'd go into the house, mother, an' 'tend to your own affairs," the old man said then. He ran his words together, and his speech was almost as inarticulate as a growl.

But the woman understood; it was her most native tongue. "I ain't goin' into the house till you tell me what them men are doin' over there in the field," said she.

Then she stood waiting. She was a small woman, short and straight-waisted like a child in her brown cotton gown. Her forehead was mild and benevolent between the smooth curves of gray hair; there were meek downward lines about her nose and mouth; but her eyes, fixed upon the old man, looked as if the meekness had been the result of her own will, never of the will of another.

They were in the barn, standing before the wide open doors. The spring air, full of the smell of growing grass and unseen blossoms, came in their faces. The deep yard in front was littered with farm wagons and piles of wood; on the edges, close to the fence and the house, the grass was a vivid green, and there were some dandelions.

The old man glanced doggedly at his wife as he tightened the last buckles on the harness. She looked as immovable to him as one of the rocks in his pasture-land, bound to the earth with generations of blackberry vines. He slapped the reins over the horse and started forth from the barn.

"Father!" said she.

The old man pulled up. "What is it?"

"I want to know what them men are diggin' over there in that field for."

"They're diggin' a cellar, I s'pose, if you've got to know."

"A cellar for what?"

"A barn."

"A barn? You ain't goin' to build a barn over there where we was goin' to have a house, father?"

The old man said not another word. He hurried the horse into the farm wagon and clattered out of the yard, jouncing as sturdily on his seat as a boy.

The woman stood a moment looking after him, then she went out of the barn across a corner of the yard to the house. The house, standing at right angles with the great barn and a long reach of sheds and out-buildings, was infinitesimal compared with them. It was scarcely as commodious for people as the little boxes under the barn eaves were for doves.

A pretty girl's face, pink and delicate as a flower, was looking out of one of the house windows. She was watching three men who were digging over in the field which bounded the yard near the road line. She turned quietly when the woman entered.

"What are they digging for, mother?" said she. "Did he tell you?"

"They're diggin' for—a cellar for a new barn."

"Oh, mother, he ain't going to build another barn?"

"That's what he says."

A boy stood before the kitchen glass combing his hair. He combed slowly and painstakingly, arranging his brown hair in a smooth hillock over his forehead. He did not seem to pay any attention to the conversation.

"Sammy, did you know father was going to build a new barn?" asked the girl.

The boy combed assiduously.

"Sammy!"

He turned and showed a face like his father's under his smooth crest of hair. "Yes, I s'pose I did," he said, reluctantly.

"How long have you known it?" asked his mother.

"'Bout three months, I guess."

"Why didn't you tell of it?"

"Didn't think 'twould do no good."

"I don't see what father wants another barn for," said the girl, in her sweet, slow voice. She turned again to the window and stared out at the digging men in the field. Her tender, sweet face was full of a gentle distress. Her forehead was as bald and innocent as a baby's, with the light hair strained back from it in a row of curl-papers. She was quite large, but her soft curves did not look as if they covered muscles.

Her mother looked sternly at the boy. "Is he goin' to buy more cows?" said she.

The boy did not reply; he was tying his shoes.

"Sammy, I want you to tell me if he's goin' to buy more cows."

"I s'pose he is."

"How many?"

"Four, I guess."

The girl went to the sink and began to wash the dishes that were piled up there. Her mother came promptly out of the pantry and shoved her aside. "You wipe 'em," said she; "I'll wash. There's a good many this mornin'."

The mother plunged her hands vigorously into the water, the girl wiped the plates slowly and dreamily. "Mother," said she, "don't you think it's too bad father's going to build that new barn, much as we need a decent house to live in?"

Her mother scrubbed a dish fiercely. "You ain't found out yet we're women-folks, Nanny Penn," said she. "You ain't seen enough of men-folks yet to. One of these days you'll find it out, an' then you'll know that we know only what men-folks think we do, so far as any use of it goes, an' how we'd ought to reckon men-folks in with Providence an' not complain of what they do any more than we do of the weather."

"I don't care; I don't believe George is anything like that, anyhow," said Nanny. Her delicate face flushed pink, her lips pouted softly, as if she were going to cry.

"You wait an' see. I guess George Eastman ain't no better than other men. You hadn't ought to judge father, though. He can't help it, 'cause he don't look at things jest the way we do. An' we've been pretty comfortable here, after all. The roof don't leak—ain't never but once—that's one thing. Father's kept it shingled right up."

"I do wish we had a parlor."

"I guess it won't hurt George Eastman any to come to see you in a nice clean kitchen. I guess a good many girls don't have as good a place as this. Nobody's ever heard me complain."

"I ain't complained either, mother."

"Well, I don't think you'd better, a good father an' a good home as you've got. S'pose your father made you go out an' work for your livin'? Lots of girls have to that ain't no stronger an' better able to than you be."

Sarah Penn washed the frying pan with a conclusive air. She scrubbed the outside of it as faithfully as the inside. She was a masterly keeper of her box of a house. Her one living-room never seemed to have in it any of the dust which the friction of life with inanimate matter produces. She swept, and there seemed to be no dirt to go before the broom; she cleaned, and one could see no difference. She was like an artist so perfect that he has apparently no art. Today she got out a mixing bowl and a board and rolled some pies, and there was no more flour upon her than upon her daughter who was doing finer work. Nanny was to be married in the fall, and she was sewing on some white cambric and embroidery. She sewed industriously while her mother cooked, her soft milk-white hands and wrists showed whiter than her delicate work.

"We must have the stove moved out in the shed before long," said Mrs. Penn. "Talk about not havin' things, it's been a real blessin' to be able to put a stove up in that shed in hot weather. Father did one good thing when he fixed that stovepipe out there."

Sarah Penn's face as she rolled her pies had that expression of meek vigor which might have characterized one of the New Testament saints. She was making mince pies. Her husband, Adoniram Penn, liked them better than any other kind. She baked twice a week. Adoniram often liked a piece of pie between meals. She hurried this morning. It had been later than usual when she began, and she wanted to have a pie baked for dinner. However deep a resentment she might be forced to hold against her husband, she would never fail in sedulous attention to his wants.

Nobility of character manifests itself at loopholes when it is not provided with large doors. Sarah Penn's showed itself today in flaky dishes of pastry. So she made the pies faithfully, while across the table she could see, when she glanced up from her work, the sight that rankled in her patient and steadfast soul—the digging of the cellar of the new barn in the place where Adoniram forty years ago had promised her their new house should stand.

The pies were done for dinner. Adoniram and Sammy were home a few minutes after twelve o'clock. The dinner was eaten with serious haste. There was never much conversation at the table in the Penn family. Adoniram asked a blessing, and they ate promptly, then rose up and went about their work.

Sammy went back to school, taking soft sly lopes out of the yard like a rabbit. He wanted a game of marbles before school and feared his father would give him some chores to do. Adoniram hastened to the door and called after him, but he was out of sight.

"I don't see what you let him go for, mother," said he. "I wanted him to help me unload that wood."

Adoniram went to work out in the yard unloading wood from the wagon. Sarah put away the dinner dishes, while Nanny took down her curl-papers and changed her dress. She was going down to the store to buy some more embroidery and thread.

When Nanny was gone, Mrs. Penn went to the door. "Father!" she called.

"Well, what is it!"

"I want to see you jest a minute, father."

"I can't leave this wood nohow. I've got to git it unloaded an' go for a load of gravel afore two o'clock. Sammy had ought to helped me. You hadn't ought to let him go to school so early."

"I want to see you jest a minute."

"I tell ye I can't, nohow, mother."

"Father, you come here." Sarah Penn stood in the door like a queen; she held her head as if it bore a crown; there was the patience which makes authority royal in her voice. Adoniram went.

Mrs. Penn led the way into the kitchen and pointed to a chair. "Sit down, father," said she; "I've got somethin' I want to say to you."

He sat down heavily; his face was quite stolid, but he looked at her with restive eyes. "Well, what is it, mother?"

"I want to know what you're buildin' that new barn for, father?"

"I ain't got nothin' to say about it."

"It can't be you think you need another barn?"

"I tell ye I ain't got nothin' to say about it, mother; an' ain't goin' to say nothin'."

"Be you goin' to buy more cows?"

Adoniram did not reply; he shut his mouth tight.

"I know you be, as well as I want to. Now, father, look here"—Sarah Penn had not sat down; she stood before her husband in the humble fashion of a Scripture woman—"I'm goin' to talk real plain to you; I never have sence I married you, but I'm goin' to now. I ain't never complained, an' I ain't goin' to complain now, but I'm goin' to talk plain. You see this room here, father; you look at it well. You see there ain't no carpet on the floor, an' you see the paper is all dirty, an' droppin' off the walls. We ain't had no new paper on it for ten years, an' then I put it on myself, an' it didn't cost but ninepence a roll. You see this room, father; it's all the one I've had to work in an' eat in an' sit in sence we was married. There ain't another woman in the whole town whose husband ain't got half the means you have but what's got better. It's all the room Nanny's got to have her company in; an' there ain't one of her mates but what's got better, an' their fathers not so able as hers is. It's all the room she'll have to be married in. What would you have thought, father, if we had had our weddin' in a room no better than this? I was married in my mother's parlor with a carpet on the floor, an' stuffed furniture, an' a mahogany card-table. An' this is all the room my daughter will have to be married in. Look here, father!"

Sarah Penn went across the room as though it were a tragic stage. She flung open a door and disclosed a tiny bedroom, only large enough for a bed and bureau, with a path between. "There, father," said she—"there's all the room I've had to sleep in forty years. All my children were born there—the two that died, an' the two that's livin'. I was sick with a fever there."

She stepped to another door and opened it. It led into the small, ill-lighted pantry. "Here," said she, "is all the buttery I've got—every place I've got for my dishes, to set away my victuals in, an' to keep my milk-pans in. Father. I've been takin' care of the milk of six cows in this place, an' now you're goin' to build a new barn, an' keep more cows, an' give me more to do in it."

She threw open another door. A narrow crooked flight of stairs wound upward from it. "There, father," said she, "I want you to look at the stairs that go up to them two unfinished chambers that are all the places our son an' daughter have had to sleep in all their lives. There ain't a prettier girl in town nor a more ladylike one than Nanny, an' that's the place she has to sleep in. It ain't so good as your horse's stall; it ain't so warm an' tight."

Sarah Penn went back and stood before her husband. "Now, father," said she, "I want to know if you think you're doin' right an' accordin' to what you profess. Here, when we was married, forty years ago, you promised me faithful that we should have a new house built in that lot over in the field before the year was out. You said you had money enough, an' you wouldn't ask me to live in no such place as this. It is forty years now, an' you've been makin' more money, an' I've been savin' of it for you ever since, an' you ain't built no house yet. You've built sheds an' cow-houses an' one new barn, an' now you're goin' to build another. Father, I want to know if you think it's right. You're lodgin' your dumb beasts better than you are your own flesh an' blood. I want to know if you think it's right."

"I ain't got nothin' to say."

"You can't say nothin' without ownin' it ain't right, father. An' there's another thing—I ain't complained; I've got along forty years, an' I s'pose I should forty more, if it wa'n't for that—if we don't have another house. Nanny she can't live with us after she's married. She'll have to go somewheres else to live away from us, an' it don't seem as if I could have it so, noways, father. She wa'n't ever strong. She's got considerable color, but there wa'n't ever any backbone to her. I've always took the heft of everything off her, an' she ain't fit to keep house an' do everything herself. She'll be all worn out inside of a year. Think of her doin' all the washin' an' ironin' an' bakin' with them soft white hands an' arms, an' sweepin'! I can't have it so, noways, father."

Mrs. Penn's face was burning; her mild eyes gleamed. She had pleaded her little cause like a Webster; she had ranged from severity to pathos; but her opponent employed that obstinate silence which makes eloquence futile with mocking echoes. Adoniram arose clumsily.

"Father, ain't you got nothin' to say?" said Mrs. Penn.

"I've got to go off after that load of gravel. I can't stan' here talkin' all day."

"Father, won't you think it over, an' have a house built there instead of a barn?"

"I ain't got nothin' to say."

Adoniram shuffled out....

Nanny came home with her embroidery and sat down with her needlework. She had taken down her curl-papers, and there was a soft roll of fair hair like an aureole over her forehead; her face was as delicately fine and clear as porcelain. Suddenly she looked up, and the tender red flamed all over her face and neck. "Mother," said she.

"What say?"

"I've been thinking—I don't see how we're goin' to have any—wedding in this room. I'd be ashamed to have his folks come if we didn't have anybody else."

"Mebbe we can have some new paper before then; I can put it on. I guess you won't have no call to be ashamed of your belongin's."

"We might have the wedding in the new barn," said Nanny, with gentle pettishness. "Why, mother, what makes you look so?"

Mrs. Penn had started and was staring at her with a curious expression. She turned again to her work and spread out a pattern carefully on the cloth. "Nothin'," said she.

Presently Adoniram clattered out of the yard in his two-wheeled dump cart, standing as proudly upright as a Roman charioteer. Mrs. Penn opened the door and stood there a minute looking out....

The barn was all completed ready for use by the third week in July. Adoniram had planned to move his stock in on Wednesday; on Tuesday he received a letter which changed his plans. He came in with it early in the morning. "Sammy's been to the post office," said he, "an' I've got a letter from Hiram." Hiram was Mrs. Penn's brother, who lived in Vermont.

"Well," said Mrs. Penn, "what does he say about the folks?"

"I guess they're all right. He says he thinks if I come up country right off there's a chance to buy jest the kind of a horse I want." He stared reflectively out of the window at the new barn.

Mrs. Penn was making pies. She went on clapping the rolling-pin into the crust, although she was very pale, and her heart beat loudly.

"I dun' know but what I'd better go," said Adoniram. "I hate to go off jest now, right in the midst of hayin', but the ten-acre lot's cut, an' I guess Rufus an' the others can git along without me three or four days. I can't get a horse round here to suit me, nohow, an' I've got to have another for all that wood-haulin' in the fall. I told Hiram to watch out, an' if he got wind of a good horse to let me know. I guess I'd better go."

"I'll get out your clean shirt an' collar," said Mrs. Penn calmly.

She laid out Adoniram's Sunday suit and his clean clothes on the bed in the little bedroom. She got his shaving-water and razor ready. At last she buttoned on his collar and fastened his black cravat.

Adoniram never wore his collar and cravat except on extra occasions. He held his head high, with a rasped dignity. When he was all ready, with his coat and hat brushed and a lunch of pie and cheese in a paper bag, he hesitated on the threshold of the door. He looked at his wife, and his manner was defiantly apologetic. "If them cows come today, Sammy can drive 'em into the new barn," said he; "an' when they bring the hay up, they can pitch it in there."

"Well," replied Mrs. Penn.

Adoniram set his shaven face ahead and started. When he had cleared the doorstep, he turned and looked back with a kind of nervous solemnity. "I shall be back by Saturday if nothin' happens," said he.

"Do be careful, father," returned his wife.

She stood in the door with Nanny at her elbow and watched him out of sight. Her eyes had a strange, doubtful expression in them; her peaceful forehead was contracted. She went in, and about her baking again. Nanny sat sewing. Her wedding day was drawing nearer, and she was getting pale and thin with her steady sewing. Her mother kept glancing at her.

"Have you got that pain in your side this mornin'?" she asked.

"A little."

Mrs. Penn's face, as she worked, changed, her perplexed forehead smoothed, her eyes were steady, her lips firmly set. She formed a maxim for herself, although incoherently with her unlettered thoughts. "Unsolicited opportunities are the guideposts of the Lord to the new roads of life," she repeated in effect, and she made up her mind to her course of action.

"S'posin' I had wrote to Hiram," she muttered once, when she was in the pantry—"s'posin' I had wrote, an' asked him if he knew of any horse? But I didn't, an' father's goin' wa'n't none of my doin'. It looks like a providence." Her voice rang out quite loud at the last.

"What you talkin' about, mother?" called Nanny.

"Nothin'."

Mrs. Penn hurried her baking; at eleven o'clock it was all done. The load of hay from the west field came slowly down the cart track and drew up at the new barn. Mrs. Penn ran out. "Stop!" she screamed—"stop!"

The men stopped and looked; Sammy upreared from the top of the load and stared at his mother.

"Stop!" she cried out again. "Don't you put the hay in that barn; put it in the old one."

"Why, he said to put it in here," returned one of the hay-makers, wonderingly. He was a young man, a neighbor's son, whom Adoniram hired by the year to help on the farm.

"Don't you put the hay in the new barn; there's room enough in the old one, ain't there?" said Mrs. Penn.

"Room enough," returned the hired man, in his thick, rustic tones. "Didn't need the new barn, nohow, far as room's concerned. Well, I s'pose he changed his mind." He took hold of the horses' bridles.

Mrs. Penn went back to the house. Soon the kitchen windows were darkened, and a fragrance like warm honey came into the room.

Nanny laid down her work. "I thought father wanted them to put the hay into the new barn?" she said, wonderingly.

"It's all right," replied her mother.

Sammy slid down from the load of hay and came in to see if dinner was ready.

"I ain't goin' to get a regular dinner today, as long as father's gone," said his mother. "I've let the fire go out. You can have some bread an' milk an' pie. I thought we could get along." She set out some bowls of milk, some bread, and a pie on the kitchen table. "You'd better eat your dinner now," said she. "You might jest as well get through with it. I want you to help me afterward."

Nanny and Sammy stared at each other. There was something strange in their mother's manner. Mrs. Penn did not eat anything herself. She went into the pantry, and they heard her moving dishes while they ate. Presently she came out with a pile of plates. She got the clothes basket out of the shed and packed them in it. Nanny and Sammy watched. She brought out cups and saucers and put them in with the plates.

"What you goin' to do, mother?" inquired Nanny, in a timid voice. A sense of something unusual made her tremble, as if it were a ghost. Sammy rolled his eyes over his pie.

"You'll see."....

At five o'clock in the afternoon, the little house in which the Penns had lived for forty years had emptied itself into the new barn.

Every builder builds somewhat for unknown purposes and is in a measure a prophet. The architect of Adoniram Penn's barn, while he designed it for the comfort of four-footed animals, had planned better than he knew for the comfort of humans. Sarah Penn saw at a glance its possibilities. These great box-stalls, with quilts hung before them, would make better bedrooms than the one she had occupied for forty years, and there was a tight carriage-room. The harness-room, with its chimney and shelves, would make a kitchen of her dreams. The great middle space would make a parlor, by and by, fit for a palace. Upstairs there was as much room as down. With partitions and windows, what a house would there be! Sarah looked at the row of stanchions before the allotted space for cows and reflected that she would have her front entry there.

At six o'clock the stove was up in the harness-room, the kettle was boiling, and the table set for tea. It looked almost as home-like as the abandoned house across the yard had ever done. The young hired man milked, and Sarah directed him calmly to bring the milk to the new barn. He came gaping, dropping little blots of foam from the brimming pails on the grass. Before the next morning, he had spread the story of Adoniram Penn's wife moving into the new barn all over the little village. Men assembled in the store and talked it over, women with shawls over their heads scuttled into each other's houses before their work was done. Any deviation from the ordinary course of life in this quiet town was enough to stop all progress in it. Everybody paused to look at the staid, independent figure on the side track. There was a difference of opinion with regard to her. Some held her to be insane; some, of a lawless and rebellious spirit.

Friday, the minister went to see her. It was in the forenoon, and she was at the barn door shelling peas for dinner. She looked up and returned his salutation with dignity, then she went on with her work. She did not invite him in. The saintly expression of her face remained fixed, but there was an angry flush over it.

The minister stood awkwardly before her and talked. She handled the peas as if they were bullets. At last she looked up, and her eyes showed the spirit that her meek front had covered for a lifetime.

"There ain't no use talkin', Mr. Hersey," said she. "I've thought it all over an' over, an' I believe I'm doin' what's right. I've made it the subject of prayer, an' it's betwixt me an' the Lord an' Adoniram. There ain't no call for nobody else to worry about it."

"Well, of course, if you have brought it to the Lord in prayer and feel satisfied that you are doing right, Mrs. Penn," said the minister, helplessly. His thin gray-bearded face was pathetic. He was a sickly man; his youthful confidence had cooled; he had to scourge himself up to some of his pastoral duties as relentlessly as a Catholic ascetic, and then he was prostrated by the smart.

"I think it's right jest as much as I think it was right for our forefathers to come over from the old country 'cause they didn't have what belonged to 'em," said Mrs. Penn. She arose. The barn threshold might have been Plymouth Rock from her bearing. "I don't doubt you mean well, Mr. Hersey," said she, "but there are things people hadn't ought to interfere with. I've been a member of the church for over forty years. I've got my own mind an' my own feet, an' I'm goin' to think my own thoughts an' go my own ways, an' nobody but the Lord is goin' to dictate to me unless I've a mind to have him. Won't you come in an' set down? How is Mis' Hersey?"

"She is well, I thank you," replied the minister. He added some more perplexed apologetic remarks; then he retreated.

Towards sunset on Saturday, when Adoniram was expected home, there was a knot of men in the road near the new barn. The hired man had milked, but he still hung around the premises. Sarah Penn had supper all ready. There were brown bread and baked beans and a custard pie; it was the supper Adoniram loved on a Saturday night. She had a clean calico, and she bore herself imperturbably. Nanny and Sammy kept close at her heels. Their eyes were large, and Nanny was full of nervous tremors. Still there was to them more pleasant excitement than anything else. An inborn confidence in their mother over their father asserted itself.

Sammy looked out of the harness-room window. "There he is," he announced, in an awed whisper. He and Nanny peeped around the casing. Mrs. Penn kept on about her work. The children watched Adoniram leave the new horse standing in the drive while he went to the house door. It was fastened. Then he went around to the shed. That door was seldom locked, even when the family was away. The thought of how her father would be confronted by the cow flashed upon Nanny. There was a hysterical sob in her throat. Adoniram emerged from the shed and stood looking about in a dazed fashion. His lips moved; he was saying something, but they could not hear what it was. The hired man was peeping around a corner of the old barn, but nobody saw him.

Adoniram took the new horse by the bridle and led him across the yard to the new barn. Nanny and Sammy slunk close to their mother. The barn doors rolled back, and there stood Adoniram, with the long mild face of the great Canadian farm horse looking over his shoulder.

Nanny kept behind her mother, but Sammy stepped suddenly forward and stood in front of her.

Adoniram stared at the group. "What on airth you all down here for?" said he. "What's the matter over to the house?"

"We've come here to live, father," said Sammy. His shrill voice quavered out bravely.

"What"—Adoniram sniffed—"what is it smells like cookin'?" said he. He stepped forward and looked in the open door of the harness-room. Then he turned to his wife. His old bristling face was pale and frightened. "What on airth does this mean, mother?" he gasped.

"You come in here, father," said Sarah. She led the way into the harness-room and shut the door. "Now, father," said she, "you needn't be scared. I ain't crazy. There ain't nothin' to be upset over. But we've come here to live, an' we're goin' to live here. We've got jest as good a right here as new horses an' cows. The house wa'n't fit for us to live in any longer, an' I made up my mind I wa'n't goin' to stay there. I've done my duty by you forty years, an' I'm goin' to do it now; but I'm goin' to live here. You've got to put in some windows and partitions, an' you'll have to buy some furniture."

"Why, mother!" the old man gasped.

"You'd better take your coat off an' get washed—there's the washbasin—an' then we'll have supper."

"Why, mother!"

Sammy went past the window, leading the new horse to the old barn. The old man saw him and shook his head speechlessly. He tried to take off his coat, but his arms seemed to lack the power. His wife helped him. She poured some water into the tin basin and put in a piece of soap. She got the comb and brush and smoothed his thin gray hair after he had washed. Then she put the beans, hot bread, and tea on the table. Sammy came in, and the family drew up. Adoniram sat looking dazedly at his plate, and they waited.

"Ain't you goin' to ask a blessin', father?" said Sarah.

And the old man bent his head and mumbled.

All through the meal he stopped eating at intervals and stared furtively at his wife, but he ate well. The home food tasted good to him, and his old frame was too sturdily healthy to be affected by his mind. But after supper he went out and sat down on the step of the smaller door at the right of the barn, through which he had meant his Jerseys to pass in stately file, but which Sarah designed for her front house door, and he leaned his head on his hands.

After the supper dishes were cleared away and the milk-pans washed, Sarah went out to him. The twilight was deepening. There was a clear green glow in the sky. Before them stretched the smooth level of field; in the distance was a cluster of haystacks like the huts of a village; the air was very cool and calm and sweet. The landscape might have been an ideal one of peace.

Sarah bent over and touched her husband on one of his thin, sinewy shoulders. "Father!"

The old man's shoulders heaved: he was weeping.

"Why, don't do so, father," said Sarah.

"I'll—put up the—partitions, an'—everything you—want, mother."

Sarah put her apron up to her face; she was overcome by her own triumph.

Adoniram was like a fortress whose walls had no active resistance and went down the instant the right besieging tools were used. "Why, mother," he said, hoarsely, "I hadn't no idee you was so set on't as all this comes to."

Close Reading Questions:

1. As you read, notice when and how each family member learns of Adoniram Penn's decision to build a new barn. What do you think each member's knowledge of the new barn suggests about his or her position in this family?

2. Throughout this story, Sarah Penn and her husband Adoniram each repeat several phrases as they converse. What is a phrase each one of these married characters repeats, and what do you think these phrases reveal about each person and their marriage?

3. Note the various reactions by Sarah's neighbors to her decision to move. What do you think the responses of the hired man, the minister, and other townspeople reveal about their expectations for nineteenth-century fathers and mothers?

Analytical Writing/Discussion:

4. As Sarah discusses men's knowledge and later Hiram's letter, she refers to "Providence," the biblical belief in divine aid for certain individuals. Using these references to Providence, what do you think is Sarah's attitude toward male authority and her decision to move? (Cultural Influences)

5. Both the title and the opening scene of the story refer to "mother." Only later does the story refer to the main character and her husband by their married names: Mrs. and Mr. Penn and then by their first names: Sarah and Adoniram. Using specific references to both Freeman's story and the expected roles in nineteenth-century families, what do you think this progression of names suggests?

6. As twenty-first-century readers of Freeman's story, many of us may be tempted to read this story as an absolute rebellion by a wife against her husband. However, when Adoniram returns, Sarah has prepared one of his favorite meals. Considering the words and deeds of each family member, what are some of the different ways to interpret the final scene, and how can you defend the interpretation you prefer? (Multiple Perspectives)

Further Options:

7. As Hareven explains in "The Nineteenth-Century Retreat" (see pp. 167–174), sons and daughters usually were raised to fulfill very different family roles in this era. In what ways are Nanny and Sammy being raised to become the traditional mothers and fathers of nineteenth-century families? Then, using specific references to the text, why do you think each child will or will not fulfill these gender-specific family roles? (Historical Trends)

8. As a relatively long short story, "The Revolt" has many detailed and sometimes ambiguous scenes. Using the double-entry notes described in Chapter 3 on Reading, select three or four of the key passages of this story, and explain each one to a classmate.

Freewrite 2: Past and Present

As this chapter's readings shift from historical texts to more recent ones, your instructor may ask you to pause and connect your own family to some of the historical trends that may have shaped your family's form and its members' roles.

Using one or more of the images of your own family from Freewrite 1, can you now place that family scene(s) in the context of the nineteenth century? In what ways and to what degree does your family conform to or diverge from the typical family of nineteenth-century America?

Once you have completed this freewrite, you may want to expand this rough writing into a more formal paper with some direct quotations from some of the historical texts by Hareven, Douglass, and Freeman.

PARENTING 101: CONSERVATIVE CHRISTIANS ON CHILDREARING

by John P. Bartkowski and Christopher Ellison

In 1979, a new conservative Christian group emerged as a powerful social and political force in the United States. Known as the Moral Majority, this conservative Christian group opposed abortion and homosexuality in favor of the "traditional" family. This advocacy group demonstrated its political muscle when it helped the 1980 Republican candidate, Ronald Reagan, defeat the incumbent, President Jimmy Carter. Although other conservative Christian groups like Focus on the Family have since eclipsed the Moral Majority, their views on family structure and child rearing continue to influence many Americans. In the following text, two sociologists contrast the child-raising practices of conservative Protestants with those of "mainstream" parents. Written by and for academics, this abridged article from 1995 draws sharp contrasts.

By John P. Bartowski and Christopher Ellison, "Divergent Models of Childrearing in Popular Manuals: Conservative Protestants Vs. the Mainstream Experts," in *Sociology of Religion*, Volume 56, Number 1 (Spring 1995) Pages 21–34. By permission of Oxford University Press.

Contemporary conflicts over the American family have attracted widespread popular commentary and academic research (Thorne and Yalom 1982; Berger and Berger 1983; Dornbusch and Strober 1988; Stacey 1990; Faludi 1991; Hunter 1991). To date, however, these and other social scientists have constructed the "battle over the family" almost exclusively in terms of debates regarding gender roles. Indeed, many have dismissed other dimensions of this conflict, including conflicts over parenting issues, asserting that they are insignificant and obfuscatory. For instance, Cohen and Katzenstein (1988) put the matter bluntly: "The debate [over the family] is fundamentally about the places in society of men and women. The discourse about what is good for children is *simply not so polarized ...*," (p. 25, emphasis added).

While we readily grant the importance of ongoing debates over gender roles, we also believe that disagreements over parent–child relations are much more fundamental and significant than previous discussions have recognized. A sharply polemical literature on parenting surfaced within conservative Protestant circles in the 1970s, extolling the virtues of "traditional" parenting techniques and challenging the views of mainstream experts. Since that time, sales of popular literature on "Christian" (generally conservative Protestant) parenting have mushroomed, and the core themes of this parenting ideology have been widely circulated via broadcast media and organizations devoted to family issues, such as Focus on the Family. Conservative Protestant writers and commentators have clearly emerged as the leading spokespersons for "traditional" hierarchical child-rearing practices.

Our study explores this conservative Protestant parenting ideology in greater detail. We argue that the parenting ideas embraced by many conservative Protestant writers are legitimated via two related theological tenets.... Our analysis suggests that conservative Protestant parenting specialists part company with their mainstream counterparts in four key areas: (1) long-term parenting goals; (2) the structure of parent–child relations; (3) the definition of parental roles; and (4) strategies of child discipline and punishment....

For mainstream and conservative Protestant specialists alike, we have focused primarily on the writings of the most prominent, best-selling child-rearing experts, as determined via sales figures and interviews with publishers' representatives.... Because we are primarily interested in the differences between conservative Protestant and mainstream parenting ideologies, our discussion necessarily downplays the inevitable heterogeneity within these camps.... Our goal is to distinguish the common parenting prescriptions and shared presuppositions of conservative Protestant writers from those of mainstream experts....

Divergent Models of Parenting: Long-Term Goals

What constitutes successful parenting? Mainstream and conservative Protestant advice manuals emphasize strikingly different outcomes. Almost without exception, leading mainstream writers focus on "healthy" personality development and social competence. Most mainstream parenting manuals underscore the importance of helping children develop desirable personality profiles: self-esteem, self-confidence, self-discipline, creativity, and intellectual curiosity. According to Lawrence Balter, the parent must be careful to foster "mastery, self-respect, and hopefulness ... [based on] a loving relationship in which empathy and support are the central motifs" (1989:36). Although it is recognized that parents must elicit compliance from youngsters in various settings, they are strongly urged to refrain from employing any child-rearing or disciplinary techniques that might undermine the development of these personality traits in their children.

...Many mainstream parenting specialists [also] stress the importance of teaching empathy and verbal communication skills. For instance, Balter (1989:85–6) suggests that teaching empathy to toddlers reduces parent–child conflicts, allows the child to become more considerate of the needs and desires of others, and promotes self-control and self-discipline. LeShan (1985:106–08) recommends that parents should teach their children to interpret the moods and actions of others effectively, because this will foster greater tolerance of human frailty. Taken together, the interrelated social skills of empathy and communication help children to create a common understanding between two interacting individuals—the very definition of a "healthy" relationship.

Although most conservative Protestant specialists grant the value of "healthy" personalities and social competence, these traits are not seen as the most important outcomes of successful parenting. Instead, conservative Protestant writers emphasize that to succeed in adult roles, children must be trained to embrace the divinely-ordained principles of authority and hierarchy. This emphasis on authority is vital because of the view that children are born with sinful natures, prone to challenge authority in all forms. Conservative Protestants contend that a child who is not taught to submit to familial authority (1) will not develop a respect for [superior] figures outside the family (e.g., teachers, employers, guardians), and (2) will be unable to exercise rightful authority when assuming a [superior] role in human relationships (e.g., as a father, parent, or employer).

Moreover, the kind of authority training advocated by conservative Protestant writers is also believed to convey a crucial spiritual lesson to children. According to these writers, Christian parents are responsible for leading their children toward righteousness and salvation. Given their belief that human nature is fundamentally sinful, conservative Protestants maintain that training children to submit their selfish desires to the will of God, the creator and supreme authority of the universe, is central to this project of salvation. In short, conservative Protestant parents are warned that abrogating their divinely ordained parenting responsibilities—i.e., failing to command respect from their child—may substantially decrease the likelihood that the developing youngster will be inclined to "humble" him/herself before the divine authority of God.

Parent-Child Relationships

Both mainstream and conservative Protestant parenting specialists strive for [consistency] between the structure of family life and the social order. Mainstream experts tend to view the family as a dynamic entity that changes in both form and content to mirror normative and organizational shifts in the broader society. In particular, many mainstream specialists believe that all human institutions—including the family—should be guided by democratic and egalitarian principles. Consequently, the dominant discourse in much of the mainstream literature centers on the "rights" and "interests" of family members. Most mainstream parenting manuals suggest that conflicts within the family should be resolved through negotiation and that ideal solutions to these conflicts are solutions that maximize the joint satisfaction of the conflicting parties....

In sharp contrast to the prevailing mainstream perspectives on the structure of parent–child relations, conservative Protestants view the family as an organic whole, rather than a compilation of potentially conflicting "rights" and "interests." Conservative Protestants assert the moral superiority of one "timeless," divinely ordained blueprint for parent–child relations, a model based on (and legitimated by) the biblical principles of authority and hierarchy that are articulated within contemporary literalist communities.

Not surprisingly, conservative Protestant parenting writers have reacted with alarm and hostility to calls for democracy within the family. Families, in their view, are characterized by specific sets of [superior] and subordinate roles. Conservative commentators cite an array of passages from Old and

New Testament sources underscoring the respective obligations of children and parents. Conservative Protestant writers frequently stress the imperative of intergenerational hierarchy within the family. They repeatedly exhort children to honor and obey parental authority, and they call attention to Old Testament writings that threaten disobedient children with familial and societal ostracism and even death. These conservative religious commentators also emphasize that parents are held strictly accountable for any deviations from biblical parenting guidelines....

Popular notions of children's "rights" especially rankle these conservative religious writers. As Dobson puts it, "I find no place in the Bible where our little ones are installed as co-discussants at a conference table, deciding what they will and will not accept from the older generation" (1978:170). Yet some religious writers appropriate the language of "rights" and "interests" in the service of conservative parenting ideals, countering that religious Scripture accords children the right to receive love, protection, religious training, and responsible leadership from their parents. These writers commonly contend that children, regardless of what they may say, actually want and expect these benefits from their parents and that these crucial children's rights are undermined by the egalitarian impulses of mainstream experts.

Further, conservative religious writers believe that popular democratic and egalitarian family models also have undesirable spiritual consequences. Virtually all of the Christian parenting specialists reviewed for this study claim that children develop their initial images of God based on the behavior of parents. This belief makes the preservation of hierarchical parent–child relations crucial. Those adults who opt for egalitarian households are denounced by conservative Protestant parenting specialists for abrogating their divinely ordained parental responsibilities and for sabotaging their youngsters' respect for parental, institutional, and (ultimately) divine authority.

Parental Roles

Perhaps the most common image of the ideal parent in mainstream parenting literature is that of the proactive tactician or manager. This ideal parent is knowledgeable about child development issues and consequently holds "reasonable" expectations of the child, consonant with the child's developmental stage. In addition, the ideal parent remains sensitive to the feelings of the child and permits him/her considerable latitude for the expression of these feelings. The mainstream literature emphasizes the importance of manipulating the child's environment in order (1) to minimize the potential for conflict between parents and child or between siblings, and (2) to facilitate the safe exploration of the physical and social world, thus building his/her self-esteem and self-confidence. The parent is advised to encourage desired behavior through love, praise, and various forms of positive reinforcement (hence the hackneyed phrase "catch 'em when they're doing good"). According to mainstream experts, competent parents plan lessons and games to communicate values and promote desired behavior, and they find ways to engage children in their own training whenever possible. Finally, the parent-as-tactician organizes household life in ways that maximize "win-win" situations among family members, instilling egalitarian values while carefully reconciling the needs and interests of various parties....

Although parenting advice has generally been directed toward mothers, on the assumption that they have primary responsibility for child care, mainstream experts have increasingly promoted ungendered parenting roles. It seems that a growing number of mainstream parenting manuals acknowledge that child rearing should be understood as a partnership between equals.... Some reason that these youngsters are better equipped to participate fully and successfully in a society experiencing slow but steady progress toward gender equality in the workplace, political arena, and other institutions. Like their mainstream counterparts, many conservative Protestant family experts urge parents to become knowledgeable about child rearing. However … Christian parents are encouraged to consult what is believed to be the most reliable parenting manual, the Bible. The lessons to be learned from Scripture apparently differ notably from the information conveyed by mainstream parenting experts.

While some conservative Protestant specialists occasionally acknowledge the value of parental cleverness, empathy, and communication…. Conservative Protestants are repeatedly advised to demonstrate firm leadership. Because children are perceived to be naturally sinful and rebellious, according to these specialists, the Christian parent should "shape the will," training the child to submit to authority figures. Parents are told to expect conflict and respond decisively, often with physical force, to the youngster's inevitable expressions of willful defiance. Dobson maintains that parents who shrink from this challenge will be hard-pressed to elicit obedience from their children thereafter.

Finally, unlike mainstream experts, conservative Protestant writers generally do not approve of ungendered parental roles…. They argue that the de-gendering of parental roles undermines the authority of the Bible as the word of God, because some scriptural passages place the father as the divinely ordained head and protector of the family The absence of a clear, biblically inspired gender hierarchy within the household is thought to undermine the child's ability to learn submission to authority…. Some worry that ungendered parental roles will erode the allegiance of youngsters to more traditional gender roles, thus exacerbating what they see as a societal devaluation of masculinity.

Discipline and Punishment

Central to the ongoing debate over parent–child relations are the sharp disagreements over appropriate strategies of discipline and punishment. Mainstream specialists overwhelmingly oppose the use of physical discipline. In place of corporal punishment, mainstream specialists advocate setting firm guidelines accompanied by various pragmatic disciplinary techniques, including combinations of positive reinforcement, logical consequences and/or natural consequences, time-outs, and empathetic communication and reasoning. Specialists who endorse these myriad strategies argue that they promote the internalization of moral judgment and self-discipline…. Harsh forms of punishment, including corporal punishment, are believed to inhibit parent–child communication and produce counterproductive degrees of guilt and aggression in youngsters.

In contrast to their mainstream counterparts, conservative Protestant parenting specialists strongly endorse the use of corporal punishment, albeit under specific conditions. In general, they recommend that physical punishment should be administered regularly: (1) on occasions of willful defiance to parental authority, (2) promptly after the defiant act, (3) with the use of a "rod," specifically designated for the purpose of physical chastisement, and (4) only to preadolescents.

Most conservative Protestant specialists support the use of corporal punishment for a variety of reasons. First, they believe that chastisement is commanded by Scripture. Indeed, they interpret some passages as indicating that chastisement is a sign of parental love and caring. Thus, in addition to serving as a behavioral corrective, corporal punishment is believed to promote youthful security by communicating both a deep concern for the child's welfare and an unswerving commitment to biblical principles.

Further, because children initially understand God in terms of parental images, conservative Protestants suggest that children will infer God's view of them based on the treatment they receive from their parents. These writers are quick to point out that parents should teach their children by example that God is loving, merciful, and forgiving. At the same time, however, because God's punishment of sin is understood as both inevitable and consistent, they also believe that parental discipline should embody these characteristics as well. Given such convictions, conservative Protestants argue that the experience of loving physical discipline helps the child to develop an appropriate, accurate image of God and underscores the importance of obedience to His authority. Thus, corporal punishment is believed to demonstrate to the young child that deviation from biblical principles will provoke consistent and inevitable reproof from authorities in this life and from God in the next....

Conclusion

...We began this study by noting that most previous analyses of the "battle over the family" have centered on the issue of gender roles and have given short shrift to debates over parenting. In contrast, we have argued that conflicts over parent–child relations should be viewed as a significant part of this contemporary cultural conflict....

A number of recent books by conservative luminaries suggest that various "threats" to the welfare of American children—ranging from drugs and "cults" to public school counseling programs—are emerging as potent themes in the current and future campaigns of New Christian Right groups. Thus, it is vitally important that sociologists of religion and the family explore these developments, and the ideologies that legitimate them, with care.

REFERENCES

Balter, L. (with A. Shreve). 1989. *Who's in control: Dr. Balter's guide to discipline without combat*. New York: Poseidon Press.

Berger, B., and P. L. Berger. 1983. *The war over the family*. Garden City, NY: Anchor Press/Doubleday.

Cohen, H. 1980. *Equal rights for children*. Totowa, NJ: Littlefield, Adams. and Co.

Cohen, S., and M. F. Katzenstein. 1988. The war over the family is not over the family. In *Feminism, children, and the new families*, edited by S. M. Dornbusch and M. Strober, 25–46. New York: Guilford Press.

Dobson, J. 1978. *The strong-willed child: Birth through adolescence*. Wheaton, IL: Living Books/Tyndale House.

Dornbusch, S., and M. Strober, eds. 1988. *Feminism, children, and the new families*. New York: Guilford Press.

Faludi, S. 1991. *Backlash: The undeclared war against American women*. New York: Basic Books.

Hunter, J. D. 1991. *Evangelicalism: The coming generation*. Chicago: University of Chicago Press.

LeShan, E. 1985. *When your child drives you crazy*. New York: St. Martin's Press.

Stacey, J. 1990. *Brave new families*. New York: Basic Books.

Thorne, B., and M. Yalom, eds. 1982. *Rethinking the family: Some feminist questions*. New York: Longman.

Wald, K. D., D. E. Owen, and S. S. Hill. 1989. Habits of the mind? The problem of authority in the New Christian Right. In *Religion and behavior in the United States*, edited by T. G. Jelen, 93–108. New York: Praeger.

Close Reading Questions:

1. Why do the authors of this sociological study believe the focus of family research should be expanded and to what new topic?

2. According to the authors, upon what biblical beliefs do the child-rearing practices of most conservative Protestants depend?

3. Although the authors want to focus on more than the gender-specific roles of parents, in what ways do the expected gender roles of parents differ between conservative Protestants and "mainstream" families? (Multiple Perspectives)

Analytical Writing/Discussion:

4. According to the authors, how do conservative Protestants' assumptions about hierarchical authority and human nature lead them to beliefs about the goals of parenting and relationships with children that diverge from "mainstream" views? (Cultural Influences)

5. If some of the child-rearing practices of conservative Protestants seem outdated to you, then in what historical period do you think these practices might belong? Why might these practices seem sensible to many Americans during this period? (Historical Trends)

6. Bartkowski and Ellison refer to parenting manuals by leading authors to create a sharp contrast between "mainstream" and conservative Protestant families. Using examples from your own childhood and/or families you know well, to what degree does your personal knowledge confirm, contradict, or complicate the researchers' conclusions about the differences between these two types of families?

Further Options:

7. The noted philosopher J. S. Mill once asserted that one who knows only his or her side of an argument knows little. What do you think he meant by this assertion, and can you apply it to the example of conservative Protestant and mainstream practices of child punishment? Using specific references to this text, can you explain why the "side" with which you do not agree believes its punishment practices are sensible and beneficial?

8. In Chapter 5 on Writing Assignments, the issue of the elaborate language of academic discourse is raised. Why do you think these sociologists use language like "establish a paradigm for social relationships that is generalized to other spheres, especially the family"? Why, in general, do you think that academics usually employ complicated language in their scholarly writing?

FINDING FAMILIES FOR AFRICAN AMERICAN CHILDREN: THE CHALLENGES OF TRANSRACIAL ADOPTION

by Susan Smith, Ruth McRoy, Madelyn Freundlich, and Joe Kroll of The Evan B. Donaldson Adoption Institute

According to the U.S. Department of Health and Human Services, nearly 500,000 children were in the foster care system in 2007. That same year, only 51,000 children left the public foster care system to join adoptive homes. The issue of race plays a salient role in the adoption process: African American children spend longer in foster care than other children and are adopted at lower rates than children of other races. In an effort to encourage the adoption of children of color, the Multiethnic Placement Act of 1994 prevents discrimination in the placement of children of color (with the exception of Native American children). The following policy paper, published by The Evan B. Donaldson Adoption Institute in 2008, examines the laws that affect the transracial adoption of African American children and the extent to which adoption across racial boundaries affects children and parents.

When children cannot grow up in their families of origin, adoption can provide new parents who can love and guide them through childhood and into adulthood. The benefits of adoption are well recognized; at the same time, it also can present complexities for children and their adoptive families that are not typically found in families of origin—issues related to separation and loss, belonging, and identity. Children may come to adoption from social, economic, and racial and cultural backgrounds that differ from those of their new parents. For many children who are adopted from a different racial or ethnic background and/or from countries other than the United States, these differences can be visibly evident.

Transracial adoption is generally defined as occurring when a child's race/ethnicity is different than that of both parents when a couple adopts or that of a single parent when only one adopts. Transracial adoption—which primarily involves White parents adopting children of color—has been the subject of discourse and debate for decades. In books, articles, and professional discussions for much of the past 50 years, it frequently has been portrayed in a polarizing manner, as either "good" or "bad" for children. The most intense discussion has centered on the placement of African American children with White parents. All sides lay claim to the "best interest of the child," with very different concepts of what that means.

In practice, transracial adoption is not inherently good or bad but, rather, is a practice that benefits some children who may not otherwise have families to raise them. At the same time, this practice clearly adds an additional layer of complexity to the issues dealt with by adoptive families. White parents adopting children of other racial or ethnic groups can provide excellent nurturance, but they need to address their sons' and daughters' racial/ethnic identity issues to fully meet their needs as they develop. Children's racial and ethnic needs and issues include the implications of the physical difference between children and parents, especially in relation to handling the reactions of others; the children's gaining understanding of and comfort with their own race/ethnicity; learning social skills to interact comfortably with peers; and learning coping skills to deal with discrimination. Adoption practitioners and policymakers therefore need to address some difficult questions relating to transracial adoption in order to best serve children and families.

The Historical Role of Race in African American Adoptions

Throughout most of the nineteenth century and beyond, transracial adoption in the United States rarely occurred and, as a result of racism institutionalized in law, it was illegal in many states. During this time, adoption was largely arranged informally and, to the extent that efforts were made to "match" children with adoptive families, religion was the most important criterion. By the mid-twentieth century, adoption had become the province of professional social workers, who assumed the responsibility for placing children. They utilized a wide range of criteria that were considered vital to a proper "match" in a social environment that required children and adoptive parents to share as many traits as possible, from physical appearance (including race) to religious and cultural background to potential talents. Within the context of the country's highly segregated social environment during the 1950s and

1960s—including antimiscegenation laws that prohibited interracial marriage—transracial adoption was rare (Freundlich, 2000).

Although there were a few transracial placements as early as the 1940s, the practice began in earnest in the 1960s as a result of two significant developments. First, the civil rights movement significantly altered societal views of racial relationships; as integration was embraced as an ideal in the 1960s, interest in transracial adoption began to grow. At the same time, changes occurred in the demographic profile of children available for adoption; that is, the number of healthy Caucasian infants relinquished for adoption began to decline as a result of changing attitudes about single parenting, the legalization of abortion, and the increased use of contraceptives. White couples continued to want to adopt, so a growing number began to seek biracial or minority infants. Adoption agencies, including some private ones that had previously discouraged the relinquishment of children of color, began to accept them for adoptive placement planning (Day, 1979), and they started being placed with White families.

From a historical perspective, racial matching has been the predominant practice. In 1958, the Adoption Standards of the Child Welfare League of America (CWLA), a national association of public and private child welfare agencies, suggested that in most cases, children with the same racial characteristics as their new parents would more easily be incorporated into the family. In the 1950s and into the 1960s, formal adoptions primarily involved the placement of White infants with White families. Stringent criteria were used to qualify parents seeking to adopt a healthy White infant, considered the "ideal adoptable child." If White couples did not qualify for such an infant (often as a result of parental age or number of children already in the home), some agencies considered the family for a "child with special needs," typically one who was Black, of mixed race, older, or with emotional, behavioral, or health issues (McRoy, 1989).

In 1968, the CWLA revised its Adoption Standards and incorporated transracial adoptions. The new standards stated that "in most communities, there are families who have the capacity to adopt a child whose racial background is different from their own. Such couples should be encouraged to consider such a child" (CWLA, 1968, p. 34). With greater acceptance of transracial adoptions, their numbers began to grow. By 1971, the number of transracially adopted Black children reportedly reached 2,574 (Simon & Altstein, 1987).

In 1972, as a result of concerns about the growing number of Black children being placed with White families, the National Association of Black Social Workers (NABSW) issued a position statement opposing transracial adoption. The NABSW stated that Black children "belong physically and psychologically and culturally in Black families where they receive the total sense of themselves and develop a sound projection of their future" (NABSW, 1972, pp. 2–3). African American leaders also expressed concern about limited efforts to recruit Black families to adopt these children. Despite the fact that Black children historically had been cared for within their families and communities and informally adopted at significant rates, agencies—which were primarily and often exclusively staffed by White caseworkers—seldom recruited from African American communities (Duncan, 2005). Concerns grew that many White workers "knew little about stable African American families or their potential as resources for the children" (Duncan, 2005, p. 2), and they assumed such families were either not available or were not interested in adopting (Sullivan, 1994).

The Impact of Transracial Adoption on Children of Color

Although he was not adopted, Barack Obama's struggle to come to terms with racial identity issues without close relationships with Black caring adults mirrors the emotional struggles of many transracially adopted individuals—though these experiences obviously vary. In describing his experience, he wrote:

Away from my mother, away from my grandparents, I was engaged in a fitful interior struggle. I was trying to raise myself to be a black man in America, and beyond the given of my appearance, no one around me seemed to know exactly what that meant. (Obama, 2004, p. 76)

Many transracially adopted individuals become highly competent in matters of race and successfully negotiate challenges regarding their racial identity and their place in the cultures of both their adoptive and birth families. Others deal with moderate difficulties that they are able to resolve as they achieve the developmental tasks of adolescence and adulthood. Yet others experience strong feelings of marginality and difficulties in self-acceptance that persist through childhood and into their later lives.

Transracially adopted children face challenges in coping with being "different." Coming to terms with a sense of difference is challenging for many adopted children in various areas of their lives and is compounded by transracial adoption. Research has not specifically addressed issues of color differences for Black children adopted from foster care, but the recent findings of a study of intercountry transracially adopted children (Juffer, 2006) shed light on transracially adopted children's perceptions. For example, based on parent reports, many of these children—particularly those with dark skin color—expressed the wish to be White....

Some studies have found transracially adopted children struggle more with acceptance and comfort with their physical appearance than do children placed in-race (Andujo, 1988; Kim, 1995). Although some children leave this feeling behind, many transracial adoptees continue to have a sense of difference into adulthood. Brooks and Barth (1999) studied 25-year-old adoptees and reported that about half of African American and Asian transracial adoptees expressed discomfort about their ethno-racial appearance. Feigelman (2000) found that appearance discomfort was linked with higher levels of adjustment difficulties in transracially adopted young adults.

Research and reports from transracially adopted adults indicate that the sense of physical difference is more intense for children of color growing up in homogeneous White communities. One Black man who grew up with White parents in a small Minnesota town described his pervasive feelings of difference while growing up: "I always felt like I had this 'A' on my forehead, this adoptee, that people could see from a far distance that I was different" (Clemetson & Nixon, 2006, p. A18). Feigelman (2000) found transracial adoptees—adopted in the early 1970s—who were raised in heavily White communities were twice as likely as adoptees living in racially mixed areas to feel discomfort with their appearance (51 percent versus 25 percent). Feigelman summarized his findings as follows:

One of the study's most striking findings showed that transracial adoptive parents' decisions on where to live had a substantial impact upon their children's adjustments. Transracial adoptive parents residing in predominately White communities tended to have adoptees who experienced more discomfort about their appearance than those who lived in integrated settings. Adoptees feeling more discomfort, in turn, were more likely to have adjustment difficulties. (p. 180)

Transracially adopted children often struggle to fit in— within their own families, their social environments, and their cultures of origin.... In a study by de Haymes and Simon (2003), transracially adopted youth described their struggles to "fit in" and their beliefs about the importance of addressing this issue:

If we lived in a different neighborhood, I'd feel more comfortable. People wouldn't ask so many questions or call me names. I feel a little more comfortable around people who are my color because I know they won't call me names. (p. 261)

Reports from transracial adoptees at times describe struggles to feel a sense of belonging within their cultures of origin. A transracially adopted African American man interviewed for a *New York Times* story said he always felt awkward around other Blacks because he did not understand their culture, trends in fashion or music, activities (such as playing the dozens), or the Black oral tradition of dueling insults (Clemetson & Nixon, 2006). Having grown up in a small town in Minnesota, few people around him could help him develop an understanding of Black culture. Others who grew up in similar situations have reported that it was not until they went to college that they began to cultivate relationships with persons of their own race. John Raible (1990), a transracial adoptee, described his struggle:

> I got to know other middle-class black students as real people who were not that different from me. I began to appreciate the variety of ways of being black.... Yet all was not smooth sailing, by any means. I felt nervous and anxious around my new black friends and peers. I was self-conscious about sounding or acting 'too white.' I felt scrutinized for having white girlfriends, and continued to fret over being rejected and not being taken seriously as an equal.... When my parents would come to visit, I was self-conscious about being seen with them. I worried about being seen too often, or in the 'wrong' places, with my white friends. I was very aware of feeling caught between two cultures, of having to tread the line between two worlds.

Raible's experience illustrates the marginal man phenomenon experienced by those who are, to a large extent, caught between two cultures.

Transracially adopted children may struggle to develop a positive racial/ethnic identity. Racial/ethnic identity, a component of personal identity, develops over the course of childhood, adolescence, and early adulthood. It is linked to some extent with a child's cognitive abilities and developmental stage. Generally, by age 4, children are aware of physical racial differences, and, by age 9, they can see themselves through the eyes of others and understand the consequences of a particular racial group membership, including prejudice (Lee & Quintana, 2005). This process has particularly important implications for African American children for whom racial/ethnic identity is salient and closely tied to self-esteem (Phinney, 1991).

Research has focused on various constructs related to the ethnic/racial identity of transracially adopted persons, including self-identification, attitudes toward one's own group, a sense of belonging to a given group, a reference group orientation, and racial preferences. McRoy and colleagues conducted one of the few early studies that included measures of both self-esteem and racial identity for same-race and transracially adopted children (McRoy et al., 1982). Although the researchers found no significant differences between transracially and in-racially adopted children on self-esteem, they found transracially adopted children scored lower on racial identity measures than their in-race counterparts. They further found that the manner in which White parents addressed race was linked with the extent to which their children acknowledged racial differences. Black children had a greater sense of racial pride when their parents acknowledged racial identity, moved to integrated neighborhoods, and provided African American role models. Black children whose White parents minimized the importance of racial identity were reluctant to identity themselves racially. Eighty percent of the transracially adopted Black children had been told that "they were not like other Blacks" (McRoy et al., 1984, p. 38). Andujo (1988) found similar results in her study of 60 Mexican American children placed with Hispanic and White families....

Three critical areas of cultural competence for transracial adoptive parenting have been identified in professional literature: racial awareness, multicultural planning, and survival skills (Vonk, 2001). The following summary discusses each area and draws on comments from transracial adoptive parents and children asked about their service needs (de Haymes & Simon, 2003):

Racial awareness: This is defined as self-awareness of one's own experiences and attitudes regarding race and difference; awareness of the roles that race, ethnicity, and culture play in children's development; and understanding of the importance of these issues in fostering a child's positive identity development.

> Transracial adoption will change your life forever.... You are not the same person you were when you adopted a child transracially. I'm not just a white, middle-class mother anymore, but the mother of two Black children. I've changed. (p. 262)

> Racism is subtle and not always overt. White families need to be tuned into the pressures that a Black child experiences. The agencies need to have classes by people who are knowledgeable in this area. They need to know about racism and how it manifests itself. It can be subtle exclusion. We had to take our son out of the preschool because he was always the one assumed to be the cause of trouble. (p. 268)

Multicultural planning: Through this process, families create ways for children to learn about their racial/ethnic groups and access relationships and experiences that afford children opportunities for positive identity development.

> Some of the biggest challenges have involved getting access to her culture, her heritage, and her people. (p. 260)

> I would advise a family who wanted to adopt transracially to find out what the neighborhood is like where they are going to live and to see what kinds of kids are there. Talk to the neighbors about racial issues first. Make sure that people will not treat the kids as outcasts, but like normal children, which is what we are. (p. 260)

Survival skills: Recognizing that children of color need specific skills in a society in which racism continues to exist, professionals prepare parents to help their children and themselves cope successfully with racial prejudice and discrimination. ("Survival skills" is a term used in the literature to refer to coping skills for overcoming discrimination.)

> As far as transracial, it is a huge responsibility, because America is extremely racist. Some parents say, 'I'm not out to change the world.' That is so naïve. You are out to change the world for your child. It's not just going to be nice. You don't want to pass it over when your child gets called a racist name, and give a sugar coating to it by saying something like 'All children get called names.' Some people [who adopted transracially] say things like 'Some children get called names because they wear glasses.' That's a whole different issue than racism (p. 263).

In some cases, both Black and White parents may express interest in adopting a specific African American child. In selecting the most appropriate family, it is essential to assess each one's strengths and abilities to meet the child's needs. Just as the assessment must address the family's ability to address any specific physical health, emotional, behavioral, or developmental issue, it must also address the family's ability to meet the child's racial/ethnic identity and socialization needs. The assessment also must take into consideration how the child will fit in with other children in the family, the parents' preferences and expectations, and their willingness to support the child in maintaining appropriate relationships with birth siblings and other family members.

Color Consciousness—Not "Color Blindness"—Adoption Policy

Race is a factor in adoption decisions. Although it should definitely not be the primary or sole basis for choosing an adoptive family, it cannot be dismissed as irrelevant to a child's healthy development and adjustment. Whether adopted by Black or White parents, children's best interests are served by ongoing connections to their racial heritage. The CWLA Standards of Excellence for Adoption (2000) state that all children deserve to be raised in families that respect their cultural heritage: "Assessing and preparing a child for a transracial/transcultural adoption should recognize the importance of culture and race to the child and his or her experiences and identification. The adoptive family selected should demonstrate an awareness of and sensitivity to the cultural resources that may be needed after placement."

When parents adopt transracially, they and their children are not well served when they do not receive preparation and training that promote racial awareness and assist them with multicultural planning and the development of survival and coping skills. Families lose critical opportunities to gauge their own preparedness to adopt transracially and to develop the awareness and skills essential to meeting their children's racial/ethnic identity and socialization needs. Failing to provide families with this preparation and training is contrary to sound and ethical social work practices and contrary to the best interests of children.

References

Andujo, E. (1988). Ethnic identity of transracially adopted Hispanic adolescents. *Social Work, 33*, 531–535.

Brooks, D., & Barth, R.P. (1999). Adult transracial and inracial adoptees: Effects of race, gender, adoptive family structure, and placement history on adjustment outcomes. *American Journal of Orthopsychiatry, 69*, 87-99.

Child Welfare League of America (1968). *Standards of Excellence for Adoption Services*. Washington, DC: Author.

Child Welfare League of America (2000). *Standards of Excellence for Adoption Services*. Washington, DC: Author.

Clemetson, L., & Nixon, R. (August 17, 2006). Breaking through adoption's racial barriers. *New York Times*.

Convention on Protection of Children & Co-operation in Respect of Intercountry Adoption. (1993). Available online at: http://hcch.e-vision.nl/index_en.php?act=conventions.text&cid=69.

Day, D. (1979). *The adoption of Black children*. Lexington, MA: Heath and Company.

De Haymes, M. V., & Simon, S. (2003). Transracial adoption: Families identify issues and needed support services. *Child Welfare, 82*(2), 251–272.

Duncan, S. (2005). Black adoption myths & realities. *Adoptalk* (Summer), North American Council on Adoptable Children, 1–5.

Feigelman, W. (2000). Adjustments of transracially and inracially adopted young adults. *Child and Adolescent Social Work Journal, 17*, 165–183.

Freundlich, M. (2000). Adoption and ethics, Volume I: *The role of race, culture, and national origin in adoption*. Washington, DC: Child Welfare League of America and Evan B. Donaldson Adoption Institute. Available online at: http://www.holtintl.org/pdfs/Survey2.pdf.

Juffer, F. (2006). Children's awareness of adoption and their problem behavior in families with 7-year-old internationally adopted children. *Adoption Quarterly, 9*(2/3), 1–22.

Kim, W. J. (1995). International adoption: A case review of Korean children. *Child Psychiatry and Human Development, 25*(3), 141–154.

Lee, D., & Quintana, S. (2005). Benefits of cultural exposure and development of Korean perspective-taking ability for transracially adopted Korean children. *Cultural Diversity and Ethnic Minority Psychology, 11*(2), 130–143.

McRoy, R. G. (1989). An organizational dilemma: The case of transracial adoptions. *Journal of Applied Behavioral Science, 25* (2) 145–160.

McRoy, R., Zurcher, L. A., Lauderdale, M. L., & Anderson, R. M. (1982). Self-esteem and racial identity in transracial adoption. *Social Work, 27*, 522–526.

McRoy, R. G., Zurcher, L. A., Lauderdale, M. L., & Anderson, R. L. (1984). The identity of transracial adoptees. *Social Casework, 65*, 34–39.

National Association of Black Social Workers. (1972, April). Position statement on transracial adoptions. Presented at the National Association of Black Social Workers Conference, Nashville, TN.

Obama, B. (2004). *Dreams from my father.* New York: Three Rivers Press.

Phinney, J. S. (1991). Ethnic identity and self-esteem: A review and integration. *Hispanic Journal of Behavioral Sciences, 13*(2), 193–208.

Raible, J. (1990). The significance of racial identity in transracially adopted young adults. Available online at: http://www.nysccc.org/T- Rarts/Articles/Raible/RacialSignigicance.html. (accessed August 16, 2007)

Simon, R. J., & Altstein, H. (1987). *Transracial adoptees and their families: A study of identity and commitment.* New York: Praeger.

Sullivan, A. (1994). On transracial adoption. *Children's Voice, 3*(3), 4–6.

Vonk, M .E. (2001). Cultural competence for transracial adoptive parents. *Social Work, 46*(3), 246–254.

Close Reading Questions:

1. According to the Donaldson report, what events helped to cause a rise in transracial adoptions?

2. According to the report, what are the three reasons that transracial adoptees struggle to identify with their adoptive parents?

3. Why does the Donaldson report suggest that white parents who want to adopt children of color should pay particular attention to "racial awareness, multicultural planning, and survival skills?"

Analytical Writing/Discussion:

4. By the 1950s, social workers were largely responsible for placing children with adoptive parents. To what extent do you think those placements were affected by existing values about race, religion, and socioeconomic status? (Cultural Influences)

5. The voices of transracial adoptees add a personal note to the Donaldson report. Making specific references to the quotations from transracial adoptees, what do you think are some of the most significant challenges they face as children and young adults?

6. Given the rise in the number of African-American children available for adoption, why do you think the position of the National Association of Black Social Workers (NABSW) is or is not still legitimate? What is the implication for children if the NABSW stance is outdated? (Historical Trends)

Further Options:

7. Using some of the methods described in Chapter 5 on Argument, how persuasive do you find some of the positions about transracial adoption made by researchers and professional organizations versus those of adoptees and their parents? What makes the positions persuasive or how do you think they could be improved? (Multiple Perspectives)

8. The Child Welfare League of America asserts, "All children deserve to be raised in families that respect their cultural heritage." Using the consensus building techniques of a Rogerian argument explained in Chapter 5 on Rhetoric (see pp. 96–98), what common ground do you think can be created on respecting the cultural heritage of transracial adoptees?

WHAT MAKES A FAMILY?

by Vanessa de la Torre

Published in the *Hartford Courant* on Nov. 21, 2014, this news report presents a recent controversy over family, housing, and zoning. As the capital city of Connecticut, Hartford (like most cities and towns) has multiple zoning areas with different kinds of housing and occupancy allowed in each area. In this reading, love, law, and biology intersect, sometimes in conflict and other times in agreement. This debate reflects the historical trends of American families as well as their contemporary variety.

A neighborhood [squabble] on one of the city's wealthiest residential streets has triggered a cease-and-desist order, fervent appeals and debate over what constitutes a family.

The controversy centers on 68 Scarborough St., a nine-bedroom brick mansion shared by eight adults and three children—an arrangement among longtime friends who share monthly expenses, chores and legal ownership of the stately home, said Julia Rosenblatt, who lives there with her husband and two kids.

The residents bought the nearly 6,000-square-foot house for $453,000 in August, although only two of the owners are listed on the mortgage and city property record. They take turns cooking dinner, have pooled money into one bank account and entertained themselves last week with a family talent show because, Rosenblatt said Thursday, "We intentionally came together as a family."

But a coalition of neighbors, while conceding that the occupants of 68 Scarborough "are nice people," have argued that the nontraditional household violates the neighborhood's zoning for single-family homes. Living in the house are two couples with children, a couple with no children and two individuals.

About three weeks ago, 68 Scarborough was hit with a cease-and-desist order from the city after zoning officials determined that the setup "doesn't meet the definition of a family," said Thomas Deller, the city's director of development services, which oversees zoning code enforcement. The city's code defines members of a family as those related by blood, marriage, civil union or legal adoption.

It was unclear Thursday whether the owners eventually would be forced to vacate the home or sell it. Rosenblatt said they have appealed the order to the Hartford Zoning Board of Appeals.

"Now it's just the waiting game," said Joshua Blanchfield, Rosenblatt's husband and a teacher at a [magnet school] in Hartford. If the residents at 68 Scarborough lose their appeal, "they need to conform to city zoning," Deller said. He added that they also have the right to sue, and "that's something they'll have to decide."

"We don't know yet what all of our steps are; we're just trying to figure this out," said Rosenblatt, a co-founder of [a local] theater company. "It's quite unnerving and upsetting. ... What is scarier than talking about losing your own home?"

The West End Civic Association convened a committee meeting Wednesday night to hear arguments from both sides. Dozens showed up to back the 68 Scarborough residents, a group that includes Blanchfield and another Hartford public school teacher, a professor at Capital Community College, employees for Charter Oak Cultural Center and the Wheeler Clinic, and a stay-at-home dad.

Rather than a fight over one mansion, neighbors who oppose the arrangement have framed their case as a broader stand against any challenges to Scarborough's single-family zoning that could chip away at the quiet character of the affluent, estate-lined street.

The University of Connecticut Foundation, Wadsworth Atheneum and [a Hartford] charter school group each own property on Scarborough. Neighbors opposed [the charter group's] now-defunct plans to use the former Hartford Medical Society building for a school.

The 68 Scarborough owners "seem like a nice group of people," said John Gale, chairman of the West End association's planning and zoning committee. On the other hand, he said, he also sympathizes with the concern that a "Pandora's box" might open without a strict interpretation of single-family homes.

In a statement to the West End Civic Association, which may decide to issue a recommendation to the city, the neighbors compared the use of a single dwelling by multiple families to "an apartment building, or a rooming house, or a fraternity house." The letter was endorsed by the residents of 16 homes on Scarborough Street and a couple who lives on neighboring Asylum Ave.

"Regrettably, over the years ... people have attempted to change properties away from single-family housing," the letter stated. "We have learned that we cannot ignore violations that will set a precedent and provide a legal standard to allow multiple other properties to be changed on the same basis."

One notable Scarborough Street resident who did not sign the letter was Hartford City Council President Shawn Wooden, who said he has not taken a public position on the controversy.

The city may have to reconcile what Blanchfield described as "contradictory" language in its zoning regulations. One section calls for a maximum density of 3.6 families per acre in Scarborough's R-8 zoning district, although it's not clear that the rule applies to single-family lots. The mansion at 68 Scarborough, built in 1921, sits on two acres.

"The house is gigantic," said Brendan Mahoney, a friend of the owners. "I've had dinner there and everybody was home. ... The house was designed to have that many people in it."

So far, the owners have spent about $20,000 to upgrade the plumbing — there are six bathrooms — and the electrical system to bring the home up to code, Blanchfield said. They have a household bank account to share the cost of groceries, utilities and mortgage payments, and have also gotten used to the emotional support.

"Even just coming home at the end of the day, from a rough day," Rosenblatt said. "Because there's so many more people to help out, and to be good to each other, it just feels a lot less lonely than I think it might otherwise be." Next week, the children are planning a night of charades, she said. "We're not trying to change the zoning law," she said. "We're trying to change the definition of a family.

Close Reading Questions:

1. Who are the members of the group living together at 68 Scarborough St.? What is your initial reaction to this group (surprise, doubt, support, etc.) and why?

2. In what ways is this group like or unlike families you know?

3. What are some of the most significant consequences of the zoning decision for the residents of 68 Scarborough St. and for their neighbors?

Analytical Writing/Discussion:

4. What inconsistencies in the zoning regulations seem to both permit and forbid the household at 68 Scarborough St.? (Multiple Perspectives)

5. The definition of family can emphasize the form of this group (i.e., "those related by blood") or its function (i.e., how member love and care for one anothe). Why do you think the legal definition of a family should emphasize the form or the function of this group? (Cultural Influences)?

6. Please read the related opinion essays that are available in the e-supplement of chapter ten (see source #6). Which one do you think offers the most persuasive defense the residents of 68 Scarborough St. and why? Which one do you think provides the most convincing opposition and why? Quote from two of these supplemental sources and explain your reaction to their pro/con arguments.

Further Options:

7. How does the example of the pre-industrial family living a 'big house' that Hareven describes in "The Nineteenth Century Retreat" (see pp. xx-yy) support the definition of family sought by Julia Rosenblatt and others in her home? Why do you think this earlier concept of family is or is not relevant to the current controversy over the residency of 68 Scarborough St.? (Historical Trends)

8. In "Suburban Communities and American Life," (see pp. xx-yy) Michael P. Marino states that Cape Cod and Ranch style houses of the 1950s were symbolic of a movement toward single family living. As it exists in the twenty-first century, how is the Scarborough St. house a departure from or continuation of those ideas?

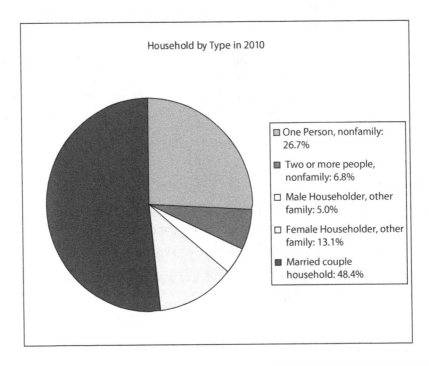

Household by Type in 2010

☐ One Person, nonfamily: 26.7%

■ Two or more people, nonfamily: 6.8%

☐ Male Householder, other family: 5.0%

☐ Female Householder, other family: 13.1%

■ Married couple household: 48.4%

FIGURE 2   The percentage of various kinds of households based on 2010 U.S. Census data. How can this information be used to support arguments for or against diverse family forms?

Freewrite 3: Televised Families

Although we do not always recognize the impact of television on our thinking, consider the influence of this media on your family's form and its members' roles. Brainstorm a list of as many television shows featuring families as you can recall. Include older shows as well as recent ones, dramas as well as comedies.

Then use freewriting and/or discussion to answer at least one of the following questions:

- How do you think the depiction of the family on television has changed from the 1950s to today?

- How similar is your own family to the most idealistic and/or the most realistic family shows?

- How have these television shows influenced, if at all, your assumptions about your own family?

Once you have completed this freewrite, you may want to expand this rough writing into a more formal paper by answering one of the questions below:

- To what degree do you think the depiction of family on television has reflected or guided the actual changes of families in American society?

- In addition to television, what are some other cultural influences on your perspective on American families?

Final Assignment 1: Defining the Family Form

For legal reasons, such as marriage, adoption, insurance, and taxation, the term "family" must be defined explicitly. For example, Douglass describes the enslavement of any child whose mother was a slave in nineteenth-century Southern families, and the Donaldson report examines the complexities of transracial adoptions in the twenty-first century. Thus, any attempt to define family must take into account these larger social contexts as well as the ability of various kinds of family forms to care for their members.

Essay Question

Given the great diversity of family forms today, how do you think "family" should be defined legally? Your definition of family must take into account the ability of various kinds of families to care for their members as well as the consequences of legal inclusion or exclusion of various families.

Write a formal and extended essay to answer this question. Be sure to include specific references and direct quotations from several readings in this chapter (see Chapter 7 on Academic Honesty on quoting and citing properly). Be sure to not only support your informed perspective but also anticipate and answer the possible objections of those who do not already agree with you. Your task is to assert your opinion and persuade others to consider it carefully.

Freewrite 4: Assignment Analysis

Before you start to answer this complex question, analyze its parts. Reread the question above and underline several phrases that represent key parts of the larger answer you will be developing. Then pick two or three of these phrases and freewrite your immediate impressions: What do you think right now? Then, pause to look for connections, contradictions, and omissions within your first response: What else do you want to discuss, what else do you want to add, and/or what order of your ideas is developing? Finally, consider the audience of your essay: Who does not agree with you already, and why might they disagree?

Reading Review

Once you have sketched some of your initial ideas, review some of the readings to find specific details and persuasive evidence to support, enrich, and possibly complicate your response. Here are some readings and post-reading questions that you may want to consider:

1. Freewrite 1
2. Hareven, Close Reading Question 1
3. Hareven, Close Reading Question 3
4. Figure 1
5. Douglass, Analytical Writing Question 6
6. de la Torre, Close Reading Question 1
7. Bartkowski and Ellison, Analytical Writing Question 6
8. Donaldson Report, Analytical Writing Question 5

Feel free to include other readings and post-reading questions. You also may want to review the suggestions for writing persuasively in Chapter 6 on Argument as well as to practice the peer response described in Chapter 4 on the Writing Process.

Final Assignment 2: Describing Parental Roles

In "The Revolt of 'Mother,'" Mary Wilkins Freeman questions the nineteenth-century concept of a mother as Sarah Penn challenges some of her husband's family decisions (see pp. 180–189). In "Parenting 101," Bartkowski and Ellison present the conservative advocacy of two-parent families with a mother and a father (see pp. 190–195). Thus, the roles of parents have been and will continue to be the subject of considerable debate.

Essay Question

Given the controversies over married, divorced, single, and homosexual parents, who do you think is capable (or not) of fathering and mothering a child well? Your description of parental roles should include both what is ideal and what is realistic in America today.

Write a formal and extended essay to answer this question. Be sure to include specific references and direct quotations from several readings in this chapter (see Chapter 7 on Academic Honesty on quoting and citing properly). Be sure to not only support your informed perspective but also anticipate and answer the possible objections of those who do not already agree with you. Your task is to assert your opinion and persuade others to consider it carefully.

Freewrite 5: Assignment Analysis

Before you start to answer this complex question, analyze its parts. Reread the question above and underline several phrases that represent key parts of the larger answer you will be developing. Then pick two or three of these phrases and freewrite your immediate impressions: What do you think right now? Then, pause to look for connections, contradictions, and omissions within your first response: What else do you want to discuss, what else do you want to add, and/or what order of your ideas is developing? Finally, consider the audience of your essay: Who does not agree with you already, and why might they disagree?

Reading Review

Once you have sketched some of your initial ideas, review some of the readings to find specific details and persuasive evidence to support, enrich, and possibly complicate your response. Here are some readings and post-reading questions that you may want to consider:

1. Hareven, Analytical Writing Question 5
2. Freeman, Analytical Writing Question 5
3. Freeman, Analytical Writing Question 6
4. Freewrite 2
5. Bartkowski and Ellison, Close Reading Question 3
6. Donaldson report, Close Reading Question 3
7. Figure 2
8. de la Torre, Analytical Writing Question 5

Feel free to include other readings and post-reading questions. You also may want to review the suggestions for writing persuasively in Chapter 6 on Argument as well as to practice the peer response described in Chapter 4 on the Writing Process.

Additional Source Suggestions

In the e-supplement of this textbook, there are several sources that will help you deepen your understanding of American families and strengthen your final assignment. These sources include videos as well as readings, and they present multiple perspectives, historical trends, and cultural influences on American families. To access these materials, see the code on the inside front cover of this textbook, which will lead you to the website for additional sources.

Education and Outcomes

CHAPTER 11

Schooles. It being one chiefe project of that old deluder Sathan, to keepe men from knowledge of the Scriptures … [it is] ordered by this Courte and Authority thereof, that euery Towneshipp within this Jurissdiction, after the Lord hath increased them to the number of fifty householders, shall then forthwith appoint one within theire Towne to teach all such children as shall resorte to him, to read and write.

—Connecticut General Court (1650)

[Education is the] great equalizer of the condition of men—the balance wheel of the social machinery.

—Horace Mann (1848)

In the field of public education, the doctrine of "separate but equal" has no place. Separate educational facilities are inherently unequal. Therefore, we hold that the plaintiffs and others similarly situated … are, by reason of the segregation complained of, deprived of the equal protection of the laws guaranteed by the Fourteenth Amendment.

—U.S. Supreme Court (Brown v. Board of Education, 1954)

Thanks to No Child Left Behind, AYP's [Annual Yearly Progress have replaced] the ABC's as the most important letters in many schools.

—Stan Karp (2004)

Introduction

In colonial America, education was recognized as vital to society. For example, in 1650, the colony in Connecticut decided that every town with more than 50 households should establish schools to teach children to read and write because it is the "chief project of that old deluder Satan to keep men and women from knowledge of the Scripture." Thus, the goal of education was to promote faith through literacy.

A century later, the aim of education was less religious and more secular, such as when Benjamin Franklin in 1749 asserted that education is "the foundation of the happiness" of individual and communities. Students should learn "those things that are likely to be most useful" in the "professions for which they are intended." The outcomes expected for various students, however, varied greatly. In more prosperous families, sons were educated to be lawyers, doctors, and clergymen, while daughters were taught to be refined wives and good mothers. And this was not the only difference in educational outcomes. Children in less privileged families received very little formal education and instead were trained for trades, such as boys becoming carpenters or blacksmiths and girls becoming servants or seamstresses. In 1848, Horace Mann hoped that education would be "the great equalizer" in American society, but to the contrary, schools often have hindered rather than promoted equal opportunity in a country created as an egalitarian democracy.

As late as the 1890s, less than seven percent of American adolescents attended high school, while most teenage children already were working in fields and factories. Fast-forward 60 years, and those fortunate enough to attend public high schools still were educated according to their expected social roles: males to be civic and economic leaders, and females to be the nurturers of offices and families. Such gender differences were not the only educational inequality that had to be confronted in the 1950s. The 1954 Supreme Court decision of *Brown v. Board of Education* rejected the racial segregation of students in what supposedly had been 'separate but equal' schools. This desegregation of public schools, however, was met with public protests and violent acts in many communities, such as Little Rock, Alabama in 1956–58 and Boston, Massachusetts in 1975–77. Despite the dreams of Horace Mann in 1848 and later of Martin Luther King in the 1960s, equal access to education has not yet been achieved in many cities and towns.

Many public schools in urban areas, with large populations of minority and/or disadvantaged students, provide inadequate education, and some are labeled as nothing more than drop-out factories. Rural schools, with their small classes, serve as a model for some, but they struggle to meet state standards for enhanced curriculum, like Advanced Placement classes, and educational facilities, such as labs and libraries. Suburban schools, populated primarily by more affluent students, are assumed by many to offer the best education. Some educators, therefore, refer to college aptitude exams, like the SAT and ACT, as little more than zip code tests: where students live determines the likely results.

The persistent inequalities in education—based on race, gender, and class—have led to the increased involvement of the federal government in local schools. In addition to the 1954 *Brown* decision, the federal government has intervened to address economic disparities (the Elementary and Secondary Education Act of 1965), sexual discrimination (Title IX in 1972), and physical and mental disabilities (All Handicapped Children Act of 1975). This federal involvement culminated with the No Child Left Behind Act of 2001 (NCLB), seeking greater accountability in public education. The emphasis on NCLB mastery tests in many schools, however, has stripped enjoyment from education for many students and their teachers. Teaching to the test unfortunately has not eliminated the achievement gap between privileged and nonprivileged students.

The three historical readings of this chapter are all relatively recent ones. The oldest ones date back to 1938 and 1984, as John Dewey and Theodore Sizer criticize traditional education, and in another, Deborah Meier encourages a return to small school districts and less federal control of education. In the contemporary readings, each author asserts the need for school reform, but they differ, for instance, on the value of mastery tests that probably dominated your own education in grades K-12.

These texts, along with the reading questions, freewriting activities, and visual elements of this chapter, are designed to develop the reading and writing abilities required for academic study. After each reading, you will find a set of questions that are divided into Close Reading Questions, Analytical Writing/Discussion, and Further Options. Some questions involve the same investigation of multiple perspectives, cultural influences, and historical trends that were introduced in Chapters 1 or 2. Answering some and discussing more of the post-reading questions will better prepare you to complete the final assignments options. These final writing assignments will ask you to assert your own, more informed perspective on education, equality, and outcomes. This chapter asks: **What do you think should be the means and ends of education?**

Freewrite 1: Initial Impressions

Describe in detail a specific scene, either one from your actual memory or a composite picture based on several recollections that represents a significant aspect of your high school education. Imagine your pen is a video camcorder and collect impressions of the setting, the characters, the actions and inactivity, and the sounds and the silences. What are your dominant thoughts and feelings toward your high school learning? What scene best represents these feelings? Where were you? What was (and was not) happening?

WHAT HIGH SCHOOL IS

by Theodore Sizer

Theodore Sizer is one of America's leading educational reformers. As the author of *Horace's Compromise: The Dilemma of the American High School* (1984) and *Horace's School: Redesigning the American High School* (1992), he has examined the goals and methods of American high schools. As chair of the Coalition of Essential Schools, Sizer has helped individual schools engage in self-examination and enact many reforms. In this reading, excerpted from *Horace's Compromise* (1984), Sizer uses an imagined student named Mark to depict the daily realities of a public high school.

Mark, sixteen, and a genial eleventh-grader, rides a bus to Franklin High School, arriving at 7:25. It is Assembly Day, so the schedule is adapted to allow for a meeting of the entire school. He hangs out with his friends, first outside school then inside, by his locker. He carries a pile of textbooks and notebooks; in all, it weighs eight and a half pounds.

From 7:30 to 8:19, with nineteen other students, he is in Room 304 for English class. The Shakespeare play being read this year for eleventh grade is *Romeo and Juliet*. The teacher, Ms. Viola, has various students in turn take parts and read out loud. Periodically, she interrupts the (usually halting) recitations to ask whether the thread of the conversation in the play is clear. Mark is entertained by the stumbling readings of some of his classmates. He hopes he will not be asked to be Romeo, particularly if his current steady, Sally, is Juliet. There is a good deal of giggling in class, and much attention is paid to who may be called on next. Ms. Viola reminds the class of a test on this part of the play to be given next week.

The bell rings at 8:19. Mark goes to the boys' room, where he sees a classmate who he thinks is a wimp but who constantly tries to be a buddy. Mark avoids the leech by rushing off. On the way, he notices two boys engaged in some sort of transaction, probably over marijuana. He pays them no attention. 8:24. Typing class. The rows of desks that embrace the big office are almost filled before the bell. Mark is uncomfortable here: typing class is girl country. The teacher constantly threatens what is to Mark a humiliating female future: "Your employer won't like these erasures." The minutes during the period are spent copying a letter from a handbook onto business stationary. Mark struggles to keep from looking at his work; the teacher wants him to watch only the material from which he is copying. Mark is frustrated, uncomfortable, and scared he will never complete his letter by the class's end, which would be embarrassing.

Nine tenths of the students present at school that day are assembled in the auditorium by the 9:18 bell. The dilatory tenth still stumble in, running down the aisles. Annoyed class deans try to get the mob settled. The curtains part; the program is a concert by a student rock group. Their electronic gear flashes under the lights, and the five boys and one girl in the group work hard at being casual. Their movements on stage are studiously at three-quarter time, and they chat with one another as though the tumultuous screaming of their classmates were totally inaudible. The girl balances on a stool; the boys crank up the music. It is very soft rock, the sanitized lyrics surely cleared with the assistant principal. The girl sings, holding the mike close to her mouth, but can scarcely be heard. Her light voice is tentative, and the lyrics indecipherable. The guitars, amplified, are tuneful, however, and the drums are played with energy.

The students around Mark—all juniors, since they are seated by class—alternately slouch in their upholstered, hinged seats, talking to one another, or sit forward, leaning on the chair backs in front of them, watching the band. A boy near Mark shouts noisily at the microphone-fondling singer, "Bite it … ohhh," but quickly subsides. A teacher walks down the aisle. Songs continue, to great applause. Assembly is over at 9:46, two minutes early.

9:53 and biology class. Mark was at a different high school last year and did not take this course as a tenth-grader. He is in it now, and all but one of his classmates are a year younger than he. He sits on the side, not taking part in the chatter that goes on after the bell. At 9:57, the public address system goes on, with the announcements of the day. After a few words from the principal (Here's today's cheers and jeers …" with a cheer for the winning basketball team and a jeer for the spectators who made a ruckus at the gymnasium), the task is taken over by the officers of ASB (Associated Student Bodies). There is an appeal for "bat bunnies." Carnations are for sale by the Girls' League. Miss Indian American is coming. Students are auctioning off their services (background catcalls are heard) to earn money for the prom. Nominees are needed for the ballot for the school bachelor and bachelorette. The announcements end with a "thought of the day. When you throw a little mud, you lose ground."

At 10:04 the biology class finally turns to science. The teacher, Mr. Robbins, has placed one of the several labeled laboratory specimens—some are pinned in frames, others swim in formaldehyde—on each of the classroom's eight laboratory tables. The three or so students whose chairs circle each of these benches are to study the specimen and make notes about it or drawings of it. After a few minutes each group of three will move to another table. The teacher points out that these specimens are of organisms already studied in previous classes. He says that the period-long test set for the following day will involve observing some of these specimens—then to be without labels—and writing an identifying paragraph on each. Mr. Robbins points out that some of the printed labels ascribe the specimens names different from those given in the textbook. He explains that biologists often give several names to the same organism.

The class now falls to peering, writing, and quiet talking. Mr. Robbins comes over to Mark, and in whispered words asks him to carry a requisition form for science department materials to the business office. Mark, because of his "older" status, is usually chosen by Robbins for this kind of errand. Robbins gives Mark the form and a green hall pass to show any teacher who might challenge him, on his way to the office, for being out of a classroom. The errand takes Mark four minutes. Meanwhile Mark's group is hard at work but gets to only three of the specimens before the bell rings at 10:42. As the students surge out, Robbins shouts a reminder about a "double" laboratory period on Thursday.

Between classes one of the seniors asks Mark whether he plans to be a candidate for schoolwide office next year. Mark says no. He starts to explain. The 10:57 bell rings, meaning that he is late for French class.

There are fifteen students in Monsieur Bates' language class. He hands out tests taken the day before: "*C'est bien fait, Etienne… c'est mieux, Marie … Tch, tch, Robert…*" Mark notes his C+ and peeks at the A- in front of Susanna, next to him. The class has been assigned seats by M. Bates; Mark resents sitting next to prissy, brainy Susanna. Bates starts by asking a student to read question and give the correct answer. "*James, question un.*" James haltingly reads the question and gives an answer that Bates now speaking English, says is incomplete. In due course: "*Mark, question cinq.*" Mark does his bit, and the sequence goes on, the eight quiz questions and answers filling about twenty minutes of time.

"Turn to page forty-nine. *Maintenant, lisez après moi …*" and Bates reads a sentence and has the class echo it. Mark is embarrassed by this and mumbles with a barely audible sound. Others, like Susanna, keep the decibels up, so Mark can hide. This I-say-and-you-repeat drill is interrupted once by the public address system, with an announcement about a meeting for cheerleaders. Bates finishes the class, almost precisely at the bell, with a homework assignment. The students are to review these sentences for a brief quiz the following day. Mark makes note of the assignment, because he knows that tomorrow will be a busy-work day in French class. Much though he dislikes oral drills, they are better than the workbook stuff that Bates hands out. Write, write, write, for Bates to throw away, Mark thinks.

11:36. Down to the cafeteria, talking noisily, hanging out, munching. Getting to Room 104 by 12:17: U. S. history. The teacher is sitting cross-legged on his desk when Mark comes in, heatedly arguing with three students over the fracas that had followed the previous night's basketball game. The teacher, Mr. Suslovic, while agreeing that the spectators from their school certainly were provoked, argues that they should neither have been so obviously obscene in yelling at the opposing cheerleaders nor have allowed Coke cans to be rolled out on the floor. The three students keep saying that "it isn't fair." Apparently they and some others had been assigned "Saturday mornings" (detentions) by the principal for the ruckus.

At 12:34, the argument begins to subside. The uninvolved students, including Mark, are in their seats, chatting amiably. Mr. Suslovic climbs off his desk and starts talking "We've almost finished this unit, chapters nine and ten …" The students stop chattering among themselves and turn toward Suslovic. Several slouch down in their chairs. Some open notebooks. Most have the five-pound textbook on their desks.

Suslovic lectures on the cattle drives, from north Texas to railroads west of St. Louis. He breaks up this narrative with questions ("Why were the railroad lines laid east to west?"), directed at nobody in particular and eventually answered by Suslovic himself. Some students take notes. Mark doesn't. A student walks in the open door, hands Mr. Suslovic a list, and starts whispering with him. Suslovic turns from the class and hears out this messenger. He then asks, "Does anyone know where Maggie Sharp is?" Some one answers, "Sick at home"; someone else says, "I thought I saw her at lunch." Genial consternation. Finally Suslovic tells the messenger, "Sorry, we can't help you," and returns to the class: "Now where are we?" He goes on for some minutes. The bell rings. Suslovic forgets to give the homework assignment.

1:11 and Algebra II. There is a commotion in the hallway: someone's locker is rumored to have been opened by the assistant principal and a narcotics agent. In the five-minute passing time, Mark hears the story three times and three ways. A locker had been broken into by another student. It was Mr. Gregory and a narc. It was the cops, and they did it without Gregory's knowing. Mrs. Ames, the mathematics, teacher, has not heard anything about it. Several of the nineteen students try to tell her and start arguing among themselves. "O.K., that's enough." She hands out the day's problem, one sheet to each student. Mark sees with dismay that it is a single, complicated "word" problem about some train that, while traveling at 84 mph, due west, passes a car that was going due east at 55 mph. Mark struggles: Is it d = rt or t = rd? The class becomes quiet, writing, while Mrs. Ames writes some additional, short problems on the blackboard. "Time's up." A sigh; some students still writing. A muffled "Shit." Mrs. Ames frowns.

"Come on, now." She collects papers, but it takes four minutes for her to corral them all.

"Copy down the problems from the board." A minute passes. "William, try number one." William suggests an approach. Mrs. Ames corrects and cajoles, and William finally gets it right. Mark watches two kids to his right passing notes; he tries to read them, but the handwriting is illegible from his distance. He hopes he is not called on, and he isn't. Only three students are asked to puzzle out an answer. The bell rings at 2:00. Mrs. Ames shouts out a homework assignment over the resulting hubbub.

Mark leaves his books in his locker. He remembers that he has homework, but figures that he can do it during English class the next day. He knows that there will be an in-class presentation of one of the *Romeo and Juliet* scenes and that he will not be in it. The teacher will not notice his homework writing, or won't do anything about it if she does.

Mark passes various friends heading toward the gym, members of the basketball team. Like most students, Mark isn't an active school athlete. However, he is associated with the yearbook staff. Although he is not taking "Yearbook" for credit as an English course, he is contributing photographs. Mark takes twenty minutes checking into the yearbook's headquarters (the classroom of its faculty advisor) and getting some assignments of pictures from his boss, the senior who is the photography editor. Mark knows that if he pleases his boss and the faculty advisor, he'll take that editor's post for the next year. He'll get English credit for his work then.

After gossiping a bit with the yearbook staff, Mark will leave school by 2:35 and go home. His grocery market bagger's job is from 4:30 to 8:00, the rush hour of the store. He'll have a snack at 4:30, and his mother will save him some supper to eat at 8:30. She will ask whether he has any homework, and he'll tell her no. Tomorrow, and virtually every other tomorrow, will be the same for Mark, save for the lack of the assembly: each period will then be five minutes longer.

Most Americans have an uncomplicated vision of what secondary education should be. Their conception of high school is remarkably uniform across the country, a striking fact, given the size and diversity of the United States and the politically decentralized character of the schools. This uniformity is of several generations' standing. It has, however, two appearances, each quite different from the other, one of words and the other of practice, a political rhetoric and Mark's world.

A California high school's general goals, set out in 1979, could serve equally well most of America's high schools, public and private. The school has as its ends:

- Fundamental scholastic achievement ... to acquire knowledge and share in the traditionally accepted academic fundamentals ... to develop the ability to make decisions, to solve problems, to reason independently, and to accept responsibility for self-evaluation and continuing self-improvement.

- Career and economic competence ...

- Citizenship and civic responsibility ...

- Competence in human and social relations ...

- Moral and ethical values ...

- Aesthetic awareness ...

- Cultural diversity ...

In addition to its optimistic rhetoric, what distinguishes this list is its comprehensiveness. The high school is to touch most aspects of an adolescent's existence—mind, body, morals, values, career. No one of these areas is given especial prominence. School people arrogate to themselves an obligation to all.

An example of the wide acceptability of these goals is found in the courts. Forced to present a detailed definition of "thorough and efficient education," elementary as well as secondary, a West Virginia judge sampled the best of conventional wisdom and concluded that

> There are eight elements of a thorough and efficient system of education: (a) Literacy, (b) The ability to add, subtract, multiply, and divide numbers, (c) Knowledge of government to the extent that the child will be equipped as a citizen to make informed choices among persons and issues that affect his own governance, (d) Self-knowledge and knowledge of his or her total environment to allow the child to intelligently choose life work—to know his or her options, (e) Work-training and advanced academic training as the child may intelligently choose, (f) Interests in all creative arts, such as music, theater, literature, and the visual arts, and (h) Social ethics, both behavioral and abstract, to facilitate compatibility with others in this society.

That these eight—now powerfully part of the debate over the purpose and practice of education in West Virginia—are reminiscent of the influential list, "The Seven Cardinal Principles of Secondary Education," promulgated in 1918 by the National Education Association, is no surprise. The rhetoric of high school purpose has been uniform and consistent for decades. Americans agree on the goals of their high schools.

That agreement is convenient, but it masks the fact that virtually all the words in these goal statements beg definition. Some schools have labored long to identify specific criteria beyond them; the result has been lists of daunting pseudospecificity and numbing earnestness. However, most leave the words undefined and let the momentum of traditional practice speak for itself. That is why analyzing how Mark spends his time is important: from watching him one uncovers the important purposes of education, the ones that shape practice. Mark's day is similar to that of other high school students across the country, as similar as the rhetoric of one goal statement to others'. Of course, there are variations, but the extent of consistency in the shape of school routine for a large and diverse adolescent population is extraordinary, indicating more graphically than any rhetoric the measure of agreement in America about what one does in high school, and by implication, what it is for.

The basic organizing structures in schools are familiar. Above all, students are grouped by age (that is freshman, sophomore, junior, and senior), and all are expected to take precisely the same time—around 720 school days over four years, to be precise, to meet the requirements for a diploma. When one is out of his grade level, he can feel odd, as Mark did in his biology class. The goals are the same for all, and the means to achieve them are also similar.

Young males and females are treated remarkably alike; the schools' goals are the same for each gender. In execution, there are differences, as those pressing sex discrimination suits have made educators intensely aware. The students in metalworking classes are mostly male; those in home economics, mostly female. But it is revealing how much less sex discrimination there is in high schools than in other American institutions. For many young women, the most liberated hours of their week are in school.

School is like a job: you start in the morning and end in the afternoon, five days a week. You don't get much of a lunch hour, so you go home early, unless you are an athlete or involved in some special school or extracurricular activity. School is conceived of as the children's workplace, and it takes young people off parents' hands and out of the labor market during prime-time work hours. Not surprisingly, many students see going to school as little more than a dogged necessity. They perceive the day-to-day routine, a Minnesota study reports, as one of "boredom and lethargy." One of the students summarizes: School is "boring, restless, tiresome, puts ya to sleep, tedious, monotonous, pain in the neck."

The school schedule is a series of units of time: the clock is king. The base time block is about fifty minutes in length. Some schools, on what they call modular scheduling, split that fifty-minute block into two or three pieces. Most schools have double periods for laboratory work, especially in the sciences, or four-hour units for smaller numbers of students involved in intensive vocational or other work-study programs. The flow of all school activity arises from or is blocked by these time units. "How much time do I have with my kids" is the teacher's key question.

Because there are many claims for those fifty-minute blocks, there is little time set aside for rest between them, usually no more than three to ten minutes, depending on how big the school is and, consequently, how far students and teachers have to walk from class to class. As a result, there is a frenetic quality to the school day, a sense of sustained restlessness. For the adolescents, there are frequent changes of room and fellow students, each change giving tempting opportunities for distraction, which are stoutly resisted by teachers. Some schools play soft music during these "passing times," to quiet the multitude, one principal told me.

Many teachers have a chance for a coffee break. Few students do so. In some city schools where security is a problem, students must be in class for seven consecutive periods, interrupted by a heavily monitored twenty-minute lunch period for small groups, starting as early as 10:30 A.M. and running to after 1:00 P.M. A high premium is placed on punctuality and on "being where you're supposed to be." Obviously, a low premium is placed on reflection and repose. The student rushes from class to class to collect knowledge. Savoring it, it is implied, is not to be done much in school, nor is such meditation really much admired. The picture that these familiar patterns yield is that of an academic supermarket. The purpose of going to school is to pick things up, in an organized and predictable way, the faster the better.

Close Reading Questions

1. Which of Mark's classes seem most similar to your own high school experiences (or those of someone you know well)? Overall, how accurate do you think Sizer's depiction of secondary education is and why?

2. At the end of this reading, Sizer offers several critiques of secondary education. Which of his critiques of high school do you think is most or least significant and why?

3. Why is Sizer troubled by the stated goals and the actual practices of most high school?

Analytical Writing/Discussion

4. With the reference to the 1918 Report (see p. 215), Sizer claims that the goals of education have not changed significantly over most of a century. Why does Sizer believe the stated goals of education have remained so constant? How much or how little do you think the goals of secondary education have changed in the three decades since Sizer made this analysis? (Historical Trends)

5. As this depiction of high school follows Mark, this reading suggests several other perspectives, such as those of more engaged students like Susanna, teachers, administrators, and parents. Focusing on another perspective or two beyond Mark's viewpoint, how can this school be seen much more positively? (Multiple Perspectives)

6. According to Sizer, attending high school is "like a job." With several references to Sizer's essay, what do you think are several ways in which the organization of the workplace influences the structure of school? (Cultural Influences)

Further Options

7. Synthesis, meaning the making of connections between two (or more) readings is central to academic writing. In the next reading, John Dewey critiques traditional education. Which of Dewey's criticisms do you think are most relevant to Mark's school day? Or conversely, what details of Mark's school day best illustrate some of Dewey's criticisms?

8. Research the goals of your former high school or current college. How similar or different are these goals with those presented by Sizer? Why do you think these similarities or differences should be considered as positive or negative?

EXPERIENCE AND EDUCATION

by John Dewey

John Dewey was one of the first and fiercest critics of traditional education in the United States. He helped lead the reform that was known as progressive education during the 1920s. Yet by the end of the next decade, he faulted progressive educators for basing their reform movement too much in opposition to traditionalism. He instead tried to rethink the basic concepts and the key relationships of education, such as educational goals and the bond between teachers and students. This reading is an excerpt from *Experience and Education*, published in 1938, after Dewey had presented these ideas on education in the Kappa Delta Pi Lecture Series.

The trouble with traditional education was not that educators took upon themselves the responsibility for providing an [educational] environment. The trouble was that they did not consider the other factor in creating an [educational] experience; namely, the powers and purposes of those taught. It was assumed that a certain set of [information] was intrinsically desirable, apart from its ability to evoke a certain quality of response in individuals. This lack of mutual adaptation made the process of teaching and learning accidental. Those to whom the provided [information was] suitable managed to learn. Others got on as best they could. Responsibility for selecting [course information] carries with it, then, the responsibility for understanding the needs and capacities of the individuals who are learning at a given time. It is not enough that certain materials and methods have proved effective with other individuals at other times. There must be a reason for thinking they will function in generating an experience that has educational quality with particular individuals at a particular time.

FIGURE 1 A Traditional Classroom

It is no reflection upon the nutritive quality of beefsteak that it is not fed to infants. It is not an invidious reflection upon trigonometry that we do not teach it in the first or fifth grade of school. It is not the subject per se that is educative or that is conducive to growth. There is no subject that is in and of itself, or without regard to the stage of growth attained by the learner, such that inherent educational value can be attributed to it. Failure to take into account adaptation to the needs and capacities of individuals was the source of the idea that certain subjects and certain methods are intrinsically cultural or intrinsically good for mental discipline. There is no such thing as educational value in the abstract. The notion that some subjects and methods and that acquaintance with certain facts and truths possess educational value in and of themselves is the reason why traditional education reduced the material of education so largely to a diet of predigested materials. According to this notion, it was enough to regulate the quantity and difficulty of the material provided, in a scheme of quantitative grading, from month to month and from year to year. Otherwise a pupil was expected to take it in doses that were prescribed from without. If the pupil left it instead of taking it, if he engaged in physical truancy, or in the mental truancy of mind-wandering and finally built up an emotional revulsion against the subject, he was held to be at fault. No question was raised as to whether the trouble might not lie in the subject-matter or in the way in which it was offered. The principle of interaction makes it clear that failure of adaptation of material to needs and capacities of individuals may cause an experience to be non-educative quite as much as failure of an individual to adapt himself to the material.

The principle of continuity in its educational application means, nevertheless, that the future has to be taken into account at every stage of the educational process. This idea is easily misunderstood and is badly distorted in traditional education. Its assumption is, that by acquiring certain skills and by learning certain subjects which would be needed later (perhaps in college or perhaps in adult life) pupils are as a matter of course made ready for the needs and circumstances of the future. Now "preparation" is a treacherous idea. In a certain sense every experience should do something to prepare a person for later experiences of a deeper and more expansive quality. That is the very meaning of growth, continuity, reconstruction of experience. But it is a mistake to suppose that the mere acquisition of a certain amount of arithmetic, geography, history, etc., which is taught and studied because it may be useful at some time in the future, has this effect, and it is a mistake to suppose that acquisition of skills in reading and figuring will automatically constitute preparation for their right and effective use under conditions very unlike those in which they were acquired.

Almost everyone has had occasion to look back upon his school days and wonder what has become of the knowledge he was supposed to have amassed during his years of schooling, and why it is that the technical skills he acquired have to be learned over again in changed form in order to stand him in good stead. Indeed, he is lucky who does not find that in order to make progress, in order to go ahead intellectually, he does not have to unlearn much of what he learned in school. These questions cannot be disposed of by saying that the subjects were not actually learned for they were learned at least sufficiently to enable a pupil to pass examinations in them. One trouble is that the subject-matter in question was learned in isolation; it was put, as it were, in a water-tight compartment. When the question is asked, then, what has become of it, where has it gone to, the right answer is that it is still there in the special compartment in which it was originally stowed away. If exactly the same conditions recurred as those under which it was acquired, it would also recur and be available. But it was segregated when it was acquired and hence is so disconnected from the rest of experience that it is not available under the actual conditions of life. It is contrary to the laws of experience that learning of this kind, no matter how thoroughly engrained at the time, should give genuine preparation.

Nor does failure in preparation end at this point. Perhaps the greatest of all pedagogical fallacies is the notion that it person learns only the particular thing he is studying at the time. Collateral learning in the way of formation of enduring attitudes, of likes and dislikes, may be and often is much more important than the spelling lesson or lesson in geography or history that is learned. For these attitudes are fundamentally what count in the future. The most important attitude that can be formed is that of desire to go on learning. If impetus in this direction is weakened instead of being intensified, something much more than mere lack of preparation takes place. The pupil is actually robbed of native capacities which otherwise would enable him to cope with the circumstances that he meets in the course of his life. We often see persons who have had little schooling and in whose case the absence of set schooling proves to be a positive asset. They have at least retained their native common sense and power of judgment, and its exercise in the actual conditions of living has given them the precious gift of ability to learn from the experiences they have. What avail is it to win prescribed amounts of information about geography and history, to win ability to read and write, if in the process the individual loses his own soul: loses his appreciation of things worthwhile, of the values to which these things are relative; if he loses desire to apply what he has learned and, above all, loses the ability to extract meaning from his future experiences as they occur?

What, then, is the true meaning of preparation in the educational scheme? In the first place, it means that a person, young or old, gets out of his present experience all that there is in it for him at the time in which he has it. When preparation is made the controlling end, then the potentialities of the present are sacrificed to a suppositious future. When this happens, the actual preparation for the future is missed or distorted. The ideal of using the present simply to get ready for the future contradicts itself. It omits, and even shuts out, the very conditions by which a person can be prepared for his future. We always live at the time we live and not at some other time, and only by extracting at each present time the full meaning of each present experience are we prepared for doing the same thing in the future. This is the only preparation which in the long run amounts to anything.

All this means that attentive care must be devoted to the conditions which give each present experience a worthwhile meaning. Instead of inferring that it doesn't make much difference what the present experience is as long as it is enjoyed, the conclusion is the exact opposite. Here is another matter where it is easy to react from one extreme to the other. Because traditional schools tended to sacrifice the present to a remote and more or less unknown future, therefore it comes to be believed that the educator has little responsibility for the kind of present experiences the young undergo. But the relation of the present and the future is not an Either-Or affair. The present affects the future anyway. The persons who should have some idea of the connection between the two are those who have achieved maturity. Accordingly, upon them devolves the responsibility for instituting the conditions for the kind of present experience which has a favorable effect upon the future. Education as growth or maturity should be an ever-present process.

Close Reading Questions

1. According to Dewey, what are two crucial factors of effective education? How does traditional education often fail to fulfill both factors?

2. What larger point do you think Dewey is trying to make using the examples of steak and trigonometry?

3. Dewey also was one of the leading philosophers of the early twentieth century so his writing often is abstract and highly theoretical. Rather than trying to comprehend of this entire reading immediately, please pick a short passage that seems very true to you and answer: why does this passage seem so significant to you?

Analytical Writing/Discussion:

4. Why does Dewey believe that some subject matter may be learned by one student but not by another? Why do you agree or disagree that the "adaptation" of material may contribute to this educational failure as well as the efforts of an individual student? (Multiple Perspectives)

5. Why are you persuaded or not by Dewey that education focused on "preparation" for the future can be a "treacherous idea"? Using some of Dewey's detailed analysis, what do you think are the best and worst ways to focus education on preparing for the future? (Historical Trends)

6. Dewey insists that although specific information may be later forgotten, the "collateral learning" of school often persists. What do you think he means by the phrase "collateral learning"? Using yourself or a student you know well, what is a positive or negative example of this collateral learning? (Cultural Influences)

Further Options

7. In question one above, you were asked to create what is known as a double-entry response to a specific passage. Now let's take this form of reading response even further: using either Freewrite 1 or the first reading by Sizer, how can you connect that text to a specific passage from this reading? In other words, how does the other text help to explain the passage by Dewey? For more on double-entry responses, see pp. 79–81 of Chapter 3.

8. In our explanation of multiple perspectives, we asserted that it is vital to test a viewpoint by considering an opposing opinion. Working away from your initial support or skepticism of Dewey's critique of traditional education and his advocacy of a revised form of progressive education, what are several aspects of the opposing opinion? In other words, why might someone else disagree with your initial reaction to Dewey? For more on multiple perspectives, see p. 8 or pp. 42–47 in Chapters 1 or 2.

SCHOOLS AND TRUST IN A DEMOCRACY

by Deborah Meier

Deborah Meier started her career in education as a kindergarten teacher in public schools in Chicago, Philadelphia, and New York City. In 1974, Meier founded and directed the alternative public Central Park East School for children from East Harlem, NYC. Meier then founded two other small public elementary schools, one named Mission Hill in Boston, participated in The Coalition of Essential Schools created by Ted Sizer, and became a leading advocate of small schools. Her books include *The Power of Ideas: Lessons from a Small School in East Harlem* (1995) and *Will Standards Save Public Schools* (2000). The following reading comes from a collection of essays, published in 2004, which she edited with George Wood, titled *Many Children Left Behind*.

The very definition of what constitutes an educated person is now dictated by federal legislation. A well-educated person is one who scores high on standardized math and reading tests. And ergo a good school is one that either has very high test scores or is moving toward them at a prescribed rate of improvement. Period.

All of this has implications for democracy, and not small ones. We worry about "public engagement" and "parental involvement," two new jargony phrases that were invented precisely as we eliminated all the natural ways in which families and citizens were engaged in their schools.

Bigger Is Not Better

The demise of small school districts was coincidental with the demise of small schools. The two phenomena together have led to a serious disconnect between young people and adults, between youth culture and adult culture.

There were good reasons to be concerned that small schools might be havens for parochial prejudices, racial bias, and insularity—and that larger consolidated school districts would be able to offer greater variety and economies of scale. Both played a role in the demise of small schools and districts, as well as the increasing role of the state and federal government in schools. We were preparing our youngsters for national and global citizenship; big schools and big districts were often seen as a way of enlarging young people's exposure to a wider range of options and offering them greater expertise and more specialized programs, as well as protecting the rights of minorities.

Furthermore, the increase over the past half-century of state and federal mandates created compliance problems in small and isolated districts. How could a small school offer the kind of library, science labs, sports programs, range of foreign language opportunities, or Advanced Placement options that would be possible in a large school?

But we embarked on that path without considering the costs, either in how adults saw their responsibility for the education of the next generation, or in the growing disconnect between school and community and its impact on children's intellectual, social, and moral development. Citizenship requires a recognition of what it means to be a member of something—and we've forgotten that kids today have precious little experience being members of anything beyond their immediate family and their self-chosen peer group.

Parochialism certainly can stunt kids' growth and impede their sharing of larger social norms and concerns. The solution to parochialism, however, isn't to destroy all small communities and institutions in favor of large, anonymous ones. When we look closely, we see that the consolidation and centralization of school districts actually made the problems they were supposed to cure even worse. Rather than expanding young people's sense of membership in the world, consolidation seriously endangered their feeling of community. And it didn't even save money: the evidence suggests that the cost per graduate of small schools is less.

Nor did the consolidation lead to other hoped-for outcomes, such as greater ethnic, racial, and social class integration. Our progress on racial separatism has been substantial, if we look back as far as 1930, but in recent years we have been losing ground. As for social class, the big difference is that far more low-income children now attend school for longer periods of time—but rarely together with rich kids. And if they do attend the same schools, they rarely study in the same classes or belong to the same subgroups. For within the new large schools, kids have recreated their own small schools, made up of their like-minded and look-alike peers. You see them in the hallways and lunchrooms and on the playgrounds.

Now NCLB does not in itself demand the consolidation of districts and the creation of bigger schools. But as I hope to show, it creates an environment in which the purpose and value of small schools [are] not allowed to flourish. In fact, it undermines small schools' most important educational characteristic: they are places where citizens and professionals can exercise judgment and build trust.

A World Designed by Strangers

Local communities are in far less danger of parochialism today than in the past. The influence of television, computers, and other technology, and the vast youth-savvy world of mass entertainment has altered the landscape of our lives, especially for children.

Few of today's youngsters lack awareness of the larger demands of society, as job requirements and college expectations are largely national in scope. We are inescapably connected by these new technologies, and there are more of them every year. It's not the Big World that kids are cut off from; increasingly, it's the one at their doorsteps—their own communities.

Education has barely acknowledged, much less begun to address, this sea change toward a new world of universalism run amok. We are not much of a match anymore for the educational impact of the national norms established, not by schools, teachers, or churches, but by that great equalizer the mass media, with its relentless drive to turn our kids into world-class consumers.

By the time they are adolescents, our children are largely cut off from relationships with adults outside their immediate families—and stuck with one another in a world designed for them by strangers. They are all educated by the music, advertisements, and products designed to sell to an international youth market. They are carefully groomed to recognize ways to enhance their status in the race to look good, get ahead, be the most. What they do not have are strong roots in any specific multiage community.

NCLB is not itself responsible for the divide between adults and children, for the breakdown of multiage communities. It merely locks these into place. Exactly at a time when we need educational policies that will counter these trends, we get NCLB, which instead amplifies their negative effects. It does so in specific ways.

By relying on standardized tests as the only measure of school quality, NCLB usurps the right of local communities to define the attributes of a sound education. Districts are further encouraged to limit any local alternatives by having schools limit their curriculum time to what will prepare children for tests .... This will ... dumb down decades of efforts to provide children with what was once offered only to the rich—a genuinely challenging and engaging program of study.

By ignoring ample evidence that the psychometric tools of testing provide limited predictions of school success, above all when it comes to children outside the mainstream (children of color, of the poor, those with handicaps or limited English proficiency), NCLB forces local districts to engage in one-size-fits-all practices that ignore the needs of these children. Districts will be encouraged to push out those so-called nonperformers in order to protect their movement toward Adequate Yearly Progress or else risk being labeled a failing school.

By suggesting that public schools can produce equity regardless of social inequity, NCLB sets up local districts for failure. This failure will lead to calls for the ultimate limitation of local, democratic authority, that is class for privatization of our public schools.

Above all, NCLB assumes that neither children, their families, their teachers, nor their communities can be trusted to make important decisions about their schools. It defines such parties as special biased self-interests, whose judgment is inferior to that of bureaucrats at the Department of Education and various testing services.

More Trust, More Democracy

We need schools where strong cross-generational relationships can be built around matters of importance in the world. Schools cannot do it alone—kids also need other non-school communities—but creating such schools is a necessary start. These schools can exist only in communities that trust them. There is no short cut. The authority needed to do the job requires trust. Trusting our schools cannot be a long-term goal in some utopian vision. If you don't trust the babysitter, no accountability scheme will make it safe to leave your child in her hands tonight. The only alternative is to stay home.

There is no way around it. We have to work harder at making our schools and teachers trustworthy. And that, in turn, means we need schoolwork we can easily see, whose governors are folks we know well, and whose graduates' lives we can track without complex databases or academic studies.

The business world offers little guidance in this task. The ways of business hardly work for business, where "buyer beware" is the primary response to the demands of accountability.

We need to return schools to our fellow citizens—yes, ordinary citizens, with all their warts. The solution to the messiness of democracy is more of it—and more time set aside to make it work. If we want to continue our grand experiment in American democracy, we are stuck depending on the people "to exercise their control with a wholesome discretion," in Thomas Jefferson's words. And if they are not enlightened enough to do so, he said, "the remedy is not to take it from them, but to inform their discretion by education."

That's what local school boards are intended to be all about. If we can't trust local citizens with matters of local K-12 schooling, whatever can we trust them with? And why would we instead trust presidents and governors or the task forces they select to replace such judgments on matters so close to the raising of our children?

How might we go about establishing greater trust? We might start by multiplying, not reducing, the number of local boards, to return to the ratio we once enjoyed. At most, no school committee that makes decisions about teaching and learning should have authority over more than perhaps 2,500 students and at most ten small schools. Maybe each school should have its own board.

Trust in schools can't grow unless principals, parents, teachers, and kids know each other well, and their work is accessible to the larger community. Likewise, the board members that oversee them must know the schools intimately—through firsthand engagement, not printouts and manipulatable bureaucratic data.

Like the private and parochial schools that the current federal government seems to favor, Mission Hill School—although part of a larger citywide system in Boston—has its own board, made up of five parent representatives, five staff representatives, five staff representatives, five public members chosen jointly, and two students. And while the Boston School Committee has ultimate power, "in-between" (which is most of the time) it's our own board that makes the important decisions on policy, budget, and personnel. That's part of the secret of our success. Maybe each school needs its own form of self-governance.

The state can set broad guidelines, and it can surely demand that schools make their standards explicit and the evidence of performance publicly accessible. It can insist on fairness for all citizens—and set out what such fairness requires. But each local board ought to be responsible for the details, including exactly how schools are held accountable to their constituents and what evidence will count toward the awarding of diplomas. There is precious little likelihood that a board will ignore what colleges and employers say, what Educational Testing Service and other credentialing bodies lay down as norms, or what the mass media and national politicians and public figures claim needs to be done.

The state might reasonably require that sample populations of students be tested to look at indicators across localities. And it might require schools to submit every few years to a review of their work by a panel of expert and lay outsiders, whose opinions and analysis would be made public. Otherwise, let there be both voice and, where possible, choice—close to where children live. While choice allows folks to vote with their feet, voice allows them to vote in the most democratic sense—by going to the polls. Both choice and voice strengthen the allegiance of communities to their schools. Not all people will get exactly what they want; but democracy is also all about compromises, building consensus, thinking about the other guy's needs and views, and a commitment to the larger community.

There will be acrimony, and there will be local fights. Hurrah, but not alas. It is the habits of mind necessary for practicing and resolving disagreements—the mental toughness that democracy rests on—that kids most need to learn about in school. If we all agreed about everything, we wouldn't need democracy; we wouldn't need to learn how people work out differences.

Local school boards need to look politicians, corporate boards, and foundation leaders in the eye and remind them: This is what America is all about. And it just so happens it's what a strong and rigorous education requires—even if we don't get it right at first or all the time. That too is what America is all about.

Rebuilding Trust

Our school boards need to turn their eyes to their real constituencies—not just to following the dictates of state and federal government bureaucrats.

Good school governance needs to keep its eyes on its real constituents—above all the kids and their families. Disappointing them is what such a board must worry about day and night. What it doesn't need to do is live in fear of state and federal government micromanagers. That's not easy, of course. But it will be the foundation of a powerful coalition of school people and local school boards creating trustworthy schools.

There is no way to give all kids a serious and high-quality education unless and until we make our schools worthy of trust.

Close Reading Questions

1. According to Meier, who defines what constitutes a good education, and what now is the definition of a well-educated person?

2. What does Meier believe are the respective benefits and disadvantages of small schools and of large schools?

3. According to Meier, why is trust essential in education, and how has trust been reduced by NCLB?

Analytical Writing/Discussion

4. Why do you agree or disagree with Meier that the typical high school student participates in a group of "like-minded and look-alike" peers? (Multiple Perspectives)

5. According to Meier, what effect does the mass media have on most students? To what degree do you think this effect contradicts Meier's fear of "look-alike" conformity among students in large schools? (Cultural Influences)

6. Why does Meier want to return to the 1930s level of local control of schools? Why do you think greater local control would be beneficial or not? (Historical Trends)

Further Options

7. Meier cites Thomas Jefferson on the role of education in a democracy. What do you think is the necessary relationship between education and democracy in the United States?

8 As explained in Chapter 6 on Rhetoric, a Rogerian argument seeks compromise and consensus among disputants by seeking, first, common ground (see p. 111). Although Deborah Meier and Anthony Consiglio (see pp. 227–232) disagree on NCLB, on what aspects of educational reform might they agree? What consensus on improving public schools do you think is possible?

Freewrite 2: Tracking Students

The division of students into different ability levels for one subject—or "tracking" them into high, middle, and low sections—is practiced in almost all of America's public high schools today. This common practice, however, once was a topic of great debate among educators. The following excerpts are from two very influential reports on education: the Committee of Ten Report from 1893 and *the American High School Today*, a second report from 1959. After you read their positions on tracking, please discuss and/or freewrite in response using the questions below.

From the 1893 Report

On one very important question of general policy that affects profoundly the preparation of all school programs, the Committee of Ten and all the Conferences are absolutely unanimous. Among the questions suggested for discussion in each Conference were the following:

1. Should the subject be treated differently for pupils who are going to college, for those who are going to a scientific school, and for those who, presumably, are going to neither?

2. At what age should this differentiation begin, if any be recommended?

The first question is answered unanimously in the negative ... [so] the second therefore needs no answer.... Every subject which is taught at all in a secondary school should be taught in the same way and to the same extent to every pupil so long as he pursues it, no matter what the probable destination of the pupil may be, or at what point his education is to cease. Thus, for all pupils who study Latin, or history, or algebra, for example, the allotment of time and the method of instruction in a given school should be the same year by year. Not that all the pupils should pursue every subject for the same number of years; but so long as they do pursue it, they should all be treated alike. It has been a very general custom in American high schools and academies to make up separate courses of study for pupils of supposed different destinations.... Each subject [should be] treated by the school in the same way by the year for all pupils.

From the 1959 Report

In the required subjects and those elected by students with a wide range of ability, the students should be grouped according to ability, subject by subject. For example, in English, American history, ninth-grade algebra, biology, and physical science, there should be at least three types of classes—one for the more able in the subject, another for the large group whose ability is about average, and another for the very slow readers who should be handled by special teachers. The middle group might be divided into two or three sections according to the students' abilities in the subject in question. This type of grouping is not to be confused with across the board grouping according to which a given student is placed in a particular section in all courses. Under the scheme here recommended, for example, a student may be in the top section in English but the middle section in history or ninth-grade algebra.

Answer one or more of the following questions by freewriting and/or discussion in order to react to these two reports:

-   How did your high school handle tracking, and how might its grouping policy have been improved by heeding one or both of these reports?

-   Rather than pick one side over another on tracking, how do you think each position can be considered a fair way to treat all students equally?

-   During the 1890s, only a fraction of American adolescents attended high school (7%), but by the 1950s, a large majority of teenagers attended high school (though all did not complete four years and graduate). How do you think the different historical circumstances of these reports can be used to explain their opposing positions on differentiated instruction and ability grouping?

EDUCATIONAL EQUALITY: RENEWING NCLB

by Anthony Consiglio

After teaching in public schools in New York and Connecticut for more than a decade, Anthony Consiglio turned to the study of law. He has combined these professional pursuits by focusing on what he terms "the noble achievement and arduous challenge of expanding access to a quality education." The following essay was originally published in the *Brigham and Young University Education and Law Journal* in 2009, and the author asked his readers to maintain an "open and searching mind."

Presidential candidates called it "unconstitutional," an "unfunded mandate." Its fiercest critics charge its intent is to undermine and dismantle public education itself .... Yet the No Child Left Behind Act of 2001 (NCLB) is hardly the subversive, far-reaching, and peremptory law that these misconceptions and attacks suggest. Rather, NCLB is divisive because it has raised penetrating questions with profound implications for the future. NCLB is a major example of a federal initiative to respond to a well-documented nationwide need, and its success or failure will influence future solutions to stubborn national problems ranging from health care to oversight of the financial industries.

As Congress considers the renewal of NCLB, it has a moral and political imperative to get it right. The greatest support for NCLB continues to come from states, communities, organizations, and families who are sensitive to its central mission: improving the academic achievement and educational opportunities in the poorest-performing schools to match more closely those in high-performing schools. When it was enacted, NCLB enjoyed broad bipartisan support and recognition of its central, civil rights objectives. Much of the public has grown disenchanted, however—"educators, legislators, and even entire states are in open revolt over NCLB"—and liberal education scholars talk of "laudable goals" and "noble agenda" overrun by inherent flaws and "unintended consequences."

Where a sound and laudable premise meets flawed design and unintended consequences, however, revolt and abandonment are not the normal nor the best response. The countless parodies and puns the name No Child Left Behind has inspired in the press and elsewhere suggest something more than a logical reaction is going on....

The Two Main Objections

There are two elemental objections to NCLB. Although they are inextricably related, the first objection expresses a policy concern about education (what government should provide and require), while the second expresses a constitutional concern about federalism (how state and federal governments should function and within what limits of control). The two arguments can be summarized as follows:

1. Complying with NCLB cripples states and schools with a sterile education policy obsessively focused on annual student testing and other superficial, shortsighted goals.

2. While NCLB is in form a federal spending program, participation in the program is optional for states in theory only—the threat of withholding federal education funds from states that have long relied on them unconstitutionally coerces their participation in NCLB. Furthermore, because the federal funding is inadequate for full compliance with NCLB's requirements, the law unconstitutionally directs states' education policy.

Both arguments sensibly address practical realities, and Congress should learn many essential points from them as it considers NCLB's future—especially as to the rigidity of NCLB's deadlines and benchmarks, the punitive nature of some of its sanctions, and its neglect of teaching methods.

Nonetheless, these arguments tend toward a negative and counterproductive logic that limits their usefulness. They draw attention to what is missing (time, money, and creative and flexible teaching), but avoid frankly weighing the states' role in presiding over the accretion of unmet need. They present a contradiction by decrying excessive federal interference and insufficient federal funding. They do not point the way forward to correcting the long intractable problem of inequality in educational opportunities, but insist that the flexibility and freedom schools have enjoyed for decades is still the solution.

The policy argument correctly maintains that the testing and data collection NCLB requires cannot effect meaningful reform without a concentrated focus on teaching and curriculum. But the implication that NCLB prevents true teaching reform is a straw man, however grounded it may be in current fiscal realities. Contrarily, the policy argument more often than not incorrectly implies that meaningful education reform can proceed without a basic system of rigorous testing and solid data collection in place. It also obscures the primary objective of equality behind NCLB's requirement that each state adopt uniform educational standards. A thorough system of assessment and accountability is the necessary basis … of any sound education policy and of any equality measure.

If NCLB is to succeed on its own terms, Congress will indeed have to partner with the states to support their development of programs for teaching and curriculum reform. By their nature, these programs require individualization and resist standardization. In the meantime, though, there is no convincing justification for denying the primacy of assessment and accountability. Those denials are, at worst, part of a uniquely American distaste for governmental discipline that has left us with financial, health care, energy, and other industries profoundly neglectful of sustainability.

NCLB's requirement of uniform standards across each state is a direct attack on the inequality inherent in our system of school financing from local property taxes. From the perspective of the Fourteenth Amendment and the perspective of antipoverty measures, equalizing opportunities should take precedence over individual communities' pursuit of excellence. Connecticut's efforts to escape some of NCLB's requirements provide an especially instructive example of this problem. Connecticut lobbied and sued the Department of Education (DOE) (the agency charged with administering NCLB) for waivers to avoid supplementing its pre-NCLB tests that were nationally recognized for their excellence, even while Connecticut was recognized as the state with the single biggest discrepancy in academic achievement between its high- and low-performing students. Connecticut is the only state that has lodged a full constitutional attack on NCLB in court. Congress [however] should remain committed to uniform standards [within] each state….

The federalism argument summarized above also has merit, especially in its perception that opting out of NCLB would amount to a politically disastrous forfeit of federal aid that could not be recaptured through other means, such as raising state taxes. There may ultimately be no satisfying answer for this problem—it may simply be a fiscal reality of the modern federal relationship and a function of the federal government's responsibility for equality measures under the Fourteenth Amendment.

Yet, the federalism argument obscures a fact of fundamental importance: NCLB does not determine a participating state's education standards; it merely requires the state to adopt standards of its choosing that are adequate and to document the uniform application of those standards. If the states' ability to opt out of NCLB is largely impractical and simply a formalism, the federalism argument is as much a rhetorical stance that puts Congress on the defensive as it is a demonstration of NCLB's coercive effects. It is telling that no state has opted out of NCLB since its inception seven years ago. Connecticut's constitutional challenge to NCLB was dismissed as premature, since the DOE had taken no enforcement actions or final decisions against Connecticut. Since it has not withdrawn from NCLB or refused to comply with any of its provisions, it may be said that Connecticut has not put its money where its mouth was. The other constitutional challenge to NCLB, *School District of Pontiac v. Secretary of the United States Department of Education*, was not joined or supported by any of the states in which the plaintiff school districts reside; furthermore, Pontiac principally alleges lack of notice rather than the fatal constitutional defect of coercion....

State Control vs. National Accountability

The United States Constitution makes no provision for education. Since the Tenth Amendment reserves all unenumerated powers for state government, the federal government has no direct control over education. Early on, the federal government provided a small amount of funding for school construction, vocational and higher education, and some specialized programs like school lunch and impact aid; in 1958, it first provided some funding for academic instruction in regular primary and secondary schools. Federal funding of education began in earnest with the Elementary and Secondary Education Act of 1965 (ESEA), a product of the civil rights and antipoverty agendas of the 1960s. The overwhelming majority of ESEA funds were appropriated under Title I for raising education spending for disadvantaged students. Although not an unconditional grant like most earlier federal education spending, the intended uses of Title I funds were loosely specified.

Funding is not the only role the federal government has in education. The federal judiciary frequently supervised the desegregation of schools after 1954, when the Supreme Court held in *Brown v. Board of Education* that, under the Fourteenth Amendment, an opportunity for education, if provided by a state, was "a right which must be made available to all on equal terms." In 1973, in *San Antonio Independent School District v. Rodriguez*, the Court declined to extend that holding to strike down long-standing school financing laws whereby local property taxes largely supplement state and federal funding in local schools and whereby even state funding may be distributed unequally in favor of wealthier districts. *San Antonio* held that there is no fundamental federal right to an education or, if there is, then not to a particular quality of education beyond a minimally adequate one. Therefore, even greatly unequal local school financing is constitutionally permissible....

NCLB requires states to adopt "challenging" and specific academic content standards in language arts, mathematics, and science and to align these with achievement standards for basic, proficient, and advanced levels. These standards must be embodied in student assessments given annually in grades 3 through 8 and once in high school. Most importantly, the standards and assessments must be uniform throughout the state. States are required to develop an accountability system that defines "adequate yearly progress" (AYP) and the methods for calculating it, together with a timeline to track annual progress toward NCLB's end goal of proficiency for all students in 2014. States must submit initial, detailed compliance plans to the DOE. The Secretary of Education has approval power over the compliance plans but is also required to utilize the assistance of a peer review process that includes parents, teachers, and state education officials. School districts and states are then required to publish annual reports of data, broken down to permit tracking of student performance by economic, racial, and other indicators. A number of remedies and sanctions are provided for schools that fail to meet AYP for any two consecutive years, ranging from offering students supplemental educational services (free tutoring) and school transfer privileges to closing and restructuring schools. Finally, NCLB requires "highly qualified teachers" in every classroom....

NCLB's lack of interest in dictating particular standards for states to adopt [is shown by] the section of the law that defines "challenging academic standards" for the states' purpose of writing the content and achievement standards for the three core content areas [language arts, math, and science] .... The requirements concern administrative specificity and informational transparency, not any particular level of academic mastery, as the subjective descriptors "coherent," "rigorous," and "advanced" indicate. Similarly, the section of the law that sets forth the parameters for defining AYP concerns the state's demonstration of "valid and reliable" statistics, "continuous and substantial academic improvement for all students" and for specific subgroups of disadvantaged students, and high school graduation rates; it does not suggest any particular level or rate of progress. NCLB expressly denies the Secretary of Education "the authority to require a State, as a condition of approval of the State plan, to include in, or delete from, such plan on progress or more specific elements of the State's academic content standards or to use specific academic assessment instruments or items."

While it is true that NCLB's emphasis on annual testing, elaboration of standards, and collection and dissemination of data are unable to effect real academic improvement without a more profound reform of curriculum, teaching methods, and teacher preparation, it is equally true that education cannot be significantly improved without a solid foundation of assessment, accountability, and tracking, such as NCLB requires. This is especially true for low-performing schools, regardless of immediate negative impacts on passing rates and missed AYP.

In fact, educators have long concentrated their efforts on curriculum and teaching methods, but without concrete and rigorous systems of assessment and accountability in place, those efforts have made little, if any, lasting impact and have often changed with the winds and little other reason. Such efforts have frequently focused on engaging and nurturing students while overlooking and neglecting their actual academic achievement. NCLB's transparency and reporting requirements, however burdensome they may be, are appropriate and necessary in an open society. Students' and parents' educational choices depend on accurate information, and so does the civic purpose of our federation of states. NCLB puts academic achievement and accountability first because they are the cornerstone of any sound education policy ....

Complaints that NCLB directs state education policy are inaccurate. Particularly misleading is any implication that NCLB imposes standards on states. In fact, NCLB requires states to develop their own standards, design their own student assessments, define proficiency and AYP, and determine how quickly their AYP will approach the 2014 goal of 100 percent proficiency. By requiring states to develop statewide standards that implement a uniform education policy, NCLB works carefully with the constitutional imperatives. It respects state control of education (as the Tenth Amendment requires), and it preserves local governments' prerogative to supplement education funding (as San Antonio requires) and hence to enrich the curriculum for local needs. Standards are, after all, only a base for teaching.

The complaint that standardized testing forces teachers to "teach to the test" and to neglect a rich curriculum has entered the commonplace. Research, it is argued, shows that "as a rule, better standardized exam results are more likely to go hand-in-hand with a shallow approach to learning than with deep understanding"; thus, "a rise in scores may be worse than meaningless: it may actually be reason for concern." But the assumption here—that preparing the most disadvantaged and struggling students to pass standardized tests saps all other time and energy for teaching and learning and precludes a rich curriculum fostering critical and imaginative thinking—is a fallacy. The prevalence of the complaint against "teaching to the test" is better interpreted as evidence of the need for radical teaching and curriculum reform. There is thus no foundation to the idea that NCLB imposes education policy on states ....

Federal enforcement of equality is necessarily at times inimical to entrenched local interests, as the history of the Fourteenth Amendment, including its application to education pursuant to *Brown*, has amply demonstrated. It is perhaps inevitable that the pursuit of equality in education manifests itself temporarily (again) as a struggle over institutional power and financial resources. ESEA, after all, "was intended to be primarily a redistributive bill. NCLB executes that intention and upsets the status quo of vastly unequal opportunities and outcomes in education."

Federal Funding and Testing Costs

Congress's actual annual appropriations have never equaled the amounts authorized under NCLB; they have been between one-half and two-thirds of the amounts originally authorized. Nevertheless, the appropriations represent a significant increase in federal funding of education—in the first year of the program, federal funding increased by 26 percent and, by 2005, the increases in federal funding that had resulted from NCLB accounted for about 2 percent of the total education spending by states, a substantial increase, especially considering that federal funding of education constitutes only about 7 or 8 percent of total education spending. NCLB's critics distort this reality with irresponsible exaggerations and inaccuracies, such as the following: "NCLB places, without remuneration, financially and bureaucratically onerous reporting duties on states, districts, and schools...."

Total federal appropriations under NCLB have covered only approximately one-third of some states' costs of compliance. Since the amounts originally authorized were only twice or less than twice the actual appropriations, it is clear that even the authorized amounts would have been insufficient to pay for compliance without the need for states to incur costs of their own. Because states design their own assessments and determine their own rates of progress, each state controls the cost of its program, as the Connecticut example demonstrates.

Before the enactment of NCLB, Connecticut Mastery Tests (CMTs) were given in grades 4, 6, and 8 and were nationally recognized as models of high-quality, comprehensive testing. To avoid the cost of developing new CMTs for grades 3, 5, and 7, Connecticut requested a waiver of NCLB's annual summative testing requirement. It proposed substituting much less expensive tests individualized by classroom and offered sound rationale for such an education policy. The Bush administration's DOE denied the request and suggested that Connecticut use multiple choice tests in grades 3, 5, and 7 to comply with NCLB's requirements while avoiding the great cost of developing and implementing new CMTs. Connecticut viewed this advice as both unsound education policy and financially unworkable. The DOE thus rejected Connecticut's policy preferences in favor of strict compliance with NCLB. Connecticut, for its part, proceeded to develop new CMTs for grades 3, 5, and 7. This sequence of events makes it clear that Connecticut took on the extra cost of developing CMTs as a policy choice, not as a requirement of NCLB or the DOE, and that reality serves to keep in perspective NCLB's true financial effects....

Connecticut's policy preferences seek to maximize academic excellence, while NCLB seeks the more mundane (and historically elusive) goal of broadening basic academic achievement. Neither goal excludes the other, although limitations of funds may require focusing on one or the other at a given time. Coming three decades after *San Antonio*, NCLB is an entirely fair swing of the pendulum.

The charge that NCLB is shortsighted is therefore a matter of perspective. NCLB's priorities are democratizing and take a long view of achieving equality. Nevertheless, NCLB in no way impedes the continued supplemental funding of local education with local property taxes. It gives an incomplete and distorted picture to attribute reduction of academic enrichment programs to the costs of NCLB and not to local communities' fiscal priorities....

Conclusion

This [essay] has argued that a sound education policy cannot exist without uniform standards and transparent accountability. It has also argued that historical forces and socio-economic realities make a federal role in education necessary to achieve equal opportunity. Such a federal role is appropriate from the viewpoint of the Fourteenth Amendment, and so is the resulting financial burden on states. Because local school districts retain the prerogative of supplementing state and federal funding of education with local property taxes, the charge that NCLB dilutes their curriculum is unconvincing.

If NCLB has diluted or qualified state control of education, it has also provided considerable new funding and carefully preserved states' choices in education policy. Weighing the proportionality of these factors is a difficult, perhaps impossible endeavor .... States should therefore reconcile themselves to NCLB's requirements, and Congress should work with them to reauthorize an improved version that moves beyond standards to encompass teaching reform as well.

Without a sustained effort to build on the foundation of an adequate education, NCLB will lose the high ground it has claimed. Initiatives to reform curriculum and teacher preparation will be much more expensive and difficult to implement than NCLB's current provisions. Congress, too, must put its money where its mouth is ....

It would be a shame if the most pervasive equality measure in decades were to lapse ... [because] education is generative of all our freedoms.

Close Reading Questions

1. According to Anthony Consiglio, what are the real reasons the No Child Left Behind law (NCLB) has been so divisive?

2. What are the two main objections to NCLB, and why does Consiglio believe these critiques are somewhat contradictory?

3. Why did the state of Connecticut sue the federal Department of Education (DOE), and what was the basis of the lawsuit?

Analytical Writing/Discussion

4. What constitutional principle controls the relationship between the federal government and state governments on school control? How has this relationship changed, and why do you consider this trend to be a positive or negative one? (Historical Trends)

5. In what ways can the NCLB's demand for accountability in education through annual assessment and transparent results be considered an unnecessary burden on school systems or an essential element of school reform? After considering both viewpoints, which one do you favor, and why? (Multiple Perspectives)

6. Using the example of local funding of schools (*State of Connecticut vs. the U.S. Department of Education*), what two goals of American education are shown? Why do you think the tensions between these two goals are inevitable or resolvable? (Cultural Influences)

Further Options:

7. In "Schools and Trust in a Democracy," Deborah Meier opposes federal control of education and a standardized curriculum in America's public schools. According to Consiglio, why does NCLB avoid promoting a national curriculum, yet why do you think such standardization in education from state to state would be beneficial or not? Why do you think Meier would or would not support this uniformity within states yet variation among states?

8. As explained in Chapter 6 on Rhetoric (see pp. 104–106), it usually is persuasive to anticipate and answer likely objections to one's position. How does Consiglio counter the criticism that NCLB controls state education policies and, in particular, forces teachers to "teach to the test"? Why are you persuaded (or not) by his counterarguments?

THE ECONOMIC COST OF THE ACHIEVEMENT GAP

by Byron G. Auguste, Bryan Hancock, and Martha Laboissière

As a leading consulting firm, McKinsey & Company advises corporations, institutions, and governments worldwide. In addition to consulting on business, marketing, and public opinion, the social sector division of McKinsey & Co. publishes reports on societal concerns, such as health care and education. The three authors of this report are McKinsey employees. The following report from 2009 focuses on the widening gap in achievement by students in the United States and other developed countries, and it stresses the financial effects on the American economy.

A persistent gap in academic achievement between children in the United States and their counterparts in other countries deprived the US economy of as much as $2.3 trillion in economic output in 2008, McKinsey research finds. Moreover, each of the long-standing achievement gaps among US students of differing ethnic origins, income levels, and school systems represents hundreds of billions of dollars in unrealized economic gains. Together, these disturbing gaps underscore the staggering economic and social cost of underutilized human potential. Yet they also create room for hope by suggesting that the widespread application of best practices could secure a better, more equitable education for the country's children—along with substantial economic gains.

How has educational achievement changed in the United States since 1983, when the publication of the seminal US government report A Nation at Risks sounded the alarm about the "rising tide of mediocrity" in American schools? To learn the answer, we interviewed leading educational researchers around the world, assessed the landscape of academic research and educational-achievement data, and built an economic model that allowed us to examine the relationships among educational achievement (represented by standardized test scores), the earnings potential of workers, and GDP.

We made three noteworthy assumptions: test scores are the best available measure of educational achievement; educational achievement and attainment (including milestones such as graduation rates) are key drivers in hiring and are positively correlated with earnings; and labor markets will hire available workers with higher skills and education. While these assumptions admittedly simplify the socioeconomic complexities and uncertainties, they allowed us to draw meaningful conclusions about the economic impact of educational gaps in the United States.

Four substantial achievement gaps emerged from our work. The first is the international one. As recently as the 1960s, the United States led the world in a variety of educational outcomes. Yet the Organisation for Economic Co-operation and Development (OECD) found that in 2006, America ranked 25th out of 30 industrialized countries in math and 24th in science. Moreover, cross-country comparisons of US students at two different ages—9–10 and 15—suggest that the closer they get to joining the labor force, the further they lag behind their international counterparts in reading, math, and science.

1. Finland	548	21. Hungary	491
Korea	547	Luxembourg	490
Netherlands	531	Norway	490
Switzerland	530	Spain	480
Canada	527	25. **United States**	474
Japan	523	Portugal	466
New Zealand	522	Italy	462
Belgium	520	Greece	459
Australia	520	Turkey	424
10. Denmark	513	Mexico	406
Czech Republic	510		
Iceland	506		
Austria	505		
Germany	504		
Sweden	502	Average Score	498
Ireland	501		
France	496		
United Kingdom	495		
Poland	495		
20. Slovak Republic	492		

FIGURE 2 Average PISA Math Scores

The gap's impact is startling: if the United States had closed it by 1998 and reached the level of the top performers, such as Finland and South Korea, the US GDP could have been $1.3 trillion to $2.3 trillion higher in 2008. To put the facts another way, the gap imposes a higher recurring annual economic cost on the US economy than the [2009] recession does. If the United States had closed educational-achievement gaps by 1998, its GDP in 2008 could have been $1.3 trillion to $2.3 trillion higher.

Next we looked at other gaps in US educational achievement. A second one emerges among US students of different ethnic origins. As researchers have long known, black and Hispanic students score, on average, two to three years behind white students of the same age on standardized tests—a gap that persists regardless of how it is measured. These differences too represent sizable missed opportunities. If the gap had been bridged by 1998, the 2008 US GDP could have been up to $525 billion higher than it was. When we looked at the implications of the achievement gap on US earnings, we found that in aggregate they could have been up to $160 billion higher in 2008 had it been eliminated. Left unchecked, the magnitude of such disparities will rise in coming years as blacks and Hispanics account for a larger share of the US population.

The two remaining achievement gaps we studied—one between students at different income levels, the other between higher- and lower-performing school systems—also appear to exact a heavy price. We define lower-income students as those eligible for free lunch through a government program. Had the achievement gap between them and other students been bridged by 1998, a decade later US GDP might have been as much as $670 billion higher than it was. If the gap between low-performing states and the US average had been closed, the 2008 US GDP could have been up to $700 billion higher. Collectively, the economic impact of the four achievement gaps we studied is significant—comparable, in their effect on the US economy, to recessions since the 1970s.

Yet there is cause for optimism amid the gloomy findings. The wide variation in performance among schools serving similar students suggests that the widespread application of best practices observed at the system level could close the gaps. California and Texas, for example, are two large, demographically similar states. But in educational attainment, students in Texas are, on average, one to two years ahead of California students of the same age, even though Texas has a lower per capita income and spends less per pupil than California does.

The same pattern holds true among school districts within states, among schools within districts, and among classrooms within schools. Indeed, the OECD finds that the variation within US schools in 2006 was 2.6 times greater than the variation across them, confirming research by McKinsey and others that consistent, high-quality teaching is a key factor determining student achievement. Moreover, international experience confirms that it is possible to make progress in closing these gaps: not only have two dozen countries made substantial progress in overall achievement, but 17 countries that exceed US performance levels also have a narrower gap among children of divergent socioeconomic backgrounds.

Close Reading Questions:

1. What are the three key assumptions about education and the economy does the report make? Which one do you find to be easiest or hardest to accept and why?

2. Along with the international comparisons, what achievement gaps among U.S. students do the authors document? Which one do you find to be most or least likely and why?

3. According to the authors, what are the economic costs of the various forms of the achievement gaps they analyze? Create a chart to present these costs.

Analytical Writing/Discussion

4. Although the report presents several problems, why do the authors also believe there are reasons for optimism? Why does their optimism make you believe that educational reform is possible? (Multiple Perspectives)

5. When did U.S. education begin to deteriorate, and what social factors do you think might have contributed to this decline? (Historical Trends)

6. Although some defenders of public education may object that schools cannot be expected to overcome social problems like poverty and poor parenting, why do you find (or not) the report's evidence on closing the achievement gap? (Cultural Influences)

Further Options:

7. Synthesis, meaning the making of connections between two (or more) readings is central to academic writing. At the start of this chapter, Horace Mann and the Supreme Court are quoted. Mann asserts, education is a "great equalizer" in society, and in 1954, the Supreme Court decided against "separate but equal" education. How could you use some evidence from the McKinsey report to argue that the U.S. has or has not made enough progress on the ideals of educational and social equality?

8. As explained in Chapter 6 on Rhetoric (see pp.xx-yy), we can be convinced using three rhetorical appeals: logic (logos), emotion (pathos), and character (ethos). Which appeal do you think is used primarily in this report, and which appeal is used primarily in Theodore Sizer's "What High School Is" (see pp. xx-yy)? What kind of person do you think would be persuaded by this report, and what kind of person do you think would be more convinced by Sizer's argument and why?

LESS COLLEGE PREP, NOT MORE, IN HIGH SCHOOLS

by Russell Rumberger

Given the title of this reading, it may surprise you to learn that its author is a vice provost in the University of California administration. Rumberger is the author of a 2011 book titled *Dropping Out: Why Students Drop Out of High School and What Can be Done About It*. The following reading is taken from a related newspaper article that originally was published in the *Boston Globe* on September 20, 2011.

What is the purpose of high school? Over the past several years America seems to have arrived at a consensus: The overarching goal of high school is to prepare students for college. The current mantra is "college ready for all," which means high school students need to be focusing on academic preparation and study skills. It's a rare issue that crosses party lines — both Republicans and Democrats can win points by pushing for a tougher, more competitive high school education.

Driven by this notion, states and districts around the country have raised high school graduation requirements by increasing the number and rigor of required academic courses and by adding exit exams. Massachusetts doesn't let students graduate unless they can pass the MCAS exam in English, math, and one science or technology subject. Americans, anxious about their competitiveness, look around the world and worry that, if anything, we're not doing enough.

But as we push harder to create more demanding high schools that are more focused on college preparation, something is also going wrong. Emerging research in the education world suggests that a tougher approach to high school academics might leave students no better prepared for college and work, while also increasing the number of high school dropouts. The National Research Council concluded that high school exit exams have decreased high school graduation rates in the United States by 2 percentage points without increasing achievement. In Chicago, a 2010 study found no positive effects on student achievement from a school reform measure that ended remedial classes and required college preparatory course work for all students. High school graduation rates declined, and there was no improvement in college enrollment and retention rates among students who did graduate.

The United States clearly needs more college graduates: We currently rank ninth in the world in four-year college graduation rates for domestic students, and President Obama has set a goal for the United States to be first in the world by 2020.

But we also need something else: more high school graduates, and better-trained ones. And to do that, we need to think differently about what high school should be: not narrowly focused on classroom achievement, but broadly designed to keep more students engaged, reward more types of thinking, and leave young people better prepared, whatever they plan to do.

To college-minded parents and educators, rethinking high school in this way might sound like a scaling back of ambition. But it can also be a more broad-minded, accommodating vision of what school is, and who it's for. It's a vision with deep roots in American history, and one that gives more students a chance to lay the groundwork for their futures.

Despite the current focus on college preparedness, American students, parents, and public officials have long seen education as having broader goals. In 1818 Thomas Jefferson stated that the purpose of public education included giving citizens information for transacting business, the ability to express ideas in writing, and an understanding of duties to neighbors and country.

Support for a broad range of educational goals continues to this day. A recent survey of the general public, elected officials, and state legislators by Richard Rothstein from the Economic Policy Institute and his colleagues showed support for eight broad goals for public education, with "basic academic goals" being the highest rated, but generating no more than one-quarter of the votes. Other goals included critical thinking, social skills and work ethic, and citizenship.

The need for schools to do more than prepare students for college is supported by studies about jobs in the future economy. A 2010 report from Georgetown University forecasts that by 2018, 63 percent of all jobs in the United States will require a postsecondary education — but that also means that more than a quarter of all jobs will not require any postsecondary education. Indeed, the Department of Labor Statistics has projected that more than one-third of all job openings in the US economy between 2008 and 2018 will not require a college degree, and in fact will require one month or less of on-the-job experience or instruction to be fully qualified in the occupation.

So for a large number of Americans, a college degree won't matter at all. What will matter, however, is graduating from high school with a set of skills that they can use to get a job, to keep learning, to live a better life.

A number of economists, including Nobel economist James Heckman, have documented the need for non-cognitive or so-called soft skills in the labor market, such as motivation, perseverance, risk aversion, self-esteem, and self-control. A 2001 report from the National Association of Manufacturers found the top skill deficiency in both current workers and job applicants was a lack of basic employability skills such as timeliness and work ethic.

Only 76 percent of public high school students in the United States earn a diploma within four years of entering the ninth grade, a rate lower than 40 years earlier. This translates into more than 1 million students who fail to earn a high school diploma each year. When these students drop out of high school, either from lack of interest or because they can't pass an academically rigorous exam, they're losing not only the chance at the diploma they'll need to get a job, but also any opportunity they might have to acquire those basic skills.

How can we keep those students in school—and better serve them when they stay? Research has shown that the key factor in student success is being engaged. Students who are not engaged are less likely to perform well in school, more likely to fail classes, and less likely to graduate. In the 2006 Civic Enterprises report, The Silent Epidemic, high school dropouts reported that the most frequent reason for leaving school was that classes were not interesting.

America's education system—and its students—would benefit from developing a broader measure of high school success, one that includes vocational and technical education as well as the arts and humanities.

Research demonstrates that career and technical education — courses that teach applied skills in agriculture, engineering, health science, and the like—increases attendance, raises completion rates, and improves earnings and employment prospects of high school graduates whether or not they attend college. International comparisons further reveal that countries offering more access to vocational options have higher high school completion rates as well as higher scores on international tests.

Such courses, if approached creatively, can also provide another way of teaching rigorous academic content. The University of California, where I work, is helping teachers design so-called integrated technical courses for high schools that meet entry requirements for the university. One example is an auto mechanics course that also teaches students college prep physics, already offered in one California high school.

A more balanced high school education would also offer students the chance to spend time in a workplace, not only learning career-specific skills, but also developing the "soft" skills needed for success. In such schools, graduation requirements could be redefined so students could succeed not just by passing MCAS-style tests, but by demonstrating mastery of an area that most interests them—whether it is math, physics, cooking, mechanics, or sports—while achieving acceptable proficiency in core academic and other areas.

High school, in short, should not just prepare adolescents for college and careers, but for successful lives as adults. And far from backing off modern notions of success, this approach actually embodies new understandings of what really helps people succeed: not just reading and math, but deeper life skills that aren't reflected on exit exams or college applications.

A long-term study by sociologist John Clausen tracked children born in the Great Depression for six decades and found that those whose lives turned out best—who obtained more education, had lower rates of divorce, had more orderly careers, achieved higher occupational status, and experienced fewer life crises such as unemployment—shared something he labeled "planful competence," a combination of dependability, intellectual involvement, and self-confidence. Those factors, he found, didn't necessarily correspond to higher education or test scores. "There's nothing that predicts better," he wrote, "than what they were like in high school."

Close Reading Questions

1. According to recent research cited by Rumberger, what are the purpose of the tougher graduation requirements and the results of these new standards?

2. Along with college preparation, how else might the goals of high school education be defined more broadly? With which of these additional goals offered by the author, do you agree most or last, and why?

3. What percentage of students is dropping out of high school now, and what are the long-term effects on their lives?

Analytical Writing/Discussion

4. How can the advocacy of broader educational goals be supported by historical evidence as well as current economics? Which evidence do you think would be most persuasive to school officials and why? (Historical Trends)

5. Along with the broadening of the goals of education, how could the courses offered in high schools also be altered? Why would you have liked to have taken some of the courses proposed or not? (Multiple Perspectives)

6. According to the sociologist John Clausen, what personal attributes make it more likely for adults to succeed at school, work, and home? To what degree do you think these qualities can be and should be taught in public high schools? (Cultural Influences)

Further Options

7. In "What High School Is," Theodore Sizer also examines the stated goals of high school education. In what specific ways do your think Sizer's and Rumberger's analyses of school goals are similar to or different from each other?

8. Using the double-entry notes explained in Chapter 3 (see pp. 79–81), answer the following question: Which of the other authors of the previous readings of this chapter: Dewey, Meier, and Consiglio, do you think is more or less likely to agree with Rumberger on broadening the goals of high school education beyond college preparation? Explain why they agree or disagree using specific quotations selected from each reading and then explain their significance.

Freewrite 3: Two Classrooms

The following excerpts from two different books provide an unusual glimpse at the act of teaching because both describe the same poem being taught to high school students. After reading both excerpts, you will be asked to respond through freewriting and/or discussion.

From *Savage Inequalities* by Jonathan Kozol:

In a sun-drenched corner room on the top floor, a female teacher and some 25 black and Hispanic children are reading a poem by Paul Laurence Dunbar. Holes in the walls and ceiling leave exposed the structural brick. The sun appears to blind the teacher. There are no shades. Sheets of torn construction paper have been taped to windowpanes, but the glare is quite relentless. The children look forlorn and sleepy.

> I know why the caged bird sings....
> It is not a carol of joy....

"This is your homework," says the teacher. "Let's get on with it."

But the children cannot seem to wake up to the words. A 15-year-old boy, wearing a floppy purple hat, white jersey, and striped baggy pants, is asked to read the lines.

> I know what the caged bird feels ....
> When the wind stirs soft through the springing grass,
> And the river flows like a stream of glass....

A 15-year-old girl with curly long red hair and many freckles reads the lines. Her T-shirt hangs down almost to her knees.

> I know why the caged bird beats his wing
> Till its blood is red on the cruel bars.

A boy named Victor, sitting at my side, whispers the words: "I know why the caged bird beats his wing.... is blood is red. He wants to spread his wings."

The teacher asks the children what the poet means or what the imagery conveys. There is no response at first. Then Victor lifts his hand. "The poem is about ancient days of slavery," he says. "The bird destroys himself because he can't escape the cage."

> "Why does he sing?" the teacher asks.
> "He sings out of the longing to be free."
> At the end of class the teacher tells me, "Forty, maybe 45 percent out of this group will graduate."

From *Reason to Believe* by Hephzibah Roskelly and Kate Ronald:

Bill Buczinsky teaches five classes: two honors ninth grade classes, one "regular" ninth grade, and two "standard" ninth grade sections. These last sections are filled with students who for one reason or another could be labeled "at risk." [These] students are more likely to be poor, to come from dangerous neighborhoods. Many—a disproportionately large number—are black. Several students speak English as a second language. Two are physically handicapped, one with a leg brace and an arm brace that Bill will adjust to aid the student's writing. One student stutters noticeably with each sentence. They are students who are in danger of getting lost in a system that seems often to have despaired of helping them. It is an old classroom with large windows and seats ranged around on three sides. [The teacher Bill] never sits. He jokes as the bell rings, takes roll quickly, cues up a tape, writes on the board, answers questions, gives directions, all at once it seems. There are twenty-six students.

[A school official] is sitting in Bill's class to observe. She sits on one side of the room watching Bill, who walks among the students as he begins the class, laughing as he talks: "Guys, if you could do a favor for me here and get started. While you're preparing for class to begin I'm going to cue up something for you." "Notice what Andrew has on his head." "Yes, I see you have that notebook open. Good." He's speaking fast and moving as he talks, commanding their attention with his goodwill. He puts on a recording of some classical music, passes out copies of the poem they will read and discuss today, and asks students to begin to read it. It is Paul Lawrence Dunbar's "Sympathy." "You may know this poem," Bill says. "You may know what the poet feels like. Before we do anything else, I want you to take five minutes and think about it. Write for five minutes. Do you ever feel trapped like the guy in the poem? Do you know why the caged bird sings?"

… When everybody is finished or close enough, Bill asks students to read aloud their responses. Predictably they begin with characterizations of school as a time to feel caged. School is a prison. Bill talks about rules, about breaking them. He tells a story about a student he's seen eating lunch off campus. He tells them what he's said to the rule breaker: "You look like a kid I know who's a junior. So he wouldn't be here at Taco Bell because only seniors can do that, of course." The students all laugh. "Why the rule about going off campus?" Bill says. "Because people won't come back." "When is it OK to break a rule in the system?" Students ask this question but don't answer it. They are finding connections between what they have written about being caged and the discussion about breaking and making rules.

As students talk and respond, read or tell what they've written, Bill watches to see who is waiting to speak, who is quiet but ready. He does this casually, calmly, seeing the whole class, attentive to both speakers at the moment and listeners. A young woman from Columbia speaks about being caged in a culture where she's not allowed to wear long hair at her school, and the other students whistle. The students ask her about her hometown in Bogata. The conversation moves to several students who sit close together and begin complaining of being in prison at home with parents who don't let them set their own curfews or don't like their friends. One or two comment on being imprisoned in their jobs, where dress codes or hours keep them trapped.

One young man has been quietly following the discussion, looking down every so often at his paper to check it, offering a comment as others have spoken up. Finally, he raises his hand and Bill catches it. Ron begins to speak, but Bill stops him. "Why don't you read it?" he says. Ron reads: "It's bad when school is a prison or when your house is. When the walls around you trap you. But that's not the worst thing." Ron tells about his life at home. His grandmother won't let him go shoot baskets in the evening at the park because "just last week they held up some kids down there." And how he won't walk to the store anymore because there [have been] three drive-by [shootings] in the last month. "You should feel free when you're outside in the air. It's the worst thing when your own neighborhood, everything around you makes you feel like you're in a prison."

Bill asks someone to read "Sympathy" aloud now and then again. He looks at Ron and says, "Ron knows 'what the caged bird feels, alas.'" Ron laughs, "I wouldn't use 'alas.'" Everybody begins to talk at once, but time—alas—is up. Students gather up their books, a few pat Ron on the back as they leave.

After reading these two texts, answer some of the following questions by freewriting and/or discussion:

- Although students in each class demonstrate some understanding of the poem, why do you think one teacher can be deemed more effective and why?

- In what ways is each poetry lesson similar to or different from the way you usually were taught to read, enjoy, and analyze literature?

- What do you think are the crucial qualities of an effective teacher?

- How have those qualities of effective teaching been fulfilled or not in these readings?

Final Assignment 1: The Ends and the Means of Education

The authors of this chapter's readings examine the means and the ends of secondary education. Sizer, for instance, points out that the stated goals of some high schools do not match their actual practices.

Essay Question

What do you think are the most important goals and the best methods of high school education? How do you think these ends and means should be coordinated? For instance, should standardized tests be used to link goals and methods?

Write a formal and extended essay to answer this question. Be sure to include specific references and direct quotations from several readings in this chapter (see Chapter 7 on Academic Honesty on quoting and citing properly). Be sure to not only support your informed perspective but also to anticipate and answer the possible objections of those who do not already agree with you. Your task is to assert your opinion and persuade others to consider it carefully.

Freewrite 4: Assignment Analysis

Before you start to answer this complex question, analyze its parts. Reread the essay question above and underline several phrases that represent key parts of the larger answer you will be developing. Then pick two or three of these phrases and freewrite your immediate impressions: What do you think right now? Then, pause to look for connections, contradictions, and omissions within your first response: what else do you want to discuss, what else do you want to add, and/or what order of your ideas is developing? Finally, consider the audience of your essay: who does not agree with you already, and why might they disagree?

Reading Review

Once you have sketched some of your initial ideas, review some of the readings to find specific details and persuasive evidence to support, enrich, and possibly complicate your response. Here are some readings and post-reading questions that you may want to consider:

1. Freewrite 1
2. Sizer, Close Reading Question 3

3. Dewey, Analytical Writing Question 5

4. Meier, Close Reading Question 1

5. Freewrite 2

6. Freewrite 3

7. Consiglio, Analytical Writing Question 5

8. Rumberger, Analytical Writing Question 5

Feel free to include other readings and post-reading questions. You also may want to review the suggestions for writing persuasively in Chapter 6 on Argument as well as practicing the peer response described in Chapter 4 on the Writing Process.

Final Assignment 2

As an educational theorist, Dewey initially believed that better schooling would lead to the social reforms he desired, such as the furthering of democracy. Yet when he tried to implement his educational theories, Dewey found his task was much more difficult than he had considered. He discovered that schools, as social institutions, are slow to change because of the "opposition of those who … realize [educational reform] would threaten their ability to use others for their own ends." Thus, the possibility of educational reform leading to social reform is complicated by the fact that schools share many of the same problems from which society in general suffers.

Essay Question

To what degree do you think high schools can be used to help resolve social problems? Or do you think schools are limited because they reflect the problems of society?

Write a formal and extended essay to answer these questions. Be sure to include specific references and direct quotations from several readings in this chapter (see Chapter 7 on Academic Honesty on quoting and citing properly). Be sure to not only support your informed perspective but also to anticipate and answer the possible objections of those who do not already agree with you. Your task is to assert your opinion and persuade others to consider it carefully.

Freewrite 5: Assignment Analysis

Before you start to answer this complex question, analyze its parts. Reread the question above and underline several phrases that represent key parts of the larger answer you will be developing. Then pick two or three of these phrases and freewrite your immediate impressions: What do you think right now? Then, pause to look for connections, contradictions, and omissions within your first response: what else do you want to discuss, what else do you want to add, and/or what order of your ideas is developing? Finally, consider the audience of your essay: who does not agree with you already, and why might they disagree?

Reading Review

Once you have sketched some of your initial ideas, review some of the readings to find specific details and persuasive evidence to support, enrich, and possibly complicate your response. Here are some readings and post-reading questions that you may want to consider:

1. Freewrite 1
2. Sizer, Analytical Writing Question 6
3. Dewey, Analytical Writing Question 6
4. Meier, Analytical Writing Question 4
5. Meier, Further Options Question 7
6. Consiglio, Analytical Writing Question 6
7. Auguste, Hancock, and Laboissiere, Analytical Writing Question 6
8. Rumberger, Close Reading Question 3

Feel free to include other readings and post-reading questions. You also may want to review the suggestions for writing persuasively in Chapter 6 on Argument as well as practicing the peer response described in Chapter 4 on the Writing Process.

Additional Source Suggestions

In the e-supplement of this textbook, there are several sources that will help you deepen your understanding of educational reform and strengthen your final assignment. These sources include videos as well as readings, and they present multiple perspectives, historical trends, and cultural influences on educational reform. To access these materials, see the code on the inside front cover of this textbook, which will lead you to the website for additional sources.

Cities and Suburbs

Those who labor in the earth are the chosen people of God. I view cities as pestilential to the morals, the health, and the liberties of man.

—*Thomas Jefferson (1800)*

A city is a place where there is no need to wait for next week to get the answer to a question, to taste the food of any country, to find new voices to listen to and familiar ones to listen to again.

—*Margaret Mead (1975)*

To millions of Americans, a house in the suburbs with a nice yard, garden, and a little open space is the American Dream. To environmentalists and urban planners, though, it is a nightmare.

—*Thomas J. DiLorenzo (2000)*

I think there are two prevailing views of the suburbs in the States: either they're this sort of tedious place, where everyone is the same, buys the same food and drives around in their little minivans, or the view is that the suburbs are extremely perverse in a humorous way.

—*Megan Abbott (2011)*

Introduction

On the MetroNorth train that leaves daily from New Haven, CT, one phrase is repeated: "the City." Teenagers talk excitedly about shopping in the City. Some riders are working on their laptops to prepare for meetings in the City. A father and his daughter discuss the pros and cons of attending college in the City. And, there always is a group of friends anxious to see a play and have lunch in the City.

New Haven is a city of 124,000 residents. To be sure, New Haven has great shopping and a robust professional community, in addition to world-class art and theater and diverse options for higher education. Yet, "the City" of which the MetroNorth riders speak is not New Haven, but the 3-mile wide borough of Manhattan. The place most associated with the name New York City, Manhattan has 1.6 million residents and hosts 45 million annual visitors. Manhattan is, many would assert, the epitome of the American city and one of the best places to live.

During the twentieth century, American cities were equated with success, adventure, and romance. Songs and nicknames underscore our love affair with cities: "Chicago. Chicago." "It's up to you, New York." "I Left My Heart in San Francisco." "The Big Easy" and "The Mile High City." Yet in the United

States, cities have historically been the subject of critics who decry urban areas as overcrowded, wrought with crime, and suffering from poor educational and employment opportunities.

If the city is excitement, many like to think the suburbs are relaxation. Danger lurks around every city corner while safety is the hallmark of suburbia. Cities teem with subways and sidewalks, while suburbs have green grass and open spaces. The suburbs, however, are not without their detractors, who bemoan the absence of houses with architectural variety, limited access to public transportation and artistic pursuits, and the lack of racial and social diversity.

By the end of the twentieth century and the beginning of the twenty-first century, American suburbs led a parallel, if not always equal, existence with cities.

Surely President Dwight Eisenhower did not envision the public policy issues that would expand and ultimately seek to close the dichotomy of urban and suburban demographics when he signed the Federal-Aid Highway Act of 1956. Eisenhower's plan was to enhance the economy by building an efficient arrangement of highways that connected roads within and across every state in the continental United States. In his memoir, Eisenhower stated that—more than any other federally funded venture—highways would "change the face of America." Indeed, they have. In the decades since the completion of this massive infrastructure project, America's highways have become a way to circumvent our cities. For those whose employment requires that they work in a city, highways allow for quick exodus from the perceived raucousness of cities for the relative tranquility of the suburbs. Thus, cities and suburbs continue to negotiate their complex and often troubled relationship.

The three historical readings of this chapter span over 100 years of the impact of urban and suburban life. The oldest one dates back to 1895, when sociologist Frederick. J. Kingsbury cited numerous reasons why cities were more healthy and rewarding than country life. The most recent historical reading is a 2011 article by Michael P. Marino that reviews the history of suburban life in the United States. In the three contemporary readings, each author discusses plans to revive cities and their outlying areas whose population changes resulted in economic, social, and educational decline. Why they do not all agree on ways to revive cities and sustain suburban areas, the authors agree that action must be taken to assure the prosperity and vitality of these urban areas.

These texts, along with the reading questions, freewriting activities, and visual elements of this chapter, are designed to develop the reading and writing abilities required for academic study. After each reading, you will find a set of questions that are divided into Close Reading Questions, Analytical Writing/ Discussion, and Further Options. Some questions involve the same investigation of multiple perspectives, cultural influences, and historical trends that were introduced in Chapters 1 or 2. Answering some and discussing more of the post-reading questions will better prepare you to complete the final assignments options. These final writing assignments will ask you to assert your own, more informed perspective on cities and suburbs. This chapter asks: **What do you think American cities and suburbs need to thrive in the twenty-first century?**

Freewrite 1: Initial Impressions

Before you read the varying opinions of the other writers in the rest of this chapter, freewrite to explore your own thoughts and experiences about urban and suburban lifestyles. Try answering some of the following questions:

- What comes to mind when you think of cities and/or when you think of suburbs?

- What are some of your most and/or least memorable times when you have visited a major American city and/or suburban town?

- Why do you think that cities are associated with excitement and suburbs are associated with relaxation?

IN DEFENSE OF THE CITY: OBSERVING URBAN PROGRESS

by Frederick J. Kingsbury

A professor of social science and president of the American Social Science Association, Frederick J. Kingsbury delivered this speech in 1895 at a national convention of social scientists. In it, he was responding to the criticisms of cities—mainly by the clergy—who thought cities were places of moral decadence. The following is an excerpt of the speech, which was published later in 1895 in the *Journal of Social Sciences* under the title "The Tendency of Men to Live in Cities."

Dr. Josiah Strong, in that vigorous presentation of the dangers of our American civilization entitled "Our Country," says: "The city has become a serious menace to our civilization, because in it each of our dangers is enhanced and all are localized.... Not only does the proportion of the poor increase with the growth of the city, but their condition becomes more wretched..."

While there has always been a strong tendency in humanity cityward, this nineteenth century sees it intensified beyond all former experience. Statistics do not make interesting public reading; but from Dr. Strong's valuable work—where there are many—we take a few in support of our position:

The population of this country as divided between city and country was in 1790, omitting fractions: country—97 percent, city—3 percent; in 1840, country—91 percent, city—9 percent; in 1890, country—71 percent, city—29 percent; and the rate of increase is itself all the while increasing.

In 1856 Chicago had a population of 90,000. In 1895 it is supposed to have 1,500,000, with several outlying districts not yet heard from. In this classification—which is taken from the United States census—towns of 8,000 and over rank as cities, while the rest is country. Of course, a line must be drawn somewhere for the purpose of statistics; but many think it might more properly have been drawn at 5,000, which would largely increase the city percentage. Dr. Strong also quotes this statement,—that in the rural districts of Wayne County, New York, there are 400 unoccupied houses, and much other valuable statistical information of a similar character. Professor Nordau also has many statistics of various European countries, all to the same purport. But the general fact of the enormous increase of the city at the expense of the country is so notorious that it needs no proof. Let us consider some of its causes.

It is well to notice, and perhaps here as well as anywhere, that, while in all countries the influence of the city has been great, it has not been equally great in all. Rome was the Roman Empire. Carthage was Phoenicia. Paris today is France; but London, big as it is, is not England, Madrid is not Spain, and certainly Berlin is not Germany. In all these cases there is a power and a public opinion, a consensus of thought, a moral, political, and social influence in the country as a whole, which does not look to nor depend upon the city as its maker, leader, and guide. It is easier to see and feel this fact than to analyze and explain it. Probably the same reasons or kinds of reasons do not apply in every case; but each has its own, some of which are easy to find and others too deep and elusive to be discovered. Accidents of early history, geographical relations, the temper and idiosyncrasies of a people and other influences, some broader and some more subtle, all combine to fix the relative position and importance of the great city and the country or the lesser town…

Ancient cities owed their existence to a variety of causes. Probably safety and convenience were, at the bottom, the reasons for aggregating the population; but any special city frequently owed its existence, so far as appears, to the mere caprice of a ruler as a passing fancy,—though he may have had his reasons,—sometimes, doubtless, to military considerations, and sometimes perhaps to accident, or to migration, or the results of natural causes, geographical or commercial. It was not until the Middle Ages that the industrial town was evolved. But the modern town seems wholly industrial in its raisan d'etre: it is therefore governed by the laws which govern industrial progress…

Aside from all questions of mutual defense and protection and mutual helpfulness in various ways, and industrial convenience, doubtless one of the very strongest of forces in the building of the city is the human instinct of gregariousness. This underlies ancient as well as modem, military as well as industrially founded, aggregations, and the hamlet or the village as well as the city. But there is always a craving to get where there are more people. The countryman, boy or girl, longs for the village, the villager for the larger town, and the dweller in the larger town for the great city; and, having once gone, they are seldom satisfied to return to a place of less size. In short, whatever man may have been or may be in his prognathous or troglodyte condition, ever since we have known much about him he has been highly gregarious, even under unfavorable conditions.

As long ago as 1870 Mr. Frederick Law Olmsted, in a paper read before this Association, said, "There can be no doubt that in all our modern civilization, as in that of the ancients, there is a strong drift townward"; and he quotes the language of an intelligent woman, whose early life had been spent in one of the most agreeable and convenient farming countries in the United States: "If I were offered a deed of the best farm I ever saw, on condition of going back to the country to live, I would not take it. I would rather face starvation in town."

The life of the great city would seem to bear hardest of all on the very poor, and the country, or at least suburban, life to present the strongest attraction, by contrast, to this class. Pure air, plenty of water, room for children to play, milk on which to feed them, room to sleep, wholesome food for adults,—these things, almost impossible to the poor in the city, are nearly all of easy attainments in the country; yet the overmastering desire for a city life seems to be stronger with this class than with any other. Perhaps you are familiar with the story of the kind lady who found a widow with a great family of children living in the depths of poverty and dirt in the city, and moved them all to a comfortable country home, where, with a moderate amount of exertion, they were sure of a living. At the end of six weeks her country agent reported that the family had suddenly disappeared, no one knew where. Going back to the neighborhood of their old haunts, she found them all re-established there in the same circumstances of dirt and destitution as of old. "Why *did* you leave that comfortable home, and come back here?" was her astonished inquiry. "Folks is more company nor sthoomps, anyhow," was the answer. Poor food, and little of it, dirt and discomfort, heat and cold,—all count as nothing in competition with this passion of gregariousness and desire for human society, even where that means more or less of a constant fight as the popular form of social intercourse.

Doubtless one of the most potent factors in the modern growth of cities has been the immense improvement in the facilities for travel, which has been such a marked characteristic of the last half-century. But, after all, what is this but saying that it has been made easier for people to go where they wished to be? Facilities for travel make it as easy to get from city to country as from country to city; but the tide, except for temporary purposes, all sets one way. Nevertheless, there is no question that this ease of locomotion has been availed of to a surprising extent in transporting each year in the summer season a very large portion, not of the rich alone, but of nearly every class, not only from our great cities, but from our moderately large towns, to the woods and lakes and seashore for a time. The class of people who, fifty years since, lived in the same house the year round, without thought of change, now deem a six or twelve weeks' residence in the country a vital necessity; and this fact is a great alleviation and antidote to some of the unfavorable influences of city life.

All modern industrial life tends to concentration as a matter of economy. It has long been remarked that the best place to establish or carry on any kind of business is where that business is already being done. For that reason we see different kinds of manufactures grouping themselves together,—textiles in one place, metals in another; and, of the textiles, cottons in one place, woolens in another; and of the metals, iron in one place, copper in another, and so on. The reason of this is obvious. In a community where a certain kind of business is carried on the whole population unconsciously become, to a certain extent, experts. They know a vast deal more of it than people who have had no such experience. Every man, woman, and child in a fishing village is much superior in his or her knowledge of fish, bait, boats, wind, and weather to the inhabitants of inland towns. This is true of all the arts, so that, besides the trained hands which may be drawn upon when needed, there is a whole population of half-trained ones ready to be drawn upon to fill their places. Then every kind of business is partly dependent on several other kinds. There must be machine-makers, blacksmiths, millwrights, and dealers in supplies of all sorts. Where there is a large business of any kind, these subsidiary trades that are supported by it naturally flock around it; whereas in an isolated situation the central establishment must support all these trades itself or go a considerable distance when it needs their assistance. Fifty or sixty years ago small manufacturing establishments in isolated situations and on small streams were scattered all through the Eastern States. The condition of trade at that time rendered this possible. Now they have almost wholly disappeared, driven out by economic necessity; and their successors are in the cities and large towns.

If you will examine any city newspaper of fifty or sixty years ago, you will find frequent advertisements for boys as clerks in stores; and almost always they read "one from the country preferred." Now you never see this. Why is it? I think mainly because the class of boys which these advertisements were expected to attract from the country are no longer there. This was really a call for the well-educated boys of the well-to-do farmers of native stock, who thought they could better themselves by going to a city. They went, and did better themselves; and those who stayed behind fell behind. The country people deteriorated, and the country boy was no longer for business purposes the equal of the boy who had been trained in city ways. Country boys still go to the city; but they are not advertised for, and have to find their own way.

Our great Civil War compelled us to find out some way in which to replace the productive power of a million men sent into the field and suddenly changed from producers into consumers. Their places had to be filled in the lines of agriculture and of all the mechanic arts, in the counting-room, in the pulpit, at the bar, and everywhere else where a soldier was to be found. A hundred thousand of these places, more or less, in shops, in mechanic industries, in counting-rooms, in the medical profession, even at the pulpit and the bar, were filled with women; and the deficit left by the remainder of the million was supplied by newly invented machinery to do their work. The result was that, when the war was over, a million of men, or as many as came back, found their places filled. They were no longer needed. In all rural occupations this was especially the case; and, being driven out of the country by want of work, they flocked to the city as the most likely place to find it...

We must remember, too, that cities as places of human habitation have vastly improved within half a century. About fifty years ago neither New York nor Boston had public water, and very few of our cities had either water or gas, and horse railroads had not been thought of. When we stop to think what this really means in sanitary matters, it seems to me that the increase of cities is no longer a matter of surprise.

A few years since the great improvement of the lift or elevator added probably 10 percent, actually, and much more than that theoretically, to the possibilities of population on a given amount of ground; and now within a very recent period three new factors have been suddenly developed which promise to exert a powerful influence on the problems of city and country life. These are the trolley, the bicycle, and the telephone. It is impossible at present to foresee just what their influence is to be on the question of the distribution of population; but this much is certain, that it adds from five to fifteen miles to the radius of every large town, bringing all this additional area into new relations to business centers. Places five or ten miles apart and all the intervening distances are rendered accessible and communicable for all the purposes of life as if they were in the next street. Already the bicycle has done more toward directing attention and effort to the improvement of ordinary highways than all that has been done before since the days of Indian paths. It is affecting the legislation of the country on the subject of roads. When we think of what this minimizing of distance means, we cannot help seeing that its influence must be immense, but just what no man can foretell. It is by such apparently unimportant, trifling, and inconspicuous forces that civilization is swayed and moulded in its evolutions and no man can foresee them or say whither they lead…

In contrast with the statements of Nordau and of others in regard to the unfavorable sanitary conditions of city life, it must be noticed that it is always in cities that those who can afford it get the best food; and, if you are living in the country, you are largely dependent on the city for your supply. The summer seashore visitor usually finds, if he takes the trouble to investigate, that his fresh fish comes from the nearest great city, also his meat, and quite likely his butter and eggs, and nearly everything except, perhaps, his milk. To be sure, they came from the country first in many cases; but they seek the best market, and are to be best found at it…

I have been fairly familiar with the streets of New York and Boston for the last fifty years, and there is no fact in that connection with which I have been more impressed than the physical improvement which has taken place in both men and women during that period. The men are more robust and more erect, the women have greatly improved both in feature and carriage; and in the care and condition of the teeth in both sexes a surprising change has taken place. In Boston streets and streetcars it seems to me that you see a hundred good-looking women where you formerly saw one. Whether this would hold good in the slums and low parts of the town may be doubted, but there of course one looks for the refuse and cast-off material of society…

It is to be noted that the attrition and constant opportunity for comparison which city life makes possible, and even compulsory, tend to make all the people who are subjected to its influence alike. They do and see and hear and smell and eat the same things. They wear similar clothes, they read the same books, and their minds are occupied with the same objects of thought. In the end they even come to look alike, as married people are sometimes said to do, so that they are at once recognized when they are seen in some other place; while people who live isolated lives think their own thoughts, pursue different objects, and are compelled to depend upon their own judgments and wills for the conduct of their daily lives. The consequence is that they develop and increase peculiarities of character and conduct to the verge of eccentricity, if not beyond it, and present all that variety and freshness of type, which we call originality, or individuality. They are much more dramatic, picturesque, and interesting in literature, perhaps not always in real life. I mention this in passing, without any attempt to estimate fully the value of either development. Doubtless something is lost and something gained in either case, and probably much could be said in favor of each. Many persons have a great desire to get, as they say, "back to nature"; while others prefer mankind in the improved state, even with some sameness.

The ideal life, time out of mind, for all who could afford it, has been the city for action, the country for repose, tranquillity, recuperation, rest…. The country is a good place to rest in, especially if one can control his surroundings. The quiet, the calm, the peace, the pleasant color, the idyllic sights and sounds, all tend to allay nervous irritation, to tranquillize the soul, to repress the intellectual, and to invigorate the animal functions in a very remarkable degree. But this is not rustic life: it is only the country life of the city resident…

IT WOULD SEEM, THEN

(1) that for economic reasons a large part of the work of the world must be done in cities, and the people who do that work must live in cities.

(2) That almost everything that is best in life can be better had in the city than elsewhere, and that, with those who can command the means, physical comforts and favorable sanitary conditions are better obtained there.

(3) That a certain amount of change from city to country is desirable, and is also very universally attainable to those who desire it, and is constantly growing more so.

(4) That the city is growing a better place to live in year by year; that in regard to the degenerate portion of mankind, the very poor, the very wicked, or the very indifferent, it is a question whether they are better off in the country; but, whether they are or not, their gregarious instincts will lead them to the city, and they must be dealt with there as part of the problem.

(5) That efforts to relieve the congested conditions of the city poor by deportation of children to the country are good and praiseworthy, but only touch the surface of things, and that city degeneration must mainly be fought on its own ground.

Close Reading Questions

1. For what reasons did ancient cities like Rome develop and thrive?

2. According to Kingsbury, what were two or three reasons for the growth of American cities in the late 1800s?

3. What inventions does Kingsbury cite as important to the function of American cities in the nineteenth century? (Cultural Influences)

Analytical Writing/Discussion

4. Kingsbury asserts that city life was "the hardest of all on the very poor." To what did he attribute that statement and do you think that city life today is still the most difficult for the poor?

5. Kingsbury talks of the tremendous improvements in sanitation, transportation, building and development, good health—and even good looks—of people in the city. What assumptions regarding such areas as human worth, economic class, and technology form the basis of his opinions? (Multiple Perspectives)

6. Consider Kingsbury's comparison of the relative well-being of the city dweller and the country dweller. Who do you think fares better now and why? (Historical Trends)

Further Options

7. Using examples from "In Defense of the City" and "The Twenty-first Century Retreat: American Families and Expanding American Dream Houses" by Tamara Hareven from Chapter 10, for what reasons do you think suburbs still are more appealing than cities for most American families?

8. Kingsbury was an academic, attached to a university, and he prepared this lecture for academics like himself. How well do you think Kingsbury addresses the audience he originally intended to address? In what ways, if any, does this audience attention make it easier or harder for a more general audience to comprehend his speech? For more on audience, see pp. 103 of Chapter 6 on Argument).

1910

Rank	City	State	Population
1	New York	New York	4,766,883
2	Chicago	Illinois	2,185,283
3	Philadelphia	Pennsylvania	1,549,008
4	St. Louis	Missouri	687,029
5	Boston	Massachusetts	670,585
6	Cleveland	Ohio	560,663
7	Baltimore	Maryland	558,485
8	Pittsburgh	Pennsylvania	533,905
9	Detroit	Michigan	465,766
10	Buffalo	New York	423,715

Source: Population of the 100 Largest Urban Places: 1910 https://www.census.gov/population/www/documentation/twps0027/tab14.txt

1950

Rank	City	State	Population
1	New York	New York	7,891,957
2	Chicago	Illinois	3,620,962
3	Philadelphia	Pennsylvania	2,071,605
4	Los Angeles	California	1,970,358
5	Detroit	Michigan	1,849,568
6	Baltimore	Maryland	949,708
7	Cleveland	Ohio	914,808
8	St. Louis	Missouri	856,796
9	Washington	District of Columbia	802,178
10	Boston	Massachusetts	801,444

Source: Population of the 100 Largest Urban Places: 1950 https://www.census.gov/population/www/documentation/twps0027/tab18.txt

2010

Rank	City	State	Population
1	New York	New York	8,175,133
2	Los Angeles	California	3,792,621
3	Chicago	Illinois	2,695,598
4	Houston	Texas	2,099,451
5	Philadelphia	Pennsylvania	1,526,006
6	Phoenix	Arizona	1,445,632
7	San Antonio	Texas	1,327,407
8	San Diego	California	1,307,402
9	Dallas	Texas	1,197,816
10	San Jose	California	945,942

Source: Population of the 100 Largest Urban Places: 2010 (table 5) https://www.census.gov/prod/cen2010/briefs/c2010br-01.pdf

FIGURE 1   Top 10 Cities in the United States: 1910–2010. According to U.S. Census Bureau, the top 10 cities in the United States have shifted westward over the past century.

Courtesy of the U.S. Census Bureau

THE METROPOLITAN AGE: URBAN AMERICAN IN THE 1920s

by Howard P. Chudacoff and Judith E. Smith

Howard P. Chudacoff is the George L. Littlefield Professor of American History and Professor of Urban Studies at Brown University. Judith E. Smith is Professor of American Studies at University of Massachusetts—Boston. The following is excerpted from their textbook, *The Evolution of American Urban Society* (2000), a survey of American urbanization from the sixteenth century through the end of the 20ᵗʰ century.

Urbanization: The Ascendance of the City

The 1920 federal census marked a milestone in American history: its figures revealed that for the first time a majority of the nation's people (51.4 percent) lived in cities. This revelation can be misleading: Massachusetts and Rhode Island—even California—had been predominantly urban long before 1920. Moreover, the bureau defined a city as a place inhabited by at least twenty-five hundred people—hardly a rigorous criterion. Nevertheless, the 1920 tallies had symbolic importance. In 1890, the Census Bureau had announced that the frontier no longer existed. Now, thirty years later, the figures confirmed that the nation had evolved into an urban society. The city, not the farm, had become the locus of national experience.

The agrarian way of life, with its slow pace, moral sobriety, and self-help ethic, had been waning ever since urbanization accelerated early in the nineteenth century. To be sure, by the 1920s the demise was far from complete. Several social reform movements and much political rhetoric looked nostalgically backward to the simple virtues of an imagined past. But everywhere signs pointed to an urban ascendance. A precipitous drop in commodity prices after 1920 spun small farmers into distress. Convinced that there was a better life elsewhere, an estimated six million Americans gave up the land and poured into cities like Pittsburgh, Detroit, Chicago, Denver, and Los Angeles. Many more pushed into nearby cities in the South. After lagging behind the rest of the nation for nearly a century, the South now became the most rapidly urbanizing region in terms of proportionate population growth. Memphis, Atlanta, and Chattanooga experienced extraordinary expansion. The epitome of southern urbanization was Birmingham, Alabama. A burgeoning steelmaking center in the late nineteenth century, Birmingham developed a diverse industrial, commercial, and service economy in the 1920s. This expansion attracted workers and their families from all over the South, who boosted the population of Birmingham's metropolitan area from 310,000 to 431,000 during the decade (the population of the city proper was 260,000 by 1930). Smaller cities, many of them created by textile companies that had left New England to take advantage of cheap southern labor and readily available hydroelectric power, also helped boost the urban population of the South to thirteen million by 1930. The depression years heightened farmers' impoverishment. Continuing declines in crop prices, drought, foreclosure, and bank failures sent hundreds of thousands more rural men and women to the cities in search of work.

The most visible contingents of native migrants from World War I onward were the millions of African Americans who moved into northern and southern cities. Pushed off tenant farms by failures in the cotton fields and attracted by jobs in labor-scarce cities, hundreds of thousands of African American families packed up and boarded the trains for Memphis, New Orleans, Chicago, Detroit, Cleveland, and New York. African Americans were already 90 percent of Birmingham's unskilled work force by 1910, half of the iron- and steelworkers, and 70 percent of the ore miners by the 1910s and 1920s. When the war cut off the influx of cheap foreign labor, some northern companies began to hire black labor. Short-term migration in search of wages in turpentine camps, sawmills, cottonseed oil mills, and other industries tied to agriculture began to acculturate young African American men to industrial labor. Young black women similarly ventured into nearby cities and towns to find work as domestics.

By the time that World War I created increasing demand for labor in northern cities, thousands of African American men and women were ready to mobilize family and personal networks, giving up the dream of autonomy based on landownership in exchange for the promise of full citizenship emanating from northern urban life and industrial employment. By 1920, four-fifths of the country's African Americans residing outside the South lived in cities. As migrations continued during the 1920s, New York's African American population increased from 152,000 to 328,000, Chicago's from 109,000 to 234,000, Philadelphia's from 134,000 to 220,000, Detroit's from 41,000 to 120,000, and Cleveland's from 34,000 to 72,000. African Americans constituted between 5 and 10 percent of the population of each of these places. This migration continued in the 1930s as New Deal crop subsidies paid to landowners prevented tenant farmers from making their customary living....

During the 1920s, urbanization took place on a wider front than ever before. Maturing industrial economies boosted the populations of many areas, particularly steel, oil, and automobile centers such as Pittsburgh, Cleveland, Detroit, Akron, Youngstown, Houston, Tulsa, and Los Angeles. New commercial and service activities primed expansion in regional centers such as Atlanta, Cincinnati, Nashville, Indianapolis, Kansas City, Minneapolis, Portland, and Seattle. The most exceptional growth, however, occurred in warm-climate resort cities. Between 1920 and 1930, the population of Miami ballooned from 29,571 to 110,637. As the prime beneficiary of the Florida real estate explosion of the twenties, Miami attracted thousands of land speculators and home builders. A citrus-crop failure and two disastrous hurricanes punctured the boom in 1927, but the expansion of warm-climate cities continued. Tampa and San Diego doubled their populations during the twenties.

Urban populations in this period revealed a decline in foreign-born residents. After World War I, momentum for restricting immigration accelerated. Support for an end to free immigration had been building since the 1880s among urban reformers as well as unions and nativist conservatives. By 1919, reformers who had formerly opposed restriction were convinced that the melting pot had not worked and that many immigrants—particularly those from southern and eastern Europe—stubbornly resisted assimilation. Labor leaders, fearful that a new flood of unskilled aliens would depress wages, looked at the high postwar unemployment rates and increased their longstanding support for restriction. At first businessmen opposed the rising clamor out of self-interest: they hoped that a new surge of foreign workers would not only aid industrial expansion but also cut wage rates and curb unionization. But by 1924, when Congress was debating whether to close the doors more tightly, many industrialists were willing to support restriction because they discovered that mechanization and native migration from farm to city enabled them to prosper without foreign-born labor.

Congressional acts of 1921, 1924, and 1929 successively reduced the numbers of immigrants who could be admitted annually. A system of quotas, ultimately based on the number of descendants from each nationality living in the United States in 1890, severely limited immigrants from southern and eastern Europe, the very groups who had dominated urban cores since 1880.

The laws left the doors open only to Western Hemisphere countries. Mexicans now became the largest foreign group entering the country. Many came to work in the fields and vineyards of the Southwest, but others streamed into the region's booming cities. By the end of the 1920s, Chicanos[1] made up more than half the population of El Paso, slightly less than half that of San Antonio, and one-fifth that of Los Angeles. Other Mexicans found employment in the automobile factories of Detroit and the steel mills, tanneries, and meat-packing plants of Gary and Chicago. By 1930, more than 15 percent of Mexican immigrants lived outside the Southwest.

Chicano women looked for work in cities as domestics and in textile and food processing factories. Crowding into old barrios or forming new ones, Chicano migrants often lacked decent city services such as sanitation, schools, and police protection. But the barrio community provided an environment where immigrants could sustain customs and values of the homeland and develop institutions to protect them from the uncertainties of urban life. In the same period, Puerto Ricans began to arrive on the American mainland in Brooklyn and Manhattan, identified by their *bodegas* (grocery stores), restaurants, and boardinghouses. Social and cultural diversity continued to be a distinctive quality of urban life that distinguished cities most sharply from the relative homogeneity of rural and small-town social relations.

Historian Alberto Camarillo has suggested that urban neighborhoods of ethnic and racial concentration in the 1920s and 1930s served as borderlands, geographical areas marking the margin between the dominant society and the newer groups that were always in flux. Many of these borderlands were typically multiethnic in their early years, although patters of institutional and racial discrimination helped to turn many of them over time into what he termed "color-line" borderlands. Barrio neighborhoods of southwestern cities such as El Paso and Los Angeles become increasingly distinct in these years as Mexican and Mexican-American migration to cities increased, although their exclusion from areas outside the barrios was never complete. An increasing reliance by realtors on the use of real estate covenants helped sharpen the lines of racial segregation form the 1920s onward, more lightly confining Mexicans, African Americans, Jews, and Asians to certain neighborhoods.

Suburbanization and Metropolitanism

Ironically, at the moment that urban life had achieved ascendancy in the United States, important patterns of suburban development challenged the city's economic viability and political centrality. For one thing, industry began to decentralize. Electric power gave factories flexibility in location and made possible the assembly line, which required sprawling one- and two-story plants, not compact multi-story ones like those in the city. Corporations began to locate beyond city limits, where land was cheaper and tax burdens less onerous. Industrial satellite suburbs like East Chicago and Hammond outside of Chicago, Lackawanna outside of Buffalo, East St. Louis and Wellston near St. Louis, Norwood and Oakley beyond the Cincinnati city limits, and Chester and Norristown near Philadelphia became the location of factory employment. As the proportion of factory employment located within city limits declined, city tax bases suffered a corresponding loss.

As industry decentralized, suburban areas were increasingly likely to reject municipal expansion through annexation and consolidation. Upper-class residential suburbs had been resisting central-city annexation since the late nineteenth century, but now corporate leaders exerted economic and political influence in local governments and in state legislatures to assure that the political independence of suburbs would be maintained. As one suburban editor explained, "Under local government we can absolutely control every objectionable thing that may try to enter our limits, but once annexed we are the mercy of City Hall." As sharp racial, ethnic, and class divisions separated city and suburbs, new laws made incorporation easier and annexation more difficult, and suburbs were able to gain access to improved

---

[1] Americans of Mexican descent

services without annexation. Newer southern, midwestern, and southwestern cities were able to annex suburban areas, ensuring that urban growth and economic vitality would continue. But older cities came to be ringed by incorporated suburbs that emphasized their distinctiveness from cities rather than their times to them.

When industry moved out of the central city, many white workers followed to be near their jobs. The availability of relatively inexpensive automobiles (by 1908, twenty-four American companies produced automobiles at relatively low prices) allowed even more [white] workers to reside beyond and between the reaches of urban mass transit. In 1908, Henry Ford unveiled his Model T, an inexpensive, durable motorcar produced by assembly-line techniques, and in 1910 moved his own auto production factory outside of Detroit to Highland Park.

Suburban real estate interests, the construction industry, the auto, rubber, and oil industries joined automobile owners in pressing for new roads to facilitate high-speed travel. Automobile wheels destroyed whatever was left of older, lower-speed gravel surfaces. But smoother pavements and wider streets encouraged even more urban residents to invest in automobiles, generating more traffic and demand for additional roads. The building of expressways and parkways encouraged still further suburban migration.

In 1920, the growth rate of suburbs exceeded that of the cities for the first time. Among the most rapidly growing suburbs in the 1920s were Elmwood Park, Berwyn, and Wilmette near Chicago; Beverly Hills and Inglewood near Los Angeles; Grosse Point and Ferndale near Detroit; and Cleveland Heights and Shaker Heights near Cleveland. Of seventy-one new towns incorporated in Illinois, Missouri, and Michigan in the 1920s, two-thirds were suburbs of Chicago, St. Louis, or Detroit. Many were residential communities for the upper and the middle classes, and others were industrial suburbs where factory workers constituted a fifth or more of the population. In contrast with this class diversity was racial homogeneity: suburban populations were overwhelmingly likely to be white.

As more and more people moved to the suburbs, retailing followed. Older secondary business centers at streetcar transfer points were paralleled by those springing up at major highway intersections. Neighborhood banks, movie theaters, office buildings, branches of major department stores, and chain stores such as Woolworth's, Kresge's, and Walgreen's brought the amenities of downtown to the periphery. The twenties witnessed the birth of the country's first suburban shopping center. In 1922, Jesse C. Nichols, a Kansan well versed in land economics, built the Country Club Shopping Center as the commercial hub of his huge real estate development in Kansas City. A few years later Sears Roebuck and Company began to build stores in outlying districts to reap sales from growing suburban populations. The major proliferation of shopping centers would occur following World War II, but throughout the twenties and thirties, doctors, saloon keepers, restauranteurs, and independent merchants followed clients and customers out to expanding residential areas until business districts speckled every quadrant of a city's metropolitan area. By the time of the economic collapse in 1929, the population of the suburbs was growing twice as fast as that of central cities. The more industry and retailing decentralized, the more roads were built; the more roads were built, the more automobiles became a social and economic necessity for suburban residents.

Streetcars, once the marvels of progress, declined as automobile suburbanization proceeded. After World War I, the cumulative effect of publicized abuses by streetcar franchises, strikes by streetcar employees, and accidents was that streetcars lost public support during precisely the period when companies were seriously strained by postwar inflation, overextended lines, and competition from automobiles. Millions of Americans continued to depend on mass transit to get to work through the 1930s, but by the end of the decade the number of white mass-transit riders began to decline, leaving public transportation in some cities increasingly dependent on African-American riders. As automobile use made central-city streets more congested, streetcars could no longer provide a convenient ride to work, and the farther away a commuter lived from downtown, the more benefits accrued from car travel. In the 1920s, cars counted for between 20 and 30 percent of daily traffic into central business districts even in large cities such as Boston, New York, and Chicago, and as much as 50 to 66 percent in smaller cities like Kansas City, Milwaukee, and Washington, D.C. Streetcar revenues began to fade, and even with rate increases, the companies could no longer earn enough to meet operating expenses.

Instead of mass transit, city and state government invested heavily in street improvement, traffic regulation, and new road construction. Highway building has been subsidized by the government in a way that mass transit, considered a private investment, has never been. By the 1920s, street and highway construction constituted the second largest item in municipal and state budgets. Between 1915 and 1930, the city of Chicago widened and opened 112 miles of streets at a cost of $114 million. New York City parkways built between 1923 and 1937 opened up for development seventeen thousand acres around the city. Urban road building failed to relieve congestion in the central business district or even keep pace with the spread of auto use, but it did encourage car travel, overloading streets and thoroughfares as soon as they were built and ultimately stimulating travel that avoided the central business district altogether.

At the same time that manufacturing was relocating outside the city, the proportion of communications, finance, management, clerical and professional services situated in downtown increased. The spreading out of factories on the periphery and the proliferation of skyscraper office buildings downtown represented a new stage in corporate organization, the separation of the production process from administrative functions. The massive corporations expanded by vertical and horizontal integration made such a separation advantageous, and transportation between offices and factories via streetcars and highways plus communication over the telephone made separation possible. By 1929, the editors of *The American City* could count 377 buildings at least twenty stories tall. Although New York claimed nearly half of the nation's skyscrapers, Syracuse, Memphis, and Tulsa also boasted of their own. Just as factories and railroad stations symbolized prosperity and growth in nineteenth-century cities, skyscrapers offered visual proof of progress in twentieth-century cities. Corporate offices, along with the banks, law offices, and advertising agencies that serviced them, now towered over downtown streets. Cleveland's 52-story Terminal Tower, Chicago's 36-story Tribune Tower, and New York's 102-story Empire State Building represented the reorientation of downtown space in the transition from industrial to corporate city....

The Problem of Planning: Competing Visions of Cities and Space

Acceptance of the new spatial specialization and especially of a suburban mentality dominated the thinking of political, social, and physical reformers who planned cities and formulated policy from the 1920s up until the 1960s. A commitment to decentralization implicit in its title characterized the Regional Planning Association of America (RPAA). Convened in 1923, the RPAA included among its members architect and former settlement-house[2] worker Clarence Stein and fellow architect Henry B. Wright, plus intellectuals Lewis Mumford and Benton McKaye. Wright and Stein asserted that uncontrolled expansion was causing unnecessary congestion and that decentralization would relieve pressures of housing and traffic. Following the English model of Ebenezer Howard's Garden Cities—new, planned communities with limited populations and surrounded by open land—the RPAA tried to prove the merits of

---

[2] The Settlement House Movement was a social movement that believed that rich and poor people should live together in poor areas cities. The Movement began in the United Kingdom in the mid-1800s and found its way to the United States, where it reached popularity in the 1920s.

decentralization by planning two projects near New York City. In 1924, it sponsored Sunnyside, a limited-dividend housing corporation in Queens planned by Wright and Stein and intended for low-income residents. Radburn, New Jersey, a genuine garden city, was begun in 1928 on a large tract seventeen miles from New York. Although Sunnyside and Radburn won much publicity for their advanced design, both were too expensive to build to offer a feasible model for low-income housing or a solution to the problems of urban over-crowding....

Regional planning was popular among planners, but seldom implemented. The New York Regional Plan was presented in 1931, and surveys were also taken for the metropolitan areas of Philadelphia, Chicago, Boston, San Francisco, and Cleveland. Civic leaders held conferences and appointed commissions to discuss regional problems of highways, land use, and water supplies, but political and economic rivalries and suburban insistence on political independence prevented substantive reforms such as consolidation of cities with their surrounding territories. Schemes to combine city and county governments by Cleveland, St. Louis, and Seattle were defeated, and efforts to integrate planning in Cook County, Illinois (the Chicago region), were tabled. Whenever it was implemented, regional planning had the impact of certifying growth as inevitable and celebrating the automobile as the best possible means of transportation, undervaluing possibilities for controlled growth and giving highways precedence over mass transit.

More narrowly defined planning strategies such as zoning and traffic control, popularized in the 1920s and 1930s, rigidified the divisions between urban and suburban space. Originally intended as a means of confinement, zoning became a tool of exclusion that still governs land-use patterns today. Copied from Germany and elsewhere abroad, zoning is a type of local police power that restricts certain types of buildings or land use to certain districts of the city. The earliest comprehensive zoning ordinance was passed by New York in 1916 to prevent skyscrapers and garment-industry lofts from encroaching on the fashionable Fifth Avenue retail district. By 1924, every major city, plus hundreds of smaller cities, had established zoning regulations. Although loopholes left room for circumvention, the laws generally controlled heights of buildings, determined boundaries of commercial and residential zones, and fixed density limitations....

Zoning laws aimed to establish stability in existing districts and orderly growth in newer regions, but they primarily protected the interests of real estate developers and owners of commercial property by ensuring that residential or commercial zones would not be invaded by unwanted features such as multiple-family dwellings and factories. Later, zoning would commonly be used to exclude "undesirable" people from the suburbs, and it therefore became a means of using spatial and economic definitions to tighten racial segregation. In the 1920s, zoning became the principal activity of the scores of planning commissions established in cities across the country. By the end of the 1920s, three-fifths of the nation's urban population lived under some kind of zoning controls. Planning staffs spent much of their time drawing maps that identified patterns of land use, traffic, health, lighting, utilities, and other aspects of the urban environment. Such projects proved helpful in systematizing policy planning, but they mainly ratified the status quo. Zoning maps could not renovate dilapidated housing, abolish want and crime, or improve the quality of life for all city dwellers.

Unplanned urban sprawl, new suburban expansion, and "automobility" drew the country and the city closer together. Automobiles quickened travel, extended distances that could be traversed easily, and gave tourists access to rural areas as a recreational playground. On weekends, thousands of cars pierced the countryside, carrying picnicking and sightseeing families, many of whom thought that farmers' fields were appropriate places for pitching tents and disposing of tin cans. Service stations, motor camps, and tourist restaurants sprouted along highways, and as farmers relied more heavily on automobiles for purchasing necessary goods, small crossroads market centers lost their general trade and service functions to larger rural towns. With access to urban stores, goods, and services, farm families became less culturally isolated from urban life.

These regional networks formed metropolitan districts—regions that included a city and its suburbs. In 1910, the Census Bureau gave the concept official recognition by identifying twenty-five areas with central-city populations of over 200,000 as metropolitan districts. By 1920, the total of metropolitan and near-metropolitan districts had grown to fifty-eight, and together they contained two-thirds of the nation's urban population. By 1930, there were ninety-three cities with populations of over 100,000. In 1933, a member of a government-sponsored study on modern social trends described the decentralization of urban space and centralization of rural space as the national paradigm:

> The large center has been able to extend the radius of its influence…. Moreover, the formerly independent towns and villages and also rural territory have become part of the enlarged city complex…. Nor is this new type of metropolitan community confined to great cities. It has become the communal unit of local relations throughout the entire nation.

The rise of urban America had been eclipsed by the metropolitan age.

Close Reading Questions

1. Why is 1920 a significant date in the census information of the United States?

2. Chudacoff and Smith note that urbanization was in part due to the influx of people from rural communities. What was one of the major consequences for cities as a result of these population surges? To what extent do you think these consequences still affect American cities today? (Historical Trends)

3. Why were shopping centers crucial to the developments of suburbs?

Analytical Writing/Discussion

4. In what ways did immigration laws of the 1920 impact industrial growth in America's cities? Which effect of these laws do you think was the most or least important and why? (Multiple Perspectives)

5. How did planning and zoning alter the use of city spaces in the 1920s and 1930s? Considering the city where you live or the city nearest your home, to what extent are some of those changes still in effect today?

6. What do you think are several key factors in the initial development of cities? To what degree do you think these factors are particular to cities in a certain region (i.e., northeast, south, west) or common to all? (Cultural Influences)

Further Options

7. Chudacoff and Smith contend that zoning laws were intended to regulate residential districts but instead were often used by real estate developers "to exclude 'undesirable' people from the suburbs." Why do you think communities like the College Hill neighborhood as detailed in Gene

Bunnell's "Providence Saves a Neighborhood" (see pp. 268–272), both benefited from and were harmed by zoning laws?

8. The African-American population in New York swelled to over 300,000 in the 1920s complete with, as Chudacoff and Smith note, "the promise of full citizenship emanating from northern urban life" (see pp. 251–257). In what ways does the "History of Fair Housing" article complicate that expectation?

SUBURBAN COMMUNITIES AND AMERICAN LIFE

by Michael P. Marino

Michael P. Marino is an Associate Professor of History at The College of New Jersey. A former high school and junior high school social studies teacher, Marino's research specialties include social studies, education, and modern European history. The following is an excerpt from the May 2011 edition of *The History Teacher*, the official publication for the Society for History Education, Inc.

Life in the Suburbs: Housing

The most distinctive and identifiable aspect of suburban life is the house, and suburban communities are mainly characterized by the homes within them. The traditional suburban home would seemingly offer little of interest to historians or students of history. Rather, it has mainly served as a metaphor for the dull and tedious nature of suburban life.[1] Many books about suburbs, for example, feature aerial photographs of suburban communities and use the repetitive similarity of the landscape to make a subtle critique about life in these neighborhoods and the people that would choose to live in them. The humble suburban home—mundane as it may look to passersby—nonetheless acts as a medium through which much can be learned about life in America after World War II. The discussion here focuses on two particular examples of suburban architecture, the "Cape Cod" and the "Ranch." These two types of homes were the most widespread architectural styles found in early post-WWII suburbs (constituting the two types built in the first Levittown, for example) and serve as a way to understand the ideology and motivations that produced suburbanization.[2] Moreover, although these styles are by today's standards somewhat dated, they have nonetheless established principles that undergird suburban housing to this day.

Cape Cod houses are distinguished by their angular roofs and graceful, symmetrical lines. Derived from architecture found in colonial New England (early examples date to the late seventeenthcentury), the name and style combine traditional American simplicity with the charm and comfort of a summer beach

---

[1] An analysis of the critiques of suburbs would create a lengthy discussion in its own right. For a survey of portrayals of suburbs in films and novels, see Robert Beuka, *Suburban Nation: Reading Suburban Landscape in Twentieth-Century Fiction and Film* (New York: Palgrave-Macmillan, 2004). Well-known critiques of suburbs written in the post-WWII era include Lewis Mumford, *The City in History: Its Origins, Its Transformation, and Its Prospects* (New York: Harcourt, Brace and World, 1961); and William Whyte, *The Organization Man* (New York: Simon and Schuster, 1956).

[2] These two models were featured in the original Long Island Levittown, for example.

house.[3] The Cape Cod design was revived in the late 1930s when architect Royal Barry Wills won a contest (against noted architect Frank Lloyd Wright) to design the perfect middle-class American home.[4] This style resonated with Americans and became extremely popular; Cape Cods were a main type of architecture used in Levittown, for example, where 6,000 units were constructed. An extremely popular design, Cape Cod houses can be found throughout America. As one architectural historian notes, "it remains the quintessential image of the American home."[5] Given its ubiquity, a case could be made that the Cape Cod design represents one of the most historically significant styles of architecture in American history.

In contrast to the Cape Cods of New England, the Ranch house is intended to evoke life in the California countryside—a simple design nestled comfortably and unobtrusively into the surrounding landscape. Described as a "shoebox with a roof," its one distinguishing feature is the large "picture window" in front, intended to turn the outside world into a changing panorama for those inside."[6]

These homes represent classic models of 1950s suburban architecture, and although non-descript and often excoriated by critics and commentators, they nonetheless offer insight into American history and American life. Perhaps the most significant theme that can be extracted from classic suburban homes is the fact that they were the product of specific and dedicated government activity. To study the history of a suburb is to gain understanding of how the American government has shaped Americans' lives in real and tangible ways. It could be argued, for example, that the most important event to occur in the United States since World War II was the massive demographic shift that occurred as a result of movement away from cities and towards suburbs. Such a process would never have happened without the actions of the United States government, and the study of suburbanization helps provide understanding of the role government has played in American history and how government action can affect the lives of its citizens.

The issue of property (and ownership of it) has been fundamental in defining American history. The American Revolution and the Civil War were both largely the result of disputes over property rights, and the U.S. government has consistently sought to create conditions to facilitate and promote land ownership. Possession of property is also a core value of America's republican ideals, as reflected in the writings and beliefs of founding fathers such as Thomas Jefferson and James Madison. During the Great Depression, homeownership was stressed as a fundamental right of all Americans, and several New Deal legislative acts and programs were created to assist in the purchase of homes. Although these programs are not as well-known as prominent New Deal measures such as social security, the National Industrial Recovery Act (NIRA), and the construction of public works, they nonetheless had a lasting and transformative impact on American history.

Prior to the Great Depression, bank lending rules and the manner in which loans were structured prevented many Americans from purchasing homes. A significant down payment was required, and loans needed to be paid off in a relatively short period of time (usually ten years). New Deal programs such as the Home Owners Loan Corporation (1933) and the National Housing Act (1934) dramatically altered the rules of home buying, however. These measures lowered the required down payment needed to purchase a home (to 3%) and lengthened a mortgage's repayment period—extending it to a maximum of thirty years. The National Housing Act also created a government agency, the Federal Housing

---

[3] G. E. Kidder Smith and Marshall B. Davidson, *A Pictorial History of Architecture in America* (New York: American Heritage Publishing Company, 1976), 39.

[4] Richard Guy Wilson, *The Colonial Revival House* (New York: Henry Abrams, 2004), 179.

[5] Allan Greenberg, *The Architecture of Democracy: American Architecture and the Legacy of the Revolution* (New York: Rizzoli International, 2006), 37.

[6] For the Ranch house, see Clifford E. Clark, "Ranch-House Suburbia: Ideals and Realities," in *Recasting America: Culture and Politics in the Age of Cold War*, ed. Lary May (Chicago, IL: University of Chicago Press, 1983), especially 178–179.

Authority, which guaranteed and underwrote mortgages issued by banks; this encouraged lending and lowered interest rates. As a result, homeownership became a realistic possibility for millions of (largely white) Americans who could not have purchased a home otherwise.[7] Like many New Deal programs, these benefits were intended mainly for white Americans, and preference was given to white homebuyers. The FHA would only underwrite mortgages for homes bought in white neighborhoods, for example. This helped begin a process that turned the United States into a rigidly segregated society, divided by race and class. The social consequences of these government actions became evident in the 1950s and 1960s, as cities became populated by poor minorities while suburbs were almost exclusively white enclaves.

Though little new home construction occurred during the Great Depression and World War II, a system was established that allowed the suburban boom of the 1950s to occur. These government actions also produced a substantial ripple effect by expanding the banking, insurance, construction, and retail industries, reshaping America's economic life in the process. As a result, the policies begun during the New Deal played a major role in reshaping and reordering American life. A suburban home is more than just shelter and a way to satisfy a basic human need. Rather, it is the product of a long historical legacy and offers evidence of how government action has transformed the lives of generations of Americans.

Although the American government worked to create conditions that would promote homeownership, houses still needed to be constructed and made available to buyers. The challenge was to build homes that were affordable for a large number of people, given that the median American household income in 1950 was approximately $4,000 (roughly $37,000 today). Traditionally, suburban homes were custom built by an owner or built in small lots by a contractor. The novelty of post-WWII suburbs was the way they were mass-produced in large numbers using innovative construction techniques. The similarity and monotony of suburban architecture was not the result of some degenerative strain in the American psyche, but rather a way to minimize costs to keep the purchase price within reach of a majority of buyers. Builders such as the Levitt family were able to achieve for homes what Henry Ford did for automobiles by minimizing expenses and maximizing production, making them affordable for people of limited means.[8] This was accomplished by using assembly line construction methods, eliminating the need for a basement (an expensive and time-consuming room to build), controlling the cost of raw materials such as lumber and concrete, and employing cheaper unskilled labor.

The end result of these innovations was that homes could be purchased so cheaply that it was more expensive to rent an apartment in a city than it was to buy a house in the suburbs. The suburban home provides evidence of the role that innovation and ingenuity have played in American life and how technology has shaped American history and culture. The means through which these houses were made affordable gives the suburban home an important place in the pantheon of inventions that have shaped the lives of Americans. As one author notes, "Levittown was the Model T of the built environment."[9] To study a suburban home is to understand a transformative moment in American history and the ways that technological innovation can produce important historical changes. Indeed, alongside the automobile, the humble, yet affordable 1950s suburban home is perhaps the greatest American invention of the twentieth century.

---

[7] The influence of the federal government in the housing market is discussed in many places, most notably Chapter 11 of Kenneth Jackson, *Crabgrass Frontier: The Suburbanization of The United States* (New York: Oxford University Press, 1985). Also Alexander Garvin, *The American City: What Works, What Doesn't*, 2nd edition. (New York: McGraw Hill, 2002), 196; Hayden, *Building Suburbia*, 123–127.

[8] For a discussion of the Levitts' building techniques and the comparison to Henry Ford, see Rosalyn Baxandall and Elizabeth Ewen, *Picture Windows: How the Suburbs Happened* (New York: Basic Books, 2000), 120.

[9] Jane Holtz Kay, *Asphalt Nation: How the Automobile Took over America and How We Can Take It Back* (Berkeley, CA: University of California Press, 1997), 227.

The architecture, design, and physical layout of a typical suburban home also help facilitate understanding of wider themes and ideas associated with American culture. Earlier, it was noted that the distinguishing feature of a Ranch-style home was the large picture window prominently displayed at the front of the house. While intended as a feature for those living in the house, a large window such as this also lets passersby look into the house and see what is inside (which is why most picture windows are barricaded with walls of curtains). Each suburban home can become, in essence, a theater offering viewers a glimpse into the lives that exist within them.[10] More than a simple piece of architecture, a suburban home is also a portal into American life and culture. In some ways, suburbs are less about homes than they are about the lives of the people who live within them. The term "suburban lifestyle" connotes specific ideals, beliefs, and assumptions that are distinctively American, and to study a suburban home is to understand values central to the American experience.

If a suburban home is a form of theater, the residents of the house must all play certain roles. In suburban folklore and history (if not necessarily in reality), these roles are rigidly defined. For one, the cast is small, by rule a family of a husband, a wife, and generally one to three children. This separates the post-WWII suburban experience from the older residential patterns of urban life, where aunts, uncles, grandparents, and extended family all lived in close proximity to one another, often in the same house.

The scale and design of prototypical 1950s architecture prevented such living arrangements, however, creating communities of small nuclear families. Each resident in such a house and family was expected to perform certain tasks and assume certain predetermined roles. In theory, the father worked and supported the household, while the mother cared for the house and raised the children.[11] Children, in turn, got to be children and enjoy their childhoods without the pressure of work; post-WWII prosperity allowed the house to be supported without their assistance, and unlike earlier generations, they did not need to toil alongside their father in a coal mine or mother in a garment factory.

The design of these homes also helped reinforce these predetermined familial and gender roles. Walking into a 1950s suburban home, the kitchen was typically on the left, with the living room on the right, and the bedrooms in the rear.[12] Locating certain rooms in front of the house conveyed their importance and focused the "action" of the house in these areas. Various design factors also helped keep residents inside the house and in their predetermined roles. The front lawn acted as a green wall of sorts, isolating the house from all around it. Whereas older homes had stoops or porches in the front, forcing residents of a community to commingle during hot nights and leisure time, in a 1950s suburb, activity happened in the backyard, a preserve isolated and walled off from outsiders.[13] Household technologies that became widespread after World War II such as the television and air conditioner also helped keep families indoors and isolated from the surrounding community.[14] Nor was there much to do in a suburb.

---

[10] On the suburban home as a form of theater, see Lynn Spigel, "From Theater to Space Ship: Metaphors of Suburban Domesticity in Postwar America," in *Visions of Suburbia*, ed. Roger Silverstone (New York: Routledge, 1997).

[11] Research indicates that gender roles in practice were less rigid than popular memory would indicate. See Stephanie Coontz, *The Way We Never Were: American Families and the Nostalgia Trap* (New York: Basic Books, 2000); Joanne Meyerowitz, *Not June Cleaver: Women and Gender in Postwar America, 1945–1960* (Philadelphia, PA: Temple University Press, 1994).

[12] For how suburban interior architecture shaped American domestic life, see Barbara M. Kelly, *Expanding the American Dream: Building and Rebuilding Levittown* (Albany, NY: SUNY Press, 1993), 70; Clark, "Ranch-House Suburbia," 179.

[13] Suburban lawns are discussed in Robert Messia, "Lawns as Artifacts: The Evolution of Social and Environmental Implications of Suburban Residential Land Use," in *Suburban Sprawl: Culture, Theory and Politics*, eds. Matthew J. Lindstrom and Hugh Bartling (Lanham, MD: Rowan and Littlefield, 2003).

[14] For the influence of the air conditioner, see Raymond Arsenault, "The End of the Long Hot Summer: The Air Conditioner and Southern Culture," in *Searching for the Sunbelt: Historical Perspectives on a Region*, ed. Raymond A. Mohl (Athens, GA: University of Georgia Press, 1993).

While a father returning from work in Brooklyn had a myriad of leisure options to keep him away from the house, a father living in a suburb had nowhere to go and was forced to spend time at home.[15]

The suburban house thus became a vehicle that forced Americans to live and behave in certain ways and adhere to predetermined roles. The design of suburban homes and the nature of family life within them came to represent values and characteristics that are distinctly American. During the first wave of post-WWII suburbanization, the suburban home became a potent Cold War weapon, used to acclaim the benefits of capitalism and the triumph of the American system. Suburban homes and families also presented an image of a domestic utopia that helped encourage and maintain American democratic values. Buying a home and raising a family promoted social responsibility and civic virtue, focusing peoples' creative energies towards the maintenance of a home and care of children and away from more radical pursuits.[16]

The 1950s suburban home serves as a means through which much can be learned about American history, society, and culture. For one, it illustrates the effect that government action can play in shaping the lives of its citizens. It also illustrates the impact that key historical events (such as the New Deal) have had on the lives of everyday people. The suburban home also serves as a symbol that illustrates a number of themes central to understanding American history. The suburban home and the methods used to construct it demonstrate the impact that technology and innovation have had on American history. Indeed, one can place the suburban home on a continuum of epochal American inventions that have together shaped the lives of generations of people. During the 1950s, the suburban home also represented an idealized vision of American life, and the architecture and design of suburban homes and communities helped promote this ideal. This vision continues to occupy an important place in American society, as buying a house and starting a family continues to serve as a benchmark of success. The study of a suburban home can help illustrate a cultural imperative that has defined America since World War II.

Life in the Suburbs: Roads and Highways

If houses constitute the dominant characteristic of a suburb, then roads and the cars that travel on them are only slightly less important. Indeed, the two have a symbiotic relationship, as suburbs could not exist without automobiles, roads, and highways and ownership of a car is a fundamental prerequisite for life in a suburban community. Much of the criticism of suburbs is predicated on this fact, and attacks on suburbs often focus on the cars so necessary to connect them to the outside world. It is argued, for example, that cars are dangerous, take up vast amounts of space, consume scarce resources, create pollution, and—because of the expenses they generate—represent a net loss for society as a whole, requiring a massive amount of resources to maintain the infrastructure that supports them.[17]

Like suburban houses, suburban roads would seem to offer little in way of wider historical understanding. A closer look reveals their significance, however. For one, there is the obvious contrast between

---

[15] For this point, see Kelly, *Expanding the American Dream,* 70.

[16] For the cultural and political significance of suburbs, see Chapter 7 of Elaine Tyler May, *Homeward Bound: American Families in the Cold War Era* (New York: Basic Books, 1999). Also see Chapter 8 of Robert Beauregard, *When America Became Suburban* (Minneapolis, MN: University of Minnesota Press, 2006).

[17] For the negative impact of automobiles and their relationship to suburbia, see Andres Duany, Elizabeth Plater-Zyberk, and Jeff Speck, *Suburban Nation: The Rise of Sprawl and the Decline of the American Dream* (New York: North Point Press, 2000); Anthony Flint, *This Land: The Battle over Sprawl and the Future of America* (Baltimore, MD: Johns Hopkins University Press, 2006); Douglas E. Moms, *It's a Sprawl World After All* (Gabriola Island, Canada: New World Publishers, 2003).

the street pattern in many American cities, which follows a rigid, geometrical pattern of perpendicular streets, with that found in suburbs, which usually consists of streets that gently curve and twist (called "curvilinear" in developer parlance), cul-de-sacs, and roads that go nowhere. The term "subdivision" is, in fact, a product of this phenomenon, as many suburban communities exist as isolated developments built off a single main road. Of these two types of road design, the gridded street pattern of cities offers certain advantages. Gridded streets are easy to negotiate and provide a sense of orientation and direction; they also help non-native speakers find their way, an important concern in communities with large immigrant populations. Suburban roads, conversely, are frustrating and confusing, and even with a map, it is difficult to know where one is going. As one study of suburban architecture notes, "unrelenting curves create an environment that is utterly disorienting."[18] These curvilinear, directionless roads serve several purposes, however. For one, they promote isolation and discourage strangers from passing through a community. Much as individual suburban homes serve an isolating function, so too do the roads that connect them to the outside world. Given how frustrating it is to navigate curving roads, only those who live in a particular place and who know where they are going will drive on them. Strangers will stay away. If suburban homes promote isolation among individual households, suburban roads accomplish the same effect for communities and subdivisions. Planners and architects have also discovered that people tend to dislike walking on curvilinear roads and that these thoroughfares exist largely to move cars from place to place. This further reinforces the often anonymous character of suburban life, and attests to the reciprocal relationship between automobiles and suburban homes. Like suburban houses, suburban roads promote a specific lifestyle and force those who live in them to live a certain way. They again testify to the nature, style, and character of suburban living—isolated, remote, and dependent on cars.

Life in suburbs is, in fact, largely about cars and America's historical obsession with this form of transportation. This fact is most evident in the rash of highway building that occurred across twentieth-century American history. These highways illustrate a number of historical themes and ideas significant to wider understandings of American history and culture. Highways served as conduits into the suburban towns, speeding development and accelerating movement into areas that were hitherto remote and inaccessible. As a result, they not only changed the way Americans live, but also shaped their eating habits, widened their entertainment options, expanded the retail industry, and helped speed the decline of urban and town centers.[19]

Like suburban homes, highways also illustrate how the government has shaped American history and the lives of its citizens. The highway system that stretches across the United States could have been built only through government intervention and largesse on a massive scale. The motivations of various levels of government (federal, state, and local) to produce this highway system reveal a number of important historical themes and concepts. To study the history of highways, for example, promotes deeper understanding of the Cold War (due to the government's desire to disperse America's population during this period), labor history (because of the need to provide jobs for the building trades), and the way America's government operates (due to the massive lobbying of the government by various industries to pass highway legislation, as well as the use of tactics such as eminent domain).

The study of highways also promotes understanding of the dramatic demographic and economic realities that shaped American society after the Second World War. Not only did highways foster

---

[18] Duany, Plater-Zyberk, and Speck, *Suburban Nation*, 34.

[19] For malls and the decline of cities, see Lizbeth Cohen, "From Town Center to Shopping Center: The Reconfiguration of Community Marketplaces in Postwar America," *The American Historical Review* 101, no. 4 (October 1996). For fast food, see Jackson, *Crabgrass Frontier*, 263–265.

suburbanization, but their construction began the slow process of decline in many American cities. Highways, for example, made it easy to relocate industries and manufacturing away from cities in the northeast and Midwest to the south and southwest.[20] When built through cities, highways also tended to eviscerate the neighborhoods in their path, further accelerating urban decline and flight to the suburbs.[21] This movement of people and business precipitated a migratory shift that has dramatically altered America's demographic composition and its political and economic life.

Finally, and most significantly, suburban roads and highways have turned the United States into a nation dependent on cars. First begun in the 1920s, by 1960, the transformation of America into a society built around the automobile was complete. During the 1950s, when gas cost 18 cents a gallon (approximately $1.61 today) and the automobile was viewed a symbol of status and prosperity, creating a society centered on automobiles seemed logical. The modern United States is, in fact, a nation whose very existence is predicated on the widespread availability of cheap gas. As a result, generations of Americans have lived their lives around the consequences of this fact.[22] The expense of cars, gas and maintenance, the inconvenience of traffic, and the need to drive as a function of everyday life is a reality nearly every American must face, and this reality clearly illustrates how historical events and processes shape life in the present day and how decisions made in the past influence life in the present.

Life in Suburbs: People and Populations

Suburbs are not only about homes and roads. Ultimately, and most importantly, they are about people, and studying how people live and function within these communities is a last important illustration of how suburbs can produce deeper understandings of American history. It has been noted that the suburbanization of America that occurred after World War II produced dramatic demographic, economic, and cultural changes. Understanding the causes and consequences of this migration to the suburbs is central to understanding life in modern America and how and why American society has evolved in the way it has. Indeed, the impact of suburban migration on American life may be the most significant issue to arise of out of the nation's history in the second half of the twentieth century.

The post-WWII period of suburbanization produced a fundamental racial reordering of American society. Due to a varied series of push-pull factors, urban white ethnic residents were drawn to suburban communities. Cities, in turn, became populated by poorer residents of Latino and African-American descent. Cities suffered due to the subsequent decline in tax revenue, the strain on social services, and the concurrent loss of blue-collar manufacturing jobs that typically provided employment for new arrivals. As a result, many American cities entered a long period of decline and became increasingly segregated by race and class from the suburbs surrounding them. Even mighty New York City entered an economic downturn in the late 1950s, as its unemployment rate began to tick upward and it shed manufacturing

---

[20] These points are drawn from Owen Gutfreund, *Twentieth-Century Sprawl: Highways and the Reshaping of the American Landscape* (New York: Oxford University Press, 2005); Tom Lewis, *Divided Highways: Building the Interstate Highway System* (New York: Penguin, 1999); Mark H. Rose, *Interstate: Express Highway Politics, 1939–1989* (Knoxville, TN: University of Tennessee Press, 1990); Thomas J. Sugrue, *The Origins of the Urban Crisis: Race and Inequality in Postwar Detroit* (Princeton, NJ: Princeton University Press, 1996).

[21] See Robert A. Caro's discussion of the impact of the Cross Bronx Expressway on the neighborhood of East Tremont in Chapter 37 of *The Power Broker: Robert Moses and the Fall of New York* (New York: Alfred A. Knopf, 1974).

[22] A discussion of this can be found in Kay, *Asphalt Nation*.

jobs in large numbers.[23] By the early 1970s, the city was borrowing money simply to pay interest on previous debts incurred. Although New York recovered from this crisis, many cities have not, and understanding the causes of urban decline and the consequences of suburban migration are vital for understanding the nature of life in modern America.

American communities are in a constant state of flux, however, and rarely do they stay the same for long. Although it is easy to think of suburbs and cities representing two diametrically opposed ways of life, the reality is not so obvious in the modern era. Studies of suburbs have shown that they have evolved significantly from their days as preserves for white urban refugees. For example, many suburban communities have become increasingly diverse and more "urban" in their demographic composition and character. Many suburbs (often called "ethno-burbs") also now have a distinct ethnic profile, making them similar to the urban enclaves of the past.[24] Moreover, the push-pull factors that lured white residents to the suburbs after World War II clearly still hold sway, and suburbs still attract people looking for better schools, the ability to own a home, and a quieter, more peaceful life.

Although suburbs are colloquially assumed to be prosperous and peaceful, in recent years, many suburban communities have experienced symptoms of decline that have traditionally impacted American urban areas. As one study notes, "suburbs as poor as any city neighborhood have emerged to disrupt the myth of suburban success."[25] In some cases, this is simply a function of geography, as suburbs that directly border cities often begin to experience many of the problems (such as crime, poverty, and housing deterioration) that impact cities. These suburbs are called "inner ring" suburbs and they are generally older communities, first settled in the years after World War II. Many of these suburbs have taken on the characteristics of depressed urban areas, and historian John Teaford refers to them as "suburban ghettos" that "exhibit all the symptoms of social disaster."[26] Researchers refer to this phenomenon as the "suburban life cycle" and suggest that as housing in a suburb ages, the community will experience deterioration, culminating in a "thinning out" of the population and a subsequent decline in tax base and services. Eventually, a suburb may reach a "crisis point" in which various factors combine to place a community in severe difficulty.[27] Today, suburban communities vary considerably from one another; they are not monolithic in their character, nor is the idea of a suburb easy to characterize with broad, sweeping observations.

Older realities about these suburban communities still remain, however. Many suburbs are still segregated (especially by class) and it is not uncommon for extremely wealthy suburban areas to exist in close proximity to poor urban ones, or for a poor suburb to border a wealthy one. The study of suburbs and their demographics can provide knowledge of how issues such as segregation and separation of wealth still impact American society. Moreover, the study of suburbs and the people that live in them also reveals the complexity of American life and how historical forces have shaped the lives of the American people.

---

[23] See Chapter 10 of Joshua B. Freeman, *Working Class New York: Life and Labor since World War II* (New York: The New Press, 2000).

[24] See Hayden, *Building Suburbia,* 12–13. A profile of an ethnic suburb in California can be found in Timothy B. Fong, *The First Suburban Chinatown: The Remaking of Monterey Park, California* (Philadelphia. PA: Temple University Press, 1994). A discussion of the experiences of recent immigrants on Long Island can be found in Sarah J. Mahler, *American Dreaming: Immigrant Life on the Margins* (Princeton, NJ: Princeton University Press, 1995).

[25] Bernadette Hanlon, *Once the American Dream: Inner-Ring Suburbs of the Metropolitan United States* (Philadelphia, PA: Temple University Press, 2010), 15.

[26] Jon Teaford, *The American Suburb: The Basics* (New York: Routledge, 2008), 46.

[27] William H. Lucy and David L. Phillips, "Suburban Decline: The Next Urban Crisis," *Issues in Science and Technology* 17, no. 1 (September 2000).

Close Reading Questions

1. Why is the Cape Cod house design regarded as "the quintessential image of the American home?"

2. What were the reasons suburban houses were built with such uniformity in the 1950s? What was the result of those specific construction decisions?

3. According to Marino, why do roads and cars "have a symbiotic relationship?"

Analytical Writing/Discussion

4. In what ways is land and home ownership linked to the history of the United States? How did twentieth century laws affect people who wanted to buy land upon which to build a home? (Cultural Influences)

5. What were some of the culturally symbolic features of 1950s suburban homes? In what ways are the features of suburban homes built in the 2000s or later a cultural reflection of the twenty-first century? (Historical Trends)

6. Do you agree or disagree with the idea that suburban migration fundamentally changed post–World War II American society? What factors support your perspective? (Multiple Perspectives)

Further Options

7. Marino states that older sections of suburban towns "experience many of the problems (such as crime, poverty, and housing deterioration)" that are most often associated with city life. To what extent can government and/or nongovernmental organizations intervene to revive these sections of suburbia, as was the case with the Billings Forge complex in Hartford, CT? (See Freewrite 3 in this chapter)

8. According to Marino, the quality of suburban schools is one of the reasons that people have—for more than 50 years—fled cities and moved to the suburbs. Examine the school system of the nearest city or suburban town. Where are the "better" schools located and how does their urban or suburban location affect their success?

Freewrite 2: History of Fair Housing

The Civil Rights Act of 1964 and 1968 are among the most important federal legislation of the 1960s. The Fair Housing Act of 1968 served a complementary function in transforming the culture of neighborhoods across the nation. After reading this historical account, published by the U.S. Department of Housing and Urban Development, freewrite on one of the questions below:

On April 11, 1968, President Lyndon Johnson signed the Civil Rights Act of 1968, which was meant as a follow-up to the Civil Rights Act of 1964. The 1968 act expanded on previous acts and prohibited discrimination concerning the sale, rental, and financing of housing based on race, religion, national origin, sex, (and as amended) handicap, and family status. Title VIII of the Act is also known as the Fair Housing Act (of 1968).

The enactment of the federal Fair Housing Act on April 11, 1968 came only after a long and difficult journey. From 1966 to 1967, Congress regularly considered the fair housing bill, but failed to garner a strong enough majority for its passage. However, when the Rev. Dr. Martin Luther King, Jr. was assassinated on April 4, 1968, President Lyndon Johnson utilized this national tragedy to urge for the bill's speedy Congressional approval. Since the 1966 open housing marches in Chicago, Dr. King's name had been closely associated with the fair housing legislation. President Johnson viewed the Act as a fitting memorial to the man's life work, and wished to have the Act passed prior to Dr. King's funeral in Atlanta.

Another significant issue during this time period was the growing casualty list from Vietnam. The deaths in Vietnam fell heaviest upon young, poor African-American and Hispanic infantrymen. However, on the home front, these men's families could not purchase or rent homes in certain residential developments on account of their race or national origin. Specialized organizations like the NAACP, the GI Forum, and the National Committee Against Discrimination in Housing lobbied hard for the Senate to pass the Fair Housing Act and remedy this inequity. Senators Edward Brooke and Edward Kennedy of Massachusetts argued deeply for the passage of this legislation. In particular, Senator Brooke, the first African-American ever to be elected to the Senate by popular vote, spoke personally of his return from World War II and inability to provide a home of his choice for his new family because of his race.

With the cities rioting after Dr. King's assassination, and destruction mounting in every part of the United States, the words of President Johnson and Congressional leaders rang the Bell of Reason for the House of Representatives, who subsequently passed the Fair Housing Act. Without debate, the Senate followed the House in its passage of the Act, which President Johnson then signed into law.

The power to appoint the first officials administering the Act fell upon President Johnson's successor, Richard Nixon. President Nixon tapped then Governor of Michigan, George Romney, for the post of Secretary of Housing and Urban Development (HUD). While serving as Governor, Secretary Romney had successfully campaigned for ratification of a state constitutional provision that prohibited discrimination in housing. President Nixon also appointed Samuel Simmons as the first Assistant Secretary for Equal Housing Opportunity.

When April 1969 arrived, HUD could not wait to celebrate the Act's first Anniversary. Within that inaugural year, HUD completed the Title VIII Field Operations Handbook, and instituted a formalized complaint process. In truly festive fashion, HUD hosted a gala event in the Grand Ballroom of New York's Plaza Hotel. From across the nation, advocates and politicians shared in this marvelous evening, including one of the organizations that started it all—the National Committee Against Discrimination in Housing.

In subsequent years, the tradition of celebrating Fair Housing Month grew larger and larger. Governors began to issue proclamations that designated April as "Fair Housing Month," and schools across the country sponsored poster and essay contests that focused upon fair housing issues. Regional winners from these contests often enjoyed trips to Washington, DC for events with HUD and their Congressional representatives.

Under former Secretaries James T. Lynn and Carla Hills, with the cooperation of the National Association of Homebuilders, National Association of Realtors, and the American Advertising Council these groups adopted fair housing as their theme and provided "free" billboard space throughout the nation. These large 20-foot by 14-foot billboards placed the fair housing message in neighborhoods, industrial centers, agrarian regions, and urban cores. Every region also had its own celebrations, meetings, dinners, contests, and radio–television shows that featured HUD, state and private fair housing experts and officials. These celebrations continue the spirit behind the original passage of the Act, and are remembered fondly by those who were there from the beginning.

After reading the History of Fair Housing, freewrite or discuss one or more the following questions:

- In what ways do you consider enacting laws, like the Fair Housing Act of 1968, to be more effective than engaging the beliefs people hold to end housing segregation?

- In the decades since the passage of the Fair Housing Act of 1968, how has the trend of racial segregation changed in many cities and/or suburbs? What do you think this change suggest about race, ethnicity, and economic class in the United States since the late 1960s?

PROVIDENCE SAVES A NEIGHBORHOOD

by Gene Bunnell

Gene Bunnell is a certified planner and an Associate Professor Department of Geography and Planning at the State University of New York at Albany. Bunnell has worked as a planning consultant as well as the planning director for the town of Northampton, MA. The following is an excerpt from the October 2002 edition of *Planning,* the trade publication of the American Planning Association.

At one time, the College Hill area of Providence, Rhode Island (where Roger Williams and his followers first settled in the 17th century), was regarded as the city's best neighborhood. But by the 1950s, College Hill had become one of the worst slums in the city-an area of badly run-down and overcrowded tenements. Five or six families lived in each building, and it was common for one basement bathroom to serve everyone.

Ironically, some of the forces that contributed to the destabilization and decline of College Hill came from the venerable educational institutions located there. According to my contacts in Providence, it was Brown University's heavy-handed institutional expansion that largely prompted the formation of the Providence Preservation Society in 1956-an organization initially formed for the initial and sole purpose of preserving the College Hill neighborhood. "Brown was the devil," said the late planner Lachlan F. Blair.

During the 1950s and 1960s, under a new president, Brown University was intent on expanding, and began to acquire property for new university buildings and parking lots. As one historic building after another on the edge of campus was demolished, concerns increased. Concerns intensified when massive new buildings of modern design, which clashed horribly with the low-scaled, historic character of the surrounding neighborhood, began to rise on cleared sites.

Property acquisitions and demolitions conducted by the Rhode Island School of Design further destabilized the neighborhood. In the fall of 1959, RISD demolished the historic Pearce House* at 225-227 Benefit Street, despite offers from individuals associated with the Providence Preservation Society to purchase and restore the building.

College Hill was threatened from another direction as well: federally funded urban renewal. College Hill could have been one of the many neighborhoods across the U.S. that were declared "blighted" and cleared. Indeed, it seemed almost inevitable that urban renewal land acquisition and clearance activities, already under way in downtown Providence, would extend well into College Hill, since College Hill was essentially part of downtown, and there was no denying that its housing stock was badly run down.

Rescuing College Hill

Few people in Providence know more about the actions that saved College Hill than Tina Regan. In addition to being an active member of the Providence Preservation Society since 1975, and staffing the society's offices, she is also chair of the city's College Hill Historic District Commission, and serves as a member of the Downcity Design Review Committee....

Providence had a City Plan Commission at the time and a small staff headed by an engineer. But the real power and control over land use and development resided in the Providence Redevelopment Authority. It wasn't until the early 1970s that the city's mayor, Joseph Doorley, established the Department of Planning and Urban Development and folded the redevelopment agency into it.

Had it not been for the fact that urban renewal and highway building were having such a devastatingly negative effect on Providence, Tina Regan probably would not have become involved in the fight to save College Hill. She knew there had to be a better way of remaking the city.

Regan is modest about the role she played in the overall effort. She credits long-time neighborhood residents who, with the help of architectural historian Antoinette Downing, formed the preservation society and initiated a remarkably well-organized and successful planning effort.

In most places where citizens have organized to opposed publicly financed urban renewal or highway projects, the central aim has been to stop something from happening. However, from the beginning in the College Hill area, the goal was to bring about positive change. Organizers and leaders of the effort to save College Hill did something else that proved crucially important: They emphasized the importance of planning, and of developing a coherent, overall development strategy rather than a series of ad hoc, crisis-driven actions.

Professionals took the lead

Over time, professionals played an increasingly important role in saving College Hill. The first "outside" consultant was Lachlan Blair, who was hired to help the group write an application for a demonstration planning grant from the U.S. Department of Housing and Urban Development. Before founding a private consulting firm with Stewart Stein in 1957, Blair had been planning chief for the state of Rhode Island and deputy planning director of Providence.

The application was successful, and the HUD demonstration planning grant of $40,000 was matched by $20,000 from the Providence Preservation Society. Blair's newly established firm got the job.

It was Blair and Stein's responsibility to direct the overall planning effort, whose purpose was to document and describe significant historic and architectural resources, and develop a detailed plan and implementation strategy for the area. To accomplish that, Blair and Stein assembled a team of professionals, including Antoinette Downing and architect-planner William Warner. Another person drawn into the project was Martin Adler, who had just earned a master's degree in planning and was awarded a student

---

* The Earle D. Pearce House was a three-story brick rowhouse built around 1820. It was built to house two families and was similar to other row houses in the neighborhood.

internship from the American Society of Planning Officials [one of the predecessors of the American Planning Association] to work on the College Hill project.

As a first step, the team studied the experience of other cities that had been leaders in preservation planning. This helped the team generate ideas about how they would approach their task in Providence. "It also helped us avoid the mistakes that others had made," Blair pointed out. Cities that had conducted surveys of historic buildings or adopted city ordinances regulating land use and structure in historic areas were identified and studied, he said.

Antoinette Downing, a tenacious advocate of historic preservation and a highly respected scholar in the field, also became involved as a consultant. It was Downing who developed the innovative survey tools and methods used at College Hill—the system of classes and categories used to describe and classify properties, the numerical system used to rate properties for the significance, and the actual survey forms used in the field.

A final report, a team effort called "College Hill: A Demonstration Study and Plan for Historic Area Renewal" (the "1959 College Hill plan"), was over 200 pages long and contained scores of maps, photographs, and illustrations.

The first part of the 1959 College Hill plan, largely written by Blair, provided a succinct but thorough overview and analysis of preservation efforts in other cities. The second part of the report, written primarily by Downing, describes the history of College Hill and the various architectural styles there. The third and final part of the report, written by Warner, detailed proposals for nine subareas within College Hill and tied them together into a 25-year plan. Several actions were proposed:

- Establish a permanent committee or organization to oversee development efforts related to the 1959 College Hill plan.
- Undertake an urban renewal project in College Hill involving selective clearance, rehabilitation, and conservation.
- Establish an historic trail along Benefit Street, and plant street trees there and elsewhere.
- Develop a national historic park at the site of the Roger Williams Spring on North Main Street.
- Adopt special zoning regulations for the protection of the historic area of College Hill (with proposed state enabling legislation provided).
- Stimulate private investment.
- Urge compliance by the universities located in College Hill.
- Undertake publicity, education, and information programs....

1959 and beyond

One year after the 1959 College Hill plan was completed, the city passed an historic district zoning ordinance creating the College Hill Historic District and establishing the College Hill Historic District Commission. After that, no building in the district could be demolished and no exterior remodeling or alteration of any building there could take place without the permission of the commission.

It did not take long for the commission's power and resolve to be tested. RISD came before the commission seeking permission to tear down the old Woods-Gerry** mansion at 62 Prospect Street. This was a controversial issue. In an attempt to find a compromise the commission found a person who was willing to repair the house and live in it, if the college provided a 20-year lease. The college said no and the issue was forced to a vote.

Antoinette Downing, who chaired the commission, recalled nearly 20 years later that she went to the climactic meeting so uncertain of the outcome of the vote that she had prepared a minority opinion. But the vote of the commission was unanimous: The demolition application was turned down. For many years, RISD did nothing with the Woods-Gerry mansion; eventually, the college restored the building, and today it houses an art gallery and faculty offices.

One reason that people remain unaware of the extent to which plans shape subsequent events is that studies and reports are rarely prepared after the plans go into effect. That was not the case in Providence.

Two years after the 1959 College Hill plan was completed, a follow-up report documented the progress made in implementing its various recommendations. "College Hill 1961" was prepared by Martin Adler. It noted the formation of a coordinating committee; the start of a federally assisted, preservation-oriented urban renewal program; the 1959 adoption of a state-enabling act for historic area zoning; the formation of the College Hill historic district and commission; the preparation of educational material and maps; legislation submitted for congressional approval to establish a national historic park along the western edge of College Hill; the purchase of 30 pre-1840 houses by private individuals and corporations interested in restoring them; and the fact that the Episcopal Diocese of Rhode Island had acquired three houses on Benefit Street and converted them into apartments for the elderly.

Nevertheless, the neighborhood still looked run down. In the minds of developers, bankers, and home buyers, College Hill remained a risky place to invest.

It starts with one

Then someone extraordinary stepped forward: Beatrice "Happy" Chace, long-time resident of Providence and a founding member of the Providence Preservation Society. She bought 15 structures in College Hill and proceeded to restore their exteriors. Through the Burnside Corporation, which she formed in the 1960s, she also built new infill housing on Pratt Street, on land that had been cleared of structures so deteriorated they couldn't be renovated.

Chace hoped to entice others to buy and renovate other historic structures in College Hill. She also hoped people would be encouraged by her renovated exteriors and would buy and renovate the interiors of her buildings. Few people stepped forward to buy the properties she had rescued. For many years, Chace owned and maintained a large number of properties in College Hill, waiting for others to follow.

It is impossible to underestimate the importance of what Chace did. Had she not made a significant investment in College Hill when the market for property was extremely weak, the physical renewal of College Hill would undoubtedly have taken even longer than it did-or might not have happened at all....

Lining up the big boys

In the decades that followed, progress was made in establishing a regulatory mechanism to help avoid the kind of head-on conflicts that were sparked when Brown University and RISD bought and demolished buildings without regard to the effect on the surrounding neighborhood. The 1959 College Hill plan specifically addressed this problem by recommending that Brown, RISD, and Bryant

---

** The Woods-Gerry house is an Italiante-style mansion built in 1860. The house was placed on the National Register of Historic Places in 1971.

College work with the city planning commission to plan the future growth of the community and the institutions.

In the spirit of that recommendation, the city's planning department drafted-and the city council approved-a special institutional overlay zoning district in 1986. It imposed special requirements and obligations on the city's seven major colleges and seven hospitals.

The boundaries of the overlay zoning district were drawn to conform exactly to the boundaries of the city's institutions as they existed in 1986. In effect, the ordinance declared that the facilities were allowed in those areas but were prohibited outside them. The only way universities or hospitals could expand in the future was to request that adjoining properties be rezoned to be included in the institutional zone. That, in turn, meant coming before the city council and having a public hearing that neighborhood people could attend....

In 1991, a revised master plan provision was adopted requiring institutions to prepare a formal, printed master plan document, and to submit it to the city plan commission for approval. That approval can only be given after a formal public hearing. Those plans and that approval process-must be completed every five years....

College Hill today

Hundreds of historically and architecturally significant structures in College Hill have now been restored. But there is another extremely positive outcome of the 1961 plan to report: It saved and rebuilt a truly unique inner-city neighborhood, and, in doing so, provided people with an opportunity to live in an extraordinary environment that is markedly different from what is typically experienced in suburban communities.

Because of the success in College Hill, over 11,000 people live in a neighborhood with a distinctly urban character and a wide array of housing, literally a stone's throw from the heart of the city. Few American cities as large as Providence (pop. 174,000) have such a large, stable, and attractive residential neighborhood so close to the downtown core.

College Hill is not for everyone. Because the streets that crisscross the neighborhood were laid out before the automobile age, they are narrow, and parking spaces are hard to find. People who have grown accustomed to private driveways and two- and three-car garages probably would not want to live there. The lots are small and buildings are close together. College Hill is a densely developed, congested place.

On the other hand, for people who like cities, value history and architecture, like to walk, and don't mind the prospect of bumping into and talking to people, there could hardly be a better place.

Some may be inclined to criticize and dismiss what was achieved in College Hill by saying that the renewal and restoration of the neighborhood displaced low-income people who had come to occupy the badly run-down but cheap tenement apartments there. However, even more widespread displacement would have occurred had the College Hill preservation plan not been adopted and implemented. The alternative to preservation was clearance.

The preservation of existing structures in College Hill had the long-term benefit of preserving and maintaining a wide array of housing types. Preservation did not simply produce elegant homes for wealthy people. Many long-time and well-to-do families live on College Hill, but the population there is remarkably varied by age, income, and household characteristics. Over one-quarter of the people who live in College Hill are students. They and their neighbors are the beneficiaries of a 40-year effort to save a place that deserved to be saved.

Close Reading Questions

1. According to Bunnell, what became of the College Hill neighborhood in the 1950s?

2. For what reasons were the historic buildings in College Hill saved? (Multiple Perspectives)

3. Why is the modern-day College Hill "not for everyone?"

Analytical/Discussion

4. What do you think was the most important component of the 1959 College Hill Plan? If such a plan were instituted for a neighborhood you know, what do you think would be most or least beneficial? (Historical Trends)

5. In what ways did residents like Antoinette Downing affect this Providence neighborhood? What do you think would have become of College Hill if not for Downing?

6. Why do you agree or disagree that Brown University and the Rhode Island College of Design "destabilized" the neighborhood? In what ways has your college and/or a local college supported or not supported the neighborhoods where they exist? (Cultural Influences)

Further Options

7. Bunnell's article focuses on preserving neighborhoods. What do you think are two or three key lessons that other American cities can learn from the example of the College Hill restoration?

8. As explained in Freewrite 3, the Billings Forge development was a solution saving a neighborhood in Hartford, CT (see pp. 282–284). How do you think College Hill would have been transformed if the neighborhood adopted the architectural and social ideas of Billings Forge?

CHICAGO DRAWS UP PLAN TO PROSPER IN 2040

by Tom Hundley

Tom Hundley is a senior editor for the Pulitzer Center on Crisis Reporting, a non-profit journalism organization. He was a reporter for the *Detroit Free Press*, a foreign correspondent for the *Chicago Tribune*, and a contributing writer for the Chicago News Cooperative, where this article first appeared in July 2010.

As the Chicago Metropolitan Agency for Planning sees it, Chicago in 2040 will no longer be battling its suburban neighbors for growth and prosperity opportunities.

Instead, the city will be part of a super-region competing with areas like China and Brazil. Two million more people will probably be crammed into the area, and Chicago may be served by a new, huge transportation hub in the West Loop with high-speed trains and other new transportation ideas.

If all goes according to the agency's "Go to 2040" plan, the Chicago area 30 years from now will have a different look and feel. But much of the plan's momentum and vision might seem familiar, thanks in large part to Daniel Burnham, Chicago's original über-planner.

His influence is on display, both in the strategy the planning agency has put together for the city's future, and literally—in the shrine-like glass display case in its office reception area, which holds a well-thumbed and slightly faded copy of Mr. Burnham's 101-year-old "Plan of Chicago."

"When you think about planning in the city of Chicago, you can't ignore Daniel Burnham's shadow," said Randall S. Blankenhorn, the planning agency's executive director.

Mr. Burnham was the architect who designed some of Chicago's earliest skyscrapers and oversaw construction of the 1893 World's Columbian Exposition. But his greatest contribution to Chicago may have been the 1909 plan that gave the city its broad boulevards, its miles of lakeshore park and an enduring sense that Chicago is still destined for great things.

"The main legacy of the Burnham plan is that it got people to believe in the idea of planning itself," said Carl Smith, an urban history scholar at Northwestern University. "It convinced them that you can intervene in history and remake a city." …

"Go to 2040" and the Burnham plan share a pedigree: Both were created at the behest of the Commercial Club of Chicago, an invitation-only conclave of the city's business leaders.

In 1996 the club set up a group called Chicago Metropolis 2020, which in 1999 published a plan so elegant that it was sold as a coffee-table book. One recommendation was the establishment of a regional planning agency, and acting on that suggestion, the Illinois legislature created the Chicago Metropolitan Agency for Planning.

The agency's 2040 draft envisions Chicago as the hub of an integrated region that, in order to prosper, will need to add two million people and one million jobs over the next 30 years.

That is the view of many experts who foresee a 21st-century global economy that revolves around a dozen or so megaregions spread across Asia, Europe and the Americas. Mr. Blankenhorn said his job was to make sure the Chicago area was one of those regions.

"It's no longer Chicago against [the Illinois cities of] Joliet and Waukegan and Elgin," he said. "It's us against India and China and Brazil."

Architects of the 2040 plan also share Mr. Burnham's belief that Chicago's principal purpose is to serve as a transportation hub.

One of the plan's key proposals incorporates Union Station into a new West Loop Transportation Center, an underground complex that would run beneath Clinton Street between Lake Street and the Eisenhower Expressway. The center would serve as a hub for commuter trains, the El[1], bus lines and a long-dreamed-of intercity high-speed rail network.

The plan also emphasizes that the movement of freight is what links Chicago to the global economy. But with government studies indicating that the already huge volume of freight handled by Chicago is likely to increase by 60 percent to 70 percent over the next 30 years, the 2040 plan focuses on modest transportation upgrades that aim simply to keep congestion at today's barely tolerable levels.

---

[1] El: The rapid transit train system serving greater Chicago

"It's unrealistic to think that congestion will go away," said Mr. Blankenhorn, the former bureau chief of urban project planning at the Illinois Department of Transportation.

In recent decades, regional planning has been driven—often to its detriment—by federally financed transportation projects.

"It became a competition for transportation dollars," said Thomas Cuculich, director of planning and development for DuPage County. "Whoever hired the best lobbyists got their project."

Mr. Cuculich, who has been involved in the planning agency's 2040 project from the start, said the new plan tried to reverse this logic. Instead of allowing the eagerness for federally financed transportation projects to shape planning priorities, the emphasis is placed on land-use considerations, conservation, green technology and job growth.

"It's a paradigm shift that needed to occur," he said.

Although the planning agency does not have authority over zoning and land use—that remains in the hands of local municipalities—it is not without influence. It has statutory power to decide which federally financed transportation projects get built.

But Mr. Blankenhorn said the key to carrying out the 2040 plan lay not in the disbursement of federal dollars, but in winning over the public.

The Chicago Plan Commission recognized the importance of that a century ago when it hired an indefatigable salesman named Walter Moody to promote the Burnham plan. Mr. Moody went on the lecture circuit with lantern slides—the PowerPoint of its day. He papered the city with pamphlets, produced a newsreel that was shown in local theaters and even managed to have the plan incorporated in the civics curriculum of public schools.

But Mr. Burnham's ideas were realized mainly because they had the financial and political backing of the Commercial Club. These days, the club no longer has that kind of clout.

"That's not necessarily a bad thing," Mr. Smith said. "Our society is more open, more democratic, which is good."

In terms of democracy, the Chicago area may get bogged down by too much of a good thing. In addition to 284 municipalities, the region encompasses more than 1,400 units of local government, the most of any region in the United States. The New York metropolitan area, by contrast, has fewer than 200.

The tension between city and suburb is often the biggest obstacle that regional planners must overcome. But even as Chicago's suburbs emerge as economic powerhouses in their own right, groups like the Metropolitan Mayors Caucus, founded by Mayor Richard M. Daley in 1997, have helped foster a spirit of cooperation, city and suburban officials say.

The 2040 plan also revives what might be called the hidden legacy of the Burnham plan. Mr. Burnham cared deeply about living conditions for ordinary citizens, and in his original, 300-page handwritten manuscript he argued for providing day care to the children of the working class and making sure the police acted in a transparent manner. He also wanted the city to be equipped with plenty of public restrooms maintained to a standard of "perfect sweetness."

These recommendations were trimmed from the plan's final version, but according to Mr. Smith, it is clear that Mr. Burnham wanted a city that was not only grand, but also livable.

The new plan makes no mention of restrooms, but it contains chapters devoted to education, nutrition, access to health care, energy conservation and other quality-of-life issues. "Livability" appears to be a main goal.

As the planning agency's staff members ponder the strategies for selling the 2040 plan to the public, they need look no further than the words on the jersey of the group's softball team: "What Would Daniel Burnham Do?"

Close Reading Questions

1. According to Hundley, why was Daniel Burnham important to the city of Chicago? (Multiple Perspectives)

2. Why are transportation issues a priority for the Chicago Metropolitan Agency for Planning (CMAP)?

3. What was the work of the Chicago Plan Commission of 1909? In what ways were its plans realized or not realized?

Analytical Writing/Discussion

4. Why do you think the CMAP wants to make Chicago "a super-region"? In what ways would a super-region make Chicago equal to cities in China and Brazil?

5. What aspects of Burnham's 1909 vision for Chicago are also a part of the Chicago 2040 plan? (Historical Trends)

6. Hundley noted that regional planners often have to deal with "tension between city and suburb." According to Hundley, what are some of those tensions? In what ways are there tensions between the urban and suburban areas where you live? (Cultural Influences)

Further Options

7. According to Hundley, the Commercial Club of Chicago had a great deal of influence in transforming Chicago. To what extent do you think the private organizations and/or regional governments—like the St. Bernard parish officials in Lizzy Ratner's "New Orleans Redraws its Color Lines" in this chapter (see pp. 277–281)—should have a say in the design and function of cities?

8. Urban scholar Carl Smith notes the vital role of city planners. What do you suppose might happen to cities like Chicago without planners? In what ways does or doesn't your city or town seem to have been developed according to a carefully designed plan?

FIGURE 2   Farm Meets City

NEW ORLEANS REDRAWS ITS COLOR LINES

by Lizzy Ratner

Lizzy Ratner is a journalist whose work has appeared in publications like the New York Observer and the New York Times. She is a co-editor of the 2008 book *The Goldstone Report: The Legacy of the Landmark Investigation of the Gaza Conflict.* Ratner is a contributing editor at *The Nation* magazine, where she manages the magazine's "Cities Rising" series of articles that focus on urban revitalization and transformation. The following excerpt is from an article that first appeared in *The Nation* in September 2008, three years after Hurricane Katrina.

The stories sound like strange echoes from another era, as if someone had wound up the old Victrola of history and let the Dixie tunes rip. They begin on a half-abandoned street in St. Bernard Parish[1], an aggressively white community on the southeastern edge of New Orleans. That is where Daphne Clark, 39, an African-American supervisor at a group home, rented a house with help from a rental voucher last year, and that is where the harassment began. First, the Confederate flag hoisted over a neighbor's house followed by stares and sneers; then the official torment by the parish government as it waged a post-Hurricane Katrina crusade against the specter of rental housing. For Clark, this took the form of a series of "notices of violation" warning her that the parish would disconnect her utilities—not because she had done anything wrong but because her landlord had failed to apply for a rental permit, as required by a new parish law. According to Hestel Stout, a white contractor working on Clark's house, the parish official who delivered one of these notices explained to him, "How would you like those types living next to you?"

Around this time, in nearby Jefferson Parish, Leatrice Hollis was enduring her own losing battle with the forces of housing prejudice. The founder and director of People's Community Subsidiary, a nonprofit housing development agency, Hollis had just completed plans for a mixed-income development that would have created forty-nine occupant-owned homes, with twenty-five going to moderate- and low-income "first responders." But just as she was ready to close the deal, Parish Councilman Chris Roberts declared that he wouldn't approve parish funding for any affordable housing in his district. The project was killed.

And then there is the tale of Maria Tejeda, 48, a receptionist and janitor who lived in the Redwood Apartments complex—in apartment L, "as in love"—before the storm[2]. Located in Kenner, the Redwood complex was a 400-unit subsidized housing development and longtime anchor for the area's Latino community. But after the storm, the city decided not to rebuild it. And in April, just two weeks after nearly 1,500 poor and mostly black and brown people lined up overnight to apply for affordable housing vouchers, the parish council unanimously passed a yearlong moratorium on the building of multifamily housing—a measure that effectively halts affordable housing construction in Kenner and leaves people like Tejeda struggling to pay market-rate rent in New Orleans, miles from her community and 12-year-old son. "Maybe in the future I could find me a nice place for me and my child to live," she sighed.

Reprinted with permission from the September 15, 2008 Issue of The Nation. Portions of each week's Nation magazine can be accessed at http://www.thenation.com

---

[1] A parish refers to the division of land in a state. Parishes, like counties, are assigned and execute governmental authority.

[2] In August 2005, Hurricane Katrina was an especially powerful storm, which devastated the Gulf Coast regions of Mississippi, Alabama, and Louisiana.

Such are the stories drifting out of New Orleans and its environs these days, dispatches from a rebuilding effort that often bears an alarming resemblance to a segregation re-enactment. Throughout the region, historically white suburbs, as well as one African-American neighborhood, have been tightening the housing noose by passing laws that restrict, limit or simply ban the building—and even renting—of homes that traditionally benefit poor and working-class people of color. Couched in the banal language of zoning and tax credits, density and permissive-use permits, these efforts often pass for legal and rarely raise eyebrows outside the small community of fair-housing monitors. But taken together—and accompanied, as they so often are, by individual acts of flagrant racism—they represent one of the most brazen and sweeping cases of housing discrimination in recent history.

"It's been like a wildfire," said Lucia Blacksher, general counsel for the Greater New Orleans Fair Housing Action Center, an advocacy group that has been leading the fight against post-Katrina housing discrimination. "Local governments have been creating legal barriers—legal, in the sense they created laws—to prevent people who are African-American from returning. And I'm saying that because we all know what we're talking about here. Affordable housing or multifamily housing is where African-Americans lived. And if you don't let that kind of housing back, you're not going to give people who are African-American or Latino an opportunity to live [here]."

The intensity of this discrimination has surprised even veteran advocates like Blacksher, who grew up in Mobile, Alabama, with a civil rights attorney father. But in many ways it was foreshadowed—though not necessarily foreordained—by the powerful racial tectonics that have shaped New Orleans and its surrounding parishes for decades. Since as far back as 1960—when New Orleans schools were ordered desegregated and its white majority rioted, resisted and fled to neighboring parishes—the region has been defined by a vigorously maintained bull's-eye shape. At the center was the black-majority city, while the outer ring belonged to the mostly white suburban parishes.

Hurricane Katrina threatened to shake everything up, both within and between parishes. With 80 percent of New Orleans flooded; with much of its poor black population uprooted and blocked from returning (witness the decision to tear down public housing); and with millions of dollars in low-income-housing tax credits flowing into the area, a rare possibility emerged: displaced New Orleanians might try to move into historically white parishes. But these parishes were not about to let that happen.

Among the first and most aggressive to take action was St. Bernard Parish, 84 percent white before the storm and working to rebuild itself that way. Barely two months into the recovery, St. Bernard's governing council passed a twelve-month ban on "the re-establishment and development" of multifamily dwellings, stalling the reconstruction of affordable housing complexes. But the council truly distinguished itself in September 2006 when it passed an ordinance that, critics said, danced about as close to legalized segregation as perhaps any law since 1972, the year Louisiana finally deleted its Jim Crow laws. Known as the "blood relative ordinance," this law prohibited homeowners from renting their properties to anyone who was not a bona fide blood relation without first obtaining a permit—a loaded concept anywhere, but particularly in St. Bernard, where the white majority owned 93 percent of the pre-storm housing.

Ultimately, the parish was forced to remove the offending "blood relative" term and pay more than $150,000 in attorneys' fees and damages, thanks to a 2006 lawsuit brought under the Fair Housing Act by Blacksher's organization. But even so, the modified law retained much of the toxic thrust. All homeowners wishing to rent their property, either to strangers or blood relatives, were required to submit to an arduous and costly permit process. If they did not, they—and their tenants—would suffer serious consequences, from fines to utility shutoffs, as Clark and others discovered during an enforcement campaign that began this past winter. Among the highlights: the flood of notices warning tenants that their utilities would be disconnected; the visits from officials demanding they vacate their properties;

the spate of utilities cutoffs (the parish denies this); reports of police officers stopping black renters as they drove to their homes in once-white neighborhoods ("Only homeowners should be in this area," one renter recalls being told by a cop); and, in the most egregious incidents, the arrest of a Nigerian-American landlord and the arson that destroyed another black landlord's property. Call it "Louisiana burning."

"They don't want the blacks back," explained Lynn Dean, 84, a quirky, self-styled "mini-mogul" who served for years on the St. Bernard Parish Council and was one of only two council members to oppose the blood relative law. "What they'd like to do now with Katrina is say, We'll wipe out all of them. They're not gonna say that out in the open, but how do you say? Actions speak louder than words. There's their action."

Such race-based "actions" have made St. Bernard notorious in the post-Katrina housing discrimination frenzy. But it has plenty of company—from Lakeview, a white, middle- and upper-income neighborhood, to New Orleans East, where the cruelties of class prejudice, perhaps more than race, have been on bold display. A traditionally middle-income African-American community with pockets of immense wealth and poverty, New Orleans East has been the site of several moratorium efforts as well as other legislative maneuvering to fend off mixed-income housing developments, Section 8 housing and anything else that might allow poor people to live there. Not surprisingly, Confederate flag waving has been absent in New Orleans East. In other ways the situation has been distressingly similar to that in other districts: the same fears of crime and the same angst about property values and blight, all emphasizing the interplay between race and class, with one occasionally trumping the other, but with the two far more often combining and amplifying each other.

Jefferson Parish is a prime case of the latter. Located just west of New Orleans, it was nearly 70 percent white before the storm and is perhaps best known as the old stomping grounds of rabid ex-Klansman David Duke (in 1989, 8,456 parish citizens elected him to the State House of Representatives). From the beginning, it was clear that the parish was going to be a problem. Just three days after Katrina, police officers from the mostly white outpost of Gretna blocked the bridge known as the Crescent City Connection as desperate New Orleanians tried to escape to drier, safer ground. Armed with shotguns, the police fired into the air over the evacuees' heads and demanded they turn back. "The only two explanations we ever received was, one, 'We're not going to have any Superdomes over here,' and 'This is not New Orleans,'" a witness told *60 Minutes*.

Three years later, the Crescent City Connection incident hasn't really ended. It continues in vigilante acts of intimidation like the one visited on Travis and Kiyanna Smith, a young African-American couple who moved into the area in May and were treated to a crude welcome: three crosses and the letters KKK burned into their lawn. And it continues in the moratoriums passed by cities like Kenner and Westwego, as well as the machinations of Councilman Roberts, an ambitious young Republican who has made a hobby of killing affordable housing proposals while mouthing off about the "ignorant" and "lazy" tenants who might live in them. Among Roberts's accomplishments: spiking plans by Volunteers of America, a century-old social service organization, to build a 200-unit housing development for low-income seniors in his district. (Roberts did not return calls seeking comment for this article.)

And yet, for all Roberts's cruel maneuvering, legislators of his ilk, if not bluntness, are disturbingly common in the annals of housing discrimination. Even before Katrina, legislators from New Orleans East and all but one other Orleans Parish district had tried to pass moratoriums on multifamily housing, and the Gulf Coast can hardly claim credit for inventing these tactics. Indeed, in the forty years since Congress passed the Fair Housing Act, which is supposed to prohibit housing discrimination on the basis of race, color, religion and national origin (as well as sex, disability and family status, thanks to later versions), exclusionary land use policy has become the preferred means of maintaining this country's stark separate-and-unequal housing patterns.

The post-Katrina orgy of ordinances and moratoriums falls squarely within this tradition. But there are some essential differences, beginning with the fact that the post-storm frenzy is fundamentally more: more overt, more excessive, more widespread. "It is extreme," said Milton Bailey, president of the Louisiana Housing Finance Agency. "If we can do away with NIMBYism[3], we can solve every single housing problem and every single social problem there is in this state. The single most interfering, stick in the mud, big hill to climb is NIMBYism."

Bailey wasn't being melodramatic. Hurricane Katrina damaged as much as 80 percent of the New Orleans area's affordable housing, leaving as many as 12,000 people homeless and tens of thousands unable to return. These people need homes, but even in a best-case scenario, the number of planned affordable housing units is expected to meet only 45 percent of the post-storm need, according to Bailey; the federal government simply didn't cough up cash for more. And now, thanks to the rash of ordinances and moratoriums—coupled with the national housing crisis—even this scenario looks distressingly unlikely.

Part of the reason for this bind goes back to the guidelines set by Congress when it allotted hundreds of millions of dollars in low-income-housing tax credits to Louisiana after the storm. Under the guidelines, the state is required to have all its tax-credit-supported projects in the ground and completed by December 31, 2010, or the government snatches the credits back. But as things stand now, more than one in five tax-credit-backed projects already in the pipeline—roughly 6,100 units—could fall victim to the combined catastrophes of housing discrimination and the capital markets crisis, according to Bailey.

"This is a very valuable resource, and for it to go unused as a result of NIMBYism is a crying shame, because we don't get to carry those tax credits forward," said Bailey. "But [the parishes] don't get it.... They refuse to see it because we are blinded by the fact that we don't want those people in our neighborhoods."

This self-destructive logic is on full display in St. Bernard Parish. With its tax base in tatters and vast swaths still uninhabited, if not uninhabitable, the parish could reasonably give medals of bravery to each person who chooses to return. But, as Okechukwu Okafor, a soft-spoken Nigerian-American, soon learned, some prejudices die harder than the will to recover.

Okafor, 29, purchased three houses in St. Bernard after the storm in the hopes of renovating and renting them. (He had initially hoped to sell them but, like many landlords, got caught in the real estate meltdown and couldn't find buyers.) Two were in the lily-white Lexington Place subdivision and one in the black-friendly neighborhood of Violet. When he began renting them out he was unaware of the rental ordinance, and when he found out he held off applying for permits because he feared the process was not genuine. "I think it was just a deliberate ploy to prevent you from having you rent it out at all," he said.

But woe to the person who defies the parish! In February, a lock was placed on the water meter of one of Okafor's Lexington Place houses, and on March 11 Okafor was arrested after he confessed to telling his water-deprived tenant that it was OK to break the meter if he was desperate. One moment Okafor was sitting in a meeting with parish officials cordially discussing the meter matter, and the next he was handcuffed and hauled off to jail, where he was questioned about whether he was in this country legally and how he got the money to purchase his properties.

Okafor's twenty-four hours behind bars culminated in two charges: theft of a utility and criminal damage to property. But curiously, he was approached shortly after his release by the chief administrative officer for St. Bernard Parish with an offer to amend those charges. According to legal documents, the administrative czar told Okafor the charges would be dropped if he would "empty the houses" of their

---

[3] NIMBY: Not In My Backyard

three tenants, which Okafor obediently did. (The charges, however, have not been dropped, and Okafor is still awaiting his day in court.)

When asked to explain these strange goings-on, Craig Taffaro, the parish president, zealously denied that they were the result of anything less than altruistic impulses. "There has been absolutely zero racial influence for what has taken place," he said, explaining that what has been cast as "prejudice" is simply economic acumen, a desire to prevent out-of-town developers from "destabilizing" the housing market and "changing the face of St. Bernard" from a "predominantly owner-occupied community" to a renters' town.

And yet, who tends to own homes in St. Bernard Parish? And who tends to rent? Certainly there are white renters in St. Bernard, and some of them have been harassed with notices. But for each story of white families caught in the anti-rental onslaught, there are many more anecdotes reeking of racial prejudice, like that of Kiana Alexander. A former Post Office employee with carefully coiffed hair and shy eyes, Alexander, 34, is among the landlords who did apply for a rental permit. She paid her application fees ($250 apiece for her three St. Bernard Parish properties), mailed notices to neighbors and, on January 22, attended a parish council meeting during which the council was supposed to vote on her application to rent her house in Buccaneer Villa, a historically white enclave. The council ended up tabling the matter—it said she'd applied too soon for the permit because she hadn't completed the renovations—but that didn't quell the group of angry parishioners who'd shown up to express their displeasure.

And then, less than five hours later, Alexander's house was in flames. For Alexander, who had no insurance, there was only one explanation for the fire that destroyed her house. "Somebody at the meeting," she said. "Because the house has been sitting there since September, so why burn it after the meeting? The day of the meeting! Why?"

Alexander is still awaiting an answer, as are dozens of other St. Bernardians who have been burned, literally or figuratively, by the parish's anti-rental campaign. In fact, the drama continues; in July, the planning commission recommended denying eighteen permit applications. And more than seventy property owners have joined a lawsuit brought this past spring by Henry Klein, a New Orleans attorney suing the parish for overregulation of land use. (In a victory for tenants, shortly after the suit was filed the parish agreed to stop threatening them with utility shutoffs.) But even if they win in court—a big question mark—it's hard to imagine much improvement as long as their fellow parishioners refuse to acknowledge even the possibility that racial prejudice has fueled such outrages as the blood relative ordinance or the arson that destroyed Alexander's house.

"Aw, that's bull," growled St. Bernard Parish fire chief Thomas Stone during a phone conversation in which he demanded to know whether *The Nation* was going to write about all the other arson cases that have afflicted the parish. He even suggested that Alexander might have set the fire "to draw attention to herself." And he added, "I don't think there's any problem with race relations at all in St. Bernard Parish—none whatsoever."

Close Reading Questions

1. Why did Ratner refer to changes in housing laws as "brazen and sweeping cases of housing discrimination?"

2. How did the need for affordable housing complicate the return of thousands of New Orleans residents in the months following Hurricane Katrina?

3. In what ways did the parishes and neighborhoods respond to requests for housing before and after the storm?

Analytical Writing/Discussion

4. To what degree can the Fair Housing Act and/or the local parish governments be blamed for the lack of housing options in New Orleans?

5. Ratner states that regulations surrounding low income and rental property are repeatedly utilized to keep neighborhoods racially segregated. What do you think are some of the least defensible reasons for the lack of affordable housing options? (Multiple Perspectives)

6. The earliest version of the St. Bernard Parish "blood relative ordinance" goes back to the 1970s. Why do you think the 2006 lawsuit was or was not an important moment for residents and elected officials of St. Bernard Parish? (Historical Trends)

Further Options

7. Review "The History of Fair Housing" in this chapter. In what ways did the actions of elected parish councilors and law enforcement officials violate the Fair Housing Act of 1968? How do stories like those of Okechukwu Okafor and Kiana Alexander exemplify those violations? (Cultural Influences)

8. Among others, Milton Bailey of the Louisiana Housing Authority pointed to NIMBYism as a prime reason for limited affordable housing construction in hurricane ravaged New Orleans. What can New Orleans learn from the revitalization of Providence, Rhode Island as detailed in Gene Bunnell's "Providence Saves a Neighborhood" (see pp. 268–272)?

Freewrite 3: Thriving on New Models for City Housing

Urban revitalization often happens within a single city block, which is the case in one neighborhood of Hartford, CT. The following—an excerpt of a 2010 article by Dan Haar, a business columnist for *The Hartford Courant*—focuses on the revival of a neighborhood in Connecticut's capitol city. After reading the excerpt, freewrite and/or discuss some of the questions below.

[Tamarra] Carson will finish work [at The Kitchen, a bakery with an attached café at the Billings Forge complex in Hartford's Frog Hollow neighborhood] soon, and her three children will arrive from school. Her gaze finds the family's third-floor, three-bedroom corner apartment just across the courtyard. She has high ceilings and a view of the state Capitol. "It's kind of like a New York City apartment," said Carson, 32…. [She] is lucky that her search for an apartment with a Section 8 voucher brought her two years ago to Billings Forge, a self-contained complex with 98 apartments, artists' studios, a community center, an upscale restaurant, community gardens and The Kitchen, where she works. She was unemployed two years ago, so let's change that to extremely lucky.

It's downright idyllic, and the key to it—one key—is a model of philanthropy that could emerge as a force in the search for workable housing answers.

Billings Forge, a mixed-income development, was already an apartment complex when The Melville Charitable Trust bought it five years ago for $5.5 million. Melville poured in another $5 million or so, and works with a nonprofit agency, Billings Forge Community Works, to operate the place, more or less breaking even on yearly costs. A mile or so away, in downtown, The Hollander at 410 Asylum St. stands as another monument to philanthropic housing development. The long-vacant building had little value and its owners, the Hollander family, decided to make a lasting gesture after it became clear they couldn't tear it down for yet another parking lot. Common Ground, a New York-based nonprofit dedicated to ending homelessness and building communities, spent $22 million on the rehab, and residents moved in last fall. Now The Hollander's 70 units are full, some at market rates and some restricted to residents making between $23,690 and $45,960 a year, typically with a subsidy.

This type of development, inspired by philanthropic owners and built in the tradition of non-profit, community-oriented housing, was among the bright ideas in urban revitalization highlighted Wednesday at a discussion organized by the Partnership for Strong Communities. The forum—part of a series at the Lyceum, also owned by Melville in Frog Hollow—looked at the great potential of city neighborhoods.

"We're not any longer talking about dumping public money into cities just to increase the concentration of poor people living in them. We're talking about attracting a mix of incomes to cities by focusing on neighborhood growth and preservation," said Timothy Bannon, executive director of the Connecticut Housing Finance Authority.

The philanthropic, community-building model of development isn't going to spread wildly. But it's a catalyst for other investment and a stabilizing force, so the effect of just a few of these projects is huge.

Will there be more? Economic conditions say yes. Building values remain low, and many are in disrepair.... Bob Hohler, executive director of The Melville Charitable Trust, said a new generation of philanthropists is poised to push ahead with the sort of "program-related investment" that Melville is doing at Billings Forge. It could pay off big-time for the foundations if the properties multiply in value. But Hohler added, "This is an investment for generations."

That means decades of work for the organizers. For the neighborhood, it means a permanent economic anchor. For Tamarra Carson, it means a stable life for her boys, a teen and a tween, and her 8-year-old girl.

After reading the Haar article, freewrite and/or discuss the following question:

- Why do you think Haar regards Billings Forge as "downright idyllic"? To what degree does Billings Forge conform to your idea of an ideal way of living?

You may choose to expand on this freewriting by linking it to the cities with which you are familiar. Answer one or more of the following questions through further writing and/or discussion:

- What effects do you think it has on an urban neighborhood when the residents are not overwhelmingly poor?

- To what degree do you think urban planning and city renewal should be led by local government and/or philanthropic organizations?

Final Assignment 1: Reviving Cities

American cities are constantly changing, yet not without conflicts. Chudacoff and Smith wrote of the competing ideas about the function of cities in the early twentieth century. By the 1950s, federal legislation allowed the destruction of entire city neighborhoods under the guise of urban renewal, forcing thousands of displaced African-Americans families to live in public housing. By the first decade of the twenty-first century, Hundley and Bunnell both suggest that careful attention to architecture, transportation, and neighborhood environments is critical for the future of cities in the United States.

Essay Question

To what extent do you think the revival of American cities should be based on social, political, economic, and/or environmental concerns? Your answer should include a discussion of the development of cities over time.

    Write a formal and extended essay to answer this question. Be sure to include specific references and direct quotations from several readings of this chapter (see Chapter 7 on Academic Honesty on quoting and citing properly). Be sure to not only support your informed perspective but also to anticipate and answer the possible objections of those who do not already agree with you. Your task is to assert your opinion and persuade others to consider it carefully.

Freewrite 4: Assignment Analysis

Before you try to start answering this complex question, analyze its parts. Reread the question above and underline several phrases that represent key parts of the larger answer you will be developing. Then pick two or three of these phrases and freewrite your immediate impressions: What do you think right now? Then, pause to look for connections, contradictions, and omissions within your first response: what else do you want to discuss, what else do you want to add, and/or what order of your ideas is developing? Finally, consider the audience of your essay: who does not agree with you already, and why might they disagree?

Reading Review

Once you have sketched some of your initial ideas, review some of the readings to find specific details and persuasive evidence to support, enrich, and possibly complicate your response. Here are some readings and post-reading questions that you may want to consider:

1. Kingsbury, Analytical Writing/Discussion question 5
2. Chudacoff and Smith, Close Reading question 2
3. Marino, Analytical Writing/Discussion question 6

4. Freewrite 3

5. Bunnell, Analytical Writing/Discussion question 7

6. Hundley, Close Reading question 2

7. Ratner, Analytical Writing/Discussion question 5

8. Figure 2

Feel free to include other readings and post-reading questions. You also may want to review the suggestions for writing persuasively in Chapter 6 on Argument as well as practice the peer response described in Chapter 4 on the Writing Process.

Final Assignment 2: Contested Spaces

For the majority of the twentieth century, government policies favored the suburbs over cities. Indeed, the History of Fair Housing article details the history of federally sanctioned segregation that made the creation of suburban towns possible. Despite legal intervention, Americans have definite ideas about where they live and where they want to live. As Marino and Hundley both state, the end of the twentieth century saw a continuation of the competing perceptions of the suburbs or cities as the best places to live in the United States.

Essay Question

To what degree do you think that the desirability of urban or suburban living is a result of unequal government policies favoring cities or suburbs? Your answer should include a discussion of the social practices and legal policies that favored cities or suburbs over time.

Write a formal and extended essay to answer this question. Be sure to include specific references and direct quotations from several readings of this chapter (see Chapter 7 on Academic Honesty on quoting and citing properly). Be sure to not only support your informed perspective but also to anticipate and answer the possible objections of those who do not already agree with you. Your task is to assert your opinion and persuade others to consider it carefully.

Freewrite 5: Assignment Analysis

Before you try to start answering this complex question, analyze its parts. Reread the question above and underline several phrases that represent key parts of the larger answer you will be developing. Then pick two or three of these phrases and fastwrite your immediate impressions: What do you think right now? Then, pause to look for connections, contradictions, and omissions within your first response: what else do you want to discuss, what else do you want to add, and/or what order of your ideas is developing? Finally, consider the audience of your essay: who does not agree with you already, and why might they disagree?

Reading Review

Once you have sketched some of your initial ideas, review some of the readings to find specific details and persuasive evidence to support, enrich, and possibly complicate your response. Here are some readings and post-reading questions that you may want to consider:

1. Freewrite 1

2. Marino, Analytical Writing/Discussion question 4

3. Figure 1

4. Bunnell, Close Reading question 2

5. Hundley, Close Reading question 3

6. Ratner, Close Reading question 2

7. Ratner, Analytical Writing/Discussion question 6

8. Freewrite 2

Feel free to include other readings and post-reading questions. You also may want to review the suggestions for writing persuasively in Chapter 6 on Argument as well as practice the peer response described in Chapter 4 on the Writing Process.

Additional Source Suggestions

In the e-supplement of this textbook, there are several sources that will help you deepen your understanding of cities and suburbs and strengthen your final assignment. These sources include videos as well as readings, and they present multiple perspectives, historical trends, and cultural influences on urban and suburban lifestyles. To access these materials, see the code on the inside front cover of this textbook, which will lead you to the website for additional sources.

Energy and Sustainability

To waste, to destroy, our natural resources, to skin and exhaust the land instead of using it so as to increase its usefulness, will result in undermining in the days of our children the very prosperity which we ought by right to hand down to them.

— *President Theodore Roosevelt (1907)*

We've got to pause and ask ourselves: How much clean air do we need?"

— *Lee Iacocca (1974)*

The trouble in corporate America is that too many people with too much power live in a box (their home), then travel the same road every day to another box (their office).

— *Faith Popcorn (1991)*

Global warming has become a new religion.

— *Dr. Ivar Giaever (2008)*

Introduction

Author Barbara Kingsolver lived a comfortable life with her husband and two children in their Arizona home. However, Kingsolver was curious as to whether her family could become more mindful of their energy usage and overall impact on the planet. So, for 1 year, Kingsolver's family moved to rural Virginia vowing to eat food grown within 100 miles of their home—including food grown in the family garden. In her 2007 memoir, *Animal, Vegetable, Miracle,* Kingsolver admits that their journey began with hope, yet was also filled with reminders of their ties to the habits she was seeking to avoid. She writes:

> As the U.S. population made an unprecedented mad dash for the Sun Belt, one carload of us paddled against the tide, heading for the Promised Land where water falls from the sky and green stuff grows all around. We were about to begin the adventure of realigning our lives with our food chain. Naturally, our first stop was to buy junk food and fossil fuel.

So many Americans are not accustomed to the frugal and environmentally aware lifestyle Kingsolver tried to create, for it means making a serious assessment of the energy usage contemporary lifestyles demand.

According to the 2009 Residential Energy Consumption Survey, the average household had at least two televisions, one computer, and two or more rechargeable devices, like cell phones and video game consoles. Most homes had washing machines and dryers, microwave ovens, and air conditioning. According to the National Household Travel Survey (NHTS), 70% of households in 1969 did not own a car; by 2009, that number dropped to less than 40%. By the end of the first decade of the twenty-first century, 91% of American households had at least one car and many had at least two cars. Less than 3% of Americans walked to work and only a few used public transit. The vast majority drove to and from work, often with one person per car. We are a nation of convenience and energy consumption.

The three historical readings of this chapter include diverse discussions about energy and sustainability. Brian C. Black's article traces the way oil became an integral part of American life, while industrial designer Raymond Loewy's commentary on the economic and environmental effects of consumer demands for 1950s automobiles.

The most recent historical reading is James Atwater's *Saturday Evening Post* article, which provides a glimpse of 1960s America, when households were brimming with energy-hogging appliances. Among the three contemporary readings, David W. Orr implores a new generation of designers to consider the environment in all aspects of building design. Michael Pollan's essay questions whether there is any reason for individuals to take small steps toward reducing the effects of global warming, while Nicolas Loris asserts such steps are not necessary, as scientists cannot agree that global warming exists. Every reading in this chapter provides perspectives on the storied history of energy usage in America and the varied attempts to create sustainable lifestyles amid an affinity for convenience and consumption.

These texts, along with the reading questions, freewriting activities, and visual elements of this chapter, are designed to develop the reading and writing abilities required for academic study. After each reading, you will find a set of questions that are divided into Close Reading Questions, Analytical Writing/ Discussion, and Further Options. Some questions involve the same investigation of multiple perspectives, cultural influences, and historical trends that were introduced in Chapter 1 or 2. Answering some and discussing more of the post-reading questions will better prepare you to complete the final assignments options. These final writing assignments will ask you to assert your own, more informed perspective on fashion and consumerism. This chapter asks: **To what extent should energy sustainability be a top priority?**

Freewrite 1: Initial Impressions

Before you read the varying opinions of the other writers in the rest of this chapter, freewrite to explore your own thoughts and experiences about energy and sustainability. Try answering some of the following questions:

- To what extent do you think your daily use of energy impacts the environment?
- Why do you think the United States should or should not reduce its dependence on oil as its primary energy source?

OIL FOR LIVING

by Brian C. Black

Brian C. Black is an associate professor of history and environmental studies at Pennsylvania State University, Altoona, and is the author of several books, including *Petrolia: The Landscape of American's First Oil Boom* and *Crude Reality: Petroleum in World History*. The following excerpt is from Black's 2012 article, "Oil for Living: Petroleum and American Conspicuous Consumption," which was published in the *Journal of American History*.

Americans proudly streamed to the 1939 World's Fair in New York City as World War II flared on the other side of the Atlantic. Not yet part of the conflict, Americans used the opportunity to escape the present and wax utopian. Although the dreams on display took many forms, they were woven together by an invisible hand—more specifically, by a basic assumption—concealed within each of the fair's scenes: bountiful supplies of cheap energy. The novelist E. L. Doctorow provides one of the most revealing descriptions of one of the fair's best-known attractions:

> We rode across the Bridge of Wheels and got out, of course, at the General Motors Building. That was everyone's first stop…. In front of us a whole world lit up, as if we were flying over it, the most fantastic sight I had ever seen, an entire city of the future, with skyscrapers and fourteen-lane highways, real little cars moving on them at different speeds, the center for the higher speeds, the lanes on the edge for the lower…. This miniature world demonstrated how everything was planned…. It was a toy that any child in the world would want to own. You could play with it forever… it was a model world.

Inside General Motors' Futurama, five million visitors rode on the "Magic Motorways" exhibit, designed by Norman Bel Geddes, that led to the "Town of Tomorrow." Details of reality—such as grocery stores and gas stations—were left out of the vision, but the nation was abuzz with the futuristic marvels such as flying sedans found on the model expressways of Ford's "Road of Tomorrow."[1] Although that dream world possessed iconic aspects that resonated for generations, its greatest appeal may have been its vision of a world in which basic aspects of everyday life occurred easily—requiring neither care nor attention. With their basic needs met, humans might occupy themselves with greater challenges or endless diversion.

Even though automobiles have, for the most part, remained grounded, many other details of that futuristic landscape materialized. The remarkable accomplishments that shaped everyday American life after World War II have many common threads that bind them together, but perhaps none is as central

From "Oil for Living: Petroleum and American Conspicuous Consumption," by Brian C. Black. *The Journal of American History*, Volume 99, Issue 1, June 2012 (Pages 40–50). Used by permission of Oxford University Press.

---

[1] E. L. Doctorow, *World's Fair* (New York, 1985), 252–53. Jeffrey L. Meikle, *Twentieth Century Limited: Industrial Design in America, 1925–1939* (Philadelphia, 1979), 200–209. For more on the 1939 World's Fair in New York City, see Robert W. Rydell and Laura Burd Schiavo, eds., *Designing Tomorrow: America's World's Fairs of the 1930s* (New Haven, 2010).

as petroleum. Measured in terms of quadrillion btus (British thermal units), which is the basis for charting energy consumption, U.S. consumption of petroleum rose from less than ten after 1945 to twenty in 1960, forty in 1975, and over forty after 2000. It was approximately 1950 when petroleum overtook coal as the nation's leading energy producer, and today the rate of petroleum consumption ranks approximately double its nearest competitors, coal and natural gas. Although the nation passed through different eras in the commodity's centrality, petroleum's ongoing predominance in American life after 1945 demands new terminology. The inculcation is so dramatic that Americans during the postwar era can be said to exist within an ecology of oil.[2]

When the French philosopher Roland Barthes sought to condemn the overconsumption and superficiality of the modern era, his symbol was the substance of many forms—plastic. Similar to the people that he condemns, Barthes overlooks the raw material that made possible the iconic plastic.[3] Before Americans could have the hula hoops and Twinkies that helped define the postwar era, there had to be a prodigious and reliable supply of crude oil. The best evidence of twentieth-century Americans' overwhelming dependence on petroleum may be that they have completely neglected to give it proper credit for enabling the nation's overall high standard of living. Even now, most Americans barely get past an elementary-level understanding of their dependence on oil. Oil does not just fuel Americans' vehicles. Oil has changed their diet, their clothes, their neighborhoods, their jobs, their fun—in fact, everything about U.S. society. Although Americans continue this profound reliance today, the nation's culture of crude has begun to shift in dramatic ways.

Taken for granted for decades, the flow of surplus crude came to a sudden halt during the 1970s when increasing imports converged with political limitations. As abundance turns to scarcity in the second decade of the twenty-first century, the American ecology of oil has come to include concepts such as resource wars, peak oil, petro-dictators, and bottom kill. This increasing appreciation of petroleum's importance and the complexity of acquiring it demands that we also revise our historical narratives—that we acknowledge the hidden hand (or nozzle) when it was most essential to American life and history.[4] This brief essay deconstructs the trope of American mass consumption after World War II to reveal two of its primary elements functioning symbiotically: consumer passion and cheap crude. From the Big Mac

---

[2] "Figure 5. Primary Energy Consumption by Source, 1775–2009," in *Annual Energy Review 2009*, by U.S. Energy Information Administration (Washington, 2010), xx. Myrna I. Santiago uses the term "ecology of oil" to describe the wholesale changes that developing crude meant to the lives of native inhabitants in her work about Mexico. See Myrna I. Santiago, *The Ecology of Oil: Environment, Labor, and the Mexican Revolution, 1900–1938* (Cambridge, Eng., 2006).

[3] Roland Barthes, *Mythologies*, trans. Annette Lavers (New York, 1972), 97–99. This book was originally published in French in 1957.

[4] On the factors relating to the 1970s oil crisis, see, for instance, Daniel Yergin, *The Prize: The Epic Quest for Oil, Money, and Power* (New York, 1991); Karen R. Merrill, *The Oil Crisis of 1973–1974: A Brief History with Documents* (New York, 2007); and Daniel Horowitz, *Jimmy Carter and the Energy Crisis of the 1970s: The "Crisis of Confidence" Speech of July 15, 1979; A Brief History with Documents* (New York, 2004). On American reaction to energy transition after the 1970s crisis, see David E. Nye, *Consuming Power: A Social History of American Energies* (Boston, 1998); Michael T. Klare, *Resource Wars: The New Landscape of Global Conflict* (New York, 2001); Kenneth S. Deffeyes, *Hubbert's Peak: The Impending World Oil Shortage* (Princeton, 2008); Paul Roberts, *The End of Oil: On the Edge of a Perilous New World* (New York, 2005); and Thomas L. Friedman, *Hot, Flat, and Crowded: Why We Need a Green Revolution—and How It Can Renew America* (New York, 2008). For efforts by historians to include energy and petroleum in the historical narrative, see Alfred W. Crosby, *Children of the Sun: A History of Humanity's Unappeasable Appetite for Energy* (New York, 2006); and J. R. McNeill, *Something New under the Sun: An Environmental History of the Twentieth-Century World* (New York, 2000). For works by journalists who have told portions of this story, see Peter Maass, *Crude World: The Violent Twilight of Oil* (New York, 2009); Lisa Margonelli, *Oil on the Brain: Adventures from the Pump to the Pipeline* (New York, 2008); and Roberts, *End of Oil*.

to Tupperware's burping bowl, petroleum provided the raw material for much of what defined consumption in postwar America.

Conspicuously Consuming Crude

In Futurama, science fiction–like visions merged with the ideas of intellects such as Lewis Mumford to take concrete form. Modernism was no longer an artistic genre restricted to the few; now, modernist design and "the new" were the stuff of the middle class. Consumer expectations—such as those shaped by the scene of Futurama—became a primary engine behind radical shifts in patterns of American living. The transformation of living patterns after World War II was so dramatic that historians have given it a name: "mass consumption." Lizabeth Cohen and other historians have demonstrated that the motivations that drove consumers and filled out the middle class were fed by the policies and politics of the Cold War.[5] But the factor behind the scenes that enabled this dramatic change has yet to be fully appreciated by historians.

In her work, Cohen reaches back to Thorstein Veblen's *The Theory of the Leisure Class* (1899), in which he developed the idea of "conspicuous consumption," to describe the power of social emulation expressed through extravagant display, particularly in the American model of capitalist society. Consumable items, in such a paradigm, can function as symbols of affluence that spur citizens to increase their economic standing. Similar arguments were made in other well-known critiques of postwar America such as David Riesman's *The Lonely Crowd* (1950), David Potter's *People of Plenty* (1954), and John Kenneth Galbraith's *The Affluent Society* (1958). Although in each case scholars ultimately criticized American emphasis on consumption, there was clear agreement that the overriding priority in America of this era was the freedom to purchase goods that fleshed out a life-style that today we refer to as middle class. A society with affordable products and consumers with discretionary income to spend became primary components of the "affluence" that defined the American standard of living after World War II. Despite its implication for ideas of race, gender, and youth—not to mention of home design and the overall construction of the human habitat—mass consumption became a symbol of American success in the Cold War. Although scholars such as Cohen argue that many of these details grew from basic policies, such as the G.I. Bill, we must also ascribe credit to the lifeblood of the affluent society that took shape after World War II: cheap energy, primarily petroleum. Even more important, the scope of the affluence that oil enabled made this higher standard of living the new normal, eventually making consumption no longer conspicuous.[6]

In *People of Plenty*, Potter sought to analyze this society by expanding our conceptions of what is included in a society's "culture." By including everyday patterns and habits associated with America's experience with mass consumption, for instance, these details could be seen as part of larger level social patterns, including efforts to stimulate unity or, contradictorily, exclusion. As a unifier, this emerging culture helped overcome class distinctions and cleared the way for one, predominant middle class. With this pattern in mind, theorists have constructed a critique of consumption as a homogenizing force. Barthes,

---

[5] On Lewis Mumford and other modernist intellectuals of this era, see Meikle, *Twentieth Century Limited*, 135, 180. Lewis Mumford, *Technics and Civilization* (1934; Chicago, 1963), 357–58. For general studies of modernism and consumption, see, for example, Gary Cross, *An All-Consuming Century: Why Commercialism Won in Modern America* (New York, 2000); and Terry Smith, *Making the Modern: Industry, Art, and Design in America* (Chicago,1993). Lizabeth Cohen, *A Consumers' Republic: The Politics of Mass Consumption in Postwar America* (New York,2003), 10–12.

[6] Thorstein Veblen, *The Theory of the Leisure Class: An Economic Study of Institutions* (New York, 1899); David Riesman, *The Lonely Crowd: A Study of the Changing American Character* (New Haven, 1950); David Potter, *People of Plenty: Economic Abundance and the American Character* (Chicago, 1954); John Kenneth Galbraith, *The Affluent Society* (Boston, 1958).

however, decried the loss of meaning and depth with such flexibility and, by the end of the twentieth century, other scholars had joined the fray. For instance, the sociologist George Ritzer and others railed against the McDonaldization (or Walmartization) of American life that took away distinct, individualized opportunities for consumption and replaced them with standardized, less personal options. Other scholars, alternatively, suggest that although the disposable society has many shortcomings, by making prosperity and comfort so accessible, it may also represent the most democratic culture that American society has thus far produced.[7] Regardless of its ultimate meaning for Americans, mass consumption, scholars agree, had made the U.S. standard of living after World War II a symbol of U.S. prosperity. Unseen in many of these consumer items, unrecognizable in its finished form, the alchemy of gallons upon gallons of cheap crude played a defining role.

So where does petroleum fit into the historical paradigm of post–World War II consumerism? Certainly, it was a critical cog in the engine that drove this consumptive society. Can one go one step further, in an era enabled by cheap petroleum, to argue that "black gold" has functioned as a democratizing element in American life? Big Oil has wrought mighty evils on societies all over the world and also on the natural environment; however, for the society that inculcated it more completely than any other, there is clear evidence that cheap oil empowered the middle class and helped the United States attain the world's greatest standard of living by, not least of all, helping Americans overcome very basic limits on the human condition. Our histories must accept this premise so that scholars might unravel the larger environmental, social, and cultural implications of our high-energy existence.

Petroleum Makes Consumption Less Conspicuous

As consumption became less conspicuous or exceptional after World War II, transportation became the preeminent example of the new ecology of oil. The use of human and animal power, the essential ways that humans had moved about, had remained fairly static for centuries. By the early 1900s, automated methods of transportation (powered by biofuels, gasoline, steam, or electricity) had become widely available. Fuel and vehicle prices made such options primarily available only to wealthy consumers. With few roads or conveniences, a drive in such a vehicle during the 1910s was almost purely a luxury. Local and state governments worked to make auto travel easier and more convenient, and entrepreneurs such as Henry Ford brought vehicle prices down to a level at which mass consumers became drivers. Seen as a societal good, driving became an emphasis of federal funding after World War II. Tax breaks and zoning regulations all spurred America's shift toward becoming a real-life version of Futurama. None of this mattered, though, if fuel was too costly for most consumers. Therefore, federal authority also maintained remarkably low gasoline prices—ensuring that the fuel became accessible to almost everyone. With this widespread access to modes of transportation, the landscape of consumption took shape after World War II.[8]

---

[7] "Traditionally, 'culture' had meant a collection of artifacts, actually or potentially on show in a museum," wrote David Potter. "But in very recent decades, it has come to mean a collection of customs, a series of habits." See Potter, *People of Plenty*, 35, 42. See also George Ritzer, *The McDonaldization of Society* (Thousand Oaks, 2004). Lizabeth Cohen has demonstrated that some of these developments have offered women and minority consumer groups, including African Americans, the opportunity to express and achieve social status from which they were previously excluded. Cohen, *Consumers' Republic*, 194–96.

[8] Clay McShane and Joel A. Tarr, *The Horse in the City: Living Machines in the Nineteenth Century* (Baltimore, 2007); Douglas Brinkley, *Wheels for the World: Henry Ford, His Company, and a Century of Progress, 1903–2003* (New York, 2003); David A. Kirsch, *The Electric Vehicle and the Burden of History* (New Brunswick, 2000); Edwin Black, *Internal Combustion: How Corporations and Governments Addicted the World to Oil and Derailed the Alternatives* (New York, 2006). Christopher W. Wells, "Fueling the Boom: Gasoline Taxes, Invisibility, and the Growth of the American Highway Infrastructure, 1919–1956," *Journal of American History*, 99 (June 2012), 72–81.

Suburbs, as Adam Rome portrays in *The Bulldozer in the Countryside*, were the anchors of the corridors of commerce for the new, postwar America. In those model environments, developers dropped housing tracts in outlying areas where real estate prices were low. Often, these suburbs first appeared marooned from essential services—a sort of man-made frontier when services were still predominantly located in cities (and many of these services, such as grocery stores, soda fountains, and Automat restaurants, had become quite advanced in their ability to deliver a variety of products reliably and rapidly). Recalibrating the human habitat for automobility remade the American land- scape after World War II. Between suburban homes and urban workplaces the economic frontier of the postwar era emerged. Of one component of the new sprawl, the historian Catherine Gudis writes: "With every coming year, automobiles could be found in more and more places, thus expanding the marketing frontier and potential location of billboard spaces to areas heretofore untouched." To manage these new corridors of consumption, an industry soon took shape, led by the trade organization Outdoor Advertising Association of America (OAAA), which proclaimed in its motto: "we have changed from essentially a 'home people' to an 'automobile … people.'"[9]

In its various forms, petroleum enabled humans to overcome limits, particularly those of time and space. Potter discussed American expansion and restlessness in this fashion: "The man best qualified for this role was the completely mobile man, moving freely from one locality to the next, from one economic position to another, or from one social level to levels above."[10] In addition to ensuring physical movement, petroleum helped bring Americans economic and social mobility through mass consumption. Along with new information technologies and advancements in production capabilities, petroleum became a primary component in allowing producers to overcome limits of supply and production. That success then allowed for massive growth in the scale of production and, ultimately, in mass production, which brought prices down and made a whole world of products and services available to middle-class American consumers.

Possibly the longest trope in the study of American culture had been to view the push and pull of technology against agriculture and, by extension, nature. In such a paradigm, technology was a "counterforce" against which Americans struggled to retain certain aspects of their original culture. As mass purchasers of goods and services, Americans no longer viewed such innovations and economic development as a "counterforce" in American life; instead, new technologies became inculcated into revamped life-styles. This modern sensibility of working cooperatively with technologies, such as the internal combustion engine, was captured by Lewis Mumford when he described the machine as a force that "simplifies the environment." He explained:

As a practical instrument, the machine has enormously complicated the environment…. [But] without standardization, without repetition, without the neutralizing effect of habit, our mechanical environment might well, by reason of its tempo and its continuous impact, be too formidable…. The machine has thus, in its aesthetic manifestations, something of the same effect that a conventional code of manners has in social intercourse: it removes the strain of contact and adjustment … it permits intercourse between persons and groups to take place without the preliminary exploration and understanding that are requisite for an ultimate adjustment.

---

[9] Adam Rome, *The Bulldozer in the Countryside: Suburban Sprawl and the Rise of American Environmentalism* (New York, 2001). Owen D. Gutfreund, *Twentieth-Century Sprawl: Highways and the Reshaping of the American Landscape* (New York, 2004); Dolores Hayden, A Field Guide to Sprawl (New York, 2004). Catherine Gudis, *Buyways: Billboards, Automobiles, and the American Landscape* (New York, 2004), 39, 49.

[10] Potter, *People of Plenty*, 96.

Mass consumption was the product of Americans internalizing the machine and domesticating it. During the Cold War era, technology was accepted as key to the nation's progress and also to keeping the Soviet Union at bay. This aesthetic was fueled by large-scale economic and social changes as well. Cohen describes this trend as the construction of a "consumer's republic" in which consumption was construed as an expression of national identity and even patriotism. She traces the emergence of "a new postwar ideal of the purchaser as citizen who simultaneously fulfilled personal desire and civic obligation by consuming."[11]

The key to this technical society—its essential element—was crude oil available at an average per-barrel price of $22–23 (in 2008 dollars) from 1869 to the present. From 1945–1970 the per-barrel price remained below $20, and U.S. society poured a cultural and social foundation that was, in hindsight, based on the assumption that Americans would always have a perpetual supply of petroleum at a stable price. Of course, things changed dramatically by the end of the twentieth century—by 2007–2008 the per-barrel price reached an all-time high of $145.[12] The availability of inexpensive crude persuaded American society to organize itself into an ecology of oil in which basic human needs—such as acquiring food—became reliant on crude.

Fast food is the obvious link between petroleum-powered transportation and the human need to acquire the calories that our bodies require—what scholars refer to as American foodways. This new method of foraging involved innovations such as that of Maurice McDonald and Richard McDonald when they intentionally located their McDonald's just off Route 66 in San Bernadino, California. Ray Kroc, a milkshake- machine salesman, then expanded that form on a massive scale.[13] From White Castle to Royce Hailey's Pig Stand, burger joints, tea houses, diners, and, eventually, strip malls defined sprawl as the new American consumer environment.

Petroleum, however, was impacting Americans' food consumption through more than their reliance on automobiles; a more insidious change is symbolized by the seemingly innocent Twinkie. Although this sweet snack seems at first simple, it is actually a high-tech piece of complex chemistry, manufacturing, and distribution with no fewer than thirty-nine ingredients (most of which were also first manufactured).[14] Food production in the twentieth century, epitomized by the lusciously nutritionally void Twinkie, was characterized by efforts to simplify and streamline crop growing and processing by supplementing and embellishing those steps with the use of cheap resources such as petroleum.

Chemists played an important role in using petroleum to expand, simplify, and, at times, enhance the food that appeared in American shopping carts. Often with petroleum hydrocarbons as a basis or active ingredient, chemicals were created to control problems associated with agriculture, including managing weeds and pests (through herbicides and pesticides). Most important to the twentieth century, though,

---

[11] Mumford, *Technics and Civilization*, esp. 357–58. For discussion of these general points, see Thomas P. Hughes, *American Genesissss A Century of Invention and Technological Enthusiasm, 1870–1970* (New York, 1989). Cohen, *Consumers' Republic*, 119.

[12] For pricing data, see "Oil Price History and Analysis," wtrg *Economics*, http://www.wtrg.com/prices.htm. After the 2007–2008 peak, crude oil prices dropped dramatically. Analysts suggest this was due to the global economic difficulty in 2008–2009. In 2011 prices began to rise again and most analysts agree that they will likely return to 2007 levels as a "new reality" or baseline in crude pricing. Peter Maass, *Crude World: The Violent Twilight of Oil* (New York, 2009), 5–8; Daniel Yergin, *The Quest: Energy, Security, and the Remaking of the Modern World* (New York, 2011), 6–10. For more historical data, see "Petroleum and Other Liquids," *U.S. Energy Information Administration*, http://www.eia.gov/petroleum/.

[13] There are a number of sources that nicely capture portions of the automobile's extension into changes in American life. For one of the most useful, see James J. Flink, *The Automobile Age* (Boston, 1988).

[14] Steve Ettlinger, *Twinkie, Deconstructed: My Journey to Discover How the Ingredients Found in Processed Foods Are Grown, Mined (Yes, Mined), and Manipulated into What America Eats* (New York, 2008), xi–xii. For a general discussion of these ideas, see Michael Pollan, *Omnivore's Dilemma: A Natural History of Four Meals* (New York, 2006); and Maurice B. Green, *Eating Oil: Energy Use in Food Production* (Boulder, 1978).

chemists also used petroleum and natural gas to create heat that manufactured and "fixed" synthetic nitrogen to enhance growing potential. The Haber-Bosch process alone increased the food production capabilities of nations throughout the world. This method for manufacturing synthetic nitrogen (as a fertilizer) has been exported to less-developed nations to enhance their ability to grow food crops. The great success of sharing this technique and other agriculture technology since 1960 is referred to as the "green revolution" and has helped avoid some famines in Africa and elsewhere.[15]

The implications of crude came in the form of the processed Twinkie as well as the seemingly organic, locally grown head of romaine lettuce. In the late twentieth century, humans (and particularly Americans) came to rely more than ever on foods acquired and prepared through the assistance of petroleum. Our histories have told many of these stories of consumption without specifically delineating the role that petroleum played in powering the autos that carried Americans to lunch or the rigs that hauled corn and other raw materials to manufacturers such as Frito-Lay. Neither have our histories clearly captured the work in chemistry laboratories that applied petroleum to an array of uses that moved innovations from the beaker to fill every shelf in local Walmart stores.[16]

Chemicals and Flexible Forms Shape a New Consumer Reality

When Barthes waxed about the capabilities of plastic, his comments were stirred by the first use of a plastic replacement valve in heart surgery in the 1950s. In fact, however, he captured the germ of the method historians might use to demonstrate the scale of the transformations in American life made possible when petroleum allowed mass consumption to become inconspicuous. We must follow Barthes and move beyond gasoline- powered engines and chemically enhanced agriculture to consider products in which the petroleum content is largely unrecognizable. The symbol of such oil-based consumer products is, of course, plastics, which enabled significant cultural and social shifts in America.

The industry now known as petrochemicals is responsible for too many consumer products to list—among them, the materials that go into heart valves and Twinkie wrappers. A remarkable statistic from *Chemistry in Context*, a standard chemistry text- book, helps reveal the wide array of applications for which the petrochemical industry is responsible: "37 of the almost 45 gallons in a typical barrel of refined crude oil is simply burned for heating and transportation. The remaining 7.6 gal is used for non-fuel purposes, including only 1.25 gal set aside to serve as nonrenewable starting materials (reactants, commercially called feedstocks) to make the myriad of plastics, pharmaceuticals, fabrics, and other carbon-based industrial products so common in our society."[17] These uses of petroleum have so intrinsically altered the ways that Americans live, that as petroleum supplies dwindle, humans will likely wish they had conserved crude not to burn but to fulfill these remarkably rare capabilities in the chemistry sector.

On its way to becoming each of those useful substances, petroleum first is transformed into feedstocks, which are used to produce plastics, drugs, detergents, and synthetic fibers. For instance, almost all

---

[15] On the use of chemicals for military purposes, see Edmund Russell, *War and Nature: Fighting Humans and Insects with Chemicals from World War I to Silent Spring* (New York, 2001). On agricultural uses, see James McCann, *Maize and Grace: Africa's Encounter with a New World Crop, 1500–2000* (Cambridge, Mass., 2007); David R. Montgomery, *Dirt: The Erosion of Civilizations* (Berkeley, 2007); Christian Anton Smedshaug, *Feeding the World in the Twenty-First* Century: A Historical Analysis of Agriculture and Society (London, 2010); and Richard P. Tucker, *Insatiable Appetite: The United States and the Ecological Degradation of the Tropical World* (New York, 2007).

[16] See, for instance, Shane Hamilton, *Trucking Country: The Road to America's Wal-Mart Economy* (Princeton, 2008); and William Cronon, *Nature's Metropolis: Chicago and the Great West* (New York, 1991).

[17] American Chemistry Society, *Chemistry in Context: Applying Chemistry to Society* (New York, 2005), 45. See also Jeffrey L. Meikle, American Plastic: A Cultural History (New Brunswick, 1995).

pharmaceuticals contain benzene rings in their chemical structure, which is refined from petroleum. In addition, such chemicals go on to serve many purposes, including refrigeration and cooling. In many of these applications, chemists initially identified alternative methods of producing the necessary compounds; petroleum entered the laboratory only later as a method for making compounds more easily and cheaply. The design historian Jeffrey Meikle describes this synthetic chemistry as, "everything and nothing."[18] As a chemical filler, petroleum was added because it cost so little, but the flexibility that it brought to chemists proved to be revolutionary.

For oil companies, the use of crude to manufacture resources for living began in the 1930s but became a corporate priority after World War II. In the case of Shell Oil, its Shell Chemical division switched from manufacturing ammonia and solvents to seeking synthetic substitutes for natural materials and then making them. Early industrial chemistry had concentrated on synthesizing molecules from coal-based feedstocks, mainly to produce chemicals such as benzene and its derivatives. With petroleum, chemists could produce such chemicals less expensively and in larger quantities while also generating more reactive hydrocarbons called olefins, including ethylene, propylene, and butylene, which became building-block chemicals of the new petrochemical industry.[19]

As Shell and other petroleum companies formed entire chemical divisions to research petrochemicals and apply them to everyday uses, the best known might have been synthetic glycerine. The limited supply of natural glycerine, a by-product of the soap and fatty acid industries, had become useful by the 1920s as a food preservative, a humectant for tobacco (to help retain moisture), and as a component in the manufacture of such diverse products as shaving cream, toothpaste, glue, soft drinks, mayonnaise, cosmetics, and paper. It also served as a mainstay for the paint industry and in the manufacture of cellophane. By the 1940s Americans used over 200 million pounds of natural glycerine each year (more than a pound per person), although very few consumers realized its presence. In the late 1940s Shell Chemical made Houston, Texas, which already served as a hub for oil shipping and refining, its focus for petrochemical development. Its $8 million synthetic glycerine plant—the world's first—went on-line at Houston Deer Park in September 1948, and by 1950 its production of synthetic glycerine equaled one-fifth of the nation's prewar output of natural glycerine.[20]

Similar developments occurred as synthetic rubber replaced natural supplies when Shell developed isoprene rubber, which duplicated the isoprene that served as the chemical building block of the natural rubber molecule. The manufacturers of automobile and truck tires began using isoprene rubber and other polymers developed from petroleum. The influence on consumer America was profound. The postwar expansion of Shell Chemical reached a high point in 1956, when chemical sales totaled a record $213 million, compared to only $24 million ten years earlier. In terms of volume, yearly sales rose from 231,000 tons to just over 1 million tons over that period.[21] These are the type of statistics that allow conspiracy theorists to claim that the inculcation of petroleum into everyday American life through chemistry was an elaborate plan by Big Oil. And there may be some truth to such a claim; however, American consumers swept up these new, cheaper products with vigor.

---

[18] Meikle, *American Plastic*, 3. See also Gail Cooper, *Air-Conditioning America: Engineers and the Controlled Environment, 1900–1960* (Baltimore, 1998).

[19] Peter H. Spitz, *Petrochemicals: The Rise of an Industry* (New York, 1988), 63–69.

[20] Kendall Beaton, *Enterprise in Oil: A History of Shell in the United States* (New York, 1957), 542–43, 676–77; "Shell Chemical Corporation," Shell News (April 1957), 19, cited in Tyler Priest, "The History of Shell Chemical," unpublished manuscript (in Tyler Priest's possession).

[21] "Torrance Takes an Opportunity," *Shell News*, 27 (May 1959), 1–3, cited in Priest, "History Shell of Chemical"; "Shell Chemical Corporation," 21–22.

"Plastics," uttered a friend of the father of Dustin Hoffman's character in *The Graduate* when asked what he foresaw as the promising future for a college graduate in the 1960s. Plastic would have thousands of applications, and some were essential to patterns of everyday human life. As one example, consider the impact of Tupperware and Saran Wrap on food preservation. Again, each innovation in this area grew from earlier resin-based materials that did not use petroleum. In large chemical companies such as DuPont, researchers worked constantly to develop any synthetic material that might prove useful. In a world filled previously only with products made of wood, clay, and a few other organic materials, by the 1930s it became a sign of progress to insert obviously man-made objects of modernity into the most mundane areas of people's everyday lives—such as food storage.[22]

Meikle writes that these materials, known as thermoplastics, were "driven not so much by market demand as by the pressure of supply, an overabundance of chemical raw materials, waiting to be exploited." After World War II, lab experiments regularly became consumer products, such as vinyl, which quickly remade cultural genres ranging from music to automobile interiors, and nylon, the elastic threads useful in many applications. In 1939 American companies produced 213 million pounds of synthetic resins. By 1945 this production reached 818 million pounds, and by 1951 2.4 billion pounds of synthetic resins were produced in the United States, partly because of the growing reliance on petroleum in the process. It was staggering growth sufficient to remake a civilization. And in the 1950s, writes Meikle, that is exactly what happened as the industry committed to such petroleum-based thermoplastics as "polyethylene that contributed to a flood of new uses—garbage pails, squeeze bottles, hula hoops—lighter, more flexible, less permanent than objects made from thermosets." The use of petroleum, in particular, allowed plastics to become "infinitely shape-shifting."[23] Infinite shapes and possibilities—a basic flexibility of form—would become a commodity in its own right if the products could fill basic human needs at extremely low cost. Throughout American consumer society, petroleum-based products fueled the ubiquity of stuff—regularizing overconsumption and making it the new normal.

Close Reading Questions

1. What made the General Motors exhibit at the 1939 World's Fair so appealing?

2. After World War II, how did transportation affect where Americans lived and worked?

3. In what ways did the abundance of crude oil impact oil companies in the 1940s and 1950s?

Analytical Writing/Discussion

4. In what ways was post–World War II affluence—especially the creation of a "middle class"—made possible by the availability of cheap sources of energy? (Multiple Perspectives)

5. To what extent do you agree or disagree with Black's assertion that petroleum changed food culture in America, particularly the development of fast food? (Historical Trends)

6. Black provides an extensive discussion of the ways chemists altered crude oil. Why is it important to understand the relationship between petrochemicals and American society? (Cultural Influences)

---

[22] *The Graduate*, dir. Mick Nichols (Embassy, 1967). Meikle, *American Plastic*, 85. See also Alison J. Clarke, *Tupperware: The Promise of Plastic in 1950s America* (Washington, 1999).
[23] Meikle, *American Plastic*, 176, 125–26, 176–77, esp. 82, 168.

Further Options

7. Previewing a text is an effective way to begin to read a lengthy article or chapter (see pp. 77–81 in Chapter 3). Review the headings in Black's article. How do the headings help you to understand the main ideas? What reading strategies would you have used if Black's article did not have headings?

8. Black discusses the concept of "planned obsolescence," noting that Americans purchase replacements for cars and household appliances, even if those products still work well. How does this relate to James Atwater's explanation of 1960s appliances in "A Household of Helpers" in this chapter (see pp. 298–305)?

A HOUSEFUL OF HELPERS

by James Atwater

> The late 1950s and early 1960s marked a period of mass consumerism for those Americans who were eager to settle into suburban lives with televisions, cars, refrigerators, and dishwashers. The following excerpt, which appeared in the December 5, 1964 edition of the *Saturday Evening Post*, chronicles the reasons why appliance makers sought to design and sell quality products to increasingly fickle consumers.

For her birthday she got earrings and perfume. So what she wants for Christmas is something that washes, dries, toasts, roasts, freezes, cuts, peels, percolates or tidies up—something that may even turn a dreary household chore into an interlude of fun. She wants a new appliance, and she knows that if she doesn't get it at Christmas, she might have to wait another year.

If the appliance-craving American housewife is anxious about Christmas, the appliance manufacturer is doubly so. Depending on his line, as much as a third of his yearly sales must be made in the month of December if they are to be made at all. Will husbands buy his elegant bonnet-style hair dryer for their wives, or will they be lured away by his rival's new cordless electric slicing knife? Can his electric hedge trimmer command attention in the stores amid the crowd of equally dazzling floor waxers, electric dehumidifiers and garbage-disposal units? Worst of all, will masses of shoppers turn their backs on the Electrical Age *in toto*[1], choosing to muddle through manually? For the volatile and hotly competitive electric-appliance industry, Christmas is seldom a time of peace on earth.

Christmas, 1964, however, promises to be good to both housewives and manufacturers. Dealers' showrooms, department stores and discount palaces are aglitter with an incredible variety of ingenious devices ready to perform magic at the flip of a switch. More to the point, the industry has every expectation of selling them in a holiday splurge that will make 1964 the biggest, richest year in its history.

As histories go, this is not too long a stretch. The iceman[2] bending beneath his burden is still a vivid recollection for middle-aged Americans: in fact, the first electric refrigerator with all its parts in a single

---

[1] *in toto*: Latin for completely; totally; entirely

unit was introduced by Frigidaire exactly half a century ago this year. The automatic electric washing machine dates back only 27 years and the dryer only 26. There are millions of women who can remember slaving over a corrugated washboard: the wife handing out the wash and the apron-clad husband helping with the dishes are only slightly archaic stereotypes of U.S. homelife.

The New American Home

But labor conditions in the average American home have obviously undergone a profound change. Uncounted billions of woman-hours of work have been cut away by laborsaving appliances; a dishwasher alone, for example, reduces the average kitchen cleanup time from an hour and 13 minutes to half an hour, according to industry statisticians. Immeasurable vistas of leisure time have opened up, with social effects no statistician can really pin down. (Do housewives use their extra time to improve their minds, get jobs, enter local politics, plump pillows or find floors to wax which they wouldn't have waxed otherwise?)

Whatever the case, there is hardly an essential household task that can't be eased or eliminated by plugging in something. Americans have shown that they will buy an appliance to perform a task they had no idea needed performing until someone suggested it. Hundreds of thousands of people will buy electric can openers this month, though the job of opening cans by hand has caused no great outcry by housewives in the past. The latest, and perhaps ultimate, model switches itself on and off. Hamilton Beach is offering a power unit with five attachments called the "Gourmet Center" which permits a gourmet to open a can, sharpen a knife, toss salad, grind meat or crush ice without expending a calorie of energy. Shoppers will also be rushing to buy electric toothbrushes, including Westinghouse's new Rocket model for children, a toothbrush shaped like an I.C.B.M.[3], which comes with accompanying launching pad and gantry crane. They will even buy some electric swizzle sticks, a highly expendable appliance which has become a pet whipping boy for critics of the affluent society.

Competition Drives the Appliance Market

In today's competitive market, appliance makers have to expand and experiment at an unprecedented pace just to keep up. The pressure is particularly keen in the small-appliance business, where manufacturers just a few years ago had little to offer but such old reliables as the coffee maker, the toaster and the iron. Now these markets are becoming saturated (80 percent of U.S. homes have toasters, 97 percent have irons), and while millions will still be sold as replacements, the need for new products has impelled companies like General Electric and Sunbeam to double the number of items in their lines in just the last few years. "The housewife's major chores have been automated," says Norman Langenfeld, a top G.E. official. "To survive today, you have to innovate. You have to work the fringe areas of the market."

Almost every small-appliance maker is putting out a bonnet-style hair dryer with a chic carrying case, and a manicure set with power-driven nail buffers. With the rise of income and the consequent nourishing of home entertainment, the industry is selling a whole rumpus room[4] full of new appliances designed specifically for this market—four-slice toasters, warming trays, party grills, and 20- and 30-cup coffee urns.

[2.] iceman: The person who delivered ice to homes and businesses. Large blocks of ice were used to chill iceboxes, which were the precursor to the electric refrigerator.

[3.] I.C.B.M.: Intercontinental Ballistic Missile. A missile designed to deliver nuclear warheads at ranges of more than 3,500 miles.

[4.] rumpus room: A room in a house designed specifically for children's recreation or play.

The newest thing in electric skillets and frying pans is Teflon, a material developed by Du Pont that keeps food from sticking to cooking surfaces and thus permits greaseless frying. New lightweight and long-life batteries are creating a whole new family of products: battery-powered shavers and clocks and mixers, rechargeable electric cigarette lighters, and even a battery-powered flour sifter. Designers are trying to hit on ideas that will make good gifts, since 30 percent of all small appliances are bought for presents. The aura of "giftability," as the trade describes it, has spurred the sales of such items as the flashy rotisserie and the electric slicing knife—appliances which easily catch the eye of the despairing husband searching for something different for his wife.

The makers of major appliances—"white goods," to the trade—do not live and die by Christmas as do small-appliance manufacturers (General Electric and Westinghouse are about the only companies which straddle the two divisions of the industry). But they, too, are counting on holiday business to top off their third consecutive year of rising sales. Frigidaire general manager Herman Lehman predicts that the industry's unit sales will run more than ten percent ahead of 1963, when a record 15.2 million major appliances were sold for $4.2 billion.

Less volatile, and nearly three times the size of the small-appliance market, the white-goods business tends more to majestic evolution than to rapid-fire innovation. Its fundamental statistics are majestic in themselves. Every 21 seconds a new household is formed in the U.S. with certain minimum needs for major pieces of hardware. Every three seconds a major appliance somewhere in the U.S. "outlives its useful life and needs replacements"—an industry researcher's expression, which suggests a ghastly undercurrent of domestic turmoil, but is probably deceptive. In any case, the net effect is that one new refrigerator, range, washer, freezer, dryer, dishwasher or air conditioner is delivered to someone's home every two seconds.

The appliances themselves are changing, of course, and there have been fundamental improvements in all of them in recent year. For example, the industry has learned to control the blasts of heat that used to shrink clothes in the dryers. Dishwasher sprays are far more powerful and better diffused. Because of new and thinner insulation, a refrigerator with 12 cubic feet inside occupies no more kitchen space than a 10-cubic-foot box did a few years back. General Electric last year introduced an oven that cleans itself (with a special device that applies superhigh heat to vaporize accumulated grease); sales have soared despite a $75 premium for the feature. This year, Frigidaire is introducing a washer with a transmission that replaces troublesome belts, pulleys and gears with a compact system of rollers and wheels, for added reliability.

Appliance Sales Miss the Mark

Despite booming sales and expanding profits, however, the white-goods business is still struggling with some serious and deep-rooted problems—problems which grew out of the fierce competitive struggles of the 1950's and which have yet to be entirely resolved.

The trouble began after World War II, when a number of large and powerful companies from out-side the business—companies like International Harvester and Admiral—rushed in to compete with the established manufacturers in satisfying postwar demands for appliances. The result was a tremendous spurt of overproduction and falling prices, which dropped even faster as the cut-rate discount house began to get a big share of the appliance business. Retail prices have dropped some 25 percent since 1947, eight percent in the last five years.

To make matters worse, sales did not hold up as expected. E.B. Barnes, Kelvinator's vice president for sales, points out that during the '50's there was a slight decline in the number of persons in the 18-to-34 bracket, the biggest buyers of appliances. In addition, the market was gradually becoming saturated, particularly in washers and refrigerators, the industry's two major items.

The result was a severe shakedown. International Harvester quit the business altogether. The Speed Queen washer was bought by McGraw-Edison. The Easy washer ended up under the control of the Hupp Corp., a Cleveland-based company, which also bought the Gibson refrigerator. Bendix, which put out the first automatic washer in 1937, eventually sold it to Philco, which later was bought by Ford. G.E. bought Hotpoint.

In this competitive jungle, quick reactions have been essential for survival. Whenever one company added a feature that seemed to help its appliance sales, every other company would race to copy it. In the mid-'50's, for example, G.E. hit it big with the lint filter for its washer. Even Maytag, a firm which traditionally has resisted fads, joined the copycats. Maytag had been disposing of lint with a system that washed it down the drain, but it bowed to the pressures of the marketplace and added a filter it didn't need. Maytag points out, in its defense, that it really did add a feature, since it managed to incorporate the filter in a device that also dispenses the detergent....

Market research shows that women want versatile machines with controls that are as simple as possible. But the dealers, who have the usual male fascination with glittering dials and winking lights, believe that a flashy instrument panel is important in helping to close sales. And so the manufacturer may load on the gadgetry which the industry calls "whistles and bells."

New Year, Slightly Different Appliance

Prodded by the dealers, the manufacturers turn out a bewildering array of models to hit every possible segment of the market. One industry consultant came home recently to discover that the family washer had broken down. "I told my wife I'd drop down to a store and buy one that night," he says. "But when I got there, there were so many models with so many features that I finally went home in disgust. It was too damn confusing—and I know something about this business. The next day I went back and bought a model of a company I admire, and that was that."

The prime example of the strong influence dealers have is the annual model change, perhaps the main source of trouble in the business, since it vastly complicates the problem of building a solid appliance and servicing it expertly.

The dealers are afraid that their sales will slip unless they can annually put on display a new product brightened by new styling and festooned with new features. Many manufacturers will admit that they don't want the annual change: it is tremendously expensive in money, time and effort. Moreover, some market research indicates that the consumer couldn't care less whether an appliance first came on the market this year or last.

In fact, there is some evidence that not even the experts can tell the difference between models put out in two consecutive years. At a meeting of the trade press Kelvinator once lined up 10 refrigerators of similar price and covered over the brand names. The display was made up of the models produced in two consecutive years by five different companies. The visitors were asked to identify the refrigerators by year and manufacturer. Half of the experts refused to take the test, and of those who tried, only 52 percent could name the brands, and only 25 percent the years.

Kelvinator abandoned the annual cycle four years ago. "We do not make changes unless they are meaningful." says sales vice president Barnes. The firm's 1964 range line, for example, is virtually identical with 1963's.

"The annual model change is senseless," says one official in the industry. "It's based on the assumption that the appliance is a status symbol, and that's just not so. You don't park your refrigerator in the driveway."

The industry's most outspoken critic of the practice of adding some chrome and changing the instrument panel to get a "new" model is Maytag, which never adopted the annual change. By stressing the reliability and long life of its washers and dryers, Maytag has prospered mightily. For the first half of 1964, its earnings were 12.8 percent of sales, far above the industry average. "We're extremely old-fashioned," says one company official. "We think it is ethically wrong to foist something on the public that is not an improvement."

The result of the annual-model flap is that the engineers are placed under impossible pressure. "You have to produce new features *and* dependability," says the director of one company's advance-engineering department. "This is what is driving the engineers nuts. The more complex a device is, the more service problems you're likely to have, no matter how well designed it is."

Skyrocketing Repair Costs

The annual model change, in fact, is the main reason that every neighborhood has its share of horror stories about the failures of refrigerators, ranges or washers, that are repeated with little tingles of terror at the morning kaffeeklatsch. In Tarrytown, N.Y., for example, the neighbors talk of what happened to David and Lorraine Epstein, who installed a brand-name combination washer-dryer in their new home in 1959.

The one-year warranty had barely expired when the door began to leak. The charge was $18.85. The Epsteins now regard this bill rather wistfully, as though it were the first mild tantrum of a child who was to turn out to be incorrigible.

On July 3, 1961, the machine failed. For 28 days Lorraine Epstein improvised with the Laundromat and the neighbors' washers. When the repairs were completed, the Epsteins had a machine with a rebuilt rear end and a bill for $75. On November 6, 1961, the thing died again. This time it was out of action for 23 days, and the bill came to $54.05. Something about a bad pump and clogged vents.

Dave Epstein, an artist, is a mild and accommodating man, but this time he picked up the phone. The servicing company settled for $35. On January 26, 1962, the drying system broke down. $11.

In time, Lorraine Epstein came to know three different crews of repairmen. Each pair would utter caustic comments about the abilities of the others while peering into the stricken machine. One repairman adopted a brusquely proprietary air toward the Epsteins. Without ringing the bell, he opened the back door one morning at 8:30 and began to dismantle the machine while Lorraine was in the bedroom down the hall.

Dave eventually became something of an expert at spotting the combo's troubles. He once retrieved an ossified door gasket, as shredded and tangled as a clump of dried spaghetti, from its lodging place in the heat vent.

On September 9, 1962, the door gave way. $18.85. On December 10, 1963, the whole rear end collapsed again, the $75 collapse, "After that," recalls Dave, "we came to an agreement. Whatever happened, I was to pay for the parts, but not the labor."

On January 17, 1964, the rear end disintegrated a third time. A man came and poked at it moodily and went away. This time it was 40 days before the thing was fixed, but this time there was no bill. In four years, counting stray odds and ends, the Epsteins have spent about $300 repairing a machine that cost $420.25.

Epic disasters like this are unavoidable in any mass-production industry—they come with the territory—but the appliance manufacturers are making a sincere effort to reduce their number. The campaign had its beginnings in the late '50's when appliances began to break down at an alarming rate. Looking back, a few executives are willing to admit that one cause was that they had let their quality-control programs slip.

To make matters worse, the housewife who was stuck with a spavined dishwasher or refrigerator often had to start a great manhunt to find someone to repair it. Not only were there too few repairmen to handle the sudden avalanche of work, but many of those who were in business boggled at any job that required much more than a screwdriver and friction tape. The industry had woefully failed to train men to repair products that were getting increasingly complex.

The result was a consumer revolt that thoroughly frightened the industry. Some executives believe that the poor sales record of the early 60's was due in part to the public's growing disenchantment with appliance makers and all their works.

To improve the quality of their servicing, many companies are conducting training courses around the country that are attended free by repairmen who work for completely independent firms or for franchised dealers. G.E. alone has a force of over 100 full-time instructors and trouble-shooters.

"By running very hard (in their training program), the manufacturers are barely able to stand still," says Frederick Schlink, technical director of Consumer's Research, an independent testing service that publishes *Consumer Bulletin*. "They have trouble catching up because of the constant innovations. The poor serviceman doesn't get the parts or manuals before the appliances get in trouble. We get letters from people whose appliances are out of action for months."

Labor now accounts for 60 to 70 percent of most repair bills, and it is not at all unusual for a homeowner to pay $7.50 or more an hour for a service call. The best way to keep down rising service costs, of course, is to make a better product. As a whole, the industry is making a strong effort to turn out appliances that are more reliable and more easily Serviced. "The service manager never used to see the product until it came off the line," says Philco's President Robert O. Fickes. "Now he's in on the creation of it from the beginning."

Quality Control for the Appliance Industry

Nearly every major manufacturer has a quality-control program that has been substantially improved in the last few years. Appliances are pulled off the line and rigorously tested at regular intervals. At Whirlpool, quality-control supervisors report directly to the president. They have the authority—the ultimate power in any manufacturing process—to shut down the line completely if their testers find a series of lemons.

This concern for a sturdy product is beginning to pay off in both small and major appliances. The Detroit Edison Co., which services 800,000 small appliances a year, is convinced that quality has improved.

Product improvement is most obvious in major appliances. "There are some indications of improved quality control in such appliances as washers and refrigerators, formerly among the worst offenders," says Morris Kaplan, technical director of Consumers Union, which publishes *Consumer Reports*. Then he adds, "but consistency of quality—what quality control tries to assure—is not necessarily equivalent to high quality. I'd like to see some manufacturer make and sell the guts and not the gleam, the stamina and not the trim. The engineer is usually required to design the product to sell at a predetermined price. He can spend a lot on fancy things like butter dishes and egg shelves and chrome and gimmicks that are supposed to sell. Or put the money into the guts of the machine."

Because quality is not as obvious as, say, a lint filter, Kaplan thinks it would have to be backed up by broad, long-term warranties patterned after those now used by the auto industry. "It would take some doing and a tremendous advertising campaign," Kaplan concludes, "but I think the appliance industry, if it wanted to, could find a way to sell quality to the public."

Here and there are scattered signs that the American public may indeed be ready to buy quality—and service—rather than going automatically for the lowest price, or falling for a cute butter compartment.

Albert Sindlinger, head of the market research firm of Sindlinger & Co., thinks that consumers are tending more and more to buy appliances from dealers who emphasize good service rather than the best price deal.

The problem of servicing is one reason that product development will continue to be more evolutionary than revolutionary: appliances are complicated enough as it is. What is more, no manufacturer wants to risk losing heavily on a long shot. "This is an industry," says one executive, "in which the companies are glad when a rival tries out a new idea—and takes a chance of falling on his face."

Perhaps most important, the housewife seems to be essentially a conservative. "Unless she sees the real advantage of a product or a feature, I don't think she'll go for it." says William L. Hullsiek, vice president in charge of Admiral's appliance division. "We have to be damned down-to-earth in what we offer."

Yet all of the major companies inevitably are experimenting with totally new and revolutionary appliances that may someday be as familiar as today's refrigerators and ranges. Some examples:

- *Sonic Cleaning.* For years the public has been hearing reports of miracle clothes and washers and dishwashers that would vibrate dirt away with bombardments of sonic waves. The principle is now used in many industries to clean metallic pans, but there are stiff problems to be overcome. Sound waves do not work too well on some soils, and in dishwashers they are blocked by the shielding effect of plates and pans. (They also have been known to clean the pattern off china, the finish off silver plate.)

- *Electronic Cooking.* The industry has been marketing small quantities of electronic ovens for some time. The oven generates microwaves that agitate the molecules of food, and the friction of the molecules produces the heat that does the actual cooking. Microwaves can bake a potato in four minutes, cook a frozen 19-pound turkey in 90 minutes, and fry an egg as soon as the oven door is closed. But the cost of this performance is high—the oven is priced at around $800. When the frozen-food business expands, as it is certain to do, the fast-action electronic oven will become more salable.

- *Home Dry Cleaning.* The popularity of coin-operated dry-cleaning machines has suggested that perhaps American homes should have their own units. Westinghouse estimates that the public might be interested in paying around $500 for a single machine that dry-cleaned as well as washed and dried clothes. So far no one in the industry has come close to reaching this figure. The main problem is finding a dry-cleaning solvent that is safe for household use, and that can be economically filtered to remove impurities.

- *Thermo-Electric Refrigeration.* For decades engineers have known that the passage of electricity from some conductors to others produces a cooling effect. A simple device with no moving parts theoretically could replace the bulky, conventional compressor of the standard refrigerator. It could also be broken up into a series of thermoelectric drawers that could be placed around the kitchen and the house where they would be most convenient. To date the process is still far too expensive for widespread use, although several companies are marketing small thermoelectric units.

- *Clothes Washing.* "Over the years the housewife has been satisfied with the progress in developing laundry equipment," says Whirlpool's Dr. Gale Cutler, director of research, "but it's time for a new step. It's time we got away from bleaching the dirt, or dyeing it with brighteners. And the only way we can do this is take the job out of her hands, make it completely automatic." Cutler is thinking of a washer that would only require the housewife to push a single button indicating the type of load. The machine would use uncanny electronic sensors lo determine such things as the hardness of the water and the amount of dirt in the clothes, then not only add precisely the right amount of detergent, chemicals and properly heated water, but set the spin and agitation cycles at precisely the right speeds. Whirlpool is now test-marketing what could be the forerunner of this genius washer—a unit with controls that allow the operator to choose a wide variety of agitation and spin speeds.

- *Water Purification.* As population grows, the shrinking supply of pure water will become an increasingly serious problem. The appliance industry is interested in developing a water system that would circulate household wastes through a sophisticated purifier that would make the water usable again, and so on around and around.

- *Home Computer.* G.E. believes that someday the household bookkeeping will be done instantly and automatically by a computer about the size of a desk. The computer will make up shopping lists, pay your bills, remind you of anniversaries and even figure your income tax. Industry is now using somewhat similar electronic brains, but the price is still far too high for the kitchen.

Whatever other duties the appliances of the future will perform, they all seem bound to make money, for today's boom market is only a rumble compared to what is coming. Within the next few years millions of war babies will marry each other and buy millions of appliances to fill millions of new homes. Appliance men are also looking forward to replacing the aging appliances now in use—over 30 million homes have refrigerators, washers and ranges that are at least 10 years old.

The industry which has always called itself the housewife's best friend hopes to reaffirm that status, promising a Utopian tomorrow when every chore is reduced to the nip of a switch and every switch, almost infallibly, will work.

Close Reading Questions

1. According to Atwater, why was Christmas 1964 a critical time for appliance manufacturers? (Cultural Influences)

2. For what reasons were makers of large appliances experiencing problems that started after World War II and continued through the early 1960s?

3. Why did some appliance manufacturers resist plans to change appliance models every year while other manufacturers embraced the practice? (Multiple Perspectives)

Analytical Writing/Discussion

4. Why do you think that consumers in the 1950s and 1960s were concerned with appliances that saved time rather than energy?

5. According to Atwater, manufacturers envisioned household products of the future that would appeal to the American consumer. To what extent do you think the descriptions of those imagined products reflect a desire for energy efficiency and/or symbols of continued affluence?

6. In what ways do you think the story of David and Lorraine Epstein exemplified middle-class consumption of the 1950s? What appliance do you think symbolizes America in the twenty-first century? (Historical Trends)

Further Options

7. Atwater states that William L. Hullsiek—vice-president of the appliance company, Admiral—believed that the 1960s American housewife would not continue to purchase an appliance "unless she sees the real advantage of a product or a feature." In what ways does this sentiment reflect the design considerations David Orr proposed in "Your Great Work" (pp. 314–317 in this chapter).

8. In the 1950s and 1960s, appliances like refrigerators and washers and dryers were marketed to men and women aged 18–34. How is this type of marketing similar to the way Facebook was marketed to young adults? See "Why I Despise Facebook" by Tom Hodgkinson (pp. 17–18 in Chapter 1.)

JUKEBOX ON WHEELS

by Raymond Loewy

Raymond Loewy was a prolific industrial designer known for such iconic designs as the Shell and Exxon logos, Studebaker and Lincoln Continental car models, and numerous household appliances, including the Sears *Coldspo*t refrigerator. Known as "The Father of Industrial Design," Loewy was famous for his dislike of consumer goods that made life challenging for the consumer. The following article was first published by The Atlantic Magazine in April 1955.

In every phase of the automotive industry certain factors have been more important than all others in relation to the way the automobile has looked. Phase One is really the Ford story[1]. Function and production were the most important considerations. The automobile was an invention, and it looked like one.

Phase Two is marked by the introduction of the steel body in mass production, and appearance became a major factor for the first time. Walter Chrysler discovered that robin's-egg blue helped sales; so all other companies tried to top Chrysler in styling. It was an era of individuality and healthy competition.

By the time of World War II, the industry had reached a point where many factors had leveled out: body types, price differences, market potential, manufacturing methods, advertising, technical developments (at least, those released to the public). Independents believed that styling, with improved function, would not only sell well but create good will for the small company.

The style factors were: good visibility, compactness, lighter weights. Big companies jumped on the "style" bandwagon, but what so-called functional factor did they select? *Bulk*—a sorry choice! Bulk gets to be habit-forming, and bulk means weight. To this manufacturers added "flash." So they got into a spiral of increased weight and ornamentation. This led to the horsepower rat-race and the chrome gadget rat-race—a costly combination. As a result, standardization—a byproduct of mass production has

---

[1] Refers to Henry T. Ford (1963-1947), founder of the Ford Motor Company. The production of the Model T Ford revolutionized the automobile industry in the 1900s. Ford's factory was the first to employ assembly line production to mass produce an affordable car.

established as today's dreamboat a vehicle that's too big for most people, too expensive, too costly to maintain, and too gaudy.

Some might say that this apparent wastefulness is indeed a blessing—that it brings about the use of more materials, more employment, prosperity. I believe the theory would be even more valid if the industry's basic product were a model—cheaper, more economical, and therefore available to more people—within reach of the wide mass market that lies at the bottom layer of the consumers' pyramid. Instead, what have we got? The total loss of distinction among all automobiles plus the finest state of jitters in the history of the automotive industry.

Designers today are briefed to "give the public what it wants," and "what the public wants" is being translated into the flashy, the gadgety, the spectacular. I refuse to believe that today's automobiles represent, stylewise, "what the public wants" any more than they reflect what we in the automotive industry want. But the result of this mistaken opinion is vulgarity and blatancy. Instead of the automobile's expressing advancement, the story is now one of external bric-a-brac[2]. This reflects a distorted notion of what is competitive.

I think that vulgarity is dangerous for many reasons. The American automobile has changed the habits of every member of modern society. In the past fifty years it has become the symbol, all over the world, of American industrial genius and enterprise. It has become so potent a force that it is very nearly the symbol of American thought and morals to people who don't know us. It is more than an object to be sold for money. The automobile is an American cultural symbol.

"Some culture," one might say as one watches the sad parade of the 1955 models. The world will soon forget that under these gaudy shells are concealed masterpieces of inspired technology. What we see today looks more like an orgiastic chrome plated brawl.

There was another great American symbol, probably exported by the GI—the jukebox. Today's jukebox moves! The automobile. This year's production includes two-tone and three-tone jukeboxes. We are probably going to have a fluorescing six-passenger jukebox before long. Seriously, aren't manufacturers doing disservice to this country if they mass-present the automobile in such misleading vulgarity? Aren't they depressing the level of American taste by saturating the market with bad taste? Is it necessary?

This point has always interested me: Big companies make two conflicting statements –"We give the public what it wants" and, also, "Whatever design we choose becomes the accepted style standard through saturation." I do not agree with this last statement. But, if it is right, isn't it the company's cultural responsibility to choose a high standard instead of a low one? I realize that I am setting myself up as an arbiter of taste, but I have helped develop a profession in this country that sells taste.

This situation in the automobile industry is the more tragic because it is so unnecessary. Without doubt there are sufficient design taste and talent in the United States to correct the situation. But someone must demand better taste and not just better sales.

I am told that cab drivers have the highest rate of duodenal ulcers. I'll bet a chrome-plated carrot that automotive stylists have them beat. Every really creative and imaginative stylist and many engineers I know seem to be frustrated in their work today. The near-shattering pressure of their repressions is relieved in constant doodling blue-sky dreaming. They rush home and make scale models in the attic. Or they long for the weekend to go road-racing in the old red Isotta-Fraschini or the souped-up pre-war Ford.

We know that the men at the top of the industry are well aware of their economic responsibilities, of their vital roles in the nation's economy. What about their cultural responsibilities? Is it responsible to camouflage one of America's most remarkable machines as a piece of gaudy merchandise? Is it possible that they don't know the merchandise is gaudy?

I don't think the automotive industry in general is showing faith in good taste today. With rare exceptions, it cannot be accused of backing design sophistication. One shocking condition is the servile copying of one company's product by the others. It seems that giants in industry are taking refuge in sameness. This is just the time when they ought to be pioneering while they have the money, the momentum, and the market. This "management by escapism" is usually a manifestation of a fearful and insecure society. Perhaps we should ask the teenagers—the consumers of tomorrow. They love automobiles—especially ones that look like automobiles. Today these kids rib what used to be the family's proudest possession. Pop buys a chrome-plated "barge" just like the one he traded in. It's a wise kid who knows his own barge.

Fixing responsibility for the present state of design and styling this year is a tricky business. It probably starts with someone's deciding that the American public really likes vulgarity. However, numbers of men in a company do decide to give the public what it is supposed to want, in spite of their own consciences in the matter. Hesitation and doubt then creep into the whole design-engineering-sales team. The result is just what you'd expect—safe, imitative, over-decorated chariots, with something for everyone laid over a basic formula design that is a copy of someone else's formula design. Form, which should be a clean-cut expression of mechanical excellence, has become sensuous and organic.

Progressive management may realize that it is losing contact with a segment of consumers and that, however spectacular the sales, the company is losing popularity. This unpopularity has not yet reduced sales. But I think resentment is growing. And resentment is never an asset.

The public may admire a corporation for its impressive size. Who in the United States doesn't? But when a business, however gigantic, gets smug enough to believe that it is sufficient only to match competition on trivial points instead of leading competition in valid matters, that business is becoming vulnerable to public disfavor.

If there should be any such thing as a cloud in the blue sky of bigness for bigness' sake, I believe it will be the loss of people's trust and not governmental interference or control.

I hear conversations like these: "Remove the chrome schmaltz and the name plates and you can't tell one from another." Or, "Leave a Ford and a Chevvy in the same garage overnight and nine months later you get a Plymouth!" Or vice versa! These aren't funny and loving remarks: they're cynical. Compare them with the old Ford jokes that invariably oozed love and respect for a great man and a practical car.

Isn't it a bit complacent on the part of management to feel that the public is satisfied with this situation? There will be loud shouts: Who's complacent? Don't we all have new bodies this year? If the present "all-new" bodies are all that can be eked out in a year like this one, then I think wrong decisions have been made in a lot of places.

Experts estimate that fifty years from now there will be 120 million automobiles on the roads for approximately 98 million Americans. What company will be on top then? Would anyone care to guess? You can be reasonably sure that surprises are ahead. We've had enough in the past five years to count on it. And whoever wins will win by more than the length of a chrome-plated Dagmar[3].

Now, what are cars in the year 2005 going to look like? I'll use the same techniques we used to predict an automobile design for *Time* magazine in 1942. A few days ago we looked at the design again and were surprised to see how many developments we had guessed correctly, including wraparound windshields, clear plastic tops, and twenty-nine other features that have since appeared in production cars.

---

[2] bric-a-brac: decorative items, sometimes called knick-knacks, often found on mantels and shelves of American homes in the 1950s.

[3] Dagmars referred to stylized chrome car bumpers, often in the shape of exaggerated, cone-shaped artillery shells.

I class the factors affecting styling as variables and constants. Among the variables are: the future state of the nation's economy; the nature and cost of the available fuel; the rate and radius of decentralization of population; the development of new metals, synthetic materials, and new techniques; the development of more compact power plants; the possibility of highway systems with resilient surfaces or some other quality of surface. The big variable, of course, is atomic conflict [4].

Let's now isolate the factors that are near-certitudes, and predict their probable effects:

1. Highways will be able to carry more traffic at greater average speeds. (We shall need better streamlining, smooth undercarriage, higher speeds, better deceleration.)

2. There will be more automobiles everywhere. (Automobiles must be made easier to maneuver in all directions.)

3. Automobiles will increase productivity in all industries. There will be more leisure, more family travel for longer distances. (Increased luggage space is indicated for the family car.)

4. Semiautomatic driving will become the rule. Driving will be easier—therefore more relaxing; therefore more dangerous. (Interior design must take into account that the occupants must be protected more carefully if the driver lapses in attention and dozes. Devices may become standard equipment to prevent this from happening.)

5. The standard of living will be more uniform. More people will be able to consider the possibility of owning two or more cars. (There will be a wider variety of body types made available at the low-cost level—possibly a utility car, of which no example exists, now; or a vacation car, combining advantages of the present station wagon with some of the more important facilities found in trailers: refrigerated compartments, cooking units, folding awning tents, and so forth.)

6. Finally—and by far the most effective factor—there must be greater emphasis laid on the safety factor in car design. At present, one out of every ten hospital beds is occupied by the victim of an automobile accident. In 1954, 36,000 or more people were killed. In fifty years, even if the rate of fatal accidents declines (as it does annually, based on the number of miles traveled), we may expect as many as 120,000 killed annually. Obviously, something will have to be done about this, by driver education—the biggest factor—and by the automotive industry itself. (This fact will affect appearance, because structural revisions may shift glazed areas, simplify instrument panels. Automobiles, like planes today, will need to be studied as human engineering problems. Style will follow function.)

Now let's see if we can visualize an ensemble. Our 2005 model has a compact engine that does not require a high hood. This engine can be placed anywhere, and the cooling intake, if any, will be small. The body encloses large luggage spaces. The car is correctly streamlined; the undercarriage is smooth. The body is built strongly to be safe in case of collision. Therefore, window arrangement will be changed, by the new type of structure. I believe the goldfish-bowl or greenhouse superstructure is on its way out, especially in the rear of the vehicle.

---

[4] Refers to the nuclear weapon capacities of the United States and the Soviet Union and the global political, economic, and military implications of the Cold War.

The doors—or rather the accessibility panels will be power-operated and will open so that one can get in and out without crouching. The car can move laterally for close parking.

Inside, the automobile will be quite changed. With emphasis on de-lethalization, air conditioning, and partial convertibility, all-new interiors are inevitable. Seats will probably incorporate a pneumatic network to control resiliency.

Various devices will have made driving a semiautomatic process. It is known that metabolic and neuro-electrical variations take place in the human body when one relaxes and goes to sleep. It is conceivable that in the next fifty years means will be found to detect these fluctuations in body condition so as to stop the car automatically whenever the danger point approaches. Perhaps the driver will wear wrist electrodes. Or the steering wheel may transmit the body impulses. That steering wheel must, by all means, be mounted on a telescoping column.

Visibility in a 360-degree-arc is assured. Inside, windows closed, the car is quiet. The roof is a light-reflecting surface that will keep the car from getting too hot inside in the sun.

The electronics industry will probably have developed a low-priced radar unit for driving in the fog. Also, I see a possibility of a return to the flat windshield, which eliminates misleading light reflections at night. The tire started tubeless, and we are now back to the tubeless tire. As to the rear window, I wouldn't be surprised if it were the type that can be opened.

But now we come back to 1955 and our automotive jukeboxes. Are we proud of them? What do you think? Nothing about the appearance of the 1955 automobiles offsets the impression that Americans must be wasteful, swaggering, insensitive people. Automotive borax offers gratuitous evidence to people everywhere that much of what they suspect about us may be true. Our values are off beat, our ostentation acute, *if* the 1955 automobile is any reflection of ourselves and our taste.

Close Reading Questions

1. After World War II, what style decisions positively impacted car design?

2. When referring to the size of 1955 car models, why did Loewy describe the size of 1995 car models as "apparent wastefulness" and "a blessing?" What changes to the automobile validates the author's use of these apparently contradictory terms?

3. What factors did Loewy believe lead to an increased resentment of the choices made by the management departments of automobile companies? Why did Loewy insist that management was "vulnerable to public disfavor?" (Multiple Perspectives)

Analytical Writing/Discussion

4. Consider the role of cars in your life in relation to the 1950s. To what extent is having a car with particular styling—like a high end audio system—symbolic of modern American culture in the way that cars in the 1950s reflected American culture?

5. What values does Loewy connect to 1950s automobile manufacturers? What do you think is the environmentally conscious equivalent of the twenty-first century? (Cultural Influences)

6. Given the 1950s view of energy conservation, which predictions of the role and structure of the car in 2005 American culture do you think came true? Why? (Historical Trends)

Further Options

7. In "Jukebox on Wheels," the author debates whether the automobile designers of the 1950s do or should fulfill public tastes for large, gaudy cars. What do you think has a greater effect on twenty-first century automobile manufactures in the United States: consumer desires for fuel efficient cars and Congressional mandates for greater fuel efficiency or consumer desires for status objects and advertisements creating those desires? For more information about research strategies, see pp. 76–81 in Chapter 3.

8. Owning a car and a home is, for many, a key part of the American Dream. In what ways can you imagine the American Dream being maintained as we seek a more sustainable way of living? To begin crafting your answer, review the ways you can collect ideas as described in Chapter 4: The Writing Process.

FIGURE 1   1970s Gasoline shortage, Long Island, NY

Source: © Associated Press

Freewrite 2: America's Responses to Energy Crises

Thomas Friedman is a Pulitzer Prize-winning author and a columnist for the *New York Times*. The following is from Friedman's 2008 book *Hot, Flat, & Crowded: Why We Need a Green Revolution—And How It Can Renew America*. After reading the excerpt, freewrite on one of the questions below.

I can think of no better example of America's lack of sustained focus to take on a big challenge than the way we have dealt with our energy crises. In the wake of the 1973-74 Arab oil embargo, the Europeans and Japanese responded by raising gasoline taxes and, in Japan's case particularly, by launching a huge drive toward energy efficiency. France invested especially heavily in nuclear energy as a state project, with the result that today France gets 78 percent of its electricity from nuclear plants and much of the waste is reprocessed and turned into energy again. Even Brazil, a developing country, launched a national program to produce ethanol from sugarcane to make itself less dependent on imported oil. Today, between Brazil's domestic oil production and its ethanol industry, it doesn't need to import crude oil.

America's initial response was significant. Urged on by Presidents Gerald Ford and Jimmy Carter, the United States implemented higher fuel economy standards for American cars and trucks. In 1975, Congress passed the Energy Policy and Conservation Act, which established corporate average fuel economy (CAFE) standards that required the gradual doubling of passenger vehicle efficiency for new cars-to 27.5 miles per gallon within ten years.

Not surprisingly, it all worked. Between 1975 and 1985, American passenger vehicle mileage went from around 13.5 miles per gallon to 27.5, while light truck mileage increased from 11.6 miles per gallon to 19.5—all of which helped to create a global oil glut from the mid-1980s to the mid-1990s, which not only weakened OPEC but also helped to unravel the Soviet Union, then the world's second-largest oil producer.

So what happened next? Did we keep our focus on the long term? No. After the original Congressional mandate of 27.5 miles per gallon took full effect in 1985, President Reagan, rather than continuing to increase the fuel economy standard to keep reducing our dependence on foreign oil, actually rolled it back to 26 miles per gallon in 1986.... In backing away from fuel economy standards, Reagan apparently thought he was giving America's then sagging domestic oil and auto industries a boost. The result: We quickly started to get readdicted to imported oil. While the Reagan administration was instrumental in bringing down the Soviet Union, it was also instrumental in building our current dependence on Saudi Arabia.

The Reagan administration was an environmental turning point too. We forget, because it was so long ago, that there was a time when Washington had a bipartisan approach to the environment. It was a Republican, Richard Nixon, who signed into law the first wave of major environmental legislation in the United States, which addressed our first generation of environmental problems—air pollution, water pollution, and toxic waste. But Reagan changed that. Reagan ran not only against government in general but against environmental regulation in particular. He and his interior secretary, James Watt, turned environmental regulation into a much more partisan and polarizing issue than it had ever been before....

In 1989, the elder Bush's administration at least moved the fuel economy standard back up to the 1985 level of 27.5 miles per gallon. It also passed substantial improvements in building standards and new appliance standards, introduced a production tax credit for renewable energy, and elevated the Solar Energy Research Institute to the status of a national institution as the National Renewable Energy Laboratory. But as soon as Bush liberated Kuwait from Saddam Hussein, and oil prices went back down, he did nothing strategic to liberate America from dependence on Middle East oil.

When the Clinton administration came into office, it looked into raising fuel economy standards further, just for light trucks. But to make sure there would be none of that, Congress, spurred on by the Michigan Congressional delegation—which is a wholly owned subsidiary of the Big Three automakers and the United Auto Workers—literally gagged and blindfolded the government when it came to improving mileage standards. Specifically, Congress inserted an appropriations rider into the fiscal year 1996-fiscal year 2001 Department of Transportation appropriations bill that expressly prohibited the use of appropriated funds for any rule-making by the National Highway Traffic Safety Administration to tighten fuel economy standards for American cars and trucks-thereby freezing the whole process. Congress effectively banned the NHTSA from taking any steps to improve mileage standards for American cars! This move blocked any mileage improvements until 2003, when the younger Bush's administration made a tiny adjustment upward in the mileage standard for light-duty trucks....

Detroit introduced the sport-utility vehicle and successfully lobbied the government to label these as light trucks so they would not have to meet the 27.5 miles per gallon standard for cars, but only the light truck standard of 20.7. So we became even more addicted to oil. When I asked Rick Wagoner, the chairman and CEO of General Motors, why his company didn't make more fuel-efficient cars, he gave me the standard answer: that GM has never succeeded in telling Americans what cars they should buy. "We build what the market wants," he said. If people want SUVs and Hummers, you have to give them what they want."

But what the Detroit executives never tell you is that one big reason the public wanted SUVs and Hummers all those years was that Detroit and the oil industry consistently lobbied Congress against raising gasoline taxes, which would have shaped public demand for something different. European governments imposed very high gasoline taxes and taxes on engine size-and kept imposing them—and guess what? Europeans demanded smaller and smaller cars. America wouldn't impose more stringent gasoline and engine taxes, so American consumers kept wanting bigger and bigger cars. Big Oil and Big Auto used their leverage in Washington to shape the market so people would ask for those cars that consumed the most oil and earned their companies the most profits—and our Congress never got in the way. It was bought off for more than two decades.

These were the years the locust ate—brought to a filling station near you by a bipartisan alliance of special interests, with Democrats supporting the auto companies and their unions and Republicans supporting the oil companies, while the groups representing the broad national interest were marginalized and derided as part of some eco-fringe. That is "dumb as we wanna be." When the public is engaged, as it was after 1973, when people were waiting in lines for gasoline, it can override the entrenched interests of the auto and oil lobbies. But the minute—and I mean the minute—the public takes its eye off the ball, those special interest lobbyists barge back into the cloakrooms of Congress, passing out political donations and calling the shots according to their needs, not the nation's. What was good for General Motors was not always good for America, but few Democrats or Republicans in high office were ready to lead the country on a different path.

And so it is with America. Alas, we are not just the people we've been waiting for. We are the people we have to overcome. We have been consuming too much, saving too little, studying too laxly, and investing not nearly enough. And our political institutions are also the institutions we have to overcome. As long as our political system and Congress and Senate seem incapable of producing the right answers to big problems, as long as our politicians can only behave like Santa Claus and give things away, and never like Abraham Lincoln and make the really hard calls, the greatness that America is capable of will elude it in this generation.

Have no doubts. The era we have entered is one of enormous social, political, and economic change— driven in part by the Market and in part by Mother Nature. If we want things to stay as they are—that is, if we want to maintain our technological, economic, and moral leadership, and a habitable planet, rich with flora and fauna, leopards and lions, and human communities that can grow in a sustainable way—things will have to change around here, and fast.

After reading Friedman's excerpt, freewrite or discuss one or more of the following questions:

- Do you think Presidents Ford, Carter, Reagan, Bush (Sr.), and Clinton acted responsibly to the energy challenges during their respective presidencies? Why or why not?

- In what ways can you support the following two positions: Detroit fulfills consumer demands for autos *and* Detroit manipulates car buyers to create the most profitable products?

- How discerning is the American public when it comes to purchasing cars? What features, including fuel efficiency, have persuaded you or someone you know to purchase a car?

- What lessons, if any, do you think can be learned from the energy policies and car manufacturing of other countries?

YOUR GREAT WORK

by David W. Orr

David W. Orr is the Paul Sears Distinguished Professor of Environmental Studies and Politics at Oberlin College, where he is also special advisor to the president. Orr is also a James Marsh Professor at the University of Vermont. He is the author of six books, including *Ecological Literacy*. Originally titled "The Designer's Challenge," Orr delivered this speech in 2007 to the graduates of the University of Pennsylvania's School of Design, challenging them to consider a multitude of factors in their work as designers.

Dean Hack, distinguished faculty of the School of Design, honored guests, and most important, you the members of the class of 2007: It is a great privilege to stand before you on your graduation day.

As a Penn alumnus I feel a deep sense of affection for this institution and for this place. My own interest in design was kindled here long ago by Ian McHarg, who as much as anyone was the founder of modern landscape design and the larger field of ecological design. His book Design with Nature remains a classic statement of the art of intelligent inhabitation. From its founding, the city of Philadelphia has been home to a great deal of innovative urban design and experimentation now carried on here in the School of Design. You are a part of a great history and have inherited a legacy of which you may be justly proud. But the work of designers is now entering its critical and most important phase.

It is said that we are entitled to hold whatever opinions we choose, but we are not entitled to whatever facts we wish. Whatever opinions you may have, there are four facts that will fundamentally shape the world in which you will live and work.

The first is the fact that we spend upwards of 95 percent of our time in houses, cars, malls, and offices. We are becoming an indoor species increasingly shut off from sky, land, forests, waters, and animals.

Nature, as a result, is becoming more and more an abstraction to us. The problem is most severe for children who now spend up to eight hours each day before a television or computer screen and less and less time outdoors in nature. Author Richard Louv describes the results as "nature deficit disorder"—the loss of our sense of rootedness in place and connection to the natural world. In some future time, it is not farfetched to think that disconnected and rootless we would become unhinged in a fundamental way and that is a spiritual crisis for which there is no precedent.

Second, when Benjamin Franklin walked the streets of Philadelphia there were fewer than one billion of us on Earth. The human population is now 6.5 billion and will likely crest at 9 or 10 billion. One-and-a-half billion live in the most abject poverty, while another billion live in considerable wealth. One billion suffer from the afflictions of eating too much while others suffer from malnutrition. When I was a graduate student at Penn the ratio of richest to poorest was said to be 35:1. It is now approaching 100:1 and growing. The problem of a more crowded world is not just about what ecologists call carrying capacity of the Earth. It also a problem of justice with more and more people competing for less and less.

A third fact has been particularly difficult for a society built on the foundation of cheap portable fossil fuels to acknowledge. We are at or near the year of peak oil extraction, the point at which we will have consumed the easy and better half of the accessible oil. The other half is harder to refine, farther out, and deeper down, and mostly located in places where people do not like us. We are not likely to run out of oil or liquid fossil fuels from one source or another, but we are nearing the end of the era of cheap oil. We have known this for decades, but we still have no coherent or farsighted energy policy. In the meantime the penalty for procrastination grows daily along with the risks of supply interruptions and volatile energy prices.

There is a fourth fact. When the University of Pennsylvania was founded the level of CO_2 in the atmosphere was about 280 parts per million. But now the level of all human-generated heat-trapping gases is 430 parts per million CO_2 equivalent. We have already warmed the Earth by .8 degrees C and are committed at least to another .6 degrees C. According to the scientists who participated in writing the Fourth Report for the Intergovernmental Panel on Climate Change we are not just warming the Earth, but destabilizing the entire planet. Climate scientist James Hansen says that we are close to making Earth a different planet and one that we will not much like.

Four facts.

- One has to do with the largeness of the human spirit and our capacity to connect to life.
- The second has to do with justice, fairness, and decency in a more crowded world.
- The third has to do with our wisdom and creativity in the face of limits to the biosphere.
- The last is about human survival on a hotter and less stable and predictable planet.

In the face of the remorseless working out of large numbers do you have reason to be optimistic? Frankly, no. Optimism is a prediction that the odds are in your favor—like being a Yankees fan with a one-run lead in the ninth inning and two outs and a two-strike count on a .200 hitter and Mariano Rivera—in his prime—on the mound. You have good reason to believe that you will win the game. That's optimism. The Red Sox fans, on the other hand, believing in the salvation of small percentages, hope for a hit to get the runner home from second base to tie the game. Optimism is a bet that the odds are in your favor; hope is the faith that things will work out whatever the odds. Hope is a verb with its sleeves rolled up. Hopeful people are actively engaged in defying the odds or changing the odds. But optimism leans back, puts its feet up, and sports a confident look knowing that the deck is stacked.

If you know enough, you cannot honestly be optimistic. But you have every reason to be hopeful and to act faithfully and competently on that hope. And what does that mean for you as designers?

My message to you is this. As designers you hold the keys to creating a far better world than that in prospect, but only if you respond creatively, smartly, wisely, and quickly to the four facts described above. Your generation does not have a choice to solve one or two of these problems. You must solve them all—rather like solving a quadratic equation. And you have no time to lose. As designers you must design so artfully and carefully as to help reconnect people to nature and to their places. You must design to promote justice in a more crowded world. You must design a world powered by efficiency and sunlight. You do not have the option of maintaining the status quo—a world dependent on ancient sunlight. And since Nature is a ruthless and unforgiving bookkeeper, you must do your work in a way that balances the carbon books. How will you do such things? The answers, fortunately, are many, but the principles of design are few. Let me suggest three.

The first has to do with the scope of your work. You must see design as a large and unifying concept—quite literally the remaking of the human presence on Earth. Design in its largest sense has to do with how we provision ourselves with food, energy, materials, shelter, livelihood, transport, water, and waste cycling. It is the calibration of human intentions with how the world works as a physical system and the awareness of how the world works to inform our intentions. And good design at all times joins our five senses (and perhaps others that we suspect) with the human fabricated world. When designers get it right, they create in ways that reinforce our common humanity at the deepest level.

Ecological design is flourishing in fields as diverse as architecture, landscape architecture, biomimicry, industrial ecology, urban planning, ecological engineering, agriculture, and forestry. It is gathering momentum, driven by necessity, better technology, and economic opportunity. Designers in diverse fields are learning how to

- use nature as the standard, as Ian McHarg proposed;

- power the world on current sunlight;

- eliminate waste;

- pay the full cost of development;

- build prosperity on a durable basis.

Design as a large concept means, in Wendell Berry's felicitous words, "solving for pattern," creating solutions that solve many problems. When you solve for pattern you will also have created resilience, which is the capacity of systems to persist in a world perturbed by human error, malevolence, and what we call "acts of God." And by solving for pattern you are also likely to learn the virtues of reparability, redundancy, locality, and simplicity....

As a corollary, you must see yourselves as the designers, not just of buildings, landscapes, and objects, but of the systems in which these are components. That means that you must reckon with economic, political, and social aspects of design. And the hardest but most important object for designers is the design of what Peter Senge calls learning organizations, in which designing ecologically becomes the default setting, not an aberration.

Second, you will need a standard for your work, rather like the Hippocratic Oath or a compass by which you chart a journey. For that I propose that designers should aim to cause no ugliness, human or ecological, somewhere else or at some later time. That standard will cause you to think upstream from the particular design project or object to the wells, mines, forests, farms, and manufacturing establishments from which materials are drawn and crystallized into the particularities of design. It will cause you, as well, to look downstream to the effects of design on climate and health of people and ecosystems. If there is ugliness, human or ecological, at either end you cannot claim success as a designer regardless of the artfulness of what you make.

As a corollary, you, as designers, ought to think of yourselves first as place makers, not merely form makers. The difference is crucial. Form making puts a premium on artistry and sometimes merely fashion. It is mostly indifferent to human and ecological costs incurred elsewhere. The first rule of place making, on the other hand, is to honor and preserve other places, however remote in space and culture. When you become accomplished designers, of course, you will have mastered the integration of both making places and making them beautiful.

Third, as designers, you will need to place your work in a larger historical context—what philosopher Thomas Berry calls, your Great Work. No generation ever asks for its Great Work. The generation of the Civil War certainly did not wish to fight and die at places like Shiloh, Antietam, Gettysburg, or the Wilderness. But their Great Work, the end of human bondage, required just that of tens of thousands of them...and they rose to do their Great Work. Those now passing from the scene that Tom Brokaw calls "The Greatest Generation" did not wish to fight and die in places like Iwo Jima or the battlefields of Europe. But their Great Work, the fight against Nazism, required them to do so and they rose to the challenge to do their Great Work as well. Your Great Work, however, is not one of fighting wars, but of extending and speeding a worldwide ecological enlightenment that joins human needs and purposes with the way the world works as a biophysical system.

Your Great Work will be no less demanding and no less complex than that of any previous generation. But in outline it is very simple. Your Great Work as designers is to:

1. Stabilize and reduce all heat trapping gases

2. Make a rapid transition to efficiency and renewable energy

3. Build a world secure by design for everyone... a world in which every child has a decent home, food, water, education, medical care

4. Preserve the best of our history and culture

5. Enable us to see our way forward to a world that is sustainable and spiritually sustaining

This challenge, your Great Work, is neither liberal nor conservative; neither Republican nor Democrat. It is, rather, the recognition that the present generation is a trustee standing midway between a distant past and the horizon of the future. As trustees we are obligated to pass on the best of our civilization and the ecological requisites on which it depends—including a stable climate and biological diversity—to future generations. The idea that we are no more than trustees was proposed long ago by Edmund Burke, the founder of modern conservatism (1790), and by one of the founders of modern revolutionary politics, Thomas Jefferson (1789), as well. It is a perspective that unites us across our present divisions in service to our posterity. Your Great Work is a sacred trust given only to your generation. If you do not rise to do your Great Work, it will not be done. We know enough now to say what no other generation could rightfully say: the price for that dereliction—not rising to do your Great Work—will be high and perhaps total. Your Great Work as designers is to honor wholeness, health, and the great holy mystery of life. No other generation before you ever had a greater challenge and none more reason to rise to greatness.

My charge to you is to do your work so well that those who will look back on your time—the beneficiaries of your Great Work—will know that this was indeed humankind's finest hour.

Close Reading Questions

1. Why do you think Orr compares the population of Philadelphia in 2007 to the Philadelphia of Benjamin Franklin's time?

2. Why does Orr say that "Nature is a ruthless and unforgiving bookkeeper"?

3. For what reasons does Orr deflect political labels when describing the tasks facing the design profession?

Analytical Writing/Discussion

4. Why do you agree or disagree with Orr's contention that designers face four facts "that will fundamentally shape the world in which [we] live and work"? Which fact strikes you as more or least critical? Why? (Multiple Perspectives)

5. In what ways do you think Orr's use of a sports analogy is an effective or ineffective way to illustrate the responsibilities of design professionals to create in environmentally conscious ways? (Cultural Influences)

6. How does Orr define the design graduates' "Great Work"? How does their Great Work compare to the nineteenth- and twentieth-century examples of Great Work? (Historical Trends)

Further Options

7. In the middle of his speech, Orr tells the graduates the unequivocal tasks ahead of them as newly minted designers. What would you imagine that students in other disciplines—like English, business, or education—would say is their plan for using their careers to maintain an environmentally conscious world?

8. Michael Pollan, in his essay "Why Bother?," is initially uncertain that his personal actions can avert damage to the environment. How do you imagine Orr would respond to Pollan's views on an individual's ability to affect change? (Cultural Influences)

THE WAY WE LIVE NOW

by Michael Pollan

Michael Pollan is the author of several books, including *The Omnivore's Dilemma: A Natural History of Four Meals* and *The Botany of Desire: A Plant's-Eye View of the World*. In 2010, Pollan was named one of *TIME Magazine's* 100 most influential people in the world. The following excerpt was first published in 2008 in *The New York Times Magazine*.

The Main Question

Why bother? That really is the big question facing us as individuals hoping to do something about climate change, and it's not an easy one to answer. I don't know about you, but for me the most upsetting moment in "An Inconvenient Truth" came long after Al Gore scared the hell out of me, constructing an utterly convincing case that the very survival of life on earth as we know it is threatened by climate change. No, the really dark moment came during the closing credits, when we are asked to … change our light bulbs. That's when it got really depressing. The immense disproportion between the magnitude of the problem Gore had described and the puniness of what he was asking us to do about it was enough to sink your heart.

But the drop-in-the-bucket issue is not the only problem lurking behind the "why bother" question. Let's say I do bother, big time. I turn my life upside-down, start biking to work, plant a big garden, turn down the thermostat so low I need the Jimmy Carter signature cardigan, forsake the clothes dryer for a laundry line across the yard, trade in the station wagon for a hybrid, get off the beef, go completely local. I could theoretically do all that, but what would be the point when I know full well that halfway around the world there lives my evil twin, some carbon-footprint doppelgänger in Shanghai or Chongqing who has just bought his first car (Chinese car ownership is where ours was back in 1918), is eager to swallow every bite of meat I forswear and who's positively itching to replace every last pound of CO_2 I'm struggling no longer to emit. So what exactly would I have to show for all my trouble?

A sense of personal virtue, you might suggest, somewhat sheepishly. But what good is that when virtue itself is quickly becoming a term of derision? And not just on the editorial pages of The Wall Street Journal or on the lips of the vice president, who famously dismissed energy conservation as a "sign of personal virtue." No, even in the pages of The New York Times and The New Yorker, it seems the epithet "virtuous," when applied to an act of personal environmental responsibility, may be used only ironically. Tell me: How did it come to pass that virtue–a quality that for most of history has generally been deemed, well, a virtue–became a mark of liberal softheadedness? How peculiar, that doing the right thing by the environment–buying the hybrid, eating like a locavore–should now set you up for the Ed Begley Jr. treatment.

And even if in the face of this derision I decide I am going to bother, there arises the whole vexed question of getting it right. Is eating local or walking to work really going to reduce my carbon footprint? According to one analysis, if walking to work increases your appetite and you consume more meat or milk as a result, walking might actually emit more carbon than driving. A handful of studies have recently suggested that in certain cases under certain conditions, produce from places as far away as New Zealand might account for less carbon than comparable domestic products. True, at least one of these studies was co-written by a representative of agribusiness interests in (surprise!) New Zealand, but even so, they make you wonder. If determining the carbon footprint of food is really this complicated, and I've got to consider not only "food miles" but also whether the food came by ship or truck and how lushly the grass grows in New Zealand, then maybe on second thought I'll just buy the imported chops at Costco, at least until the experts get their footprints sorted out.

A Crisis of Character

There are so many stories we can tell ourselves to justify doing nothing, but perhaps the most insidious is that, whatever we do manage to do, it will be too little too late. Climate change is upon us, and it has arrived well ahead of schedule. Scientists' projections that seemed dire a decade ago turn out to have been unduly optimistic: the warming and the melting is occurring much faster than the models predicted. Now truly terrifying feedback loops threaten to boost the rate of change exponentially, as the shift from white ice to blue water in the Arctic absorbs more sunlight and warming soils everywhere become more biologically active, causing them to release their vast stores of carbon into the air. Have you looked into the eyes of a climate scientist recently? They look really scared.

So do you still want to talk about planting gardens?

I do.

Whatever we can do as individuals to change the way we live at this suddenly very late date does seem utterly inadequate to the challenge. It's hard to argue with Michael Specter, in a recent New Yorker piece on carbon footprints, when he says: "Personal choices, no matter how virtuous [N.B.!], cannot do enough. It will also take laws and money." So it will. Yet it is no less accurate or hardheaded to say that laws and money cannot do enough, either; that it will also take profound changes in the way we live. Why? Because the climate-change crisis is at its very bottom a crisis of lifestyle–of character, even. The Big Problem is nothing more or less than the sum total of countless little everyday choices, most of them made by us (consumer spending represents 70 percent of our economy), and most of the rest of them made in the name of our needs and desires and preferences.

For us to wait for legislation or technology to solve the problem of how we're living our lives suggests we're not really serious about changing–something our politicians cannot fail to notice. They will not move until we do. Indeed, to look to leaders and experts, to laws and money and grand schemes, to save us from our predicament represents precisely the sort of thinking–passive, delegated, dependent for solutions on specialists–that helped get us into this mess in the first place. It's hard to believe that the same sort of thinking could now get us out of it.

Thirty years ago, Wendell Berry, the Kentucky farmer and writer, put forward a blunt analysis of precisely this mentality. He argued that the environmental crisis of the 1970s–an era innocent of climate change; what we would give to have back that environmental crisis!–was at its heart a crisis of character and would have to be addressed first at that level: at home, as it were. He was impatient with people who wrote checks to environmental organizations while thoughtlessly squandering fossil fuel in their everyday lives–the 1970s equivalent of people buying carbon offsets to atone for their Tahoes and Durangos. Nothing was likely to change until we healed the "split between what we think and what we do." For Berry, the "why bother" question came down to a moral imperative: "Once our personal connection to what is wrong becomes clear, then we have to choose: we can go on as before, recognizing our dishonesty and living with it the best we can, or we can begin the effort to change the way we think and live."

For Berry, the deep problem standing behind all the other problems of industrial civilization is "specialization," which he regards as the "disease of the modern character." Our society assigns us a tiny number of roles: we're producers (of one thing) at work, consumers of a great many other things the rest of the time, and then once a year or so we vote as citizens. Virtually all of our needs and desires we delegate to specialists of one kind or another–our meals to agribusiness, health to the doctor, education to the teacher, entertainment to the media, care for the environment to the environmentalist, political action to the politician.

As Adam Smith and many others have pointed out, this division of labor has given us many of the blessings of civilization. Specialization is what allows me to sit at a computer thinking about climate change. Yet this same division of labor obscures the lines of connection–and responsibility–linking our everyday acts to their real-world consequences, making it easy for me to overlook the coal-fired power plant that is lighting my screen, or the mountaintop in Kentucky that had to be destroyed to provide the coal to that plant, or the streams running crimson with heavy metals as a result.

The Reality of Cheap Energy

Of course, what made this sort of specialization possible in the first place was cheap energy. Cheap fossil fuel allows us to pay distant others to process our food for us, to entertain us and to (try to) solve our problems, with the result that there is very little we know how to accomplish for ourselves. Think for a moment of all the things you suddenly need to do for yourself when the power goes out–up to and including entertaining yourself. Think, too, about how a power failure causes your neighbors–your community–to suddenly loom so much larger in your life. Cheap energy allowed us to leapfrog community by making it possible to sell our specialty over great distances as well as summon into our lives the specialties of countless distant others.

Here's the point: Cheap energy, which gives us climate change, fosters precisely the mentality that makes dealing with climate change in our own lives seem impossibly difficult. Specialists ourselves, we can no longer imagine anyone but an expert, or anything but a new technology or law, solving our problems. Al Gore asks us to change the light bulbs because he probably can't imagine us doing anything much more challenging, like, say, growing some portion of our own food. We can't imagine it, either, which is probably why we prefer to cross our fingers and talk about the promise of ethanol and nuclear power–new liquids and electrons to power the same old cars and houses and lives.

The "cheap-energy mind," as Wendell Berry called it, is the mind that asks, "Why bother?" because it is helpless to imagine–much less attempt–a different sort of life, one less divided, less reliant. Since the cheap-energy mind translates everything into money, its proxy, it prefers to put its faith in market-based solutions–carbon taxes and pollution-trading schemes. If we could just get the incentives right, it believes, the economy will properly value everything that matters and nudge our self-interest down the proper channels. The best we can hope for is a greener version of the old invisible hand. Visible hands it has no use for.

But while some such grand scheme may well be necessary, it's doubtful that it will be sufficient or that it will be politically sustainable before we've demonstrated to ourselves that change is possible. Merely to give, to spend, even to vote, is not to do, and there is so much that needs to be done–without further delay. In the judgment of James Hansen, the NASA climate scientist who began sounding the alarm on global warming 20 years ago, we have only 10 years left to start cutting–not just slowing–the amount of carbon we're emitting or face a "different planet." Hansen said this more than two years ago, however; two years have gone by, and nothing of consequence has been done. So: eight years left to go and a great deal left to do.

Living Green for the Greater Good

Which brings us back to the "why bother" question and how we might better answer it. The reasons not to bother are many and compelling, at least to the cheap-energy mind. But let me offer a few admittedly tentative reasons that we might put on the other side of the scale:

If you do bother, you will set an example for other people. If enough other people bother, each one influencing yet another in a chain reaction of behavioral change, markets for all manner of green products and alternative technologies will prosper and expand. (Just look at the market for hybrid cars.) Consciousness will be raised, perhaps even changed: new moral imperatives and new taboos might take root in the culture. Driving an S.U.V. or eating a 24-ounce steak or illuminating your McMansion like an airport runway at night might come to be regarded as outrages to human conscience. Not having things might become cooler than having them. And those who did change the way they live would acquire the moral standing to demand changes in behavior from others–from other people, other corporations, even other countries.

All of this could, theoretically, happen. What I'm describing (imagining would probably be more accurate) is a process of viral social change, and change of this kind, which is nonlinear, is never something anyone can plan or predict or count on. Who knows, maybe the virus will reach all the way to Chongqing and infect my Chinese evil twin. Or not. Maybe going green will prove a passing fad and will lose steam after a few years, just as it did in the 1980s, when Ronald Reagan took down Jimmy Carter's solar panels from the roof of the White House.

Going personally green is a bet, nothing more or less, though it's one we probably all should make, even if the odds of it paying off aren't great. Sometimes you have to act as if acting will make a difference, even when you can't prove that it will. That, after all, was precisely what happened in Communist Czechoslovakia and Poland, when a handful of individuals like Vaclav Havel and Adam Michnik resolved that they would simply conduct their lives "as if" they lived in a free society. That improbable bet created a tiny space of liberty that, in time, expanded to take in, and then help take down, the whole of the Eastern bloc.

So what would be a comparable bet that the individual might make in the case of the environmental crisis? Havel himself has suggested that people begin to "conduct themselves as if they were to live on this earth forever and be answerable for its condition one day." Fair enough, but let me propose a slightly less abstract and daunting wager. The idea is to find one thing to do in your life that doesn't involve spending or voting, that may or may not virally rock the world but is real and particular (as well as symbolic) and that, come what may, will offer its own rewards. Maybe you decide to give up meat, an act that would reduce your carbon footprint by as much as a quarter. Or you could try this: determine to observe the Sabbath. For one day a week, abstain completely from economic activity: no shopping, no driving, no electronics.

But the act I want to talk about is growing some–even just a little–of your own food. Rip out your lawn, if you have one, and if you don't–if you live in a high-rise, or have a yard shrouded in shade–look into getting a plot in a community garden. Measured against the Problem We Face, planting a garden sounds pretty benign, I know, but in fact it's one of the most powerful things an individual can do–to reduce your carbon footprint, sure, but more important, to reduce your sense of dependence and dividedness: to change the cheap-energy mind.

Small Steps

A great many things happen when you plant a vegetable garden, some of them directly related to climate change, others indirect but related nevertheless. Growing food, we forget, comprises the original solar technology: calories produced by means of photosynthesis. Years ago the cheap-energy mind discovered that more food could be produced with less effort by replacing sunlight with fossil-fuel fertilizers and pesticides, with a result that the typical calorie of food energy in your diet now requires about 10 calories of fossil-fuel energy to produce. It's estimated that the way we feed ourselves (or rather, allow ourselves to be fed) accounts for about a fifth of the greenhouse gas for which each of us is responsible.

Yet the sun still shines down on your yard, and photosynthesis still works so abundantly that in a thoughtfully organized vegetable garden (one planted from seed, nourished by compost from the kitchen and involving not too many drives to the garden center), you can grow the proverbial free lunch–CO_2-free and dollar-free. This is the most-local food you can possibly eat (not to mention the freshest, tastiest and most nutritious), with a carbon footprint so faint that even the New Zealand lamb council dares not challenge it. And while we're counting carbon, consider too your compost pile, which shrinks the heap of garbage your household needs trucked away even as it feeds your vegetables and sequesters carbon in your soil. What else? Well, you will probably notice that you're getting a pretty good workout there in your garden, burning calories without having to get into the car to drive to the gym. (It is one of the absurdities of the modern division of labor that, having replaced physical labor with fossil fuel, we now have to burn even more fossil fuel to keep our unemployed bodies in shape.) Also, by engaging both body and mind, time spent in the garden is time (and energy) subtracted from electronic forms of entertainment.

You begin to see that growing even a little of your own food is, as Wendell Berry pointed out 30 years ago, one of those solutions that, instead of begetting a new set of problems–the way "solutions" like ethanol or nuclear power inevitably do–actually beget other solutions, and not only of the kind that save carbon. Still more valuable are the habits of mind that growing a little of your own food can yield. You quickly learn that you need not be dependent on specialists to provide for yourself–that your body is still good for something and may actually be enlisted in its own support. If the experts are right, if both oil and time are running out, these are skills and habits of mind we're all very soon going to need. We may also need the food. Could gardens provide it? Well, during World War II, victory gardens supplied as much as 40 percent of the produce Americans ate.

But there are sweeter reasons to plant that garden, to bother. At least in this one corner of your yard and life, you will have begun to heal the split between what you think and what you do, to commingle your identities as consumer and producer and citizen. Chances are, your garden will re-engage you with your neighbors, for you will have produce to give away and the need to borrow their tools. You will have reduced the power of the cheap-energy mind by personally overcoming its most debilitating weakness: its helplessness and the fact that it can't do much of anything that doesn't involve division or subtraction. The garden's season-long transit from seed to ripe fruit–will you get a load of that zucchini?!–suggests that the operations of addition and multiplication still obtain, that the abundance of nature is not exhausted. The single greatest lesson the garden teaches is that our relationship to the planet need not be zero-sum, and that as long as the sun still shines and people still can plan and plant, think and do, we can, if we bother to try, find ways to provide for ourselves without diminishing the world.

Close Reading Questions

1. For what reasons is Pollan skeptical about his own efforts to affect climate change?

2. Considering your lifestyle and those of people you know, to what degree do you follow or resist what Wendell Berry calls "the cheap-energy mind"? Why do you agree or disagree that this energy mind-set represents a "crisis of lifestyle"?

3. Consider the contemporary connotation of the word "viral." What is Pollan suggesting when he mentions the need for viral social change?

Analytical Writing/Discussion

4. To what extent does Pollan believe that affecting climate change cannot rely solely on legislation? What do you think are the most or least persuasive examples he provides to support this idea? (Multiple Perspectives)

5. Why do you think that writer Wendell Berry connected the climate crisis of the 1970s to "specialization"? To what degree is it possible to decrease specialization in the twenty-first century? (Historical Trends)

6. The French writer and philosopher Voltaire asserted, late in his life, that significant changes start in one's own life. Speaking both literally and metaphorically, he asserted that we tend our own "gardens." According to Pollan, what are several immediate and indirect benefits of growing at least some of one's own food? Which of the benefits do you find most or least compelling? (Cultural Influences)

Further Options

7. Why do you believe or not believe that K-12 education should teach children to live in environmentally responsible ways? What lessons do you think children should learn about digital literacy technologies (see Nicholas Carr's "Is Google Making us Stupid?" on pp. 361–365 in Chapter 14) and experimental urban housing developments like the Billings Forge complex (pp. 282–283 in Chapter 12)?

8. Pollan is clearly an advocate of growing your own food. Using some of the suggestions on analyzing rhetorical appeals on pp. 102–106 in Chapter 6, how can you persuade people to plant gardens, no matter where they live?

HOW THE "SCIENTIFIC CONSENSUS" ON GLOBAL WARMING AFFECTS AMERICAN BUSINESS—AND CONSUMERS

by Nicolas Loris

Nicolas Loris is a policy analyst in the Thomas A. Roe Institute for Economic Policy Studies at The Heritage Foundation, a research and educational think tank. Loris's work has also appeared in publications like *The Wall Street Journal*, *The Washington Times*, and *Investor's Business Daily*. The following excerpt is from a 2010 article written partly in response to the 2007 report by the United Nations about greenhouse gas emissions.

For years businesses and the general public have been told by mainstream climatologists that the planet is warming due to human activity and that immediate action is necessary to avoid a global catastrophe. The U.S. government relied heavily on a 2007 report by the United Nations' Intergovernmental Panel on Climate Change (IPCC) to justify the need to reduce emissions of carbon dioxide (CO_2) and other greenhouse gases (GHGs) created anthropogenically[1]. Over time, Congress enacted numerous policies to increase clean energy production, such as mandates for renewable fuels, expanded tax credits for renewable energy, and new energy efficiency targets for vehicles and appliances. All of these policies had the goal of reducing America's carbon footprint. Congress is now seeking to expand and create new policies

---

[1] created or caused by human activity

aimed at further reducing emissions by placing a national cap on carbon emissions and enforcing a federal mandate for renewable energy production. Meanwhile, the Environmental Protection Agency is on its own regulatory path to decrease CO_2.

The business landscape consequently changed, and not for the better. Energy producers became vested stakeholders and lobbied for handouts to produce what Congress determined to be cleaner energy from cleaner sources, such as windmills, solar panels, and ethanol. Major oil companies invested in renewable energy technology to capitalize on subsidies and tax breaks while enhancing their image. Most businesses factored the threat of global warming into their daily operations and became cognizant of the threat of higher energy prices caused by government policies.

Despite vigorous dissension among the scientific community concerning the effects of anthropogenic warming, the climatologists who believe the warming to be a serious problem controlled the message for years. Simply put, they convinced the general public that global warming posed an imminent threat and drastic cuts in greenhouse gas emissions were necessary to prevent a catastrophe. Recent flaws discovered in the scientific assessment of climate change have shown that the scientific consensus is not as settled as the public had been led to believe. Leaked e-mails from the University of East Anglia's Climate Research Unit in the U.K. revealed conspiracy, exaggerated warming data, possibly illegal destruction and manipulation of data, and attempts to freeze out dissenting scientists from publishing their work in reputable journals. Furthermore, gaffes exposed in the IPCC report have only increased skepticism among businesses and the public, and raised serious questions about sacrificing economic activity to reduce CO_2 emissions.

Policy should never rest on a shaky set of assumptions, particularly when it can have far-reaching implications for American businesses and everyday Americans, and could therefore fundamentally alter decisions in ways that harm America's productive system of free enterprise. While the government can pick winners and prop them up with subsidies, every winner comes at the expense of the taxpayer and discourages the innovation necessary to discover new and economically competitive sources of energy. Moreover, business uncertainty created by the government's wavering on more climate change policy is stunting America's economic recovery. With such inconclusive scientific evidence, Congress should not implement any new GHG-reduction policies, and it should prohibit the EPA from doing the same.

The Shifting Consensus

The alleged scientific consensus on climate change holds that the planet is warming at a dramatic rate. But not long ago, scientists thought that global *cooling* was a threat to the planet. As recently as 1975, *The New York Times* ran an article titled, "A Major Cooling Widely Considered to Be Inevitable." Some proposals even included covering the polar ice caps with black soot to melt them. Only six years later, climatologists predicted that global warming was inevitable, and the issue gained more traction throughout the 1980s and 1990s. The IPCC published multiple reports, the first in 1990, pronouncing that human activities, predominately fossil fuel use, were warming the planet. A supplementary report followed in 1992, the second report appeared in 1995, and the third in 2001—all presenting "newer and stronger" evidence that the planet's surface was heating due to human activity.

The message that warming was incontrovertible continually gained momentum and exploded in 2006 when former Vice President Al Gore released his book and documentary film *An Inconvenient Truth*, claiming that the planet would witness more Hurricane Katrina-like disasters and rising sea levels if humans do not drastically reduce man-made greenhouse gas emissions. The 2007 IPCC report became Al Gore's *magnum opus* on climate change and the main source for the "evidence" he relentlessly pitched to Congress. The 2007 report declared that global warming is "unequivocal," and the frequency and intensity of natural disasters is likely to increase. The report's "Summary for Policymakers" warned that carbon emissions from fossil fuel production and nitrous oxide, and methane emissions from agricultural production, are significantly contributing to global warming. Government officials in the U.S. and around the world continually use and exaggerate the IPCC report to justify the need for carbon reduction policies, creating a large disparity between hype and reality. For instance, even the IPCC projection of sea level rising over the next century is a modest 7 to 23 inches, with the lower end of that projection occurring over the past two centuries.

Is There a Scientific Consensus?

Several recent events, including revelations that forced the IPCC to retract parts of its 2007 report, have called the scientific consensus into question. Although the study puts the probability of Himalayan glaciers melting by 2035 at "very high," the authors acknowledged that they based this and other claims on speculation. Further, the IPCC's assessment of reductions in mountain ice in the Andes, Alps, and Africa came from two dubious sources. One was from a magazine that discussed anecdotal evidence from mountain climbers; the other came from a student dissertation. The IPCC also acknowledged overstating crop loss in Africa, depletion of the Amazon rain forest, sea level increases in the Netherlands, and damage from weather catastrophes.

Climate data sets are also raising questions. Hackers leaked thousands of e-mails and other documents from the University of East Anglia's Climate Research Unit that detailed how these climatologists, many with important roles in promulgating the official U.N. science, refused to share data, plotted to keep dissenting scientists from being published in leading journals, and discarded original data. Some have resigned and others have been investigated for breaching data laws under the Freedom of Information Act. Russian climatologists blamed the scandal-laden Climate Research Unit (CRU) for omitting cooler data points from its data set. In the U.S., computer programmer E. Michael Smith and meteorologist Joseph D'Aleo detailed how the National Climatic Data Center (NCDC) dropped thousands of data points from its climate data set—data points that were in cooler regions around the globe.

A few errors in the three-volume, almost 1,000-page IPCC report may not warrant dismissal of the entire study, but climatologists questioned the IPCC's findings before these gaffes. University of Virginia professor Fred Singer recently published an 800-page report titled, "Climate Change Reconsidered," which questions and debunks many of the IPCC conclusions and emphasizes that there is no scientific consensus on climate change. Richard Lindzen, professor of meteorology at the Massachusetts Institute of Technology, notes that the IPCC's models fail to take into account naturally occurring cycles such as El Niño, the Pacific decadal oscillation, or the Atlantic multidecadal oscillation. Other prominent scientists called political action "irresponsible and immoral" because of the lack of credible evidence. When the IPCC released its report in 2007, 400 climate experts disputed the findings; that number has since grown to more than 700 scientists, including several current and former IPCC scientists.

The profusion of scientific dissent should have been sufficient evidence for policymakers to call the alleged consensus into question, and these recent events should raise even more red flags, especially in light of the economic costs that policies to mitigate greenhouse gases carry.

Government Plans to Reduce Greenhouse Gases

Despite these revelations about scientific research on global warming, the U.S. government has aggressively pursued climate change policies to reduce carbon dioxide emissions. During the past two decades, the federal government has spent more than $79 billion on climate change policies, "including science and technology research, administration, education campaigns, foreign aid, and tax breaks." Legislation signed into law in 2005 and 2007 included more steps to transition from fossil fuels and improve energy efficiency to reduce CO_2 emissions. More recently, the Obama Administration has attempted to tip the balance in favor of renewable energy by advocating a cap-and-trade system, CO_2 regulations, renewable electricity mandates, and additional billions of dollars in government spending for government-picked "clean-energy" sources. Key legislative and regulatory steps are:

2005 and 2007 Energy Bills and 2009 Green Stimulus. Over the past five years, the government implemented two key policies to support renewable energy production, and passed a stimulus bill in 2009 with billions allocated to renewable energy projects. The Energy Policy Act (EPACT) of 2005 contained loan guarantees for technologies, such as nuclear energy carbon capture, and sequestration, that would reduce greenhouse gas output by increasing the supply of carbon-free energy, as well as a host of subsidies and policies to increase renewable energy production. The act also included the first requirement that renewable fuels be mixed into the gasoline supply. The Energy Independence and Security Act (EISA) of 2007 increased the renewable fuel mandate from 7.5 billion gallons in 2012 to 36 billion gallons by 2022, and included more tax credits for wind power, solar energy, and small irrigation power. Congress implemented a number of other energy-efficiency mandates for vehicles, buildings, and appliances to reduce energy consumption and consumers' carbon footprint....

The 2009 American Recovery and Reinvestment Act included funding for renewable energy as well. Also known as the stimulus bill, the $814 billion package allocates nearly $47 billion for renewable energy sources, smart grids, and energy-efficiency programs. Congress granted an additional $20 billion to manufacturers of renewable energy technology in the form of tax credits. The reason these sources of energy need government help is that they are too uncompetitive to reach the market otherwise. To the extent that there is a valid economic case for wind energy, solar energy, and ethanol fuel, industry will provide them even in the absence of government dictates and subsidies. Moreover, government-mandated energy-efficiency programs may sound good to consumers, but it is rarely good when Washington controls the market, since the forced energy-efficiency standards can result in decreased product performance, features, or reliability, which destroys value for the consumer. Mandatory improvements in efficiency usually raise the purchase price of appliances; sometimes the increase is more than enough to negate the energy savings.

Cap and Trade. One way to make clean energy more competitive is to tax fossil fuels to make them more expensive through a cap-and-trade system. Under cap and trade, emitters of greenhouse gases, primarily carbon dioxide derived from fossil fuel production, would be required to obtain permits (also known as allowances) for each ton of CO_2 emitted. The price of the allowances, in essence the tax on energy, is determined by supply and demand. As the carbon cuts become more stringent, the government allocates fewer permits, thus driving up the price for the energy-intensive sectors required to buy them. By taxing fossil-fuel-derived energy with artificial caps on carbon dioxide, clean energy artificially becomes more economically viable. In July 2009, the House of Representatives passed a cap-and-trade bill to reduce greenhouse gases 83 percent below 2005 levels by 2050. Since nearly 85 percent of America's energy needs come from fossil fuels, capping carbon dioxide amounts to an enormous tax on energy consumption.

EPA Regulations. With Congress unable to deliver a final cap-and-trade bill to the President, the Environmental Protection Agency (EPA) has been working on a backdoor policy to regulate greenhouse gas emissions much like cap and trade. A 2007 Supreme Court case decided that carbon dioxide and five other GHGs are pollutants and can be regulated under the Clean Air Act. The court ordered the EPA administrator to determine whether these GHG emissions were dangerous to human health and the environment and whether the scientific consensus on the effects of GHGs was settled. In April 2009, the EPA issued an endangerment finding, saying that current and future greenhouse gas emissions pose a serious threat to public health and safety. The EPA relied on the 2007 IPCC report as well as data from the NCDC to establish this finding. Thus, questionable science is guiding major changes in economic regulation. Under this approach, almost any activity that emits carbon dioxide and other greenhouse gases could be regulated under the Clean Air Act. Like cap and trade, regulating CO_2 emissions under the Clean Air Act would similarly burden the economy with higher energy costs, and would also include higher administrative compliance costs for businesses, higher bureaucratic costs for enforcing the regulations, and higher legal costs from the inevitable litigation.

Business Responds to Government

Recognizing policymakers' commitment to reducing greenhouse gases, businesses shaped their plans around government policies, despite the fact they are based on poor scientific evidence. Companies worldwide are taking climate change into consideration when making short-term and long-term business decisions. A June 2009 PricewaterhouseCoopers global survey asked 1,124 CEOs how their respective businesses were responding to climate change policies. In a series of yes or no questions, when asked about making changes to the products and services provided due to climate change policies, 46 percent said they were already making changes to day-to-day operations, and 40 percent are already changing how they manage risk.

Businesses are not just changing day-to-day operations and preparing for higher energy costs, but also how they invest for the future. Johnson & Johnson is investing in renewable energy and now uses the most hybrid vehicles of any company in America. Wal-Mart CEO Scott Lee made a pledge that each of his stores would eventually run on 100 percent renewable energy. Coca Cola's environmental initiative focuses not only on water stewardship and sustainable packaging, but also climate protection. Goldman Sachs invested $1.5 billion in wind, solar, and ethanol projects in 2006.

There is nothing wrong with these business decisions if they are made voluntarily. But if they are made in response to government policies favoring renewable energy over other sources, especially on questionable scientific grounds, it misallocates private resources, crowds out innovation, and wastes taxpayer money. In Spain, solar companies enjoyed lucrative subsidies for years; when the global recession forced the Spanish government to cut back its handouts, the Spanish solar market crashed.

In a free market, the private sector should bear the risk and, therefore, reap the reward or suffer the consequences of an investment decision. If the government dictates these decisions by subsidizing a portion of the project, businesses receive all rewards with minimal risk. With start-up companies and large corporations alike receiving money from the government through stimulus funds or tax credits, firms will divert investments to clean-energy technology away from other—potentially more profitable and value-creating—investments.

As the government moves more actively toward funding renewable technology, investors are waiting to determine who the government winners will be before they spend more of their own money on innovative ideas, expanding their businesses, and hiring more employees. As Darryl Siry, former head of marketing at Tesla Motors, put it, "The existence of an 800-pound gorilla putting massive capital behind select start-ups is sucking the air away from the rest of the venture-capital ecosystem. Being anointed by DOE [U.S. Department of Energy] has become everything for companies looking to move ahead."

Large corporations also flooded the halls of Congress with thousands of lobbyists to ask for preferential treatment on energy policy. In 2007, 10 of the largest companies in the U.S. formed the United States

Climate Action Partnership (USCAP) urging the government to cut GHG emissions. USCAP has since grown to 28 businesses and environmental organizations. Businesses heavily ramped up lobbying efforts in the past decade. More than 1,700 firms and groups sent lobbyists to work in the area of energy in 2009, up from 1,300 the year before, and 900 in 2006....

Politics governed by special interests typically worsens conditions for the consumer. Consumers are the ones who bear the costs of these government policies; meanwhile, industry receives a seemingly free windfall. The more that government becomes involved in energy decisions, the more money will be used for special interest politicking. As founding father Ben Franklin said, "When the people find that they can vote themselves money, that will herald the end of the republic."

Congressional Action Required

Congress has spent years and billions of dollars building policy around an alleged scientific consensus, and is on a path to spend billions more as well as implement policies that would significantly reduce this country's economic potential. Congress should instead focus on the following measures to prevent more unnecessary economic damage and promote sound energy policy that would create jobs and increase energy supply:

1. **Refrain from Legislating for the Purpose of Reducing GHGs.** Congress should not pursue policies, such as cap and trade, a renewable electricity standard, or subsidies for "clean energy" as long as grave scientific disputes remain. Even if a scientific consensus emerges, Congress should still refrain from taking any action unless the economic cost of climate change mitigation justifies any benefits.

2. **Prohibit EPA Regulations.** Congress should rein in the EPA's regulatory authority by amending the Clean Air Act to exclude carbon dioxide and other greenhouse gases from coming under the EPA's purview.

3. **Focus Energy Policy on Energy, not GHGs.** Instead of artificially propping up certain energy sources with subsidies and mandates based on a false scientific consensus, Congress should focus on creating a regulatory and legal framework for all energy policies to succeed or fail on their own merit by removing subsidies and reducing regulatory red tape that prevents the development of all energy sources.

Uncertain Science, Certain Cost

If the scientific consensus behind global warming is crumbling, so, too, should the economically harmful policies that stem from it. When asked about the scientific consensus on climate change, Phil Jones, former climate-research director at the University of East Anglia, said, "I don't believe the vast majority of climate scientists think this. This is not my view. There is still much that needs to be undertaken to reduce uncertainties, not just for the future, but for the instrumental (and especially the paleoclimatic) past as well." If the vast majority of climatologists do not believe that the debate on climate change is over, politicians should not be pushing for greenhouse gas reduction policies that not only have significant economic costs, but will also deeply alter the business landscape of the United States.

Close Reading Questions

1. How did the business community initially respond to warnings about global warming? What does the business community now say about global warming? (Historical Trends)

2. According to Loris, why are consumers negatively affected by government-mandated energy programs?

3. How are some businesses planning for higher energy costs created by climate change policies?

Analytical Writing/Discussion

4. As Loris questions the validity of climate-change warnings, how do the phrases he uses to describe the science involved change and develop? What do you think this series of phrases reveals about Loris's argument?

5. Loris cites Ben Franklin on "people … [voting] themselves money" to promote free enterprise by businesses and oppose lobbying by special interests. To what degree do you think large corporations in energy or other economic sectors, such as medicine, agriculture, and national defense, should refrain from lobbying and engage in true competition? (Cultural Influences)

6. Loris states that Congress should focus on specific measures that create jobs and foster sensible energy policies. Which of the three suggestions by Loris do you believe are the most or least likely to occur, and why? (Multiple Perspectives)

Further Options

7. In James Atwater's article "A Household of Helpers," he notes that the post–World War II economy encouraged American families to purchase a variety of household appliances. In what ways would those energy-dependent purchases—and thus, the American economy—have been affected by what Loris calls "questionable science"?

8. As explained in Chapter 6 on Rhetoric, a Rogerian argument seeks compromise and consensus among disputants by seeking, first, common ground (see p. 110). Loris discusses several contradictory reports of the existence of global warming, including the 1975 *New York Times* article and the 2006 documentary. What aspects of climate change do these opposing sides agree upon? How might these areas of consensus affect the perspective of writers like Loris?

Freewrite 3: Becoming "No Impact Man"

The following is from the 2009 book No Impact Man by blogger and author Colin Beavan, who in 2006, decided to try to live without significantly impacting the environment. After reading this excerpt, freewrite on one of the questions below:

For one year, my wife, baby daughter, and I, while residing in the middle of New York City, attempted to live without making any net impact on the environment. Ultimately, this meant we did our best to

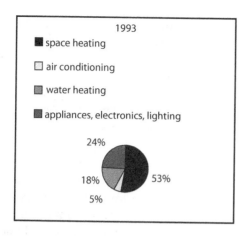
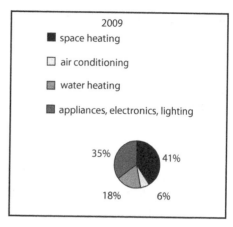

FIGURE 2 U.S. Household Energy Use

Source: U.S. Energy Information Administration, Residential Energy Consumption Survey.
Courtesy of U.S. Energy Information Administration

create no trash (so no take-out food), cause no carbon dioxide emissions (so no driving or flying), pour no toxins in the water (so no laundry detergent), buy no produce from distant lands (so no New Zealand fruit). Not to mention: no elevators, no subway, no products in packaging, no plastics, no air conditioning, no TV, no buying anything new ... I planned to write a book about what I was doing, and in the meantime I'd keep a blog on the Internet. I would breach the norms of our normally consumptive society inside a transparent bubble, into which, I imagined, a small number of blog readers and, later, a larger number of book readers would eventually get to look....

For all my grand ideas about saving the world and figuring out a happier way of life and changing people's minds and living according to my principles and—let's face it—being way overearnest, it turns out that becoming No Impact Man does not mean running into a phone booth and coming out transformed into some sort of eco-hero with my underwear stretched over my trousers. It doesn't, in fact, feel heroic at all. What it feels like, waking up at 6:00 a.m. and hoping to get just a little more shut-eye before your eighteen-month-old greets the day by jumping up and 'down on your head, is enforced martyrdom of the most trivial and ridiculous kind. Because day one starts with me standing in my skivvies, looking through the purple dawn light and into the bathroom closet at a roll of paper towel (which I've always preferred to flimsy tissues), really needing to blow my nose, and suddenly realizing I'm not supposed to use the paper towel.

Today is the first day of my environmental lifestyle experiment. The one that is supposed to make me feel like I'm not contributing to the planet's destruction. The one that I have decided to ease myself into by starting with the seemingly simple first step of not making trash. The one, in other words, that means that I should not use a paper towel to blow my nose. So what do I do now that I am officially No Impact Man? Now that I have chosen a nom de guerre that makes me sound like an environmental superhero? Now that I have begun living in a self-imposed blog, book, and documentary bubble where for the next

364 days, 23 hours, and 50 frigging minutes anyone can look and judge how well I'm living up to my public declaration about making no negative environmental impact? What would anybody do? I reach for the paper towel. I tear off a piece, blow my nose, realize what an awful mess I've gotten myself into with this project, start feeling depressed before I even wake up, turn around, and shuffle back to the bedroom. I discover Isabella standing in the crib, opening and closing her hands and saying, "Uppie, Daddy, uppie." Instantly my self-recrimination begins: I'm selfish. I blew my nose on a dead tree. And now God has punished me by making the sound of my honking wake up Isabella so. that she can jump up and down on my head....

No one can live without making *some* environmental impact. Even breathing creates carbon dioxide. You can turn your own lights out, but residing in a culture that provides street lighting means you still have an impact. The very fact that I had chosen to call this project No Impact went to the underlying point: I was naive and idealistic. I was not an environmentalist or an activist. I had no credentials. All I had was the knowledge that world events were freaking me out and the faith that we could do better. I knew nothing, at that stage, about environmental living or environmental choices or carbon offsets or green spin or the relative worth of individual versus political action or, for that matter, anything else relevant to the question of maintaining a safe habitat for humanity. Hell, I still didn't know the answer to the paper-or-plastic question. But that was the point. The idea was not to become an environmental expert and then apply what I'd learned. The idea was to start from scratch—with not a clue about how to deal with our planetary emergency—and stumble forward. To see what I could find out. To see how I evolved. What I learned in that moment in the yoga grocery store was that I would find no well-blazed path to follow. I would have to figure out my extreme eco-lifestyle for myself.

Lack of well-sourced information mixed with a surfeit of corporate PR resulted only in confusion. I'd hear of one study saying that the energy used washing ceramic cups damages the environment as much as the use of disposable plastic cups that won't degrade for a thousand years. I'd hear of another that said using hot water and detergent to wash cloth rags harms the planet more than cutting down trees to make paper towels. If I listened to the promulgated wisdom, it seemed that everything was as bad as everything else. The spin merchants seemed to want to convince me that trying to make any difference was futile. I might as well give up. Toss away another plastic cup. Forget about electric cars because of the deleterious effects of disposing of their worn-out batteries. Go on, guzzle, the spurious wisdom seemed to say. There *is* no right way to live lightly on the land....

[T]here didn't seem to be any reliable environmental-living road map to follow. The "science" did not seem to be so much about making things clear, but more about confusing us and wearing us down so that we just carried on the way things were. "Stasis through obfuscation," my wife, Michelle, called it.

I read an article in *The New York Times* about the corporate rush to label products "green." Companies were slapping environmentally friendly labels on everything from tree-killing chainsaws that used less gas to highly toxic bug sprays. "Greenwashing" abounded, and to obsessively try to figure out which products truly harmed the planet less seemed like a fast path to an ulcer.

Then I began to wonder: Instead of driving ourselves nuts trying to find a way through the maze of product spin, might it not be simpler just to climb out of the maze? The trick to environmental living might not be in choosing *different* products. Instead—at least for profligate citizens of the United States and Western Europe—it might partly be about choosing *fewer* products. It might not just be about using different resources. It might be about using *fewer* resources.

As the ancient Chinese *Tao Te Ching* says, "The man who knows that enough is enough will always have enough."

After reading about Beavan's plans to reduce his family's impact on the environment, freewrite or discuss one or more the following questions:

- What are two or three reasons that Beavan does not feel like "some sort of eco-hero?" Which of the concerns about his project do you find the least or most convincing and why?

- Why does Beavan's No Impact project make you feel optimistic or pessimistic about being environmentally responsible?

- How do you think science experts, product manufacturers, and/or the media have confused, rather than clarified, methods for living an environmentally sustainable life?

Final Assignment 1: Prioritizing Energy

The American love affair with consumption has soured with rising energy costs and their environmental implications. Black suggests that the post–World War II years were the beginning of an energy-dependent lifestyle for millions of Americans. That lifestyle was at the center of Americans' need for oil during the 1973 oil embargo and continues today. Although there is not always agreement about energy-related topics—as is the case with Loris and Orr, who have opposing views on the presence of climate change—scientists, environmentalists, researchers, and corporate leaders agree that it is important to continue the debates about energy use.

Essay Question

Given the rate of energy consumption in the United States, in what ways do you think that the perspectives of government, business, consumers, and science can and/or cannot be reconciled in debates about energy usage? Your answer should include a discussion of American energy usage in the twentieth and twenty-first centuries.

Write a formal and extended essay to answer this question. Be sure to include specific references and direct quotations from several readings of this chapter (see Chapter 7 on Academic Honesty and Its Conventions on quoting and citing properly). Be sure to not only support your informed perspective but also anticipate and answer the possible objections of those who do not already agree with you. Your task is to assert your opinion and persuade others to consider it carefully.

Freewrite 4: Assignment Analysis

Before you start to answer this complex question, analyze its parts. Reread the question above and underline several phrases that represent key parts of the larger answer you will be developing. Then pick two or three of these phrases and fastwrite your immediate impressions: What do you think right now? Then, pause to look for connections, contradictions, and omissions within your first response: What else do you want to discuss, what else do you want to add, and/or what order of your ideas is developing?

Finally, consider the audience of your essay: Who does not agree with you already, and why might they disagree?

Reading Review

Once you have sketched some of your initial ideas, review some of the readings to find specific details and persuasive evidence to support, enrich, and possibly complicate your response. Here are some readings and post-reading questions that you may want to consider:

1. Black, Close Reading Question 3
2. Figure 1
3. Atwater, Analytical Writing/Discussion Question 5
4. Loewy, Close Reading Question 2
5. Freewrite 2
6. Loris, Close Reading Question 2
7. Loris, Analytical Writing/Discussion Question 6
8. Orr, Close Reading Question 2

Feel free to include other readings and post-reading questions. You also may want to review the suggestions for writing persuasively in Chapter 6 on Rhetoric and Arguments as well as practice the peer response described in Chapter 4 on the Writing Process.

Final Assignment 2: Lessons about Sustainability

The quest to live a sustainable life in the United States can be difficult, especially because the United States has a history of producing more goods than any other nation on earth. Thomas Friedman offered a reality check of sorts in his reflection on America's addiction to cars and oil knowing that it can be painful to change habits, even if the environment would be better for it. Pollan and Beavan are intrigued by the idea of living a sustainable life, yet even Pollan doubts that the efforts of one person can make the planet a greener place.

Essay Question

To what degree do you think that the possibility of living a sustainable lifestyle is complicated by the perspective that sustainable efforts are only a trend and not a serious commitment on the part of some Americans? Your answer should include a discussion of the sustainability efforts in the United States during the second half of the twentieth century and the beginning of the twenty-first century.

Write a formal and extended essay to answer this question. Be sure to include specific references and direct quotations from several readings of this chapter (see Chapter 6 on Academic Honesty and Its Conventions on quoting and citing properly). Be sure to not only support your informed perspective but also anticipate and answer the possible objections of those who do not already agree with you. Your task is to assert your opinion and persuade others to consider it carefully.

Freewrite 5: Assignment Analysis

Before you start to answer this complex question, analyze its parts. Reread the question above and underline several phrases that represent key parts of the larger answer you will be developing. Then pick two or three of these phrases and fastwrite your immediate impressions: What do you think right now? Then, pause to look for connections, contradictions, and omissions within your first response: What else do you want to discuss, what else do you want to add, and/or what order of your ideas is developing? Finally, consider the audience of your essay: Who does not agree with you already, and why might they disagree?

Reading Review

Once you have sketched some of your initial ideas, review some of the readings to find specific details and persuasive evidence to support, enrich, and possibly complicate your response. Here are some readings and post-reading questions that you may want to consider:

1. Black, Analytical Writing/Discussion Question 5
2. Loewy, Analytical Writing/Discussion Question 6
3. Freewrite 2
4. Orr, Close Reading Question 3
5. Pollan, Close Reading Question 1
6. Pollan, Analytical Writing/Discussion Question 5
7. Freewrite 3
8. Figure 2

Feel free to include other readings and post-reading questions. You also may want to review the suggestions for writing persuasively in Chapter 6 on Rhetoric and Arguments as well as practice the peer response described in Chapter 4 on the Writing Process.

Additional Source Suggestions

In the e-supplement of this textbook, there are several sources that will help you deepen your understanding of energy and sustainability and strengthen your final assignment. These sources include videos as well as readings, and they present multiple perspectives, historical trends, and cultural influences on sources of energy and sustainability efforts. To access these materials, see the code on the inside front cover of this textbook, which will lead you to the website for additional sources.

Literacy and Technology

CHAPTER 14

There is no Frigate like a Book/To Take us Lands Away…
How frugal is the Chariot/That bears the Human soul.

—Emily Dickinson (1873)

Describing computer technology as either beneficial or detrimental, either good or bad … [limits] our understanding…. With such as simple [dichotomous] representation, … [we] are encouraged to take a side—for or against technology—rather than to understand the complex ways in which technology has become linked with our conception of literacy.

—Cynthia Selfe (1999)

Between 1982 and 2002, the percentage of Americans who read literature declined not only in every age group but in every generation…. We are reading less as we age, and we are reading less than people who were our age ten or twenty years ago…. [S]ome sociologists speculate that the reading books for pleasure will one day be the province of a special "reading class," much as it was before the arrival of mass literacy in the second half of the nineteenth century.

—Caleb Crain (2007)

Young people write far more than any generation before them. That's because so much socializing takes place online, and it almost always involves text…. Students [are] remarkably adept at … assessing their audience and adapting their tone and technique to best get their point across.

—Clive Owens (2009)

Introduction

When most of us consider literacy *and* technology, we probably think of computers first. Computers are a primary link between our ability to read and write and our use of technology. Computers, of course, now include an array of associated technologies, such as the Internet, websites, e-readers, tablets, word processing, spell check, Facebook, and Twitter. You may be able to add more examples to this list, or some items may not be very familiar to you. Perhaps you have heard of them, but you have never tried them. You may even be wary of one or two of these literacy technologies. They may strike you as silly or strange.

It may be hard to imagine that many of the older literacy technologies we now take for granted once struck some in the past as too new, too strange. For instance, in the nineteenth century, some teachers worried that attaching erasers to the then new, mass-produced pencils would ruin students' handwriting. For if students could eliminate their penmanship errors with a quick rub of an eraser, how would they ever learn to write neatly? Now very few people consider the eraser to be a dangerous development or even to be a literacy technology.

The history of literacy includes many technological developments that we never stop to consider:

- Clay tablets
- Papyrus paper
- Wood pulp paper
- Quill pens and inkwells
- The printing press
- The fountain pen
- The pencil
- The typewriter
- Carbon copy paper
- The disposable plastic pen
- The "Xerox" copier

In their time, some of these developments were just as controversial as a pencil with an eraser. For example, in 1874, Samuel Clemens (Mark Twain) wrote that he was struggling "to get the hang of this new fangled writing machine," but he marveled, that it "piles an awful stack of words on one page … [without scattering] ink blots around." This now obsolete technology altered the office work of nineteenth-century companies because they could keep detailed records much more easily (especially with the additional invention of carbon paper). Typewriters also allowed authors like Clemens to draft and deliver their manuscripts with greater efficiency. But as one critic of new literacy technologies named Nicholas Carr reports, the technology of the typewriter may also have affected not only how a text was written but also what was written. For example, another early user of the typewriter, the German writer Frederick Nietzsche, felt that his writing became more direct and more compact when he changed from handwriting to typing. Now, Carr poses a similar question about computer technologies: Does how we read affect what we can (and cannot) comprehend?

Those who are very comfortable with the latest literacy technologies may be tempted to dismiss those critics as elders unable to embrace the new and afraid of change. However, even one of the inventors of the virtual reality of the Internet, Jaron Lanier, now worries that the social networks of the more interactive Web 2.0 promote shallow thinking and stifle individual creativity. This chapter consists of current readings on literacy and technology, such as Nick Bilton's defense of digital literacy, and historical ones like William Powers' analysis of centuries-old paper. These texts, along with reading questions, freewriting activities, and visual elements, are designed to develop the reading and writing abilities required for academic study. After each reading, you will find a set of questions that are divided into Close Reading Questions, Analytical Writing/Discussion, and Further Options. Some questions involve the same investigation of multiple perspectives, cultural influences, and historical trends that were introduced in Chapters 1 and 2. Answering some and discussing more of the post-reading questions will prepare you to complete the final assignment options. These final writing assignments will ask you to assert your own, more informed perspective on this topic. This chapter asks: **What do you think are the effects of computer technologies on our literacy practices?**

Freewrite 1: Initial Impressions

Before you read the conflicting and often vehement opinions of the writers in the rest of this chapter, freewrite to explore your own thoughts and experiences. Try answering some of the following questions:

- How often do you rely on the computer and its associated technologies, such as web pages and word processing, when you read and write?

- What are some of your most and least favorite various ways to use new media technologies when you read and write?

- When and why do you rely on paper and print sources when you write and read?

- What effects, if any, do you think new technologies have had on your literacy? In other words, how might your reading and writing practices be different if you did not use these newer technologies?

THE GUTENBERG ELEGIES: THE FATE OF READING IN AN ELECTRONIC AGE

by Sven Birkerts

As computers became household items during the 1980s and the Internet became widely used in the 1990s, concerns about their effect on our reading practices developed. Sven Birkerts captured this cautious spirit in his highly regarded book *The Gutenberg Elegies: The Fate of Reading in an Electronic Age.* As an essayist, a professor, and a literary critic, Birkerts has continued to express the joys of literature as well as his concerns about our reading habits in such works as *Reading Life: Books for the Ages* (2007) and "Resisting the Kindle" (2009). This excerpt is taken from *The Gutenberg Elegies,* published in 1994.

In the fall of 1992, I taught a course called "The American Short Story" to undergraduates at a local college. I assembled a set of readings that I thought would appeal to the tastes of the average undergraduate and felt relatively confident. We would begin with Washington Irving, then move on quickly to Hawthorne, Poe, James, and Jewett, before connecting with the progressively more accessible works of our century. I had expected that my students would enjoy "The Legend of Sleepy Hollow," be amused by its caricatures and ghost-story element. Nothing of the kind. Without exception they found the story over long, verbose, a chore. I wrote their reactions off to the fact that it was the first assignment and that most students would not have hit their reading stride yet. When we got to Hawthorne and Poe, I had the illusion that things were going better.

But then came Henry James' "Brooksmith" and I was completely derailed. I began the class, as I always do, by soliciting casual responses of the "I liked it" and "I hated it" sort. My students could barely muster the energy for a thumbs-up-or-down. It was as though some pneumatic pump had sucked out the last dregs of their spirits. "Bad day, huh?" I ventured. Persistent questioning revealed that it was the reading that had undone them. But why? What was the problem? I had to get to the bottom of their stupefaction before this relatively—I thought—available tale.

I asked: Was it a difficulty with the language, the style of writing? Nods all around. Well, let's be more specific. Was it vocabulary, sentence length, syntax? "Yeah, sort of," said one student, "but it was more just the whole thing." Hmmmmm. Well then, I said, we should consider this. I questioned whether they understood the basic plot. Sure, they said. A butler's master dies and the butler can't find another place as good. He loses one job after another—usually because he quits—then falls into despair and disappears, probably to end it all. "You don't find this moving?" One or two students conceded the pathos of the situation, but then the complaints resurfaced, with the original complainer chiming in again that it was not the story so much as "the whole thing."

The whole thing. What whole thing? My tone must have reflected my agitation, my impatience with their imprecision. But then, after endless going around, it stood revealed: These students were entirely defeated by James's prose—the medium of it—as well as by the assumptions that underlie it. It was not the vocabulary, for they could make out most of the words; and not altogether the syntax, although they admitted to discomfort, the occasional abandoned sentences. What they really could not abide was what the vocabulary, the syntax, the ironic indirection, and so forth, were communicating. *They didn't get it,* and their not getting it angered them, and they expressed their anger by drawing around themselves a cowl of ill-tempered apathy. Students whom I knew to be quick and resourceful in other situations suddenly retreated into glum illiteracy. "I dunno," said the spokesman. "the who thing just bugged me—I couldn't get into it."

Disastrous though the class had been, I drove home in an excited mood. What had happened, I started to realize, was that I had encountered a conceptual ledge, one that may mark a break in historical continuity. This was more than just a bad class—it was a corroboration of something I had been on the verge of grasping for years. You could have drawn a lightbulb over my head and turned it on.

What is this ledge, and what does it have to do with the topic I have embarked upon? To answer the second question: Everything. As I wrote before: the world we have known, the world of our myths and references and shared assumptions, is being changed by powerful forces. We are living in the midst of a momentous paradigm shift. My classroom experience, which in fact represents hundreds of classroom experiences, can be approached diagnostically.

This is not a simple case of students versus Henry James. We are not concerned with an isolated clash of sensibilities, his and theirs. Rather we are standing in one spot along a ledge—or, better, a fault line—dividing one order from another. In place of James we could as easily put Joyce or Woolf or Shakespeare or Ralph Ellison. It would be the same. The point is that the collective experience of these students, most of whom were born in the early 1970s, has rendered a vast portion of our cultural heritage utterly alien. *That* is the breaking point: it describes where their understandings and aptitudes give out. What is at issue is not diction, not syntax, but everything that diction and syntax serve. Which is to say, an entire system of beliefs, values, and cultural aspirations.

In Henry James are distilled many of the elements I would discuss. He is inward and subtle, a master of ironies and indirections; his work manifests a care for the range of moral distinctions. And one cannot "get" him without paying heed to the twist and turn of the language. James's world, and the dramas that take place in that world, are predicated on the idea of individuals in an organic relationship with their societies. In his universe, each one of those individuals are still surrounded by an aura of importance; their actions and decisions are felt to count for something.

I know that the society of James's day was also repressive to many, and was, further, invested in certain now-discredited assumptions of empire. I am not going to argue for its return, certainly not in that form. But this was not the point, at least not in the discussions I pursued with my students. For we did, after our disastrous James session, begin to question not only our various readings, but also the reading act itself and their relation to it. And what emerged was this: that they were not, with a few exceptions, readers—never had been; that they had always occupied themselves with music, TV, and videos; that they had difficulty slowing down enough to concentrate on prose of any density; that they had problems with what they thought of as archaic diction, with allusions, with vocabulary that seemed "pretentious"; that they were especially uncomfortable with indirect or interior passages, indeed with any deviations from straight plot; and that they were put off by ironic tone because it flaunted superiority and made them feel that they were missing something. The list is partial.

All of this confirmed my longstanding suspicion that, having grown up in an electronic culture, my students would naturally exhibit certain aptitudes and lack others. But the implications, as I began to realize, were rather staggering, especially if one thinks of this not as a temporary generational disability, but rather a permanent turn. If this were true of my twenty-five undergraduates, I reasoned, many of them from relatively advantaged backgrounds, then it was probably true for most of their generation. And not only theirs, but for generations on either side of them as well. What this meant was not, narrowly, that a large sector of our population would not be able to enjoy certain works of literature, but that a much more serious situation was developing. For, in fact, our entire collective subjective history—the soul of our societal body—is encoded in print. Is encoded, and has for countless generations been passed along by way of the word, mainly through books. I'm not talking about facts and information here, but the somewhat more elusive soft data, the expressions that tell us who we are and who we have been, that are the record of individuals living in different epochs—that are, in effect, the cumulative speculations of the species. If a person turns from print—finding it too slow, too hard, irrelevant to the excitements of the present—then what happens to that person's sense of culture and continuity?

These issues are too large for mere analysis; they are over-determined. There is no way to fish one strand and think it through. Yet think we must, even if we have to be clumsy and obvious at times. We are living in a society and culture that is in dissolution. Pack this paragraph with your headlines about crime, eroded values, educational decline, what have you. There are many causes, many explanations. But behind them all, vague and menacing, is this recognition: that the understandings and assumptions that were formerly operative in society no longer feel valid. Things have shifted; they keep shifting. We all feel a desire for connection, for meaning, but we don't seem to know what to connect with what, and we are utterly at sea about our places as individuals in the world at large. The maps no longer describe the terrain we inhabit. There is no clear path to the future. We trust that the species will blunder on, and we don't know where to. We feel imprisoned in a momentum that is not of our own making.

I am not about to suggest that all of this comes of not reading Henry James. But I will say that of all this comes not being *able* to read James or any other emissary from that recent but rapidly vanishing world.

Our historically sudden transition into the electronic culture has thrust us into a place of unknowing. We have been stripped not only of familiar habits and ways, but of familiar points of moral and psychological reference. Looking at our society, we see no real leaders, no real figures of wisdom. Not a brave new world at all, but a fearful one.

Close Reading Questions

1. Beyond representing an admittedly "disastrous" class, what larger concerns does Birkerts think this classroom example represents? In other words, what do you think is the thesis of this reading?

2. Using annotated comments or double-entry notes (for more, see pp. 79–80 in Chapter 3 on Reading), what are two or three assertions by Birkerts with which you strongly agree or disagree?

3. Birkerts concludes this excerpt with a claim for which he provides little evidence. What examples can you provide for his conclusion that we live in a "fearful" world, and how can you connect these supports to his concern about the reading habits of his students?

Analytical Writing/Discussion

4. Birkerts admits that his students, who grew up in an electronic culture of televisions and computers, "exhibit certain aptitudes and lack others." What abilities does he think they specifically lack, and what positive aptitudes do you think they might possess? (Multiple Perspectives)

5. As an excerpt from the first chapter of Birkerts' book, this reading includes several strong assertions about major cultural changes. Pick one of Birkerts' statements about these changes, and why do you think this "permanent turn" is or is not underway? (Cultural Influences)

6. In Chapter 3 on Reading, a brief history of literacy standards is presented (see p. 73). How do you think that history, and the graph of rising standards in particular, can be used to support or challenge Birkerts? (Historical Trends)

Further Options

7. In Chapter 6 on Rhetoric, the three appeals by ethos (character), pathos (emotions), and logos (reason) are explained. Which of these three appeals do you think Birkerts uses most or least effectively, and why?

8. Writing in 1994, Birkerts could not consider the increased access to books, and great literature in particular, created by e-reading devices, such as the Kindle. However, later in 2009, he wrote in opposition of e-readers, fearing the "page-to-screen transfer." Read his essay titled "Resisting the Kindle" (*The Atlantic* 3/2/09) found in the e-supplement of this chapter. Why do you find his more recent argument to be convincing or not?

FROM PENCILS TO PIXELS: THE STAGES OF LITERACY TECHNOLOGY

by Dennis Baron

As a professor who has studied digital technologies and regularly writes a blog on this topic, Baron is a highly regarded expert in this field. As his title suggests, Baron traces the development of such literacy technologies as pencils and the pixel-filled screens of computer monitors. Baron has expanded this article from 2000 into a book titled *A Better Pencil: Readers, Writers, and the Digital Revolution* (2009).

The computer, the latest development in writing technology, promises, or threatens, to change literacy practices for better or worse, depending on your point of view. For many of us, the computer revolution came long ago, and it has left its mark on the way we do things with words. We take word processing as a given. We don't have typewriters in our offices anymore....

I will not join in the hyperbole of predictions about what the computer will or will not do for literacy, though I will be the first to praise computers, to acknowledge the importance of the computer in the last fifteen years of my own career as a writer and to predict that in the future the computer will be put to communications uses we cannot now even begin to imagine....

The Stages of Literacy Technologies

Each new literacy technology begins with a restricted communications function and is available only to a small number of initiates. Because of the high cost of the technology and general ignorance about it, practitioners keep it to themselves at first—either on purpose or because nobody else has any use for it—and then, gradually, they begin to mediate the technology for the general public. The technology expands beyond this "priestly" class when it is adapted to familiar functions often associated with an older, accepted form of communication. As costs decrease and the technology becomes better able to mimic more ordinary or familiar communications, a new literacy spreads across a population. Only then does the technology come into its own, no longer imitating the previous forms given us by the earlier communications technology but creating new forms and new possibilities for communication.... [Most literacy] technologies, including writing itself, were initially met with suspicion as well as enthusiasm.

The pencil may be old, but like the computer today ... , it is an indisputable example of a communications technology.... [As Bill Henderson explains, Henry David] Thoreau's father founded "the first quality pencil [factory] in America." In Thoreau's day, a good pencil was hard to find, and until Thoreau's father and uncle began making pencils in the New World, the best ones were imported from Europe. The family fortune was built on the earnings of the Thoreau Pencil Company, and Thoreau not only supported his sojourn at Walden Pond and his trip to the Maine woods with pencil profits, he himself perfected some of the techniques of pencil-making that made Thoreau pencils so desirable.

The pencil may seem a simple device in contrast to the computer, but although it has fewer parts, it too is an advanced technology. The engineer Henry Petroski (1990) portrays the development of the wood-cased pencil as a paradigm of the engineering process, hinging on the solution of two essential problems: finding the correct blend of graphite and clay so that the "lead" is not too soft or too brittle; and getting the lead into the cedar wood case so that it doesn't break when the point is sharpened or when pressure is applied during use. Pencil technologies involve advanced design techniques, the preparation and purification of graphite, the mixing of graphite with various clays, the baking and curing of the lead mixture, its extrusion into leads, and the preparation and finishing of the wood casings. Petroski observes that pencil-making also involves a knowledge of dyes, shellacs, resins, clamps, solvents, paints, woods, rubber, glue, printing ink, waxes, lacquer, cotton, drying equipment, impregnating processes, high-temperature furnaces, abrasives, and mixing (Petroski, 12). These are no simple matters. A hobbyist cannot decide to make a wood-cased pencil at home and go out to the craft shop for a set of instructions. Pencil-making processes were from the outset proprietary secrets as closely guarded as any Macintosh code.

The development of the pencil is also a paradigm of the development of literacy. In the two hundred fifty years between its invention, in the 1560s, and its perfection at John Thoreau and Company, as well as in the factories of Conte in France, and Staedtler and Faber in Germany, the humble wood pencil underwent several changes in form, greatly expanded its functions, and developed from a curiosity of use to cabinet-makers, artists, and note-takers into a tool so universally employed for writing that we seldom give it any thought.

The Technology of Writing

Of course the first writing technology was writing itself. Just like … the computer, writing itself was once an innovation strongly resisted by traditionalists because it was unnatural and untrustworthy. Plato was one leading thinker who spoke out strongly against writing, fearing that it would weaken our memories. Pessimistic complaints about new literacy technologies, like those made by Plato, by Bill Henderson, and by Henderson's idol, Henry David Thoreau, are balanced by inflated predictions of how technologies will change our lives for the better. According to one school of anthropology, the invention of writing triggered a cognitive revolution in human development (for a critique of this so-called Great Divide theory of writing, see Street 1984). Historians of print are fond of pointing to the invention of the printing press in Europe as the second great cognitive revolution (Eisenstein 1979). The spread of electric power, the invention of radio, and later television, all promised similar bio-cultural progress. Now, the influence of computers on more and more aspects of our existence has led futurologists to proclaim that another technological threshold is at hand. Computer gurus offer us a brave new world of communications where we will experience cognitive changes of a magnitude never before known. Of course, [some] … think otherwise.

Both the supporters and the critics of new communication technologies like to compare them to the good, or bad, old days. Jay Bolter disparages the typewriter as nothing more than a machine for duplicating text, and as such, he argues, it has not changed writing at all. In contrast, Bolter characterizes the computer as offering a paradigm shift not seen since the invention of the printing press, or for that matter, since the invention of writing itself. But when the typewriter first began to sweep across America's offices, it too promised to change writing radically, in ways never before imagined. So threatening was the typewriter to the traditional literacies that in 1938 the *New York Times* editorialized against the machine that depersonalized writing, usurping the place of "writing with one's own hand."

The development of writing itself illustrates the stages of technological spread. We normally assume that writing was invented to transcribe speech, but that is not strictly correct. The earliest Sumerian inscriptions, dating from ca. 3500 BCE, record not conversations, incantations, or other sorts of oral utterances, but land sales, business transactions, and tax accounts (Crystal 1987). Clay tokens bearing similar marks appear for several thousand years before these first inscriptions. It is often difficult to tell when we are dealing with writing and when with art (the recent discovery of 10,000-year-old stone carvings in Syria has been touted as a possible missing link in the art-to-writing chain), but the tokens seem to have been used as a system of accounting from at least the 9th millennium BCE [9000 BCE]. They are often regarded as the first examples of writing, and it is clear that they are only distantly related to actual speech.... So far as we know, writing itself begins not as speech transcription but as a relatively restricted and obscure record-keeping shorthand.

As innovative uses for the literacy technology are tried out, practitioners may also adapt it to older, more familiar forms in order to gain acceptance from a wider group. Although writing began as a tool of the bean counters, it eventually added a second, magical/religious function, also restricted and obscure as a tool of priests. For writing to spread into a more general population in the ancient world, it had first to gain acceptance by approximating spoken language. Once writers—in a more "modern" sense of the word—discovered what writing could do, there was no turning back.... Of course writing never spread very greatly in the ancient world. William Harris (1989) argues convincingly that no more than 10 percent of the classical Greek or Roman populations could have been literate. One reason for this must be that writing technology remained both cumbersome and expensive: writing instruments, paints, and inks had to be handmade, and writing surfaces like clay tablets, wax tablets, and papyrus had to be laboriously prepared. Writing therefore remained exclusive, until cheap paper became available, and the printing press made mass production of written texts more affordable and less labor-intensive....

The Pencil as Technology

Just as writing was not designed initially as a way of recording speech, the pencil was not invented to be a writing device. The ancient lead-pointed stylus was used to scribe lines—the lead made a faint pencil-like mark on a surface, suitable for marking off measurements but not for writing. The modern pencil, which holds not lead but a piece of graphite encased in a wooden handle, doesn't come on the scene until the 1560s....

The sixteenth-century pencil consists of a piece of graphite snapped or shaved from a larger block, then fastened to a handle for ease of use. The first pencils were made by joiners, woodworkers specializing in making furniture, to scribe measurements in wood. Unlike the traditional metal-pointed scribing tools, pencils didn't leave a permanent dent in the wood. By the time Gesner observed the pencil, it had been adopted as a tool by note-takers, natural scientists, or others who needed to write, sketch, or take measurements in the field. Carrying pens and ink pots outdoors was cumbersome. Early pencils had knobs at one end so that they could be fastened with string or chain to a notebook, creating the precursor to the laptop computer.

Pencils were also of use to artists. In fact the word pencil means "little tail" and refers not only to the modern wood-cased pencil but to the artist's brush. Ink and paint are difficult to erase: they must be scraped off a surface with a knife or painted over. But graphite pencil marks were more easily erased by using bread crumbs, and of course later by erasers made of rubber—in fact the eraser substance (caoutchouc, the milky juice of tropical plants such as ficus) was called *rubber* because it was used to rub out pencil marks....

Thoreau set about to improve his father's pencil. According to Petroski, Thoreau began his research in the Harvard Library. But then, as now, there was little written on pencil manufacture. Somehow, Thoreau learned to grind graphite more finely than had been done before and to mix it with clay in just the right proportion…. [H]is improvements on the pencil-making process, combined with the high import duty imposed on British pencils after the War of 1812, led to great demand for Thoreau pencils…. His pencils sold for seventy-five cents a dozen, higher than other brands….

The Computer and the Pattern of Literacy Technology

Writing was not initially speech transcription, and pencils were first made for woodworkers, not writers. Similarly, the mainframe computer when it was introduced was intended to perform numerical calculations too tedious or complex to do by hand. Personal computers were not initially meant for word-processing either, though that has since become one of their primary functions.

Mainframe line editors were so cumbersome that even computer programmers preferred to write their code with pencil and paper. Computer operators actually scorned the thought of using their powerful number-crunchers to process mere words. Those who braved the clumsy technology to type text were condemned to using a system that seemed diabolically designed to slow a writer down well below anything that could be done on an IBM [electric typewriter] or even with a pencil….

Early word-processing software for personal computers did little to improve the situation. At last, in the early 1980s, programs like WordStar began to produce text that looked more like the typing that many writers had become used to. Even so, writers had to put up with screens cluttered with formatting characters…. [P]aragraphs had to be reformatted every time they were revised. Furthermore, printed versions of text seldom matched what was on the computer screen, turning page design into a laborious trial-and-error session. Adding to the writer's problems was the fact that the screen itself looked nothing like the piece of paper the text would ultimately be printed on. The first PC screens were grayish-black with green phosphor letters, displaying considerably less than a full page of text…. Today we expect displays not only with black on white, just like real paper, and high resolution text characters, but also with color, which takes us a step beyond what we could do with ordinary typing paper.

If the initial technical obstacles to word processing on a PC weren't enough to keep writers away from the new technology, they still had to come up with the requisite $5,000 or more … for an entry-level personal computer. Only die-hards and visionaries considered computer word processing worth pursuing, and even they held on to their [electric typewriters] and their Bic [pens] just in case…. The next generation of word processors gave us WYSIWYG: "what you see is what you get" and that helped less-adventurous writers make the jump to computers. Only when Macintosh and Windows operating systems allowed users to create on-screen documents that looked and felt like the old, familiar documents they were used to creating on electric typewriters did word-processing really become popular. At the same time, start-up costs decreased significantly and with new, affordable hardware, computer writing technology quickly moved from the imitation of typing to the inclusion of graphics.

Of course that, too, was not an innovation in text production. We've been pasting up text and graphics for ages. The decorated medieval charters of eleventh-century England are a perfect parallel to our computerized graphics a millennium later. But just as writing in the middle ages was able to move beyond earlier limitations, computer word processing has now moved beyond the texts made possible by earlier technologies by adding not just graphics, but animation, video, and sound to documents. In addition, Hypertext and HTML allow us to create links between documents or paths within them, both of which offer restructured alternatives to linear reading….

Conclusion

As the old technologies become automatic and invisible, we find ourselves more concerned with fighting or embracing what's new. Ten years ago math teachers worried that if students were allowed to use calculators, they wouldn't learn their arithmetic tables. Regardless of the value parents and teachers still place on knowing math facts, calculators are now indispensable in math class. When we began to use computers in university writing classes, instructors didn't tell students about the spell-check programs on their word processors, fearing the students would forget how to spell. The hackers found the spelling checkers anyway, and now teachers complain if their students don't run the spell check before they turn their papers in.

Even the pencil itself didn't escape the wrath of educators. One of the major technological advances in pencil-making occurred in the early twentieth century, when manufacturers learned to attach rubber tips to inexpensive wood pencils by means of a brass clamp. But American schools allowed no crossing out. Teachers preferred pencils without erasers, arguing that students would do better, more premeditated work if they didn't have the option of revising. The students won this one, too: eraserless pencils are now extremely rare. Artists use them, because artists need special erasers in their work; golfers use pencils without erasers, too, perhaps to keep themselves honest. As for the no-crossing-out rule, writing teachers now routinely warn students that writers never get it right the first time, and we expect them to revise their work endlessly until it is polished to perfection.

The computer has indeed changed the ways some of us do things with words, and the rapid changes in technological development suggest that it will continue to do so in ways we cannot yet foresee.... [R]esearchers tend to look at the cutting edge when they examine how technology affects literacy. But technology has a trailing edge as well as a down side, and studying how computers are put to use raises serious issues in the politics of work and the mechanisms of social control. Andrew Sledd pessimistically views the computer as actually reducing the amount of literacy needed for the low end of the workplace: "As for ordinary kids, they will get jobs ... dragging computerized Cheerios boxes across computerized check-out counters."

Despite Sledd's legitimate fear that in the information age computers will increase the gap between active text production and routine, alienating, assembly-line text processing, in the United States we live in an environment that is increasingly surrounded by text.... The simplest one-word Web search returns pages of documents, which themselves link to the expanding universe of text in cyberspace....

We have a way of getting so used to writing technologies that we come to think of them as natural rather than technological. We assume that pencils are a natural way to write because they are old—or at least because we have come to think of them as being old.... Whether the computer will one day be as taken-for-granted as the pencil is an intriguing question. One thing is clear: were Thoreau alive today he would not be writing with a pencil of his own manufacture.... More likely, he would be keyboarding his complaints about the information superhighway on a personal computer that he assembled from spare parts in his garage.

References

Crystal, David. 1987. *The Cambridge Encyclopedia of Language*. Cambridge: Cambridge Univ. Press, p. 196.
Eisenstein, Elizabeth L. 1979. *The Printing Press as an Agent of Change*. Cambridge: Cambridge Univ. Press.
Harris, William V. 1989. *Ancient Literacy*. Cambridge: Harvard Univ. Press.
Henderson, Bill. 1994. "No E-Mail from Walden." *New York Times* (March 16), p. A15.

Petroski, Henry. 1990. *The Pencil: A History of Design and Circumstance*. New York: Alfred A. Knopf.
Sledd, Andrew. 1988. Readin' not Riotin': The Politics of Literacy. *College English* 50: 495–507.
Street, Brian V. 1984. *Literacy in Theory and Practice*. Cambridge: Cambridge Univ. Press.

Close Reading Questions

1. Baron explains that we tend to become "so used to writing technologies that we come to think of them as natural." What is one detail about writing itself and another on the pencil that surprised you?

2. To understand the pencil as a writing technology, consider its manufacture. According to Baron, what are several of the distinct steps required in the making of a pencil?

3. Neither the pencil nor the computer are being used now primarily for their original purpose. What were the original purposes of the pencil and the computer? Why do you think the later, innovative use led to the widespread acceptance of each technology? (Historical Trends)

Analytical Writing/Discussion

4. Pick a quotation from Baron that either describes or contradicts your experiences with the computer. Then present this quotation using a signal phrase, such as "According to Dennis Baron, ..." Cite it properly and elaborate on its meaning (see pp. 120 of Chapter 7 for more on Quotations and Citation). In what ways does this quotation describe or contradict your experiences?

5. Each new literacy technology is considered by its critics to be a negative influence. What do you think were some of the most or least significant criticisms of writing and later the computer? Why do you think each technology has been met with criticism from some skeptics? (Cultural Influences)

6. How can you use the pattern of technological resistance to support or oppose the detractors of computers and the Internet, such as Bauerlein? (Multiple Perspectives)

Further Options

7. In an argument, the writer's character and tone are crucial to his or her ability to be persuasive (see pp. 103 on "ethos" in Chapter 6). In what ways, if any, do you think the tone of the arguments by Baron and Bauerlein differs? Why do you think (or not) that one of these arguments is more persuasive?

8. Baron, along with many others concerned about computers, worry that a "digital divide" exists between those that have easy access to computers and those that do not. Using some of the strategies presented in Chapter 8, research the development and distribution of inexpensive computers to less privileged people both in the United States and other countries. To what degree do you think the digital divide can and should be overcome by further technological and political developments?

FIGURE 1   The Technological Advances of Paper and Pencil

THE PERSISTENCE OF PAPER

by William Powers

As part of the Discussion Paper Series at Harvard University, William Powers wrote an extended essay of 75 pages titled "Hamlet's Blackberry: Why Paper Is Eternal." The essay from 2007 was received so well that Powers, a media critic for the *National Journal*, has written a related book: *Hamlet's BlackBerry: A Practical Philosophy for Building a Good Life in the Digital Age* (2010). In the following excerpt from the original essay, Powers helps his audience take a second look at paper, a literacy technology that most of us never stop to consider, and he argues that some of the apparent limitations of paper actually constitute its strengths for readers.

The condition of American journalism in the first decade of the twenty-first century can be expressed in a single unhappy word: crisis. Whether it's a plagiarism scandal at a leading newspaper, the fall from grace of a network anchorman, or a reporter behind bars, the news about the news seems to be one emergency after another. But the crisis that has the greatest potential to undermine what the craft does best is a quiet one that rarely draws the big headlines: the crisis of paper. Paper's long career as a medium of human communication, and in particular as a purveyor of news, may be ending....

There is a sense in the culture, inchoate but unmistakable, that all print media, including magazines and books, are careening toward obsolescence. This is hardly a new idea. Since the advent of the computer in the mid-twentieth century, futurists have been foretelling the death of paper-based communication.

So far the obituaries have all been wrong or at least premature. Time and again, advances in computer technology that were supposed to make hard-copy media obsolete failed to do so. Paper lived on.

But with the rise of the Internet, the popularity of online media outlets, and the proliferation of devices to conveniently access those outlets—personal computers, cell phones, personal digital assistants, e-books, etc.—a paperless media world often seems not just possible or likely but inevitable. After all, in countless other ways, paper already has either surrendered to the newer media or is in rapid retreat. Most financial transactions ... can now be done online. The personal letter, which handily survived the advent of the telephone, has been largely done in by email. Even libraries, those seeming bastions of paper culture, are conspirators in paper's demise. Most public and university libraries long ago traded their card catalogs for electronic databases.... And the content of the libraries themselves has been moving online, too, as librarians rush, often with outside partners, such as Google, to create digital doppelgangers of their holdings....

In short, paper is an increasingly subordinate medium. Like a brain-dead patient on life support, it lives because other technologies allow it to live. The only question, it seems, is when we will put paper out of its misery.... [P]aper's days are most certainly numbered.

Or are they? We live in an age obsessed with new technologies. The sophisticated modern consumer knows the fine points of all the latest media devices. Comparisons between competing technologies—PC versus Mac, plasma versus LCD, Blackberry versus iPhone, satellite versus terrestrial radio—are a staple of consumer culture. There are countless popular magazines dedicated to helping us stay abreast of our media devices, and they cover every imaginable kind of technology except the one on which the magazines themselves are printed. Paper is the most successful communications innovation of the last 2000 years, the one that has lasted the longest and had the profoundest effect on civilization. One can easily make the case that without the technology that is paper, there would be no civilization. Yet most of the time, we don't even think of paper as a technology. And so we don't ask the questions we routinely ask about other technologies: How does it work? What are its strengths and weaknesses? Is it easy and enjoyable to use?

Taking A Second Look at Paper

Paper doesn't seem to require much consideration because it's so simple: a thin, flexible material that reflects light, crisply displaying any marks you make on it. What more is there to say? It has no circuits or chips, no ports, touchpad, speakers, or screen. It doesn't link to any networks or "sync" with other devices. It won't download files, burn CDs, or play movies. It just sits there, mute and passive, like a dog that knows one trick, waiting to perform it again....

Although paper appears to be a relatively "dumb" medium, it too performs tasks that require special abilities. And many of paper's tricks, the useful purposes it serves, are similarly products of its long relationship with people. There are cognitive, cultural, and social dimensions to the human–paper dynamic that come into play every time any kind of paper, from a tiny Post-it note to a groaning Sunday newspaper, is used to convey, retrieve, or store information. Paper does these jobs in a way that pleases us, which is why, for centuries we have liked having it around. It's also why we will never give it up as a medium, not completely. For some of the roles paper currently fulfills in our media lives, there is no better alternative currently available. And the most promising candidates are technologies that are striving to be more, not less, like paper....

From the end of World War II through 1990—a period that coincides exactly with the rise of the computer—U.S. consumption of paper grew dramatically. Even in the last fifteen years, as the Internet has made the networking of computers seamless, and email and electronic documents have proliferated, consumption of paper for communications (writing and printing) has not declined. One late twentieth-century study found that when offices began using email, paper consumption increased by an average of 40 percent. "The World Wide Web, far from decreasing paper consumption, served to increase the amount of printing done at home and in the office," wrote Abigail J. Sellen and Richard H. R. Harper in their 2002 book, *The Myth of the Paperless Office*. "With the Web, people could access more information more easily than before, but though they used digital means to find and retrieve information, they still preferred to print it out on paper when they wanted to read it." ...

The persistence of paper flies in the face of a widely held popular assumption about technology, propagated over the years by breathless futurists and science-fiction writers. This is the notion that newer, more advanced devices inevitably kill off older ones, as the automobile famously did to the buggy whip. Paul Duguid of the University of California at Berkeley calls this concept "supersession," meaning "the idea that each new technological type vanquishes or subsumes its predecessors." ... Obviously, some technologies do supersede others. Paper itself is a case in point. When it first appeared about 2,000 years ago, it was an astonishing new gizmo, the iPod of its day. Tradition credits the invention to a Chinese official named Cai Lun, a eunuch of the imperial court. Hoping to improve on the silk-based tissuey medium that the Chinese then used for writing, he experimented with various fibrous materials including tree bark, hemp, old rags, and fish nets. These were macerated to a pulp, which was then mixed with water and drained through some kind of screen. When the resulting soggy mat dried, it was paper.

Cai Lun introduced his innovation to the court in 105 A.D and the Chinese became the first great papermaking culture. But the new technology did not immediately race across the world and triumph over existing media. It spread slowly, first to Korea and Japan, then west across Central Asia. In the year 751 A.D., the Chinese lost a battle in Turkestan. Some of the Chinese soldiers who were taken prisoner knew how to make paper and turned over the secret to their Turkish captors, and soon papermaking was underway in Samarkand. From there, the technology moved around the Middle East and finally, at some point around 1,000 A.D., it reached Western Europe. The oldest known example of Western paper is *The Missal of Silos*, a church manuscript from the eleventh century preserved in a Benedictine abbey in central Spain.

When paper arrived in a given society, rather than wiping out the existing communications media—which were, principally, papyrus and parchment—it moved in beside them. It was accepted and embraced to varying degrees, and over different stretches of time, depending on social, cultural, and political circumstances. In Egypt, for instance, it appears that paper was quickly recognized as an improvement over the relatively inflexible and less durable parchment....

Even as paper thrived in the Middle East, Europeans received it tepidly. "The early paper of Europe was regarded with disfavour," writes historian Dard Hunter, "as not only was it higher in price and more fragile than parchment, which had been used for bookmaking, but it was distrusted on account of its introduction by Jews and Arabs." In 1221, the Holy Roman Emperor Frederick II issued a decree forbidding the use of paper for public documents. The suspect medium eventually caught on in Europe, of course, and ultimately superseded the older media that were there when it arrived. But that happened over many hundreds of years. By the middle of the fifteenth century, when Johannes Gutenberg invented the movable-type printing press, paper had been in use on the Continent for more than four centuries. Yet of the 180 bibles Gutenberg is thought to have printed, about one-quarter had pages made of vellum, a parchment made of animal skin that was still preferred for important documents because of its beauty and durability.

In With the New

In the literature of media studies, there is a determinist school, which holds that technologies shape society. Whether it's the printing press, the telegraph, or the cell phone, the new device sets the tune and people basically dance along. This is an appealingly facile way of organizing history, but in practice things are far more complicated. New technologies do not come out of nowhere. They are human creations in the first place, and they succeed, or not, to the extent that they meet human needs. In other words, as much as communications media influence the way people of a particular time and place live, the reverse is also true: People have tremendous influence over how technologies evolve. Why do we still listen to the radio when television offers both sound and images? Why did the Apple Newton fail miserably, while the Palm Pilot succeeded? When it comes to communication, we are a finicky, eccentric species. As a result, information media evolve unpredictably, not in a straight line but a wild zigzag.

For instance, Gutenberg's printing press famously changed the course of history, setting the stage for the Reformation and countless other social, political, and cultural shifts. What's less well known is that the arrival of print set off a tremendous explosion in writing itself—the old-fashioned kind of writing, by hand. The handwritten books of the pre-Gutenberg era were time consuming and costly to produce, and the class of people that was exposed to such things on a regular basis was a relatively small elite. The press made printed matter widely available, which in turn popularized and democratized the idea of written expression itself. Manuscripts were still produced in great numbers. And important new inventions for writing by hand, including graphite pencils and fountain pens, appeared…. In short, even as the world-changing new technology was taking hold—and in some ways because it was taking hold—the older one gained new life….

From One Function to Another

When a book is open on a reader's lap it is communicating; when it's sitting on a library shelf, it is storing the contents of its pages until the next reader comes along. In the last thirty years, computers and other digital devices have taken over much of the storage work that used to be paper's job…. In 1992, futurist Paul Saffo described how paper was giving up its storage role and becoming mainly an "interface." In his insightful essay, "The Electronic Piñata," Saffo wrote: "Paper today has become an increasingly volatile, disposable medium for viewing information on demand. We are solidly on our way to a future where we create and store information electronically, reducing it to paper only when we're ready to read it." …

Why does this functional change matter? Because it points to a fallacy in the popular "container" theory of newspapers and other paper media. As I mentioned earlier, this theory holds that it doesn't matter what vehicle is used to deliver information, as long as the information reaches its intended recipient. Of course, the main purpose of a container is storage. A Tupperware container stores last night's leftovers, and a newspaper stores news for the journey it must make between the printing plant and the reader's doorstep. But the argument that hard-copy newspapers are just containers implies that of the two roles paper performs, only one has value: the storage role. Since that happens to be the role paper is losing over time, it's no wonder that, by the lights of the container school, paper appears doomed. Although paper's work has been shifting away from storage and toward communication, for some reason we seldom think or talk about what exactly happens when paper communicates. This is because media communication appears to be a form of transportation: Like UPS trucks, information technologies simply move the product from one place to another. However, there is one important way in which they are not like trucks at all. After information arrives at its destination, something else has to happen for the communication to be complete: The individual must interact with the medium, using his or her senses and cognitive abilities to understand the content. In the case of paper, this is the moment when we pick up a sheet, or dozens of sheets joined together to form a newspaper, magazine, or book, and begin reading. If we could get to the bottom of that moment—which we take for granted, although it's a profound, almost magical event—we might be able to say why paper has endured this far into the age of electronic media....

What is paper? A thin, flexible, opaque material that's very good at reflecting light. We think of it as coming from trees, but it actually can be made of many different things.... [T]he essence of paper resides not in how it's made or what it's made from, but what it does. And this is where things get interesting. Like any tool, paper does some jobs well and some not so well. And our perception of its "talents" has changed over time. When paper first appeared, it was valued for its lightness and portability, as well as the efficient way it stored information. But relative to electronic media, paper is heavy and slow, and, as discussed earlier, it is no longer the default choice for information storage. In a digital world, paper actually has quite a few limitations: (1) It takes up physical space; (2) It can only be in one place at a time (virtual media can be accessed from anywhere); (3) It is difficult to alter or edit; (4) It does not play moving images or sound; and (5) It cannot network or connect to other media. The mystery is why a medium with so many disadvantages is still all around us....

Conventional wisdom says paper lingers out of habit. The medium has been with us for more than 2,000 years, and we are having trouble letting go. In this view, paper effectively is what child psychologists call a "transitional object," a security blanket we carry around to help us feel better during the rocky passage to a more advanced, "grown-up" media future. The flaw in this thinking is the assumption that paper is inherently inferior to newer technologies.... A wiser approach is to make no assumption whatsoever about paper's worth, relative status, or future, and focus instead on how it does its job, right now in the real world.

Why Paper Persists

In the last decade or so, a handful of researchers have looked at what happens when people interact with paper and, in some cases, compared that dynamic to human interactions with other media. Their findings suggest that paper has intrinsic properties that (1) make it easy and enjoyable to work with, (2) help us make sense of information, and (3) are conducive to certain kinds of reading and thinking....

In the mid-1990s, Abigail J. Sellen and Richard H. R. Harper ... conducted a study of how employees of the International Monetary Fund in Washington, D.C., managed the flow of information in their daily work. The IMF was chosen because it is a "knowledge-centered" organization that uses a lot of documents and because it had invested heavily in technology.... The study found that paper has inherent characteristics that make it useful. These are called "affordances" because they afford particular tasks. As it happens, many of paper's affordances are rooted in its limitations—its physicality, the fact that it can only be in one place, etc. In other words, its weaknesses are also its strengths. The IMF employees liked holding documents in their hands as they worked with them. They said that marking up and editing their work was easier and clearer on paper than on a screen. When working in face-to-face meetings with colleagues, they liked the way that paper documents could be conveniently passed around and discussed, something that's harder to do with a computer screen, even the smallest, lightest kind. They even appreciated the fact that paper takes up space, explaining that the clutter of paper in their offices was not as random as it appeared. Rather, the stacks and piles helped in the "thinking and planning" department by forming "a temporary holding pattern ... that serves as a way of keeping available the inputs and ideas they might have use for in their current projects. This clutter also provides important contextual clues to remind them of where they were in their space of ideas." That is, the paper served as a physical representation of what was going on in their minds, giving abstract thoughts and plans "a persistent presence" in their lives.

Among the comments the IMF workers gave the researchers, the most striking one came from an employee whose job it was to review other people's written reports. This person explained why paper was better suited to that task than a computer screen. "You've got to print it out to do it properly. You have to settle down behind your desk and get into it." Those phrases, "settle down" and "get into it" suggest a state of mind associated with a particular kind of reading—the full-immersion, deep-dive kind that occurs when a reader is able to shut out the world and truly focus. Does reading on paper somehow help create that state? In a different study that looked at how people in various professions read, Sellen and Harper found that paper has four affordances that specifically assist reading:

Tangibility: This refers to the way that we navigate a paper document or book using our eyes and hands together. "When a document is on paper, we can see how long it is, we can flick through the pages ... we can bend over a corner while searching for a section elsewhere. In other words, paper helps us work our way through documents."

Spatial Flexibility: When working with multiple paper texts, they can be spread out around a large area or reduced to fit a smaller space, depending on our needs.

Tailorability. With paper it's easy to underline, scribble in the margins, and otherwise annotate the text we are reading.

Manipulability. Because paper can be moved around, one can shuffle effectively among different paper sources, for example, putting one page aside in order to concentrate on another.

Newspapers got some of their best qualities from the paper they were printed on, [and] the good news is the medium itself is not going anywhere. Paper is all around us, quietly doing the same work it's been doing for centuries.

Close Reading Questions

1. What surprises you about the acceptance of paper by different cultures? How do some of these surprises support Powers' assertion that "People have a tremendous influence over how technologies evolve"? (Multiple Perspectives)

2. How does the effect of the printing press on handwriting disprove the concept of supersession?

3. According to Powers, what are some of the apparent weaknesses of paper in comparison to digital texts? Then why are these flaws actually some of the strengths of paper?

Analytical Writing/Discussion

4. According to Powers, we err if we consider paper only in terms of its function as a container to store information. Why do you agree or disagree that we also should consider the value of paper as based on its function of communication with readers? (Cultural Influences)

5. Although Powers joins Bauerlein in promoting print literacy, in what ways does his argument strike you as different from the one made by Bauerlein?

6. As part of his advocacy of paper, Powers ends with four of its special qualities or affordances. Which of the four affordances of reading a paper text seem most or least important to you and why?

Further Options

7. Like Powers, Baron invites his readers to consider the history of two other literacy technologies: the pencil as well as the computer (see "From Pencils to Pixels" in this chapter). In what ways do you think Powers' history of paper parallels Baron's analyses of the pencil and the computer? For example, what do you think is each writer's purpose as he presents this complex and sometimes quirky history? (Historical Trends)

8. Powers challenges the "determinist" thinking that "technology shapes society" but not the reverse: society influences technology. He asserts instead that society and technology influence each other. In what ways could you use his anti-determinist thinking to challenge Bauerlein's negative assumptions about digital literacy?

Freewrite 2: Using Technology

Using one or more of your experiences with a literacy technology, such as a pencil, a pen, a paper, or a computer, try thinking about it more critically by employing the forms introduced in the first chapter.

Historical Trends

Using some of your knowledge gained from Birkerts, Baron, and Powers, how can you place your use of this literacy technology in a historical context? How has your use of this technology changed from or remained the same with its use by others in the past?

Once you have completed this freewrite, you may want to expand this rough writing into a more formal paper with some direct quotations from some of the historical texts by Bauerlein, Baron, and Kirschenbaum.

Cultural Influences

We often fail to recognize the cultural conditions that support the rise of and the continued use of literacy technologies. Pick a literacy technology, such as a pencil, a pen, a paper, or a computer, and use some of your knowledge gained from Birkerts, Baron, and Powers to freewrite a response to one or more of the following questions:

- What cultural conditions do you think supported the rise of this technology?

- What cultural influences do you think support its continued use?

- What change in cultural conditions do you think might lead to an increase or a decrease in its use?

Once you have completed this freewrite, you may want to expand this rough writing into a more formal paper with some direct quotations from some of the historical texts by Birkerts, Baron, and Powers.

HOW READING IS BEING REIMAGINED

by Matthew Kirschenbaum

As a graduate student pursuing a Ph.D., Kirschenbaum wrote one of the first electronic dissertations in the nation. Now a professor specializing in the use of digital technologies in English studies, he helps direct the Maryland Institute for Technology in the Humanities. The following article originally appeared in the *Chronicle of Higher Education* (2007). Kirschenbaum examines some of the history of book reading as well as the current controversy over its future.

There is no doubt that it is time for a serious conversation about reading, not least because books themselves are changing.

Google, in cooperation with several dozen research libraries worldwide, is digitizing books at the rate of 3,000 a day. The noncommercial Open Content Alliance is scanning at a more modest pace but gaining ground, especially among institutions who chafe at some of the restrictions imposed by Google and its competitors. LibraryThing, an online book catalog that allows readers to list their books and find other readers with (sometimes uncannily) similar tastes, has almost 300,000 users who have collectively tagged some 20 million books. Newsweek ran a cover story on "The Future of Reading" in their November 26 issue. And on Monday, the same day that the National Endowment for the Arts released *To Read or Not to Read: A Question of National Consequence*, the follow-up to its controversial 2004 *Reading at Risk: A Survey of Literary Reading in America* report, Amazon.com launched Kindle, an e-book reader device that the *Newsweek* story describes as the "iPod of reading."

My purpose is not to debunk the NEA's most recent report, which synthesizes a number of studies to conclude that Americans—especially younger ones—are reading less, that they are reading "less well," and that these trends have disturbing implications for culture, civics, and even the national economy. The data are significant to anyone who cares about reading and its place in a 21st-century society, and deserve to be treated seriously. But clearly the report comes to us at a moment when reading and conversations about reading are in a state of flux. It's worth taking a moment to account for this broader context. High-profile projects like Google's and new devices like Kindle suggest what I call the remaking of reading, meaning that reading is being both reimagined and re-engineered, made over creatively as well as technologically.

Historically, we've placed very different values on different kinds of reading. The reading of novels and other "literary" works—precisely the core concern of the earlier NEA report—has not always enjoyed the pride of place it has in the current cultural canon. When Cervantes sent poor, mad Don Quixote on his delirious adventures at the beginning of the 17th century, there existed a popular prejudice surrounding the reading of chivalric romances. Until well into the 19th century, novel-reading was regarded in Europe as a pastime fit mostly for women and the indolent—and a potentially dangerous one, since women, especially, could not be trusted to distinguish fiction from reality. But both the 2004 and the current report are curiously devoid of historical awareness, as though there is but a single, idealized model of reading from which we have strayed.

To Read or Not to Read deploys its own self-consistent iconography to tell us what reading is. In the pages of the report we find images of an adolescent male bent over a book, a female student sitting alone reading against a row of school lockers, and a white-collar worker studying a form. These still lives of the literate represent reading as self-evident—we know it when we see it. Yet they fail to acknowledge that such images have coexisted for centuries with other kinds of reading that have their own iconography and accouterments: Medieval and early modern portraits of scholars and scribes at work at their desks show them adorned with many books (not just one), some of them bound and splayed on exotic devices for keeping them open and in view; Thomas Jefferson famously designed a lazy susan to rotate books in and out of his visual field. That kind of reading values comparison and cross-checking as much as focus and immersion—lateral reading as much as reading for depth.

That is the model of reading that seems compatible with the Web and other new electronic media. Yet it also raises fundamental questions about what it means to read, and what it means to have read something. When can we claim a book to have been read? What is the dividing line between reading and skimming? Must we consume a book in its entirety—start to finish, cover to cover—to say we have read it? Pierre Bayard, a literature professor in France, recently made a stir with a naughty little volume called *How to Talk About Books You Haven't Read*. When I read it (well, most of it), the book provoked the most intense author envy I have ever felt—not because I too secretly enjoy perpetuating literary frauds, but because Bayard speaks to a dilemma that will be familiar to every literate person: namely, that there are far more books in the world (50 million or 60 million by the estimates I've seen) than any of us will ever have time to read. Reading, Bayard says, is as much about mastering a system of relationships among texts and ideas as it is about reading any one text in great depth. He quotes the extreme case of the fictional librarian in Robert Musil's *The Man Without Qualities* (a book Bayard admits to having only skimmed): The librarian resolutely reads no books whatsoever for fear that undue attention to any one of them will compromise the integrity of his relation to them all.

The structure of *To Read or Not to Read* presents itself as tacit acknowledgment that not all of its own text will likely be read by any one reader, since it is clearly designed to be "not read" in at least some of the ways that accord with Bayard's observations. The report is accompanied by an Executive Summary, a condensed version of the major findings. Its internal organization is carefully laid out, with summary points at the head of each chapter, topic sentences, extensive notes, sidebars, and sections labeled as conclusions.

The authors of the report would doubtlessly insist that the kind of person who reads (or doesn't read) books by French intellectuals writing about books they haven't read (or have only skimmed) is not the kind of reader who has them much worried. It's the people, especially the young ones, who are simply not reading at all that are cause for alarm. But the new report also places extreme emphasis on what it repeatedly terms "voluntary" reading. Reading that one does for work or for school doesn't "count" in this regard. While one can appreciate the motivations here—the NEA is interested in people who read because they choose to, not because they have to—it seems oddly retrograde. How many of us who count ourselves as avid readers are able to maintain clear boundaries between work and leisure anymore?

Likewise, while the authors of the report repeatedly emphasize that they include online reading in their data, the report sounds most clumsy and out of touch when referring to new media. The authors of the report tend to homogenize "the computer" without acknowledging the diversity of activity—and the diversity of reading—that takes place on its screen. Our screens are spaces where new forms like blogs and e-mail and chats commingle with remediations of older forms, like newspapers and magazines—or even poems, stories, and novels. Reading your friend's blog is not likely a replacement for reading Proust, but some blogs have been a venue for extraordinary writing, and we are not going to talk responsibly or well about what it means to read online until we stop conflating genre with value.

The report also fails to acknowledge the extent to which reading and writing have become commingled in electronic venues. The staccato rhythms of a real-time chat session are emblematic in this regard: Reading and writing all but collapse into a single unified activity. But there is a spectrum of writing online, just as there is a spectrum of reading, and more and more applications blur the line between the two. Many electronic book interfaces allow users to annotate their texts, for example; some allow users to share those notes and annotations with others (CommentPress, from the Institute for the Future of the Book, is exemplary in this regard, as is Zotero, from the Center for History and New Media at George Mason University). Alph, a project directed by Nancy Kaplan at the University of Baltimore, is developing new online reading interfaces for children; the ability to leave notes and marks behind for these young readers' peers is a signature design feature. Book Glutton, a Web service still in beta mode, provides adult users with a shared electronic library; readers write notes for other readers in the margins of the books, and this virtual marginalia persists over time, accreting in Talmudic fashion. Moreover, readers can choose to chat in real time with other readers perusing the same chapter that is on their screens.

What kind of activity is taking place here? What are the new metrics of screen literacy? I don't have that data, it's not my field, but anecdotally my instinct is that computer users are capable of projecting the same aura of deep concentration and immersion as the stereotypical bookworm. Walk into your favorite coffee shop and watch the people in front of their screens. Rather than bug-eyed, frenzied jittering, you are more likely to see calm, meditative engagement—and hear the occasional click of fingers on keyboards as the readers write.

Close Reading Questions

1. Why does the date November 26, 2007 represent the current debate over digital literacy? What event do you think a supporter or a critic of digital literacy would emphasize and why?

2. In what ways can the lateral and rapid reading associated with today's "new" Web pages actually be considered quite "old"? In other words, what historical parallels exist between today's digital reading patterns and older reading practices? (Historical Trends)

3. What do you think Kirschenbaum means when he asserts, "We are not going to talk responsibly … about what it means to read online until we stop conflating genre with value?" (If needed, please consult a dictionary, such as on the meaning of genre.) Why do you agree or disagree with Kirschenbaum's assertion?

Analytical Writing/Discussion

4. What historical information on literary reading does Kirschenbaum provide that would complicate Bauerlein's argument (see pp. 363–367)? Why do you think this historical information is enough (or not) to counter Bauerlein's pessimism? (Multiple Perspectives)

5. Kirschenbaum describes several "electronic book interfaces" for text annotation and reader interaction. Why do you agree or disagree that these programs can maintain and reinforce some of the best practices of print literacy? (Cultural Influences)

6. Reread the final paragraphs of Kirschenbaum's and Bauerlein's texts (see pp. 363–367). How can their conclusions be used as part of the larger debate over print and digital literacy?

Further Options

7. Please reread the three opening paragraphs of Kirschenbaum's essay with some of the principles of argument in mind (see pp. 103 of Chapter 6). How does Kirschenbaum use a concession as well as a rebuttal to engage readers who are skeptical of digital literacy?

8. Kirschenbaum warns against the assumption of a "single, idealized model of reading from which we have strayed." Looking back at the first two readings of this chapter by Bauerlein and Baron, which writer do you think has best heeded or most failed to heed Kirschenbaum's warning? And why?

ONLINE LITERACY IS A LESSER KIND

by Mark Bauerlein

With a book titled *The Dumbest Generation: How the Digital Age Stupefies Young Americans* (2008), Bauerlein is not afraid to create controversy. He is a blunt critic of digital literacy, who has argued that because the typical teenager sends more than 2,000 text messages a month, he or she is less prepared to engage in face-to-face social interactions. In this article, Bauerlein examines the habits of people as they read Web pages and the effects these habits have on education today. This article from 2008 originally appeared in the *Chronicle of Higher Education*, which is read by college professors and administrators.

When Jakob Nielsen, a Web researcher, tested 232 people for how they read pages on screens, a curious disposition emerged. Dubbed by *The New York Times* "the guru of Web page 'usability,'" Nielsen has gauged user habits and screen experiences for years, charting people's online navigations and aims, using eye-tracking tools to map how vision moves and rests. In this study, he found that people took in hundreds of pages "in a pattern that's very different from what you learned in school." It looks like a capital letter F. At the top, users read all the way across, but as they proceed their descent quickens and horizontal sight contracts, with a slowdown around the middle of the page. Near the bottom, eyes move almost vertically, the lower-right corner of the page largely ignored. It happens quickly, too. "F for fast," Nielsen wrote in a column. "That's how users read your precious content."

The F-pattern isn't the only odd feature of online reading that Nielsen has uncovered in studies conducted through the consulting business Nielsen Norman Group (Donald A. Norman is a cognitive scientist who came from Apple; Nielsen was at Sun Microsystems). A decade ago, he issued an "alert" entitled "How Users Read on the Web." It opened bluntly: "They don't."

In the eye-tracking test, only one in six subjects read Web pages linearly, sentence by sentence. The rest jumped around chasing keywords, bullet points, visuals, and color and typeface variations. In another experiment on how people read e-newsletters, informational e-mail messages, and news feeds, Nielsen exclaimed, "'Reading' is not even the right word." The subjects usually read only the first two words in headlines, and they ignored the introductory sections. They wanted the "nut" and nothing else. A 2003 Nielsen warning asserted that a PDF file strikes users as a "content blob," and they won't read it unless they print it out. A "booklike" page on screen, it seems, turns them off and sends them away. Another Nielsen test found that teenagers skip through the Web even faster than adults do, but with a lower success rate for completing tasks online (55 percent compared to 66 percent). Nielsen writes: "Teens have a short attention span and want to be stimulated. That's also why they leave sites that are difficult to figure out." For them, the Web isn't a place for reading and study and knowledge. It spells the opposite. "Teenagers don't like to read a lot on the Web. They get enough of that at school."

Computers in Schools

Those and other trials by Nielsen amount to an important research project that helps explain one of the great disappointments of education in our time. I mean the huge investment schools have made in technology, and the meager returns such funds have earned. Ever since the Telecommunications Act of 1996, money has poured into public-school classrooms. At the same time, colleges have raced to out-technologize one another. But while enthusiasm swells, e-bills are passed, smart classrooms multiply, and students cheer—the results keep coming back negative. When the Texas Education Agency evaluated its Technology Immersion Pilot, a $14-million program to install wireless tools in middle schools, the conclusion was unequivocal: "There were no statistically significant effects of immersion in the first year on either reading or mathematics achievement." When University of Chicago economists evaluated California schools before and after federal technology subsidies (the E-Rate program) had granted 30 percent more schools in the state Internet access, they determined that "the additional investments in technology generated by E-Rate had no immediate impact on measured student outcomes." In March 2007, the National Center for Education Evaluation and Regional Assistance evaluated 16 award-winning education technologies and found that "test scores were not significantly higher in classrooms using selected reading and mathematics software products." Last spring a New York State school district decided to drop its laptop program after years of offering it. The school-board president announced why: "After seven years, there was literally no evidence it had any impact on student achievement—none."

Those conclusions apply to middle-school and high-school programs, not to higher education (which has yet to produce any similarly large-scale evaluations). Nevertheless, the results bear consideration by those pushing for more e-learning on campuses.

Backers, providers, and fans of new technology explain the disappointing measures as a matter of circumstance. Teachers didn't get enough training, they say, or schoolwide coordination was spotty, parents not sufficiently involved. Maybe so, to some extent, but Nielsen's studies indicate another source. Digitized classrooms don't come through for an off-campus reason, a factor largely overlooked by educators. When they add laptops to classes and equip kids with on-campus digital tools, they add something else, too: the reading habits kids have developed after thousands of hours with those same tools in leisure time.

To teachers and professors, a row of glistening new laptops in their classroom after a dozen years with nothing but chalk and blackboard, or a podium that has been transformed from a wooden stand into a multimedia console, can appear a stunning conversion. But to the average freshman walking through the door and finding a seat, it's nothing new. Our students have worked and played with computers for years. The Horatio Alger Association found that students in high school use the Internet four and a half hours per week for help with homework (*The State of Our Nation's Youth*, 2008–2009), while the National School Boards Association measures social networking at nine hours per week, much of it spent on homework help. The gap between viewpoints is huge. Educators envision a whole new pedagogy with the tools, but students see only the chance to extend long-established postures toward the screen. If digitized classrooms did pose strong, novel intellectual challenges to students, we should see some pushback on their part, but few of them complain about having to learn in new ways.

Student Reading Practices

Once again, this is not so much about the content students prefer—Facebook, YouTube, etc.—or whether they use the Web for homework or not. It is about the reading styles they employ. They race across the surface, dicing language and ideas into bullets and graphics, seeking what they already want and shunning the rest. They convert history, philosophy, literature, civics, and fine art into information, material to retrieve and pass along.

That's the drift of screen reading. Yes, it's a kind of literacy, but it breaks down in the face of a dense argument, a Modernist poem, a long political tract, and other texts that require steady focus and linear attention—in a word, slow reading. Fast scanning doesn't foster flexible minds that can adapt to all kinds of texts, and it doesn't translate into academic reading. If it did, then in a 2006 *Chronicle* survey of college professors, fully 41 percent wouldn't have labeled students "not well prepared" in reading (48 percent rated them "somewhat well prepared"). We would not find that the percentage of college graduates who reached "proficiency" literacy in 1992 was 40 percent, while in 2003 only 31 percent scored "proficient." We would see reading scores inching upward, instead of seeing, for instance, that the percentage of high-school students who reached proficiency dropped from 40 percent to 35 percent from 1992 to 2005.

And we wouldn't see even the better students struggling with "slow reading" tasks. In an "Introduction to Poetry" class awhile back, when I asked students to memorize 20 lines of verse and recite them to the others at the next meeting, a voice blurted, "Why?" The student wasn't being impudent or sullen. She just didn't see any purpose or value in the task. Canny and quick, she judged the plodding process of recording others' words a primitive exercise. Besides, if you can call up the verse any time with a click, why remember it? Last year when I required students in a literature survey course to obtain obituaries of famous writers without using the Internet, they stared in confusion. Checking a reference book, asking a librarian, and finding a microfiche didn't occur to them. So many free deliveries through the screen had sapped that initiative.

This is to say that advocates of e-learning in higher education pursue a risky policy, striving to unite liberal-arts learning with the very devices of acceleration that hinder it. Professors think they can help students adjust to using tools in a more sophisticated way than scattershot e-reading, but it's a lopsided battle.

To repeat, college students have spent thousands of hours online acquiring faster and faster eyes and fingers before they even enter college, and they like the pace. It is unrealistic to expect 19-year-olds to perch before a screen and brake the headlong flight, even if it is the Declaration of Independence in hypertext coming through, not a buddy's message.

Some educators spot the momentum and shrug their shoulders, elevating screen scanning to equal status with slow reading. A notable instance occurred last year, when in an essay in *The New York Times*, Leah Price, a professor of English at Harvard University, criticized a report from the National Endowment for the Arts—"To Read or Not to Read" (to which I contributed)—precisely for downgrading digital scanning. Her article contained some errors of fact, such as that the 2004 NEA report "Reading at Risk" excluded nonfiction, but correctly singled out the NEA distinction between screen reading and print reading. To Price, it's a false one: "Bafflingly, the NEA's time-use charts classify 'e-mailing' and 'surfing Web sites' as competitors to reading, not subsets of it." Indeed, she said, to do so smacks of guile: "It takes some gerrymandering to make a generation logging ever more years in school, and ever more hours on the BlackBerry, look like nonreaders." (In truth, high-school students do no more in-class reading today than they did 20 years ago, according to a 2004 Department of Education report.)

Resisting A Lesser Kind of Reading

What we are seeing is a strange flattening of the act of reading. It equates handheld screens with *Madame Bovary*, as if they made the same cognitive demands and inculcated the same habits of attention. It casts peeking at a text message and plowing through *Middlemarch* as subsets of one general activity. And it treats those quick bursts of words and icons as fully sufficient to sustain the reading culture. The long book may go, Price concluded, but reading will carry on just as it did before: "The file, the list, the label, the memo: These are the genres that will keep reading alive."

The step not taken here is a crucial one, namely to determine the relative effects of reading different "genres." We need an approach that doesn't let teachers and professors so cavalierly violate their charge as stewards of literacy. We must recognize that screen scanning is but one kind of reading, a lesser one, and that it conspires against certain intellectual habits requisite to liberal-arts learning. The inclination to read a huge Victorian novel, the capacity to untangle a metaphor in a line of verse, the desire to study and emulate a distant historical figure, the urge to ponder a concept such as Heidegger's ontic-ontological difference over and over and around and around until it breaks through as a transformative insight—those dispositions melt away with every 100 hours of browsing, blogging, IMing, Twittering, and Facebooking. The shape and tempo of online texts differ so much from academic texts that e-learning initiatives in college classrooms can't bridge them. Screen reading is a mind-set, and we should accept its variance from academic thinking. Nielsen concisely outlines the difference: "I continue to believe in the linear, author-driven narrative for educational purposes. I just don't believe the Web is optimal for delivering this experience. Instead, let's praise old narrative forms like books and sitting around a flickering campfire—or its modern-day counterpart, the PowerPoint projector," he says. "We should accept that the Web is too fast-paced for big-picture learning. No problem; we have other media, and each has its strengths. At the same time, the Web is perfect for narrow, just-in-time learning of information nuggets—so long as the learner already has the conceptual framework in place to make sense of the facts."

So let's restrain the digitizing of all liberal-arts classrooms. More than that, given the tidal wave of technology in young people's lives, let's frame a number of classrooms and courses as slow-reading (and slow-writing) spaces. Digital technology has become an imperial force, and it should meet more antagonists. Educators must keep a portion of the undergraduate experience disconnected, unplugged, and logged off. Pencils, blackboards, and books are no longer the primary instruments of learning, true, but they still play a critical role in the formation of intelligence, as countermeasures to information-age mores. That is a new mission for educators parallel to the mad rush to digitize learning, one that may seem reactionary and retrograde, but in fact strives to keep students' minds open and literacy broad. Students need to decelerate, and they can't do it by themselves, especially if every inch of the campus is on the grid.

Close Reading Questions

1. Bauerlein cites Jakob Nielsen's studies of online literacy. In your own words, what exactly is the F-pattern of reading Web pages, and why does Nielsen state "F [is] for fast"?

2. According to several studies, what have been the short- and long-term results of computer technologies on student learning in middle and high schools? (Cultural Influences)

3. Bauerlein asserts that for teenagers, "the Web isn't a place for reading and study and knowledge." He believes that it instead is a site for social networking, such as by Facebook, and viewing entertainment, such as on YouTube. To what degree do your experiences and those of your friends match his assertions about adolescents' use of the Web?

Analytical Writing/Discussion

4. Bauerlein refers to the "flattening … of reading," and he uses many other compelling phrases like "dicing language and ideas into bullets and graphics," "sapped that initiative," "violate their charge as stewards of literacy," and "conspire against certain intellectual habits." Why do you think these phrases strengthen or weaken his argument for a reader still undecided on this topic?

5. Bauerlein distinguishes academic print literacy from leisurely digital reading. How does he then use this distinction to explain the failure of computer technologies to improve student learning in schools? Why do you find his explanation to be convincing or not?

6. Bauerlein relies heavily on Neilsen's research in order to insist that digital reading or "screen scanning is but one kind of reading, a lesser one." Neilsen, however, asserts that for various media, such as print and Web pages, "each has its strengths." As explained by Neilsen, what are the strengths of each one, and why do you believe (or not) that differences between print and digital literacies necessarily mean that one is "a lesser kind" than the other? (Multiple Perspectives)

Further Options

7. Neilsen reports that a book-like PDF file strikes many digital readers as a "content blob," and they have to print out this text in order to read it thoroughly. According to Powers (see pp. 353–358 in this chapter), what are some of the advantages of reading a difficult text in print? Why do you agree or disagree that these traits of paper promote better reading comprehension?

8. Later in this chapter, Kirschenbaum cautions that we should not define reading based on one particular historical model of reading (see pp. 360–362). He explains that the slow, linear comprehension of literary reading once was distrusted. How can you use this historical information to complicate the significant drop of college graduates that demonstrate proficient literacy (from 40% in 1992 to 31% in 2003)? (Historical Trends)

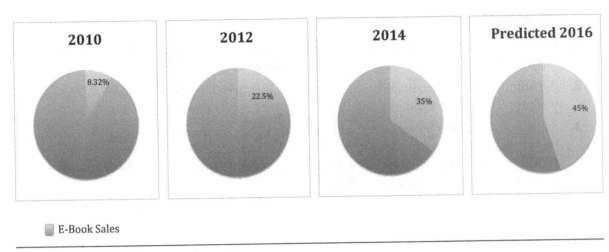

■ E-Book Sales

FIGURE 2   The Increasing Sales of e-Books

DON'T FEAR THE FUTURE … AGAIN

by Nick Bilton

Nick Bilton is a technology writer and blogger for the *New York Times*; he has been a key contributor to the paper's efforts to deliver the news online. The following excerpt comes from his book *I Live in the Future and Here's How it Works* (2011), and Bilton addresses the fears of those who doubt digital literacy. He relies on historical precedents and recent scientific investigations to counter some of the concerns of critics like Matthew Bauerlein and Nicholas Carr.

In the summer of 2008, Nicholas Carr, an author and writer for *The Atlantic* magazine, felt his brain slipping ever so slightly from its moorings. In the past, he wrote, "Immersing myself in a book or lengthy article used to be easy."

Not anymore. "Now my concentration often starts to drift after two or three pages. I get fidgety, lost the thread, begin looking for something else to do," he said. "I feel as if I'm always dragging my wayward brain back to the text."

The problem, he concluded, was the Internet generally and Google quite specifically. In a piece titled "Is Google Making Us Stupid?" and later in the book *The Shallows: What the Internet is Doing to Our Brains*, he frets that having snippets of massive amounts of information right at our fingertips may be eroding our ability to concentrate and contemplate.

Déjà vu all over again, don't you think?

In fairness, Carr recognizes that the printing press caused similar hand-wringing. And even though some of the predictions came true—the press actually did undermine religious authority, for instance—the many advantages of printing far outweighed the concerns. So he admits that he may be wrong and "a golden age of intellectual discovery and universal wisdom" may emerge from the text, tweets, bytes, and snacks of today's online world. But he still worries that deep thinking and serious reflection will be forever lost in the date stream of information the Web affords.

Although Carr is fatalistic about the future, his balanced, well-researched article offers a thoughtful perspective. Most of those who are skeptical about the shift aren't so reflective. In a *San Francisco Chronicle* article headlined "Attention Loss Feared as High-Tech Rewires Brain," the author, Benny Evangelista, citing some mental health experts, saw interpersonal relationships breaking down and attention deficit disorder increasing as more people found themselves unable to separate from email, Facebook, and Twitter.

How bad is the attention loss? The inability to detach oneself from electronic updates has spread from the office to the restaurant to the car—and now has reached into the bedroom. The story quotes a survey that found that 36 percent of people age thirty-five or younger used Facebook or Twitter after having sex. "Men," the story noted, "were twice a s likely [as women] to tweet or post status updates after sex."

Said an executive who commissioned the survey: "It's the new cigarette."

Other news stories and books drip with angst over how new technologies may be destroying us, ruining our intellect, quashing our ability to converse face-to-face, and fundamentally changing relationships for both kids and adults. "Anti-social Networking?" a *New York Times* story asked, questioning whether time online diminishes intimacy and destroys the natural give-and-take of relationships. "Scientists warn of Twitter dangers," said CNN.com, stating that researches had found "social-networking tools such as Twitter could numb our sense of morality and make us indifferent to human suffering. A number of books, such as *The Dumbest Generation: How the Digital Age Stupefies Young Americans and Jeopardizes Our Future* and the previously mentioned *Distracted: The Erosion of Attention and the Coming Dark Age*, add fuel to the fire.

But it doesn't stop there: There's a recent, oft-quoted study, "Emails 'Hurt IQ More than Pot.'" A survey of more than a thousand Britons found that the IQ of those trying to juggle messages and work fell ten points, more than double the drop seen after smoking pot.

Over and over at speeches and conferences, I hear the same kinds of fears and anxieties that new technologies and developments have generated for decades: Our brains weren't wired for all this fast-paced stuff. We're too distracted to do meaningful and thorough work. At the same time, our entertainment is also dangerous and damaging, people tell me. Video games will destroy our children's brains and their relationships—if Twitter and Facebook don't do so first. We cannot effectively multitask or jump from email to writing to video, and we never will be able to.

There may be some truth to some of this; we may well be fundamentally different when this is all over. But for the most part, I believe it's bunk. Just as well-meaning scientists and consumers feared that trains and comic books and television would rot our brains and spoil our minds, I believe many of the skeptics and worrywarts today are missing the bigger picture, the greater value that access to new and faster information is bringing us. For the most past, our brains will adapt in a constructive way to this new online world, just as we formed communities to help us sort information.

Why do I believe this? Because we've learned how to do so many things already, including learning how to read.

Learning to Read

Some argue that our brains aren't designed to consume information on screens, or play video games, or consume real-time information. But the same argument holds true for the words you're reading now. It's true: Your brain wasn't built to read. Several thousand years ago, someone created symbols, which ultimately became an alphabet. That alphabet formed into a written language with its own set of unique rules. As a result, the organization of the human brain changed dramatically. But the human brain doesn't come automatically equipped with the ability to read these symbols. It's something that has to be rewired in the circuitry every time it happens. Our brains are designed to communicate and to tell stories with language. But reading letters and words is essentially man-made, just like video games and screens.

Even today, when children learn their letters and form them into words and sentences and big, powerful ideas, their brains still have to re-form and readapt to make the information fall into place.

Stanislas Dehaene, chair of Experimental Cognitive Neurology at the Collège de France, has spent most of his career in neuroscience exploring how our brains learn to read and calculate numbers. He explains that human brains are better wired to communicate by speaking. In the first year of life, babies begin to pick up words and sounds simply from hearing them. Sure, they need some help identifying that a cup is a cup and Mommy is Mommy. But by two years old, most children are talking and applying labels to objects without any special lessons or drills.

This is not the case with reading. Most children, even if they share books with their parents and hear stories every single day, won't pick up reading on their own. Instead, they must learn to recognize letters one by one and put them together into sounds or words before recognizing whole sentences and thoughts. They must learn to decode the symbols.

Some research suggests that in doing this, children and even adults actually develop a new area within the brain. Manuel Carreiras at the Basque Center on Cognition, Brain and Language has taken research on language into other complex areas. Carreiras's work over the years has been focused on the neural processes of human language and the way humans comprehend differently when reading and when interpreting sign language. When he wanted a better understanding of how people learn to read, he decided he needed to find illiterate adults to see how their brains adapt before and after learning how to read words.

At first Carreiras had trouble finding a group of adults who really didn't have any reading skill, but finally, he recruited forty-two veterans of the Colombian guerrilla wars. Twenty of the ex-fights had recently completed a Spanish literacy training program to teach them to read. The other ex-fighters still needed to take the course and were for the most part illiterate. The former fighters were tested, taught to read, and then tested again. In the process, areas of the brain actually grew and formed connections that had not existed earlier. The brain had rewired itself while the guerrillas learned how to read.

Carreiras found that the brain changes its structure when someone properly learns to read, particularly in the white matter, which creates connections and helps information move between different areas of the brain. He explained, "We found that the literate members of our group have more white matter in the splenium … a structure that connects the brain's left and right hemispheres—than did the illiterate members." As the former guerrillas learned to read, the scientists used imaging techniques to measure what was happening. They saw that reading triggered brain functions in the same areas that had grown over the course of the study. In other words, even adults were able to create new neural pathways as they learned a difficult new skill.

The Brain's Adaptability

What's significant in this example is that our brains are something like a muscle, which can grow stronger and more powerful with practice and work. Today, technology is building new connections as our brains interpret content and receive stimulation. There's a constant and simplistic iterative adaptation taking place in our brains as we use our computers, mobile phones, and e-readers. Our brains are learning how to navigate these gadgets, just as they do when we learn how to read.

There's one piece of this puzzle that's important to point out. With the use of computers and digital technologies, our brains are not evolving. Human beings evolve at much slower pace than do new communication mechanisms and the technologies we invent and create. Neuroscientists I spoke with explained that a brain from five hundred years ago or even ten thousand years ago would look pretty much the way it does today, just as humans look pretty much the way they did a few thousand years ago.

To illustrate this point, let's hypothetically travel back two thousand years and find a newborn baby. Imagine taking that baby and transporting him through our time machine forward to today. This child would be raised in our technology-rich society, growing up in a world of iPods, video games, the Internet, mobile phones, GPS, robotic Elmo toys, banner ads, and more. I asked several neuroscientists if this baby born two thousand years ago, would likely grow up differently than a child born today. The resounding answer was "no." A newborn's brain from two thousand years ago, I was told, would likely look and work exactly like the same as a brain does today.

But if you took an adult—let's say a thirty-year-old man from two thousand years ago—and dropped him a the middle of Times Square. He might well experience a panic attack from all the crowds, cars, flashing lights, and stimulation. But, neuroscientists said, his brain would begin to adapt. He might never get to a point where he could talk and simultaneously send text messages, but numerous research studies show that our brains are capable of substantial adaptation in about two weeks and in some instances seven days. Our two-thousand-year-old man would be just fine. His adaptation to society and the new stimuli would just take brain training, and not as much as you might think.

What Research Studies Show

How do our magnificent minds adapt? In 2008, a group of neuroscience researchers from UCLA's Semel Institute studied the brain activity of twenty-four volunteers when the subjects were reading a book of surfing the Web to see if the Web was rewiring the way our brains function.

The volunteers were divided on the basis of how much experiences they had using computers and the Internet. Twelve of the participants were labeled "Net Naive" because they used the Internet or computers once a month at most. Asked to rate their tech savvy, they gave themselves a rating of minimal to none. The other twelve participants were labeled "Net Savvy." Those in this group used a computer at least once a day, and most of them were online numerous times throughout the day. The members of this group considered themselves moderate to expert on computers and the Internet.

The researchers showed volunteers different types of content while monitoring them using functional magnetic resonance imaging (fMRI) scanners, special machines that allow the research subjects to watch screens or perform certain tasks while the scanner records the blood flow in their brains and how the brain handles its processing.

First, volunteers were shown a table of contents from a book and given fifteen seconds to pick the chapter they wanted to read. Then they had just under thirty seconds to read a page of the book. Next, the same participants were shown a search page from Google and asked to decide on a search and enter a word in the search box within fifteen seconds. The display took them to a website that corresponded with their search, and they were asked to read the page for an additional thirty seconds. To make sure they were paying attention, the participants were told they would be tested on their reading of both the print and digital versions.

When reading the printed page, the Net Naïve and Net Savvy brains reacted the same way. Those brains were slightly stimulated, although there was a little less activity in the brains of the Net Savvy while reading the printed text. But during the online searching and reading tests, the Net Savvy brains were much more active. In fact, the Net Savvy group showed almost twice as much activity while online compared with reading a book. The reading task stimulated parts of their brain used for language and reading, memory, and visual abilities. In comparison, the Web surfing task activated the same areas of the brain as reading, but in addition, the brain was involved in decision making, complex reasoning, and vision detection.

Even more interesting, the volunteers weren't a bunch of young kids with malleable brains. Rather, the group consisted of people between fifty-five and seventy-six years old, all of them digital immigrants with varying degrees of success in adapting to the online world. The Internet wasn't even around in a meaningful way until they were in their late thirties or early forties to mid-fifties, yet the brains of the Net Savvy rewired and sprang into action to work with this new stimulation.

What was happening with those brains is a process called neuroplasticity, a theory that our brains' 100 billion neurons, or nerve cells, can re-form, or create new cells and new connections, as we learn and grow.

Many new activities we engage in on a daily basis can make this happen, from touching something hot for the first time to using the Internet or even juggling, as Bogdan Draganski and a group of scientists from the department of neurology at the University of Regensburg, Germany, discovered.

Draganski, with previous brain research as a foundation, developed a hypothesis that our brains must act differently when they learn something new. After watching a group of kids text messaging on their mobile phones at dramatic speeds, he wondered if sending hundreds of messages made the thumbs work differently. He theorized that the brain correlations that operate these functions should look differently from what they look like in people who rarely text.

To explore this theory further, Draganski told me in a phone interview, he got permission to scan the brains of a small group of young people. The initial results showed that the heavy texters had a large area of mass in the portion of the brain that controls the right hand, but that other areas were similar to the normal brains he had studied earlier. Draganski believed that this larger area most likely signified heightened use of the right hand used for texting. His original goal was to understand if brain growth would become more obvious over time as more kids learned to text. But, he said in an interview, wit so many people already familiar with texting, he decided to switch to a different task that involved a clear and steep learning curve: juggling.

Draganski and his researchers took a group of participants who had never juggled before and mea-sured the gray matter, the neurons, in each of their brains as they gradually learned to juggle with three and then four balls. As Draganski predicted, he saw significant areas of growth in gray matter in cer-tain areas. The motor areas of the brain actually grew over a three-month period of learning. When the participants stopped juggling, however, their gray matter began to recede and return to its previous size and shape.

Another group of researchers in a different study found that when a completely new task is learned, changes in brain shape are visible after a mere seven days of practice.

When these theories were tested in a later study by the UCLA researchers in late 2009, it was found that Net Naïve Web surfers could catch up to the Net Savvy. When the Net Naïve repeatedly used the Internet over a one-week period, the brain scans showed that they, too, started to adapt and respond to the online experience in a very similar fashion to the Net Savvy. Their brains also began to show twice as much stimulation from reading a Web page as from reading a printed page.

Gary Small, director of UCLA's Semel Institute for Neuroscience & Human Behavior and one of the nation's leading experts on memory and aging, was one of the key researchers in this study. He said the brains were learning, benefiting from practice and experience. In theory, Small said, as we learn, the brain should show less activity. For example, when we get a new phone, it takes a while to figure out where all the functions are hidden. "At first I'll show a lot of activity in my brain," he said, but then, once he gets used to the experience and better at navigating the device, the activity should slow down. At that point, he said, the brain's "synapses … will grow, become strengthened, and then become efficient," and less activity should be required.

But that isn't what happened when he watched people become experienced digital surfers. Instead, his research found, our brains work completely differently while reading online that while reading a printed page, making numerous decisions based on the many options, menus, photos, text, and links on each page. In fact, the first study concluded, "Internet searching appears much more stimulating than reading."

Close Reading Questions

1. According to Bilton, what are some of the fears about digital literacy? What concerns do you think are most or least valid? (Cultural Influences)

2. Why does Bilton believe our brains are not designed to learn how to read?

3. What does Bilton state would happen if a newborn or an adult from 2000 years ago somehow were to be transported to Times Square in New York City? What is the significance of these hypothetical examples? (Historical Trends)

Analytical Writing/Discussion

4. Why do you think Bilton mentions Carr's concern in particular and then adds many other examples? Is he trying to commend and/or dismiss Carr's viewpoint?

5. How does Bilton use learning to talk versus learning to read to create a new perspective on reading? Why do you find this perspective on reading the printed page to be compelling or not? (Multiple Perspectives)

6. Which of the studies cited on brain adaptation do you find to be most or least persuasive and why? (Cultural Influences)

Further Options

7. Synthesis, meaning the making of connections between two (or more) readings, is central to academic writing. Select a quotation from Bilton and another by a critic like Bauerlein. Then present each quotation using a signal phrase (as explained in Chapter 8 on pp. 141) and elaborate on each writer's perspective. How exactly do you think these writers disagree?

8. As defined by Aristotle, rhetoric is "the discovery of the available means of persuasion" (see p. 102 of Chapter 6). Both Bilton and Powers refer to fears of whatever technology is considered to be "new," such as the Internet or paper. How does each writer use these fears to support of his perspective? Which author's argument do you find to be more persuasive and why?

Freewrite 3: e-Book Sales

See Figure 2 on p. 368, then freewrite to answer some of the following questions:

- What first strikes you about these visuals?

- When you consider the progression of these visuals, what do you think is shown?

- What information do you think those who defend digital literacy, like Kirchenbaum, and those who oppose it, Bauerlein, would emphasize from these charts?

Final Assignment 1: Evidence of a Problem and Its Implications

As explained in Chapter 6, an argument is supported by evidence, and this evidence can come in many forms.

Essay Question

The authors of this chapter's readings offer various kinds of evidence ranging from personal experiences and observations to historical analysis and research studies. What do you think is some of the most persuasive evidence of a literacy problem in this chapter? Then, what do you think is the best response to this problem: a retreat from digital texts, a rush to adopt them, the appropriate use of both print and digital texts, or some other option? Why?

Write a formal and extended essay to answer these questions. Be sure to include specific references and direct quotations from several readings in this chapter (see Chapter 7 on Academic Honesty on quoting and citing properly). Be sure to not only support your informed perspective but also anticipate and answer the possible objections of those who do not already agree with you. Your task is to assert your opinion and persuade others to consider it carefully.

Freewrite 4: Assignment Analysis

Before you start to answer this complex question, analyze its parts. Reread the questions above and underline several phrases that represent key parts of the larger answer you will be developing. Then pick two or three of these phrases and freewrite your immediate impressions: What do you think right now? Then, pause to look for connections, contradictions, and omissions within your first response: What else do you want to discuss, what else do you want to add, and/or what order of your ideas is developing? Finally, consider the audience of your essay: Who does not agree with you already, and why might they disagree?

Reading Review

Once you have sketched some of your initial ideas, review some of the readings to find specific details and persuasive evidence to support, enrich, and possibly complicate your response. Here are some readings and post-reading questions that you may want to consider:

1. Birkerts, Close Reading Question 1
2. Baron, Analytical Writing Question 6
3. Powers, Analytical Writing Question 5
4. Kirschenbaum, Close Reading Question 2
5. Kirschenbaum, Further Options Question 7
6. Bauerlein, Close Reading Question 2
7. Bauerlein, Close Reading Question 3
8. Bilton, Further Option Question 8

Feel free to include other readings and post-reading questions. You also may want to review the suggestions for writing persuasively in Chapter 6 on Argument as well as practice the peer response described in Chapter 4 on the Writing Process.

Final Assignment 2: Using the Best of Both

Another writer named Sven Birkerts was one of the first critics to warn that reading is being "changed by powerful forces. We are living in the midst of a momentous paradigm shift." Kirschenbaum too acknowledges that reading is being "reimagined and re-engineered," but he also asserts that various kinds of reading "have coexisted for centuries." He believes that readers are not facing some "momentous … shift," instead they can continue to enjoy the best of print and digital literacies.

Essay Question

Instead of framing this issue as an either/or choice, the debate over print and digital literacy can be considered a strategic alternation: Sometimes it is more appropriate to rely on print literacy, and at others, it is better to use digital texts. What do you think are the best uses of print and digital texts? Why do you think it is better to use each literacy in certain circumstances?

Write a formal and extended essay to answer this question. Be sure to include specific references and direct quotations from several readings in this chapter (see Chapter 7 on Academic Honesty on quoting and citing properly). Be sure to not only support your informed perspective but also anticipate and answer the possible objections of those who do not already agree with you. Your task is to assert your opinion and persuade others to consider it carefully.

Freewrite 5: Assignment Analysis

Before you start to answer this complex question, analyze its parts. Reread the question above and underline several phrases that represent key parts of the larger answer you will be developing. Then pick two or three of these phrases and freewrite your immediate impressions: What do you think right now? Then, pause to look for connections, contradictions, and omissions within your first response: What else do you want to discuss, what else do you want to add, and/or what order of your ideas is developing? Finally, consider the audience of your essay: Who does not agree with you already, and why might they disagree?

Reading Review

Once you have sketched some of your initial ideas, review some of the readings to find specific details and persuasive evidence to support, enrich, and possibly complicate your response. Here are some readings and post-reading questions that you may want to consider:

1. Freewrite 1
2. Birkerts, Analytical Writing Question 4
3. Baron, Close Reading Question 2
4. Powers, Analytical Writing Question 6
5. Kirschenbaum, Analytical Writing Question 6

6.   Bauerlein, Analytical Writing Question 6

7.   Bilton, Close Reading Question 1

8.   Bilton, Analytical Writing Question 6

Feel free to include other readings and post-reading questions. You also may want to review the suggestions for writing persuasively in Chapter 6 on Argument as well as practice the peer response described in Chapter 4 on the Writing Process.

Additional Source Suggestions

In the e-supplement of this textbook, there are several sources that will help you deepen your understanding of print as well as digital literacies and strengthen your final assignment. These sources include videos as well as readings, and they present multiple perspectives, historical trends, and cultural influences on print and digital literacy. To access these materials, see the code on the inside front cover of this textbook, which will lead you to the website for additional sources.

INDEX